WILLIAM MORRIS

CENTENARY EDITION

WILLIAM MORRIS

Stories in Prose ★ *Stories in Verse*

Shorter Poems

Lectures and Essays

Edited by G. D. H. Cole for

the Nonesuch Press, London, 1948

New York : Random House

First edition March 1934

PRINTED IN GREAT BRITAIN BY ROBERT MACLEHOSE AND CO. LTD.
THE UNIVERSITY PRESS, GLASGOW

THE CONTENTS

A 2

SHORTER POEMS—continued:

LECTURES AND ESSAYS:

"News from Nowhere" and
all the items in this book are
printed in full.

*The endpapers are reproduced from a
wallpaper design by William Morris.*

BIOGRAPHICAL NOTE

1834. March 24th. William Morris born at Elm House, Clay Hill, Walthamstow.

1848–51. At school at Marlborough.

1853–55. At Exeter College, Oxford, with Burne-Jones.

1856. *The Oxford and Cambridge Magazine.* Morris's contributions include poems and romantic stories, among them *The Story of the Unknown Church* (p. 274); articled to Street, intending to become an architect; moves to London with Burne-Jones, (end of year) gives up architecture and decides, under Rossetti's influence, to become a painter.

1857. With others, paints frescoes for the new Hall of the Oxford Union.

1858. *The Defence of Guenevere* (p. 411).

1859. April 26th. Marries Jane Burden, of Oxford. Begins to build The Red House, Upton, to Philip Webb's design, and to furnish and decorate it to suit himself. This is the origin of Morris & Company, decorators.

1860. Moves into The Red House.

1861. April. Morris, Marshall, Faulkner & Co. founded. Jane Morris born.

1862. May Morris born.

1865. Moves to Queen Square, Bloomsbury. The Red House sold.

1867. *The Life and Death of Jason.*

1868–70. *The Earthly Paradise.*

1869. Translates Grettis Saga (with E. Magnússon)— first of Icelandic translations.

1870. Begins making illuminated books.

vii

1871. Takes lease of Kelmscott Manor, Oxfordshire,
at first with Rossetti.
Visits Iceland, and writes a journal of his visit.

1873. *Love is Enough*.

1875. Morris & Company reorganised under his sole
control. Takes up dyeing.
Translation of Vergil's *Æneid*.

1876. First political activity, as Liberal, on the Turkish
question (Bulgarian atrocities).

1877. *The Story of Sigurd the Volsung*—his best long poem.
Founds the Society for the Protection of Ancient
Buildings, known as "Anti-Scrape."
Gives his first lecture, *The Decorative Arts*, pub-
lished as a pamphlet, and, later, as *The Lesser
Arts* (p. 494).

1878. Active in the Eastern Question Association.
Writes first political poem, *Wake, London Lads*.
Moves to Kelmscott House, Upper Mall, Ham-
mersmith (keeping Kelmscott Manor as well).

1880. Severs connection with Liberal Party.

1881. Moves Morris & Company's works to Merton
Abbey.

1882. *Hopes and Fears for Art*.

1883. Is made Honorary Fellow of Exeter College,
Oxford. Joins Democratic (later Social
Democratic) Federation.

1884. Contributes largely to *Justice* (journal of S.D.F.),
and begins speaking on Socialism at street-
corners.

1884–5. *Chants for Socialists* (p. 459). Quarrels with S.D.F.,
and helps to found Socialist League.

1885–90. Edits and contributes largely to *The Commonweal*
(journal of Socialist League).

1885. Arrested in police court disturbance over Socialist
meeting, but discharged.

1886. *The Pilgrims of Hope*, privately re-printed from *The Commonweal* (p. 355).

1887. Translation of Homer's *Odyssey*.
"Bloody Sunday" (November 13), police break up meeting in Trafalgar Square. Alfred Linnell killed. Morris writes *A Death Song* (p. 465).

1888. *A Dream of John Ball* and *A King's Lesson* (pp. 198, 267).
Signs of Change (p. 565).
The House of the Wolfings—his first long prose romance.
Takes active part in Arts and Crafts Exhibition Society.

1889. *The Roots of the Mountains.*

1890. *News from Nowhere* appears in *The Commonweal* (in book form in 1891) (p. 3).
Leaves Socialist League and founds Hammersmith Socialist Society.

1890-1. Founds Kelmscott Press (the first book printed at the Kelmscott Press was his *Story of the Glittering Plain* in 1891).

1891. Serious illness in spring—never wholly recovers his health.
Poems by the Way (p. 466).
Volume I of *The Saga Library*—translations from the Icelandic, with E. Magnússon.

1892. On Tennyson's death is asked whether he will accept the office of Poet Laureate, and refuses.

1893. *Socialism, its Growth and Outcome* (with E. Belfast Bax).

1895. Translations of *Beowulf.*

1896. October 3rd. Dies, aged sixty-three.

The standard life of Morris is that of J. W. Mackail (1899). See also *William Morris, His Art, His Writings, and His Public Life*, by Aymer Vallance (1897), *The Art of William Morris*, by Lewis F. Day (*Art Journal* Extra

Number, 1899), *William Morris and the Early Days of the Socialist Movement*, by J. Bruce Glasier (1921), *A Brief Sketch of the Morris Movement* (privately printed for Morris & Company, 1911), and the prefaces to the twenty-four volumes of his *Collected Works*. For a bibliography, see *The Books of William Morris*, by H. Buxton Forman (1897) and *A Note by William Morris on his aims in starting the Kelmscott Press: together with facts concerning the press, and an annot ted list of all the books there printed*, compiled by S. C. Cockerell

INTRODUCTION

WILLIAM MORRIS had busy hands—hands that could never be still. He was a man who must always be making something; and in his time he made many sorts of things. Above all else he was a craftsman and a designer, with deep pleasure in fashioning shapes, playing with colours, making pretty pictures by blending shapes and colours together. He made pictures in his mind; but he was never happy until he had set them out for others to see. Pictures in tapestry, pictures in glass, pictures in wall-paper or cretonne, pictures in wood or stone —and, when he was not making pictures in these material forms, pictures in words.

For much of Morris's writing is really picture. His prose romances are mostly woven tapestries of words. *The Earthly Paradise* has much the character of a series of Pre-Raphaelite paintings. Some of his early poems remind one of an illuminated missal. When he was not making pictures, in one medium or another, he liked talking about them. For most of his life he wrote best, in prose, when he was writing about art —best of all when he was writing of the decorative arts, which were his own field of work.

This picture-making explains why the greater part of Morris's writing has dropped out of fashion. Our age, unlike the Victorian, does not want pretty pictures: it is suspicious of them. It demands, instead, significance; for it is an age of critical and highly intellectualised appreciations. Most of Morris's work is not in the least intellectual: it is simply sensuous. His temper was not critical, but appreciative. He wanted to like things, more than to understand them. He denounced many things, hotly and yet with a determined attempt to understand when and why they had gone wrong. Doubtless at times he enjoyed denouncing them; for he had a quick temper. But he did not enjoy picking holes as an exercise in intellectual subtlety. He did not like finding things hollow when they pretended to be solid. He had no special feeling for clever people, and no desire to be clever. He wanted to make beautiful things, and find beautiful things around him; and he was ready to be generous in his appreciation of beauty.

For the taste of to-day, however, Morris's conception of beauty had in it too much of prettiness. He preferred softness and roundness to hardness and angularity. He liked to invest things with a romantic colourfulness that illuminated without exposing. And, though he wrote much about heroism, and was himself under the impulsion to be ceaselessly up and doing, his ideal world was one in which there would be not much scope for heroism, but much for being pleasantly idle. He wanted a world without problems, in which everybody would have room to be happy in his own way, without jostling the others.

An atmosphere of easiness, or even languor, clings about much of his writing—especially his early writing—and spoils some of his designs. This is true of a good deal of his verse, partly because he wrote verses so easily, and partly because he seldom gave to writing them more than a fraction of himself. Writing poetry was for him one among many occupations. He would turn to it after a day at the works, spent perhaps in designing a wallpaper, or experimenting with a new dye; and he would come to all these tasks in much the same mood. His attitude was that of craftsman and designer, not of psychologist or metaphysician or imaginative artist determined to get at the heart of the world's meaning. Good verse can be written so, but hardly the greatest poetry.

Yet, if much of William Morris's work falls short of greatness, there is about the man something great. It is easy to see that a great deal of his writing is in a certain sense imitative. Not that he merely copied what other men were doing. His early poetry often shows Browning's influence; but no one will ever accuse Morris of merely copying Browning. For the most part his imitativeness, if that is the right word, was the outcome of his desire to act as the interpreter of forgotten beauty. To bring back the beauty of the Middle Ages, he drew on old French poetry and romance and upon Chaucer, whose influence pervades *The Earthly Paradise*. As the interpreter of a very different beauty he wanted to make his contemporaries appreciate the Northern Sagas—so he translated the *Volsunga Saga* and many besides, and wrote *Sigurd the Volsung*. As a designer, he revived old patterns as well as made new ones, largely under the influence of the old. In all this he was as much interpreter as original artist. Only in his Socialist writings, above all in *News from Nowhere* and *The Pilgrims of Hope*, does he allow himself to create things that are wholly new.

But, as a man, Morris was very definitely himself. In his life there was no imitation, but an abundant impulse to live and to create. One can get this impression of him most by taking his works, not one by one, but all together, and reading or looking at them against the background of his life. Moreover, among his writings, those over which he took least literary trouble most record the man. Scribbling hard for *The Commonweal*, in a cause that had hold of him in his deepest and most intimate faith, he put more stuff, though less finish, into his writing than when he was simply making pictures. Only a little of his poetry has this quality—most of all, I think, the section called "Mother and Son" in *The Pilgrims of Hope*.

So it comes about that in this selection from Morris's writings I have included only a few of his poems—half a dozen or so from *The Defence of Guenevere*, one story from *The Earthly Paradise*, a sprinkling of later poems, and his Socialist story-poem about the Paris Commune, *The Pilgrims of Hope*, of which more anon. With one exception, the leaving out of the rest cost me no pang—for those who want them can easily find them for themselves. But this exception is important. Morris wrote one long poem which seems to me, as poetry, to be head and shoulders above *Jason* or *The Earthly Paradise*, pleasantly easy, gently beautiful as these are. That one poem is *Sigurd the Volsung*; and it is impossible to represent it by selection. In *Sigurd*, and there alone, Morris wrote a long, finished poem which escaped altogether from the taint of prettiness. *The Pilgrims of Hope* is not pretty, either; but, as verse, it is mostly far less finished. Morris dashed it off, and never revised it. But *Sigurd* is a finished work; and it is not like anything else I know in English. Morris did manage, in *Sigurd*, to get the spirit of the Norse Sagas into English verse; and he did there reveal a side of himself that is not in any of his other poetry.

The attraction which Iceland and Icelandic literature had for Morris calls for comment in view of what I have said of his work and his ideals. For the theme of the sagas is sheer struggle and heroism, in a bare, bleak setting as far removed as possible from the colourful Greek and medieval settings that otherwise he chiefly loved. I think he found in the sagas—in translating and interpreting them, and in putting their spirit into English verse—compensation for his mind, the vision of another part of life he was conscious of leaving out in his earlier tales and romances. There was realism here, an imaginative realism of high living under hard conditions that formed no part of the Utopia of which he dreamed, and yet had in it a fineness and heroism that compelled his imagination. When he went to Iceland, nothing struck home to him so much as the contrast between the small lives men lived now amid those cold, bleak hills, scratching a bare living from an unfriendly soil, and the greatness of the past. He put down that contrast in his *Journal*, one of the most revealing things he wrote. His Utopia was to be a place of smooth and easy living; but those old heroes had lived greatly under conditions whose very hardness and roughness had been the stuff of which greatness is made.

Morris never resolved this contrast. He did not alter his ideal, though in his later years, when he had become a Socialist, he altered very greatly his view of how it was to be achieved. But, without changing his aim, he drew strength from his contemplation of this very different way of life. It helped him to turn from an art reformer into a Socialist, and enabled him to face without shrinking the prospect of a hard struggle to set the world to rights—a struggle not without compensations in the heroism and endurance for which it would call. *The Pilgrims of Hope* has in it that sense of heroic struggle; and I doubt if Morris could have written *The Pilgrims of Hope* unless he had written *Sigurd*, or at any rate drawn new understanding from the sagas of the North.

I should have liked dearly to include *Sigurd*; but I had to leave it out, and Morris's *Journal* of his visit to Iceland as well. But I have put into this volume at any rate one poem that tells of Morris's feeling for the Northern heroism. *Iceland First Seen* must stand here for all that vital part of his work.

What else has been chosen, besides the poems? Four prose stories, *News from Nowhere*, *A Dream of John Ball*, *A King's Lesson*, and *The Story of an Unknown Church*, and what some may hold to be an unduly large selection from Morris's essays and lectures. *News from Nowhere*, of course, chose itself. It is the best known, the most revealing, and the widest in its appeal, of all Morris's writings. As a vision of a coming Socialist society, it is easy enough to pick holes in. Never on earth could human affairs run so smoothly as all that, with so little clanking of the machinery, and with so little machinery to clank. Never could the job of getting the world's work done be reduced to quite that idyllic simplicity, even if men and women did limit their wants to what they really wanted and their quarrels to matters really worth quarrelling about. Never could the weather be quite so fine, all the colours quite so bright, all the people quite so healthy, good-looking, and good-humoured. Never could life be quite so easy-going, or man or nature quite so kind.

Morris knew that. *News from Nowhere* was neither a prophecy nor a promise, but the expression of a personal preference. Morris was saying, "Here is the sort of society I feel I should like to live in. Now tell me yours." He was letting himself dream of a society that would let him do without stint everything he thought worth doing, and would not upset his pleasure in what he did by the sense that others were lacking a like freedom. He wanted to be free to make beautiful things, not merely for ornament, but for everyday use, and not merely for a fortunate few who could afford to buy them, but for everyone who would get pleasure out of having and using them. Through most of his life, nothing hurt him so constantly as the knowledge that his pretty things were out of the reach of most who liked them—except the sense that most people had not been given a chance of finding out whether they liked them or not. He believed in his bones that the appreciation of beauty was a vitally important part of the art of living, and that a people devoid of artistic appreciation was inevitably a dead people, destined to slavery and decay. He believed that it came natural to men to have this sense of beauty in the everyday things of common use, and that a society in which they had it not was fundamentally "unnatural"—a society out of which half the pleasure and happiness had been banished. He believed that the quality of beauty in these common things, and in man's relation to them, affected the whole way of living, impoverishing any society that went without it, however men might pile up material riches. He believed that the ordinary things men made ought to be so made as to be "a joy to the maker and to the user," and that where most men spent their working days joylessly making ugly things, the death of civilisation was at hand.

All this Morris set down in *News from Nowhere*, in the form of a Socialist Utopia. He thought that a man who wrote a "Utopia" ought, above all else, to set down in it his personal estimate of the quality of living, and to leave others to put beside it other estimates; for it takes many sorts to make a world, and each man's task in making it is to clear space for the things he values. We must judge *News from Nowhere*, not as a complete picture of a possible society, but as a picture of something that a decent society will have to include, and to foster.

But, within this limitation, *News from Nowhere* is far more than a craftsman's paradise. In its opening chapters there is the plain foreshadowing of the struggle through which men must come to whatever new society they choose to make; and through it all there is, refreshingly and abundantly, the sense of

human equality and fellowship. The message of the
sermon John Ball preached at the Cross permeates
Morris's dream of the future. Men do live, in Nowhere, with an equality that is not a cold uniformity
of rights and duties, but a warm fellowship of mind
and habit.

After *News from Nowhere* comes *A Dream of John Ball*,
a Nowhere of the past instead of the future. Perhaps
its medieval setting puts some of us off in these days;
for we cannot quite believe in Morris's Middle Ages.
We can picture London as "small," but hardly as
quite so "white and clean" as he would have it; and
we get a feeling of unreality from these hearty,
healthy, straight-spoken villagers to whom we are
introduced. If Morris's "future" is never to be,
equally his "past" never was.

Yet . . . does it matter? *A Dream of John Ball* is not
a historical essay, but a sermon, with John Ball's
sermon set within it. Even if London never was clean,
cannot we make it cleaner? Even if John Ball was
but a hedge-priest, and not a prophet, need that spoil
his sermon for us? Even if the oppressed never were
quite such splendid fellows, were they, or are they,
the less oppressed and in need of a crusade? Let us
forget Dr. Coulton's very different picture for a moment, and take Morris's parable for what it is—clean,
chiselled prose telling a good story, and none the
worse for having an excellent moral.

Then follows another parable, *A King's Lesson*,
shorter this time, but also an admirable example of
Morris's best prose style, free from the over-artificiality
of his tapestry romances and yet far more polished
than his occasional writing. Thereafter comes yet
another story, *The Unknown Church*, one of Morris's
earliest works, a *juvenilium* from his undergraduate
days, published originally in the *Oxford and Cambridge
Magazine* when he was only twenty-three. It is the

best, I think, of these early stories, written long before
his Socialist days, while he was still wholly under the
influences that were making the Pre-Raphaelites, and
yet foreshadowing, in its keen sense of the joy of
craftsmanship, much of his later growth.

Next comes the poetry, of which I have spoken
already; and thereafter the essays and lectures chosen
from what many would regard—and perhaps Morris
himself regarded—as his "unliterary" work. Certainly the style is here less polished; but it has plenty
of vigour and expressiveness, and a good deal of music
as well. Morris wrote these talks often in haste, for
delivery at some assembly of artists or school of art,
or perhaps at a Socialist meeting; and, though he
revised most of them for publication, he let them
stand substantially as they were spoken. I have said
that I shall be accused of according to this part of
Morris's writings too generous a measure in this
volume; but I have no apology to make. For I think
Morris is alive even more on account of what he stood
for and attempted than of what he accomplished;
and in these occasional writings he gives a clear and
telling presentation of what he was trying to do.

John Ruskin's influence stands out very plainly in
these writings on art in its relation to the art of living;
and Morris whole-heartedly acknowledged the debt.
Ruskin's chapter on "The Nature of Gothic" seemed
to him to go to the root of the matter: he said as much
in his introduction when, by way of tribute, he reprinted it at the Kelmscott Press. For Ruskin, more
than anyone else, had stressed the relation between
the quality of work and the quality of life; and
Morris's gospel of "Useful Work *versus* Useless Toil"
was based on Ruskin's teaching. But before long he
went, in his interpretation of Ruskin's doctrine, far
beyond his master. He came to realise that the
squalor and ugliness that he hated would not yield

to a merely artistic crusade, or to a venture in private philanthropy or personal example, that these things were inseparable from the social and economic system in which they were set, and that the regeneration of the arts and of the art of living was at bottom a political rather than an artistic matter. He came to hold that it would be better for the arts to die out altogether, surely to be reborn in a new social environment, than for their preservation to be made the excuse for the survival of a system founded on exploitation and the denial of fellowship. Morris became in fact not merely a Socialist, but a revolutionary Socialist, putting his faith in the good nature and good fellowship of the working-class movement as the creative force to make the new society.

Yet, in becoming a Socialist, Morris did not yield up his belief in the overmastering importance of the arts. His creed was that the arts must be made again the possession of common men, and that common men must be given again, or rather must take for themselves, the means of expressing their creative impulses in their daily work. This brought him up against machinery—not all machinery, for he realised that machines could be used to lighten labour—but against machines that made the lives of those who tended them a dead monotony of irksome routine. He wanted men to enjoy, as he enjoyed, making things; to have the chance of making beautiful things; to learn by this to know and value beauty in things of common use. In this rebellion against the machine he went, no doubt, too far, exaggerating the ease with which all could be supplied with the means of good living without its extensive use, and blind, for the most part, to the pleasure which a man can take in a machine that he helps to do its intricate work well. He pressed too far his desire for the "hand-made," as if handwork were the only form of craftsmanship.

But this does not invalidate his essential point—that if a man be compelled to spend the best part of his days in irksome toil, making things that it yields him no pleasure to make, then it shall go hard with a civilisation that uses men so; for the men will not escape to their hours of leisure unscathed by the influence of the hours of work. That Morris saw clearly how to put pleasure into most men's labour I do not suggest; but that he saw labour without pleasure as men's curse was not merely a pathetic fallacy of the artist, but clear vision of the truth. For the time, he looked for men to get compensation in the social struggle, finding in the "cause" that which would give joy and creative purpose to their lives. But beyond the struggle he envisaged them coming again to demand, as their right, work pleasant in the doing, and casting out those machines, however productive, that must make their attendants into slaves.

Was he wrong in this? Will not men, as they get their freedom, use machines more and more to do the rough and dirty work, but claim back from the machine the making of those things which it is a pleasure to fashion as well as to use, if they are fashioned with individual care and skill? There is no fixed line between the spheres of handcraft and machine work; but will not men, as it grows easier to make enough, claim back more and more the pleasure of skilful making? I think, with Morris, that they will; but I think also, with him, that there will be more machinery before there can be less.

Through these lectures runs the reiterated protest against the divorce between craftsman and designer, which came in with the Renaissance and has become more extreme with every advance of mechanisation. William Morris hated this divorce, because he saw in it a force making for human inequality and the degradation of labour. He wanted the builder to be again an architect, and the craftsman to design: at the least he demanded that the class-difference between creative artist and executant should disappear. In this it may be held that he was kicking against the pricks, and that the divorce does not really matter, because only a very few have in them the impulse to create. Morris denied this with fury: he believed the creative impulse to be profoundly natural, suppressed in men and turned aside from its expression in the work of their hands, but by no means torn up out of their natures. He held, accordingly, that economic freedom would of itself bring back the creative impulse into industry, and that industry, under Socialism, would have to be adapted to the needs of men, instead of breaking them upon its inhuman wheels. Here again perhaps he went too far, mistaking the creative impulse that was so strong in him for a common possession of all mankind in equal measure. But will anyone who knows the arts and crafts of simpler peoples deny that he had warrant for his faith?

The lectures, then, expound Morris's social gospel, now from an artistic and now from a Socialist angle; and I have thought fit to include enough of them to let him explain himself clearly both as craftsman and as Socialist. What men will make of his gospel will doubtless differ greatly from what he expected them to make of it; for men brought up on machinery learn to regard machinery in a new way, and the mechanic can be no less a craftsman than the tool-using artificer. Machinery is not men's curse; the curse lies in how it is abused and its user exploited. That Morris partly saw this the tract, *A Factory as it Might Be*, plainly shows. I have included it the more gladly because it is omitted from the standard edition of his works.

With so much preface, let this selection speak for itself. It does not include, or attempt to include, nearly all of Morris's writing that is worth keeping alive: nor, of course, does it touch the other parts of his creative work. Of this other work, a good deal "dates." It is important as a landmark in the history of modern craftsmanship and design rather than for the positive pleasure it still has power to give. In printing, for example, Morris did wonderful work at the Kelmscott Press, and every fine modern printer is in his debt. But of his types, the "Troy" is over-elaborate; and only the "Golden" is really a type to be *read* with pleasure now. Of his wallpapers, chintzes, and cretonnes, many have lost their appeal; but the best, the "Woodpecker" and the "Strawberry Thief," aided by Philip Webb's birds, still make most modern designs look foolish or tawdry. I have had the "Strawberry Thief" in my house for more than fifteen years; and it gives me as much pleasure to-day as ever it did—fresh, lively pleasure, not mere recollection; and of how many designs could that be said? Moreover, Morris's fabrics *wear*: in that, fully as much as in design, he set a standard.

Yet of Morris, less than of any other great artist I know of, can it be said that here or there, in any one work of his hands, he expressed the essence of what was in him. He had great force; but he dissipated it over so many things that it was never fully concentrated anywhere. Could he have concentrated it more, he might have been a greater artist; and yet the concentration would have been a misfortune. For it was William Morris's mission to throw himself into a great many arts, exhausting none, but creating everywhere things at the least passably beautiful, and at the best also powerfully influential for good. I like best to think of him as the man who, loving beauty, wanted to make beauty a common possession of all mankind, and, realising how much stood in the way, did not shrink from giving battle to giants. In short,

I like to think of him as the creative artist who was also a Socialist, and was artist and Socialist, not as two separate things, but as aspects of one and the same faith in human fellowship.

G. D. H. COLE

Oxford, February, 1934.

STORIES IN PROSE

NEWS FROM NOWHERE *was published first in* The Commonweal, *the organ of the Socialist League, which was founded and edited by Morris. It appeared in instalments from January to October 1890. In the same year it was issued in book form in the United States by Robert Brothers of Boston.[1] This unauthorised reprint is the* editio princeps. *The authorised edition was published in London by Reeves and Turner in 1891.[2] In 1892 Morris reprinted it at the Kelmscott Press, using the "Golden" type.[3] There have been many later editions.*

> [1] pp. vi + 278. Crown 8vo., with cartoon, "Labour's May-Day," by Walter Crane.
> [2] pp. 238. Large paper issue, tall crown 8vo. Ordinary issue $7\frac{1}{2} \times 4\frac{1}{2}$ in paper and cloth.
> [3] pp. 306. 8vo. Limp vellum binding. Frontispiece of Kelmscott Press. Binder by Morris.

A DREAM OF JOHN BALL *was published first in* The Commonweal, *between November 1886 and January 1887. It appeared first in book form in 1888, accompanied by* A King's Lesson, *with the "Adam and Eve" frontispiece by Burne-Jones.[1] The same two works were reprinted by Morris at the Kelmscott Press in 1892.[2] The Burne-Jones frontispiece, etched for the first edition, was reproduced as a woodcut for the Kelmscott Press edition. The "Golden" type was used. There are many later editions.*

> [1] pp. 8 + 144. Royal 16mo. Also large paper edition, post quarto, in half-vellum.
> [2] pp. 124. Quarto (crown 8vo. size). Limp vellum binding by Morris.

A KING'S LESSON *was published first in* The Commonweal *in September 1886, under the title* An Old Story Re-told. *For its subsequent history see under* A Dream of John Ball. *It also appeared separately as a pamphlet, published by James Leatham in Aberdeen, in 1891.*

THE STORY OF THE UNKNOWN CHURCH *first appeared in* The Oxford and Cambridge Magazine *in 1856, when Morris was only twenty-one. It was the first of his stories to be published. It was reprinted, with other stories, under the collective title,* The Hollow Land and other Contributions to the Oxford and Cambridge Magazine, *in 1903, at the Chiswick Press, the Kelmscott "Golden" type being used.*

NEWS FROM NOWHERE

CHAPTER I

DISCUSSION & BED

UP at the League, says a friend, there had been one night a brisk conversational discussion, as to what would happen on the Morrow of the Revolution, finally shading off into a vigorous statement by various friends of their views on the future of the fully-developed new society.

Says our friend: Considering the subject, the discussion was good-tempered; for those present being used to public meetings and after-lecture debates, if they did not listen to each others' opinions (which could scarcely be expected of them), at all events did not always attempt to speak all together, as is the custom of people in ordinary polite society when conversing on a subject which interests them. For the rest, there were six persons present, and consequently six sections of the party were represented, four of which had strong but divergent Anarchist opinions. One of the sections, says our friend, a man whom he knows very well indeed, sat almost silent at the beginning of the discussion, but at last got drawn into it, and finished by roaring out very loud, and damning all the rest for fools; after which befell a period of noise, and then a lull, during which the aforesaid section, having said good-night very amicably, took his way home by himself to a western suburb, using the means of travelling which civilisation has forced upon us like a habit. As he sat in that vapour-bath of hurried and discontented humanity, a carriage of the underground railway, he, like others, stewed discontentedly, while in self-reproachful mood he turned over the many excellent and conclusive arguments which, though they lay at his fingers' ends, he had forgotten in the just past discussion. But this frame of mind he was so used to, that it didn't last him long, and after a brief discomfort, caused by disgust with himself for having lost his temper (which he was also well used to), he found himself musing on the subject-matter of discussion, but still discontentedly and unhappily. "If I could but see a day of it," he said to himself; "if I could but see it!"

As he formed the words, the train stopped at his station, five minutes' walk from his own house, which stood on the banks of the Thames, a little way above an ugly suspension bridge. He went out of the station, still discontented and unhappy, muttering "If I could but see it! if I could but see it!" but had not gone many steps towards the river before (says our friend who tells the story) all that discontent and trouble seemed to slip off him.

It was a beautiful night of early winter, the air just sharp enough to be refreshing after the hot room and the stinking railway carriage. The wind, which had lately turned a point or two north of west, had blown the sky clear of all cloud save a light fleck or two which went swiftly down the heavens. There was a young moon halfway up the sky, and as the home-farer caught sight of it, tangled in the branches of a tall old elm, he could scarce bring to his mind the shabby London suburb where he was, and he felt as if he were in a pleasant country place—pleasanter, indeed, than the deep country was as he had known it.

He came right down to the river-side, and lingered a little, looking over the low wall to note the moonlit river, near upon high water, go swirling and glittering up to Chiswick Eyot; as for the ugly bridge below, he did not notice it or think of it, except when for a moment (says our friend) it struck him that he missed the row of lights down-stream. Then he turned to his house door and let himself in; and even as he shut the door to, disappeared all remembrance of that brilliant logic and foresight which had so illuminated the recent discussion; and of the discussion itself there remained no trace, save a vague hope, that was now become a pleasure, for days of peace and rest, and cleanness and smiling goodwill.

In this mood he tumbled into bed, and fell asleep after

his wont, in two minutes' time; but (contrary to his wont) woke up again not long after in that curiously wide-awake condition which sometimes surprises even good sleepers; a condition under which we feel all our wits preternaturally sharpened, while all the miserable muddles we have ever got into, all the disgraces and losses of our lives, will insist on thrusting themselves forward for the consideration of those sharpened wits.

In this state he lay (says our friend) till he had almost begun to enjoy it: till the tale of his stupidities amused him, and the entanglements before him, which he saw so clearly, began to shape themselves into an amusing story for him.

He heard one o'clock strike, then two and then three; after which he fell asleep again. Our friend says that from that sleep he awoke once more, and afterwards went through such surprising adventures that he thinks that they should be told to our comrades and indeed the public in general, and therefore proposes to tell them now. But, says he, I think it would be better if I told them in the first person, as if it were myself who had gone through them; which, indeed, will be the easier and more natural to me, since I understand the feelings and desires of the comrade of whom I am telling better than any one else in the world does.

CHAPTER II

A MORNING BATH

WELL, I awoke, and found that I had kicked my bed-clothes off; and no wonder, for it was hot and the sun shining brightly. I jumped up and washed and hurried on my clothes, but in a hazy and half-awake condition, as if I had slept for a long, long while, and could not shake off the weight of slumber. In fact, I rather took it for granted that I was at home in my own room than saw that it was so.

When I was dressed, I felt the place so hot that I made haste to get out of the room and out of the house; and my first feeling was a delicious relief caused by the fresh air and pleasant breeze; my second, as I began to gather my wits together, mere measureless wonder: for it was winter when I went to bed the last night, and now, by witness of the river-side trees, it was summer, a beautiful bright morning seemingly of early June. However, there was still the Thames sparkling under the sun, and near high water, as last night I had seen it gleaming under the moon.

I had by no means shaken off the feeling of oppression, and wherever I might have been should scarce have been quite conscious of the place; so it was no wonder that I felt rather puzzled in despite of the familiar face of the Thames. Withal I felt dizzy and queer; and remembering that people often got a boat and had a swim in mid-stream, I thought I would do no less. It seems very early, quoth I to myself, but I daresay I shall find some one at Biffin's to take me. However, I didn't get as far as Biffin's, or even turn to my left thitherward, because just then I began to see that there was a landing-stage right before me in front of my house: in fact, on the place where my next-door neighbour had rigged one up, though somehow it didn't look like that either. Down I went on to it, and sure enough among the empty boats moored to it lay a man on his sculls in a solid-looking tub of a boat clearly meant for bathers. He nodded to me, and bade me good-morning as if he expected me, so I jumped in without any words, and he paddled away quietly as I peeled for my swim. As we went, I looked down on the water, and couldn't help saying:

"How clear the water is this morning!"

"Is it?" said he; "I didn't notice it. You know the flood-tide always thickens it a bit."

"H'm," said I, "I have seen it pretty muddy even at half-ebb."

He said nothing in answer, but seemed rather astonished; and as he now lay just stemming the tide, and I had my clothes off, I jumped in without more ado. Of course when I had my head above water again I turned towards the tide, and my eyes naturally sought for the bridge, and so utterly astonished was I by what I saw, that I forgot to strike out, and went spluttering under water again, and when I came up made straight for the boat; for I felt that I must ask some questions of my waterman, so bewildering had been the half-sight I had seen from the face of the river with the water hardly out of my eyes; though by this time I was quit of the slumbrous and dizzy feeling, and was wide-awake and clear-headed.

As I got in up the steps which he had lowered, and he held out his hand to help me, we went drifting speedily up towards Chiswick; but now he caught up the sculls and brought her head round again, and said:

"A short swim, neighbour; but perhaps you find the water cold this morning, after your journey. Shall I put you ashore at once, or would you like to go down to Putney before breakfast?"

He spoke in a way so unlike what I should have expected from a Hammersmith waterman, that I stared at him, as I answered, "Please to hold her a little; I want to look about me a bit."

"All right," he said; "it's no less pretty in its way here than it is off Barn Elms; it's jolly everywhere this time in the morning. I'm glad you got up early; it's barely five o'clock yet."

If I was astonished with my sight of the river banks, I was no less astonished at my waterman, now that I had time to look at him and see him with my head and eyes clear.

He was a handsome young fellow, with a peculiarly pleasant and friendly look about his eyes,—an expression which was quite new to me then, though I soon became familiar with it. For the rest, he was dark-haired and berry-brown of skin, well-knit and strong, and obviously used to exercising his muscles, but with nothing rough or coarse about him, and clean as might be. His dress was not like any modern work-a-day clothes I had seen, but would have, served very well as a costume for a picture of fourteenth-century life: it was of dark blue cloth, simple enough, but of fine web, and without a stain on it. He had a brown leather belt round his waist, and I noticed that its clasp was of damascened steel beautifully wrought. In short, he seemed to be like some specially manly and refined young gentleman, playing waterman for a spree, and I concluded that this was the case.

I felt that I must make some conversation; so I pointed to the Surrey bank, where I noticed some light plank stages running down the foreshore, with windlasses at the landward end of them, and said, "What are they doing with those things here? If we were on the Tay, I should have said that they were for drawing the salmon-nets; but here——"

"Well," said he, smiling, "of course that is what they *are* for. Where there are salmon, there are likely to be salmon-nets, Tay or Thames; but of course they are not always in use; we don't want salmon *every* day of the season."

I was going to say, "But is this the Thames?" but held my peace in my wonder, and turned my bewildered eyes eastward to look at the bridge again, and thence to the shores of the London river; and surely there was enough to astonish me. For though there was a bridge across the stream and houses on its banks, how all was changed from last night! The soap-works with their smoke-vomiting chimneys were gone; the engineer's works gone; the lead-works gone; and no sound of riveting and hammering came down the west wind from Thorneycroft's. Then the bridge! I had perhaps dreamed of such a bridge, but never seen such an one out of an illuminated manuscript; for not even the Ponte Vecchio at Florence came anywhere near it. It was of stone arches, splendidly solid, and as graceful as they were strong; high enough also to let ordinary river traffic through easily. Over the parapet showed quaint and fanciful little buildings, which I supposed to be booths or shops, beset with painted and gilded vanes and spirelets. The stone was a little weathered, but showed no marks of the grimy sootiness which I was used to on every London building more than a year old. In short, to me a wonder of a bridge.

The sculler noted my eager astonished look, and said, as if in answer to my thoughts:

"Yes, it *is* a pretty bridge, isn't it? Even the up-stream bridges, which are so much smaller, are scarcely daintier, and the down-stream ones are scarcely more dignified and stately."

I found myself saying, almost against my will, "How old is it?"

"O, not very old," he said; "it was built, or at least

opened, in 2003. There used to be a rather plain timber bridge before then."

The date shut my mouth as if a key had been turned in a padlock fixed to my lips; for I saw that something inexplicable had happened, and that if I said much, I should be mixed up in a game of cross questions and crooked answers. So I tried to look unconcerned, and to glance in a matter-of-course way at the banks of the river, though this is what I saw up to the bridge and a little beyond; say as far as the site of the soap-works. Both shores had a line of very pretty houses, low and not large, standing back a little way from the river; they were mostly built of red brick and roofed with tiles, and looked, above all, comfortable, and as if they were, so to say, alive and sympathetic with the life of the dwellers in them. There was a continuous garden in front of them, going down to the water's edge, in which the flowers were now blooming luxuriantly, and sending delicious waves of summer scent over the eddying stream. Behind the houses, I could see great trees rising, mostly planes, and looking down the water there were the reaches towards Putney almost as if they were a lake with a forest shore, so thick were the big trees; and I said aloud, but as if to myself:

"Well, I'm glad that they have not built over Barn Elms."

I blushed for my fatuity as the words slipped out of my mouth, and my companion looked at me with a half smile which I thought I understood; so to hide my confusion I said, "Please take me ashore now: I want to get my breakfast."

He nodded, and brought her head round with a sharp stroke, and in a trice we were at the landing-stage again. He jumped out and I followed him; and of course I was not surprised to see him wait, as if for the inevitable after-piece that follows the doing of a service to a fellow-citizen. So I put my hand into my waistcoat-pocket, and said, "How much?" though still with the uncomfortable feeling that perhaps I was offering money to a gentleman.

He looked puzzled, and said, "How much? I don't quite understand what you are asking about. Do you mean the tide? If so, it is close on the turn now."

I blushed, and said, stammering, "Please don't take it
amiss if I ask you; I mean no offence: but what ought I to
pay you? You see I am a stranger, and don't know your
customs—or your coins."

And therewith I took a handful of money out of my
pocket, as one does in a foreign country. And by the way,
I saw that the silver had oxydised. and was like a black-
leaded stove in colour.

He still seemed puzzled, but not at all offended; and he
looked at the coins with some curiosity. I thought, Well
after all, he *is* a waterman, and is considering what he may
venture to take. He seems such a nice fellow that I'm sure
I don't grudge him a little over-payment. I wonder, by
the way, whether I couldn't hire him as a guide for a day
or two, since he is so intelligent.

Therewith my new friend said thoughtfully:

"I think I know what you mean. You think that I have
done you a service; so you feel yourself bound to give me
something which I am not to give to a neighbour, unless
he has done something special for me. I have heard of this
kind of thing: but pardon me for saying, that it seems to us
a troublesome and roundabout custom; and we don't know
how to manage it. And you see this ferrying and giving
people casts about the water is my *business*, which I would
do for anybody; so to take gifts in connection with it would
look very queer. Besides, if one person gave me something,
then another might, and another, and so on; and I hope
you won't think me rude if I say that I shouldn't know
where to stow away so many mementos of friendship."

And he laughed loud and merrily, as if the idea of being
paid for his work was a very funny joke. I confess I began
to be afraid that the man was mad, though he looked sane
enough; and I was rather glad to think that I was a good
swimmer, since we were so close to a deep swift stream.
However, he went on by no means like a madman:

"As to your coins, they are curious, but not very old;
they seem to be all of the reign of Victoria; you might give
them to some scantily-furnished museum. Ours has enough
of such coins, besides a fair number of earlier ones, many o
which are beautiful, whereas these nineteenth century ones
are so beastly ugly, ain't they? We have a piece of Edward

III, with the king in a ship, and little leopards and fleurs-de-lys all along the gunwale, so delicately worked. You see," he said, with something of a smirk, "I am fond of working in gold and fine metals; this buckle here is an early piece of mine."

No doubt I looked a little shy of him under the influence of that doubt as to his sanity. So he broke off short, and said in a kind voice:

"But I see that I am boring you, and I ask your pardon. For, not to mince matters, I can tell that you *are* a stranger, and must come from a place very unlike England. But also it is clear that it won't do to overdose you with information about this place, and that you had best suck it in little by little. Further, I should take it as very kind in you if you would allow me to be the showman of our new world to you, since you have stumbled on me first. Though indeed it will be a mere kindness on your part, for almost anybody would make as good a guide, and many much better."

There certainly seemed no flavour in him of Colney Hatch; and besides I thought I could easily shake him off if it turned out that he really was mad; so I said:

"It is a very kind offer, but it is difficult for me to accept it, unless——" I was going to say, Unless you will let me pay you properly; but fearing to stir up Colney Hatch again, I changed the sentence into, "I fear I shall be taking you away from your work—or your amusement."

"O," he said, "don't trouble about that, because it will give me an opportunity of doing a good turn to a friend of mine, who wants to take my work here. He is a weaver from Yorkshire, who has rather overdone himself between his weaving and his mathematics, both indoor work, you see; and being a great friend of mine, he naturally came to me to get him some outdoor work. If you think you can put up with me, pray take me as your guide."

He added presently: "It is true that I have promised to go up-stream to some special friends of mine, for the hay-harvest; but they won't be ready for us for more than a week: and besides, you might go with me, you know, and see some very nice people, besides making notes of our ways in Oxfordshire. You could hardly do better if you want to see the country."

I felt myself obliged to thank him, whatever might come of it; and he added eagerly:

"Well, then, that's settled. I will give my friend a call; he is living in the Guest House like you, and if he isn't up yet, he ought to be this fine summer morning."

Therewith he took a little silver bugle-horn from his girdle and blew two or three sharp but agreeable notes on it; and presently from the house which stood on the site of my old dwelling (of which more hereafter) another young man came sauntering towards us. He was not so well-looking or so strongly made as my sculler friend, being sandy-haired, rather pale, and not stout-built; but his face was not wanting in that happy and friendly expression which I had noticed in his friend. As he came up smiling towards us, I saw with pleasure that I must give up the Colney Hatch theory as to the waterman, for no two mad-men ever behaved as they did before a sane man. His dress also was of the same cut as the first man's, though somewhat gayer, the surcoat being light green with a golden spray embroidered on the breast, and his belt being of filigree silver-work.

He gave me good-day very civilly, and greeting his friend joyously, said:

"Well, Dick, what is it this morning? Am I to have my work, or rather your work? I dreamed last night that we were off up the river fishing."

"All right, Bob," said my sculler; "you will drop into my place, and if you find it too much, there is George Bright-ling on the look-out for a stroke of work, and he lives close handy to you. But see, here is a stranger who is willing to amuse me to-day by taking me as his guide about our countryside, and you may imagine I don't want to lose the opportunity; so you had better take to the boat at once. But in any case I shouldn't have kept you out of it for long, since I am due in the hayfields in a few days."

The newcomer rubbed his hands with glee, but turning to me, said in a friendly voice:

"Neighbour, both you and friend Dick are lucky, and will have a good time to-day, as indeed I shall too. But you had better both come in with me at once and get something to eat, lest you should forget your dinner in your amusement.

I suppose you came into the Guest House after I had gone to bed last night?"

I nodded, not caring to enter into a long explanation which would have led to nothing, and which in truth by this time I should have begun to doubt myself. And we all three turned toward the door of the Guest House.

CHAPTER III

THE GUEST HOUSE
AND BREAKFAST THEREIN

I LINGERED a little behind the others to have a stare at this house, which, as I have told you, stood on the site of my old dwelling.

It was a longish building with its gable ends turned away from the road, and long traceried windows coming rather low down set in the wall that faced us. It was very handsomely built of red brick with a lead roof; and high up above the windows there ran a frieze of figure subjects in baked clay, very well executed, and designed with a force and directness which I had never noticed in modern work before. The subjects I recognised at once, and indeed was very particularly familiar with them.

However, all this I took in in a minute; for we were presently within doors, and standing in a hall with a floor of marble mosaic and an open timber roof. There were no windows on the side opposite to the river, but arches below leading into chambers, one of which showed a glimpse of a garden beyond, and above them a long space of wall gaily painted (in fresco, I thought) with similar subjects to those of the frieze outside; everything about the place was handsome and generously solid as to material; and though it was not very large (somewhat smaller than Crosby Hall perhaps), one felt in it that exhilarating sense of space and freedom which satisfactory architecture always gives to an unanxious man who is in the habit of using his eyes.

In this pleasant place, which of course I knew to be the hall of the Guest House, three young women were flitting to and fro. As they were the first of the sex I had seen on this eventful morning, I naturally looked at them very attentively, and found them at least as good as the gardens, the architecture, and the male men. As to their dress, which of course I took note of, I should say that they were decently veiled with drapery, and not bundled up with millinery; that they were clothed like women, not upholstered like arm-chairs, as most women of our time are. In short, their dress was somewhat between that of the ancient classical costume and the simpler forms of the fourteenth-century garments, though it was clearly not an imitation of either: the materials were light and gay to suit the season. As to the women themselves, it was pleasant indeed to see them, they were so kind and happy-looking in expression of face, so shapely and well-knit of body, and thoroughly healthy-looking and strong. All were at least comely, and one of them very handsome and regular of feature. They came up to us at once merrily and without the least affectation of shyness, and all three shook hands with me as if I were a friend newly come back from a long journey: though I could not help noticing that they looked askance at my garments; for I had on my clothes of last night, and at the best was never a dressy person.

A word or two from Robert the weaver, and they bustled about on our behoof, and presently came and took us by the hands and led us to a table in the pleasantest corner of the hall, where our breakfast was spread for us; and, as we sat down, one of them hurried out by the chambers aforesaid, and came back again in a little while with a great bunch of roses, very different in size and quality to what Hammersmith had been wont to grow, but very like the produce of an old country garden. She hurried back thence into the buttery, and came back once more with a delicately made glass, into which she put the flowers and set them down in the midst of our table. One of the others, who had run off also, then came back with a big cabbage-leaf filled with strawberries, some of them barely ripe, and said as she set them on the table, "There, now; I thought of that before I got up this morning; but looking at the stranger here getting into your boat, Dick, put it out of my head; so that I was not before *all* the blackbirds: however, there are a few about as good as you will get them anywhere in Hammersmith this morning."

Robert patted her on the head in a friendly manner; and we fell to on our breakfast, which was simple enough, but most delicately cooked, and set on the table with much daintiness. The bread was particularly good, and was of several different kinds, from the big, rather close, dark-coloured, sweet-tasting farmhouse loaf, which was most to my liking, to the thin pipe-stems of wheaten crust, such as I have eaten in Turin.

As I was putting the first mouthfuls into my mouth, my eye caught a carved and gilded inscription on the panelling, behind what we should have called the High Table in an Oxford college hall, and a familiar name in it forced me to read it through. Thus it ran:

"*Guests and neighbours, on the site of this Guest-hall
once stood the lecture-room of the Hammersmith Socialists.
Drink a glass to the memory ! May 1962.*"

It is difficult to tell you how I felt as I read these words, and I suppose my face showed how much I was moved, for both my friends looked curiously at me, and there was silence between us for a little while.

Presently the weaver, who was scarcely so well mannered a man as the ferryman, said to me rather awkwardly:

"Guest, we don't know what to call you: is there any indiscretion in asking you your name?"

"Well," said I, "I have some doubts about it myself; so suppose you call me Guest, which is a family name, you know, and add William to it if you please."

Dick nodded kindly to me; but a shade of anxiousness passed over the weaver's face, and he said:

"I hope you don't mind my asking, but would you tell me where you come from? I am curious about such things for good reasons, literary reasons."

Dick was clearly kicking him underneath the table; but he was not much abashed, and awaited my answer somewhat eagerly. As for me, I was just going to blurt out "Hammersmith," when I bethought me what an entanglement of cross purposes that would lead us into; so I took time to invent a lie with circumstance, guarded by a little truth, and said:

"You see, I have been such a long time away from Europe that things seem strange to me now; but I was born and bred on the edge of Epping Forest; Walthamstow and Woodford, to wit."

"A pretty place too," broke in Dick; "a very jolly place, now that the trees have had time to grow again since the great clearing of houses in 1955."

Quoth the irrepressible weaver: "Dear neighbour, since you knew the Forest some time ago, could you tell me what truth there is in the rumour that in the nineteenth century the trees were all pollards?"

This was catching me on my archæological natural-history side, and I fell into the trap without any thought of where and when I was; so I began on it, while one of the girls, the handsome one, who had been scattering little twigs of lavender and other sweet-smelling herbs about the floor, came near to listen, and stood behind me with her hand on my shoulder, in which she held some of the plant that I used to call balm: its strong sweet smell brought back to my mind my very early days in the kitchen-garden at Woodford, and the large blue plums which grew on the wall beyond the sweet-herb patch,—a connection of memories which all boys will see at once.

I started off: "When I was a boy, and for long after, except for a piece about Queen Elizabeth's Lodge, and for the part about High Beech, the Forest was almost wholly made up of pollard hornbeams mixed with holly thickets. But when the Corporation of London took it over about twenty-five years ago, the topping and lopping, which was a part of the old commoners' rights, came to an end, and the trees were let to grow. But I have not seen the place now for many years, except once, when we Leaguers went a-pleasuring to High Beech. I was very much shocked then to see how it was built-over and altered; and the other day we heard that the philistines were going to landscape-garden it. But what you were saying about the building being stopped and the trees growing is only too good news; —only you know——"

At that point I suddenly remembered Dick's date, and

stopped short rather confused. The eager weaver didn't notice my confusion, but said hastily, as if he were almost aware of his breach of good manners, "But, I say, how old are you?"

Dick and the pretty girl both burst out laughing, as if Robert's conduct were excusable on the grounds of eccentricity; and Dick said amidst his laughter:

"Hold hard, Bob; this questioning of guests won't do. Why, much learning is spoiling you. You remind me of the radical cobblers in the silly old novels, who, according to the authors, were prepared to trample down all good manners in the pursuit of utilitarian knowledge. The fact is, I begin to think that you have so muddled your head with mathematics, and with grubbing into those idiotic old books about political economy (he he!), that you scarcely know how to behave. Really, it is about time for you to take to some open-air work, so that you may clear away the cobwebs from your brain."

The weaver only laughed good-humouredly; and the girl went up to him and patted his cheek and said laughingly "Poor fellow! he was born so."

As for me, I was a little puzzled, but I laughed also, partly for company's sake, and partly with pleasure at their unanxious happiness and good temper; and before Robert could make the excuse to me which he was getting ready, I said:

"But, neighbours" (I had caught up that word), "I don't in the least mind answering questions, when I can do so: ask me as many as you please; it's fun for me. I will tell you all about Epping Forest when I was a boy, if you please; and as to my age, I'm not a fine lady, you know, so why shouldn't I tell you? I'm hard on fifty-six."

In spite of the recent lecture on good manners, the weaver could not help giving a long "whew" of astonishment, and the others were so amused by his *naïveté* that the merriment flitted all over their faces, though for courtesy's sake they forbore actual laughter; while I looked from one to the other in a puzzled manner, and at last said:

"Tell me, please, what is amiss: you know I want to learn from you. And please laugh; only tell me."

Well, they *did* laugh, and I joined them again, for the

above-stated reasons. But at last the pretty woman said coaxingly:

"Well, well, he *is* rude, poor fellow! but you see I may as well tell you what he is thinking about: he means that you look rather old for your age. But surely there need be no wonder in that, since you have been travelling; and clearly from all you have been saying, in unsocial countries. It has often been said, and no doubt truly, that one ages very quickly if one lives amongst unhappy people. Also they say that southern England is a good place for keeping good looks." She blushed and said: "How old am I, do you think?"

"Well," quoth I, "I have always been told that a woman is as old as she looks, so without offence or flattery, I should say that you were twenty."

She laughed merrily, and said, "I am well served out for fishing for compliments, since I have to tell you the truth, to wit, that I am forty-two."

I stared at her, and drew musical laughter from her again; but I might well stare, for there was not a careful line on her face; her skin was as smooth as ivory, her cheeks full and round, her lips as red as the roses she had brought in; her beautiful arms, which she had bared for her work, firm and well-knit from shoulder to wrist. She blushed a little under my gaze, though it was clear that she had taken me for a man of eighty; so to pass it off I said:

"Well, you see, the old saw is proved right again, and I ought not to have let you tempt me into asking you a rude question."

She laughed again, and said: "Well, lads, old and young, I must get to my work now. We shall be rather busy here presently; and I want to clear it off soon, for I began to read a pretty old book yesterday, and I want to get on with it this morning: so good-bye for the present."

She waved a hand to us, and stepped lightly down the hall, taking (as Scott says) at least part of the sun from our table as she went.

When she was gone, Dick said, "Now, guest, won't you ask a question or two of our friend here? It is only fair that you should have your turn."

"I shall be very glad to answer them," said the weaver.

"If I ask you any questions, sir," said I, "they will not be very severe; but since I hear that you are a weaver, I should like to ask you something about that craft, as I am—or was—interested in it."

"O," said he, "I shall not be of much use to you there, I'm afraid. I only do the most mechanical kind of weaving, and am in fact but a poor craftsman, unlike Dick here. Then besides the weaving, I do a little with machine printing and composing, though I am little use at the finer kinds of printing; and moreover machine printing is beginning to die out, along with the waning of the plague of bookmaking, so I have had to turn to other things that I have a taste for, and have taken to mathematics; and also I am writing a sort of antiquarian book about the peaceable and private history, so to say, of the end of the nineteenth century,—more for the sake of giving a picture of the country before the fighting began than for anything else. That was why I asked you those questions about Epping Forest. You have rather puzzled me, I confess, though your information was so interesting. But later on, I hope, we may have some more talk together, when our friend Dick isn't here. I know he thinks me rather a grinder, and despises me for not being very deft with my hands: that's the way nowadays. From what I have read of the nineteenth-century literature (and I have read a good deal), it is clear to me that this is a kind of revenge for the stupidity of that day, which despised everybody who *could* use his hands. But, Dick, old fellow, *Ne quid nimis!* Don't overdo it!"

"Come now," said Dick, "am I likely to? Am I not the most tolerant man in the world? Am I not quite contented so long as you don't make me learn mathematics, or go into your new science of æsthetics, and let me do a little practical æsthetics with my gold and steel, and the blowpipe and the nice little hammer? But, hillo! here comes another questioner for you, my poor guest. I say, Bob, you must help me to defend him now."

"Here, Boffin," he cried out, after a pause; "here we are, if you must have it!"

I looked over my shoulder, and saw something flash and gleam in the sunlight that lay across the hall; so I turned round, and at my ease saw a splendid figure slowly sauntering over the pavement; a man whose surcoat was embroidered most copiously as well as elegantly, so that the sun flashed back from him as if he had been clad in golden armour. The man himself was tall, dark-haired, and exceedingly handsome, and though his face was no less kindly in expression than that of the others, he moved with that somewhat haughty mien which great beauty is apt to give to both men and women. He came and sat down at our table with a smiling face, stretching out his long legs and hanging his arm over the chair in the slowly graceful way which tall and well-built people may use without affectation. He was a man in the prime of life, but looked as happy as a child who has just got a new toy. He bowed gracefully to me and said:

"I see clearly that you are the guest, of whom Annie has just told me, who have come from some distant country that does not know of us, or our ways of life. So I daresay you would not mind answering me a few questions; for you see——"

Here Dick broke in: "No, please, Boffin! let it alone for the present. Of course you want the guest to be happy and comfortable; and how can that be if he has to trouble himself with answering all sorts of questions while he is still confused with the new customs and people about him? No, no: I am going to take him where he can ask questions himself, and have them answered; that is, to my great-grandfather in Bloomsbury: and I am sure you can't have anything to say against that. So instead of bothering, you had much better go out to James Allen's and get a carriage for me, as I shall drive him up myself; and please tell Jim to let me have the old grey, for I can drive a wherry much better than a carriage. Jump up, old fellow, and don't be disappointed; our guest will keep himself for you and your stories."

I stared at Dick; for I wondered at his speaking to such a dignified-looking personage so familiarly, not to say curtly; for I thought that this Mr. Boffin, in spite of his well-known name out of Dickens, must be at the least a senator of these strange people. However, he got up and said, "All right, old oar-wearer, whatever you like; this is not one of my busy days; and though" (with a condescending bow to me) "my pleasure of a talk with this learned guest is put off, I admit that he ought to see your worthy kinsman as soon as possible. Besides, perhaps he will be the better able to answer *my* questions after his own have been answered."

And therewith he turned and swung himself out of the hall.

When he was well gone, I said: "Is it wrong to ask what Mr. Boffin is? whose name, by the way, reminds me of many pleasant hours passed in reading Dickens."

Dick laughed. "Yes, yes," said he, "as it does us, I see you take the allusion. Of course his real name is not Boffin, but Henry Johnson; we only call him Boffin as a joke, partly because he is a dustman, and partly because he will dress so showily, and get as much gold on him as a baron of the Middle Ages. As why should he not if he likes? only we are his special friends, you know, so of course we jest with him."

I held my tongue for some time after that; but Dick went on:

"He is a capital fellow, and you can't help liking him; but he has a weakness: he will spend his time in writing reactionary novels, and is very proud of getting the local colour right, as he calls it; and as he thinks you come from some forgotten corner of the earth, where people are un-happy, and consequently interesting to a story-teller, he thinks he might get some information out of you. O, he will be quite straightforward with you, for that matter. Only for your own comfort beware of him!"

" Well, Dick," said the weaver, doggedly, "I think his novels are very good."

"Of course you do," said Dick; "birds of a feather flock together; mathematics and antiquarian novels stand on much the same footing. But here he comes again."

And in effect the Golden Dustman hailed us from the hall-door; so we all got up and went into the porch, before which, with a strong grey horse in the shafts, stood a carriage ready for us which I could not help noticing. It was light and handy, but had none of that sickening vulgarity which I had known as inseparable from the carriages of our time, especially the "elegant" ones, but was as graceful and pleasant in line as a Wessex waggon. We got in, Dick and

I. The girls, who had come into the porch to see us off, waved their hands to us; the weaver nodded kindly; the dustman bowed as gracefully as a troubadour; Dick shook the reins, and we were off.

CHAPTER IV

A MARKET BY THE WAY

WE turned away from the river at once, and were soon in the main road that runs through Hammersmith. But I should have had no guess as to where I was, if I had not started from the waterside; for King Street was gone, and the highway ran through wide sunny meadows and garden-like tillage. The Creek, which we crossed at once, had been rescued from its culvert, and as we went over its pretty bridge we saw its waters, yet swollen by the tide, covered with gay boats of different sizes. There were houses about, some on the road, some amongst the fields with pleasant lanes leading down to them, and each surrounded by a teeming garden. They were all pretty in design, and as solid as might be, but countrified in appearance, like yeomen's dwellings; some of them of red brick like those by the river, but more of timber and plaster, which were by the necessity of their construction so like mediæval houses of the same materials that I fairly felt as if I were alive in the fourteenth century; a sensation helped out by the costume of the people that we met or passed, in whose dress there was nothing "modern." Almost everybody was gaily dressed, but especially the women, who were so well-looking, or even so handsome, that I could scarcely refrain my tongue from calling my companion's attention to the fact. Some faces I saw that were thoughtful, and in these I noticed great nobility of expression, but none that had a glimmer of unhappiness, and the greater part (we came upon a good many people) were frankly and openly joyous.

I thought I knew the Broadway by the lie of the roads that still met there. On the north side of the road was a range of buildings and courts, low, but very handsomely built and ornamented, and in that way forming a great contrast to the unpretentiousness of the houses round about; while above this lower building rose the steep lead-covered roof and the buttresses and higher part of the wall of a great hall, of a splendid and exuberant style of architecture, of which one can say little more than that it seemed to me to embrace the best qualities of the Gothic of northern Europe with those of the Saracenic and Byzantine, though there was no copying of any one of these styles. On the other, the south side, of the road was an octagonal building with a high roof, not unlike the Baptistry at Florence in outline, except that it was surrounded by a lean-to that clearly made an arcade or cloisters to it: it also was most delicately ornamented.

This whole mass of architecture which we had come upon so suddenly from amidst the pleasant fields was not only exquisitely beautiful in itself, but it bore upon it the expression of such generosity and abundance of life that I was exhilarated to a pitch that I had never yet reached. I fairly chuckled for pleasure. My friend seemed to understand it, and sat looking on me with a pleased and affectionate interest. We had pulled up amongst a crowd of carts, wherein sat handsome healthy-looking people, men, women, and children very gaily dressed, and which were clearly market carts, as they were full of very tempting-looking country produce.

I said, "I need not ask if this is a market, for I see clearly that it is; but what market is it that it is so splendid? And what is the glorious hall there, and what is the building on the south side?"

"O," said he, "it is just our Hammersmith market; and I am glad you like it so much, for we are really proud of it. Of course the hall inside is our winter Mote-House; for in summer we mostly meet in the fields down by the river opposite Barn Elms. The building on our right hand is our theatre: I hope you like it."

"I should be a fool if I didn't," said I.

He blushed a little as he said: "I am glad of that, too, because I had a hand in it; I made the great doors, which are of damascened bronze. We will look at them later in the day, perhaps: but we ought to be getting on now. As to the market, this is not one of our busy days; so we shall do better with it another time, because you will see more people."

I thanked him, and said: "Are these the regular country people? What very pretty girls there are amongst them."

As I spoke, my eye caught the face of a beautiful woman, tall, dark-haired, and white-skinned, dressed in a pretty light-green dress in honour of the season and the hot day, who smiled kindly on me, and more kindly still, I thought, on Dick; so I stopped a minute, but presently went on:

"I ask because I do not see any of the country-looking people I should have expected to see at a market—I mean selling things there."

"I don't understand," said he, "what kind of people you would expect to see; nor quite what you mean by 'country' people. These are the neighbours, and that like they run in the Thames valley. There are parts of these islands which are rougher and rainier than we are here, and there people are rougher in their dress; and they themselves are tougher and more hard-bitten than we are to look at. But some people like their looks better than ours; they say they have more character in them—that's the word. Well, it's a matter of taste.—Anyhow, the cross between us and them generally turns out well," added he, thoughtfully.

I heard him, though my eyes were turned away from him, for that pretty girl was just disappearing through the gate with her big basket of early peas, and I felt that disappointed kind of feeling which overtakes one when one has seen an interesting or lovely face in the streets which one is never likely to see again; and I was silent a little. At last I said: "What I mean is, that I haven't seen any poor people about—not one."

He knit his brows, looked puzzled, and said: "No, naturally; if anybody is poorly, he is likely to be within doors, or at best crawling about the garden: but I don't know of any one sick at present. Why should you expect to see poorly people on the road?"

"No, no," I said; "I don't mean sick people. I mean poor people, you know; rough people."

"No," said he, smiling merrily, "I really do not know.

The fact is, you must come along quick to my great-grand-father, who will understand you better than I do. Come on, Greylocks!" Therewith he shook the reins, and we jogged along merrily eastward.

CHAPTER V

CHILDREN ON THE ROAD

PAST the Broadway there were fewer houses on either side. We presently crossed a pretty little brook that ran across a piece of land dotted over with trees, and awhile after came to another market and town-hall, as we should call it. Although there was nothing familiar to me in its surroundings, I knew pretty well where we were, and was not surprised when my guide said briefly, "Kensington Market."

Just after this we came into a short street of houses; or rather, one long house on either side of the way, built of timber and plaster, and with a pretty arcade over the footway before it.

Quoth Dick: "This is Kensington proper. People are apt to gather here rather thick, for they like the romance of the wood; and naturalists haunt it, too; for it is a wild spot even here, what there is of it; for it does not go far to the south: it goes from here northward and west right over Paddington and a little way down Notting Hill: thence it runs north-east to Primrose Hill, and so on; rather a narrow strip of it gets through Kingsland to Stoke-Newing-ton and Clapton, where it spreads out along the heights above the Lea marshes; on the other side of which, as you know, is Epping Forest holding out a hand to it. This part we are just coming to is called Kensington Gardens; though why 'gardens' I don't know."

I rather longed to say, "Well, *I* know"; but there were so many things about me which I did *not* know, in spite of his assumptions, that I thought it better to hold my tongue.

The road plunged at once into a beautiful wood spreading out on either side, but obviously much further on the north side, where even the oaks and sweet chestnuts were of a good growth; while the quicker-growing trees (amongst which I thought the planes and sycamores too numerous) were very big and fine-grown.

It was exceedingly pleasant in the dappled shadow, for the day was growing as hot as need be, and the coolness and shade soothed my excited mind into a condition of dreamy pleasure, so that I felt as if I should like to go on for ever through that balmy freshness. My companion seemed to share in my feelings, and let the horse go slower and slower as he sat inhaling the green forest scents, chief amongst which was the smell of the trodden bracken near the way-side.

Romantic as this Kensington wood was, however, it was not lonely. We came on many groups both coming and going, or wandering in the edges of the wood. Amongst these were many children from six or eight years old up to sixteen or seventeen. They seemed to me to be especially fine specimens of their race, and were clearly enjoying themselves to the utmost; some of them were hanging about little tents pitched on the greensward, and by some of these fires were burning, with pots hanging over them gipsy fashion. Dick explained to me that there were scattered houses in the forest, and indeed we caught a glimpse of one or two. He said they were mostly quite small, such as used to be called cottages when there were slaves in the land, but they were pleasant enough and fitting for the wood.

"They must be pretty well stocked with children," said I, pointing to the many youngsters about the way.

"O," said he, "these children do not all come from the near houses, the woodland houses, but from the countryside generally. They often make up parties, and come to play in the woods for weeks together in summer-time, living in tents, as you see. We rather encourage them to it; they learn to do things for themselves, and get to notice the wild creatures; and, you see, the less they stew inside houses the better for them. Indeed, I must tell you that many grown people will go to live in the forests through the summer; though they for the most part go to the bigger ones, like Windsor, or the Forest of Dean, or the northern wastes. Apart from the other pleasures of it, it gives them a little rough work, which I am sorry to say is getting somewhat scarce for these last fifty years."

He broke off, and then said, "I tell you all this, because I see that if I talk I must be answering questions, which you are thinking, even if you are not speaking them out; but my kinsman will tell you more about it."

I saw that I was likely to get out of my depth again, and so merely for the sake of tiding over an awkwardness and to say something, I said:

"Well, the youngsters here will be all the fresher for school when the summer gets over and they have to go back again."

"School?" he said; "yes, what do you mean by that word? I don't see how it can have anything to do with children. We talk, indeed, of a school of herring, and a school of painting, and in the former sense we might talk of a school of children—but otherwise," said he, laughing, "I must own myself beaten."

Hang it! thought I, I can't open my mouth without digging up some new complexity. I wouldn't try to set my friend right in his etymology; and I thought I had best say nothing about the boy-farms which I had been used to call schools, as I saw pretty clearly that they had disappeared; and so I said after a little fumbling, "I was using the word in the sense of a system of education."

"Education?" said he, meditatively, "I know enough Latin to know that the word must come from *educere*, to lead out; and I have heard it used; but I have never met anybody who could give me a clear explanation of what it means."

You may imagine how my new friends fell in my esteem when I heard this frank avowal; and I said, rather contemptuously, "Well, education means a system of teaching young people."

"Why not old people also?" said he with a twinkle in his eye. "But," he went on, "I can assure you our children learn, whether they go through a 'system of teaching' or not. Why, you will not find one of these children about here, boy or girl, who cannot swim, and every one of them has been used to tumbling about the little forest ponies—there's one of them now! They all of them know how to cook; the bigger

lads can mow; many can thatch and do odd jobs at carpen-
tering; or they know how to keep shop. I can tell you they
know plenty of things."

"Yes, but their mental education, the teaching of their
minds," said I, kindly translating my phrase.

"Guest," said he, "perhaps you have not learned to do
these things I have been speaking about; and if that's the
case, don't you run away with the idea that it doesn't take
some skill to do them, and doesn't give plenty of work for
one's mind: you would change your opinion if you saw a
Dorsetshire lad thatching, for instance. But, however, I
understand you to be speaking of book-learning; and as to
that, it is a simple affair. Most children, seeing books lying
about, manage to read by the time they are four years old;
though I am told it has not always been so. As to writing,
we do not encourage them to scrawl too early (though
scrawl a little they will), because it gets them into a habit of
ugly writing; and what's the use of a lot of ugly writing being
done, when rough printing can be done so easily. You
understand that handsome writing we like, and many
people will write their books out when they make them, or
get them written; I mean books of which only a few copies
are needed—poems, and such like, you know. However, I am
wandering from my lambs; but you must excuse me, for I am
interested in this matter of writing, being myself a fair writer."

"Well," said I, "about the children; when they know
how to read and write, don't they learn something else—
languages, for instance?"

"Of course," he said; "sometimes even before they can
read, they can talk French, which is the nearest language
talked on the other side of the water; and they soon get to
know German also, which is talked by a huge number of
communes and colleges on the mainland. These are the
principal languages we speak in these islands, along with
English or Welsh, or Irish, which is another form of Welsh;
and children pick them up very quickly, because their elders
all know them; and besides our guests from oversea often
bring their children with them, and the little ones get
together, and rub their speech into one another."

"And the older languages?" said I.

"O yes," said he, " they mostly learn Latin and Greek

along with the modern ones, when they do anything more than merely pick up the latter."

"And history?" said I; "how do you teach history?"

"Well," said he, "when a person can read, of course he reads what he likes to; and he can easily get some one to tell him what are the best books to read on such or such a subject, or to explain what he doesn't understand in the books when he is reading them."

"Well," said I, "what else do they learn? I suppose they don't all learn history?"

"No, no," said he; "some don't care about it; in fact, I don't think many do. I have heard my great-grandfather say that it is mostly in periods of turmoil and strife and confusion that people care much about history; and you know," said my friend, with an amiable smile, "we are not like that now. No; many people study facts about the make of things and the matters of cause and effect, so that knowledge increases on us, if that be good; and some, as you heard about friend Bob yonder, will spend time over mathematics. 'Tis no use forcing people's tastes."

Said I: "But you don't mean that children learn all these things?"

Said he: "That depends on what you mean by children; and also you must remember how much they differ. As a rule, they don't do much reading, except for a few story-books, till they are about fifteen years old; we don't encourage early bookishness, though you will find some children who *will* take to books very early; which perhaps is not good for them; but it's no use thwarting them; and very often it doesn't last long with them, and they find their level before they are twenty years old. You see, children are mostly given to imitating their elders, and when they see most people about them engaged in genuinely amusing work, like house-building and street-paving, and gardening, and the like, that is what they want to be doing; so I don't think we need fear having too many book-learned men."

What could I say? I sat and held my peace, for fear of fresh entanglements. Besides, I was using my eyes with all my might, wondering as the old horse jogged on, when I should come into London proper, and what it would be like now.

But my companion couldn't let his subject quite drop, and went on meditatively:

"After all, I don't know that it does them much harm, even if they do grow up book-students. Such people as that, 'tis a great pleasure seeing them so happy over work which is not much sought for. And besides, these students are generally such pleasant people; so kind and sweet-tempered; so humble, and at the same time so anxious to teach everybody all that they know. Really, I like those that I have met prodigiously."

This seemed to me such *very* queer talk that I was on the point of asking him another question; when just as we came to the top of a rising ground, down a long glade of the wood on my right I caught sight of a stately building whose outline was familiar to me, and I cried out, "Westminster Abbey!"

"Yes," said Dick, "Westminster Abbey—what there is left of it."

"Why, what have you done with it?" quoth I in terror.

"What have *we* done with it?" said he; "nothing much, save clean it. But you know the whole outside was spoiled centuries ago: as to the inside, that remains in its beauty after the great clearance, which took place over a hundred years ago, of the beastly monuments to fools and knaves, which once blocked it up, as great-grandfather says."

We went on a little further, and I looked to the right again, and said, in rather a doubtful tone of voice, "Why, there are the Houses of Parliament! Do you still use them?"

He burst out laughing, and was some time before he could control himself; then he clapped me on the back and said:

"I take you, neighbour; you may well wonder at our keeping them standing, and I know something about that, and my old kinsman has given me books to read about the strange game that they played there. Use them! Well, yes, they are used for a sort of subsidiary market, and a storage place for manure, and they are handy for that, being on the water-side. I believe it was intended to pull them down quite at the beginning of our days; but there was, I am told, a queer antiquarian society, which had done some service in past times, and which straightway set up its pipe against their destruction, as it has done with many other buildings, which most people looked upon as worthless, and public nuisances; and it was so energetic, and had such good reasons to give, that it generally gained its point; and I must say that when all is said I am glad of it: because you know at the worst these silly old buildings serve as a kind of foil to the beautiful ones which we build now. You will see several others in these parts; the place my great-grandfather lives in, for instance, and a big building called St. Paul's. And you see, in this matter we need not grudge a few poorish buildings standing, because we can always build elsewhere; nor need we be anxious as to the breeding of pleasant work in such matters, for there is always room for more and more work in a new building, even without making it pretentious. For instance, elbow-room *within* doors is to me so delightful that if I were driven to it I would almost sacrifice out-door space to it. Then, of course, there is the ornament, which, as we must all allow, may easily be overdone in mere living houses, but can hardly be in mote-halls and markets, and so forth. I must tell you, though, that my great-grandfather sometimes tells me I am a little cracked on this subject of fine building; and indeed I *do* think that the energies of mankind are chiefly of use to them for such work; for in that direction I can see no end to the work, while in many others a limit does seem possible."

CHAPTER VI

A LITTLE SHOPPING

AS he spoke, we came suddenly out of the woodland into a short street of handsomely built houses, which my companion named to me at once as Piccadilly: the lower part of these I should have called shops, if it had not been that, as far as I could see, the people were ignorant of the arts of buying and selling. Wares were displayed in their finely designed fronts, as if to tempt people in, and people stood and looked at them, or went in and came out with parcels under their arms, just like the real thing. On each side of the street ran an elegant arcade to protect foot-passengers, as in some of the old Italian cities. About half-way down, a huge building of the kind I was now prepared to expect told me that this also was a centre of some kind, and had its special public buildings.

Said Dick: "Here, you see, is another market on a different plan from most others: the upper stories of these houses are used for guest-houses; for people from all about the country are apt to drift up hither from time to time, as folk are very thick upon the ground, which you will see evidence of presently, and there are people who are fond of crowds, though I can't say that I am."

I couldn't help smiling to see how long a tradition would last. Here was the ghost of London still asserting itself as a centre,—an intellectual centre, for aught I knew. However, I said nothing, except that I asked him to drive very slowly, as the things in the booths looked exceedingly pretty.

"Yes," said he, "this is a very good market for pretty things, and is mostly kept for the handsomer goods, as the Houses-of-Parliament market, where they set out cabbages and turnips and such like things, along with beer and the rougher kind of wine, is so near."

Then he looked at me curiously, and said, "Perhaps you would like to do a little shopping, as 'tis called?"

I looked at what I could see of my rough blue duds, which I had plenty of opportunity of contrasting with the gay attire of the citizens we had come across; and I thought that if, as seemed likely, I should presently be shown about as a curiosity for the amusement of this most unbusinesslike people, I should like to look a little less like a discharged ship's purser. But in spite of all that had happened, my hand went down into my pocket again, where to my dismay it met nothing metallic except two rusty old keys, and I remembered that amidst our talk in the guest hall at Hammersmith I had taken the cash out of my pocket to show to the pretty Annie, and had left it lying there. My face fell fifty per cent., and Dick, beholding me, said rather sharply:

"Hilloa, Guest! what's the matter now? Is it a wasp?"

"No," said I, "but I've left it behind."

"Well," said he, "whatever you have left behind, you can get in this market again, so don't trouble yourself about it."

I had come to my senses by this time, and remembering the astounding customs of this country, had no mind for another lecture on social economy and the Edwardian coinage; so I said only:

"My clothes— Couldn't I? You see— What do you think could be done about them?"

He didn't seem in the least inclined to laugh, but said quite gravely:

"O don't get new clothes yet. You see, my great-grandfather is an antiquarian, and he will want to see you just as you are. And, you know, I mustn't preach to you, but surely it wouldn't be right for you to take away people's pleasure of studying your attire, by just going and making yourself like everybody else. You feel that, don't you?" said he, earnestly.

I did *not* feel it my duty to set myself up for a scarecrow amidst this beauty-loving people, but I saw I had got across some ineradicable prejudice, and that it wouldn't do to quarrel with my new friend. So I merely said, "O certainly, certainly."

"Well," said he, pleasantly, "you may as well see what the inside of these booths is like: think of something you want."

Said I: "Could I get some tobacco and a pipe?"

"Of course," said he; "what was I thinking of, not asking you before? Well, Bob is always telling me that we non-smokers are a selfish lot, and I'm afraid he is right. But come along; here is a place just handy."

Therewith he drew rein and jumped down, and I followed. A very handsome woman, splendidly clad in figured silk, was slowly passing by, looking into the windows as she went. To her quoth Dick: "Maiden, would you kindly hold our horse while we go in for a little?" She nodded to us with a kind smile, and fell to patting the horse with her pretty hand.

"What a beautiful creature!" said I to Dick as we entered.

"What, old Greylocks?" said he, with a sly grin.

"No, no," said I; "Goldylocks,—the lady."

"Well, so she is," said he. "'Tis a good job there are so many of them that every Jack may have his Jill: else I fear that we should get fighting for them. Indeed," said he, becoming very grave, "I don't say that it does not happen.

C

even now, sometimes. For you know love is not a very reasonable thing, and perversity and self-will are commoner than some of our moralists think." He added, in a still more sombre tone: "Yes, only a month ago there was a mishap down by us, that in the end cost the lives of two men and a woman, and, as it were, put out the sunlight for us for a while. Don't ask me about it just now; I may tell you about it later on."

By this time we were within the shop or booth, which had a counter, and shelves on the walls, all very neat, though without any pretence of showiness, but otherwise not very different to what I had been used to. Within were a couple of children—a brown-skinned boy of about twelve, who sat reading a book, and a pretty little girl of about a year older, who was sitting also reading behind the counter; they were obviously brother and sister.

"Good morning, little neighbours," said Dick. "My friend here wants tobacco and a pipe; can you help him?"

"O yes, certainly," said the girl with a sort of demure alertness which was somewhat amusing. The boy looked up, and fell to staring at my outlandish attire, but presently reddened and turned his head, as if he knew that he was not behaving prettily.

"Dear neighbour," said the girl, with the most solemn countenance of a child playing at keeping shop, "what tobacco is it you would like?"

"Latakia," quoth I, feeling as if I were assisting at a child's game, and wondering whether I should get anything but make-believe.

But the girl took a dainty little basket from a shelf beside her, went to a jar, and took out a lot of tobacco and put the filled basket down on the counter before me, where I could both smell and see that it was excellent Latakia.

"But you haven't weighed it," said I, "and—and how much am I to take?"

"Why," she said, "I advise you to cram your bag, because you may be going where you can't get Latakia. Where is your bag?"

I fumbled about, and at last pulled out my piece of cotton print which does duty with me for a tobacco pouch. But the girl looked at it with some disdain, and said:

"Dear neighbour, I can give you something much better than that cotton rag." And she tripped up the shop and came back presently, and as she passed the boy whispered something in his ear, and he nodded and got up and went out. The girl held up in her finger and thumb a red morocco bag, gaily embroidered, and said, "There, I have chosen one for you, and you are to have it: it is pretty, and will hold a lot."

Therewith she fell to cramming it with the tobacco, and laid it down by me and said, "Now for the pipe: that also you must let me choose for you; there are three pretty ones just come in."

She disappeared again, and came back with a big-bowled pipe in her hand, carved out of some hard wood very elaborately, and mounted in gold sprinkled with little gems. It was, in short, as pretty and gay a toy as I had ever seen; something like the best kind of Japanese work, but better.

"Dear me!" said I, when I set eyes on it, "this is altogether too grand for me, or for anybody but the Emperor of the World. Besides, I shall lose it: I always lose my pipes."

The child seemed rather dashed, and said, " Don't you like it, neighbour?"

"O yes," I said, "of course I like it."

"Well, then, take it," said she, "and don't trouble about losing it. What will it matter if you do? Somebody is sure to find it, and he will use it, and you can get another."

I took it out of her hand to look at it, and while I did so, forgot my caution, and said, "But however am I to pay for such a thing as this?"

Dick laid his hand on my shoulder as I spoke, and turning I met his eyes with a comical expression in them, which warned me against another exhibition of extinct commercial morality; so I reddened and held my tongue, while the girl simply looked at me with the deepest gravity, as if I were a foreigner blundering in my speech, for she clearly didn't understand me a bit.

"Thank you so very much," I said at last, effusively, as I put the pipe in my pocket, not without a qualm of doubt as to whether I shouldn't find myself before a magistrate presently.

"O, you are so very welcome," said the little lass, with an

affectation of grown-up manners at their best which was very quaint. "It is such a pleasure to serve dear old gentlemen like you; specially when one can see at once that you have come from far over sea."

"Yes, my dear," quoth I, "I have been a great traveller."

As I told this lie from pure politeness, in came the lad again, with a tray in his hands, on which I saw a long flask and two beautiful glasses. "Neighbours," said the girl (who did all the talking, her brother being very shy, clearly), "please to drink a glass to us before you go, since we do not have guests like this every day."

Therewith the boy put the tray on the counter and solemnly poured out a straw-coloured wine into the long bowls. Nothing loth, I drank, for I was thirsty with the hot day; and thinks I, I am yet in the world, and the grapes of the Rhine have not yet lost their flavour; for if ever I drank good Steinberg, I drank it that morning; and I made a mental note to ask Dick how they managed to make fine wine when there were no longer labourers compelled to drink rot-gut instead of the fine wine which they themselves made.

"Don't you drink a glass to us, dear little neighbours?" said I.

"I don't drink wine," said the lass; "I like lemonade better: but I wish your health!"

"And I like ginger-beer better," said the little lad.

Well, well, thought I, neither have children's tastes changed much. And therewith we gave them good day and went out of the booth.

To my disappointment, like a change in a dream, a tall old man was holding our horse instead of the beautiful woman. He explained to us that the maiden could not wait, and that he had taken her place; and he winked at us and laughed when he saw how our faces fell, so that we had nothing for it but to laugh also.

"Where are you going?" said he to Dick.

"To Bloomsbury," said Dick.

"If you two don't want to be alone, I'll come with you," said the old man.

"All right," said Dick, "tell me when you want to get down and I'll stop for you. Let's get on."

So we got under way again; and I asked if children generally waited on people in the markets. "Often enough," said he, "when it isn't a matter of dealing with heavy weights, but by no means always. The children like to amuse themselves with it, and it is good for them, because they handle a lot of diverse wares and get to learn about them, how they are made, and where they come from, and so on. Besides, it is such very easy work that anybody can do it. It is said that in the early days of our epoch there were a good many people who were hereditarily afflicted with a disease called Idleness, because they were the direct descendants of those who in the bad times used to force other people to work for them—the people, you know, who are called slave-holders or employers of labour in the history books. Well, these Idleness-stricken people used to serve booths *all* their time, because they were fit for so little. Indeed, I believe that at one time they were actually *compelled* to do some such work, because they, especially the women, got so ugly and produced such ugly children if their disease was not treated sharply, that the neighbours couldn't stand it. However, I am happy to say that all that is gone by now; the disease is either extinct, or exists in such a mild form that a short course of aperient medicine carries it off. It is sometimes called the Blue-devils now, or the Mulleygrubs. Queer names, ain't they?"

"Yes," said I, pondering much. But the old man broke in:

"Yes, all that is true, neighbour; and I have seen some of those poor women grown old. But my father used to know some of them when they were young; and he said that they were as little like young women as might be: they had hands like bunches of skewers, and wretched little arms like sticks; and waists like hour glasses, and thin lips and peaked noses and pale cheeks; and they were always pretending to be offended at anything you said or did to them. No wonder they bore ugly children, for no one except men like them could be in love with them—poor things!"

He stopped, and seemed to be musing on his past life, and then said:

"And do you know, neighbours, that once on a time people were still anxious about that disease of Idleness: at one time we gave ourselves a great deal of trouble in trying to cure people of it. Have you not read any of the medical books on the subject?"

"No," said I; for the old man was speaking to me.

"Well," said he, "it was thought at the time that it was the survival of the old mediæval disease of leprosy: it seems it was very catching, for many of the people afflicted by it were much secluded, and were waited upon by a special class of diseased persons queerly dressed up, so that they might be known. They wore amongst other garments, breeches made of worsted velvet, that stuff which used to be called plush some years ago."

All this seemed very interesting to me, and I should like to have made the old man talk more. But Dick got rather restive under so much ancient history: besides, I suspect he wanted to keep me as fresh as he could for his great-grandfather. So he burst out laughing at last, and said: "Excuse me, neighbours, but I can't help it. Fancy people not liking to work !—it's too ridiculous. Why, even you like to work, old fellow—sometimes," said he, affectionately patting the old horse with the whip. "What a queer disease! it may well be called Mulleygrubs!"

And he laughed out again most boisterously; rather too much so, I thought, for his usual good manners; and I laughed with him for company's sake, but from the teeth outward only; for I saw nothing funny in people not liking to work, as you may well imagine.

CHAPTER VII

TRAFALGAR SQUARE

AND now again I was busy looking about me, for we were quite clear of Piccadilly Market, and were in a region of elegantly-built much ornamented houses, which I should have called villas if they had been ugly and pretentious, which was very far from being the case. Each house stood in a garden carefully cultivated, and running over with flowers. The blackbirds were singing their best amidst the

garden-trees, which, except for a bay here and there, and
occasional groups of limes, seemed to be all fruit trees:
there were a great many cherry trees, now all laden with
fruit, and several times as we passed by a garden we were
offered baskets of fine fruit by children and young girls.
Amidst all these gardens and houses it was of course
impossible to trace the sites of the old streets, but it seemed
to me that the main roadways were the same as of old.

We came presently into a large open space, sloping somewhat toward the south, the sunny site of which had been
taken advantage of for planting an orchard, mainly, as I
could see, of apricot trees, in the midst of which was a pretty
gay little structure of wood, painted and gilded, that looked
like a refreshment stall. From the southern side of the said
orchard ran a long road, chequered over with the shadow of
tall old pear trees, at the end of which showed the high
tower of the Parliament House, or Dung Market.

A strange sensation came over me; I shut my eyes to keep
out the sight of the sun glittering on this fair abode of
gardens, and for a moment there passed before them a
phantasmagoria of another day. A great space surrounded
by tall ugly houses, with an ugly church at the corner and
a nondescript ugly cupolaed building at my back; the roadway thronged with a sweltering and excited crowd, dominated by omnibuses crowded with spectators. In the
midst a paved be-fountained square, populated only by a
few men dressed in blue, and a good many singularly ugly
bronze images (one on top of a tall column). The said
square guarded up to the edge of the roadway by a four-
fold line of big men clad in blue, and across the southern
roadway the helmets of a band of horse-soldiers, dead white
in the greyness of the chilly November afternoon——

I opened my eyes to the sunlight again and looked
round me, and cried out among the whispering trees and
odorous blossoms, "Trafalgar Square!"

"Yes," said Dick, who had drawn rein again, "so it is.
I don't wonder at your finding the name ridiculous: but
after all, it was nobody's business to alter it, since the name
of a dead folly doesn't bite. Yet sometimes I think we
might have given it a name which would have commem-
orated the great battle which was fought on the spot itself

in 1952,—*that* was important enough, if the historians don't lie."

"Which they generally do, or at least did," said the old man. "For instance, what can you make of this, neighbours? I have read a muddled account in a book—O a stupid book!—called James' Social Democratic History, of a fight which took place here in or about the year 1887 (I am bad at dates). Some people, says this story, were going to hold a ward-mote here, or some such thing, and the Government of London, or the Council, or the Commission, or what not other barbarous half-hatched body of fools, fell upon these citizens (as they were then called) with the armed hand. That seems too ridiculous to be true; but according to this version of the story, nothing much came of it, which certainly *is* too ridiculous to be true."

"Well," quoth I, "but after all your Mr. James is right so far, and it *is* true; except that there was no fighting, merely unarmed and peaceable people attacked by ruffians armed with bludgeons."

"And they put up with that?" said Dick, with the first unpleasant expression I had seen on his good-tempered face.

Said I, reddening: "We *had* to put up with it; we couldn't help it."

The old man looked at me keenly, and said: "You seem to know a great deal about it, neighbour! And is it really true that nothing came of it?"

"This came of it," said I, "that a good many people were sent to prison because of it."

"What, of the bludgeoners?" said the old man. "Poor devils!"

"No, no," said I, "of the bludgeoned."

Said the old man rather severely: "Friend, I expect that you have been reading some rotten collection of lies, and have been taken in by it too easily."

"I assure you," said I, "what I have been saying is true."

"Well, well, I am sure you think so, neighbour," said the old man, "but I don't see why you should be so cocksure."

As I couldn't explain why, I held my tongue. Meanwhile Dick, who had been sitting with knit brows, cogitating, spoke at last, and said gently and rather sadly:

"How strange to think that there have been men like

ourselves, and living in this beautiful and happy country, who I suppose had feelings and affections like ourselves, who could yet do such dreadful things."

"Yes," said I, in a didactic tone; "yet after all, even those days were a great improvement on the days that had gone before them. Have you not read of the Mediæval period, and the ferocity of its criminal laws; and how in those days men fairly seemed to have enjoyed tormenting their fellow-men?—nay, for the matter of that, they made their God a tormentor and a jailer rather than anything else."

"Yes," said Dick, "there are good books on that period also, some of which I have read. But as to the great improvement of the nineteenth century, I don't see it. After all, the Mediæval folk acted after their conscience, as your remark about their God (which is true) shows, and they were ready to bear what they inflicted on others; whereas the nineteenth century ones were hypocrites and pretended to be humane, and yet went on tormenting those whom they dared to treat so by shutting them up in prison, for no reason at all, except that they were what they themselves, the prison-masters, had forced them to be. O, it's horrible to think of!"

" But perhaps," said I, " they did not know what the prisons were like."

Dick seemed roused, and even angry. "More shame for them," said he, "when you and I know it all these years afterwards. Look you, neighbour, they couldn't fail to know what a disgrace a prison is to the Commonwealth at the best, and that their prisons were a good step on towards being at the worst."

Quoth I: "But have you no prisons at all now?"

As soon as the words were out of my mouth, I felt that I had made a mistake, for Dick flushed red and frowned, and the old man looked surprised and pained; and presently Dick said angrily, yet as if restraining himself somewhat:

"Man alive! how can you ask such a question? Have I not told you that we know what a prison means by the undoubted evidence of really trustworthy books, helped out by our own imaginations? And haven't you specially called me to notice that the people about the roads and streets look happy? and how could they look happy if they knew that their neighbours were shut up in prison, while they bore such things quietly? And if there were people in prison, you couldn't hide it from folk, like you may an occasional man-slaying; because that isn't done of set purpose, with a lot of people backing up the slayer in cold blood, as this prison business is. Prisons, indeed! O no, no, no!"

He stopped, and began to cool down, and said in a kind voice: "But forgive me! I needn't be so hot about it, since there are *not* any prisons: I'm afraid you will think the worse of me for losing my temper. Of course, you, coming from the outlands, cannot be expected to know about these things. And now I'm afraid I have made you feel uncomfortable."

In a way he had; but he was so generous in his heat, that I liked him the better for it, and I said: "No, really 'tis all my fault for being so stupid. Let me change the subject, and ask you what the stately building is on our left just showing at the end of that grove of plane trees?"

"Ah," he said, "that is an old building built before the middle of the twentieth century, and as you see, in a queer fantastic style not over beautiful; but there are some fine things inside it, too, mostly pictures, some very old. It is called the National Gallery; I have sometimes puzzled as to what the name means: anyhow, nowadays wherever there is a place where pictures are kept as curiosities permanently it is called a National Gallery, perhaps after this one. Of course there are a good many of them up and down the country."

I didn't try to enlighten him, feeling the task too heavy; but I pulled out my magnificent pipe and fell a-smoking, and the old horse jogged on again. As we went, I said:

"This pipe is a very elaborate toy, and you seem so reasonable in this country, and your architecture is so good, that I rather wonder at your turning out such trivialities."

It struck me as I spoke that this was rather ungrateful of me, after having received such a fine present; but Dick didn't seem to notice my bad manners, but said:

"Well, I don't know; it *is* a pretty thing, and since nobody need make such things unless they like, I don't see why they shouldn't make them, *if* they like. Of course, if carvers were scarce they would all be busy on the architecture, as you call it, and then these 'toys' (a good word) would not be made; but since there are plenty of people who can carve—in fact, almost everybody, and as work is somewhat scarce, or we are afraid it may be, folk do not discourage this kind of petty work."

He mused a little, and seemed somewhat perturbed; but presently his face cleared, and he said: "After all, you must admit that the pipe is a very pretty thing, with the little people under the trees all cut so clean and sweet;—too elaborate for a pipe, perhaps, but—well, it is very pretty."

"Too valuable for its use, perhaps," said I.

"What's that?" said he; "I don't understand."

I was just going in a helpless way to try to make him understand, when we came by the gates of a big rambling building, in which work of some sort seemed going on. "What building is that?" said I, eagerly; for it was a pleasure amidst all these strange things to see something a little like what I was used to: "it seems to be a factory."

"Yes," he said, "I think I know what you mean, and that's what it is; but we don't call them factories now, but Banded-workshops; that is, places where people collect who want to work together."

"I suppose," said I, "power of some sort is used there?"

"No, no," said he. "Why should people collect together to use power, when they can have it at the places where they live, or hard by, any two or three of them; or any one, for the matter of that? No; folk collect in these Banded-workshops to do hand-work in which working together is necessary or convenient; such work is often very pleasant. In there, for instance, they make pottery and glass,—there, you can see the tops of the furnaces. Well, of course it's handy to have fair-sized ovens and kilns and glass-pots, and a good lot of things to use them for: though of course there are a good many such places, as it would be ridiculous if a man had a liking for pot-making or glass-blowing that he should have to live in one place or be obliged to forego the work he liked."

"I see no smoke coming from the furnaces," said I.

"Smoke?" said Dick; "why should you see smoke?"

I held my tongue, and he went on: "It's a nice place

inside, though as plain as you see outside. As to the crafts, throwing the clay must be jolly work: the glass-blowing is rather a sweltering job; but some folk like it very much indeed; and I don't much wonder: there is such a sense of power, when you have got deft in it, in dealing with the hot metal. It makes a lot of pleasant work," said he, smiling, "for however much care you take of such goods, break they will, one day or another, so there is always plenty to do."

I held my tongue and pondered.

We came just here on a gang of men road-mending, which delayed us a little; but I was not sorry for it; for all I had seen hitherto seemed a mere part of a summer holiday; and I wanted to see how this folk would set to on a piece of real necessary work. They had been resting, and had only just begun work again as we came up; so that the rattle of the picks was what woke me from my musing. There were about a dozen of them, strong young men, looking much like a boating party at Oxford would have looked in the days I remembered, and not more troubled with their work: their outer raiment lay on the road-side in an orderly pile under the guardianship of a six-year-old boy, who had his arm thrown over the neck of a big mastiff, who was as happily lazy as if the summer day had been made for him alone. As I eyed the pile of clothes, I could see the gleam of gold and silk embroidery on it, and judged that some of these workmen had tastes akin to those of the Golden Dust-man of Hammersmith. Beside them lay a good big basket that had hints about it of cold pie and wine: a half-dozen of young women stood by watching the work or the workers, both of which were worth watching, for the latter smote great strokes and were very deft in their labour, and as handsome clean-built fellows as you might find a dozen of in a summer day. They were laughing and talking merrily with each other and the women, but presently their foreman looked up and saw our way stopped. So he stayed his pick and sang out, "Spell ho, mates! here are neighbours want to get past." Whereon the others stopped also, and drawing around us, helped the old horse by easing our wheels over the half undone road, and then, like men with a pleasant task on hand, hurried back to their work, only stopping to give us a smiling good-day; so that the sound of the picks broke out again before Greylocks had taken to his jog-trot. Dick looked back over his shoulder at them and said:

"They are in luck to-day: it's right down good sport trying how much pick-work one can get into an hour; and I can see those neighbours know their business well. It is not a mere matter of strength getting on quickly with such work; is it, guest?"

"I should think not," said I, "but to tell you the truth, I have never tried my hand at it."

"Really?" said he gravely, "that seems a pity; it is good work for hardening the muscles, and I like it; though I admit it is pleasanter the second week than the first. Not that I am a good hand at it: the fellows used to chaff me at one job where I was working, I remember, and sing out to me, 'Well rowed, stroke!' 'Put your back into it, bow!'"

"Not much of a joke," quoth I.

"Well," said Dick, "everything seems like a joke when we have a pleasant spell of work on, and good fellows merry about us; we feel so happy, you know." Again I pondered silently.

CHAPTER VIII

AN OLD FRIEND

WE now turned into a pleasant lane where the branches of great plane trees nearly met overhead, but behind them lay low houses standing rather close together.

"This is Long Acre," quoth Dick; "so there must once have been a cornfield here. How curious it is that places change so, and yet keep their old names! Just look how thick the houses stand! and they are still going on building, look you!"

"Yes," said the old man, "but I think the cornfields must have been built over before the middle of the nineteenth century. I have heard that about here was one of the thickest parts of the town. But I must get down here, neighbours; I have got to call on a friend who lives in the gardens behind this Long Acre. Good-bye and good luck, Guest!"

And he jumped down and strode away vigorously, like a young man.

"How old should you say that neighbour will be?" said I to Dick as we lost sight of him; for I saw that he was old, and yet he looked dry and sturdy like a piece of old oak; a type of old man I was not used to seeing.

"O, about ninety, I should say," said Dick.

"How long-lived your people must be!" said I.

"Yes," said Dick, "certainly we have beaten the three-score-and-ten of the old Jewish proverb-book. But then you see that was written of Syria, a hot dry country, where people live faster than in our temperate climate. However, I don't think it matters much, so long as a man is healthy and happy while he *is* alive. But now, Guest, we are so near to my old kinsman's dwelling-place that I think you had better keep all future questions for him."

I nodded a yes; and therewith we turned to the left, and went down a gentle slope through some beautiful rose-gardens, laid out on what I took to be the site of Endell Street. We passed on, and Dick drew rein an instant as we came across a long straightish road with houses scantily scattered up and down it. He waved his hand right and left, and said, "Holborn that side, Oxford Road that. This was once a very important part of the crowded city outside the ancient walls of the Roman and Mediæval burg: many of the feudal nobles of the Middle Ages, we are told, had big houses on either side of Holborn. I daresay you remember that the Bishop of Ely's house is mentioned in Shakespeare's play of King Richard II.; and there are some remains of that still left. However, this road is not of the same importance, now that the ancient city is gone, walls and all."

He drove on again, while I smiled faintly to think how the nineteenth century, of which such big words have been said, counted for nothing in the memory of this man, who read Shakespeare and had not forgotten the Middle Ages.

We crossed the road into a short narrow lane between the gardens, and came out again into a wide road, on one side of which was a great and long building, turning its

gables away from the highway, which I saw at once was
another public group. Opposite to it was a wide space of
greenery, without any wall or fence of any kind. I looked
through the trees and saw beyond them a pillared portico
quite familiar to me—no less old a friend, in fact, than the
British Museum. It rather took my breath away, amidst
all the strange things I had seen; but I held my tongue and
let Dick speak. Said he:

"Yonder is the British Museum, where my great-grandfather mostly lives; so I won't say much about it. The
building on the left is the Museum Market, and I think we
had better turn in there for a minute or two; for Greylocks
will be wanting his rest and his oats; and I suppose you will
stay with my kinsman the greater part of the day; and to
say the truth, there may be some one there whom I particularly want to see, and perhaps have a long talk with."

He blushed and sighed, not altogether with pleasure, I
thought; so of course I said nothing, and he turned the
horse under an archway which brought us into a very large
paved quadrangle, with a big sycamore tree in each corner
and a plashing fountain in the midst. Near the fountain
were a few market stalls, with awnings over them of gay
striped linen cloth, about which some people, mostly
women and children, were moving quietly, looking at the
goods exposed there. The ground floor of the building
round the quadrangle was occupied by a wide arcade or
cloister, whose fanciful but strong architecture I could not
enough admire. Here also a few people were sauntering or
sitting reading on the benches.

Dick said to me apologetically: "Here as elsewhere there
is little doing to-day; on a Friday you would see it thronged,
and gay with people, and in the afternoon there is generally
music about the fountain. However, I daresay we shall
have a pretty good gathering at our mid-day meal."

We drove through the quadrangle and by an archway,
into a large handsome stable on the other side, where we
speedily stalled the old nag and made him happy with
horse-meat, and then turned and walked back again
through the market, Dick looking rather thoughtful, as it
seemed to me.

I noticed that people couldn't help looking at me rather

hard; and considering my clothes and theirs, I didn't wonder; but whenever they caught my eye they made me a very friendly sign of greeting.

We walked straight into the forecourt of the Museum, where, except that the railings were gone, and the whispering boughs of the trees were all about, nothing seemed changed; the very pigeons were wheeling about the building and clinging to the ornaments of the pediment as I had seen them of old.

Dick seemed grown a little absent, but he could not forbear giving me an architectural note, and said:

"It is rather an ugly old building, isn't it? Many people have wanted to pull it down and rebuild it: and perhaps if work does really get scarce we may yet do so. But, as my great-grandfather will tell you, it would not be quite a straightforward job; for there are wonderful collections in there of all kinds of antiquities, besides an enormous library with many exceedingly beautiful books in it, and many most useful ones as genuine records, texts of ancient works and the like; and the worry and anxiety, and even risk, there would be in moving all this has saved the buildings themselves. Besides, as we said before, it is not a bad thing to have some record of what our forefathers thought a handsome building. For there is plenty of labour and material in it."

"I see there is," said I, "and I quite agree with you. But now hadn't we better make haste to see your great-grandfather?"

In fact, I could not help seeing that he was rather dallying with the time. He said, "Yes, we will go into the house in a minute. My kinsman is too old to do much work in the Museum, where he was a custodian of the books for many years; but he still lives here a good deal; indeed I think," said he, smiling, "that he looks upon himself as a part of the books, or the books a part of him, I don't know which."

He hesitated a little longer, then flushing up, took my hand, and saying, "Come along, then!" led me toward the door of one of the old official dwellings.

CHAPTER IX

CONCERNING LOVE

"YOUR kinsman doesn't much care for beautiful buildings, then," said I, as we entered the rather dreary
classical house; which indeed was as bare as need be, except
for some big pots of the June flowers which stood about
here and there: though it was very clean and nicely whitewashed.

"O, I don't know," said Dick, rather absently. "He is
getting old, certainly, for he is over a hundred and five,
and no doubt he doesn't care about moving. But of course
he could live in a prettier house if he liked: he is not obliged
to live in one place any more than any one else. This way,
Guest."

And he led the way upstairs, and opening a door we went
into a fair-sized room of the old type, as plain as the rest
of the house, with a few necessary pieces of furniture, and
those very simple and even rude, but solid and with a good
deal of carving about them, well designed but rather
crudely executed. At the furthest corner of the room, at a
desk near the window, sat a little old man in a roomy oak
chair, well be-cushioned. He was dressed in a sort of
Norfolk-jacket of blue serge worn threadbare, with breeches
of the same, and grey worsted stockings. He jumped up
from his chair, and cried out in a voice of considerable
volume for such an old man, "Welcome, Dick, my lad;
Clara is here, and will be more than glad to see you; so
keep your heart up."

"Clara here?" quoth Dick; "if I had known, I would not
have brought— At least, I mean I would——"

He was stuttering and confused, clearly because he was
anxious to say nothing to make me feel one too many.
But the old man, who had not seen me at first, helped
him out by coming forward and saying to me in a kind
tone:

"Pray pardon me, for I did not notice that Dick, who is
big enough to hide anybody, you know, had brought a
friend with him. A most hearty welcome to you! All the
more, as I almost hope that you are going to amuse an old

man by giving him news from over sea, for I can see that you are come from over the water and far-off countries."

He looked at me thoughtfully, almost anxiously, as he said in a changed voice, "Might I ask you where you come from, as you are so clearly a stranger?"

I said in an absent way: "I used to live in England, and now I am come back again; and I slept last night at the Hammersmith Guest House."

He bowed gravely, but seemed, I thought, a little disappointed with my answer. As for me, I was now looking at him harder than good manners allowed of, perhaps; for in truth his face, dried-apple-like as it was, seemed strangely familiar to me; as if I had seen it before—in a looking-glass it might be, said I to myself.

"Well," said the old man, "wherever you come from, you are come among friends. And I see my kinsman Richard Hammond has an air about him as if he had brought you here for me to do something for you. Is that so, Dick?"

Dick, who was getting still more absent-minded and kept looking uneasily at the door, managed to say, "Well, yes, kinsman: our guest finds things much altered, and cannot understand it; nor can I; so I thought I would bring him to you, since you know more of all that has happened within the last two hundred years than anybody else does.—What's that?"

And he turned toward the door again. We heard footsteps outside; the door opened, and in came a very beautiful young woman, who stopped short on seeing Dick, and flushed as red as a rose, but faced him nevertheless. Dick looked at her hard, and half reached out his hand toward her, and his whole face quivered with emotion.

The old man did not leave them long in this shy discomfort, but said, smiling with an old man's mirth: "Dick, my lad, and you, my dear Clara, I rather think that we two oldsters are in your way; for I think you will have plenty to say to each other. You had better go into Nelson's room up above; I know he has gone out; and he has just been covering the walls all over with mediæval books, so it will be pretty enough even for you two and your renewed pleasure."

The girl reached out her hand to Dick, and taking his led

him out of the room, looking straight before her; but it was easy to see that her blushes came from happiness, not anger; as, indeed, love is far more self-conscious than wrath.

When the door had shut on them the old man turned to me, still smiling, and said:

"Frankly, my dear guest, you will do me a great service if you are come to set my old tongue wagging. My love of talk still abides with me, or rather grows on me; and though it is pleasant enough to see these youngsters moving about and playing together so seriously, as if the whole world depended on their kisses (as indeed it does somewhat), yet I don't think my tales of the past interest them much. The last harvest, the last baby, the last knot of carving in the market-place, is history enough for them. It was different, I think, when I was a lad, when we were not so assured of peace and continuous plenty as we are now— Well, well! Without putting you to the question, let me ask you this: Am I to consider you as an enquirer who knows a little of our modern ways of life, or as one who comes from some place where the very foundations of life are different from ours,—do you know anything or nothing about us?"

He looked at me keenly and with growing wonder in his eyes as he spoke; and I answered in a low voice:

"I know only so much of your modern life as I could gather from using my eyes on the way here from Hammersmith, and from asking some questions of Richard Hammond, most of which he could hardly understand."

The old man smiled at this. "Then," said he, "I am to speak to you as——"

"As if I were a being from another planet," said I.

The old man, whose name, by the bye, like his kinsman's, was Hammond, smiled and nodded, and wheeling his seat round to me, bade me sit in a heavy oak chair, and said, as he saw my eyes fix on its curious carving:

"Yes, I am much tied to the past, *my* past, you understand. These very pieces of furniture belong to a time before my early days; it was my father who got them made; if they had been done within the last fifty years they would have been much cleverer in execution; but I don't think I should have liked them the better. We were almost beginning again in those days: and they were brisk, hot-headed times. But you hear how garrulous I am: ask me questions, ask me questions about anything, dear guest; since I *must* talk, make my talk profitable to you."

I was silent for a minute, and then I said, somewhat nervously: "Excuse me if I am rude; but I am so much interested in Richard, since he has been so kind to me, a perfect stranger, that I should like to ask a question about him."

"Well," said old Hammond, "if he were not 'kind,' as you call it, to a perfect stranger he would be thought a strange person, and people would be apt to shun him. But ask on, ask on! don't be shy of asking."

Said I: "That beautiful girl, is he going to be married to her?"

"Well," said he, "yes, he is. He has been married to her once already, and now I should say it is pretty clear that he will be married to her again."

"Indeed," quoth I, wondering what that meant.

"Here is the whole tale," said old Hammond; "a short one enough; and now I hope a happy one: they lived together two years the first time; were both very young; and then she got it into her head that she was in love with somebody else. So she left poor Dick; I say *poor* Dick, because he had not found any one else. But it did not last long, only about a year. Then she came to me, as she was in the habit of bringing her troubles to the old carle, and asked me how Dick was, and whether he was happy, and all the rest of it. So I saw how the land lay, and said that he was very unhappy, and not at all well; which last at any rate was a lie. There, you can guess the rest. Clara came to have a long talk with me to-day, but Dick will serve her turn much better. Indeed, if he hadn't chanced in upon me to-day I should have had to have sent for him to-morrow."

"Dear me," said I. "Have they any children?"

"Yes," said he, "two; they are staying with one of my daughters at present, where, indeed, Clara has mostly been. I wouldn't lose sight of her, as I felt sure they would come together again: and Dick, who is the best of good fellows, really took the matter to heart. You see, he had no other love to run to, as she had. So I managed it all; as I have done with such-like matters before."

"Ah," said I, "no doubt you wanted to keep them out of the Divorce Court: but I suppose it often has to settle such matters."

"Then you suppose nonsense," said he. "I know that there used to be such lunatic affairs as divorce courts. But just consider; all the cases that came into them were matters of property quarrels: and I think, dear guest," said he, smiling, "that though you do come from another planet, you can see from the mere outside look of our world that quarrels about private property could not go on amongst us in our days."

Indeed, my drive from Hammersmith to Bloomsbury, and all the quiet happy life I had seen so many hints of, even apart from my shopping, would have been enough to tell me that "the sacred rights of property," as we used to think of them, were now no more. So I sat silent while the old man took up the thread of the discourse again, and said:

"Well, then, property quarrels being no longer possible, what remains in these matters that a court of law could deal with? Fancy a court for enforcing a contract of passion or sentiment! If such a thing were needed as a *reductio ad absurdum* of the enforcement of contract, such a folly would do that for us."

He was silent again a little, and then said: "You must understand once for all that we have changed these matters; or rather, that our way of looking at them has changed, as we have changed within the last two hundred years. We do not deceive ourselves, indeed, or believe that we can get rid of all the trouble that besets the dealings between the sexes. We know that we must face the unhappiness that comes of man and woman confusing the relations between natural passion, and sentiment, and the friendship which, when things go well, softens the awakening from passing illusions: but we are not so mad as to pile up degradation on that unhappiness by engaging in sordid squabbles about livelihood and position, and the power of tyrannising over the children who have been the result of love or lust."

Again he paused awhile, and again went on: "Calf love, mistaken for a heroism that shall be life-long, yet early waning into disappointment; the inexplicable desire that comes on a man of riper years to be the all-in-all to some one woman, whose ordinary human kindness and human beauty he has idealised into superhuman perfection, and made the one object of his desire; or lastly the reasonable longing of a strong and thoughtful man to become the most intimate friend of some beautiful and wise woman, the very type of the beauty and glory of the world which we love so well,—as we exult in all the pleasure and exaltation of spirit which goes with these things, so we set ourselves to bear the sorrow which not unseldom goes with them also; remembering those lines of the ancient poet (I quote roughly from memory one of the many translations of the nineteenth century):

'For this the Gods have fashioned man's grief and evil day
That still for man hereafter might be the tale and the lay.'

"Well, well, 'tis little likely anyhow that all tales shall be lacking, or all sorrow cured."

He was silent for some time, and I would not interrupt him. At last he began again: "But you must know that we of these generations are strong and healthy of body, and live easily; we pass our lives in reasonable strife with nature, exercising not one side of ourselves only, but all sides, taking the keenest pleasure in all the life of the world. So it is a point of honour with us not to be self-centred; not to suppose that the world must cease because one man is sorry; therefore we should think it foolish, or if you will, criminal, to exaggerate these matters of sentiment and sensibility: we are no more inclined to eke out our sentimental sorrows than to cherish our bodily pains; and we recognise that there are other pleasures besides love-making. You must remember, also, that we are long-lived, and that therefore beauty both in man and woman is not so fleeting as it was in the days when we were burdened so heavily by self-inflicted diseases. So we shake off these griefs in a way which perhaps the sentimentalists of other times would think contemptible and unheroic, but which we think necessary and manlike. As on the other hand, therefore, we have ceased to be commercial in our love-matters, so also we have ceased to be *artificially* foolish. The folly which comes by nature, the unwisdom of the immature man, or the older man caught in a trap, we must put up with that, nor are we much ashamed of it; but to be conventionally sensitive or sentimental—my friend, I am old and perhaps disappointed, but at least I think we have cast off *some* of the follies of the older world."

He paused, as if for some words of mine; but I held my peace: then he went on: "At least, if we suffer from the tyranny and fickleness of nature or our own want of experience, we neither grimace about it, nor lie. If there must be sundering betwixt those who meant never to sunder, so it must be: but there need be no pretext of unity when the reality of it is gone: nor do we drive those who well know that they are incapable of it to profess an undying sentiment which they cannot really feel: thus it is that as that monstrosity of venal lust is no longer possible, so also it is no longer needed. Don't misunderstand me. You did not seem shocked when I told you that there were no law-courts to enforce contracts of sentiment or passion; but so curiously are men made, that perhaps you will be shocked when I tell you that there is no code of public opinion which takes the place of such courts, and which might be as tyrannical and unreasonable as they were. I do not say that people don't judge their neighbours' conduct, sometimes, doubtless, unfairly. But I do say that there is no unvarying conventional set of rules by which people are judged; no bed of Procrustes to stretch or cramp their minds and lives; no hypocritical excommunication which people are *forced* to pronounce, either by unconsidered habit, or by the unexpressed threat of the lesser interdict if they are lax in their hypocrisy. Are you shocked now?"

"N-o—no," said I, with some hesitation. "It is all so different."

"At any rate," said he, "one thing I think I can answer for: whatever sentiment there is, it is real—and general; it is not confined to people very specially refined. I am also pretty sure, as I hinted to you just now, that there is not by a great way as much suffering involved in these matters either to men or to women as there used to be. But excuse me for being so prolix on this question! You know you asked to be treated like a being from another planet."

"Indeed I thank you very much," said I. "Now may I ask you about the position of women in your society?"

He laughed very heartily for a man of his years, and said: "It is not without reason that I have got a reputation as a careful student of history. I believe I really do understand 'the Emancipation of Women movement' of the nineteenth century. I doubt if any other man now alive does."

"Well?" said I, a little bit nettled by his merriment.

"Well," said he, "of course you will see that all that is a dead controversy now. The men have no longer any opportunity of tyrannising over the women, or the women over the men; both of which things took place in those old times. The women do what they can do best, and what they like best, and the men are neither jealous of it or injured by it. This is such a commonplace that I am almost ashamed to state it."

I said, "O; and legislation? do they take any part in that?"

Hammond smiled and said: "I think you may wait for an answer to that question till we get on to the subject of legislation. There may be novelties to you in that subject also."

"Very well," I said; "but about this woman question? I saw at the Guest House that the women were waiting on the men: that seems a little like reaction, doesn't it?"

"Does it?" said the old man; "perhaps you think housekeeping an unimportant occupation, not deserving of respect. I believe that was the opinion of the 'advanced' women of the nineteenth century, and their male backers. If it is yours, I recommend to your notice an old Norwegian folk-lore tale called How the Man minded the House, or some such title; the result of which minding was that, after various tribulations, the man and the family cow balanced each other at the end of a rope, the man hanging half-way up the chimney, the cow dangling from the roof, which, after the fashion of the country, was of turf and sloping down low to the ground. Hard on the cow, *I* think. Of course no such mishap could happen to such a superior person as yourself," he added, chuckling.

I sat somewhat uneasy under this dry gibe. Indeed, his manner of treating this latter part of the question seemed to me a little disrespectful.

"Come, now, my friend," quoth he, "don't you know that it is a great pleasure to a clever woman to manage a house skilfully, and to do it so that all the house-mates about her look pleased, and are grateful to her? And then, you know, everybody likes to be ordered about by a pretty woman: why, it is one of the pleasantest forms of flirtation You are not so old that you cannot remember that. Why, I remember it well."

And the old fellow chuckled again, and at last fairly burst out laughing.

"Excuse me," said he, after a while; "I am not laughing at anything you could be thinking of, but at that silly nineteenth-century fashion, current amongst rich so-called cultivated people, of ignoring all the steps by which their daily dinner was reached, as matters too low for their lofty intelligence. Useless idiots! Come, now, I am a 'literary man,' as we queer animals used to be called, yet I am a pretty good cook myself."

"So am I," said I.

"Well, then," said he, "I really think you can understand me better than you would seem to do, judging by your words and your silence."

Said I: "Perhaps that is so; but people putting in practice commonly this sense of interest in the ordinary occupations of life rather startles me. I will ask you a question or two presently about that. But I want to return to the position of women amongst you. You have studied the 'emancipation of women' business of the nineteenth century: don't you remember that some of the 'superior' women wanted to emancipate the more intelligent part of their sex from the bearing of children?"

The old man grew quite serious again. Said he: "I *do* remember about that strange piece of baseless folly, the result, like all other follies of the period, of the hideous class tyranny which then obtained. What do we think of it now? you would say. My friend, that is a question easy to answer. How could it possibly be but that maternity should be highly honoured amongst us? Surely it is a matter of course that the natural and necessary pains which the mother must go through form a bond of union between man and woman, an extra stimulus to love and affection between them, and that this is universally recognised. For the rest, remember that all the *artificial* burdens of motherhood are now done

away with. A mother has no longer any mere sordid
anxieties for the future of her children. They may indeed
turn out better or worse; they may disappoint her highest
hopes; such anxieties as these are a part of the mingled
pleasure and pain which goes to make up the life of mankind. But at least she is spared the fear (it was most commonly the certainty) that artificial disabilities would make
her children something less than men and women: she knows
that they will live and act according to the measure of their
own faculties. In times past, it is clear that the 'Society' of
the day helped its Judaic god, and the 'Man of Science' of
the time, in visiting the sins of the father upon the children.
How to reverse this process, how to take the sting out of hered-
ity, has for long been one of the most constant cares of the
thoughtful men amongst us. So that, you see, the ordinarily
healthy woman (and almost all our women are both healthy
and at least comely), respected as a child-bearer and rearer
of children, desired as a woman, loved as a companion, unanxious for the future of her children, has far more instinct
for maternity than the poor drudge and mother of drudges
of past days could ever have had; or than her sister of the
upper classes, brought up in affected ignorance of natural
facts, reared in an atmosphere of mingled prudery and
prurience."

"You speak warmly," I said, "but I can see that you are
right."

"Yes," he said, "and I will point out to you a token of all
the benefits which we have gained by our freedom. What
did you think of the looks of the people whom you have
come across to-day?"

Said I: "I could hardly have believed that there could be
so many good-looking people in any civilised country."

He crowed a little, like the old bird he was. "What! are
we still civilised?" said he. "Well, as to our looks, the English and Jutish blood, which on the whole is predominant
here, used not to produce much beauty. But I think we
have improved it. I know a man who has a large collection
of portraits printed from photographs of the nineteenth century, and going over those and comparing them with the
everyday faces in these times, puts the improvement in our
good looks beyond a doubt. Now, there are some people

who think it not too fantastic to connect this increase of beauty directly with our freedom and good sense in the matters we have been speaking of: they believe that a child born from the natural and healthy love between a man and a woman, even if that be transient, is likely to turn out better in all ways, and especially in bodily beauty, than the birth of the respectable commercial marriage bed, or of the dull despair of the drudge of that system. They say, Pleasure begets pleasure. What do you think?"

"I am much of that mind," said I.

CHAPTER X

QUESTIONS AND ANSWERS

"WELL," said the old man, shifting in his chair, "you must get on with your questions, Guest; I have been some time answering this first one."

Said I: "I want an extra word or two about your ideas of education; although I gathered from Dick that you let your children run wild and didn't teach them anything; and in short, that you have so refined your education, that now you have none."

"Then you gathered left-handed," quoth he. "But of course I understand your point of view about education, which is that of times past, when 'the struggle for life,' as men used to phrase it (*i.e.*, the struggle for a slave's rations on one side, and for a bouncing share of the slave-holders' privilege on the other), pinched 'education' for most people into a niggardly dole of not very accurate information; something to be swallowed by the beginner in the art of living whether he liked it or not, and was hungry for it or not: and which had been chewed and digested over and over again by people who didn't care about it in order to serve it out to other people who didn't care about it."

I stopped the old man's rising wrath by a laugh, and said: "Well, *you* were not taught that way, at any rate, so you may let your anger run off you a little."

"True, true," said he, smiling. "I thank you for correcting

my ill-temper: I always fancy myself as living in any period of which we may be speaking. But, however, to put it in a cooler way: you expected to see children thrust into schools when they had reached an age conventionally supposed to be the due age, whatever their varying faculties and dispositions might be, and when there, with like disregard to facts, to be subjected to a certain conventional course of 'learning.' My friend, can't you see that such a proceeding means ignoring the fact of *growth*, bodily and mental? No one could come out of such a mill uninjured; and those only would avoid being crushed by it who would have the spirit of rebellion strong in them. Fortunately most children have had that at all times, or I do not know that we should ever have reached our present position. Now you see what it all comes to. In the old times all this was the result of *poverty*. In the nineteenth century, society was so miserably poor, owing to the systematised robbery on which it was founded, that real education was impossible for anybody. The whole theory of their so-called education was that it was necessary to shove a little information into a child, even if it were by means of torture, and accompanied by twaddle which it was well known was of no use, or else he would lack information lifelong: the hurry of poverty forbade anything else. All that is past; we are no longer hurried, and the information lies ready to each one's hand when his own inclinations impel him to seek it. In this as in other matters we have become wealthy: we can afford to give ourselves time to grow."

"Yes," said I, "but suppose the child, youth, man, never wants the information, never grows in the direction you might hope him to do: suppose, for instance, he objects to learning arithmetic or mathematics; you can't force him when he *is* grown; can't you force him while he is growing, and oughtn't you to do so?"

"Well," said he, "were you forced to learn arithmetic and mathematics?"

"A little," said I.

"And how old are you now?"

"Say fifty-six," said I.

"And how much arithmetic and mathematics do you know now?" quoth the old man, smiling rather mockingly.

Said I: "None whatever, I am sorry to say."

Hammond laughed quietly, but made no other comment on my admission, and I dropped the subject of education, perceiving him to be hopeless on that side.

I thought a little, and said: "You were speaking just now of households: that sounded to me a little like the customs of past times; I should have thought you would have lived more in public."

"Phalangsteries, eh?" said he. "Well, we live as we like, and we like to live as a rule with certain house-mates that we have got used to. Remember, again, that poverty is extinct, and that the Fourierist phalangsteries and all their kind, as was but natural at the time, implied nothing but a refuge from mere destitution. Such a way of life as that could only have been conceived of by people surrounded by the worst form of poverty. But you must understand therewith, that though separate households are the rule amongst us, and though they differ in their habits more or less, yet no door is shut to any good-tempered person who is content to live as the other house-mates do: only of course it would be unreasonable for one man to drop into a household and bid the folk of it to alter their habits to please him, since he can go elsewhere and live as he pleases. However, I need not say much about all this, as you are going up the river with Dick, and will find out for yourself by experience how these matters are managed."

After a pause, I said: "Your big towns, now; how about them? London, which—which I have read about as the modern Babylon of civilisation, seems to have disappeared."

"Well, well," said old Hammond, "perhaps after all it is more like ancient Babylon now than the 'modern Babylon' of the nineteenth century was. But let that pass. After all, there is a good deal of population in places between here and Hammersmith; nor have you seen the most populous part of the town yet."

"Tell me, then," said I, "how is it towards the east?"

Said he: "Time was when if you mounted a good horse and rode straight away from my door here at a round trot for an hour and a half, you would still be in the thick of London, and the greater part of that would be 'slums,' as they were called; that is to say, places of torture for innocent men and women; or worse, stews for rearing and breeding men and women in such degradation that that torture should seem to them mere ordinary and natural life."

"I know, I know," I said, rather impatiently. "That was what was; tell me something of what is. Is any of that left?"

"Not an inch," said he; "but some memory of it abides with us, and I am glad of it. Once a year, on May-day, we hold a solemn feast in those easterly communes of London to commemorate The Clearing of Misery, as it is called. On that day we have music and dancing, and merry games and happy feasting on the site of some of the worst of the old slums, the traditional memory of which we have kept. On that occasion the custom is for the prettiest girls to sing some of the old revolutionary songs, and those which were the groans of the discontent, once so hopeless, on the very spots where those terrible crimes of class-murder were committed day by day for so many years. To a man like me, who has studied the past so diligently, it is a curious and touching sight to see some beautiful girl, daintily clad, and crowned with flowers from the neighbouring meadows, standing amongst the happy people, on some mound where of old time stood the wretched apology for a house, a den in which men and women lived packed amongst the filth like pilchards in a cask; lived in such a way that they could only have endured it, as I said just now, by being degraded out of humanity—to hear the terrible words of threatening and lamentation coming from her sweet and beautiful lips, and she unconscious of their real meaning: to hear her, for instance, singing Hood's Song of the Shirt, and to think that all the time she does not understand what it is all about—a tragedy grown inconceivable to her and her listeners. Think of that, if you can, and of how glorious life is grown!"

"Indeed," said I, "it is difficult for me to think of it."

And I sat watching how his eyes glittered, and how the fresh life seemed to glow in his face, and I wondered how at his age he should think of the happiness of the world, or indeed anything but his coming dinner.

"Tell me in detail," said I, "what lies east of Blooms-bury now?"

Said he: "There are but few houses between this and the outer part of the old city; but in the city we have a thickly-dwelling population. Our forefathers, in the first clearing of the slums were not in a hurry to pull down the houses in what was called at the end of the nineteenth century the business quarter of the town, and what later got to be known as the Swindling Kens. You see, these houses, though they stood hideously thick on the ground, were roomy and fairly solid in building, and clean, because they were not used for living in, but as mere gambling booths; so the poor people from the cleared slums took them for lodgings and dwelt there, till the folk of those days had time to think of something better for them; so the buildings were pulled down so gradually that people got used to living thicker on the ground there than in most places; therefore it remains the most populous part of London, or perhaps of all these islands. But it is very pleasant there, partly because of the splendour of the architecture, which goes further than what you will see elsewhere. However, this crowding, if it may be called so, does not go further than a street called Aldgate, a name which perhaps you may have heard of. Beyond that the houses are scattered wide about the meadows there, which are very beautiful, especially when you get on to the lovely river Lea (where old Isaak Walton used to fish, you know) about the places called Stratford and Old Ford, names which of course you will not have heard of, though the Romans were busy there once upon a time."

Not heard of them! thought I to myself. How strange! that I who had seen the very last remnant of the pleasantness of the meadows by the Lea destroyed, should have heard them spoken of with pleasantness come back to them in full measure.

Hammond went on: "When you get down to the Thames side you come on the Docks, which are works of the nineteenth century, and are still in use, although not so thronged as they once were, since we discourage centralisation all we can, and we have long ago dropped the pretension to be the market of the world. About these Docks are a good few houses, which, however, are not inhabited by many people permanently; I mean, those who use them come and go a good deal, the place being too low and marshy for pleasant dwelling. Past the Docks eastward and landward it is all flat pasture, once marsh, except for a few gardens, and there are very few permanent dwellings there: scarcely anything but a few sheds, and cots for the men who come to look after the great herds of cattle pasturing there. But however, what with the beasts and the men, and the scattered red-tiled roofs and the big hayricks, it does not make a bad holiday to get a quiet pony and ride about there on a sunny after-noon of autumn, and look over the river and the craft pass-ing up and down, and on to Shooters' Hill and the Kentish uplands, and then turn round to the wide green sea of the Essex marshland, with the great domed line of the sky, and the sun shining down in one flood of peaceful light over the long distance. There is a place called Canning's Town, and further out, Silvertown, where the pleasant meadows are at their pleasantest: doubtless they were once slums, and wretched enough."

The names grated on my ear, but I could not explain why to him. So I said: "And south of the river, what is it like?"

He said: "You would find it much the same as the land about Hammersmith. North, again, the land runs up high, and there is an agreeable and well-built town called Hamp-stead, which fitly ends London on that side. It looks down on the north-western end of the forest you passed through."

I smiled. "So much for what was once London," said I. "Now tell me about the other towns of the country."

He said: "As to the big murky places which were once, as we know, the centres of manufacture, they have, like the brick and mortar desert of London, disappeared; only, since they were centres of nothing but 'manufacture,' and served no purpose but that of the gambling market, they have left less signs of their existence than London. Of course, the great change in the use of mechanical force made this an easy matter, and some approach to their break-up as centres would probably have taken place, even if we had not changed our habits so much: but they being such as they were, no sacrifice would have seemed too great a price to pay for getting rid of the 'manufacturing districts,' as they used to be called. For the rest, whatever coal or mineral we need is brought to grass and sent whither it is needed with as little as possible of dirt, confusion, and the distressing of quiet people's lives. One is tempted to believe from what one has read of the condition of those districts in the nineteenth century, that those who had them under their power worried, befouled, and degraded men out of malice prepense: but it was not so; like the miseducation of which we were talking just now, it came of their dreadful poverty. They were obliged to put up with everything, and even pretend that they liked it; whereas we can now deal with things reasonably, and refuse to be saddled with what we do not want."

I confess I was not sorry to cut short with a question his glorifications of the age he lived in. Said I: "How about the smaller towns? I suppose you have swept those away entirely?"

"No, no," said he, "it hasn't gone that way. On the contrary, there has been but little clearance, though much rebuilding, in the smaller towns. Their suburbs, indeed, when they had any, have melted away into the general country, and space and elbow-room has been got in their centres: but there are the towns still with their streets and squares and market-places; so that it is by means of these smaller towns that we of to-day can get some kind of idea of what the towns of the older world were like;—I mean to say at their best."

"Take Oxford, for instance," said I.

"Yes," said he, "I suppose Oxford was beautiful even in the nineteenth century. At present it has the great interest of still preserving a great mass of precommercial building, and is a very beautiful place, yet there are many towns which have become scarcely less beautiful."

Said I: "In passing, may I ask if it is still a place of learning?"

"Still?" said he, smiling. "Well, it has reverted to some of its best traditions; so you may imagine how far it is from its nineteenth-century position. It is real learning, knowledge cultivated for its own sake—the Art of Knowledge, in short—which is followed there, not the Commercial learning of the past. Though perhaps you do not know that in the nineteenth century Oxford and its less interesting sister Cambridge became definitely commercial. They (and

D

especially Oxford) were the breeding places of a peculiar class of parasites, who called themselves cultivated people; they were indeed cynical enough, as the so-called educated classes of the day generally were; but they affected an exaggeration of cynicism in order that they might be thought knowing and worldly-wise. The rich middle classes (they had no relation with the working classes) treated them with the kind of contemptuous toleration with which a mediæval baron treated his jester; though it must be said that they were by no means so pleasant as the old jesters were, being, in fact, *the* bores of society. They were laughed at, despised —and paid. Which last was what they aimed at."

Dear me! thought I, how apt history is to reverse contemporary judgments. Surely only the worst of them were as bad as that. But I must admit that they were mostly prigs, and that they *were* commercial. I said aloud, though more to myself than to Hammond, "Well, how could they be better than the age that made them?"

"True," he said, "but their pretensions were higher."

"Were they?" said I, smiling.

"You drive me from corner to corner," said he, smiling in turn. "Let me say at least that they were a poor sequence to the aspirations of Oxford of 'the barbarous Middle Ages.' "

"Yes, that will do," said I.

"Also," said Hammond, "what I have been saying of them is true in the main. But ask on!"

I said: "We have heard about London and the manufacturing districts and the ordinary towns: how about the villages?"

Said Hammond: "You must know that toward the end of the nineteenth century the villages were almost destroyed, unless where they became mere adjuncts to the manufacturing districts, or formed a sort of minor manufacturing district themselves. Houses were allowed to fall into decay and actual ruin; trees were cut down for the sake of the few shillings which the poor sticks would fetch; the building became inexpressibly mean and hideous. Labour was scarce; but wages fell nevertheless. All the small country arts of life which once added to the little pleasures of country people were lost. The country produce which passed through the hands of the husbandman never got so far as their mouths. Incredible shabbiness and niggardly pinching reigned over the fields and acres which, in spite of the rude and careless husbandry of the times, were so kind and bountiful. Had you any inkling of all this?"

"I have heard that it was so," said I; "but what followed?"

"The change," said Hammond, "which in these matters took place very early in our epoch, was most strangely rapid. People flocked into the country villages, and, so to say, flung themselves upon the freed land like a wild beast upon his prey; and in a very little time the villages of England were more populous than they had been since the fourteenth century, and were still growing fast. Of course, this invasion of the country was awkward to deal with, and would have created much misery, if the folk had still been under the bondage of class monopoly. But as it was, things soon righted themselves. People found out what they were fit for, and gave up attempting to push themselves into occupations in which they must needs fail. The town invaded the country; but the invaders, like the warlike invaders of early days, yielded to the influence of their surroundings, and became country people; and in their turn, as they became more numerous than the townsmen, influenced them also; so that the difference between town and country grew less and less; and it was indeed this world of the country vivified by the thought and briskness of town-bred folk which has produced that happy and leisurely but eager life of which you have had a first taste. Again I say, many blunders were made, but we have had time to set them right. Much was left for the men of my earlier life to deal with. The crude ideas of the first half of the twentieth century, when men were still oppressed by the fear of poverty, and did not look enough to the present pleasure of ordinary daily life, spoilt a great deal of what the commercial age had left us of external beauty: and I admit that it was but slowly that men recovered from the injuries they had inflicted on themselves even after they became free. But slowly as the recovery came, it *did* come; and the more you see of us, the clearer it will be to you that we are happy.

That we live amidst beauty without any fear of becoming effeminate; that we have plenty to do, and on the whole enjoy doing it. What more can we ask of life?"

He paused, as if he were seeking for words with which to express his thought. Then he said:

"This is how we stand. England was once a country of clearings amongst the woods and wastes, with a few towns interspersed, which were fortresses for the feudal army, markets for the folk, gathering places for the craftsmen. It then became a country of huge and foul workshops and fouler gambling-dens, surrounded by an ill-kept, poverty-stricken farm, pillaged by the masters of the workshops. It is now a garden, where nothing is wasted and nothing is spoilt, with the necessary dwellings, sheds, and workshops scattered up and down the country, all trim and neat and pretty. For, indeed, we should be too much ashamed of ourselves if we allowed the making of goods, even on a large scale, to carry with it the appearance, even, of desolation and misery. Why, my friend, those housewives we were talking of just now would teach us better than that."

Said I: "This side of your change is certainly for the better. But though I shall soon see some of these villages, tell me in a word or two what they are like, just to prepare me."

"Perhaps," said he, "you have seen a tolerable picture of these villages as they were before the end of the nineteenth century. Such things exist."

"I have seen several of such pictures," said I.

"Well," said Hammond, "our villages are something like the best of such places, with the church or mote-house of the neighbours for their chief building. Only note that there are no tokens of poverty about them: no tumble-down picturesque: which, to tell you the truth, the artist usually availed himself of to veil his incapacity for drawing architecture. Such things do not please us, even when they indicate no misery. Like the mediævals, we like everything trim and clean, and orderly and bright; as people always do when they have any sense of architectural power; because then they know that they can have what they want, and they won't stand any nonsense from Nature in their dealings with her."

"Besides the villages, are there any scattered country houses?" said I.

"Yes, plenty," said Hammond; "in fact, except in the wastes and forests and amongst the sand-hills (like Hindhead in Surrey), it is not easy to be out of sight of a house; and where the houses are thinly scattered they run large, and are more like the old colleges than ordinary houses as they used to be. That is done for the sake of society, for a good many people can dwell in such houses, as the country dwellers are not necessarily husbandmen; though they almost all help in such work at times. The life that goes on in these big dwellings in the country is very pleasant, especially as some of the most studious men of our time live in them, and altogether there is a great variety of mind and mood to be found in them which brightens and quickens the society there."

"I am rather surprised," said I, "by all this, for it seems to me that after all the country must be tolerably populous."

"Certainly," said he; "the population is pretty much the same as it was at the end of the nineteenth century; we have spread it, that is all. Of course, also, we have helped to populate other countries—where we were wanted and were called for."

Said I: "One thing, it seems to me, does not go with your word of 'garden' for the country. You have spoken of wastes and forests, and I myself have seen the beginning of your Middlesex and Essex forest. Why do you keep such things in a garden? and isn't it very wasteful to do so?"

"My friend," he said, "we like these pieces of wild nature, and can afford them, so we have them; let alone that as to the forests, we need a great deal of timber, and suppose that our sons and sons' sons will do the like. As to the land being a garden, I have heard that they used to have shrubberies and rockeries in gardens once; and though I might not like the artificial ones, I assure you that some of the natural rockeries of our garden are worth seeing. Go north this summer and look at the Cumberland and Westmoreland ones,—where, by the way, you will see some sheep feeding, so that they are not so wasteful as you think; not so wasteful as forcing-grounds for fruit out of season, I think. Go and have a look at the sheep-walks high up the slopes between Ingleborough and Pen-y-gwent, and tell me if you think we *waste* the land there by not covering it with factories for making things that nobody wants, which was the chief business of the nineteenth century."

"I will try to go there," said I.

"It won't take much trying," said he.

CHAPTER XI

CONCERNING GOVERNMENT

"NOW," said I, "I have come to the point of asking questions which I suppose will be dry for you to answer and difficult for you to explain; but I have foreseen for some time past that I must ask them, will I nill I. What kind of a government have you? Has republicanism finally triumphed? or have you come to a mere dictatorship, which some persons in the nineteenth century used to prophesy as the ultimate outcome of democracy? Indeed, this last question does not seem so very unreasonable, since you have turned your Parliament House into a dung-market. Or where do you house your present Parliament?"

The old man answered my smile with a hearty laugh, and said: "Well, well, dung is not the worst kind of corruption ; fertility may come of that, whereas mere dearth came from the other kind, of which those walls once held the great supporters. Now, dear guest, let me tell you that our present parliament would be hard to house in one place, because the whole people is our parliament."

"I don't understand," said I.

"No, I suppose not," said he. "I must now shock you by telling you that we have no longer anything which you, a native of another planet, would call a government."

"I am not so much shocked as you might think," said I, "as I know something about governments. But tell me, how do you manage, and how have you come to this state of things?"

Said he: "It is true that we have to make some arrangements about our affairs, concerning which you can ask presently; and it is also true that everybody does not always agree with the details of these arrangements; but, further, it is true that a man no more needs an elaborate system of government, with its army, navy, and police, to force him to give way to the will of the majority of his *equals*, than he wants a similar machinery to make him understand that his head and a stone wall cannot occupy the same space at the same moment. Do you want further explanation?"

"Well, yes, I do," quoth I.

Old Hammond settled himself in his chair with a look of enjoyment which rather alarmed me, and made me dread a scientific disquisition: so I sighed and abided. He said:

"I suppose you know pretty well what the process of government was in the bad old times?"

"I am supposed to know," said I.

(Hammond) What was the government of those days? Was it really the Parliament or any part of it?

(I) No.

(H.) Was not the Parliament on the one side a kind of watch-committee sitting to see that the interests of the Upper Classes took no hurt; and on the other side a sort of blind to delude the people into supposing that they had some share in the management of their own affairs?

(I) History seems to show us this.

(H.) To what extent did the people manage their own affairs?

(I) I judge from what I have heard that sometimes they forced the Parliament to make a law to legalise some alteration which had already taken place.

(H.) Anything else?

(I) I think not. As I am informed, if the people made any attempt to deal with the *cause* of their grievances, the law stepped in and said, this is sedition, revolt, or what not, and slew or tortured the ringleaders of such attempts.

(H.) If Parliament was not the government then, nor the people either, what was the government?

(I) Can you tell me?

(H.) I think we shall not be far wrong if we say that government was the Law-Courts, backed up by the executive, which handled the brute force that the deluded people allowed them to use for their own purposes; I mean the army, navy, and police.

(I) Reasonable men must needs think you are right.

(H.) Now as to those Law-Courts. Were they places of fair dealing according to the ideas of the day? Had a poor man a good chance of defending his property and person in them?

(I) It is a commonplace that even rich men looked upon a law-suit as a dire misfortune, even if they gained the case; and as for a poor one—why, it was considered a miracle of justice and beneficence if a poor man who had once got into the clutches of the law escaped prison or utter ruin.

(H.) It seems, then, my son, that the government by law-courts and police, which was the real government of the nineteenth century, was not a great success even to the people of that day, living under a class system which proclaimed inequality and poverty as the law of God and the bond which held the world together.

(I) So it seems, indeed.

(H.) And now that all this is changed, and the "rights of property," which mean the clenching the fist on a piece of goods and crying out to the neighbours, You shan't have this!—now that all this has disappeared so utterly that it is no longer possible even to jest upon its absurdity, is such a Government possible?

(I) It is impossible.

(H.) Yes, happily. But for what other purpose than the protection of the rich from the poor, the strong from the weak, did this Government exist?

(I) I have heard that it was said that their office was to defend their own citizens against attack from other countries.

(H.) It was said; but was any one expected to believe this? For instance, did the English Government defend the English citizen against the French?

(I) So it was said.

(H.) Then if the French had invaded England and conquered it, they would not have allowed the English workman to live well?

(I, laughing) As far as I can make out, the English masters of the English workmen saw to that: they took from their workmen as much of their livelihood as they dared, because they wanted it for themselves.

(H.) But if the French had conquered, would they not have taken more still from the English workmen?

(I) I do not think so; for in that case the English workmen would have died of starvation; and then the French conquest would have ruined the French, just as if the English horses and cattle had died of under-feeding. So that after all, the English *workmen* would have been no worse off for the conquest: their French masters could have got no more from them than their English masters did.

(H.) This is true; and we may admit that the pretensions of the government to defend the poor (*i.e.*, the useful) people against other countries come to nothing. But that is but natural; for we have seen already that it was the function of government to protect the rich against the poor. But did not the government defend its rich men against other nations?

(I) I do not remember to have heard that the rich needed defence; because it is said that even when two nations were at war, the rich men of each nation gambled with each other pretty much as usual, and even sold each other weapons wherewith to kill their own countrymen.

(H.) In short, it comes to this, that whereas the so-called government of protection of property by means of the law-courts meant destruction of wealth, this defence of the citizens of one country against those of another country by means of war or the threat of war meant pretty much the same thing.

(I) I cannot deny it.

(H.) Therefore the government really existed for the destruction of wealth?

(I) So it seems. And yet——

(H.) Yet what?

(I) There were many rich people in those times.

(H.) You see the consequences of that fact?

(I) I think I do. But tell me out what they were.

(H.) If the government habitually destroyed wealth, the country must have been poor?

(I) Yes, certainly.

(H.) Yet amidst this poverty the persons for the sake of whom the government existed insisted on being rich whatever might happen?

(I) So it was.

(H.) What *must* happen if in a poor country some people insist on being rich at the expense of the others?

(I) Unutterable poverty for the others. All this misery then, was caused by the destructive government of which we have been speaking?

(H.) Nay, it would be incorrect to say so. The government itself was but the necessary result of the careless, aimless tyranny of the times; it was but the machinery of tyranny. Now tyranny has come to an end, and we no longer need such machinery; we could not possibly use it since we are free. Therefore in your sense of the word we have no government. Do you understand this now?

(I) Yes, I do. But I will ask you some more questions as to how you as free men manage your affairs.

(H.) With all my heart. Ask away.

CHAPTER XII

CONCERNING THE ARRANGEMENT
OF LIFE

"WELL," I said, "about those 'arrangements' which you spoke of as taking the place of government, could you give me any account of them?"

"Neighbour," he said, "although we have simplified our lives a great deal from what they were, and have got rid of many conventionalities and many sham wants, which used to give our forefathers much trouble, yet our life is too complex for me to tell you in detail by means of words how it is arranged; you must find that out by living amongst us. It is true that I can better tell you what we don't do, than what we do do."

"Well?" said I.

"This is the way to put it," said he: "We have been living for a hundred and fifty years, at least, more or less in our present manner, and a tradition or habit of life has been growing on us; and that habit has become a habit of acting on the whole for the best. It is easy for us to live without robbing each other. It would be possible for us to contend with and rob each other, but it would be harder for us than refraining from strife and robbery. That is in short the foundation of our life and our happiness."

"Whereas in the old days," said I, "it was very hard to live without strife and robbery. That's what you mean, isn't it, by giving me the negative side of your good conditions?"

"Yes," he said, "it was so hard, that those who habitually acted fairly to their neighbours were celebrated as saints and heroes, and were looked up to with the greatest reverence."

"While they were alive?" said I.

"No," said he, "after they were dead."

"But as to these days," I said; "you don't mean to tell me that no one ever transgresses this habit of good fellowship?"

"Certainly not," said Hammond, "but when the transgressions occur, everybody, transgressors and all, know them for what they are; the errors of friends, not the habitual actions of persons driven into enmity against society."

"I see," said I: "you mean that you have no 'criminal' classes."

"How could we have them," said he, "since there is no rich class to breed enemies against the state by means of the injustice of the state?"

Said I: "I thought that I understood from something that fell from you a little while ago that you had abolished civil law. Is that so, literally?"

"It abolished itself, my friend," said he. "As I said before, the civil law courts were upheld for the defence of private property, for nobody ever pretended that it was possible to make people act fairly to each other by means of brute force. Well, private property being abolished, all the laws and all the legal 'crimes' which it had manufactured of course came to an end. Thou shalt not steal, had to be translated into, Thou shalt work in order to live happily. Is there any need to enforce that commandment by violence?"

"Well," said I, "that is understood, and I agree with it; but how about the crimes of violence? would not their occurrence (and you admit that they occur) make criminal law necessary?"

Said he: "In your sense of the word, we have no criminal law either. Let us look at the matter closer, and see whence crimes of violence spring. By far the greater part of these in past days were the result of the laws of private property, which forbade the satisfaction of their natural desires to all but a privileged few, and of the general visible coercion which came of those laws. All *that* cause of violent crime is gone. Again, many violent acts came from the artificial perversion of the sexual passions, which caused overweening jealousy and the like miseries. Now, when you look carefully into these, you will find that what lay at the bottom of them was mostly the idea (a law-made idea) of the woman being the property of the man, whether he were husband, father, brother, or what not. That idea has of course vanished with private property, as well as certain follies about the 'ruin' of women for following their natural desires in an illegal way, which of course was a convention caused by the laws of private property.

"Another cognate cause of crimes of violence was the family tyranny, which was the subject of so many novels and stories of the past, and which once more was the result of private property. Of course that is all ended, since families are held together by no bond of coercion, legal or social, but by mutual liking and affection, and everybody is free to come or go as he or she pleases. Furthermore, our standards of honour and public estimation are very different from the old ones; success in besting our neighbours is a road to renown now closed, let us hope for ever. Each man is free to exercise his special faculty to the utmost, and every one encourages him in so doing. So that we have got rid of the scowling envy, coupled by the poets with hatred, and surely with good reason; heaps of unhappiness and ill-blood were caused by it, which with irritable and passionate men—*i.e.*, energetic and active men—often led to violence."

I laughed, and said: "So that you now withdraw your admission, and say that there is no violence amongst you?"

"No," said he, "I withdraw nothing: as I told you, such things will happen. Hot blood will err sometimes. A man may strike another, and the stricken strike back again, and the result be a homicide, to put it at the worst. But what then? Shall we the neighbours make it worse still? Shall we think so poorly of each other as to suppose that the slain man calls on us to revenge him, when we *know* that if he had been maimed, he would, when in cold blood and able to weigh all the circumstances, have forgiven his maimer? Or will the death of the slayer bring the slain man to life again and cure the unhappiness his loss has caused?"

"Yes," I said, "but consider, must not the safety of society be safeguarded by some punishment?"

"There, neighbour!" said the old man, with some exultation. "You have hit the mark. That *punishment* of which men used to talk so wisely and act so foolishly, what was it but the expression of their fear? And they had need to fear, since *they—i.e.*, the rulers of society—were dwelling like an armed band in a hostile country. But we who live amongst our friends need neither fear nor punish. Surely if we, in dread of an occasional rare homicide, an occasional rough blow, were solemnly and legally to commit homicide and violence, we could only be a society of ferocious cowards. Don't you think so, neighbour?"

"Yes, I do, when I come to think of it from that side," said I.

"Yet you must understand," said the old man, "that when any violence is committed, we expect the transgressor to make any atonement possible to him, and he himself expects it. But again, think if the destruction or serious injury of a man momentarily overcome by wrath or folly can be any atonement to the commonwealth? Surely it can only be an additional injury to it."

Said I: "But suppose the man has a habit of violence—kills a man a year, for instance?"

"Such a thing is unknown," said he. "In a society where there is no punishment to evade, no law to triumph over, remorse will certainly follow transgression."

"And lesser outbreaks of violence," said I, "how do you deal with them? for hitherto we have been talking of great tragedies, I suppose?"

Said Hammond: "If the ill-doer is not sick or mad (in

which case he must be restrained till his sickness or madness is cured) it is clear that grief and humiliation must follow the ill-deed; and society in general will make that pretty clear to the ill-doer if he should chance to be dull to it; and again, some kind of atonement will follow,—at the least, an open acknowledgment of the grief and humiliation. Is it so hard to say, I ask your pardon, neighbour?—Well, sometimes it is hard—and let it be."

"You think that enough?" said I.

"Yes," said he, "and moreover it is all that we *can* do. If in addition we torture the man, we turn his grief into anger, and the humiliation he would otherwise feel for *his* wrong-doing is swallowed up by a hope of revenge for *our* wrong-doing to him. He has paid the legal penalty, and can 'go and sin again' with comfort. Shall we commit such a folly, then? Remember Jesus had got the legal penalty remitted before he said 'Go and sin no more.' Let alone that in a society of equals you will not find any one to play the part of torturer or jailer, though many to act as nurse or doctor."

"So," said I, "you consider crime a mere spasmodic disease, which requires no body of criminal law to deal with it?"

"Pretty much so," said he; "and since, as I told you, we are a healthy people generally, so we are not likely to be much troubled with *this* disease."

" Well, you have no civil law, and no criminal law. But have you no laws of the market, so to say—no regulation for the exchange of wares? for you must exchange, even if you have no property."

Said he: "We have no obvious individual exchange, as you saw this morning when you went a-shopping; but of course there are regulations of the markets, varying according to the circumstances and guided by general custom. But as these are matters of general assent, which nobody dreams of objecting to, so also we have made no provision for enforcing them: therefore I don't call them laws. In law, whether it be criminal or civil, execution always follows judgment, and some one must suffer. When you see the judge on his bench, you see through him, as clearly as if he were made of glass, the policeman to emprison, and the soldier to slay some actual living person. Such follies would make an agreeable market, wouldn't they?"

"Certainly," said I, "that means turning the market into a mere battlefield, in which many people must suffer as much as in the battlefield of bullet and bayonet. And from what I have seen I should suppose that your marketing, great and little, is carried on in a way that makes it a pleasant occupation."

"You are right, neighbour," said he. "Although there are so many, indeed by far the greater number amongst us, who would be unhappy if they were not engaged in actually making things, and things which turn out beautiful under their hands,—there are many, like the housekeepers I was speaking of, whose delight is in administration and organisation, to use long-tailed words; I mean people who like keeping things together, avoiding waste, seeing that nothing sticks fast uselessly. Such people are thoroughly happy in their business, all the more as they are dealing with actual facts, and not merely passing counters round to see what share they shall have in the privileged taxation of useful people, which was the business of the commercial folk in past days. Well, what are you going to ask me next?"

CHAPTER XIII

CONCERNING POLITICS

SAID I: "How do you manage with politics?"

Said Hammond, smiling: "I am glad that it is of *me* that you ask the question: I do believe that anybody else would make you explain yourself, or try to do so, till you were sickened of asking questions. Indeed, I believe I am the only man in England who would know what you mean; and since I know, I will answer your question briefly by saying that we are very well off as to politics,—because we have none. If ever you make a book out of this conversation, put this in a chapter by itself, after the model of old Horrebow's Snakes in Iceland."

"I will," said I.

CHAPTER XIV

HOW MATTERS ARE MANAGED

SAID I: "How about your relations with foreign nations?"

"I will not affect not to know what you mean," said he, "but I will tell you at once that the whole system of rival and contending nations which played so great a part in the 'government' of the world of civilisation has disappeared along with the inequality betwixt man and man in society."

"Does not that make the world duller?" said I.

"Why?" said the old man.

"The obliteration of national variety," said I.

"Nonsense," he said, somewhat snappishly. "Cross the water and see. You will find plenty of variety: the landscape, the building, the diet, the amusements, all various. The men and women varying in looks as well as in habits of thought; the costume far more various than in the commercial period. How should it add to the variety or dispel the dulness, to coerce certain families or tribes, often heterogeneous and jarring with one another, into certain artificial and mechanical groups, and call them nations, and stimulate their patriotism—*i.e.*, their foolish and envious prejudices?"

"Well—I don't know how," said I.

"That's right," said Hammond cheerily; "you can easily understand that now we are freed from this folly it is obvious to us that by means of this very diversity the different strains of blood in the world can be serviceable and pleasant to each other, without in the least wanting to rob each other: we are all bent on the same enterprise, making the most of our lives. And I must tell you whatever quarrels or misunderstandings arise, they very seldom take place between people of different race; and consequently since there is less unreason in them, they are the more readily appeased."

"Good," said I, "but as to those matters of politics; as to general differences of opinion in one and the same community. Do you assert that there are none?"

"No, not at all," said he, somewhat snappishly: "but I do say that differences of opinion about real solid things need not, and with us do not, crystallise people into parties permanently hostile to one another, with different theories as to the build of the universe and the progress of time. Isn't that what politics used to mean?"

"H'm, well," said I, "I am not so sure of that."

Said he: "I take you, neighbour; they only *pretended* to this serious difference of opinion; for if it had existed they could not have dealt together in the ordinary business of life; couldn't have eaten together, bought and sold together, gambled together, cheated other people together, but must have fought whenever they met: which would not have suited them at all. The game of the masters of politics was to cajole or force the public to pay the expense of a luxurious life and exciting amusement for a few cliques of ambitious persons: and the *pretence* of serious difference of opinion, belied by every action of their lives, was quite good enough for that. What has all that got to do with us?"

Said I: "Why, nothing, I should hope. But I fear— In short, I have been told that political strife was a necessary result of human nature."

"Human nature!" cried the old boy, impetuously: "what human nature? The human nature of paupers, of slaves, of slave-holders, or the human nature of wealthy freemen? Which? Come, tell me that!"

"Well," said I, "I suppose there would be a difference according to circumstances in people's action about these matters."

"I should think so, indeed," said he. "At all events, experience shows that it is so. Amongst us, our differences concern matters of business, and passing events as to them, and could not divide men permanently. As a rule, the immediate outcome shows which opinion on a given subject is the right one; it is a matter of fact, not of speculation. For instance, it is clearly not easy to knock up a political party on the question as to whether haymaking in such and such a countryside shall begin this week or next, when all men agree that it must at latest begin the week after next, and when any man can go down into the fields himself and see whether the seeds are ripe enough for the cutting."

Said I: "And you settle these differences, great and small, by the will of the majority, I suppose?"

"Certainly," said he; "how else could we settle them? You see in matters which are merely personal which do not affect the welfare of the community—how a man shall dress, what he shall eat and drink, what he shall write and read, and so forth—there can be no difference of opinion, and everybody does as he pleases. But when the matter is of common interest to the whole community, and the doing or not doing something affects everybody, the majority must have their way; unless the minority were to take up arms and show by force that they were the effective of real majority; which, however, in a society of men who are free and equal is little likely to happen; because in such a community the apparent majority *is* the real majority, and the others, as I have hinted before, know that too well to obstruct from mere pigheadedness; especially as they have had plenty of opportunity of putting forward their side of the question."

"How is that managed?" said I.

"Well," said he, "let us take one of our units of management, a commune, or a ward, or a parish (for we have all three names, indicating little real distinction between them now, though time was there was a good deal). In such a district, as you would call it, some neighbours think that something ought to be done or undone: a new town-hall built; a clearance of inconvenient houses; or say a stone bridge substituted for some ugly old iron one,—there you have undoing and doing in one. Well, at the next ordinary meeting of the neighbours, or Mote, as we call it, according to the ancient tongue of the times before bureaucracy, a neighbour proposes the change, and of course, if everybody agrees, there is an end of discussion, except about details. Equally, if no one backs the proposer—'seconds him,' it used to be called—the matter drops for the time being; a thing not likely to happen amongst reasonable men, however, as the proposer is sure to have talked it over with others before the Mote. But supposing the affair proposed and seconded, if a few of the neighbours disagree to it, if they think that the beastly iron bridge will serve a little longer and they don't want to be bothered with building a new one just then, they don't count heads that time, but put off the formal discussion to the next Mote; and meantime arguments *pro* and *con* are flying about, and some get printed, so that everybody knows what is going on; and when the Mote comes together again there is a regular discussion and at last a vote by show of hands. If the division is a close one, the question is again put off for further discussion; if the division is a wide one, the minority are asked if they will yield to the more general opinion, which they often, nay, most commonly do. If they refuse, the question is debated a third time, when, if the minority has not perceptibly grown, they always give way; though I believe there is some half-forgotten rule by which they might still carry it on further; but I say, what always happens is that they are convinced, not perhaps that their view is the wrong one, but they cannot persuade or force the community to adopt it."

"Very good," said I, "but what happens if the divisions are still narrow?"

Said he: "As a matter of principle and according to the rule of such cases, the question must then lapse, and the majority, if so narrow, has to submit to sitting down under the *status quo*. But I must tell you that in point of fact the minority very seldom enforces this rule, but generally yields in a friendly manner."

"But do you know," said I, "that there is something in all this very like democracy; and I thought that democracy was considered to be in a moribund condition many, many years ago."

The old boy's eyes twinkled. "I grant you that our methods have that drawback. But what is to be done? We can't get *any one* amongst us to complain of his not always having his own way in the teeth of the community, when it is clear that *everybody* cannot have that indulgence. What *is* to be done?"

"Well," said I, "I don't know."

Said he: "The only alternatives to our method that I can conceive of are these. First, that we should choose out, or breed, a class of superior persons capable of judging on all matters without consulting the neighbours; that, in short, we should get for ourselves what used to be called an aristocracy of intellect; or, secondly, that for the purpose of safeguarding the freedom of the individual will, we should revert to a system of private property again, and have slaves and slave-holders once more. What do you think of those two expedients?"

"Well," said I, "there is a third possibility—to wit, that every man should be quite independent of every other, and that thus the tyranny of society should be abolished."

He looked hard at me for a second or two, and then burst out laughing very heartily; and I confess that I joined him. When he recovered himself he nodded at me, and said: "Yes, yes, I quite agree with you—and so we all do."

"Yes," I said, "and besides, it does not press hardly on the minority: for, take this matter of the bridge, no man is obliged to work on it if he doesn't agree to its building. At least, I suppose not."

He smiled, and said: "Shrewdly put; and yet from the point of view of the native of another planet. If the man of the minority does find his feelings hurt, doubtless he may relieve them by refusing to help in building the bridge. But, dear neighbour, that is not a very effective salve for the wound caused by the 'tyranny of a majority' in our society; because all work that is done is either beneficial or hurtful to every member of society. The man is benefited by the bridge-building if it turns out a good thing, and hurt by it if it turns out a bad one, whether he puts a hand to it or not; and meanwhile he is benefiting the bridge-builders by his work, whatever that may be. In fact, I see no help for him except the pleasure of saying 'I told you so' if the bridge-building turns out to be a mistake and hurts him; if it benefits him he must suffer in silence. A terrible tyranny our Communism, is it not? Folk used often to be warned against this very unhappiness in times past, when for every well-fed, contented person you saw a thousand miserable starvelings. Whereas for us, we grow fat and well-liking on the tyranny; a tyranny, to say the truth, not to be made visible by any microscope I know. Don't be afraid, my friend; we are not going to seek for troubles by calling our peace and plenty and happiness by ill names whose very meaning we have forgotten!"

He sat musing for a little, and then started and said: "Are there any more questions, dear guest? The morning is waning fast amidst my garrulity."

CHAPTER XV

ON THE LACK OF INCENTIVE TO LABOUR IN A COMMUNIST SOCIETY

"YES," said I. "I was expecting Dick and Clara to make their appearance any moment: but is there time to ask just one or two questions before they come?"

"Try it, dear neighbour—try it," said old Hammond. "For the more you ask me the better I am pleased; and at any rate if they do come and find me in the middle of an answer, they must sit quiet and pretend to listen till I come to an end. It won't hurt them; they will find it quite amusing enough to sit side by side, conscious of their proximity to each other."

I smiled, as I was bound to, and said: "Good; I will go on talking without noticing them when they come in. Now, this is what I want to ask you about—to wit, how you get people to work when there is no reward of labour, and especially how you get them to work strenuously?"

"No reward of labour?" said Hammond, gravely. "The reward of labour is *life*. Is that not enough?"

"But no reward for especially good work," quoth I.

"Plenty of reward," said he—"the reward of creation. The wages which God gets, as people might have said time agone. If you are going to ask to be paid for the pleasure of creation, which is what excellence in work means, the next thing we shall hear of will be a bill sent in for the begetting of children."

"Well, but," said I, "the man of the nineteenth century would say there is a natural desire towards the procreation of children, and a natural desire not to work."

"Yes, yes," said he, "I know the ancient platitude,—wholly untrue; indeed, to us quite meaningless. Fourier, whom all men laughed at, understood the matter better."

"Why is it meaningless to you?" said I.

He said: "Because it implies that all work is suffering, and we are so far from thinking that, that, as you may have noticed, whereas we are not short of wealth, there is a kind of fear growing up amongst us that we shall one day be short of work. It is a pleasure which we are afraid of losing, not a pain."

"Yes," said I, "I have noticed that, and I was going to ask you about that also. But in the meantime, what do you positively mean to assert about the pleasurableness of work amongst you?"

"This, that *all* work is now pleasurable; either because of the hope of gain in honour and wealth with which the work is done, which causes pleasurable excitement, even when the actual work is not pleasant; or else because it has grown into a pleasurable *habit*, as in the case with what you may call mechanical work; and lastly (and most of our work is of this kind) because there is conscious sensuous pleasure in the work itself; it is done, that is, by artists."

"I see," said I. "Can you now tell me how you have come to this happy condition? For, to speak plainly, this change from the conditions of the older world seems to me far greater and more important than all the other changes you have told me about as to crime, politics, property, marriage."

"You are right there," said he. "Indeed, you may say rather that it is this change which makes all the others possible. What is the object of Revolution? Surely to make people happy. Revolution having brought its foredoomed change about, how can you prevent the counter-revolution from setting in except by making people happy? What! shall we expect peace and stability from unhappiness? The gathering of grapes from thorns and figs from thistles is a reasonable expectation compared with that! And happiness without happy daily work is impossible."

"Most obviously true," said I: for I thought the old boy was preaching a little. "But answer my question, as to how you gained this happiness."

"Briefly," said he, "by the absence of artificial coercion, and the freedom for every man to do what he can do best, joined to the knowledge of what productions of labour we really want. I must admit that this knowledge we reached slowly and painfully."

"Go on," said I, "give me more detail; explain more fully. For this subject interests me intensely."

"Yes, I will," said he; "but in order to do so I must weary you by talking a little about the past. Contrast is necessary for this explanation. Do you mind?"

"No, no," said I.

Said he, settling himself in his chair again for a long talk: "It is clear from all that we hear and read, that in the last age of civilisation men had got into a vicious circle in the matter of production of wares. They had reached a wonderful facility of production, and in order to make the most of that facility they had gradually created (or allowed to grow, rather) a most elaborate system of buying and selling, which has been called the World-Market; and that World-Market, once set a-going, forced them to go on making more and more of these wares, whether they needed them or not. So that while (of course) they could not free themselves from the toil of making real necessaries, they created in a never-ending series sham or artificial necessaries, which became, under the iron rule of the aforesaid World-Market, of equal importance to them with the real necessaries which supported life. By all this they burdened themselves with a prodigious mass of work merely for the sake of keeping their wretched system going."

"Yes—and then?" said I.

"Why, then, since they had forced themselves to stagger along under this horrible burden of unnecessary production, it became impossible for them to look upon labour and its results from any other point of view than one—to wit, the ceaseless endeavour to expend the least possible amount of labour on any article made, and yet at the same time to make as many articles as possible. To this 'cheapening of production,' as it was called, everything was sacrificed: the happiness of the workman at his work, nay, his most elementary comfort and bare health, his food, his clothes, his dwelling, his leisure, his amusement, his education—his life, in short—did not weigh a grain of sand in the balance against this dire necessity of 'cheap production' of things, a great part of which were not worth producing at all. Nay, we are told, and we must believe it, so overwhelming is the evidence, though many of our people scarcely *can* believe it, that even rich and powerful men, the masters of the poor devils aforesaid, submitted to live amidst sights and sounds and smells which it is in the very nature of man to abhor and flee from, in order that their riches might bolster up this supreme folly. The whole community, in fact, was cast into the jaws of this ravening monster, 'the cheap production' forced upon it by the World-Market.''

"Dear me!" said I. "But what happened? Did not their cleverness and facility in production master this chaos of misery at last? Couldn't they catch up with the World-Market, and then set to work to devise means for relieving themselves from this fearful task of extra labour?"

He smiled bitterly. "Did they even try to?" said he. "I am not sure. You know that according to the old saw the beetle gets used to living in dung; and these people, whether they found the dung sweet or not, certainly lived in it.''

His estimate of the life of the nineteenth century made me catch my breath a little; and I said feebly, "But the labour-saving machines?"

"Heyday!" quoth he. "What's that you are saying? the labour-saving machines? Yes, they were made to 'save labour' (or, to speak more plainly, the lives of men) on one piece of work in order that it might be expended—I will say wasted—on another, probably useless, piece of work. Friend, all their devices for cheapening labour simply resulted in increasing the burden of labour. The appetite of the World-Market grew with what it fed on: the countries within the ring of 'civilisation' (that is, organised misery) were glutted with the abortions of the market, and force and fraud were used unsparingly to 'open up' countries *outside* that pale. This process of 'opening up' is a strange one to those who have read the professions of the men of that period and do not understand their practice; and perhaps shows us at its worst the great vice of the nineteenth century, the use of hypocrisy and cant to evade the responsibility of vicarious ferocity. When the civilised World-Market coveted a country not yet in its clutches, some transparent pretext was found—the suppression of a slavery different from, and not so cruel as that of commerce; the pushing of a religion no longer believed in by its promoters; the 'rescue' of some desperado or homicidal madman whose misdeeds had got him into trouble amongst the natives of the 'barbarous' country—any stick, in short, which would

beat the dog at all. Then some bold, unprincipled, ignorant adventurer was found (no difficult task in the days
of competition), and he was bribed to 'create a market' by
breaking up whatever traditional society there might be in
the doomed country, and by destroying whatever leisure or
pleasure he found there. He forced wares on the natives
which they did not want, and took their natural products in
'exchange,' as this form of robbery was called, and thereby
he 'created new wants,' to supply which (that is, to be
allowed to live by their new masters) the hapless, helpless
people had to sell themselves into the slavery of hopeless
toil so that they might have something wherewith to
purchase the nullities of 'civilisation.' Ah," said the old
man, pointing to the Museum, "I have read books and
papers in there, telling strange stories indeed of the dealings
of civilisation (or organised misery) with 'non-civilisation';
from the time when the British Government deliberately
sent blankets infected with small-pox as choice gifts to
inconvenient tribes of Red-skins, to the time when Africa
was infested by a man named Stanley, who——"

"Excuse me," said I, "but as you know, time presses; and
I want to keep our question on the straightest line possible;
and I want at once to ask this about these wares made for
the World-Market—how about their quality; these people
who were so clever about making goods, I suppose they
made them well?"

"Quality!" said the old man crustily, for he was rather
peevish at being cut short in his story; "how could they
possibly attend to such trifles as the quality of the wares they
sold? The best of them were of a lowish average, the worst
were transparent make-shifts for the things asked for, which
nobody would have put up with if they could have got anything else. It was a current jest of the time that the wares
were made to sell and not to use; a jest which you, as coming
from another planet, may understand, but which our folk
could not."

Said I: "What! did they make nothing well?"

"Why, yes," said he, "there was one class of goods which
they did make thoroughly well, and that was the class of
machines which were used for making things. These were
usually quite perfect pieces of workmanship, admirably

adapted to the end in view. So that it may be fairly said that the great achievement of the nineteenth century was the making of machines which were wonders of invention, skill, and patience, and which were used for the production of measureless quantities of worthless make-shifts. In truth, the owners of the machines did not consider anything which they made as wares, but simply as means for the enrichment of themselves. Of course, the only admitted test of utility in wares was the finding of buyers for them—wise men or fools, as it might chance."

"And people put up with this?" said I.

"For a time," said he.

"And then?"

"And then the overturn," said the old man, smiling, "and the nineteenth century saw itself as a man who has lost his clothes whilst bathing, and has to walk naked through the town."

"You are very bitter about that unlucky nineteenth century," said I.

"Naturally," said he, "since I know so much about it."

He was silent a little, and then said: "There are traditions —nay, real histories—in our family about it: my grandfather was one of its victims. If you know something about it, you will understand what he suffered when I tell you that he was in those days a genuine artist, a man of genius, and a revolutionist."

"I think I do understand," said I: "but now, as it seems, you have reversed all this?"

"Pretty much so," said he. "The wares which we make are made because they are needed: men make for their neighbours' use as if they were making for themselves, not for a vague market of which they know nothing, and over which they have no control: as there is no buying and selling, it would be mere insanity to make goods on the chance of their being wanted; for there is no longer any one who can be *compelled* to buy them. So that whatever is made is good, and thoroughly fit for its purpose. Nothing *can* be made except for genuine use; therefore no inferior goods are made. Moreover, as aforesaid, we have now found out what we want, so we make no more than we want; and as we are not driven to make a vast quantity of useless things, we have time and resources enough to consider our pleasure in making them. All work which would be irksome to do by hand is done by immensely improved machinery; and in all work which it is a pleasure to do by hand machinery is done without. There is no difficulty in finding work which suits the special turn of mind of everybody; so that no man is sacrificed to the wants of another. From time to time, when we have found out that some piece of work was too disagreeable or troublesome, we have given it up and done altogether without the thing produced by it. Now, surely you can see that under these circumstances all the work that we do is an exercise of the mind and body more or less pleasant to be done: so that instead of avoiding work everybody seeks it: and, since people have got defter in doing the work generation after generation, it has become so easy to do, that it seems as if there were less done, though probably more is produced. I suppose this explains that fear, which I hinted at just now, of a possible scarcity in work, which perhaps you have already noticed, and which is a feeling on the increase, and has been for a score of years."

"But do you think," said I, "that there is any fear of a work-famine amongst you?"

"No, I do not," said he, "and I will tell why; it is each man's business to make his own work pleasanter and pleasanter, which of course tends towards raising the standard of excellence, as no man enjoys turning out work which is not a credit to him, and also to greater deliberation in turning it out; and there is such a vast number of things which can be treated as works of art, that this alone gives employment to a host of deft people. Again, if art be inexhaustible, so is science also; and though it is no longer the only innocent occupation which is thought worth an intelligent man spending his time upon, as it once was, yet there are, and I suppose will be, many people who are excited by its conquest of difficulties, and care for it more than for anything else. Again, as more and more of pleasure is imported into work, I think we shall take up kinds of work which produce desirable wares, but which we gave up because we could not carry them on pleasantly. Moreover, I think that it is only in parts of Europe which are more advanced than the rest of the world that you will hear this talk of the fear of a work-famine. Those lands which were once the colonies of Great Britain, for instance, and especially America—that part of it, above all, which was once the United States—are now and will be for a long while a great resource to us. For these lands, and, I say, especially the northern parts of America, suffered so terribly from the full force of the last days of civilisation, and became such horrible places to live in, that they are now very backward in all that makes life pleasant. Indeed, one may say that for nearly a hundred years the people of the northern parts of America have been engaged in gradually making a dwelling-place out of a stinking dust-heap; and there is still a great deal to do, especially as the country is so big."

"Well," said I, "I am exceedingly glad to think that you have such a prospect of happiness before you. But I should like to ask a few more questions, and then I have done for to-day."

CHAPTER XVI

DINNER IN THE HALL OF THE BLOOMSBURY MARKET

AS I spoke, I heard footsteps near the door; the latch yielded, and in came our two lovers, looking so handsome that one had no feeling of shame in looking on at their little-concealed love-making; for indeed it seemed as if all the world must be in love with them. As for old Hammond, he looked on them like an artist who has just painted a picture nearly as well as he thought he could when he began it, and was perfectly happy. He said:

"Sit down, sit down, young folk, and don't make a noise. Our guest here has still some questions to ask me."

"Well, I should suppose so," said Dick; "you have only been three hours and a half together; and it isn't to be hoped that the history of two centuries could be told in three hours and a half: let alone that, for all I know, you may have been wandering into the realms of geography and craftsmanship."

"As to noise, my dear kinsman," said Clara, "you will very soon be disturbed by the noise of the dinner-bell, which I should think will be very pleasant music to our guest, who breakfasted early, it seems, and probably had a tiring day yesterday."

I said: "Well, since you have spoken the word, I begin to feel that it is so; but I have been feeding myself with wonder this long time past: really, it's quite true," quoth I, as I saw her smile, O so prettily!

But just then from some tower high up in the air came the sound of silvery chimes playing a sweet clear tune, that sounded to my unaccustomed ears like the song of the first blackbird in the spring, and called a rush of memories to my mind, some of bad times, some of good, but all sweetened now into mere pleasure.

"No more questions now before dinner," said Clara; and she took my hand as an affectionate child would, and led me out of the room and down stairs into the forecourt of the Museum, leaving the two Hammonds to follow as they pleased.

We went into the market-place which I had been in before, a thinnish stream of elegantly[1] dressed people going in along with us. We turned into the cloister and came to a richly moulded and carved doorway, where a very pretty dark-haired young girl gave us each a beautiful bunch of summer flowers, and we entered a hall much bigger than that of the Hammersmith Guest House, more elaborate in its architecture and perhaps more beautiful. I found it difficult to keep my eyes off the wall-pictures (for I thought it bad manners to stare at Clara all the time, though she was quite worth it). I saw at a glance that their subjects were taken from queer old-world myths and imaginations which in yesterday's world only about half a dozen people in the country knew anything about; and when the two Hammonds sat down opposite to us, I said to the old man, pointing to the frieze:

"How strange to see such subjects here!"

"Why?" said he. "I don't see why you should be

[1] "Elegant," I mean, as a Persian pattern is elegant; not like a rich "elegant" lady out for a morning call. I should rather call that *genteel*.

surprised; everybody knows the tales; and they are graceful and pleasant subjects, not too tragic for a place where
people mostly eat and drink and amuse themselves, and yet
full of incident."

I smiled, and said: "Well, I scarcely expected to find
record of the Seven Swans and the King of the Golden
Mountain and Faithful Henry, and such curious pleasant
imaginations as Jacob Grimm got together from the childhood of the world, barely lingering even in his time: I should
have thought you would have forgotten such childishness
by this time."

The old man smiled, and said nothing; but Dick turned
rather red, and broke out:

"What *do* you mean, guest? I think them very beautiful,
I mean not only the pictures, but the stories; and when we
were children we used to imagine them going on in every
wood-end, by the bight of every stream: every house in the
fields was the Fairyland King's House to us. Don't you
remember, Clara?"

"Yes," she said; and it seemed to me as if a slight cloud
came over her fair face. I was going to speak to her on the
subject, when the pretty waitresses came to us smiling, and
chattering sweetly like reed warblers by the river-side, and
fell to giving us our dinner. As to this, as at our breakfast,
everything was cooked and served with a daintiness which
showed that those who had prepared it were interested in
it; but there was no excess either of quantity or of gourman-
dise; everything was simple, though so excellent of its kind;
and it was made clear to us that this was no feast, only an
ordinary meal. The glass, crockery, and plate were very
beautiful to my eyes, used to the study of mediæval art; but
a nineteenth-century club-haunter would, I daresay, have
found them rough and lacking in finish; the crockery being
lead-glazed pot-ware, though beautifully ornamented; the
only porcelain being here and there a piece of old oriental
ware. The glass, again, though elegant and quaint, and
very varied in form, was somewhat bubbled and hornier
in texture than the commercial articles of the nineteenth
century. The furniture and general fittings of the hall were
much of a piece with the table-gear, beautiful in form and
highly ornamented, but without the commercial "finish" of

the joiners and cabinet-makers of our time. Withal, there was a total absence of what the nineteenth century calls "comfort"—that is, stuffy inconvenience; so that, even apart from the delightful excitement of the day, I had never eaten my dinner so pleasantly before.

When we had done eating, and were sitting a little while, with a bottle of very good Bordeaux wine before us, Clara came back to the question of the subject-matter of the pictures, as though it had troubled her.

She looked up at them, and said: "How is it that though we are so interested with our life for the most part, yet when people take to writing poems or painting pictures they seldom deal with our modern life, or if they do, take good care to make their poems or pictures unlike that life? Are we not good enough to paint ourselves? How is it that we find the dreadful times of the past so interesting to us—in pictures and poetry?"

Old Hammond smiled. "It always was so, and I suppose always will be," said he, "however it may be explained. It is true that in the nineteenth century, when there was so little art and so much talk about it, there was a theory that art and imaginative literature ought to deal with contemporary life; but they never did so; for, if there was any pretence of it, the author always took care (as Clara hinted just now) to disguise, or exaggerate, or idealise, and in some way or another make it strange; so that, for all the verisimilitude there was, he might just as well have dealt with the times of the Pharaohs."

"Well," said Dick, "surely it is but natural to like these things strange; just as when we were children, as I said just now, we used to pretend to be so-and-so in such-and-such a place. That's what these pictures and poems do; and why shouldn't they?"

"Thou hast hit it, Dick," quoth old Hammond; "it is the child-like part of us that produces works of imagination. When we are children time passes so slow with us that we seem to have time for everything."

He sighed, and then smiled and said: "At least let us rejoice that we have got back our childhood again. I drink to the days that are!"

"Second childhood," said I in a low voice, and then

blushed at my double rudeness, and hoped that he hadn't heard. But he had, and turned to me smiling, and said: "Yes, why not? And for my part, I hope it may last long; and that the world's next period of wise and unhappy manhood, if that should happen, will speedily lead us to a third childhood: if indeed this age be not our third. Meantime, my friend, you must know that we are too happy, both individually and collectively, to trouble ourselves about what is to come hereafter."

"Well, for my part," said Clara, "I wish we were interesting enough to be written or painted about."

Dick answered her with some lover's speech, impossible to be written down, and then we sat quiet a little.

CHAPTER XVII

HOW THE CHANGE CAME

DICK broke the silence at last, saying: "Guest, forgive us for a little after-dinner dulness. What would you like to do? Shall we have out Greylocks and trot back to Hammersmith? or will you come with us and hear some Welsh folk sing in a hall close by here? or would you like presently to come with me into the City and see some really fine building? or—what shall it be?"

"Well," said I, "as I am a stranger, I must let you choose for me."

In point of fact, I did not by any means want to be "amused" just then; and also I rather felt as if the old man, with his knowledge of past times, and even a kind of inverted sympathy for them caused by his active hatred of them, was as it were a blanket for me against the cold of this very new world, where I was, so to say, stripped bare of every habitual thought and way of acting; and I did not want to leave him too soon. He came to my rescue at once, and said:

"Wait a bit, Dick; there is some one else to be consulted besides you and the guest here, and that is I. I am not going to lose the pleasure of his company just now, especially as I know he has something else to ask me. So go to your Welshmen, by all means; but first of all bring us

another bottle of wine to this nook, and then be off as soon
as you like; and come again and fetch our friend to go
westward, but not too soon."

Dick nodded smilingly, and the old man and I were soon
alone in the great hall, the afternoon sun gleaming on the
red wine in our tall quaint-shaped glasses. Then said
Hammond:

"Does anything especially puzzle you about our way of
living, now you have heard a good deal and seen a little
of it?"

Said I: "I think what puzzles me most is how it all came
about."

"It well may," said he, "so great as the change is. It
would be difficult indeed to tell you the whole story, perhaps impossible: knowledge, discontent, treachery, disappointment, ruin, misery, despair—those who worked for
the change because they could see further than other people
went through all these phases of suffering; and doubtless
all the time the most of men looked on, not knowing what
was doing, thinking it all a matter of course, like the rising
and setting of the sun—and indeed it was so."

"Tell me one thing, if you can," said I. "Did the change,
the 'revolution' it used to be called, come peacefully?"

"Peacefully?" said he; "what peace was there amongst
those poor confused wretches of the nineteenth century? It
was war from beginning to end: bitter war, till hope and
pleasure put an end to it."

"Do you mean actual fighting with weapons?" said I, "or
the strikes and lock-outs and starvation of which we have
heard?"

"Both, both," he said. "As a matter of fact, the history
of the terrible period of transition from commercial slavery
to freedom may thus be summarised. When the hope of
realising a communal condition of life for all men arose,
quite late in the nineteenth century, the power of the middle
classes, the then tyrants of society, was so enormous and
crushing, that to almost all men, even those who had, you
may say despite themselves, despite their reason and judgment, conceived such hopes, it seemed a dream. So much
was this the case that some of those more enlightened men
who were then called Socialists, although they well knew,

E

and even stated in public, that the only reasonable condition of Society was that of pure Communism (such as you now see around you), yet shrunk from what seemed to them the barren task of preaching the realisation of a happy dream. Looking back now, we can see that the great motive-power of the change was a longing for freedom and equality, akin if you please to the unreasonable passion of the lover; a sickness of heart that rejected with loathing the aimless solitary life of the well-to-do educated men of that time: phrases, my dear friend, which have lost their meaning to us of the present day; so far removed we are from the dreadful facts which they represent.

"Well, these men, though conscious of this feeling, had no faith in it, as a means of bringing about the change. Nor was that wonderful: for looking around them they saw the huge mass of the oppressed classes too much burdened with the misery of their lives, and too much overwhelmed by the selfishness of misery, to be able to form a conception of any escape from it except by the ordinary way prescribed by the system of slavery under which they lived; which was nothing more than a remote chance of climbing out of the oppressed into the oppressing class.

"Therefore, though they knew that the only reasonable aim for those who would better the world was a condition of equality; in their impatience and despair they managed to convince themselves that if they could by hook or by crook get the machinery of production and the management of property so altered that the 'lower classes' (so the horrible word ran) might have their slavery somewhat ameliorated, they would be ready to fit into this machinery, and would use it for bettering their condition still more and still more, until at last the result would be a practical equality (they were very fond of using the word 'practical'), because 'the rich' would be forced to pay so much for keeping 'the poor' in a tolerable condition that the condition of riches would become no longer valuable and would gradually die out. Do you follow me?"

"Partly," said I. "Go on."

Said old Hammond: "Well, since you follow me, you will see that as a theory this was not altogether unreasonable; but 'practically,' it turned out a failure."

"How so?" said I.

"Well, don't you see," said he, "because it involved the making of a machinery by those who didn't know what they wanted the machines to do. So far as the masses of the oppressed class furthered this scheme of improvement, they did it to get themselves improved slave-rations—as many of them as could. And if those classes had really been incapable of being touched by that instinct which produced the passion for freedom and equality aforesaid, what would have happened, I think, would have been this: that a certain part of the working classes would have been so far improved in condition that they would have approached the condition of the middling rich men; but below them would have been a great class of most miserable slaves, whose slavery would have been far more hopeless than the older class-slavery had been."

"What stood in the way of this?" said I.

"Why, of course," said he, "just that instinct for freedom aforesaid. It is true that the slave-class could not conceive the happiness of a free life. Yet they grew to understand (and very speedily too) that they were oppressed by their masters, and they assumed, you see how justly, that they could do without them, though perhaps they scarce knew how; so that it came to this, that though they could not look forward to the happiness or peace of the freeman, they did at least look forward to the war which a vague hope told them would bring that peace about."

"Could you tell me rather more closely what actually took place?" said I; for I thought *him* rather vague here.

"Yes," he said, "I can. That machinery of life for the use of people who didn't know what they wanted of it, and which was known at the time as State Socialism, was partly put in motion, though in a very piecemeal way. But it did not work smoothly; it was, of course, resisted at every turn by the capitalists; and no wonder, for it tended more and more to upset the commercial system I have told you of, without providing anything really effective in its place. The result was growing confusion, great suffering amongst the working classes, and, as a consequence, great discontent. For a long time matters went on like this. The power of the upper classes had lessened, as their command over wealth lessened, and they could not carry things wholly by the high hand as they had been used to in earlier days. So far the State Socialists were justified by the result. On the other hand, the working classes were ill-organised, and growing poorer in reality, in spite of the gains (also real in the long run) which they had forced from the masters. Thus matters hung in the balance, the masters could not reduce their slaves to complete subjection, though they put down some feeble and partial riots easily enough. The workers forced their masters to grant them ameliorations, real or imaginary, of their condition, but could not force freedom from them. At last came a great crash. To explain this you must understand that very great progress had been made amongst the workers, though as before said but little in the direction of improved livelihood."

I played the innocent and said: "In what direction could they improve, if not in livelihood?"

Said he: "In the power to bring about a state of things in which livelihood would be full, and easy to gain. They had at last learned how to combine after a long period of mistakes and disasters. The workmen had now a regular organisation in the struggle against, their masters a struggle which for more than half a century had been accepted as an inevitable part of the conditions of the modern system of labour and production. This combination had now taken the form of a federation of all or almost all the recognised wage-paid employments, and it was by its means that those betterments of the condition of the workmen had been forced from the masters: and though they were not seldom mixed up with the rioting that happened, especially in the earlier days of their organisation, it by no means formed an essential part of their tactics; indeed at the time I am now speaking of they had got to be so strong that most commonly the mere threat of a 'strike' was enough to gain any minor point: because they had given up the foolish tactics of the ancient trades unions of calling out of work a part only of the workers of such and such an industry, and supporting them while out of work on the labour of those that remained in. By this time they had a biggish fund of money for the support of strikes, and could stop a certain industry altogether for a time if they so determined."

Said I: "Was there not a serious danger of such moneys being misused—of jobbery, in fact?"

Old Hammond wriggled uneasily on his seat, and said: "Though all this happened so long ago, I still feel the pain of mere shame when I have to tell you that it was more than a danger: that such rascality often happened; indeed more than once the whole combination seemed dropping to pieces because of it: but at the time of which I am telling, things looked so threatening, and to the work-men at least the necessity of their dealing with the fast-gathering trouble which the labour-struggle had brought about, was so clear, that the conditions of the times had begot a deep seriousness amongst all reasonable people; a determination which put aside all non-essentials, and which to thinking men was ominous of the swiftly-approaching change: such an element was too dangerous for mere traitors and self-seekers, and one by one they were thrust out and mostly joined the declared reactionaries."

"How about those ameliorations," said I; "what were they? or rather of what nature?"

Said he: "Some of them, and these of the most practical importance to the men's livelihood, were yielded by the masters by direct compulsion on the part of the men; the new conditions of labour so gained were indeed only cus-tomary, enforced by no law: but, once established, the masters durst not attempt to withdraw them in face of the growing power of the combined workers. Some again were steps on the path of 'State Socialism'; the most important of which can be speedily summed up. At the end of the nineteenth century the cry arose for compelling the masters to employ their men a less number of hours in the day: this cry gathered volume quickly, and the masters had to yield to it. But it was, of course, clear that unless this meant a higher price for work per hour, it would be a mere nullity, and that the masters, unless forced, would reduce it to that. Therefore after a long struggle another law was passed fixing a minimum price for labour in the most important industries; which again had to be supplemented by a law fixing the maximum price on the chief wares then considered necessary for a workman's life."

"You were getting perilously near to the late Roman

poor-rates," said I, smiling, "and the doling out of bread to the proletariat."

"So many said at the time," said the old man drily; "and it has long been a commonplace that that slough awaits State Socialism in the end, if it gets to the end, which as you know it did not with us. However, it went further than this minimum and maximum business, which by the bye we can now see was necessary. The government now found it imperative on them to meet the outcry of the master class at the approaching destruction of commerce (as desirable, had they known it, as the extinction of the cholera, which has since happily taken place). And they were forced to meet it by a measure hostile to the masters, the establishment of government factories for the production of necessary wares, and markets for their sale. These measures taken altogether did do something: they were in fact of the nature of regulations made by the commander of a beleaguered city. But of course to the privileged classes it seemed as if the end of the world were come when such laws were enacted.

"Nor was that altogether without a warrant: the spread of communistic theories, and the partial practice of State Socialism had at first disturbed, and at last almost paralysed the marvellous system of commerce under which the old world had lived so feverishly, and had produced for some few a life of gambler's pleasure, and for many, or most, a life of mere misery: over and over again came 'bad times' as they were called, and indeed they were bad enough for the wage-slaves. The year 1952 was one of the worst of these times; the workmen suffered dreadfully: the partial inefficient government factories, which were terribly jobbed, all but broke down, and a vast part of the population had for the time being to be fed on undisguised 'charity' as it was called.

"The Combined Workers watched the situation with mingled hope and anxiety. They had already formulated their general demands; but now by a solemn and universal vote of the whole of their federated societies, they insisted on the first step being taken toward carrying out their demands: this step would have led directly to handing over the management of the whole natural resources of the country, together with the machinery for using them, into the power of the Combined Workers, and the reduction of the privileged classes into the position of pensioners obviously dependent on the pleasure of the workers. The 'Resolutior,' as it was called, which was widely published in the newspapers of the day, was in fact a declaration of war, and was so accepted by the master class. They began henceforward to prepare for a firm stand against the 'brutal and ferocious communism of the day,' as they phrased it. And as they were in many ways still very powerful, or seemed so to be, they still hoped by means of brute force to regain some of what they had lost, and perhaps in the end the whole of it. It was said amongst them on all hands that it had been a great mistake of the various governments not to have resisted sooner; and the liberals and radicals (the name as perhaps you may know of the more democratically inclined part of the ruling classes) were much blamed for having led the world to this pass by their mis-timed pedantry and foolish sentimentality: and one Gladstone, or Gledstein (probably, judging by this name, of Scandinavian descent), a notable politician of the nineteenth century, was especially singled out for reprobation in this respect. I need scarcely point out to you the absurdity of all this. But terrible tragedy lay hidden behind this grinning through a horse-collar of the reactionary party. 'The insatiable greed of the lower classes must be repressed'—'The people must be taught a lesson'—these were the sacramental phrases current amongst the reactionists, and ominous enough they were."

The old man stopped to look keenly at my attentive and wondering face, and then said:

"I know, dear guest, that I have been using words and phrases which few people amongst us could understand without long and laborious explanation; and not even then perhaps. But since you have not yet gone to sleep, and since I am speaking to you as to a being from another planet, I may venture to ask you if you have followed me thus far?"

"O yes," said I, "I quite understand: pray go on; a great deal of what you have been saying was common-place with us—when—when——"

"Yes," said he gravely, "when you were dwelling in the other planet. Well, now for the crash aforesaid.

"On some comparatively trifling occasion a great meeting was summoned by the workmen leaders to meet in Trafalgar Square (about the right to meet in which place there had for years and years been bickering). The civic bourgeois guard (called the police) attacked the said meeting with bludgeons, according to their custom; many people were hurt in the *mêlée*, of whom five in all died, either trampled to death on the spot, or from the effects of their cudgelling; the meeting was scattered, and some hundred of prisoners cast into gaol. A similar meeting had been treated in the same way a few days before at a place called Manchester, which has now disappeared. Thus the 'lesson' began. The whole country was thrown into a ferment by this; meetings were held which attempted some rough organisation for the holding of another meeting to retort on the authorities. A huge crowd assembled in Trafalgar Square and the neighbourhood (then a place of crowded streets), and was too big for the bludgeon-armed police to cope with; there was a good deal of dry-blow fighting; three or four of the people were killed, and half a score of policemen were crushed to death in the throng, and the rest got away as they could. This was a victory for the people as far as it went. The next day all London (remember what it was in those days) was in a state of turmoil. Many of the rich fled into the country; the executive got together soldiery, but did not dare to use them; and the police could not be massed in any one place, because riots or threats of riots were everywhere. But in Manchester, where the people were not so courageous or not so desperate as in London, several of the popular leaders were arrested. In London a convention of leaders was got together from the Federation of Combined Workmen, and sat under the old revolutionary name of the Committee of Public Safety; but as they had no drilled and armed body of men to direct, they attempted no aggressive measures, but only placarded the walls with somewhat vague appeals to the workmen not to allow themselves to be trampled upon. However, they called a meeting in Trafalgar Square for the day fortnight of the last-mentioned skirmish.

"Meantime the town grew no quieter, and business came pretty much to an end. The newspapers—then, as always hitherto, almost entirely in the hands of the masters—clamoured to the Government for repressive measures; the rich citizens were enrolled as an extra body of police, and armed with bludgeons like them; many of these were strong, well-fed, full-blooded young men, and had plenty of stomach for fighting; but the Government did not dare to use them, and contented itself with getting full powers voted to it by the Parliament for suppressing any revolt, and bringing up more and more soldiers to London. Thus passed the week after the great meeting; almost as large a one was held on the Sunday, which went off peaceably on the whole, as no opposition to it was offered, and again the people cried 'victory.' But on the Monday the people woke up to find that they were hungry. During the last few days there had been groups of men parading the streets asking (or, if you please, demanding) money to buy food; and what for goodwill, what for fear, the richer people gave them a good deal. The authorities of the parishes also (I haven't time to explain that phrase at present) gave willy-nilly what provisions they could to wandering people; and the Government, by means of its feeble national workshops, also fed a good number of half-starved folk. But in addition to this, several bakers' shops and other provision stores had been emptied without a great deal of disturbance. So far, so good. But on the Monday in question the Committee of Public Safety, on the one hand afraid of general unorganised pillage, and on the other emboldened by the wavering conduct of the authorities, sent a deputation provided with carts and all necessary gear to clear out two or three big provision stores in the centre of the town, leaving papers with the shop managers promising to pay the price of them; and also in the part of the town where they were strongest they took possession of several bakers' shops and set men at work in them for the benefit of the people;—all of which was done with little or no disturbance, the police assisting in keeping order at the sack of the stores, as they would have done at a big fire.

"But at this last stroke the reactionaries were so alarmed, that they were determined to force the executive into action. The newspapers next day all blazed into the fury of frightened people, and threatened the people, the Government, and everybody they could think of, unless 'order were at once restored.' A deputation of leading commercial people waited on the Government and told them that if they did not at once arrest the Committee of Public Safety, they themselves would gather, a body of men, arm them, and fall on 'the incendiaries,' as they called them.

"They, together with a number of the newspaper editors, had a long interview with the heads of the Government and two or three military men, the deftest in their art that the country could furnish. The deputation came away from that interview, says a contemporary eye-witness, smiling and satisfied, and said no more about raising an anti-popular army, but that afternoon left London with their families for their country seats or elsewhere.

"The next morning the Government proclaimed a state of siege in London,—a thing common enough amongst the absolutist governments on the Continent, but unheard of in England in those days. They appointed the youngest and cleverest of their generals to command the proclaimed district; a man who had won a certain sort of reputation in the disgraceful wars in which the country had been long engaged from time to time. The newspapers were in ecstasies, and all the most fervent of the reactionaries now came to the front; men who in ordinary times were forced to keep their opinions to themselves or their immediate circle, but who began to look forward to crushing once for all the Socialist, and even democratic tendencies, which, said they, had been treated with such foolish indulgence for the last sixty years.

"But the clever general took no visible action; and yet only a few of the minor newspapers abused him; thoughtful men gathered from this that a plot was hatching. As for the Committee of Public Safety, whatever they thought of their position, they had now gone too far to draw back; and many of them, it seems, thought that the Government would not act. They went on quietly organising their food supply, which was a miserable driblet when all is said; and also as a retort to the state of siege, they armed as many men as they could in the quarter where they were strongest, but did not attempt to drill or organise them, thinking, perhaps, that they could not at the best turn them into trained soldiers till they had some breathing space. The clever general, his soldiers, and the police did not meddle with all this in the least in the world; and things were quieter in London that week-end; though there were riots in many places of the provinces, which were quelled by the authorities without much trouble. The most serious of these were at Glasgow and Bristol.

"Well, the Sunday of the meeting came, and great crowds came to Trafalgar Square in procession, the greater part of the Committee amongst them, surrounded by their band of men armed somehow or other. The streets were quite peaceful and quiet, though there were many spectators to see the procession pass. Trafalgar Square had no body of police in it; the people took quiet possession of it, and the meeting began. The armed men stood round the principal platform, and there were a few others armed amidst the general crowd; but by far the greater part were unarmed.

"Most people thought the meeting would go off peaceably; but the members of the Committee had heard from various quarters that something would be attempted against them; but these rumours were vague, and they had no idea of what threatened. They soon found out.

"For before the streets about the Square were filled, a body of soldiers poured into it from the north-west corner and took up their places by the houses that stood on the west side. The people growled at the sight of the red-coats; the armed men of the Committee stood undecided, not knowing what to do; and indeed this new influx so jammed the crowd together that, unorganised as they were, they had little chance of working through it. They had scarcely grasped the fact of their enemies being there, when another column of soldiers, pouring out of the streets which led into the great southern road going down to the Parliament House (still existing, and called the Dung Market), and also from the embankment by the side of the Thames, marched up, pushing the crowd into a denser and denser mass, and formed along the south side of the Square. Then any of those who could see what was going on, knew at once that they were in a trap, and could only wonder what would be done with them.

"The closely-packed crowd would not or could not budge, except under the influence of the height of terror, which was soon to be supplied to them. A few of the armed men struggled to the front, or climbed up to the base of the monument which then stood there, that they might face the wall of hidden fire before them; and to most men (there were many women amongst them) it seemed as if the end of the world had come, and to-day seemed strangely different from yesterday. No sooner were the soldiers drawn up aforesaid than, says an eye-witness, 'a glittering officer on horseback came prancing out from the ranks on the south, and read something from a paper which he held in his hand; which something, very few heard; but I was told afterwards that it was an order for us to disperse, and a warning that he had legal right to fire on the crowd else, and that he would do so. The crowd took it as a challenge of some sort, and a hoarse threatening roar went up from them; and after that there was comparative silence for a little, till the officer had got back into the ranks. I was near the edge of the crowd, towards the soldiers,' says this eye-witness, 'and I saw three little machines being wheeled out in front of the ranks, which I knew for mechanical guns. I cried out, "Throw yourselves down! they are going to fire!" But no one scarcely could throw himself down, so tight as the crowd were packed. I heard a sharp order given, and wondered where I should be the next minute; and then— It was as if the earth had opened, and hell had come up bodily amidst us. It is no use trying to describe the scene that followed. Deep lanes were mowed amidst the thick crowd; the dead and dying covered the ground, and the shrieks and wails and cries of horror filled all the air, till it seemed as if there was nothing else in the world but murder and death. Those of our armed men who were still unhurt cheered wildly and opened a scattering fire on the soldiers. One or two soldiers fell; and I saw the officers going up and down the ranks urging the men to fire again; but they received the orders in sullen silence, and let the butts of their guns fall. Only one sergeant ran to a machine-gun and began to set it going; but a tall young man, an officer too, ran out of the ranks and dragged him back by the collar; and the soldiers stood there motionless whilst the horror-stricken crowd, nearly wholly unarmed (for most of the armed men had fallen in that first discharge), drifted out of the Square. I was told afterwards that the soldiers on the west side had fired also, and done their part of the slaughter. How I got out of the Square I scarcely know: I went, not feeling the ground under me, what with rage and terror and despair.'

"So says our eye-witness. The number of the slain on the side of the people in that shooting during a minute was prodigious; but it was not easy to come at the truth about it; it was probably between one and two thousand. Of the soldiers, six were killed outright, and a dozen wounded."

I listened, trembling with excitement. The old man's eyes glittered and his face flushed as he spoke, and told the tale of what I had often thought might happen. Yet I wondered that he should have got so elated about a mere massacre, and I said:

"How fearful! And I suppose that this massacre put an end to the whole revolution for that time?"

"No, no," cried old Hammond; "it began it!"

He filled his glass and mine, and stood up and cried out, "Drink this glass to the memory of those who died there, for indeed it would be a long tale to tell how much we owe them."

I drank, and he sat down again and went on.

"That massacre of Trafalgar Square began the civil war, though, like all such events, it gathered head slowly, and people scarcely knew what a crisis they were acting in.

"Terrible as the massacre was, and hideous and over-powering as the first terror had been, when the people had time to think about it, their feeling was one of anger rather than fear; although the military organisation of the state of siege was now carried out without shrinking by the clever young general. For though the ruling-classes when the news spread next morning felt one gasp of horror and even dread, yet the Government and their immediate backers felt that now the wine was drawn and must be drunk. However, even the most reactionary of the capitalist papers, with two exceptions, stunned by the tremendous news, simply gave an account of what had taken place, without making any comment upon it. The exceptions were one, a so-called 'Liberal' paper (the Government of the day was of that complexion), which, after a preamble in which it declared its undeviating sympathy with the cause of labour, proceeded to point out that in times of revolutionary disturbance it behoved the Government to be just but firm, and that by far the most merciful way of dealing with the poor madmen who were attacking the very foundations of society (which had made them mad and poor) was to shoot them at once, so as to stop others from drifting into a position in which they would run a chance of being shot. In short, it praised the determined action of the Government as the *acmé* of human wisdom and mercy, and exulted in the inauguration of an epoch of reasonable democracy free from the tyrannical fads of Socialism.

"The other exception was a paper thought to be one of the most violent opponents of democracy, and so it was; but the editor of it found his manhood, and spoke for himself and not for his paper. In a few simple, indignant words he asked people to consider what a society was worth which had to be defended by the massacre of unarmed citizens, and called on the Government to withdraw their state of siege and put the general and his officers who fired on the people on their trial for murder. He went further, and declared that whatever his opinion might be as to the doctrines of the Socialists, he for one should throw in his lot with the people, until the Government atoned for their atrocity by showing that they were prepared to listen to the demands of men who knew what they wanted, and whom the decrepitude of society forced into pushing their demands in some way or other.

"Of course, this editor was immediately arrested by the military power; but his bold words were already in the hands of the public, and produced a great effect: so great an effect that the Government, after some vacillation, withdrew the state of siege; though at the same time it strengthened the military organisation and made it more stringent. Three of the Committee of Public Safety had been slain in Trafalgar Square: of the rest, the greater part went back to their old place of meeting, and there awaited the event calmly. They were arrested there on the Monday morning, and would have been shot at once by the general, who was a

mere military machine, if the Government had not shrunk
before the responsibility of killing men without any trial.
There was at first a talk of trying them by a special commission of judges, as it was called—*i.e.*, before a set of men
bound to find them guilty, and whose business it was to do
so. But with the Government the cold fit had succeeded to
the hot one; and the prisoners were brought before a jury
at the assizes. There a fresh blow awaited the Government;
for in spite of the judge's charge, which distinctly instructed
the jury to find the prisoners guilty, they were acquitted,
and the jury added to their verdict a presentment, in which
they condemned the action of the soldiery, in the queer
phraseology of the day, as 'rash, unfortunate, and unnecessary.' The Committee of Public Safety renewed its sittings,
and from thenceforth was a popular rallying-point in opposition to the Parliament. The Government now gave way
on all sides, and made a show of yielding to the demands
of the people, though there was a widespread plot for
effecting a *coup d'état* set on foot between the leaders of the
two so-called opposing parties in the parliamentary faction
fight. The well-meaning part of the public was overjoyed,
and thought that all danger of a civil war was over. The
victory of the people was celebrated by huge meetings held
in the parks and elsewhere, in memory of the victims of the
great massacre.

"But the measures passed for the relief of the workers,
though to the upper classes they seemed ruinously revolutionary, were not thorough enough to give the people food
and a decent life, and they had to be supplemented by un-
written enactments without legality to back them. Although the Government and Parliament had the law-courts,
the army, and 'society' at their backs, the Committee of
Public Safety began to be a force in the country, and really
represented the producing classes. It began to improve
immensely in the days which followed on the acquittal of
its members. Its old members had little administrative
capacity, though with the exception of a few self-seekers
and traitors, they were honest, courageous men, and many
of them were endowed with considerable talent of other
kinds. But now that the times called for immediate action,
came forward the men capable of setting it on foot; and

a new network of workmen's associations grew up very speedily, whose avowed single object was the tiding over of the ship of the community into a simple condition of Communism; and as they practically undertook also the management of the ordinary labour-war, they soon became the mouthpiece and intermediary of the whole of the working classes; and the manufacturing profit-grinders now found themselves powerless before this combination; unless *their* committee, Parliament, plucked up courage to begin the civil war again, and to shoot right and left, they were bound to yield to the demands of the men whom they employed, and pay higher and higher wages for shorter and shorter day's work. Yet one ally they had, and that was the rapidly approaching breakdown of the whole system founded on the World-Market and its supply; which now became so clear to all people, that the middle classes, shocked for the moment into condemnation of the Government for the great massacre, turned round nearly in a mass, and called on the Government to look to matters, and put an end to the tyranny of the Socialist leaders.

"Thus stimulated, the reactionist plot exploded probably before it was ripe; but this time the people and their leaders were forewarned, and, before the reactionaries could get under way, had taken the steps they thought necessary.

"The Liberal Government (clearly by collusion) was beaten by the Conservatives, though the latter were nominally much in the minority. The popular representatives in the House understood pretty well what this meant, and after an attempt to fight the matter out by divisions in the House of Commons, they made a protest, left the House, and came in a body to the Committee of Public Safety: and the civil war began again in good earnest.

"Yet its first act was not one of mere fighting. The new Tory Government determined to act, yet durst not re-enact the state of siege, but it sent a body of soldiers and police to arrest the Committee of Public Safety in the lump. They made no resistance, though they might have done so, as they had now a considerable body of men who were quite prepared for extremities. But they were determined to try first a weapon which they thought stronger than street fighting.

"The members of the Committee went off quietly to prison; but they had left their soul and their organisation behind them. For they depended not on a carefully arranged centre with all kinds of checks and counter-checks about it, but on a huge mass of people in thorough sympathy with the movement, bound together by a great number of links of small centres with very simple instructions. These instructions were now carried out.

"The next morning, when the leaders of the reaction were chuckling at the effect which the report in the newspapers of their stroke would have upon the public—no newspapers appeared; and it was only towards noon that a few straggling sheets, about the size of the gazettes of the seventeenth century, worked by policemen, soldiers, managers, and press-writers, were dribbled through the streets. They were greedily seized on and read; but by this time the serious part of their news was stale, and people did not need to be told that the GENERAL STRIKE had begun. The railways did not run, the telegraph-wires were unserved; flesh, fish, and green stuff brought to market was allowed to lie there still packed and perishing; the thousands of middle-class families, who were utterly dependent for the next meal on the workers, made frantic efforts through their more energetic members to cater for the needs of the day, and amongst those of them who could throw off the fear of what was to follow, there was, I am told, a certain enjoyment of this unexpected picnic—a forecast of the days to come, in which all labour grew pleasant.

"So passed the first day, and towards evening the Government grew quite distracted. They had but one resource for putting down any popular movement—to wit, mere brute-force; but there was nothing for them against which to use their army and police: no armed bodies appeared in the streets; the offices of the Federated Workmen were now, in appearance, at least, turned into places for the relief of people thrown out of work, and under the circumstances, they durst not arrest the men engaged in such business, all the more, as even that night many quite respectable people applied at these offices for relief, and swallowed down the charity of the revolutionists along with their supper. So the Government massed soldiers and police here and there—

and sat still for that night, fully expecting on the morrow some manifesto from 'the rebels,' as they now began to be called, which would give them an opportunity of acting in some way or another. They were disappointed. The ordinary newspapers gave up the struggle that morning, and only one very violent reactionary paper (called the *Daily Telegraph*) attempted an appearance, and rated 'the rebels' in good set terms for their folly and ingratitude in tearing out the bowels of their 'common mother,' the English Nation, for the benefit of a few greedy paid agitators, and the fools whom they were deluding. On the other hand, the Socialist papers (of which three only, representing somewhat different schools, were published in London) came out full to the throat of well-printed matter. They were greedily bought by the whole public, who, of course, like the Government, expected a manifesto in them. But they found no word of reference to the great subject. It seemed as if their editors had ransacked their drawers for articles which would have been in place forty years before, under the technical name of educational articles. Most of these were admirable and straightforward expositions of the doctrines and practice of Socialism, free from haste and spite and hard words, and came upon the public with a kind of May-day freshness amidst the worry and terror of the moment; and though the knowing well understood that the meaning of this move in the game was mere defiance, and a token of irreconcilable hostility to the then rulers of society, and though, also, they were meant for nothing else by 'the rebels,' yet they really had their effect as 'educational articles.' However, 'education' of another kind was acting upon the public with irresistible power, and probably cleared their heads a little.

"As to the Government, they were absolutely terrified by this act of 'boycotting' (the slang word then current for such acts of abstention). Their counsels became wild and vacillating to the last degree: one hour they were for giving way for the present till they could hatch another plot; the next they all but sent an order for the arrest in the lump of all the workmen's committees; the next they were on the point of ordering their brisk young general to take any excuse that offered for another massacre. But when they called to mind that the soldiery in that 'Battle' of Trafalgar Square were so daunted by the slaughter which they had made, that they could not be got to fire a second volley, they shrank back again from the dreadful courage necessary for carrying out another massacre. Meantime the prisoners, brought the second time before the magistrates under a strong escort of soldiers, were the second time remanded.

"The strike went on this day also. The workmen's committees were extended, and gave relief to great numbers of people, for they had organised a considerable amount of production of food by men whom they could depend upon. Quite a number of well-to-do people were now compelled to seek relief of them. But another curious thing happened: a band of young men of the upper classes armed themselves, and coolly went marauding in the streets, taking what suited them of such eatables and portables that they came across in the shops which had ventured to open. This operation they carried out in Oxford Street, then a great street of shops of all kinds. The Government, being at that hour in one of their yielding moods, thought this a fine opportunity for showing their impartiality in the maintenance of 'order,' and sent to arrest these hungry rich youths; who, however, surprised the police by a valiant resistance, so that all but three escaped. The Government did not gain the reputation for impartiality which they expected from this move; for they forgot that there were no evening papers; and the account of the skirmish spread wide indeed, but in a distorted form; for it was mostly told simply as an exploit of the starving people from the East-end; and everybody thought it was but natural for the Government to put them down when and where they could.

"That evening the rebel prisoners were visited in their cells by *very* polite and sympathetic persons, who pointed out to them what a suicidal course they were following, and how dangerous these extreme courses were for the popular cause. Says one of the prisoners: 'It was great sport comparing notes when we came out anent the attempt of the Government to "get at" us separately in prison, and how we answered the blandishments of the highly "intelligent and refined" persons set on to pump us. One laughed; another told extravagant long-bow stories to the envoy; a third held a sulky silence; a fourth damned the polite spy and bade him hold his jaw—and that was all they got out of us.'

"So passed the second day of the great strike. It was clear to all thinking people that the third day would bring on the crisis; for the present suspense and ill-concealed terror was unendurable. The ruling classes, and the middle-class non-politicians who had been their real strength and support, were as sheep lacking a shepherd; they literally did not know what to do.

"One thing they found they had to do: try to get the 'rebels' to do something. So the next morning, the morning of the third day of the strike, when the members of the Committee of Public Safety appeared again before the magistrate, they found themselves treated with the greatest possible courtesy—in fact, rather as envoys and ambassadors than prisoners. In short, the magistrate had received his orders; and with no more to do than might come of a long stupid speech which might have been written by Dickens in mockery, he discharged the prisoners, who went back to their meeting-place and at once began a due sitting. It was high time. For this third day the mass was fermenting indeed. There was, of course, a vast number of working people who were not organised in the least in the world: men who had been used to act as their masters drove them, or rather as the system drove, of which their másters were a part. That system was now falling to pieces, and the old pressure of the master having been taken off these poor men' it seemed likely that nothing but the mere animal necessities and passions of men would have any hold on them, and that mere general overturn would be the result. Doubtless this would have happened if it had not been that the huge mass had been leavened by Socialist opinion in the first place, and in the second place by actual contact with declared Socialists, many or indeed most of whom were members of those bodies of workmen above said.

"If anything of this kind had happened some years before, when the masters of labour were still looked upon as the natural rulers of the people, and even the poorest and most ignorant men leaned upon them for support, while they sub-mitted to their fleecing, the entire break-up of all society would have followed. But the long series of years during which the workmen had learned to despise their rulers, had done away with their dependence upon them, and they were now beginning to trust (somewhat dangerously, as events proved) in the non-legal leaders whom events had thrust forward; and though most of these were now become mere figure-heads, their names and reputations were useful in this crisis as a stop gap.

"The effect of the news, therefore, of the release of the Committee gave the Government some breathing time: for it was received with the greatest joy by the workers, and even the well-to-do saw in it a respite from the mere destruction which they had begun to dread, and the fear of which most of them attributed to the weakness of the Government. As far as the passing hour went, perhaps they were right in this."

"How do you mean?" said I. "What could the Government have done? I often used to think that they would be helpless in such a crisis."

Said old Hammond: "Of course I don't doubt that in the long run matters would have come about as they did. But if the Government could have treated their army as a real army, and used them strategically as a general would have done, looking on the people as a mere open enemy to be shot at and dispersed wherever they turned up, they would probably have gained the victory at the time."

"But would the soldiers have acted against the people in this way?" said I.

Said he: "I think from all I have heard that they would have done so if they had met bodies of men armed however badly, and however badly they had been organised. It seems also as if before the Trafalgar Square massacre they might as a whole have been depended upon to fire upon an unarmed crowd, though they were much honeycombed by Socialism. The reason for this was that they dreaded the use by apparently unarmed men of an explosive called dynamite, of which many loud boasts were made by the workers on the eve of these events; although it turned out to be of little use as a material for war in the way that was expected. Of course the officers of the soldiery fanned this fear to the utmost, so that the rank and file probably thought on that occasion that they were being led into a desperate battle with men who were really armed, and whose weapon was the more dreadful, because it was concealed. After that massacre, however, it was at all times doubtful if the regular soldiers would fire upon an unarmed or half-armed crowd."

Said I: "The regular soldiers? Then there were other combatants against the people?"

"Yes," said he, "we shall come to that presently."

"Certainly," I said, "you had better go on straight with your story. I see that time is wearing."

Said Hammond: "The Government lost no time in coming to terms with the Committee of Public Safety; for indeed they could think of nothing else than the danger of the moment. They sent a duly accredited envoy to treat with these men, who somehow had obtained dominion over people's minds, while the formal rulers had no hold except over their bodies. There is no need at present to go into the details of the truce (for such it was) between these high contracting parties, the Government of the empire of Great Britain and a handful of working-men (as they were called in scorn in those days), amongst whom, indeed, were some very capable and 'square-headed' persons, though, as aforesaid, the abler men were not then the recognised leaders. The upshot of it was that all the definite claims of the people had to be granted. We can now see that most of these claims were of themselves not worth either demanding or resisting; but they were looked on at that time as most important, and they were at least tokens of revolt against the miserable system of life which was then beginning to tumble to pieces. One claim, however, was of the utmost immediate importance, and this the Government tried hard to evade; but as they were not dealing with fools, they had to yield at last. This was the claim of recognition and formal status for the Committee of Public Safety, and all the associations which it fostered under its wing. This it is clear meant two things: first, amnesty for 'the rebels,' great and small, who, without a distinct act of civil war, could no longer be attacked; and next, a continuance of the organised revolution. Only one point the Government could gain, and that was a name. The dreadful revolutionary title was dropped, and the body, with its branches,

acted under the respectable name of the 'Board of Concili-
ation and its local offices.' Carrying this name, it became
the leader of the people in the civil war which soon
followed."

"O," said I, somewhat startled, "so the civil war went on,
in spite of all that had happened?"

"So it was," said he. "In fact, it was this very legal
recognition which made the civil war possible in the
ordinary sense of war; it took the struggle out of the element
of mere massacres on one side, and endurance plus strikes
on the other."

"And can you tell me in what kind of way the war was
carried on?" said I.

"Yes," he said; "we have records and to spare of all that;
and the essence of them I can give you in a few words. As
I told you, the rank and file of the army was not to be
trusted by the reactionists; but the officers generally were
prepared for anything, for they were mostly the very
stupidest men in the country. Whatever the Government
might do, a great part of the upper and middle classes were
determined to set on foot a counter revolution; for the Communism which now loomed ahead seemed quite unendurable to them. Bands of young men, like the marauders in
the great strike of whom I told you just now, armed themselves and drilled, and began on any opportunity or pretence to skirmish with the people in the streets. The Government neither helped them nor put them down, but stood
by, hoping that something might come of it. These 'Friends
of Order,' as they were called, had some successes at first,
and grew bolder; they got many officers of the regular army
to help them, and by their means laid hold of munitions of
war of all kinds. One part of their tactics consisted in their
guarding and even garrisoning the big factories of the
period: they held at one time, for instance, the whole of
that place called Manchester which I spoke of just now.
A sort of irregular war was carried on with varied success
all over the country; and at last the Government, which at
first pretended to ignore the struggle, or treat it as mere
rioting, definitely declared for 'the Friends of Order,' and
joined to their bands whatsoever of the regular army
they could get together, and made a desperate effort to

overwhelm 'the rebels,' as they were now once more called, and as indeed they called themselves.

"It was too late. All ideas of peace on a basis of compromise had disappeared on either side. The end, it was seen clearly, must be either absolute slavery for all but the privileged, or a system of life founded on equality and Communism. The sloth, the hopelessness, and, if I may say so, the cowardice of the last century, had given place to the eager, restless heroism of a declared revolutionary period. I will not say that the people of that time foresaw the life we are leading now, but there was a general instinct amongst them towards the essential part of that life, and many men saw clearly beyond the desperate struggle of the day into the peace which it was to bring about. The men of that day who were on the side of freedom were not unhappy, I think, though they were harassed by hopes and fears, and sometimes torn by doubts, and the conflict of duties hard to reconcile."

"But how did the people, the revolutionists, carry on the war? What were the elements of success on their side?"

I put this question, because I wanted to bring the old man back to the definite history, and take him out of the musing mood so natural to an old man.

He answered: "Well, they did not lack organisers; for the very conflict itself, in days when, as I told you, men of any strength of mind cast away all consideration for the ordinary business of life, developed the necessary talent amongst them. Indeed, from all I have read and heard, I much doubt whether, without this seemingly dreadful civil war, the due talent for administration would have been developed amongst the working men. Anyhow, it was there, and they soon got leaders far more than equal to the best men amongst the reactionaries. For the rest, they had no difficulty about the material of their army; for that revolutionary instinct so acted on the ordinary soldier in the ranks that the greater part, certainly the best part, of the soldiers joined the side of the people. But the main element of their success was this, that wherever the working people were not coerced, they worked, not for the reactionists, but for 'the rebels.' The reactionists could get no work done for them outside the districts where they were all-powerful: and even in those districts they were harassed by continual risings; and in all cases and everywhere got nothing done without obstruction and black looks and sulkiness; so that not only were their armies quite worn out with the difficulties which they had to meet, but the non-combatants who were on their side were so worried and beset with hatred and a thousand little troubles and annoyances that life became almost unendurable to them on those terms. Not a few of them actually died of the worry; many committed suicide. Of course, a vast number of them joined actively in the cause of reaction, and found some solace to their misery in the eagerness of conflict. Lastly, many thousands gave way and submitted to 'the rebels'; and as the numbers of these latter increased, it at last became clear to all men that the cause which was once hopeless, was now triumphant, and that the hopeless cause was that of slavery and privilege."

CHAPTER XVIII

THE BEGINNING OF THE NEW LIFE

"WELL," said I, "so you got clear out of all your trouble. Were people satisfied with the new order of things when it came?"

"People?" he said. "Well, surely all must have been glad of peace when it came; especially when they found, as they must have found, that after all, they—even the once rich—were not living very badly. As to those who had been poor, all through the war, which lasted about two years, their condition had been bettering, in spite of the struggle; and when peace came at last, in a very short time they made great strides towards a decent life. The great difficulty was that the once-poor had such a feeble conception of the real pleasure of life: so to say, they did not ask enough, did not know how to ask enough, from the new state of things. It was perhaps rather a good than an evil thing that the necessity for restoring the wealth destroyed during the war forced them into working at first almost as hard as they had been used to before the Revolution. For all historians are agreed that there never was a war in which there was so much destruction of wares, and instruments for making them as in this civil war."

"I am rather surprised at that," said I.

"Are you? I don't see why," said Hammond.

"Why," I said, "because the party of order would surely look upon the wealth as their own property, no share of which, if they could help it, should go to their slaves, supposing they conquered. And on the other hand, it was just for the possession of that wealth that 'the rebels' were fighting, and I should have thought, especially when they saw that they were winning, that they would have been careful to destroy as little as possible of what was so soon to be their own."

"It was as I have told you, however," said he. "The party of order, when they recovered from their first cowardice of surprise—or, if you please, when they fairly saw that, whatever happened, they would be ruined, fought with great bitterness, and cared little what they did, so long as they injured the enemies who had destroyed the sweets of life for them. As to 'the rebels,' I have told you that the outbreak of actual war made them careless of trying to save the wretched scraps of wealth that they had. It was a common saying amongst them, Let the country be cleared of everything except valiant living men, rather than that we fall into slavery again!"

He sat silently thinking a little while, and then said:

"When the conflict was once really begun, it was seen how little of any value there was in the old world of slavery and inequality. Don't you see what it means? In the times which you are thinking of, and of which you seem to know so much, there was no hope; nothing but the dull jog of the mill-horse under compulsion of collar and whip; but in that fighting-time that followed, all was hope: 'the rebels' at least felt themselves strong enough to build up the world again from its dry bones,—and they did it, too!" said the old man, his eyes glittering under his beetling brows. He went on: "And their opponents at least and at last learned something about the reality of life, and its sorrows, which they—their class, I mean—had once known nothing of. In short, the two combatants, the workman and the gentleman, between them——"

"Between them," said I, quickly, "they destroyed commercialism!"

"Yes, yes, YES," said he; "that is it. Nor could it have been destroyed otherwise; except, perhaps, by the whole of society gradually falling into lower depths, till it should at last reach a condition as rude as barbarism, but lacking both the hope and the pleasures of barbarism. Surely the sharper, shorter remedy was the happiest?"

"Most surely," said I.

"Yes," said the old man, "the world was being brought to its second birth; how could that take place without a tragedy? Moreover, think of it. The spirit of the new days, of our days, was to be delight in the life of the world; intense and overweening love of the very skin and surface of the earth on which man dwells, such as a lover has in the fair flesh of the woman he loves; this, I say, was to be the new spirit of the time. All other moods save this had been exhausted: the unceasing criticism, the boundless curiosity in the ways and thoughts of man, which was the mood of the ancient Greek, to whom these things were not so much a means, as an end, was gone past recovery; nor had there been really any shadow of it in the so-called science of the nineteenth century, which, as you must know, was in the main an appendage to the commercial system; nay, not seldom an appendage to the police of that system. In spite of appearances, it was limited and cowardly, because it did not really believe in itself. It was the outcome, as it was the sole relief, of the unhappiness of the period which made life so bitter even to the rich, and which, as you may see with your bodily eyes, the great change has swept away. More akin to our way of looking at life was the spirit of the Middle Ages, to whom heaven and the life of the next world was such a reality, that it became to them a part of the life upon the earth; which accordingly they loved and adorned, in spite of the ascetic doctrines of their formal creed, which bade them contemn it.

"But that also, with its assured belief in heaven and hell as two countries in which to live, has gone, and now we do, both in word and in deed, believe in the continuous life of the world of men, and as it were, add every day of that common life to the little stock of days which our own mere individual experience wins for us: and consequently we are happy. Do you wonder at it? In times past, indeed, men were told to love their kind, to believe in the religion of humanity and so forth. But look you, just in the degree that a man had elevation of mind and refinement enough to be able to value this idea, was he repelled by the obvious aspect of the individuals composing the mass which he was to worship; and he could only evade that repulsion by making a conventional abstraction of mankind that had little actual or historical relation to the race; which to his eyes was divided into blind tyrants on the one hand and apathetic degraded slaves on the other. But now, where is the difficulty in accepting the religion of humanity, when the men and women who go to make up humanity are free, happy, and energetic at least, and most commonly beautiful of body also, and surrounded by beautiful things of their own fashioning, and a nature bettered and not worsened by contact with mankind? This is what this age of the world has reserved for us."

"It seems true," said I, "or ought to be, if what my eyes have seen is a token of the general life you lead. Can you now tell me anything of your progress after the years of the struggle?"

Said he: "I could easily tell you more than you have time to listen to; but I can at least hint at one of the chief difficulties which had to be met: and that was, that when men began to settle down after the war, and their labour had pretty much filled up the gap in wealth caused by the destruction of that war, a kind of disappointment seemed coming over us, and the prophecies of some of the reactionists of past times seemed as if they would come true, and a dull level of utilitarian comfort be the end for a while of our aspirations and success. The loss of the competitive spur to exertion had not, indeed, done anything to interfere with the necessary production of the community, but how if it should make men dull by giving them too much time for thought or idle musing? But, after all, this dull thundercloud only threatened us, and then passed over. Probably, from what I have told you before, you will have a guess at the remedy for such a disaster; remembering always that many of the things which used to be produced—slave-wares

for the poor and mere wealth-wasting wares for the rich—
ceased to be made. That remedy was, in short, the production of what used to be called art, but which has no
name amongst us now, because it has become a necessary
part of the labour of every man who produces."

Said I: "What! had men any time or opportunity for
cultivating the fine arts amidst the desperate struggle for
life and freedom that you have told me of?"

Said Hammond: "You must not suppose that the new
form of art was founded chiefly on the memory of the art
of the past; although, strange to say, the civil war was much
less destructive of art than of other things, and though what
of art existed under the old forms, revived in a wonderful
way during the latter part of the struggle, especially as
regards music and poetry. The art or work-pleasure, as one
ought to call it, of which I am now speaking, sprung up
almost spontaneously, it seems, from a kind of instinct
amongst people, no longer driven desperately to painful
and terrible overwork, to do the best they could with the
work in hand—to make it excellent of its kind; and when
that had gone on for a little, a craving for beauty seemed
to awaken in men's minds, and they began rudely and
awkwardly to ornament the wares which they made; and
when they had once set to work at that, it soon began to
grow. All this was much helped by the abolition of the
squalor which our immediate ancestors put up with so
coolly; and by the leisurely, but not stupid, country-life
which now grew (as I told you before) to be common
amongst us. Thus at last and by slow degrees we got pleasure into our work; then we became conscious of that pleasure, and cultivated it, and took care that we had our fill
of it; and then all was gained, and we were happy. So may
it be for ages and ages!"

The old man fell into a reverie, not altogether without
melancholy I thought; but I would not break it. Suddenly
he started, and said: "Well, dear guest, here are come Dick
and Clara to fetch you away, and there is an end of my
talk; which I daresay you will not be sorry for; the long day
is coming to an end, and you will have a pleasant ride back
to Hammersmith."

CHAPTER XIX

THE DRIVE BACK TO HAMMERSMITH

I SAID nothing, for I was not inclined for mere politeness to him after such very serious talk; but in fact I should like to have gone on talking with the older man, who could understand something at least of my wonted ways of looking at life, whereas, with the younger people, in spite of all their kindness, I really was a being from another planet. However, I made the best of it, and smiled as amiably as I could on the young couple; and Dick returned the smile by saying, "Well, guest, I am glad to have you again, and to find that you and my kinsman have not quite talked yourselves into another world; I was half suspecting as I was listening to the Welshmen yonder that you would presently be vanishing away from us, and began to picture my kinsman sitting in the hall staring at nothing and finding that he had been talking a while past to nobody."

I felt rather uncomfortable at this speech, for suddenly the picture of the sordid squabble, the dirty and miserable tragedy of the life I had left for a while, came before my eyes; and I had, as it were, a vision of all my longings for rest and peace in the past, and I loathed the idea of going back to it again. But the old man chuckled and said:

"Don't be afraid, Dick. In any case, I have not been talking to thin air; nor, indeed to this new friend of ours only. Who knows but I may not have been talking to many people? For perhaps our guest may some day go back to the people he has come from, and may take a message from us which may bear fruit for them, and consequently for us."

Dick looked puzzled, and said: "Well, gaffer, I do not quite understand what you mean. All I can say is, that I hope he will not leave us: for don't you see, he is another kind of man to what we are used to, and somehow he makes us think of all kind of things; and already I feel as if I could understand Dickens the better for having talked with him."

"Yes," said Clara, "and I think in a few months we shall

make him look younger; and I should like to see what he was like with the wrinkles smoothed out of his face. Don't you think he will look younger after a little time with us?"

The old man shook his head, and looked earnestly at me, but did not answer her, and for a moment or two we were all silent. Then Clara broke out:

"Kinsman, I don't like this: something or another troubles me, and I feel as if something untoward were going to happen. You have been talking of past miseries to the guest, and have been living in past unhappy times, and it is in the air all round us, and makes us feel as if we were longing for something that we cannot have."

The old man smiled on her kindly, and said: "Well, my child, if that be so, go and live in the present, and you will soon shake it off." Then he turned to me, and said: "Do you remember anything like that, guest, in the country from which you come?"

The lovers had turned aside now, and were talking together softly, and not heeding us; so I said, but in a low voice: "Yes, when I was a happy child on a sunny holiday, and had everything that I could think of."

"So it is," said he. "You remember just now you twitted me with living in the second childhood of the world. You will find it a happy world to live in; you will be happy there—for a while."

Again I did not like his scarcely veiled threat, and was beginning to trouble myself with trying to remember how I had got amongst this curious people, when the old man called out in a cheery voice: "Now, my children, take your guest away, and make much of him; for it is your business to make him sleek of skin and peaceful of mind: he has by no means been as lucky as you have. Farewell, guest!" and he grasped my hand warmly.

"Good-bye," said I, "and thank you very much for all that you have told me. I will come and see you as soon as I come back to London. May I?"

"Yes," he said, "come by all means—if you can."

"It won't be for some time yet," quoth Dick, in his cheery voice; "for when the hay is in up the river, I shall be for taking him a round through the country between hay and wheat harvest, to see how our friends live in the north country. Then in the wheat harvest we shall do a good stroke of work, I should hope,—in Wiltshire by preference; for he will be getting a little hard with all the open-air living, and I shall be as tough as nails."

"But you will take me along, won't you, Dick?" said Clara, laying her pretty hand on his shoulder.

"Will I not?" said Dick, somewhat boisterously. "And we will manage to send you to bed pretty tired every night; and you will look so beautiful with your neck all brown, and your hands too, and you under your gown as white as privet, that you will get some of those strange discontented whims out of your head, my dear. However, our week's haymaking will do all that for you."

The girl reddened very prettily, and not for shame but for pleasure; and the old man laughed, and said:

"Guest, I see that you will be as comfortable as need be; for you need not fear that those two will be too officious with you: they will be so busy with each other, that they will leave you a good deal to yourself, I am sure, and that is a real kindness to a guest, after all. O, you need not be afraid of being one too many, either: it is just what these birds in a nest like, to have a good convenient friend to turn to, so that they may relieve the ecstasies of love with the solid common-place of friendship. Besides, Dick, and much more Clara, likes a little talking at times; and you know lovers do not talk unless they get into trouble, they only prattle. Good-bye, guest; may you be happy!"

Clara went up to old Hammond, threw her arms about his neck and kissed him heartily, and said: "You are a dear old man, and may have your jest about me as much as you please; and it won't be long before we see you again; and you may be sure we shall make our guest happy; though, mind you, there is some truth in what you say."

Then I shook hands again, and we went out of the hall and into the cloisters, and so in the street found Greylocks in the shafts waiting for us. He was well looked after; for a little lad of about seven years old had his hand on the rein and was solemnly looking up into his face; on his back, withal, was a girl of fourteen, holding a three-year-old sister on before her; while another girl, about a year older than the boy, hung on behind. The three were occupied partly with eating cherries, partly with patting and punching Greylocks, who took all their caresses in good part, but pricked up his ears when Dick made his appearance. The girls got off quietly, and going up to Clara, made much of her and snuggled up to her. And then we got into the carriage, Dick shook the reins, and we got under way at once, Greylocks trotting soberly between the lovely trees of the London streets, that were sending floods of fragrance into the cool evening air; for it was now getting toward sunset.

We could hardly go but fair and softly all the way, as there were a great many people abroad in that cool hour. Seeing so many people made me notice their looks the more; and I must say, my taste, cultivated in the sombre greyness, or rather brownness, of the nineteenth century, was rather apt to condemn the gaiety and brightness of the raiment; and I even ventured to say as much to Clara. She seemed rather surprised, and even slightly indignant, and said: "Well, well, what's the matter? They are not about any dirty work; they are only amusing themselves in the fine evening; there is nothing to foul their clothes. Come, doesn't it all look very pretty? It isn't gaudy, you know."

Indeed that was true; for many of the people were clad in colours that were sober enough, though beautiful, and the harmony of the colours was perfect and most delightful.

I said, "Yes, that is so; but how can everybody afford such costly garments? Look! there goes a middle-aged man in a sober grey dress; but I can see from here that it is made of very fine woollen stuff, and is covered with silk embroidery."

Said Clara: "He could wear shabby clothes if he pleased,—that is, if he didn't think he would hurt people's feelings by doing so."

"But please tell me," said I, "how can they afford it?"

As soon as I had spoken I perceived that I had got back to my old blunder; for I saw Dick's shoulders shaking with laughter; but he wouldn't say a word, but handed me over to the tender mercies of Clara, who said:

"Why, I don't know what you mean. Of course we can afford it, or else we shouldn't do it. It would be easy enough for us to say, we will only spend our labour on making our clothes comfortable: but we don't choose to stop there. Why

F

do you find fault with us? Does it seem to you as if we starved ourselves of food in order to make ourselves fine clothes? or do you think there is anything wrong in liking to see the coverings of our bodies beautiful like our bodies are? —just as a deer's or an otter's skin has been made beautiful from the first? Come, what is wrong with you?"

I bowed before the storm, and mumbled out some excuse or other. I must say, I might have known that people who were so fond of architecture generally, would not be backward in ornamenting themselves; all the more as the shape of their raiment, apart from its colour, was both beautiful and reasonable—veiling the form, without either muffling or caricaturing it.

Clara was soon mollified; and as we drove along toward the wood before mentioned, she said to Dick:

"I tell you what, Dick: now that kinsman Hammond the Elder has seen our guest in his queer clothes, I think we ought to find him something decent to put on for our journey to-morrow: especially since, if we do not, we shall have to answer all sorts of questions as to his clothes and where they came from. Besides," she said slyly, "when he is clad in handsome garments he will not be so quick to blame us for our childishness in wasting our time in making ourselves look pleasant to each other."

"All right, Clara," said Dick; "he shall have everything that you—that he wants to have. I will look something out for him before he gets up to-morrow."

CHAPTER XX

THE HAMMERSMITH GUEST-HOUSE AGAIN

AMIDST such talk, driving quietly through the balmy evening, we came to Hammersmith, and were well received by our friends there. Boffin, in a fresh suit of clothes, welcomed me back with stately courtesy; the weaver wanted to button-hole me and get out of me what old Hammond had said, but was very friendly and cheerful when Dick warned him off; Annie shook hands with me, and hoped I had had a pleasant day—so kindly, that I felt a slight pang as our hands parted; for to say the truth, I liked her better than Clara, who seemed to be always a little on the defensive, whereas Annie was as frank as could be, and seemed to get honest pleasure from everything and everybody about her without the least effort.

We had quite a little feast that evening, partly in my honour, and partly, I suspect, though nothing was said about it, in honour of Dick and Clara coming together again. The wine was of the best; the hall was redolent of rich summer flowers; and after supper we not only had music (Annie, to my mind, surpassing all the others for sweetness and clearness of voice, as well as for feeling and meaning), but at last we even got to telling stories, and sat there listening, with no other light but that of the summer moon streaming through the beautiful traceries of the windows, as if we had belonged to time long passed, when books were scarce and the art of reading somewhat rare. Indeed, I may say here, that, though, as you will have noted, my friends had mostly something to say about books, yet they were not great readers, considering the refinement of their manners and the great amount of leisure which they obviously had. In fact, when Dick, especially, mentioned a book, he did so with an air of a man who has accomplished an achievement; as much as to say, "There, you see, I have actually read that!"

The evening passed all too quickly for me; since that day, for the first time in my life, I was having my fill of the pleasure of the eyes without any of that sense of incongruity, that dread of approaching ruin, which had always beset me hitherto when I had been amongst the beautiful works of art of the past, mingled with the lovely nature of the present; both of them, in fact, the result of the long centuries of tradition, which had compelled men to produce the art, and compelled nature to run into the mould of the ages. Here I could enjoy everything without an after-thought of the injustice and miserable toil which made my leisure; the ignorance and dulness of life which went to make my keen appreciation of history; the tyranny and the struggle full of fear and mishap which went to make my romance. The only weight I had upon my heart was a vague fear as it drew toward bed-time concerning the place where I should wake on the morrow: but I choked that down, and went to bed happy, and in a very few moments was in a dreamless sleep.

CHAPTER XXI

GOING UP THE RIVER

WHEN I did wake, to a beautiful sunny morning, I leapt out of bed with my over-night apprehension still clinging to me, which vanished delightfully however in a moment as I looked around my little sleeping chamber and saw the pale but pure-coloured figures painted on the plaster of the wall, with verses written underneath them which I knew somewhat over-well. I dressed speedily, in a suit of blue laid ready for me, so handsome that I quite blushed when I had got into it, feeling as I did so that excited pleasure of anticipation of a holiday, which, well remembered as it was, I had not felt since I was a boy, new come home for the summer holidays.

It seemed quite early in the morning, and I expected to have the hall to myself when I came into it out of the corridor wherein was my sleeping chamber; but I met Annie at once, who let fall her broom and gave me a kiss, quite meaningless I fear, except as betokening friendship, though she reddened as she did it, not from shyness, but from friendly pleasure, and then stood and picked up her broom again, and went on with her sweeping, nodding to me as if to bid me stand out of the way and look on; which, to say the truth, I thought amusing enough, as there were five other girls helping her, and their graceful figures engaged in the leisurely work were worth going a long way to see, and their merry talk and laughing as they swept in quite a scientific manner was worth going a long way to hear. But Annie presently threw me back a word or two as she went on to the other end of the hall: "Guest," she said, "I am glad that you are up early, though we wouldn't disturb you; for our Thames is a lovely river at half-past six on a June morning: and as it would be a pity for you to lose it, I am told just to give you a cup of milk and a bit of bread outside there, and put you into the boat: for Dick and Clara are all ready now. Wait half a minute till I have swept down this row."

So presently she let her broom drop again, and came and took me by the hand and led me out on to the terrace above the river, to a little table under the boughs, where my bread and milk took the form of as dainty a breakfast as any one could desire, and then sat by me as I ate. And in a minute or two Dick and Clara came to me, the latter looking most fresh and beautiful in a light silk embroidered gown, which to my unused eyes was extravagantly gay and bright; while Dick was also handsomely dressed in white flannel prettily embroidered. Clara raised her gown in her hands as she gave me the morning greeting, and said laughingly: "Look, guest! you see we are at least as fine as any of the people you felt inclined to scold last night; you see we are not going to make the bright day and the flowers feel ashamed of themselves. Now scold me!"

Quoth I: "No, indeed; the pair of you seem as if you were born out of the summer day itself; and I will scold you when I scold it."

"Well, you know," said Dick, "this is a special day—all these days are, I mean. The hay-harvest is in some ways better than corn-harvest because of the beautiful weather; and really, unless you had worked in the hay-field in fine weather, you couldn't tell what pleasant work it is. The women look so pretty at it, too," he said, shyly; "so all things considered, I think we are right to adorn it in a simple manner."

"Do the women work at it in silk dresses?" said I, smiling.

Dick was going to answer me soberly; but Clara put her hand over his mouth, and said, "No, no, Dick; not too much information for him, or I shall think that you are your old kinsman again. Let him find out for himself: he will not have long to wait."

"Yes," quoth Annie, "don't make your description of the picture too fine, or else he will be disappointed when the curtain is drawn. I don't want him to be disappointed. But now it's time for you to be gone, if you are to have the best of the tide, and also of the sunny morning. Good-bye, guest."

She kissed me in her frank friendly way, and almost took away from me my desire for the expedition thereby; but I had to get over that, as it was clear that so delightful a woman would hardly be without a due lover of her own age. We went down the steps of the landing-stage, and got into a pretty boat, not too light to hold us and our belongings comfortably, and handsomely ornamented; and just as we got in, down came Boffin and the weaver to see us off. The former had now veiled his splendour in a due suit of working clothes, crowned with a fantail hat, which he took off, however, to wave us farewell with his grave old-Spanish-like courtesy. Then Dick pushed off into the stream, and bent vigorously to his sculls, and Hammersmith, with its noble trees and beautiful water-side houses, began to slip away from us.

As we went, I could not help putting beside his promised picture of the hay-field as it was then the picture of it as I remembered it, and especially the images of the women engaged in the work rose up before me: the row of gaunt figures, lean, flat-breasted, ugly, without a grace of form or face about them; dressed in wretched skimpy print gowns, and hideous flapping sun-bonnets, moving their rakes in a listless mechanical way. How often had that marred the loveliness of the June day to me; how often had I longed to see the hay-fields peopled with men and women worthy of the sweet abundance of midsummer, of its endless wealth of beautiful sights, and delicious sounds and scents. And now, the world had grown old and wiser, and I was to see my hope realised at last.

CHAPTER XXII

HAMPTON COURT. AND A PRAISER
OF PAST TIMES

SO on we went, Dick rowing in an easy tireless way, and Clara sitting by my side admiring his manly beauty and heartily good-natured face, and thinking, I fancy, of nothing else. As we went higher up the river, there was less difference between the Thames of that day and the Thames as I remembered it; for setting aside the hideous vulgarity of the cockney villas of the well-to-do, stockbrokers and other such, which in older time marred the beauty of the bough-hung banks, even this beginning of the country Thames was always beautiful; and as we slipped between the lovely summer greenery, I almost felt my youth come back to me, and as if I were on one of those water excursions which I used to enjoy so much in days when I was too happy to think that there could be much amiss anywhere.

At last we came to a reach of the river where on the left hand a very pretty little village with some old houses in it came down to the edge of the water, over which was a ferry; and beyond these houses the elm-beset meadows ended in a fringe of tall willows, while on the right hand went the tow-path and a clear space before a row of trees, which rose up behind huge and ancient, the ornaments of a great park: but these drew back still further from the river at the end of the reach to make way for a little town of quaint and pretty houses, some new, some old dominated by the long walls and sharp gables of a great red-brick pile of building, partly of the latest Gothic, partly of the court-style of Dutch William, but so blended together by the bright sun and beautiful surroundings, including the bright blue river, which it looked down upon, that even amidst the beautiful buildings of that new happy time it had a strange charm about it. A great wave of fragrance, amidst which the lime-tree blossom was clearly to be distinguished, came down to us from its unseen gardens, as Clara sat up in her place, and said:

"O Dick, dear, couldn't we stop at Hampton Court for to-day, and take the guest about the park a little, and show him those sweet old buildings? Somehow, I suppose because you have lived so near it, you have seldom taken me to Hampton Court."

Dick rested on his oars a little, and said: "Well, well Clara, you are lazy to-day. I didn't feel like stopping short of Shepperton for the night; suppose we just go and have our dinner at the Court, and go on again about five o'clock?"

"Well," she said, "so be it; but I should like the guest to have spent an hour or two in the Park."

"The Park!" said Dick; "why, the whole Thames-side is a park this time of the year; and for my part, I had rather lie under an elm-tree on the borders of a wheat-field, with the bees humming about me and the corn-crake crying from furrow to furrow, than in any park in England. Besides——"

"Besides," said she, "you want to get on to your dearly-loved upper Thames, and show your prowess down the heavy swathes of the mowing grass."

She looked at him fondly, and I could tell that she was seeing him in her mind's eye showing his splendid form at its best amidst the rhymed strokes of the scythes; and she looked down at her own pretty feet with a half sigh, as though she were contrasting her slight woman's beauty with his man's beauty; as women will when they are really in love, and are not spoiled with conventional sentiment.

As for Dick, he looked at her admiringly a while, and then said at last: "Well, Clara, I do wish we were there! But, hilloa! we are getting back way." And he set to work sculling again, and in two minutes we were all standing on the gravelly strand below the bridge, which, as you may imagine, was no longer the old hideous iron abortion, but a handsome piece of very solid oak framing.

We went into the Court and straight into the great hall, so well remembered, where there were tables spread for dinner, and everything arranged much as in Hammersmith Guest Hall. Dinner over, we sauntered through the ancient rooms, where the pictures and tapestry were still preserved, and nothing was much changed, except that the people whom we met there had an indefinable kind of look of being at home and at ease, which communicated itself to me, so that I felt that the beautiful old place was mine in the best sense of the word; and my pleasure of past days seemed to add itself to that of to-day, and filled my whole soul with content.

Dick (who, in spite of Clara's gibe, knew the place very well) told me that the beautiful old Tudor rooms, which I remembered had been the dwellings of the lesser fry of Court flunkies, were now much used by people coming and going; for, beautiful as architecture had now become, and although the whole face of the country had quite recovered its beauty, there was still a sort of tradition of pleasure and beauty which clung to that group of buildings, and people thought going to Hampton Court a necessary summer outing, as they did in the days when London was so grimy and miserable. We went into some of the rooms looking into the old garden, and were well received by the people in them, who got speedily into talk with us, and looked with politely half-concealed wonder at my strange face. Besides these birds of passage, and a few regular dwellers in the place, we saw out in the meadows near the garden, down "the Long Water," as it used to be called, many gay tents with men, women, and children round about them. As it seemed, this pleasure-loving people were fond of tent-life with all its inconveniences, which, indeed, they turned into pleasure also.

We left this old friend by the time appointed, and I made some feeble show of taking the sculls; but Dick repulsed me, not much to my grief, I must say, as I found I had quite enough to do between the enjoyment of the beautiful time and my own lazily blended thoughts.

As to Dick, it was quite right to let him pull, for he was as strong as a horse, and had the greatest delight in bodily exercise, whatever it was. We really had some difficulty in getting him to stop when it was getting rather more than dusk, and the moon was brightening just as we were off Runnymede. We landed there, and were looking about for a place whereon to pitch our tents (for we had brought two with us), when an old man came up to us, bade us good-evening, and asked if we were housed for that night; and finding that we were not, bade us home to his house. Nothing loth, we went with him, and Clara took his hand in a coaxing way which I noticed she used with old men; and as we went on our way, made some commonplace remark about the beauty of the day. The old man stopped short, and looked at her and said: "You really like it then?"

"Yes," she said, looking very much astonished, "don't you?"

"Well," said he, "perhaps I do. I did, at any rate, when I was younger; but now I think I should like it cooler."

She said nothing, and went on, the night growing about as dark as it would be; till just at the rise of the hill we came to a hedge with a gate in it, which the old man unlatched and led us into a garden, at the end of which we could see a little house, one of whose little windows was already yellow with candlelight. We could see even under the doubtful light of the moon and the last of the western glow that the garden was stuffed full of flowers; and the fragrance it gave out in the gathering coolness was so wonderfully sweet, that it seemed the very heart of the delight of the June dusk; so that we three stopped instinctively, and Clara gave forth a little sweet "O," like a bird beginning to sing.

"What's the matter?" said the old man, a little testily, and pulling at her hand. "There's no dog; or have you trodden on a thorn and hurt your foot?"

"No, no, neighbour," she said; "but how sweet, how sweet it is!"

"Of course it is," said he, "but do you care so much for that?"

She laughed out musically, and we followed suit in our gruffer voices; and then she said: "Of course I do, neighbour; don't you?"

"Well, I don't know," quoth the old fellow; then he added, as if somewhat ashamed of himself; "Besides, you know, when the waters are out and all Runnymede is flooded, it's none so pleasant."

"*I* should like it," quoth Dick. "What a jolly sail one would get about here on the floods on a bright frosty January morning!"

"*Would* you like it?" said our host. "Well, I won't argue with you, neighbour; it isn't worth while. Come in and have some supper."

We went up a paved path between the roses, and straight into a very pretty room, panelled and carved, and as clean as a new pin; but the chief ornament of which was a young woman, light-haired and grey-eyed, but with her face and hands and bare feet tanned quite brown with the sun. Though she was very lightly clad, that was clearly from choice, not from poverty, though these were the first cottage-dwellers I had come across; for her gown was of silk, and on her wrists were bracelets that seemed to me of great value. She was lying on a sheep-skin near the window, but jumped up as soon as we entered, and when she saw the guests behind the old man, she clapped her hands and cried out with pleasure, and when she got us into the middle of the room, fairly danced round us in delight of our company.

"What!" said the old man, "you are pleased, are you, Ellen?"

The girl danced up to him and threw her arms round him, and said: "Yes I am, and so ought you to be, grandfather."

"Well, well, I am," said he, "as much as I can be pleased. Guests, please be seated."

This seemed rather strange to us; stranger, I suspect, to my friends than to me; but Dick took the opportunity of both the host and his grand-daughter being out of the room to say to me, softly: "A grumbler: there are a few of them still. Once upon a time, I am told, they were quite a nuisance."

The old man came in as he spoke and sat down beside us with a sigh, which, indeed, seemed fetched up as if he wanted us to take notice of it; but just then the girl came in with the victuals, and the carle missed his mark, what between our hunger generally and that I was pretty busy watching the grand-daughter moving about as beautiful as a picture.

Everything to eat and drink, though it was somewhat different to what we had had in London, was better than good, but the old man eyed rather sulkily the chief dish on the table, on which lay a leash of fine perch, and said:

"H'm, perch! I am sorry we can't do better for you, guests. The time was when we might have had a good piece of salmon up from London for you; but the times have grown mean and petty."

"Yes, but you might have had it now," said the girl, giggling, "if you had known that they were coming."

"It's our fault for not bringing it with us, neighbours," said Dick, good-humouredly. "But if the times have grown petty, at any rate the perch haven't; that fellow in the middle there must have weighed a good two pounds when he was showing his dark stripes and red fins to the minnows

yonder. And as to the salmon, why, neighbour, my friend
here, who comes from the outlands, was quite surprised
yesterday morning when I told him we had plenty of salmon
at Hammersmith. I am sure I have heard nothing of the
times worsening."

He looked a little uncomfortable. And the old man,
turning to me, said very courteously:

"Well, sir, I am happy to see a man from over the water;
but I really must appeal to you to say whether on the whole
you are not better off in your country; where I suppose,
from what our guest says, you are brisker and more alive,
because you have not wholly got rid of competition. You
see, I have read not a few books of the past days, and
certainly. *they* are much more alive than those which are
written now; and good sound unlimited competition was
the condition under which they were written,—if we didn't
know that from the record of history, we should know it
from the books themselves. There is a spirit of adventure in
them, and signs of a capacity to extract good out of evil
which our literature quite lacks now; and I cannot help
thinking that our moralists and historians exaggerate hugely
the unhappiness of the past days, in which such splendid
works of imagination and intellect were produced."

Clara listened to him with restless eyes, as if she were
excited and pleased; Dick knitted his brow and looked still
more uncomfortable, but said nothing. Indeed, the old man
gradually, as he warmed to his subject, dropped his sneering manner, and both spoke and looked very seriously. But
the girl broke out before I could deliver myself of the answer
I was framing:

"Books, books! always books, grandfather! When will
you understand that after all it is the world we live in which
interests us; the world of which we are a part, and which
we can never love too much? Look!" she said, throwing
open the casement wider and showing us the white light
sparkling between the black shadows of the moonlit garden,
through which ran a little shiver of the summer night-wind,
"look! these are our books in these days!—and these," she
said, stepping lightly up to the two lovers and laying a hand
on each of their shoulders; "and the guest there, with his
oversea knowledge and experience;—yes, and even you,

grandfather" (a smile ran over her face as she spoke), "with all your grumbling and wishing yourself back again in the good old days,—in which, as far as I can make out, a harmless and lazy old man like you would either have pretty nearly starved, or have had to pay soldiers and people to take the folk's victuals and clothes and houses away from them by force. Yes, these are our books; and if we want more, can we not find work to do in the beautiful buildings that we raise up all over the country (and I know there was nothing like them in past times), wherein a man can put forth whatever is in him, and make his hands set forth his mind and his soul."

She paused a little, and I for my part could not help staring at her, and thinking that if she were a book, the pictures in it were most lovely. The colour mantled in her delicate sunburnt cheeks; her grey eyes, light amidst the tan of her face, kindly looked on us all as she spoke. She paused, and said again:

"As for your books, they were well enough for times when intelligent people had but little else in which they could take pleasure, and when they must needs supplement the sordid miseries of their own lives with imaginations of the lives of other people. But I say flatly that in spite of all their cleverness and vigour, and capacity for story-telling, there is something loathsome about them. Some of them, indeed, do here and there show some feeling for those whom the history-books call 'poor,' and of the misery of whose lives we have some inkling; but presently they give it up, and towards the end of the story we must be contented to see the hero and heroine living happily in an island of bliss on other people's troubles; and that after a long series of sham troubles (or mostly sham) of their own making, illustrated by dreary introspective nonsense about their feelings and aspirations, and all the rest of it; while the world must even then have gone on its way, and dug and sewed and baked and built and carpentered round about these useless—animals."

"There!" said the old man, reverting to his dry sulky manner again. "There's eloquence! I suppose you like it?"

"Yes," said I, very emphatically.

"Well," said he, "now the storm of eloquence has lulled

for a little, suppose you answer my question?—that is, if you like, you know," quoth he, with a sudden access of courtesy.

"What question?" said I. For I must confess that Ellen's strange and almost wild beauty had put it out of my head.

Said he: "First of all (excuse my catechising), is there competition in life, after the old kind, in the country whence you come?"

"Yes," said I, "it is the rule there." And I wondered as I spoke what fresh complications I should get into as a result of this answer.

"Question two," said the carle: "Are you not on the whole much freer, more energetic—in a word, healthier and happier—for it?"

I smiled. "You wouldn't talk so if you had any idea of our life. To me you seem here as if you were living in heaven compared with us of the country from which I came."

"Heaven?" said he: "you like heaven, do you?"

"Yes," said I—snappishly, I am afraid; for I was beginning rather to resent his formula.

"Well, I am far from sure that I do," quoth he. "I think one may do more with one's life than sitting on a damp cloud and singing hymns."

I was rather nettled by this inconsequence. and said: "Well, neighbour, to be short, and without using metaphors, in the land whence I come, where the competition which produced those literary works which you admire so much is still the rule, most people are thoroughly unhappy; here, to me at least, most people seem thoroughly happy."

"No offence, guest—no offence," said he; "but let me ask you; you like that, do you?"

His formula, put with such obstinate persistence, made us all laugh heartily; and even the old man joined in the laughter on the sly. However, he was by no means beaten, and said presently:

"From all I can hear, I should judge that a young woman so beautiful as my dear Ellen yonder would have been a lady, as they called it in the old time, and wouldn't have had to wear a few rags of silk as she does now, or to have browned herself in the sun as she has to do now. What do you say to that, eh?"

Here Clara, who had been pretty much silent hitherto, struck in, and said: "Well, really, I don't think that you would have mended matters, or that they want mending. Don't you see that she is dressed deliciously for this beautiful weather? And as for the sun-burning of your hay-fields, why, I hope to pick up some of that for myself when we get a little higher up the river. Look if I don't need a little sun on my pasty white skin!"

And she stripped up the sleeve from her arm and laid it beside Ellen's who was now sitting next her. To say the truth, it was rather amusing to me to see Clara putting herself forward as a town-bred fine lady, for she was as well-knit and clean-skinned a girl as might be met with anywhere at the best. Dick stroked the beautiful arm rather shyly, and pulled down the sleeve again, while she blushed at his touch; and the old man said laughingly: "Well, I suppose you *do* like that; don't you?"

Ellen kissed her new friend, and we all sat silent for a little, till she broke out into a sweet shrill song, and held us all entranced with the wonder of her clear voice; and the old grumbler sat looking at her lovingly. The other young people sang also in due time; and then Ellen showed us to our beds in small cottage chambers, fragrant and clean as the ideal of the old pastoral poets; and the pleasure of the evening quite extinguished my fear of the last night, that I should wake up in the old miserable world of worn-out pleasures, and hopes that were half fears.

CHAPTER XXIII

AN EARLY MORNING BY RUNNYMEDE

THOUGH there were no rough noises to wake me, I could not lie long abed the next morning, where the world seemed so well awake, and, despite the old grumbler, so happy; so I got up, and found that, early as it was, some one had been stirring, since all was trim and in its place in the little parlour, and the table laid for the morning meal. Nobody was afoot in the house as then, however, so I went out a-doors, and after a turn or two round the superabundant garden, I wandered down over the meadow to the river-side, where lay our boat, looking quite familiar and friendly to me. I walked up-stream a little, watching the light mist curling up from the river till the sun gained power to draw it all away; saw the bleak speckling the water under the willow boughs, whence the tiny flies they fed on were falling in myriads; heard the great chub splashing here and there at some belated moth or other, and felt almost back again in my boyhood. Then I went back again to the boat, and loitered there a minute or two, and then walked slowly up the meadow towards the little house. I noted now that there were four more houses of about the same size on the slope away from the river. The meadow in which I was going was not up for hay; but a row of flake-hurdles ran up the slope not far from me on each side, and in the field so parted off from ours on the left they were making hay busily by now, in the simple fashion of the days when I was a boy. My feet turned that way instinctively, as I wanted to see how haymakers looked in these new and better times, and also I rather expected to see Ellen there. I came to the hurdles and stood looking over into the hay-field, and was close to the end of the long line of haymakers who were spreading the low ridges to dry off the night dew. The majority of these were young women clad much like Ellen last night, though not mostly in silk, but in light woollen most gaily embroidered; the men being all clad in white flannel embroidered in bright colours. The meadow looked like a gigantic tulip-bed because of them. All hands were working deliberately but well and steadily, though they were as noisy with merry talk as a grove of autumn starlings. Half a dozen of them, men and women, came up to me and shook hands, gave me the sele of the morning, and asked a few questions as to whence and whither, and wishing me good luck, went back to their work. Ellen, to my disappointment, was not amongst them, but presently I saw a light figure come out of the hay-field higher up the slope, and make for our house; and that was Ellen, holding a basket in her hand. But before she had come to the garden gate, out came Dick and Clara, who, after a minute's pause, came down to meet me, leaving Ellen in the garden; then we three went down to the boat, talking mere morning prattle. We stayed there a little, Dick arranging some of the matters in her, for we had only taken up to the house such things as we thought the dew might damage; and then we went toward the house again; but when we came near the garden, Dick stopped us by laying a hand on my arm and said:

"Just look a moment."

I looked, and over the low hedge saw Ellen, shading her eyes against the sun as she looked toward the hay-field, a light wind stirring in her tawny hair, her eyes like light jewels amidst her sunburnt face, which looked as if the warmth of the sun were yet in it.

"Look, guest," said Dick; "doesn't it all look like one of those very stories out of Grimm that we were talking about up in Bloomsbury? Here are we two lovers wandering about the world, and we have come to a fairy garden, and there is the very fairy herself amidst of it: I wonder what she will do for us."

Said Clara demurely, but not stiffly: "Is she a good fairy, Dick?"

"O yes," said he; "and according to the card, she would do better, if it were not for the gnome or wood-spirit, our grumbling friend of last night."

We laughed at this; and I said, "I hope you see that you have left me out of the tale."

"Well," said he, "that's true. You had better consider that you have got the cap of darkness, and are seeing everything, yourself invisible."

That touched me on my weak side of not feeling sure of my position in this beautiful new country; so in order not to make matters worse, I held my tongue, and we all went into the garden and up to the house together. I noticed by the way that Clara must really rather have felt the contrast between herself as a town madam and this piece of the summer country that we all admired so, for she had rather dressed after Ellen that morning as to thinness and scantiness, and went barefoot also, except for light sandals.

The old man greeted us kindly in the parlour, and said:

"Well, guests, so you have been looking about to search into the nakedness of the land: I suppose your illusions of last night have given way a bit before the morning light? Do you still like it, eh?"

"Very much," said I, doggedly; "it is one of the prettiest places on the lower Thames."

"Oho!" said he; "so you know the Thames, do you?"

I reddened, for I saw Dick and Clara looking at me, and scarcely knew what to say. However, since I had said in our early intercourse with my Hammersmith friends that I had known Epping Forest, I thought a hasty generalisation might be better in avoiding complications than a downright lie; so I said:

"I have been in this country before; and I have been on the Thames in those days."

"O," said the old man, eagerly, "so you have been in this country before. Now really, don't you *find* it (apart from all theory, you know) much changed for the worse?"

"No, not at all," said I; "I find it much changed for the better."

"Ah," quoth he, "I fear that you have been prejudiced by some theory or another. However, of course the time when you were here before must have been so near our own days that the deterioration might not be very great: as then we were, of course, still living under the same customs as we are now. I was thinking of earlier days than that."

"In short," said Clara, "you have *theories* about the change which has taken place."

"I have facts as well," said he. "Look here! from this hill you can see just four little houses, including this one. Well, I know for certain that in old times, even in the summer, when the leaves were thickest, you could see from the same place six quite big and fine houses; and higher up the water, garden joined garden right up to Windsor; and there were big houses in all the gardens. Ah! England was an important place in those days."

I was getting nettled, and said: "What you mean is that you de-cockneyised the place, and sent the damned flunkies packing, and that everybody can live comfortably and happily, and not a few damned thieves only, who were centres of vulgarity and corruption wherever they were, and who, as to this lovely river, destroyed its beauty morally, and had almost destroyed it physically, when they were thrown out of it."

There was silence after this outburst, which for the life of me I could not help, remembering how I had suffered from cockneyism and its cause on those same waters of old time. But at last the old man said, quite coolly:

"My dear guest, I really don't know what you mean by either cockneys, or flunkies, or thieves, or damned; or how only a few people could live happily and comfortably in a wealthy country. All I can see is that you are angry, and I fear with me: so if you like we will change the subject."

I thought this kind and hospitable in him, considering his obstinacy about his theory; and hastened to say that I did not mean to be angry, only emphatic. He bowed gravely, and I thought the storm was over, when suddenly Ellen broke in:

"Grandfather, our guest is reticent from courtesy; but really what he has in his mind to say to you ought to be said; so as I know pretty well what it is, I will say it for him: for as you know, I have been taught these things by people who——"

"Yes," said the old man, "by the sage of Bloomsbury, and others."

"O," said Dick, "so you know my old kinsman Hammond?"

"Yes," said she, "and other people too, as my grandfather says, and they have taught me things: and this is the upshot of it. We live in a little house now, not because we have nothing grander to do than working in the fields, but because we please; for if we liked, we could go and live in a big house amongst pleasant companions."

Grumbled the old man: "Just so! As if I would live among those conceited fellows; all of them looking down upon me!"

She smiled on him kindly, but went on as if he had not spoken. "In the past times, when those big houses of which grandfather speaks were so plenty, we *must* have lived in a cottage whether we had liked it or not; and the said cottage instead of having in it everything we want, would have been bare and empty. We should not have got enough to eat; our clothes would have been ugly to look at, dirty and frowsy. You, grandfather, have done no hard work for years now, but wander about and read your books and have nothing to worry you; and as for me, I work hard when I like it, because I like it, and think it does me good, and knits up my muscles, and makes me prettier to look at, and healthier and happier. But in those past days you, grandfather, would have had to work hard after you were old; and would have been always afraid of having to be shut up in a kind of prison along with other old men, half-starved and without amusement. And as for me, I am twenty years old. In those days my middle age would be beginning now, and in a few years I should be pinched, thin, and haggard, beset with troubles and miseries, so that no one could have guessed that I was once a beautiful girl.

"Is this what you have had in your mind, guest?" said she, the tears in her eyes at thought of the past miseries of people like herself.

"Yes," said I, much moved; "that and more. Often—in my country I have seen that wretched change you have spoken of, from the fresh handsome country lass to the poor draggle-tailed country woman."

The old man sat silent for a little, but presently recovered himself and took comfort in his old phrase of "Well, you like it so, do you?"

"Yes," said Ellen, "I love life better than death."

"O, you do, do you?" said he. "Well, for my part I like reading a good old book with plenty of fun in it, like Thackeray's 'Vanity Fair.' Why don't you write books like that now? Ask that question of your Bloomsbury sage."

Seeing Dick's cheeks reddening a little at this sally, and noting that silence followed, I thought I had better do something. So I said: "I am only the guest, friends; but I know you want to show me your river at its best, so don't you think we had better be moving presently, as it is certainly going to be a hot day?"

CHAPTER XXIV

UP THE THAMES

THE SECOND DAY

THEY were not slow to take my hint; and indeed, as to the mere time of day, it was best for us to be off, as it was past seven o'clock, and the day promised to be very hot. So we got up and went down to our boat—Ellen thoughtful and abstracted; the old man very kind and courteous, as if to make up for his crabbedness of opinion. Clara was cheerful and natural, but a little subdued, I thought; and she at least was not sorry to be gone, and often looked shyly and timidly at Ellen and her strange wild beauty. So we got into the boat, Dick saying as he took his place, "Well, it *is* a fine day!" and the old man answering, "What! you like that, do you?" once more; and presently Dick was sending the bows swiftly through the slow weed-checked stream. I turned round as we got into mid-stream, and waving my hand to our hosts, saw Ellen leaning on the old man's shoulder, and caressing his healthy apple-red cheek, and quite a keen pang smote me as I thought how I should never see the beautiful girl again. Presently I insisted on taking the sculls, and I rowed a good deal that day; which no doubt accounts for the fact that we got very late to the place which Dick had aimed at. Clara was particularly affectionate to Dick, as I noticed from the rowing thwart; but as for him, he was as frankly kind and merry as ever; and I was glad to see it, as a man of his temperament could not have taken her caresses cheerfully and without embarrassment if he had been at all entangled by the fairy of our last night's abode.

I need say little about the lovely reaches of the river here. I duly noted that absence of cockney villas which the old man had lamented; and I saw with pleasure that my old enemies the "Gothic" cast-iron bridges had been replaced by handsome oak and stone ones. Also the banks of the forest that we passed through had lost their courtly game-keeperish trimness, and were as wild and beautiful as need be, though the trees were clearly well seen to. I thought it best, in order to get the most direct information, to play the innocent about Eton and Windsor; but Dick volunteered his knowledge to me as we lay in Datchet lock about the first. Quoth he:

"Up yonder are some beautiful old buildings, which were built for a great college or teaching-place by one of the mediæval kings—Edward the Sixth, I think" (I smiled to myself at his rather natural blunder). "He meant poor people's sons to be taught there what knowledge was going in his days; but it was a matter of course that in the times of which you seem to know so much they spoilt whatever good there was in the founder's intentions. My old kinsman says that they treated them in a very simple way, and instead of teaching poor men's sons to know something, they taught rich men's sons to know nothing. It seems from what he says that it was a place for the 'aristocracy' (if you know what that word means; I have been told its meaning) to get rid of the company of their male children for a great part of the year. I daresay old Hammond would give you plenty of information in detail about it."

"What is it used for now?" said I.

"Well," said he, "the buildings were a good deal spoilt by the last few generations of aristocrats, who seem to have had a great hatred against beautiful old buildings, and indeed all records of past history; but it is still a delightful place. Of course, we cannot use it quite as the founder intended, since our ideas about teaching young people are so changed from the ideas of his time; so it is used now as a dwelling for people engaged in learning; and folk from round about come and get taught things that they want to learn; and there is a great library there of the best books. So that I don't think that the old dead king would be much hurt if he were to come to life and see what we are doing there."

"Well," said Clara, laughing, "I think he would miss the boys."

"Not always, my dear," said Dick, "for there are often plenty of boys there, who come to get taught; and also," said he, smiling, "to learn boating and swimming. I wish we could stop there: but perhaps we had better do that coming down the water."

The lock-gates opened as he spoke, and out we went, and on. And as for Windsor, he said nothing till I lay on my oars (for I was sculling then) in Clewer reach, and looking up, said, "What is all that building up there?"

Said he: "There, I thought I would wait till you asked, yourself. That is Windsor Castle: that also I thought I would keep for you till we come down the water. It looks fine from here, doesn't it? But a great deal of it has been built or skinned in the time of the Degradation, and we wouldn't pull the buildings down, since they were there; just as with the buildings of the Dung Market. You know, of course, that it was the palace of our old mediæval kings, and was used later on for the same purpose by the parliamentary commercial sham-kings, as my old kinsman calls them."

"Yes," said I, "I know all that. What is it used for now?"

"A great many people live there," said he, "as, with all drawbacks, it is a pleasant place; there is also a well-arranged store of antiquities of various kinds that have seemed worth keeping—a museum, it would have been called in the times you understand so well."

I drew my sculls through the water on that last word, and pulled as if I were fleeing from those times which I understood so well; and we were soon going up the once sorely be-cockneyed reaches of the river about Maidenhead, which now looked as pleasant and enjoyable as the up-river reaches.

The morning was now getting on, the morning of a jewel of a summer day; one of those days which, if they were commoner in these islands, would make our climate the best of all climates, without dispute. A light wind blew from the west; the little clouds that had arisen at about our breakfast time had seemed to get higher and higher in the heavens; and in spite of the burning sun we no more longed for rain than we feared it. Burning as the sun was, there was a fresh feeling in the air that almost set us a-longing for the rest of the hot afternoon, and the stretch of blossoming wheat seen from the shadow of the boughs. No one unburdened with very heavy anxieties could have felt otherwise than happy that morning: and it must be said that whatever anxieties might lie beneath the surface of things, we didn't seem to come across any of them.

We passed by several fields where haymaking was going on, but Dick, and especially Clara, were so jealous of our up-river festival that they would not allow me to have much to say to them. I could only notice that the people in the fields looked strong and handsome, both men and women, and that so far from there being any appearance of sordidness about their attire, they seemed to be dressed specially for the occasion—lightly, of course, but gaily and with plenty of adornment.

Both on this day as well as yesterday we had, as you may think, met and passed and been passed by many craft of one kind and another. The most part of these were being rowed like ourselves, or were sailing, in the sort of way that sailing is managed on the upper reaches of the river; but every now and then we came on barges, laden with hay or other country produce, or carrying bricks, lime, timber, and the like, and these were going on their way without any means of propulsion visible to me—just a man at the tiller, with often a friend or two laughing and talking with him. Dick, seeing on one occasion this day that I was looking rather hard on one of these, said: "That is one of our force-barges; it is quite as easy to work vehicles by force by water as by land."

I understood pretty well that these "force vehicles" had taken the place of our old steam-power carrying; but I took good care not to ask any questions about them, as I knew well enough both that I should never be able to understand how they were worked, and that in attempting to do so I should betray myself, or get into some complication impossible to explain; so I merely said, "Yes, of course, I understand."

We went ashore at Bisham, where the remains of the old Abbey and the Elizabethan house that had been added to them yet remained, none the worse for many years of careful and appreciative habitation. The folk of the place, however, were mostly in the fields that day, both men and women; so we met only two old men there, and a younger one who had stayed at home to get on with some literary work, which I imagine we considerably interrupted. Yet I also think that the hard-working man who received us was not very sorry for the interruption. Anyhow, he kept on pressing us to stay over and over again, till at last we did not get away till the cool of the evening.

However, that mattered little to us; the nights were light, for the moon was shining in her third quarter, and it was all one to Dick whether he sculled or sat quiet in the boat: so we went away a great pace. The evening sun shone bright on the remains of the old buildings at Medmenham; close beside which arose an irregular pile of building which Dick told us was a very pleasant house; and there were plenty of houses visible on the wide meadows opposite, under the hill; for, as it seems that the beauty of Hurley had compelled people to build and live there a good deal. The sun very low down showed us Henley little altered in outward aspect from what I remembered it. Actual daylight failed us as we passed through the lovely reaches of Wargrave and Shiplake; but the moon rose behind us presently. I should like to have seen with my eyes what success the new order of things had had in getting rid of the sprawling mess with which commercialism had littered the banks of the wide stream about Reading and Caversham: certainly everything smelt too deliciously in the early night for there to be any of the old careless sordidness of so-called manufacture; and in answer to my question as to what sort of a place Reading was, Dick answered:

"O, a nice town enough in its way; mostly rebuilt within the last hundred years; and there are a good many houses, as you can see by the lights just down under the hills yonder. In fact, it is one of the most populous places on the Thames round about here. Keep up your spirits, guest! we are close to our journey's end for the night. I ought to ask your pardon for not stopping at one of the houses here or higher up; but a friend, who is living in a very pleasant house in the Maple-Durham meads, particularly wanted me and Clara to come and see him on our way up the Thames; and I thought you wouldn't mind this bit of night travelling."

He need not have adjured me to keep up my spirits, which were as high as possible; though the strangeness and excitement of the happy and quiet life which I saw everywhere around me was, it is true, a little wearing off, yet a deep content, as different as possible from languid acquiescence, was taking its place, and I was, as it were, really new-born.

We landed presently just where I remembered that river making an elbow to the north towards the ancient house of the Blunts; with the wide meadows spreading on the right-hand side, and on the left the long line of beautiful old trees overhanging the water. As we got out of the boat, I said to Dick:

"Is it the old house we are going to?"

"No," he said, "though that is standing still in green old age, and is well inhabited. I see, by the way, that you know your Thames well. But my friend Walter Allen, who asked me to stop here, lives in a house, not very big, which has been built here lately, because these meadows are so much liked, especially in summer, that there was getting to be rather too much of tenting on the open field; so the parishes here about, who rather objected to that, built three houses between this and Caversham, and quite a large one at Basildon, a little higher up. Look, yonder are the lights of Walter Allen's house!"

So we walked over the grass of the meadows under a flood of moonlight, and soon came to the house, which was low and built round a quadrangle big enough to get plenty of sunshine in it. Walter Allen, Dick's friend, was leaning against the jamb of the doorway waiting for us, and took us into the hall without overplus of words. There were not many people in it, as some of the dwellers there were away at the haymaking in the neighbourhood, and some, as Walter told us, were wandering about the meadow enjoying the beautiful moonlit night. Dick's friend looked to be a man of about forty; tall, black-haired, very kind-looking and thoughtful; but rather to my surprise there was a shade of melancholy on his face, and he seemed a little abstracted and inattentive to our chat, in spite of obvious efforts to listen.

Dick looked on him from time to time, and seemed troubled; and at last he said: "I say, old fellow, if there is anything the matter which we didn't know of when you wrote to me, don't you think you had better tell us about it at once? or else we shall think we have come here at an unlucky time, and are not quite wanted."

Walter turned red, and seemed to have some difficulty in restraining his tears, but said at last: "Of course everybody here is very glad to see you, Dick, and your friends; but it is true that we are not at our best, in spite of the fine weather and the glorious hay-crop. We have had a death here."

Said Dick: "Well, you should get over that, neighbour: such things must be."

"Yes," Walter said, "but this was a death by violence and it seems likely to lead to at least one more; and somehow it makes us feel rather shy of one another; and to say the truth, that is one reason why there are so few of us present to-night."

"Tell us the story, Walter," said Dick; "perhaps telling it will help you to shake off your sadness."

Said Walter: "Well, I will; and I will make it short enough, though I daresay it might be spun out into a long one, as used to be done with such subjects in the old novels. There is a very charming girl here whom we all like, and whom some of us do more than like; and she very naturally liked one of us better than anybody else. And another of us (I won't name him) got fairly bitten with love-madness, and used to go about making himself as unpleasant as he could —not of malice prepense, of course; so that the girl, who liked him well enough at first, though she didn't love him, began fairly to dislike him. Of course, those of us who knew him best—myself amongst others—advised him to go away, as he was making matters worse and worse for himself every day. Well, he wouldn't take our advice (that also, I suppose, was a matter of course), so we had to tell him that he *must* go, or the inevitable sending to Coventry would follow; for his individual trouble had so overmastered him that we felt that *we* must go if he did not.

"He took that better than we expected, when something or other—an interview with the girl, I think, and some hot words with the successful lover following close upon it— threw him quite off his balance; and he got hold of an axe and fell upon his rival when there was no one by; and in the struggle that followed the man attacked hit him an unlucky blow and killed him. And now the slayer in his turn is so upset that he is like to kill himself; and if he does, the girl will do as much, I fear. And all this we could no more help than the earthquake of the year before last."

"It is very unhappy," said Dick; "but since the man is dead, and cannot be brought to life again, and since the slayer had no malice in him, I cannot for the life of me see why he shouldn't get over it before long. Besides, it was the right man that was killed and not the wrong. Why should a man brood over a mere accident for ever? And the girl?"

"As to her," said Walter, "that whole thing seems to have inspired her with terror rather than grief. What you say about the man is true, or it should be; but then, you see, the excitement and jealousy that was the prelude to this tragedy had made an evil and feverish element round about him, from which he does not seem to be able to escape. However, we have advised him to go away—in fact, to cross the seas; but he is in such a state that I do not think he *can* go unless some one *takes* him, and I think it will fall to my lot to do so; which is scarcely a cheerful outlook for me."

"O, you will find a certain kind of interest in it," said Dick. "And of course he *must* soon look upon the affair from a reasonable point of view sooner or later."

"Well, at any rate," quoth Walter, "now that I have eased my mind by making you uncomfortable, let us have an end of the subject for the present. Are you going to take your guest to Oxford?"

"Why, of course we must pass through it," said Dick, smiling, "as we are going into the upper waters: but I thought that we wouldn't stop there, or we shall be belated as to the haymaking up our way. So Oxford and my learned lecture on it, all got at second-hand from my old kinsman, must wait till we come down the water a fortnight hence."

I listened to this story with much surprise, and could not help wondering at first that the man who had slain the other had not been put in custody till it could be proved that he killed his rival in self-defence only. However, the more I thought of it, the plainer it grew to me that no amount of examination of witnesses, who had witnessed nothing but the ill-blood between the two rivals, would have done anything to clear up the case. I could not help thinking, also, that the remorse of this homicide gave point to what old Hammond had said to me about the way in which this strange people dealt with what I had been used to hear called crimes. Truly, the remorse was exaggerated; but it was quite clear that the slayer took the whole consequences of the act upon himself, and did not expect society to whitewash him by punishing him. I had no fear any longer that "the sacredness of human life" was likely to suffer amongst my friends from the absence of gallows and prison.

CHAPTER XXV

THE THIRD DAY ON THE THAMES

AS we went down to the boat next morning, Walter could not quite keep off the subject of last night, though he was more hopeful than he had been then, and seemed to think that if the unlucky homicide could not be got to go over-sea, he might at any rate go and live somewhere in the neighbourhood pretty much by himself; at any rate, that was what he himself had proposed. To Dick, and I must say to me also, this seemed a strange remedy; and Dick said as much. Quoth he:

"Friend Walter, don't set the man brooding on the tragedy by letting him live alone. That will only strengthen his idea that he has committed a crime, and you will have him killing himself in good earnest."

Said Clara: "I don't know. If I may say what I think of it, it is that he had better have his fill of gloom now, and, so to say, wake up presently to see how little need there has been for it; and then he will live happily afterwards. As for his killing himself, you need not be afraid of that; for, from all you tell me, he is really very much in love with the woman; and to speak plainly, until his love is satisfied, he will not only stick to life as tightly as he can, but will also make the most of every event of his life—will, so to say, hug himself up in it; and I think that this is the real explanation of his taking the whole matter with such an excess of tragedy."

Walter looked thoughtful, and said: "Well, you may be

right; and perhaps we should have treated it all more lightly: but you see, guest" (turning to me), "such things happen so seldom, that when they do happen, we cannot help being much taken up with it. For the rest, we are all inclined to excuse our poor friend for making us so unhappy, on the ground that he does it out of an exaggerated respect for human life and its happiness. Well, I will say no more about it; only this: will you give me a cast upstream, as I want to look after a lonely habitation for the poor fellow, since he will have it so, and I hear that there is one which would suit us very well on the downs beyond Streatley; so if you will put me ashore there I will walk up the hill and look to it."

"Is the house in question empty?" said I.

"No," said Walter, "but the man who lives there will go out of it, of course, when he hears that we want it. You see, we think that the fresh air of the downs and the very emptiness of the landscape will do our friend good."

"Yes," said Clara, smiling, "and he will not be so far from his beloved that they cannot easily meet if they have a mind to—as they certainly will."

This talk had brought us down to the boat, and we were presently afloat on the beautiful broad stream, Dick driving the prow swiftly through the windless water of the early summer morning, for it was not yet six o'clock. We were at the lock in a very little time; and as we lay rising and rising on the in-coming water, I could not help wondering that my old friend the pound-lock, and that of the very simplest and most rural kind, should hold its place there; so I said:

"I have been wondering, as we passed lock after lock, that you people, so prosperous as you are, and especially since you are so anxious for pleasant work to do, have not invented something which would get rid of this clumsy business of going upstairs by means of these rude contrivances."

Dick laughed. "My dear friend," said he, "as long as water has the clumsy habit of running down hill, I fear we must humour it by going upstairs when we have our faces turned from the sea. And really I don't see why you should fall foul of Maple-Durham lock, which I think a very pretty place."

There was no doubt about the latter assertion, I thought,
as I looked up at the overhanging boughs of the great trees,
with the sun coming glittering through the leaves, and
listened to the song of the summer blackbirds as it mingled
with the sound of the backwater near us. So not being able
to say why I wanted the locks away—which, indeed, I
didn't do at all—I held my peace. But Walter said:

"You see, guest, this is not an age of inventions. The last
epoch did all that for us, and we are now content to use
such of its inventions as we find handy, and leaving those
alone which we don't want. I believe, as a matter of fact,
that some time ago (I can't give you a date) some elaborate
machinery was used for the locks, though people did not
go so far as try to make the water run uphill. However, it
was troublesome, I suppose, and the simple hatches, and
the gates, with a big counterpoising beam, were found to
answer every purpose, and were easily mended when
wanted with material always to hand: so here they are, as
you see."

"Besides," said Dick, "this kind of lock is pretty, as you
can see; and I can't help thinking that your machine-lock,
winding up like a watch, would have been ugly and would
have spoiled the look of the river: and that is surely reason
enough for keeping such locks as these. Good-bye, old
fellow!" said he to the lock, as he pushed us out through
the now open gates by a vigorous stroke of the boat-hook.
May you live long, and have your green old age renewed
for ever!"

On we went; and the water had the familiar aspect to
me of the days before Pangbourne had been thoroughly
cockneyfied, as I have seen it. It (Pangbourne) was distinctly a village still—i.e. a definite group of houses, and as
pretty as might be. The beech-woods still covered the hill
that rose above Basildon; but the flat fields beneath them
were much more populous than I remembered them, as
there were five large houses in sight, very carefully designed
so as not to hurt the character of the country. Down on the
green lip of the river, just where the water turns toward
the Goring and Streatley reaches, were half a dozen girls
playing about on the grass. They hailed us as we were
about passing them, as they noted that we were travellers

and we stopped a minute to talk with them. They had been bathing and were light clad and barefooted, and were bound for the meadows on the Berkshire side, where the haymaking had begun, and were passing the time merrily enough till the Berkshire folk came in their punt to fetch them. At first nothing would content them but we must go with them into the hay-field, and breakfast with them; but Dick put forward his theory of beginning the hay-harvest higher up the water, and not spoiling my pleasure therein by giving me a taste of it elsewhere, and they gave way, though unwillingly. In revenge they asked me a great many questions about the country I came from and the manners of life there, which I found rather puzzling to answer; and doubtless what answers I did give were puzzling enough to them. I noticed both with these pretty girls and with everybody else we met, that in default of serious news, such as we had heard at Maple-Durham, they were eager to discuss all the little details of life: the weather, the hay-crop, the last new house, the plenty or lack of such and such birds, and so on; and they talked of these things not in a fatuous and conventional way, but as taking, I say, real interest in them. Moreover, I found that the women knew as much about all these things as the men: could name a flower, and knew its qualities; could tell you the habitat of such and such birds and fish, and the like.

It is almost strange what a difference this intelligence made in my estimate of the country life of that day; for it used to be said in past times, and on the whole truly, that outside their daily work country people knew little of the country, and at least could tell you nothing about it; while here were these people as eager about all the goings on in the fields and woods and downs as if they had been Cockneys newly escaped from the tyranny of bricks and mortar.

I may mention as a detail worth noticing that not only did there seem to be a great many more birds about of the non-predatory kinds, but their enemies the birds of prey were also commoner. A kite hung over our heads as we passed Medmenham yesterday; magpies were quite common in the hedgerows; I saw several sparrow-hawks, and I think a merlin; and now just as we were passing the pretty bridge which had taken the place of Basildon railway-bridge, a couple of ravens croaked above our boat, as they sailed off to the higher ground of the downs. I concluded from all this that the days of the gamekeeper were over, and did not even need to ask Dick a question about it.

CHAPTER XXVI

THE OBSTINATE REFUSERS

BEFORE we parted from these girls we saw two sturdy young men and a woman putting off from the Berkshire shore, and then Dick bethought him of a little banter of the girls, and asked them how it was that there was nobody of the male kind to go with them across the water, and where their boats were gone to. Said one, the youngest of the party: "O, they have got the big punt to load stone from up the water."

"Who do you mean by 'they,' dear child?" said Dick.

Said an older girl, laughing: "You had better go and see them. Look there," and she pointed north-west, "don't you see building going on there?"

"Yes," said Dick, "and I am rather surprised at this time of the year; why are they not haymaking with you?"

The girls all laughed at this, and before their laugh was over, the Berkshire boat had run on to the grass and the girls stepped in lightly, still sniggering, while the newcomers gave us the sele of the day. But before they were under way again, the tall girl said: "Excuse us for laughing, dear neighbours, but we have had some friendly bickering with the builders up yonder, and as we have no time to tell you the story, you had better go and ask them: they will be glad to see you—if you don't hinder their work."

They all laughed again at that, and waved us a pretty farewell as the punters set them over toward the other shore, and left us standing on the bank beside our boat.

"Let us go and see them," said Clara; "that is, if you are not in a hurry to get to Streatley, Walter?"

"O no," said Walter, "I shall be glad of the excuse to have a little more of your company."

G

So we left the boat moored there, and went on up the slow slope of the hill; but I said to Dick on the way, being somewhat mystified: "What was all that laughing about? what was the joke?"

"I can guess pretty well," said Dick; "some of them up there have got a piece of work which interests them, and they won't go to the haymaking, which doesn't matter at all, because there are plenty of people to do such easy-hard work as that; only, since haymaking is a regular festival, the neighbours find it amusing to jeer good-humouredly at them."

"I see," said I, "much as if in Dickens's time some young people were so wrapped up in their work that they wouldn't keep Christmas."

"Just so," said Dick, "only these people need not be young either."

"But what did you mean by easy-hard work?" said I.

Quoth Dick: "Did I say that? I mean work that tries the muscles and hardens them and sends you pleasantly weary to bed, but which isn't trying in other ways: doesn't harass you, in short. Such work is always pleasant if you don't overdo it. Only, mind you, good mowing requires some little skill. I'm a pretty good mower."

This talk brought us up to the house that was a-building, not a large one, which stood at the end of a beautiful orchard surrounded by an old stone wall. "O yes, I see," said Dick; "I remember, a beautiful place for a house: but a starveling of a nineteenth-century house stood there: I am glad they are rebuilding: it's all stone, too, though it need not have been in this part of the country: my word, though, they are making a neat job of it: but I wouldn't have made it all ashlar."

Walter and Clara were already talking to a tall man clad in his mason's blouse, who looked about forty, but was, I daresay, older, who had his mallet and chisel in hand; there were at work in the shed and on the scaffold about half a dozen men and two women, blouse-clad like the carles, while a very pretty woman who was not in the work but was dressed in an elegant suit of blue linen came saunter- ing up to us with her knitting in her hand. She welcomed us and said, smiling: "So you are come up from the water to see the Obstinate Refusers: where are you going hay-making, neighbours?"

"O, right up above Oxford," said Dick; "it is rather a late country. But what share have you got with the Refusers, pretty neighbour?"

Said she, with a laugh: "O, I am the lucky one who doesn't want to work; though sometimes I get it, for I serve as model to Mistress Philippa there when she wants one: she is our head carver; come and see her."

She led us up to the door of the unfinished house, where a rather little woman was working with mallet and chisel on the wall near by. She seemed very intent on what she was doing, and did not turn round when we came up; but a taller woman, quite a girl she seemed, who was at work near by, had already knocked off, and was standing looking from Clara to Dick with delighted eyes. None of the others paid much heed to us.

The blue-clad girl laid her hand on the carver's shoulder and said: "Now, Philippa, if you gobble up your work like that, you will soon have none to do; and what will become of you then?"

The carver turned round hurriedly and showed us the face of a woman of forty (or so she seemed), and said rather pettishly, but in a sweet voice:

"Don't talk nonsense, Kate, and don't interrupt me if you can help it." She stopped short when she saw us, then went on with the kind smile of welcome which never failed us. "Thank you for coming to see us, neighbours; but I am sure that you won't think me unkind if I go on with my work, especially when I tell you that I was ill and unable to do anything all through April and May; and this open air and the sun and the work together, and my feeling well again too, make a mere delight of every hour to me; and excuse me, I must go on."

She fell to work accordingly on a carving in low relief of flowers and figures, but talked on amidst her mallet strokes: "You see, we all think this the prettiest place for a house up and down these reaches; and the site has been so long encumbered with an unworthy one, that we masons were determined to pay off fate and destiny for once, and build the prettiest house we could compass here—and so—and so——"

Here she lapsed into mere carving, but the tall foreman came up and said: "Yes, neighbours, that is it: so it is going to be all ashlar because we want to carve a kind of a wreath of flowers and figures all round it; and we have been much hindered by one thing or other—Philippa's illness amongst others,—and though we could have managed our wreath without her——"

"Could you, though?" grumbled the last-named from the face of the wall.

"Well, at any rate, she is our best carver, and it would not have been kind to begin the carving without her. So you see," said he, looking at Dick and me, "we really couldn't go haymaking, could we, neighbours? But you see, we are getting on so fast now with this splendid weather, that I think we may well spare a week or ten days at wheat-harvest; and won't we go at *that* work then! Come down then to the acres that lie north and by west at our backs and you shall see good harvesters, neighbours."

"Hurrah, for a good brag!" called a voice from the scaffold above us; "our foreman thinks that an easier job than putting one stone on another!"

There was a general laugh at this sally, in which the tall foreman joined; and with that we saw a lad bringing out a little table into the shadow of the stone-shed, which he set down there, and then going back, came out again with the inevitable big wickered flask and tall glasses, whereon the foreman led us up to due seats on blocks of stone, and said:

"Well, neighbours, drink to my brag coming true, or I shall think you don't believe me! Up there!" said he, hailing the scaffold, "are you coming down for a glass?" Three of the workmen came running down the ladder as men with good "building legs" will do; but the others didn't answer, except the joker (if he must so be called), who called out without turning round: "Excuse me, neighbours, for not getting down. I must get on: my work is not super-intending, like the gaffer's yonder; but, you fellows, send us up a glass to drink the haymakers' health." Of course, Philippa would not turn away from her beloved work; but the other woman carver came; she turned out to be Philippa's daughter, but was a tall strong girl, black-haired and gipsey-like of face and curiously solemn of manner. The rest gathered round us and clinked glasses, and the men on the scaffold turned about and drank to our healths; but the busy little woman by the door would have none of it all, but only shrugged her shoulders when her daughter came up to her and touched her.

So we shook hands and turned our backs on the Obstinate Refusers, went down the slope to our boat, and before we had gone many steps heard the full tune of tinkling trowels mingle with the humming of the bees and the singing of the larks above the little plain of Basildon.

CHAPTER XXVII

THE UPPER WATERS

WE set Walter ashore on the Berkshire side, amidst all the beauties of Streatley, and so went our ways into what once would have been the deeper country under the foot-hills of the White Horse; and though the contrast between half-cockneyfied and wholly unsophisticated country existed no longer, a feeling of exultation rose within me (as it used to do) at sight of the familiar and still unchanged hills of the Berkshire range.

We stopped at Wallingford for our midday meal; of course, all signs of squalor and poverty had disappeared from the streets of the ancient town, and many ugly houses had been taken down and many pretty new ones built, but I thought it curious, that the town still looked like the old place I remembered so well; for indeed it looked like that ought to have looked.

At dinner we fell in with an old, but very bright and intelligent man, who seemed in a country way to be another edition of old Hammond. He had an extraordinary detailed knowledge of the ancient history of the country-side from the time of Alfred to the days of the Parliamentary Wars, many events of which, as you may know, were enacted round about Wallingford. But, what was more interesting to us, he had detailed record of the period of the change to the present state of things, and told us a great deal about it, and especially of that exodus of the people from the town to the country, and the gradual recovery by the town-bred people on one side, and the country-bred people on the other, of those arts of life which they had each lost; which loss, as he told us, had at one time gone so far that not only was it impossible to find a carpenter or a smith in a village or small country town, but that people in such places had even forgotten how to bake bread, and that at Wallingford, for instance, the bread came down with the newspapers by an early train from London, worked in some way, the explanation of which I could not understand. He told us also that the townspeople who came into the country used to pick up the agricultural arts by carefully watching the way in which the machines worked, gathering an idea of handicraft from machinery; because at that time almost everything in and about the fields was done by elaborate machines used quite unintelligently by the labourers. On the other hand, the old men amongst the labourers managed to teach the younger ones gradually a little artisanship, such as the use of the saw and the plane, the work of the smithy, and so forth; for once more, by that time it was as much as —or rather, more than—a man could do to fix an ash pole to a rake by handiwork; so that it would take a machine worth a thousand pounds, a group of workmen, and half a day's travelling, to do five shillings' worth of work. He showed us, among other things, an account of a certain village council who were working hard at all this business; and the record of their intense earnestness in getting to the bottom of some matter which in time past would have been thought quite trivial, as, for example, the due proportions of alkali and oil for soap-making for the village wash, or the exact heat of the water into which a leg of mutton should be plunged for boiling—all this, joined to the utter absence of anything like party feeling, which even in a village assembly would certainly have made its appearance in an earlier epoch, was very amusing, and at the same time instructive.

This old man, whose name was Henry Morsom, took us, after our meal and a rest, into a biggish hall which contained a large collection of articles of manufacture and art from the last days of the machine period to that day; and he went over them with us, and explained them with great care. They also were very interesting, showing the transition from the makeshift work of the machines (which was at about its worst a little after the Civil War before told of) into the first years of the new handicraft period. Of course, there was much overlapping of the periods: and at first the new handwork came in very slowly.

"You must remember," said the old antiquary, "that the handicraft was not the result of what used to be called material necessity: on the contrary, by that time the machines had been so much improved that almost all necessary work might have been done by them: and indeed many people at that time, and before it, used to think that machinery would entirely supersede handicraft; which certainly, on the face of it, seemed more than likely. But there was another opinion, far less logical, prevalent amongst the rich people before the days of freedom, which did not die out at once after that epoch had begun. This opinion, which from all I can learn seemed as natural then, as it seems absurd now, was, that while the ordinary daily work of the world would be done entirely by automatic machinery, the energies of the more intelligent part of mankind would be set free to follow the higher forms of the arts, as well as science and the study of history. It was strange, was it not, that they should thus ignore that aspiration after complete equality which we now recognise as the bond of all happy human society?"

I did not answer, but thought the more. Dick looked thoughtful, and said:

"Strange, neighbour? Well, I don't know. I have often heard my old kinsman say the one aim of all people before our time was to avoid work, or at least they thought it was; so of course the work which their daily life *forced* them to do, seemed more like work than that which they *seemed* to choose for themselves."

"True enough," said Morsom. "Anyhow, they soon began to find out their mistake, and that only slaves and slave-holders could live solely by setting machines going."

Clara broke in here, flushing a little as she spoke: "Was not their mistake once more bred of the life of slavery that they had been living?—a life which was always looking upon

everything, except mankind, animate and inanimate—
'nature,' as people used to call it—as one thing, and mankind as another. It was natural to people thinking in this
way, that they should try to make 'nature' their slave, since
they thought 'nature' was something outside them.''

"Surely," said Morsom; "and they were puzzled as to
what to do, till they found the feeling against a mechanical
life, which had begun before the Great Change amongst
people who had leisure to think of such things, was spreading
insensibly; till at last under the guise of pleasure that was not
supposed to be work, work that was pleasure began to push
out the mechanical toil, which they had once hoped at the
best to reduce to narrow limits indeed, but never to get rid
of; and which, moreover, they found they could not limit
as they had hoped to do."

"When did this new revolution gather head?" said I.

"In the half-century that followed the Great Change,"
said Morsom, "it began to be noteworthy; machine after
machine was quietly dropped under the excuse that the
machines could not produce works of art, and that works of
art were more and more called for. Look here," he said,
"here are some of the works of that time—rough and un-
skilful in handiwork, but solid and showing some sense of
pleasure in the making."

"They are very curious," said I, taking up a piece of
pottery from amongst the specimens which the antiquary
was showing us; "not a bit like the work of either savages or
barbarians, and yet with what would once have been called
a hatred of civilisation impressed upon them."

"Yes," said Morsom, "you must not look for delicacy
there: in that period you could only have got that from a
man who was practically a slave. But now, you see," said
he, leading me on a little, "we have learned the trick of
handicraft, and have added the utmost refinement of workmanship to the freedom of fancy and imagination."

I looked, and wondered indeed at the deftness and
abundance of beauty of the work of men who had at last
learned to accept life itself as a pleasure, and the satisfaction
of the common needs of mankind and the preparation for
them, as work fit for the best of the race. I mused silently;
but at last I said:

"What is to come after this?"

The old man laughed. "I don't know," said he; "we will meet it when it comes."

"Meanwhile," quoth Dick, "we have got to meet the rest of our day's journey; so out into the street and down to the strand! Will you come a turn with us, neighbour? Our friend is greedy of your stories."

"I will go as far as Oxford with you," said he; "I want a book or two out of the Bodleian Library. I suppose you will sleep in the old city?"

"No," said Dick, "we are going higher up; the hay is waiting us there, you know."

Morsom nodded, and we all went into the street together, and got into the boat a little above the town bridge. But just as Dick was getting the sculls into the rowlocks, the bows of another boat came thrusting through the low arch. Even at first sight it was a gay little craft indeed—bright green, and painted over with elegantly drawn flowers. As it cleared the arch, a figure as bright and gay-clad as the boat rose up in it; a slim girl dressed in light blue silk that fluttered in the draughty wind of the bridge. I thought I knew the figure, and sure enough, as she turned her head to us, and showed her beautiful face, I saw with joy that it was none other than the fairy godmother from the abundant garden on Runny-mede—Ellen, to wit.

We all stopped to receive her. Dick rose in the boat and cried out a genial good morrow; I tried to be as genial as Dick, but failed; Clara waved a delicate hand to her; and Morsom nodded and looked on with interest. As to Ellen, the beautiful brown of her face was deepened by a flush, as she brought the gunwale of her boat alongside ours, and said:

" You see, neighbours, I had some doubt if you would all three come back past Runnymede, or if you did, whether you would stop there; and besides, I am not sure whether we— my father and I— shall not be away in a week or two, for he wants to see a brother of his in the north country, and I should not like him to go without me. So I thought I might never see you again, and that seemed uncomfortable to me, and—and so I came after you."

"Well," said Dick, "I am sure we are all very glad of that;

although you may be sure that as for Clara and me, we should have made a point of coming to see you, and of coming the second time, if we had found you away the first. But, dear neighbour, there you are alone in the boat, and you have been sculling pretty hard, I should think, and might find a little quiet sitting pleasant; so we had better part our company into two."

"Yes," said Ellen, "I thought you would do that, so I have brought a rudder for my boat: will you help me to ship it, please?"

And she went aft in her boat and pushed along our side till she had brought the stern close to Dick's hand. He knelt down in our boat and she in hers, and the usual fumbling took place over hanging the rudder on its hooks; for, as you may imagine, no change had taken place in the arrangement of such an unimportant matter as the rudder of a pleasure-boat. As the two beautiful young faces bent over the rudder, they seemed to me to be very close together, and though it only lasted a moment, a sort of pang shot through me as I looked on. Clara sat in her place and did not look round, but presently she said, with just the least stiffness in her tone:

"How shall we divide? Won't you go into Ellen's boat, Dick, since, without offence to our guest, you are the better sculler?"

Dick stood up and laid his hand on her shoulder, and said: "No, no; let Guest try what he can do—he ought to be getting into training now. Besides, we are in no hurry: we are not going far above Oxford; and even if we are be-nighted, we shall have the moon, which will give us nothing worse of a night than a greyer day."

"Besides," said I, "I may manage to do a little more with my sculling than merely keeping the boat from drifting down-stream."

They all laughed at this, as if it had been a very good joke; and I thought that Ellen's laugh, even amongst the others, was one of the pleasantest sounds I had ever heard.

To be short, I got into the new-come boat, not a little elated, and taking the sculls, set to work to show off a little. For—must I say it?—I felt as if even that happy world were made the happier for my being so near this strange girl;

although I must say that of all the persons I had seen in that world renewed, she was the most unfamiliar to me, the most unlike what I could have thought of. Clara, for instance, beautiful and bright as she was, was not unlike a *very* pleasant and unaffected young lady; and the other girls also seemed nothing more than specimens of very much improved types which I had known in other times. But this girl was not only beautiful with a beauty quite different from that of "a young lady," but was in all ways so strangely interesting; so that I kept wondering what she would say or do next to surprise and please me. Not, indeed, that there was anything startling in what she actually said or did; but it was all done in a new way, and always with that indefinable interest and pleasure of life, which I had noticed more or less in everybody, but which in her was more marked and more charming that in any one else that I had seen.

We were soon under way and going at a fair pace through the beautiful reaches of the river, between Bensington and Dorchester. It was now about the middle of the afternoon, warm rather than hot, and quite windless; the clouds high up and light, pearly white, and gleaming, softened the sun's burning, but did not hide the pale blue in most places, though they seemed to give it height and consistency; the sky, in short, looked really like a vault, as poets have sometimes called it, and not like mere limitless air, but a vault so vast and full of light that it did not in any way oppress the spirits. It was the sort of afternoon that Tennyson must have been thinking about, when he said of the Lotos-Eaters' land that it was a land where it was always afternoon.

Ellen leaned back in the stern and seemed to enjoy herself thoroughly. I could see that she was really looking at things and let nothing escape her, and as I watched her, an uncomfortable feeling that she had been a little touched by love of the deft, ready and handsome Dick, and that she had been constrained to follow us because of it, faded out of my mind; since if it had been so, she surely could not have been so excitedly pleased, even with the beautiful scenes we were passing through. For some time she did not say much, but at last, as we had passed under Shillingford Bridge (new built, but somewhat on its old lines), she bade me hold the boat while she had a good look at the landscape through the graceful arch. Then she turned about to me and said:

"I do not know whether to be sorry or glad that this is the first time that I have been in these reaches. It is true that it is a great pleasure to see all this for the first time; but if I had had a year or two of memory of it, how sweetly it would all have mingled with my life, waking or dreaming! I am so glad Dick has been pulling slowly, so as to linger out the time here. How do you feel about your first visit to these waters?"

I do not suppose she meant a trap for me, but anyhow I fell into it, and said: "My first visit! It is not my first visit by many a time. I know these reaches well; indeed, I may say that I know every yard of the Thames from Hammersmith to Cricklade."

I saw the complication that might follow, as her eyes fixed mine with a curious look in them, that I had seen before at Runnymede, when I had said something which made it difficult for others to understand my present position amongst these people. I reddened, and said, in order to cover my mistake: "I wonder you have never been up so high as this, since you live on the Thames, and moreover row so well that it would be no great labour to you. Let alone," quoth I, insinuatingly, "that anybody would be glad to row you."

She laughed, clearly not at my compliment (as I am sure she need not have done, since it was a very commonplace fact), but at something which was stirring in her mind; and she still looked at me kindly, but with the above-said keen look in her eyes, and then she said:

"Well, perhaps it is strange, though I have a good deal to do at home, what with looking after my father, and dealing with two or three young men who have taken a special liking to me, and all of whom I cannot please at once. But you, dear neighbour; it seems to me stranger that you should know the upper river, than that I should not know it; for, as I understand, you have only been in England a few days. But perhaps you mean that you have read about it in books, and seen pictures of it?—though that does not come to much, either."

"Truly," said I. "Besides, I have not read any books

about the Thames: it was one of the minor stupidities of our time that no one thought fit to write a decent book about what may fairly be called our only English river."

The words were no sooner out of my mouth than I saw that I had made another mistake; and I felt really annoyed with myself, as I did not want to go into a long explanation just then, or begin another series of Odyssean lies. Somehow, Ellen seemed to see this, and she took no advantage of my slip; her piercing look changed into one of mere frank kindness, and she said:

"Well, anyhow I am glad that I am travelling these waters with you, since you know our river so well, and I know little of it past Pangbourne, for you can tell me all I want to know about it." She paused a minute, and then said: "Yet you must understand that the part I do know, I know as thoroughly as you do. I should be sorry for you to think that I am careless of a thing so beautiful and interesting as the Thames."

She said this quite earnestly, and with an air of affectionate appeal to me which pleased me very much; but I could see that she was only keeping her doubts about me for another time.

Presently we came to Day's Lock, where Dick and his two sitters had waited for us. He would have me go ashore, as if to show me something which I had never seen before; and nothing loth I followed him, Ellen by my side, to the well-remembered Dykes, and the long church beyond them, which was still used for various purposes by the good folk of Dorchester: where, by the way, the village guest-house still had the sign of the Fleur-de-luce which it used to bear in the days when hospitality had to be bought and sold. This time, however, I made no sign of all this being familiar to me: though as we sat for a while on the mound of the Dykes looking up at Sinodun and its clear-cut trench, and its sister *mamelon* of Whittenham, I felt somewhat uncomfortable under Ellen's serious attentive look, which almost drew from me the cry, "How little anything is changed here!"

We stopped again at Abingdon, which, like Wallingford, was in a way both old and new to me, since it had been lifted out of its nineteenth-century degradation, and otherwise was as little altered as might be.

Sunset was in the sky as we skirted Oxford by Oseney; we stopped a minute or two hard by the ancient castle to put Henry Morsom ashore. It was a matter of course that so far as they could be seen from the river, I missed none of the towers and spires of that once don-beridden city; but the meadows all round, which, when I had last passed through them, were getting daily more and more squalid, more and more impressed with the seal of the "stir and intellectual life of the nineteenth century," were no longer intellectual, but had once again become as beautiful as they should be, and the little hill of Hinksey, with two or three very pretty stone houses new-grown on it (I use the word advisedly; for they seemed to belong to it) looked down happily on the full streams and waving-grass, grey now, but for the sunset, with its fast-ripening seeds.

The railway having disappeared, and therewith the various level bridges over the streams of Thames, we were soon through Medley Lock and in the wide water that washes Port Meadow, with its numerous population of geese nowise diminished; and I thought with interest how its name and use had survived from the older imperfect communal period, through the time of the confused struggle and tyranny of the rights of property, into the present rest and happiness of complete Communism.

I was taken ashore again at Godstow, to see the remains of the old nunnery, pretty nearly in the same condition as I had remembered them; and from the high bridge over the cut close by, I could see, even in the twilight, how beautiful the little village with its grey stone houses had become; for we had now come into the stone-country, in which every house must be either built, walls and roof, of grey stone or be a blot on the landscape.

We still rowed on after this. Ellen taking the sculls in my boat; we passed a weir a little higher up, and about three miles beyond it came by moonlight again to a little town, where we slept at a house thinly inhabited, as its folk were mostly tented in the hay-fields.

CHAPTER XXVIII

THE LITTLE RIVER

WE started before six o'clock the next morning, as we were still twenty-five miles from our resting-place, and Dick wanted to be there before dusk. The journey was pleasant, though to those who do not know the upper Thames, there is little to say about it. Ellen and I were once more together in her boat, though Dick, for fairness' sake, was for having me in his, and letting the two women scull the green toy. Ellen, however, would not allow this, but claimed me as the interesting person of the company. "After having come so far," said she, "I will not be put off with a companion who will be always thinking of somebody else than me: the guest is the only person who can amuse me properly. I mean that really," said she, turning to me, "and have not said it merely as a pretty saying."

Clara blushed and looked very happy at all this; for I think up to this time she had been rather frightened of Ellen. As for me I felt young again, and strange hopes of my youth were mingling with the pleasure of the present; almost destroying it, and quickening it into something like pain.

As we passed through the short and winding reaches of the now quickly lessening stream, Ellen said: "How pleasant this little river is to me, who am used to a great wide wash of water; it almost seems as if we shall have to stop at every reach-end. I expect before I get home this evening I shall have realised what a little country England is, since we can so soon get to the end of its biggest river."

"It is not big," said I, "but it is pretty."

"Yes," she said, "and don't you find it difficult to imagine the times when this little pretty country was treated by its folk as if it had been an ugly characterless waste, with no delicate beauty to be guarded, with no heed taken of the ever fresh pleasure of the recurring seasons, and changeful weather, and diverse quality of the soil, and so forth? How could people be so cruel to themselves?"

"And to each other," said I. Then a sudden resolution took hold of me, and I said: "Dear neighbour, I may as well tell you at once that I find it easier to imagine all that ugly past than you do, because I myself have been part of it. I see both that you have divined something of this in me; and also I think you will believe me when I tell you of it, so that I am going to hide nothing from you at all."

She was silent a little, and then she said: "My friend, you have guessed right about me; and to tell you the truth I have followed you up from Runnymede in order that I might ask you many questions, and because I saw that you were not one of us; and that interested and pleased me, and I wanted to make you as happy as you could be. To say the truth, there was a risk in it," said she, blushing—" I mean as to Dick and Clara; for I must tell you, since we are going to be such close friends, that even amongst us, where there are so many beautiful women, I have often troubled men's minds disastrously. That is one reason why I was living alone with my father in the cottage at Runny-mede. But it did not answer on that score; for of course people came there, as the place is not a desert, and they seemed to find me all the more interesting for living alone like that, and fell to making stories of me to themselves— like I know you did, my friend. Well, let that pass. This evening, or to-morrow morning, I shall make a proposal to you to do something which would please me very much, and I think would not hurt you."

I broke in eagerly, saying that I would do anything in the world for her; for indeed, in spite of my years and the too obvious signs of them (though that feeling of renewed youth was not a mere passing sensation, I think)—in spite of my years, I say, I felt altogether too happy in the company of this delightful girl, and was prepared to take her confidences for more than they meant perhaps.

She laughed now, but looked very kindly on me. "Well," she said, "meantime for the present we will let it be; for I must look at this new country that we are passing through. See how the river has changed character again; it is broad now, and the reaches are long and very slow-running. And look, there is a ferry!"

I told her the name of it, as I slowed off to put the ferry-chain over our heads; and on we went passing by a bank

clad with oak trees on our left hand, till the stream narrowed again and deepened, and we rowed on between
walls of tall reeds, whose population of reed sparrows and
warblers were delightfully restless, twittering and chuckling
as the wash of the boats stirred the reeds from the water
upwards in the still, hot morning.

She smiled with pleasure, and her lazy enjoyment of the
new scene seemed to bring out her beauty doubly as she
leaned back amidst the cushions, though she was far from
languid; her idleness being the idleness of a person, strong
and well-knit both in body and mind, deliberately resting.

"Look!" she said, springing up suddenly from her place
without any obvious effort, and balancing herself with
exquisite grace and ease; "look at the beautiful old bridge
ahead!"

"I need scarcely look at that," said I, not turning my
head away from her beauty. "I know what it is; though"
(with a smile) "we used not to call it the Old Bridge time
agone."

She looked down upon me kindly, and said, "How well
we get on now you are no longer on your guard against
me!"

And she stood looking thoughtfully at me still, till she had
to sit down as we passed under the middle one of the row
of little pointed arches of the oldest bridge across the
Thames.

"O the beautiful fields!" she said; "I had no idea of the
charm of a very small river like this. The smallness of the
scale of everything, the short reaches, and the speedy change
of the banks, give one a feeling of going somewhere, of
coming to something strange, a feeling of adventure which
I have not felt in bigger waters."

I looked up at her delightedly; for her voice, saying the
very thing which I was thinking, was like a caress to me.
She caught my eye and her cheeks reddened under their
tan, and she said simply:

"I must tell you, my friend, that when my father leaves
the Thames this summer he will take me away to a place
near the Roman wall in Cumberland; so that this voyage
of mine is farewell to the south; of course with my good will
in a way; and yet I am sorry for it. I hadn't the heart to

tell Dick yesterday that we were as good as gone from the Thames-side; but somehow to you I must needs tell it."

She stopped and seemed very thoughtful for a while, and then said, smiling:

"I must say that I don't like moving about from one home to another; one gets so pleasantly used to all the detail of the life about one; it fits so harmoniously and happily into one's own life, that beginning again, even in a small way, is a kind of pain. But I daresay in the country which you come from, you would think this petty and unadventurous, and would think the worse of me for it."

She smiled at me caressingly as she spoke, and I made haste to answer: "O no, indeed; again you echo my very thoughts. But I hardly expected to hear you speak so. I gathered from all I have heard that there was a great deal of changing of abode amongst you in this country."

"Well," she said, "of course people are free to move about; but except for pleasure-parties, especially in harvest and hay-time, like this of ours, I don't think they do so much. I admit that I also have other moods than that of stay-at-home, as I hinted just now, and I should like to go with you all through the west country—thinking of nothing," concluded she, smiling.

"I should have plenty to think of," said I.

<h2 style="text-align:center">CHAPTER XXIX</h2>

<h1 style="text-align:center">A RESTING-PLACE
ON THE UPPER THAMES</h1>

PRESENTLY at a place where the river flowed round a headland of the meadows, we stopped a while for rest and victuals, and settled ourselves on a beautiful bank which almost reached the dignity of a hill-side: the wide meadows spread before us, and already the scythe was busy amidst the hay. One change I noticed amidst the quiet beauty of the fields—to wit, that they were planted with trees here and there, often fruit-trees, and that there was none of the niggardly begrudging of space to a handsome tree which I remembered too well; and though the willows were often polled (or shrowded, as they call it in that country-side), this was done with some regard to beauty: I mean that there was no polling of rows on rows so as to destroy the pleasantness of half a mile of country, but a thoughtful sequence in the cutting, that prevented a sudden bareness anywhere. To be short, the fields were everywhere treated as a garden made for the pleasure as well as the livelihood of all, as old Hammond told me was the case.

On this bank or bent of the hill, then, we had our mid-day meal; somewhat early for dinner, if that mattered, but we had been stirring early: the slender stream of the Thames winding below us between the garden of a country I have been telling of; a furlong from us was a beautiful little islet begrown with graceful trees; on the slopes westward of us was a wood of varied growth overhanging the narrow meadow on the south side of the river; while to the north was a wide stretch of mead rising very gradually from the river's edge. A delicate spire of an ancient building rose up from out of the trees in the middle distance, with a few grey houses clustered about it; while nearer to us, in fact not half a furlong from the water, was a quite modern stone house—a wide quadrangle of one story, the buildings that made it being quite low. There was no garden between it and the river, nothing but a row of pear-trees still quite young and slender; and though there did not seem to be much ornament about it, it had a sort of natural elegance, like that of the trees themselves.

As we sat looking down on all this in the sweet June day, rather happy than merry, Ellen, who sat next me, her hand clasped about one knee, leaned sideways to me, and said in a low voice which Dick and Clara might have noted if they had not been busy in happy wordless love-making: "Friend, in your country were the houses of your field-labourers anything like that?"

I said: "Well, at any rate the houses of our rich men were not; they were mere blots upon the face of the land."

"I find that hard to understand," she said. "I can see why the workmen, who were so oppressed, should not have been able to live in beautiful houses; for it takes time and leisure, and minds not over-burdened with care, to make beautiful dwellings; and I quite understand that these poor people were not allowed to live in such a way as to have these (to us) necessary good things. But why the rich men, who had the time and the leisure and the materials for building, as it would be in this case, should not have housed themselves well, I do not understand as yet. I know what you are meaning to say to me," she said, looking me full in the eyes and blushing, "to wit that their houses and all belonging to them were generally ugly and base, unless they chanced to be ancient like yonder remnant of our fore-fathers' work" (pointing to the spire); "that they were—let me see; what is the word?"

"Vulgar," said I. "We used to say," said I, "that the ugliness and vulgarity of the rich men's dwellings was a necessary reflection from the sordidness and bareness of life which they forced upon the poor people."

She knit her brows as in thought; then turned a bright-ened face on me, as if she had caught the idea, and said: "Yes, friend, I see what you mean. We have sometimes—those of us who look into these things—talked this very matter over; because, to say the truth, we have plenty of record of the so-called arts of the time before Equality of Life; and there are not wanting people who say that the state of that society was not the cause of all that ugliness; that they were ugly in their life because they liked to be, and could have had beautiful things about them if they had chosen; just as a man or a body of men now may, if they please, make things more or less beautiful—— Stop! I know what you are going to say."

"Do you?" said I, smiling, yet with a beating heart.

"Yes," she said; "you are answering me, teaching me, in some way or another, although you have not spoken the words aloud. You were going to say that in times of in-equality it was an essential condition of the life of these rich men that they should not themselves make what they wanted for the adornment of their lives, but should force those to make them whom they forced to live pinched and sordid lives; and that as a necessary consequence the sordid-ness and pinching, the ugly barrenness of those ruined lives, were worked up into the adornment of the lives of the rich, and art died out amongst men? Was that what you would say, my friend?"

"Yes, yes," I said, looking at her eagerly; for she had risen and was standing on the edge of the bent, the light wind stirring her dainty raiment, one hand laid on her bosom, the other arm stretched downward and clenched in her earnestness.

"It is true," she said, "it is true! We have proved it true!"

I think amidst my—something more than interest in her, and admiration for her, I was beginning to wonder how it would all end. I had a glimmering of fear of what might follow; of anxiety as to the remedy which this new age might offer for the missing of something one might set one's heart on. But now Dick rose to his feet and cried out in his hearty manner: "Neighbour Ellen, are you quarrelling with the guest, or are you worrying him to tell you things which he cannot properly explain to our ignorance?"

"Neither, dear neighbour," she said. "I was so far from quarrelling with him that I think I have been making him good friends both with himself and me. Is it so, dear guest?" she said, looking down at me with a delightful smile of confidence in being understood.

"Indeed it is," said I.

"Well, moreover," she said, "I must say for him that he has explained himself to me very well indeed, so that I quite understand him."

"All right," quoth Dick. "When I first set eyes on you at Runnymede I knew that there was something wonderful in your keenness of wits. I don't say that as a mere pretty speech to please you," said he quickly, "but because it is true; and it made me want to see more of you. But, come, we ought to be going; for we are not half way, and we ought to be in well before sunset."

And therewith he took Clara's hand, and led her down the bent. But Ellen stood thoughtfully looking down for a little, and as I took her hand to follow Dick, she turned round to me and said:

"You might tell me a great deal and make many things clear to me, if you would."

"Yes," said I, "I am pretty well fit for that,—and for nothing else—an old man like me."

She did not notice the bitterness which, whether I liked it or not, was in my voice as I spoke, but went on: "It is not so much for myself; I should be quite content to dream about past times, and if I could not idealise them, yet at least idealise some of the people who lived in them. But I think sometimes people are too careless of the history of the past—too apt to leave it in the hands of old learned men like Hammond. Who knows? happy as we are, times may alter; we may be bitten with some impulse towards change, and many things may seem too wonderful for us to resist, too exciting not to catch at, if we do not know that they are but phases of what has been before; and withal ruinous, deceitful, and sordid."

As we went slowly down toward the boats she said again: "Not for myself alone, dear friend; I shall have children; perhaps before the end a good many;—I hope so. And though of course I cannot force any special kind of knowledge upon them, yet, my friend, I cannot help thinking that just as they might be like me in body, so I might impress upon them some part of my ways of thinking; that is, indeed, some of the essential part of myself; that part which was not mere moods, created by the matters and events round about me. What do you think?"

Of one thing I was sure, that her beauty and kindness and eagerness combined, forced me to think as she did, when she was not earnestly laying herself open to receive my thoughts. I said, what at the time was true, that I thought it most important; and presently stood entranced by the wonder of her grace as she stepped into the light boat, and held out her hand to me. And so on we went up the Thames still—or whither?

CHAPTER XXX

THE JOURNEY'S END

ON we went. In spite of my new-born excitement about Ellen, and my gathering fear of where it would land me, I could not help taking abundant interest in the condition of the river and its banks; all the more as she never seemed weary of the changing picture, but looked at every yard of flowery bank and gurgling eddy with the same kind of affectionate interest which I myself once had so fully, as I used to think, and perhaps had not altogether lost even in this strangely changed society with all its wonders. Ellen seemed delighted with my pleasure at this, that, or the other piece of carefulness in dealing with the river: the nursing of pretty corners; the ingenuity in dealing with difficulties of water-engineering, so that the most obviously useful works looked beautiful and natural also. All this, I say, pleased me hugely, and she was pleased at my pleasure—but rather puzzled too.

"You seem astonished," she said, just after we had passed a mill[1] which spanned all the stream save the waterway for traffic, but which was as beautiful in its way as a Gothic cathedral—"you seem astonished at this being so pleasant to look at."

"Yes," I said, "in a way I am; though I don't see why it should not be."

"Ah!" she said, looking at me admiringly, yet with a lurking smile in her face, "you know all about the history of the past. Were they not always careful about this little stream which now adds so much pleasantness to the country-side? It would always be easy to manage this little river. Ah! I forgot, though," she said, as her eye caught mine, "in the days we are thinking of, pleasure was wholly neglected in such matters. But how did they manage the river in the days that you——" Lived in she was going to say; but correcting herself, said: "in the days of which you have record?"

"They mismanaged it," quoth I. "Up to the first half of the nineteenth century, when it was still more or less of a highway for the country people, some care was taken of the river and its banks; and though I don't suppose any one troubled himself about its aspect, yet it was trim and beautiful. But when the railways—of which no doubt you have heard—came into power, they would not allow the

---

[1] I should have said that all along the Thames there were abundance of mills used for various purposes; none of which were in any degree unsightly, and many strikingly beautiful; and the gardens about them marvels of loveliness.

people of the country to use either the natural or artificial waterways, of which latter there were a great many. I suppose when we get higher up we shall see one of these: a very important one, which one of these railways entirely closed to the public, so that they might force people to send their goods by their private road, and so tax them as heavily as they could.

Ellen laughed heartily. "Well," she said, "that is not stated clearly enough in our history books, and it is worth knowing. But certainly the people of those days must have been a curiously lazy set. We are not either fidgety or quarrelsome now, but if any one tried such a piece of folly on us, we should use the said waterways, whoever gainsaid us: surely that would be simple enough. However, I remember other cases of this stupidity: when I was on the Rhine two years ago, I remember they showed us ruins of old castles, which, according to what we heard, must have been made for pretty much the same purpose as the railways were. But I am interrupting your history of the river: pray go on."

"It is both short and stupid enough," said I. "The river having lost its practical or commercial value—that is, being of no use to make money of——"

She nodded. "I understand what that queer phrase means," said she. "Go on!"

"Well, it was utterly neglected, till at last it became a nuisance——"

"Yes," quoth Ellen, "I understand: like the railways and the robber knights. Yes?"

"So then they turned the makeshift business on to it, and handed it over to a body up in London, who from time to time, in order to show that they had something to do, did some damage here and there,—cut down trees, destroying the banks thereby; dredged the river (where it was not needed always), and threw the dredgings on the fields so as to spoil them; and so forth. But for the most part they practised 'masterly inactivity,' as it was then called—that is, they drew their salaries, and let things alone."

"Drew their salaries," she said. "I know that means that they were allowed to take an extra lot of other people's goods for doing nothing. And if that had been all, it really might have been worth while to let them do so, if you couldn't find any other way of keeping them quiet; but it seems to me that being so paid, they could not help doing something, and that something was bound to be mischief,— because," said she, kindling with sudden anger, "the whole business was founded on lies and false pretensions. I don't mean only these river-guardians, but all these master-people I have read of."

"Yes," said I, "how happy you are to have got out of the parsimony of oppression!"

"Why do you sigh?" she said, kindly and somewhat anxiously. "You seem to think that it will not last?"

"It will last for you," quoth I.

"But why not for you?" said she. "Surely it is for all the world; and if your country is somewhat backward, it will come into line before long. Or," she said quickly, "are you thinking that you must soon go back again? I will make my proposal which I told you of at once, and so perhaps put an end to your anxiety. I was going to propose that you should live with us where we are going. I feel quite old friends with you, and should be sorry to lose you." Then she smiled on me, and said: "Do you know, I begin to suspect you of wanting to nurse a sham sorrow, like the ridiculous characters in some of those queer old novels that I have come across now and then."

I really had almost begun to suspect it myself, but I refused to admit so much; so I sighed no more, but fell to giving my delightful companion what little pieces of history I knew about the river and its borderlands; and the time passed pleasantly enough; and between the two of us (she was a better sculler than I was, and seemed quite tireless) we kept up fairly well with Dick, hot as the afternoon was, and swallowed up the way at a great rate. At last we passed under another ancient bridge; and through meadows bordered at first with huge elm-trees mingled with sweet chestnut of younger but very elegant growth; and the meadows widened out so much that it seemed as if the trees must now be on the bents only, or about the houses, except for the growth of willows on the immediate banks; so that the wide stretch of grass was little broken here. Dick got very much excited now, and often stood up in the boat to cry out to us that this was such and such a field, and so forth; and we caught fire at his enthusiasm for the hay-field and its harvest, and pulled our best.

At last as we were passing through a reach of the river where on the side of the towing-path was a highish bank with a thick whispering bed of reeds before it, and on the other side a higher bank, clothed with willows that dipped into the stream and crowned by ancient elm-trees, we saw bright figures coming along close to the bank, as if they were looking for something; as, indeed, they were, and we —that is, Dick and his company—were what they were looking for. Dick lay on his oars, and we followed his example. He gave a joyous shout to the people on the bank, which was echoed back from it in many voices, deep and sweetly shrill; for there were above a dozen persons, both men, women, and children. A tall handsome woman, with black wavy hair and deep set grey eyes, came forward on the bank and waved her hand gracefully to us, and said:

"Dick, my friend, we have almost had to wait for you! What excuse have you to make for your slavish punctuality? Why didn't you take us by surprise, and come yesterday?"

"O," said Dick, with an almost imperceptible jerk of his head toward our boat, "we didn't want to come too quick up the water; there is so much to see for those who have not been up here before."

"True, true," said the stately lady, for stately is the word that must be used for her; "and we want them to get to know the wet way from the east thoroughly well, since they must often use it now. But come ashore at once, Dick, and you, dear neighbours; there is a break in the reeds and a good landing-place just round the corner. We can carry up your things, or send some of the lads after them."

"No, no," said Dick; "it is easier going by water, though it is but a step. Besides, I want to bring my friend here to the proper place. We will go on to the Ford; and you can talk to us from the bank as we paddle along."

He pulled his sculls through the water, and on we went, turning a sharp angle and going north a little. Presently we saw before us a bank of elm-trees, which told us of a house amidst them, though I looked in vain for the grey walls that I expected to see there. As we went, the folk on the bank talked indeed, mingling their kind voices with the cuckoo's song, the sweet strong whistle of the blackbirds, and the ceaseless note of the corn-crake as he crept through the long grass of the mowing-field; whence came waves of fragrance from the flowering clover amidst of the ripe grass.

In a few minutes we had passed through a deep eddying pool into the sharp stream that ran from the ford, and beached our craft on a tiny strand of limestone-gravel, and stepped ashore into the arms of our up river friends, our journey done.

I disentangled myself from the merry throng, and mounting on the cart-road that ran along the river some feet above the water, I looked round about me. The river came down through a wide meadow on my left, which was grey now with the ripened seeding grasses; the gleaming water was lost presently by a turn of the bank, but over the meadow I could see the mingled gables of a building where I knew the lock must be, and which now seemed to combine a mill with it. A low wooded ridge bounded the river-plain to the south and south-east, whence we had come, and a few low houses lay about its feet and up its slope. I turned a little to my right, and through the hawthorn sprays and long shoots of the wild roses could see the flat country spreading out far away under the sun of the calm evening, till something that might be called hills with a look of sheep-pastures about them bounded it with a soft blue line. Before me, the elm-boughs still hid most of what houses there might be in this river-side dwelling of men; but to the right of the cart-road a few grey buildings of the simplest kind showed here and there.

There I stood in a dreamy mood, and rubbed my eyes as if I were not wholly awake, and half expected to see the gay-clad company of beautiful men and women change to two or three spindle-legged back-bowed men and haggard, hollow-eyed, ill-favoured women, who once wore down the soil of this land with their heavy hopeless feet, from day to day, and season to season, and year to year. But no change came as yet, and my heart swelled with joy as I thought of all the beautiful grey villages, from the river to the plain and the plain to the uplands, which I could picture to myself so well, all peopled now with this happy and lovely folk, who had cast away riches and attained to wealth.

CHAPTER XXXI

AN OLD HOUSE
AMONGST NEW FOLK

A S I stood there Ellen detached herself from our happy friends who still stood on the little strand and came up to me. She took me by the hand, and said softly, "Take me on to the house at once; we need not wait for the others: I had rather not."

I had a mind to say that I did not know the way thither, and that the river-side dwellers should lead; but almost without my will my feet moved on along the road they knew. The raised way led us into a little field bounded by a back-water of the river on one side; on the right hand we could see a cluster of small houses and barns, new and old, and before us a grey stone barn and a wall partly overgrown with ivy, over which a few grey gables showed. The village road ended in the shallow of the aforesaid backwater. We crossed the road, and again almost without my will my hand raised the latch of a door in the wall, and we stood presently on a stone path which led up to the old house to which fate in the shape of Dick had so strangely brought me in this new world of men. My companion gave a sigh of pleased surprise and enjoyment; nor did I wonder, for the garden between the wall and the house was redolent of the June flowers, and the roses were rolling over one another with that delicious super-abundance of small well-tended gardens which at first sight takes away all thought from the beholder save that of beauty. The blackbirds were singing their loudest, the doves were cooing on the roof-ridge, the rooks in the high elm-trees beyond were garrulous among the young leaves, and the swifts wheeled whining about the gables. And the house itself was a fit guardian for all the beauty of this heart of summer.

Once again Ellen echoed my thoughts as she said: "Yes, friend, this is what I came out for to see; this many-gabled old house built by the simple country-folk of the long-past times, regardless of all the turmoil that was going on in cities and courts, is lovely still amidst all the beauty which these latter days have created: and I do not wonder at our friends tending it carefully and making much of it. It seems to me as if it had waited for these happy days, and held in it the gathered crumbs of happiness of the confused and turbulent past."

She led me up close to the house, and laid her shapely sun browned hand and arm on the lichened wall as if to embrace it, and cried out, " O me! O me! How I love the earth, and the seasons, and weather, and all things that deal with it, and all that grows out of it,—as this has done !"

I could not answer her, or say a word. Her exultation and pleasure was so keen and exquisite, and her beauty, so delicate, yet so interfused with energy, expressed it so fully, that any added word would have been commonplace and futile. I dreaded lest the others should come in suddenly and break the spell she had cast about me; but we stood there a while by the corner of the big gable of the house, and no one came. I heard the merry voices some way off presently, and knew that they were going along the river to the great meadow on the other side of the house and garden.

We drew back a little, and looked up at the house: the door and the windows were open to the fragrant sun-cured air: from the upper window-sills hung festoons of flowers in honour of the festival, as if the others shared in the love for the old house.

"Come in," said Ellen. "I hope nothing will spoil it inside; but I don't think it will. Come! we must go back presently to the others. They have gone on to the tents; for surely they must have tents pitched for the haymakers— the house would not hold a tithe of the folk, I am sure."

She led me on to the door, murmuring little above her breath as she did so, "The earth and the growth of it and the life of it! If I could but say or show how I love it!"

We went in, and found no soul in any room as we wandered from room to room,—from the rose-covered porch to the strange and quaint garrets amongst the great timbers of the roof, where of old time the tillers and herdsmen of the manor slept, but which a-nights seemed now, by the small size of the beds, and the litter of useless and disregarded matters—bunches of dying flowers, feathers of birds, shells

of starlings' eggs, caddis worms in mugs, and the like—
seemed to be inhabited for the time by children.

Everywhere there was but little furniture, and that only
the most necessary, and of the simplest forms. The extravagant love of ornament which I had noted in this people
elsewhere seemed here to have given place to the feeling that
the house itself and its associations was the ornament of the
country life amidst which it had been left stranded from old
times, and that to re-ornament it would but take away its
use as a piece of natural beauty.

We sat down at last in a room over the wall which Ellen
had caressed, and which was still hung with old tapestry,
originally of no artistic value, but now faded into pleasant
grey tones which harmonised thoroughly well with the quiet
of the place, and which would have been ill supplanted
by brighter and more striking decoration.

I asked a few random questions of Ellen as we sat there,
but scarcely listened to her answers, and presently became
silent, and then scarce conscious of anything, but that I was
there in that old room, the doves crooning from the roofs
of the barn and dovecot beyond the window opposite to
me.

My thought returned to me after what I think was but a
minute or two, but which, as in a vivid dream, seemed as if
it had lasted a long time, when I saw Ellen sitting, looking
all the fuller of life and pleasure and desire from the contrast
with the grey faded tapestry with its futile design, which
was now only bearable because it had grown so faint and
feeble.

She looked at me kindly, but as if she read me through
and through. She said: "You have begun again your never-
ending contrast between the past and this present. Is it not
so?"

"True," said I. "I was thinking of what you, with your
capacity and intelligence, joined to your love of pleasure,
and your impatience of unreasonable restraint—of what you
would have been in that past. And even now, when all is
won and has been for a long time, my heart is sickened with
thinking of all the waste of life that has gone on for so many
years!"

"So many centuries," she said, "so many ages!"

"True," I said; "too true," and sat silent again.

She rose up and said: "Come, I must not let you go off into a dream again so soon. If we must lose you, I want you to see all that you can see first before you go back again."

"Lose me?" I said—"go back again? Am I not to go up to the North with you? What do you mean?"

She smiled somewhat sadly, and said: "Not yet; we will not talk of that yet. Only, what were you thinking of just now?"

I said falteringly: "I was saying to myself, The past, the present? Should she not have said the contrast of the present with the future: of blind despair with hope?"

"I knew it," she said. Then she caught my hand and said excitedly, "Come, while there is yet time! Come!" And she led me out of the room; and as we were going downstairs and out of the house into the garden by a little side door which opened out of a curious lobby, she said in a calm voice, as if she wished me to forget her sudden nervousness: "Come! we ought to join the others before they come here looking for us. And let me tell you, my friend, that I can see you are too apt to fall into mere dreamy musing: no doubt because you are not yet used to our life of repose amidst of energy; of work which is pleasure and pleasure which is work."

She paused a little, and as we came out into the lovely garden again, she said: "My friend, you were saying that you wondered what I should have been if I had lived in those past days of turmoil and oppression. Well, I think I have studied the history of them to know pretty well. I should have been one of the poor, for my father when he was working was a mere tiller of the soil. Well, I could not have borne that; therefore my beauty and cleverness and bright-ness" (she spoke with no blush or simper of false shame) "would have been sold to rich men, and my life would have been wasted indeed; for I know enough of that to know that I should have had no choice, no power of will over my life; and that I should never have bought pleasure from the rich men, or even opportunity of action, whereby I might have won some true excitement. I should have been wrecked and wasted in one way or another, either by penury or by luxury. Is it not so?"

"Indeed it is," said I.

She was going to say something else, when a little gate in the fence, which led into a small elm-shaded field, was opened, and Dick came with hasty cheerfulness up the garden path, and was presently standing between us, a hand laid on the shoulder of each. He said: "Well, neighbours, I thought you two would like to see the old house quietly without a crowd in it. Isn't it a jewel of a house after its kind? Well, come along, for it is getting towards dinner-time. Perhaps you, guest, would like a swim before we sit down to what I fancy will be a pretty long feast?"

"Yes," I said, "I should like that."

"Well, good-bye for the present, neighbour Ellen," said Dick. "Here comes Clara to take care of you, as I fancy she is more at home amongst our friends here."

Clara came out of the fields as he spoke; and with one look at Ellen I turned and went with Dick, doubting, if I must say the truth, whether I should see her again.

CHAPTER XXXII

THE FEAST'S BEGINNING—
THE END

DICK brought me at once into the little field which, as I had seen from the garden, was covered with gaily-coloured tents arranged in orderly lanes, about which were sitting and lying on the grass some fifty or sixty men, women, and children, all of them in the height of good temper and enjoyment—with their holiday mood on; so to say.

"You are thinking that we don't make a great show as to numbers," said Dick; "but you must remember that we shall have more to-morrow; because in this haymaking work there is room for a great many people who are not over-skilled in country matters: and there are many who lead sedentary lives, whom it would be unkind to deprive of their pleasure in the hay-field—scientific men and close students generally: so that the skilled workmen, outside those who are wanted as mowers, and foremen of the haymaking, stand aside, and take a little downright rest, which you know is good for them, whether they like it or not: or else they go to other countrysides, as I am doing here. You see, the scientific men and historians, and students generally, will not be wanted till we are fairly in the midst of the tedding, which of course will not be till the day after to-morrow." With that he brought me out of the little field on to a kind of causeway above the riverside meadow, and thence turning to the left on to a path through the mowing grass, which was thick and very tall, led on till we came to the river above the weir and its mill. There we had a delightful swim in the broad piece of water above the lock, where the river looked much bigger than its natural size from its being dammed up by the weir.

"Now we are in a fit mood for dinner," said Dick, when we had dressed and were going through the grass again; "and certainly of all the cheerful meals in the year, this one of haysel is the cheerfullest; not even excepting the corn-harvest feast; for then the year is beginning to fail, and one cannot help having a feeling behind all the gaiety, of the coming of the dark days, and the shorn fields and empty gardens; and the spring is almost too far off to look forward to. It is, then, in the autumn, when one almost believes in death."

"How strangely you talk," said I, "of such a constantly recurring and consequently commonplace matter as the sequence of the seasons." And indeed these people were like children about such things, and had what seemed to me a quite exaggerated interest in the weather, a fine day, a dark night, or a brilliant one, and the like.

"Strangely?" said he. "Is it strange to sympathise with the year and its gains and losses?"

"At anyrate," said I, "if you look upon the course of the year as a beautiful and interesting drama, which is what I think you do, you should be as much pleased and interested with the winter and its trouble and pain as with this wonderful summer luxury."

"And am I not?" said Dick, rather warmly; "only I can't look upon it as if I were sitting in a theatre seeing the play going on before me, myself taking no part of it. It is difficult," said he, smiling good-humouredly, "for a non-literary man like me to explain myself properly, like that

H

dear girl Ellen would; but I mean that I am part of it all, and feel the pain as well as the pleasure in my own person. It is not done for me by somebody else, merely that I may eat and drink and sleep; but I myself do my share of it."

In his way also, as Ellen in hers, I could see that Dick had that passionate love of the earth which was common to but few people at least, in the days I knew; in which the prevailing feeling amongst intellectual persons was a kind of sour distaste for the changing drama of the year, for the life of earth and its dealings with men. Indeed, in those days it was thought poetic and imaginative to look upon life as a thing to be borne, rather than enjoyed.

So I mused till Dick's laugh brought me back into the Oxfordshire hay-fields. "One thing seems strange to me," said he—"that I must needs trouble myself about the winter and its scantiness, in the midst of the summer abundance. If it hadn't happened to me before, I should have thought it was your doing, guest; that you had thrown a kind of evil charm over me. Now, you know," said he, suddenly, "that's only a joke, so you mustn't take it to heart."

"All right," said I; "I don't." Yet I did feel somewhat uneasy at his words, after all.

We crossed the causeway this time, and did not turn back to the house, but went along a path beside a field of wheat now almost ready to blossom. I said: "We do not dine in the house or garden, then?—as indeed I did not expect to do. Where do we meet, then? for I can see that the houses are mostly very small."

"Yes," said Dick, "you are right, they are small in this countryside: there are so many good old houses left, that people dwell a good deal in such small detached houses. As to our dinner, we are going to have our feast in the church. I wish, for your sake, it were as big and handsome as that of the old Roman town to the west, or the forest town to the north;[1] but, however, it will hold us all; and though it is a little thing, it is beautiful in its way."

This was somewhat new to me, this dinner in a church and I thought of the church-ales of the Middle Ages; but I said nothing, and presently we came out into the road which ran through the village. Dick looked up and down

[1] Cirencester and Burford he must have meant.

it, and seeing only two straggling groups before us, said:
"It seems as if we must be somewhat late; they are all gone
on; and they will be sure to make a point of waiting for
you, as the guest of guests, since you come from so far."

He hastened as he spoke, and I kept up with him, and
presently we came to a little avenue of lime-trees which led
us straight to the church porch, from whose open door
came the sound of cheerful voices and laughter, and varied
merriment.

"Yes," said Dick, "it's the coolest place for one thing,
this hot evening. Come along; they will be glad to see
you."

Indeed, in spite of my bath, I felt the weather more
sultry and oppressive than on any day of our journey yet.

We went into the church, which was a simple little building with one little aisle divided from the nave by three
round arches, a chancel, and a rather roomy transept for so
small a building, the windows mostly of the graceful Oxfordshire fourteenth-century type. There was no modern
architectural decoration in it; it looked, indeed, as if none
had been attempted since the Puritans whitewashed the
mediæval saints and histories on the wall. It was, however,
gaily dressed up for this latter-day festival, with festoons of
flowers from arch to arch, and great pitchers of flowers
standing about on the floor; while under the west window
hung two cross scythes, their blades polished white, and
gleaming from out of the flowers that wreathed them. But
its best ornament was the crowd of handsome, happy-
looking men and women that were set down to table, and
who, with their bright faces and rich hair over their gay
holiday raiment, looked, as the Persian poet puts it, like a
bed of tulips in the sun. Though the church was a small
one, there was plenty of room; for a small church makes a
biggish house; and on this evening there was no need to set
cross tables along the transepts; though doubtless these
would be wanted next day, when the learned men of whom
Dick had been speaking should be come to take their more
humble part in the haymaking.

I stood on the threshold with the expectant smile on my
face of a man who is going to take part in a festivity which
he is really prepared to enjoy. Dick, standing by me, was

looking round the company with an air of proprietorship in them, I thought. Opposite me sat Clara and Ellen, with Dick's place open between them: they were smiling, but their beautiful faces were each turned towards the neighbours on either side, who were talking to them, and they did not seem to see me. I turned to Dick, expecting him to lead me forward, and he turned his face to me; but strange to say, though it was as smiling and cheerful as ever, it made no response to my glance—nay, he seemed to take no heed at all of my presence, and I noticed that none of the company looked at me. A pang shot through me, as of some disaster long expected and suddenly realised. Dick moved on a little without a word to me. I was not three yards from the two women who, though they had been my companions for such a short time, had really, as I thought, become my friends. Clara's face was turned full upon me now, but she also did not seem to see me, though I know I was trying to catch her eye with an appealing look. I turned to Ellen, and she *did* seem to recognise me for an instant; but her bright face turned sad directly, and she shook her head with a mournful look, and the next moment all consciousness of my presence had faded from her face.

I felt lonely and sick at heart past the power of words to describe. I hung about a minute longer, and then turned and went out of the porch again and through the lime avenue into the road, while the blackbirds sang their strongest from the bushes about me in the hot June evening.

Once more without any conscious effort of will I set my face toward the old house by the ford, but as I turned round the corner which led to the remains of the village cross, I came upon a figure strangely contrasting with the joyous, beautiful people I had left behind in the church. It was a man who looked old, but whom I knew from habit, now half-forgotten, was really not much more than fifty. His face was rugged, and grimed rather than dirty; his eyes dull and bleared; his body bent, his calves thin and spindly, his feet dragging and limping. His clothing was a mixture of dirt and rags long over-familiar to me. As I passed him he touched his hat with some real goodwill and courtesy, and much servility.

Inexpressibly shocked, I hurried past him and hastened along the road that led to the river and the lower end of the village; but suddenly I saw as it were a black cloud rolling along to meet me, like a nightmare of my childish days; and for a while I was conscious of nothing else than being in the dark, and whether I was walking, or sitting, or lying down, I could not tell.

.   .   .   .

I lay in my bed in my house at dingy Hammersmith thinking about it all; and trying to consider if I was over-whelmed with despair at finding I had been dreaming a dream; and strange to say, I found that I was not so despairing.

Or indeed *was* it a dream? If so, why was I so conscious all along that I was really seeing all that new life from the outside, still wrapped up in the prejudices, the anxieties, the distrust of this time of doubt and struggle?

All along, though those friends were so real to me, I had been feeling as if I had no business amongst them: as though the time would come when they would reject me, and say, as Ellen's last mournful look seemed to say, "No, it will not do; you cannot be of us; you belong so entirely to the unhappiness of the past that our happiness even would weary you. Go back again, now you have seen us, and your outward eyes have learned that in spite of all the infallible maxims of your day there is yet a time of rest in store for the world, when mastery has changed into fellowship—but not before. Go back again, then, and while you live you will see all round you people engaged in making others live lives which are not their own, while they themselves care nothing for their own real lives—men who hate life though they fear death. Go back and be the happier for having seen us, for having added a little hope to your struggle. Go on living while you may, striving, with whatsoever pain and labour needs must be, to build up little by little the new day of fellowship, and rest, and happiness."

Yes, surely! and if others can see it as I have seen it, then it may be called a vision rather than a dream.

THE END

A DREAM OF JOHN BALL

CHAPTER I

THE MEN OF KENT

SOMETIMES I am rewarded for fretting myself so much about present matters by a quite unasked-for pleasant dream. I mean when I am asleep. This dream is as it were a present of an architectural peep-show. I see some beautiful and noble building new made, as it were for the occasion, as clearly as if I were awake; not vaguely or absurdly, as often happens in dreams, but with all the detail clear and reasonable. Some Elizabethan house with its scrap of earlier fourteenth-century building, and its later degradations of Queen Anne and Silly Billy and Victoria, marring but not destroying it, in an old village once a clearing amid the sandy woodlands of Sussex. Or an old and unusually curious church, much churchwardened, and beside it a fragment of fifteenth-century domestic architecture amongst the not unpicturesque lath and plaster of an Essex farm, and looking natural enough among the sleepy elms and the meditative hens scratching about in the litter of the farmyard, whose trodden yellow straw comes up to the very jambs of the richly carved Norman doorway of the church. Or sometimes 'tis a splendid collegiate church, untouched by restoring parson and architect, standing amid an island of shapely trees and flower-beset cottages of thatched grey stone and cob, amidst the narrow stretch of bright green water-meadows that wind between the sweeping Wiltshire downs, so well beloved of William Cobbett. Or some new-seen and yet familiar cluster of houses in a grey village of the upper Thames over-topped by the delicate tracery of a fourteenth-century church; or even sometimes the very buildings of the past untouched by the degradation of the sordid utilitarianism that cares not and knows not of beauty and history: as once, when I was journeying (in a dream of the night) down the well-remembered reaches of the Thames betwixt Streatley and Wallingford, where the foothills of the White Horse fall back from the broad stream, I came upon a clear-seen mediæval town standing up with roof and tower and spire within its walls, grey and ancient, but untouched from the days of its builders of old. All this I have seen in the dreams of the night clearer than I can force myself to see them in dreams of the day. So that it would have been nothing new to me the other night to fall into an architectural dream if that were all, and yet I have to tell of things strange and new that befell me after I had fallen asleep. I had begun my sojourn in the Land of Nod by a very confused attempt to conclude that it was all right for me to have an engagement to lecture at Manchester and Mitcham Fair Green at half-past eleven at night on one and the same Sunday, and that I could manage pretty well. And then I had gone on to try to make the best of addressing a large open-air audience in the costume I was really then wearing—to wit, my night-shirt, reinforced for the dream occasion by a pair of braceless trousers. The consciousness of this fact so bothered me, that the earnest faces of my audience—who would *not* notice it, but were clearly preparing terrible anti-Socialist posers for me—began to fade away and my dream grew thin, and I awoke (as I thought) to find myself lying on a strip of wayside waste by an oak copse just outside a country village.

I got up and rubbed my eyes and looked about me, and the landscape seemed unfamiliar to me, though it was, as to the lie of the land, an ordinary English low-country, swelling into rising ground here and there. The road was narrow, and I was convinced that it was a piece of Roman road from its straightness. Copses were scattered over the country, and there were signs of two or three villages and hamlets in sight besides the one near me, between which and me there was some orchard-land, where the early apples were beginning to redden on the trees. Also, just on the other side of the road and the ditch which ran along it, was a small close of about a quarter of an acre, neatly hedged with quick, which was nearly full of white poppies, and, as far as I could see for the hedge, had also a good few rose-bushes of the bright-red nearly single kind, which I had

heard are the ones from which rose-water used to be dis-
tilled. Otherwise the land was quite unhedged, but all under tillage of various kinds, mostly in small strips. From the
other side of a copse not far off rose a tall spire white and
brand-new, but at once bold in outline and unaffectedly
graceful and also distinctly English in character. This,
together with the unhedged tillage and a certain unwonted
trimness and handiness about the enclosures of the garden
and orchards, puzzled me for a minute or two, as I did not
understand, new as the spire was, how it could have been
designed by a modern architect; and I was of course used
to the hedged tillage and tumble-down bankrupt-looking
surroundings of our modern agriculture. So that the
garden-like neatness and trimness of everything surprised
me. But after a minute or two that surprise left me entirely;
and if what I saw and heard afterwards seems strange to
you, remember that it did not seem strange to me at the
time except where now and again I shall tell you of it. Also,
once for all, if I were to give you the very words of those
who spoke to me you would scarcely understand them, although their language was English too, and at the time I
could understand them at once.

Well, as I stretched myself and turned my face toward the
village, I heard horse-hoofs on the road, and presently a
man and horse showed on the other end of the stretch of
road and drew near at a swinging trot with plenty of clash
of metal. The man soon came up to me, but paid me no
more heed than throwing me a nod. He was clad in armour
of mingled steel and leather, a sword girt to his side, and
over his shoulder a long-handled bill-hook. His armour was
fantastic in form and well wrought; but by this time I was
quite used to the strangeness of him, and merely muttered
to myself, "He is coming to summon the squire to the leet;"
so I turned toward the village in good earnest. Nor, again,
was I surprised at my own garments, although I might well
have been from their unwontedness. I was dressed in a
black cloth gown reaching to my ankles, neatly embroidered about the collar and cuffs, with wide sleeves gathered
in at the wrists; a hood with a sort of bag hanging down
from it was on my head, a broad red leather girdle round
my waist, on one side of which hung a pouch embroidered

very prettily and a case made of hard leather chased with a hunting scene, which I knew to be a pen and ink case; on the other side a small sheath-knife, only an arm in case of dire necessity.

Well, I came into the village, where I did not see (nor by this time expected to see) a single modern building, although many of them were nearly new, notably the church, which was large, and quite ravished my heart with its extreme beauty, elegance, and fitness. The chancel of this was so new that the dust of the stone still lay white on the midsummer grass beneath the carvings of the windows. The houses were almost all built of oak frame-work filled with cob or plaster well whitewashed; though some had their lower stories of rubble-stone, with their windows and doors of well-moulded free-stone. There was much curious and inventive carving about most of them; and though some were old and much worn, there was the same look of deftness and trimness, and even beauty, about every detail in them which I noticed before in the field-work. They were all roofed with oak shingles, mostly grown as grey as stone; but one was so newly built that its roof was yet pale and yellow. This was a corner house, and the corner post of it had a carved niche wherein stood a gaily painted figure holding an anchor— St. Clement to wit, as the dweller in the house was a blacksmith. Half a stone's throw from the east end of the churchyard wall was a tall cross of stone, new like the church, the head beautifully carved with a crucifix amidst leafage. It stood on a set of wide stone steps, octagonal in shape, where three roads from other villages met and formed a wide open space on which a thousand people or more could stand together with no great crowding.

All this I saw, and also that there was a goodish many people about, women and children, and a few old men at the doors, many of them somewhat gaily clad, and that men were coming into the village street by the other end to that by which I had entered, by twos and threes, most of them carrying what I could see were bows in cases of linen yellow with wax or oil; they had quivers at their backs, and most of them a short sword by their left side, and a pouch and knife on the right; they were mostly dressed in red or brightish green or blue cloth jerkins, with a hood on the head generally

of another colour. As they came nearer I saw that the
cloth of their garments was somewhat coarse, but stout and
serviceable. I knew, somehow, that they had been shooting
at the butts, and, indeed, I could still hear a noise of men
thereabout, and even now and again when the wind set
from that quarter the twang of the bowstring and the plump
of the shaft in the target.

I leaned against the churchyard wall and watched these
men, some of whom went straight into their houses and some
loitered about still; they were rough-looking fellows, tall and
stout, very black some of them, and some red-haired, but
most had hair burnt by the sun into the colour of tow; and,
indeed, they were all burned and tanned and freckled
variously. Their arms and buckles and belts and the finish-
ings and hems of their garments were all what we should
now call beautiful, rough as the men were; nor in their
speech was any of that drawling snarl or thick vulgarity
which one is used to hear from labourers in civilisation; not
that they talked like gentlemen either, but full and round
and bold, and they were merry and good-tempered enough;
I could see that, though I felt shy and timid amongst them.

One of them strode up to me across the road, a man some
six feet high, with a short black beard and black eyes and
berry-brown skin, with a huge bow in his hand bare of the
case, a knife, a pouch, and a short hatchet, all clattering
together at his girdle.

"Well, friend," said he, "thou lookest partly mazed;
what tongue hast thou in thine head?"

"A tongue that can tell rhymes," said I.

"So I thought," said he. "Thirstest thou any?"

"Yea, and hunger," said I.

And therewith my hand went into my purse, and came
out again with but a few small and thin silver coins with a
cross stamped on each, and three pellets in each corner of
the cross. The man grinned.

"Aha!" said he, "is it so? Never heed it, mate. It shall be
a song for a supper this fair Sunday evening. But first,
whose man art thou?"

"No one's man," said I, reddening angrily; "I am my
own master."

He grinned again.

"Nay, that's not the custom of England, as one time belike it will be. Methinks thou comest from heaven down, and hast had a high place there too."

He seemed to hesitate a moment, and then leant forward and whispered in my ear: "*John the Miller, that ground small, small, small,*" and stopped and winked at me, and from between my lips without my mind forming any meaning came the words, "*The king's son of heaven shall pay for all.*"

He let his bow fall on to his shoulder, caught my right hand in his and gave it a great grip, while his left hand fell among the gear at his belt, and I could see that he half drew his knife.

"Well, brother," said he, "stand not here hungry in the highway when there is flesh and bread in the Rose yonder. Come on."

And with that he drew me along toward what was clearly a tavern door, outside which men were sitting on a couple of benches and drinking meditatively from curiously shaped earthen pots glazed green and yellow, some with quaint devices on them.

CHAPTER II

THE MAN FROM ESSEX

I ENTERED the door and started at first with my old astonishment, with which I had woke up, so strange and beautiful did this interior seem to me, though it was but a pothouse parlour. A quaintly-carved sideboard held an array of bright pewter pots and dishes and wooden and earthen bowls; a stout oak table went up and down the room, and a carved oak chair stood by the chimney-corner, now filled by a very old man dim-eyed and white-bearded. That, except the rough stools and benches on which the company sat, was all the furniture. The walls were panelled roughly enough with oak boards to about six feet from the floor, and about three feet of plaster above that was wrought in a pattern of a rose stem running all round the room, freely and roughly done, but with (as it seemed to my unused eyes) wonderful skill and spirit. On the hood of the great chimney a huge rose was wrought in the plaster and brightly painted in its proper colours. There were a dozen or more of the men I had seen coming along the street sitting there, some eating and all drinking; their cased bows leaned against the wall, their quivers hung on pegs in the panelling, and in a corner of the room I saw half-a-dozen bill-hooks that looked made more for war than for hedge-shearing, with ashen handles some seven foot long. Three or four children were running about among the legs of the men, heeding them mighty little in their bold play, and the men seemed little troubled by it, although they were talking earnestly and seriously too. A well-made comely girl leaned up against the chimney close to the gaffer's chair, and seemed to be in waiting on the company: she was clad in a close-fitting gown of bright blue cloth, with a broad silver girdle, daintily wrought, round her loins; a rose wreath was on her head and her hair hung down unbound; the gaffer grumbled a few words to her from time to time, so that I judged he was her grandfather.

The men all looked up as we came into the room, my mate leading me by the hand, and he called out in his rough, good-tempered voice, "Here, my masters, I bring you tidings and a tale; give it meat and drink that it may be strong and sweet."

"Whence are thy tidings, Will Green?" said one.

My mate grinned again with the pleasure of making his joke once more in a bigger company: "It seemeth from heaven, since this good old lad hath no master," said he.

"The more fool he to come here," said a thin man with a grizzled beard, amidst the laughter that followed, "unless he had the choice given him between hell and England."

"Nay," said I, "I come not from heaven, but from Essex."

As I said the word a great shout sprang from all mouths at once, as clear and sudden as a shot from a gun. For I must tell you that I knew somehow, but I know not how, that the men of Essex were gathering to rise against the poll-groat bailiffs and the lords that would turn them all into villeins again, as their grandfathers had been. And the people was weak and the lords were poor; for many a mother's son had fallen in the war in France in the old king's time, and the Black Death had slain a many; so that the lords had bethought them: "We are growing poorer, and these upland-bred villeins are growing richer, and the guilds of craft are waxing in the towns, and soon what will there be left for us who cannot weave and will not dig? Good it were if we fell on all who are not guildsmen or men of free land, if we fell on soccage tenants and others, and brought both the law and the strong hand on them, and made them all villeins in deed as they are now in name; for now these rascals make more than their bellies need of bread, and their backs of homespun, and the overplus they keep to themselves; and we are more worthy of it than they. So let us get the collar on their necks again, and make their day's work longer and their bever-time shorter, as the good statute of the old king bade. And good it were if the Holy Church were to look to it (and the Lollards might help herein) that all these naughty and wearisome holidays were done away with; or that it should be unlawful for any man below the degree of a squire to keep the holy days of the church, except in the heart and the spirit only, and let the body labour meanwhile; for does not the Apostle say, 'If a man work not, neither should he eat'? And if such things were done, and such an estate of noble rich men and worthy poor men upholden for ever, then would it be good times in England, and life were worth the living."

All this were the lords at work on, and such talk I knew was common not only among the lords themselves, but also among their sergeants and very serving-men. But the people would not abide it; therefore, as I said, in Essex they were on the point of rising, and word had gone how that at St. Albans they were wellnigh at blows with the Lord Abbot's soldiers; that north away at Norwich John Litster was wiping the woad from his arms, as who would have to stain them red again, but not with grain or madder; and that the valiant tiler of Dartford had smitten a poll-groat bailiff to death with his lathe-rending axe for mishandling a young maid, his daughter; and that the men of Kent were on the move.

Now, knowing all this I was not astonished that they shouted at the thought of their fellows the men of Essex, but rather that they said a little more about it; only Will Green saying quietly, "Well, the tidings shall be told when our fellowship is greater; fall-to now on the meat, brother, that we may the sooner have thy tale." As he spoke the blue-clad damsel bestirred herself and brought me a clean trencher—that is, a square piece of thin oak board scraped clean—and a pewter pot of liquor. So without more ado, and as one used to it, I drew my knife out of my girdle and cut myself what I would of the flesh and bread on the table. But Will Green mocked at me as I cut, and said, "Certes, brother, thou hast not been a lord's carver, though but for thy word thou mightest have been his reader. Hast thou seen Oxford, scholar?"

A vision of grey-roofed houses and a long winding street and the sound of many bells came over me at that word as I nodded "Yes" to him, my mouth full of salt pork and rye-bread; and then I lifted my pot and we made the clattering mugs kiss and I drank, and the fire of the good Kentish mead ran through my veins and deepened my dream of things past, present, and to come, as I said: "Now hearken a tale since ye will have it so. For last autumn I was in Suffolk at the good town of Dunwich, and thither came the keels from Iceland, and on them were some men of Iceland, and many a tale they had on their tongues; and with these men I foregathered, for I am in sooth a gatherer of tales, and this that is now at my tongue's end is one of them."

So such a tale I told them, long familiar to me; but as I told it the words seemed to quicken and grow, so that I knew not the sound of my own voice, and they ran almost into rhyme and measure as I told it; and when I had done there was silence awhile, till one man spake, but not loudly:

"Yea, in that land was the summer short and the winter long; but men lived both summer and winter; and if the trees grew ill and the corn throve not, yet did the plant called man thrive and do well. God send us such men even here."

"Nay," said another, "such men have been and will be, and belike are not far from this same door even now."

"Yea," said a third, "hearken a stave of Robin Hood; maybe that shall hasten the coming of one I wot of." And he fell to singing in a clear voice, for he was a young man, and to a sweet wild melody, one of those ballads which in an incomplete and degraded form you have read perhaps. My heart rose high as I heard him, for it was concerning the struggle against tyranny for the freedom of life, how that the wildwood and the heath, despite of wind and weather, were better for a free man than the court and the cheaping-town; of the taking from the rich to give to the poor; of the life of a man doing his own will and not the will of another man commanding him for the commandment's sake. The men all listened eagerly, and at whiles took up as a refrain a couplet at the end of a stanza with their strong and rough, but not unmusical voices. As they sang, a picture of the wild-woods passed by me, as they were indeed, no park-like dainty glades and lawns, but rough and tangled thicket and bare waste and heath, solemn under the morning sun, and dreary with the rising of the evening wind and the drift of the night-long rain.

When he had done, another began in something of the same strain, but singing more of a song than a story ballad; and thus much I remember of it:

> The Sheriff is made a mighty lord,
>   Of goodly gold he hath enow,
> And many a sergeant girt with sword;
>   But forth will we and bend the bow.
>   We shall bend the bow on the lily lea
>   Betwixt the thorn and the oaken tree.
>
> With stone and lime is the burg wall built,
>   And pit and prison are stark and strong,
> And many a true man there is spilt,
>   And many a right man doomed by wrong.
>   So forth shall we and bend the bow
>   And the king's writ never the road shall know.
>
> Now yeomen walk ye warily,
>   And heed ye the houses where ye go,
> For as fair and as fine as they may be,
>   Lest behind your heels the door clap to.
>   Fare forth with the bow to the lily lea
>   Betwixt the thorn and the oaken tree.
>
> Now bills and bows! and out a-gate!
>   And turn about on the lily lea!
> And though their company be great
>   The grey-goose wing shall set us free.
>   Now bent is the bow in the green abode
>   And the king's writ knoweth not the road.

So over the mead and over the hithe,
  And away to the wild-wood wend we forth;
There dwell we yeomen bold and blithe
  Where the Sheriff's word is nought of worth.
    Bent is the bow on the lily lea
    Betwixt the thorn and the oaken tree.

But here the song dropped suddenly, and one of the men
held up his hand as who would say, Hist! Then through the
open window came the sound of another song, gradually
swelling as though sung by men on the march. This time
the melody was a piece of the plain-song of the church,
familiar enough to me to bring back to my mind the great
arches of some cathedral in France and the canons singing
in the choir.

All leapt up and hurried to take their bows from wall
and corner; and some had bucklers withal, circles of leather,
boiled and then moulded into shape and hardened: these
were some two hand-breadths across, with iron or brass
bosses in the centre. Will Green went to the corner where
the bills leaned against the wall and handed them round
to the first-comers as far as they would go, and out we all
went gravely and quietly into the village street and the
fair sunlight of the calm afternoon, now beginning to turn
towards evening. None had said anything since we first
heard the new-come singing, save that as we went out of
the door the ballad-singer clapped me on the shoulder and
said:

"Was it not sooth that I said, brother, that Robin Hood
should bring us John Ball?"

CHAPTER III

THEY MEET AT THE CROSS

THE street was pretty full of men by then we were
out in it, and all faces turned toward the cross. The
song still grew nearer and louder, and even as we looked
we saw it turning the corner through the hedges of the
orchards and closes, a good clump of men, more armed,
as it would seem, than our villagers, as the low sun flashed

back from many points of bright iron and steel. The words of the song could now be heard, and amidst them I could pick out Will Green's late challenge to me and my answer; but as I was bending all my mind to disentangle more words from the music, suddenly from the new white tower behind us clashed out the church bells, harsh and hurried at first, but presently falling into measured chime; and at the first sound of them a great shout went up from us and was echoed by the new-comers, "John Ball hath rung our bell!" Then we pressed on, and presently we were all mingled together at the cross.

Will Green had good-naturedly thrust and pulled me forward, so that I found myself standing on the lowest step of the cross, his seventy-two inches of man on one side of me. He chuckled while I panted, and said:

"There's for thee a good hearing and seeing stead, old lad. Thou art tall across thy belly and not otherwise, and thy wind, belike, is none of the best, and but for me thou wouldst have been amidst the thickest of the throng, and have heard words muffled by Kentish bellies and seen little but swinky woollen elbows and greasy plates and jacks. Look no more on the ground, as though thou sawest a hare, but let thine eyes and thine ears be busy to gather tidings to bear back to Essex—or heaven!"

I grinned good-fellowship at him but said nothing, for in truth my eyes and ears were as busy as he would have them to be. A buzz of general talk went up from the throng amidst the regular cadence of the bells, which now seemed far away and as it were that they were not swayed by hands, but were living creatures making that noise of their own wills.

I looked around and saw that the new-comers mingled with us must have been a regular armed band; all had bucklers slung at their backs, few lacked a sword at the side. Some had bows, some "staves"—that is, bills, pole-axes, or pikes. Moreover, unlike our villagers, they had defensive arms. Most had steel-caps on their heads, and some had body armour, generally a "jack," or coat into which pieces of iron or horn were quilted; some had also steel or steel-and-leather arm or thigh pieces. There were a few mounted men among them, their horses being big-boned hammer-headed beasts, that looked as if they had been taken from plough or waggon, but their riders were well armed with steel armour on their heads, legs, and arms. Amongst the horsemen I noted the man that had ridden past me when I first awoke; but he seemed to be a prisoner, as he had a woollen hood on his head instead of his helmet, and carried neither bill, sword, nor dagger. He seemed by no means ill-at-ease, however, but was laughing and talking with the men who stood near him.

Above the heads of the crowd, and now slowly working towards the cross, was a banner on a high-raised cross-pole, a picture of a man and woman half-clad in skins of beasts seen against a background of green trees, the man holding a spade and the woman a distaff and spindle rudely done enough, but yet with a certain spirit and much meaning; and underneath this symbol of the early world and man's first contest with nature were the written words:

> When Adam delved and Eve span
> Who was then the gentleman.

The banner came on and through the crowd, which at last opened where we stood for its passage, and the banner-bearer turned and faced the throng and stood on the first step of the cross beside me.

A man followed him, clad in a long dark-brown gown of coarse woollen, girt with a cord, to which hung a "pair of beads" (or rosary, as we should call it to-day) and a book in a bag. The man was tall and big-boned, a ring of dark hair surrounded his priest's tonsure; his nose was big but clear cut and with wide nostrils; his shaven face showed a longish upper lip and a big but blunt chin; his mouth was big and the lips closed firmly; a face not very noteworthy but for his grey eyes well opened and wide apart, at whiles lighting up his whole face with a kindly smile, at whiles set and stern, at whiles resting in that look as if they were gazing at something a long way off, which is the wont of the eyes of the poet or enthusiast.

He went slowly up the steps of the cross and stood at the top with one hand laid on the shaft, and shout upon shout broke forth from the throng. When the shouting died away into a silence of the human voices, the bells were still quietly chiming with that far-away voice of theirs, and the long-winged dusky swifts, by no means scared by the concourse, swung round about the cross with their wild squeals; and the man stood still for a little, eyeing the throng, or rather looking first at one and then another man in it, as though he were trying to think what such an one was thinking of, or what he were fit for. Sometimes he caught the eye of one or other, and then that kindly smile spread over his face, but faded off it into the sternness and sadness of a man who has heavy and great thoughts hanging about him.

But when John Ball first mounted the steps of the cross a lad at some one's bidding had run off to stop the ringers, and so presently the voice of the bells fell dead, leaving on men's minds that sense of blankness or even disappointment which is always caused by the sudden stopping of a sound one has got used to and found pleasant. But a great expectation had fallen by now on all that throng, and no word was spoken even in a whisper, and all men's hearts and eyes were fixed upon the dark figure standing straight up now by the tall white shaft of the cross, his hands stretched out before him, one palm laid upon the other. And for me, as I made ready to hearken, I felt a joy in my soul that I had never yet felt.

CHAPTER IV

THE VOICE OF JOHN BALL

SO now I heard John Ball; how he lifted up his voice and said:

"Ho, all ye good people! I am a priest of God, and in my day's work it cometh that I should tell you what ye should do, and what ye should forbear doing, and to that end I am come hither: yet first, if I myself have wronged any man here, let him say wherein my wrongdoing lieth, that I may ask his pardon and his pity."

A great hum of good-will ran through the crowd as he spoke; then he smiled as in a kind of pride, and again he spoke:

"Wherefore did ye take me out of the archbishop's prison but three days agone, when ye lighted the archbishop's house for the candle of Canterbury, but that I might speak to you and pray you: therefore I will not keep silence, whether I have done ill, or whether I have done well. And herein, good fellows and my very brethren, I would have you to follow me; and if there be such here, as I know full well there be some, and may be a good many, who have been robbers of their neighbours ('And who is my neighbour?' quoth the rich man), or lechers, or despiteful haters, or talebearers, or fawners on rich men for the hurt of the poor (and that is the worst of all)—Ah, my poor brethren who have gone astray, I say not to you, go home and repent lest you mar our great deeds, but rather come afield and there repent. Many a day have ye been fools, but hearken unto me and I shall make you wise above the wisdom of the earth; and if ye die in your wisdom, as God wot ye well may, since the fields ye wend to bear swords for daisies, and spears for bents, then shall ye be, though men call you dead, a part and parcel of the living wisdom of all things, very stones of the pillars that uphold the joyful earth.

"Forsooth, ye have heard it said that ye shall do well in this world that in the world to come ye may live happily for ever; do ye well then, and have your reward both on earth and in heaven; for I say to you that earth and heaven are not two but one; and this one is that which ye know, and are each one of you a part of, to wit, the Holy Church, and in each one of you dwelleth the life of the Church, unless ye slay it. Forsooth, brethren, will ye murder the Church any one of you, and go forth a wandering man and lonely, even as Cain did who slew his brother? Ah, my brothers, what an evil doom is this, to be an outcast from the Church, to have none to love you and to speak with you, to be without fellowship! Forsooth, brothers, fellowship is heaven, and lack of fellowship is hell: fellowship is life, and lack of fellowship is death: and the deeds that ye do upon the earth, it is for fellowship's sake that ye do them, and the life that is in it, that shall live on and on for ever, and each one of you part of it, while many a man's life upon the earth from the earth shall wane.

"Therefore, I bid you not dwell in hell but in heaven, or

while ye must, upon earth, which is a part of heaven, and forsooth no foul part.

"Forsooth, he that waketh in hell and feeleth his heart fail him, shall have memory of the merry days of earth, and how that when his heart failed him there, he cried on his fellow, were it his wife or his son or his brother or his gossip or his brother sworn in arms, and how that his fellow heard him and came and they mourned together under the sun, till again they laughed together and were but half sorry between them. This shall he think on in hell, and cry on his fellow to help him, and shall find that therein is no help because there is no fellowship, but every man for himself. Therefore, I tell you that the proud, despiteous rich man, though he knoweth it not, is in hell already, because he hath no fellow; and he that hath so hardy a heart that in sorrow he thinketh of fellowship, his sorrow is soon but a story of sorrow—a little change in the life that knows not ill."

He left off for a little; and indeed for some time his voice had fallen, but it was so clear and the summer evening so soft and still, and the silence of the folk so complete, that every word told. His eyes fell down to the crowd as he stopped speaking, since for some little while they had been looking far away into the blue distance of summer; and the kind eyes of the man had a curious sight before him in that crowd, for amongst them were many who by this time were not dry-eyed, and some wept outright in spite of their black beards, while all had that look as if they were ashamed of themselves, and did not want others to see how deeply they were moved, after the fashion of their race when they are strongly stirred. I looked at Will Green beside me: his right hand clutched his bow so tight, that the knuckles whitened; he was staring straight before him, and the tears were running out of his eyes and down his big nose as though without his will, for his face was stolid and un-moved all the time, till he caught my eye, and then he screwed up the strangest face, of scowling brow, weeping eyes, and smiling mouth, while he dealt me a sounding thump in the ribs with his left elbow, which, though it would have knocked me down but for the crowd, I took as an esquire does the accolade which makes a knight of him.

But while I pondered all these things, and how men fight and lose the battle, and the thing that they fought for comes about in spite of their defeat, and when it comes turns out not to be what they meant, and other men have to fight for what they meant under another name—while I pondered all this, John Ball began to speak again in the same soft and clear voice with which he had left off.

"Good fellows, it was your fellowship and your kindness that took me out of the archbishop's prison three days agone, though God wot ye had nought to gain by it save outlawry and the gallows; yet lacked I not your fellowship before ye drew near me in the body, and when between me and Canterbury street was yet a strong wall, and the turnkeys and sergeants and bailiffs.

" For hearken my friends and helpers; many days ago, when April was yet young, I lay there, and the heart that I had strung up to bear all things because of the fellow-ship of men and the blessed saints and the angels and those that are, and those that are to be, this heart, that I had strung up like a strong bow, fell into feebleness, so that I lay there a longing for the green fields and the white-thorn bushes and the lark singing over the corn, and the talk of good fellows round the ale-house bench, and the babble of the little children, and the team on the road and the beasts afield, and all the life of earth; and I alone all the while, near my foes and afar from my friends, mocked and flouted and starved with cold and hunger; and so weak was my heart that though I longed for all these things yet I saw them not, nor knew them but as names; and I longed so sore to be gone that I chided myself that I had once done well; and I said to myself:

"Forsooth, hadst thou kept thy tongue between thy teeth thou mightest have been something, if it had been but a parson of a town, and comfortable to many a poor man; and then mightest thou have clad here and there the naked back, and filled the empty belly, and holpen many, and men would have spoken well of thee, and of thyself thou hadst thought well; and all this hast thou lost for lack of a word here and there to some great man, and a little winking of the eyes amidst murder and wrong and unruth; and now thou art nought and helpless, and the hemp for thee is sown and grown and heckled and spun, and lo there, the rope for thy gallows-tree!—all for nought, for nought.

"Forsooth, my friends, thus I thought and sorrowed in my feebleness that I had not been a traitor to the Fellowship of the Church, for e'en so evil was my foolish imagination.

"Yet, forsooth, as I fell a pondering over all the comfort and help that I might have been and that I might have had, if I had been but a little of a trembling cur to creep and crawl before abbot and bishop and baron and bailiff, came the thought over me of the evil of the world wherewith I, John Ball, the rascal hedge-priest, had fought and striven in the Fellowship of the saints in heaven and poor men upon earth.

"Yea, forsooth, once again I saw as of old, the great treading down the little, and the strong beating down the weak, and cruel men fearing not, and kind men daring not, and wise men caring not; and the saints in heaven forbearing and yet bidding me not to forbear; forsooth, I knew once more that he who doeth well in fellowship, and because of fellowship, shall not fail though he seem to fail to-day, but in days hereafter shall he and his work yet be alive, and men be holpen by them to strive again, and yet again; and yet indeed even that was little, since, forsooth, to strive was my pleasure and my life.

"So I became a man once more, and I rose up to my feet and went up and down my prison what I could for my hopples, and into my mouth came words of good cheer, even such as we to-day have sung, and stoutly I sang them, even as we now have sung them; and then did I rest me, and once more thought of those pleasant fields where I would be, and all the life of man and beast about them, and I said to myself that I should see them once more before I died, if but once it were.

"Forsooth, this was strange, that whereas before I longed for them and yet saw them not, now that my longing was slaked my vision was cleared, and I saw them as though the prison walls opened to me and I was out of Canterbury street and amidst the green meadows of April; and therewithal along with me folk that I have known and who are dead, and folk that are living; yea, and all those of the Fellowship on earth and in heaven; yea, and all that are here this day. Overlong were the tale to tell of them, and of the time that is gone.

"So thenceforward I wore through the days with no such faint heart, until one day the prison opened verily and in the daylight, and there were ye, my fellows, in the door—your faces glad, your hearts light with hope, and your hands heavy with wrath; then I saw and understood what was to do. Now, therefore, do ye understand it!"

His voice was changed, and grew louder than loud now, as he cast his hands abroad towards that company with those last words of his; and I could feel that all shame and fear was falling from those men, and that mere fiery manhood was shining through their wonted English shamefast stubbornness, and that they were moved indeed and saw the road before them. Yet no man spoke, rather the silence of the men folk deepened, as the sun's rays grew more level and more golden, and the swifts wheeled about shriller and louder than before.

Then again John Ball spoke and said, "In good sooth, I deem ye wot no worse than I do what is to do—and first that somewhat we shall do—since it is for him that is lonely or in prison to dream of fellowship, but for him that is of a fellowship to do and not to dream.

"And next, ye know who is the foeman, and that is the proud man, the oppressor, who scorneth fellowship, and himself is a world to himself and needeth no helper nor helpeth any, but, heeding no law, layeth law on other men because he is rich; and surely every one that is rich is such an one, nor may be other.

"Forsooth in the belly of every rich man dwelleth a devil of hell, and when the man would give his goods to the poor, the devil within him gainsayeth it, and saith, 'Wilt thou then be of the poor, and suffer cold and hunger and mocking as they suffer, then give thou thy goods to them, and keep them not.' And when he would be compassionate, again saith the devil to him, 'If thou heed these losels and turn on them a face like to their faces, and deem of them as men, then shall they scorn thee, and evil shall come of it, and even one day they shall fall on thee to slay thee when they have learned that thou art but as they be.'

"Ah, woe worth the while! too oft he sayeth sooth, as the wont of the devil is, that lies may be born of the barren truth; and sooth it is that the poor deemeth the rich to be other than he, and meet to be his master, as though, forsooth the poor were come of Adam, and the rich of him that made Adam, that is God; and thus the poor man oppresseth the poor man, because he feareth the oppressor. Nought such are ye, my brethren; or else why are ye gathered here in harness to bid all bear witness of you that ye are the sons of one man and one mother, begotten of the earth?"

As he said the words there came a stir among the weapons of the throng, and they pressed closer round the cross, yet withheld the shout as yet which seemed gathering in their bosoms.

And again he said:

"Forsooth, too many rich men there are in this realm; and yet if there were but one, there would be one too many, for all should be his thralls. Hearken, then, ye men of Kent. For overlong belike have I held you with words; but the love of you constrained me, and the joy that a man hath to babble to his friends and his fellows whom he hath not seen for a long season.

"Now, hearken, I bid you: To the rich men that eat up a realm there cometh a time when they whom they eat up, that is the poor, seem poorer than of wont, and their complaint goeth up louder to the heavens; yet it is no riddle to say that oft at such times the fellowship of the poor is waxing stronger, else would no man have heard his cry. Also at such times the rich man become fearful, and so waxeth in cruelty, and of that cruelty do people misdeem that it is power and might waxing. Forsooth, ye are stronger than your fathers, because ye are more grieved than they, and ye should have been less grieved than they had ye been horses and swine; and then, forsooth, would ye have been stronger to bear; but ye, ye are not strong to bear, but to do.

"And wot ye why we are come to you this fair eve of holiday? and wot ye why I have been telling of fellowship to you? Yea, forsooth, I deem ye wot well, that it is for this cause, that ye might bethink you of your fellowship with the men of Essex."

His last word let loose the shout that had been long on all men's lips, and great and fierce it was as it rang shattering through the quiet upland village. But John Ball held up his hand, and the shout was one and no more.

Then he spoke again:

"Men of Kent, I wot well that ye are not so hard bested as those of other shires, by the token of the day when behind the screen of leafy boughs ye met Duke William with bill and bow as he wended Londonward from that woeful field of Senlac; but I have told of fellowship, and ye have hearkened and understood what the Holy Church is, whereby ye know that ye are fellows of the saints in heaven and the poor men of Essex; and as one day the saints shall call you to the heavenly feast, so now do the poor men call you to the battle.

"Men of Kent, ye dwell fairly here, and your houses are framed of stout oak beams, and your own lands ye till; unless some accursed lawyer with his false lying sheepskin and forged custom of the Devil's Manor hath stolen it from you; but in Essex slaves they be and villeins, and worse they shall be, and the lords swear that ere a year be over ox and horse shall go free in Essex, and man and woman shall draw the team and the plough; and north away in the east countries dwell men in poor halls of wattled reeds and mud, and the north-east wind from off the fen whistles through them; and poor they be to the letter; and there him whom the lord spareth, the bailiff squeezeth, and him whom the bailiff forgetteth, the Easterling Chapman sheareth; yet be these stout men and valiant, and your very brethren.

"And yet if there be any man here so base as to think that a small matter, let him look to it that if these necks abide under the yoke, Kent shall sweat for it ere it be long; and ye shall lose acre and close and woodland, and be servants in your own houses, and your sons shall be the lords' lads, and your daughters their lemans, and ye shall buy a bold word with many stripes, and an honest deed with a leap from the gallows-tree.

"Bethink ye, too, that ye have no longer to deal with Duke William, who, if he were a thief and a cruel lord, was yet a prudent man and a wise warrior; but cruel are these, and headstrong, yea, thieves and fools in one—and ye shall lay their heads in the dust."

A shout would have arisen again, but his eager voice rising higher yet, restrained it as he said:

"And how shall it be then when these are gone? What else shall ye lack when ye lack masters? Ye shall not lack for the fields ye have tilled, nor the houses ye have built, nor the cloth ye have woven; all these shall be yours, and whatso ye will of all that the earth beareth; then shall no man mow the deep grass for another, while his own kine lack cow-meat; and he that soweth shall reap, and the reaper shall eat in fellowship the harvest that in fellowship he hath won; and he that buildeth a house shall dwell in it with those that he biddeth of his free will; and the tithe barn shall garner the wheat for all men to eat of when the seasons are untoward, and the raindrift hideth the sheaves in August; and all shall be without money and without price. Faithfully and merrily then shall all men keep the holidays of the Church in peace of body and joy of heart. And man shall help man, and the saints in heaven shall be glad, because men no more fear each other; and the churl shall be ashamed, and shall hide his churlishness till it be gone, and he be no more a churl; and fellowship shall be established in heaven and on the earth."

CHAPTER V

THEY HEAR TIDINGS OF BATTLE AND MAKE THEM READY

HE left off as one who had yet something else to say; and, indeed, I thought he would give us some word as to the trysting-place, and whither the army was to go from it; because it was now clear to me that this gathering was but a band of an army. But much happened before John Ball spoke again from the cross, and it was on this wise.

When there was silence after the last shout that the crowd had raised a while ago, I thought I heard a thin sharp noise far away, somewhat to the north of the cross, which I took rather for the sound of a trumpet or horn, than for the voice of a man or any beast. Will Green also seemed to have heard it, for he turned his head sharply and then back again, and looked keenly into the crowd as though seeking to catch some one's eye. There was a very tall man standing by the prisoner on the horse near the outskirts of the crowd, and holding his bridle. This man, who was well-armed, I saw look up and say something to the prisoner, who stooped down and seemed to whisper him in turn. The tall man nodded his head and the prisoner got off his horse, which was a cleaner-limbed, better-built beast than the others belonging to the band, and the tall man quietly led him a little way from the crowd, mounted him, and rode off northward at a smart pace.

Will Green looked on sharply at all this, and when the man rode off, smiled as one who is content, and deems that all is going well, and settled himself down again to listen to the priest.

But now when John Ball had ceased speaking, and after another shout, and a hum of excited pleasure and hope that followed it, there was silence again, and as the priest addressed himself to speaking once more, he paused and turned his head towards the wind, as if he heard something, which certainly I heard, and belike every one in the throng, though it was not over-loud, far as sounds carry in clear quiet evenings. It was the thump-a-thump of a horse drawing near at a hand-gallop along the grassy upland road; and I knew well it was the tall man coming back with tidings, the purport of which I could well guess.

I looked up at Will Green's face. He was smiling as one pleased, and said softly as he nodded to me, "Yea, shall we see the grey-goose fly this eve?"

But John Ball said in a great voice from the cross, "Hear ye the tidings on the way, fellows! Hold ye together and look to your gear; yet hurry not, for no great matter shall this be. I wot well there is little force between Canterbury and Kingston, for the lords are looking north of Thames toward Wat Tyler and his men. Yet well it is, well it is!"

The crowd opened and spread out a little, and the men moved about in it, some tightening a girdle, some getting their side arms more within reach of their right hands, and those who had bows stringing them.

Will Green set hand and foot to the great shapely piece of polished red yew, with its shining horn tips, which he carried, and bent it with no seeming effort; then he reached out his hand over his shoulder and drew out a long arrow, smooth, white, beautifully balanced, with a barbed iron head at one end, a horn nock and three strong goose feathers at the other. He held it loosely between the finger and thumb of his right hand, and there he stood with a thoughtful look on his face, and in his hands one of the most terrible weapons which a strong man has ever carried, the English long-bow and cloth-yard shaft.

But all this while the sound of the horse's hoofs was growing nearer, and presently from the corner of the road amidst the orchards broke out our long friend, his face red in the sun near sinking now. He waved his right hand as he came in sight of us, and sang out, "Bills and bows! bills and bows!" and the whole throng turned towards him and raised a great shout.

He reined up at the edge of the throng, and spoke in a loud voice, so that all might hear him:

"Fellows, these are the tidings; even while our priest was speaking we heard a horn blow far off; so I bade the sergeant we have taken, and who is now our fellow-in-arms, to tell me where away it was that there would be folk a-gathering, and what they were; and he did me to wit that may happen Sir John Newton was stirring from Rochester Castle; or, maybe, it was the sheriff and Rafe Hopton with him; so I rode off what I might towards Hartlip, and I rode warily, and that was well, for as I came through a little wood between Hartlip and Guildstead, I saw beyond it a gleam of steel, and lo in the field there a company, and a pennon of Rafe Hopton's arms, and that is blue and thereon three silver fish: and a pennon of the sheriff's arms, and that is a green tree; and withal another pennon of three red kine, and whose they be I know not.[1]

[1] Probably one of the Calverlys, a Cheshire family, one of whom was a noted captain in the French Wars.

"There tied I my horse in the middle of the wood, and myself I crept along the dyke to see more and to hear somewhat; and no talk I heard to tell of save at whiles a big knight talking to five or six others, and saying somewhat, wherein came the words London and Nicholas Bramber, and King Richard; but I saw that of men-at-arms and sergeants there might be a hundred, and of bows not many, but of those outland arbalests maybe a fifty; and so, what with one and another of servants and tip-staves and lads, some three hundred, well armed, and the men-at-arms of the best. Forsooth, my masters, there had I been but a minute, ere the big knight broke off his talk, and cried out to the music to blow up, 'And let us go look on these villeins,' said he; and withal the men began to gather in a due and ordered company, and their faces turned hitherward; forsooth, I got to my horse, and led him out of the wood on the other side, and so to saddle and away along the green roads; neither was I seen or chased. So look ye to it, my masters, for these men will be coming to speak with us; nor is there need for haste, but rather for good speed; for in some twenty or thirty minutes will be more tidings to hand."

By this time one of our best-armed men had got through the throng and was standing on the cross beside John Ball. When the long man had done, there was confused noise of talk for a while, and the throng spread itself out more and more, but not in a disorderly manner; the bowmen drawing together toward the outside, and the bill-men forming behind them. Will Green was still standing beside me and had hold of my arm, as though he knew both where he and I were to go.

"Fellows," quoth the captain from the cross, "belike this stour shall not live to be older than the day, if ye get not into a plump together for their arbalestiers to shoot bolts into, and their men-at-arms to thrust spears into. Get you to the edge of the crofts and spread out there six feet between man and man, and shoot, ye bowmen, from the hedges, and ye with the staves keep your heads below the level of the hedges, or else for all they be thick a bolt may win its way in."

He grinned as he said this, and there was laughter enough in the throng to have done honour to a better joke.

Then he sung out, "Hob Wright, Rafe Wood, John

Pargetter, and thou Will Green, bestir ye and marshal the bowshot; and thou Nicholas Woodyer shall be under me Jack Straw in ordering of the staves. Gregory Tailor and John Clerk, fair and fine are ye clad in the arms of the Canterbury bailiffs; ye shall shine from afar; go ye with the banner into the highway, and the bows on either side shall ward you; yet jump, lads, and over the hedge with you when the bolts begin to fly your way! Take heed, good fellows all, that our business is to bestride the highway, and not let them get in on our flank the while; so half to the right, half to the left of the highway. Shoot straight and strong, and waste no breath with noise; let the loose of the bow-string cry for you! and look you! think it no loss of manhood to cover your bodies with tree and bush; for one of us who know is worth a hundred of those proud fools. To it, lads, and let them see what the grey goose bears between his wings! Abide us here, brother John Ball, and pray for us if thou wilt; but for me, if God will not do for Jack Straw what Jack Straw would do for God were he in like case, I can see no help for it."

"Yea, forsooth," said the priest, "here will I abide you my fellows if ye come back; or if ye come not back, here will I abide the foe. Depart, and the blessing of the Fellowship be with you."

Down then leapt Jack Straw from the cross, and the whole throng set off without noise or hurry, soberly and steadily in outward seeming. Will Green led me by the hand as if I were a boy, yet nothing he said, being forsooth intent on his charge. We were some four hundred men in all; but I said to myself that without some advantage of the ground we were lost men before the men-at-arms that long Gregory Tailor had told us of; for I had not seen as yet the yard-long shaft at its work.

We and somewhat more than half of our band turned into the orchards on the left of the road, through which the level rays of the low sun shone brightly. The others took up their position on the right side of it. We kept pretty near to the road till we had got through all the closes save the last, where we were brought up by a hedge and a dyke, beyond which lay a wide-open nearly treeless space, not of tillage, as at the other side of the place, but of pasture, the common

grazing ground of the township. A little stream wound
about through the ground, with a few willows here and
there; there was only a thread of water in it in this hot
summer tide, but its course could easily be traced by the
deep blue-green of the rushes that grew plenteously in the
bed. Geese were lazily wandering about and near this
brook, and a herd of cows, accompanied by the town bull,
were feeding on quietly, their heads all turned one way;
while half a dozen calves marched close together side by
side like a plump of soldiers, their tails swinging in a kind of
measure to keep off the flies, of which there was great
plenty. Three or four lads and girls were sauntering about,
heeding or not heeding the cattle. They looked up toward
us as we crowded into the last close, and slowly loitered off
toward the village. Nothing looked like battle; yet battle
sounded in the air; for now we heard the beat of the horse-
hoofs of the men-at-arms coming on towards us like the
rolling of distant thunder, and growing louder and louder
every minute; we were none too soon in turning to face them.
Jack Straw was on our side of the road, and with a few
gestures and a word or two he got his men into their places.
Six archers lined the hedge along the road where the banner
of Adam and Eve, rising above the grey leaves of the apple-
trees, challenged the new-comers; and of the billmen also he
kept a good few ready to guard the road in case the enemy
should try to rush it with the horsemen. The road, not being
a Roman one, was, you must remember, little like the firm
smooth country roads that you are used to; it was a mere
track between the hedges and fields, partly grass-grown, and
cut up by the deep-sunk ruts hardened by the drought of
summer. There was a stack of fagot and small wood on the
other side, and our men threw themselves upon it and set to
work to stake the road across for a rough defence against the
horsemen.

What befell more on the road itself I had not much time
to note, for our bowmen spread themselves out along the
hedge that looked into the pasture-field, leaving some six
feet between man and man; the rest of the billmen went
along with the bowmen, and halted in clumps of some half-
dozen along their line, holding themselves ready to help the
bowmen if the enemy should run up under their shafts, or to

run on to lengthen the line in case they should try to break in on our flank. The hedge in front of us was of quick. It had been strongly plashed in the past February, and was stiff and stout. It stood on a low bank; moreover, the level of the orchard was some thirty inches higher than that of the field, and the ditch some two foot deeper than the face of the field. The field went winding round to beyond the church, making a quarter of a circle about the village, and at the western end of it were the butts whence the folk were coming from shooting when I first came into the village street.

Altogether, to me who knew nothing of war the place seemed defensible enough. I have said that the road down which Long Gregory came with his tidings went north; and that was its general direction; but its first reach was nearly east, so that the low sun was not in the eyes of any of us, and where Will Green took his stand, and I with him, it was nearly at our backs.

CHAPTER VI

THE BATTLE AT
THE TOWNSHIP'S END

OUR men had got into their places leisurely and coolly enough, and with no lack of jesting and laughter. As we went along the hedge by the road, the leaders tore off leafy twigs from the low oak bushes therein, and set them for a rallying sign in their hats and headpieces, and two or three of them had horns for blowing.

Will Green, when he got into his place, which was thirty yards from where Jack Straw and the billmen stood in the corner of the two hedges, the road hedge and the hedge between the close and field, looked to right and left of him a moment, then turned to the man on the left and said:

"Look you, mate, when you hear our horns blow ask no more questions, but shoot straight and strong at whatso cometh towards us, till ye hear more tidings from Jack Straw or from me. Pass that word onward."

Then he looked at me and said:

"Now, lad from Essex, thou hadst best sit down out of the
I

way at once: forsooth I wot not why I brought thee hither. Wilt thou not back to the cross, for thou art little of a fighting-man?"

"Nay," said I, "I would see the play. What shall come of it?"

"Little," said he; "we shall slay a horse or twain maybe. I will tell thee, since thou hast not seen a fight belike, as I have seen some, that these men-at-arms cannot run fast either to the play or from it, if they be a-foot; and if they come on a horseback, what shall hinder me to put a shaft into the poor beast? But down with thee on the daisies, for some shot there will be first."

As he spoke he was pulling off his belts and other gear and his coat, which done, he laid his quiver on the ground, girt him again, did his axe and buckler on to his girdle, and hung up his other attire on the nearest tree behind us. Then he opened his quiver and took out of it some two dozen of arrows, which he stuck in the ground beside him ready to his hand. Most of the bowmen within sight were doing the like.

As I glanced toward the houses I saw three or four bright figures moving through the orchards, and presently noted that they were women, all clad more or less like the girl in the Rose, except that two of them wore white coifs on their heads. Their errand there was clear, for each carried a bundle of arrows under her arm.

One of them came straight up to Will Green, and I could see at once that she was his daughter. She was tall and strongly made, with black hair like her father, somewhat comely, though no great beauty; but as they met, her eyes smiled even more than her mouth, and made her face look very sweet and kind, and the smile was answered back in a way so quaintly like to her father's face, that I too smiled for goodwill and pleasure.

"Well, well, lass," said he, "dost thou think that here is Crecy field toward, that ye bring all this artillery? Turn back, my girl, and set the pot on the fire; for that shall we need when we come home, I and this ballad-maker here."

"Nay," she said, nodding kindly at me, "if this is to be no Crecy, then may I stop to see as well, as the ballad-maker, since he hath neither sword nor staff?"

"Sweetling," he said, "get thee home in haste. This play is but little, yet mightest thou be hurt in it: and trust me the time may come, sweetheart, when even thou and such as thou shalt hold a sword or a staff. Ere the moon throws a shadow we shall be back."

She turned away lingering, not without tears on her face, laid the sheaf of arrows at the foot of the tree, and hastened off through the orchard. I was going to say something, when Will Green held up his hand as who would bid us hearken. The noise of the horse hoofs, after growing nearer and nearer, had ceased suddenly, and a confused murmur of voices had taken the place of it.

"Get thee down, and take cover, old lad," said Will Green; "the dance will soon begin, and ye shall hear the music presently."

Sure enough as I slipped down by the hedge close to which I had been standing, I heard the harsh twang of the bow-strings, one, two, three, almost together, from the road, and even the whew of the shafts, though that was drowned in a moment by a confused but loud and threatening shout from the other side, and again the bowstrings clanged, and this time a far-off clash of arms followed, and therewithal that cry of a strong man that comes without his will, and is so different from his wonted voice that one has a guess thereby of the change that death is. Then for a while was almost silence; nor did our horns blow up, though some half-dozen of the billmen had leapt into the road when the bows first shot. But presently came a great blare of trumpets and horns from the other side, and therewith as it were a river of steel and bright coats poured into the field before us, and still their horns blew as they spread out toward the left of our line; the cattle in the pasture-field, heretofore feeding quietly, seemed frightened silly by the sudden noise, and ran about tail in air and lowing loudly; the old bull with his head a little lowered, and his stubborn legs planted firmly, growling threateningly; while the geese about the brook waddled away gobbling and squeaking; all which seemed so strange to us along with the threat of sudden death that rang out from the bright array over against us, that we laughed outright, the most of us, and Will Green put down his head in mockery of the bull and grunted like

him, whereat we laughed yet more. He turned round to me
as he nocked his arrow, and said:

"I would they were just fifty paces nigher, and they move
not. Ho! Jack Straw, shall we shoot?"

For the latter-named was nigh us now; he shook his head
and said nothing as he stood looking at the enemy's line.

"Fear not but they are the right folk, Jack," quoth Will
Green.

"Yea, yea," said he, "but abide awhile; they could make
nought of the highway, and two of their sergeants had a
message from the grey-goose feather. Abide, for they have
not crossed the road to our right hand, and belike have not
seen our fellows on the other side, who are now for a bush-
ment to them."

I looked hard at the man. He was a tall, wiry, and broad-
shouldered fellow, clad in a handsome armour of bright
steel that certainly had not been made for a yeoman, but
over it he had a common linen smock-frock or gabardine,
like our field workmen wear now or used to wear, and in his
helmet he carried instead of a feather a wisp of wheaten
straw. He bore a heavy axe in his hand besides the sword he
was girt with, and round his neck hung a great horn for
blowing. I should say that I knew that there were at least
three "Jack Straws" among the fellowship of the discontented, one of whom was over in Essex.

As we waited there, every bowman with his shaft nocked
on the string, there was a movement in the line opposite,
and presently came from it a little knot of three men, the
middle one on horseback, the other two armed with long-
handled glaives; all three well muffled up in armour. As
they came nearer I could see that the horseman had a
tabard over his armour, gaily embroidered with a green
tree on a gold ground, and in his hand a trumpet.

"They are come to summon us. Wilt thou that he speak,
Jack?" said Will Green.

"Nay," said the other; "yet shall he have warning first.
Shoot when my horn blows!"

And therewith he came up to the hedge, climbed over,
slowly because of his armour, and stood some dozen yards
out in the field. The man on horseback put his trumpet to
his mouth and blew a long blast, and then took a scroll into

his hand and made as if he were going to read; but Jack Straw lifted up his voice and cried out:

"Do it not, or thou art but dead! We will have no accursed lawyers and their sheep-skins here! Go back to those that sent thee——"

But the man broke in in a loud harsh voice:

"Ho! YE PEOPLE! what will ye gathering in arms?"

Then cried Jack Straw:

"Sir Fool, hold your peace till ye have heard me, or else we shoot at once. Go back to those that sent thee, and tell them that we free men of Kent are on the way to London to speak with King Richard, and to tell him that which he wots not; to wit, that there is a certain sort of fools and traitors to the realm who would put collars on our necks and make beasts of us, and that it is his right and his devoir to do as he swore when he was crowned and anointed at Westminster on the Stone of Doom, and gainsay these thieves and traitors; and if he be too weak, then shall we help him; and if he will not be king, then shall we have one who will be, and that is the King's Son of Heaven. Now, therefore, if any withstand us on our lawful errand as we go to speak with our own king and lord, let him look to it. Bear back this word to them that sent thee. But for thee, hearken, thou bastard of an inky sheep-skin! get thee gone and tarry not; three times shall I lift up my hand, and the third time look to thyself, for then shalt thou hear the loose of our bow-strings, and after that nought else till thou hearest the devil bidding thee welcome to hell!"

Our fellows shouted, but the summoner began again, yet in a quavering voice·

"Ho! YE PEOPLE! what will ye gathering in arms? Wot ye not that ye are doing or shall do great harm, loss, and hurt to the king's lieges——"

He stopped; Jack Straw's hand was lowered for the second time. He looked to his men right and left, and then turned rein and turned tail, and scuttled back to the main body at his swiftest. Huge laughter rattled out all along our line as Jack Straw climbed back into the orchard grinning also.

Then we noted more movement in the enemy's line. They were spreading the archers and arbalestiers to our left, and the men-at-arms and others also spread somewhat under the three pennons of which Long Gregory had told us, and which were plain enough to us in the clear evening. Presently the moving line faced us, and the archers set off at a smart pace toward us, the men-at-arms holding back a little behind them. I knew now that they had been within bowshot all along, but our men were loth to shoot before their first shots would tell, like those half-dozen in the road when, as they told me afterwards, a plump of their men-at-arms had made a show of falling on.

But now as soon as those men began to move on us directly in face, Jack Straw put his horn to his lips and blew a loud rough blast that was echoed by five or six others along the orchard hedge. Every man had his shaft nocked on the string; I watched them, and Will Green specially; he and his bow and its string seemed all of a piece, so easily by seeming did he draw the nock of the arrow to his ear. A moment, as he took his aim, and then—O then did I understand the meaning of the awe with which the ancient poet speaks of the loose of the god Apollo's bow, for terrible indeed was the mingled sound of the twanging bowstring and the whirring shaft so close to me.

I was now on my knees right in front of Will and saw all clearly; the arbalestiers (for no long-bow men were over against our stead) had all of them bright headpieces, and stout body-armour of boiled leather with metal studs, and as they came towards us, I could see over their shoulders great wooden shields hanging at their backs. Further to our left their long-bow men had shot almost as soon as ours, and I heard or seemed to hear the rush of the arrows through the apple-boughs and a man's cry therewith; but with us the long-bow had been before the cross-bow; one of the arbalestiers fell outright, his great shield clattering down on him, and moved no more; while three others were hit and were crawling to the rear. The rest had shouldered their bows and were aiming, but I thought unsteadily; and before the triggers were drawn again Will Green had nocked and loosed, and not a few others of our folk; then came the wooden hail of the bolts rattling through the boughs, but all overhead and no one hit.

The next time Will Green nocked his arrow he drew with

a great shout, which all our fellows took up; for the arbales-tiers instead of turning about in their places covered by their great shields and winding up their cross-bows for a second shot, as is the custom of such soldiers, ran huddling together toward their men-at-arms, our arrows driving thump-thump into their shields as they ran: I saw four lying on the field dead or sore wounded.

But our archers shouted again, and kept on each plucking the arrows from the ground, and nocking and loosing swiftly but deliberately at the line before them; indeed now was the time for these terrible bowmen, for as Will Green told me afterwards they always reckoned to kill through cloth or leather at five hundred yards, and they had let the cross-bow men come nearly within three hundred, and these were now all mingled and muddled up with the men-at-arms at scant five hundred yards' distance; and belike, too, the latter were not treating them too well, but seemed to be belabouring them with their spear-staves in their anger at the poorness of the play; so that as Will Green said it was like shooting at hay-ricks.

All this you must understand lasted but a few minutes, and when our men had been shooting quite coolly, like good workmen at peaceful work, for a few minutes more, the enemy's line seemed to clear somewhat; the pennon with the three red kine showed in front and three men armed from head to foot in gleaming steel, except for their short coats bright with heraldry, were with it. One of them (and he bore the three kine on his coat) turned round and gave some word of command, and an angry shout went up from them, and they came on steadily towards us, the man with the red kine on his coat leading them, a great naked sword in his hand: you must note that they were all on foot; but as they drew nearer I saw their horses led by grooms and pages coming on slowly behind them.

Sooth said Will Green that the men-at-arms run not fast either to or fro the fray; they came on no faster than a hasty walk, their arms clashing about them and the twang of the bows and whistle of the arrows never failing all the while, but going on like the push of the westerly gale, as from time to time the men-at arms shouted, "Ha! ha! out! out! Kentish thieves!"

But when they began to fall on, Jack Straw shouted out, "Bills to the field! bills to the field!"

Then all our billmen ran up and leapt over the hedge into the meadow and stood stoutly along the ditch under our bows, Jack Straw in the forefront handling his great axe. Then he cast it into his left hand, caught up his horn and winded it loudly. The men-at-arms drew near steadily, some fell under the arrow-storm, but not a many; for though the target was big, it was hard, since not even the cloth-yard shaft could pierce well-wrought armour of plate, and there was much armour among them. Withal the arbalestiers were shooting again, but high and at a venture, so they did us no hurt.

But as these soldiers made wise by the French war were now drawing near, and our bowmen were casting down their bows and drawing their short swords, or handling their axes, as did Will Green, muttering, "Now must Hob Wright's gear end this play"—while this was a-doing, lo, on a sudden a flight of arrows from our right on the flank, of the sergeants' array, which stayed them somewhat; not because it slew many men, but because they began to bethink them that their foes were many and all around them; then the road-hedge on the right seemed alive with armed men, for whatever could hold sword or staff amongst us was there; every bowman also leapt our orchard-hedge sword or axe in hand, and with a great shout, billmen, archers, and all, ran in on them; half-armed, yea, and half-naked some of them; strong and stout and lithe and light withal, the wrath of battle and the hope of better times lifting up their hearts till nothing could withstand them. So was all mingled together, and for a minute or two was a confused clamour over which rose a clatter like the riveting of iron plates, or the noise of the street of coppersmiths at Florence; then the throng burst open and the steel-clad sergeants and squires and knights ran huddling and shuffling towards their horses; but some cast down their weapons and threw up their hands and cried for peace and ransom: and some stood and fought desperately, and slew some till they were hammered down by many strokes, and of these were the bailiffs and tipstaves, and the lawyers and their men, who could not run and hoped for no mercy.

I looked as on a picture and wondered, and my mind was at strain to remember something forgotten, which yet had left its mark on it. I heard the noise of the horse-hoofs of the fleeing men-at-arms (the archers and arbalestiers had scattered before the last minutes of the play), I heard the confused sound of laughter and rejoicing down in the meadow, and close by me the evening wind lifting the lighter twigs of the trees, and far away the many noises of the quiet country, till light and sound both began to fade from me and I saw and heard nothing.

I leapt up to my feet presently and there was Will Green before me as I had first seen him in the street with coat and hood and the gear at his girdle and his unstrung bow in his hand; his face smiling and kind again, but maybe a thought sad.

"Well," quoth I, "what is the tale for the ballad-maker?"

"As Jack Straw said it would be," said he, " 'the end of the day and the end of the fray' "; and he pointed to the brave show of the sky over the sunken sun; "the knights fled and the sheriff dead: two of the lawyer kind slain afield, and one hanged: and cruel was he to make them cruel: and three bailiffs knocked on the head—stout men, and so witless, that none found their brains in their skulls; and five arbalestiers and one archer slain, and a score and a half of others, mostly men come back from the French wars, men of the Companions there, knowing no other craft than fighting for gold; and this is the end they are paid for. Well, brother, saving the lawyers who belike had no souls, but only parchment deeds and libels of the same, God rest their souls!"

He fell a musing; but I said, "And of our Fellowship were any slain?"

"Two good men of the township," he said, "Hob Horner and Antony Webber, were slain outright, Hob with a shaft and Antony in the hand-play, and John Pargetter hurt very sore on the shoulder with a glaive: and five more men of the Fellowship slain in the hand play, and some few hurt, but not sorely. And as to those slain, if God give their souls rest it is well: for little rest they had on the earth belike; but for me, I desire rest no more."

I looked at him and our eyes met with no little love; and

I wondered to see how wrath and grief within him were contending with the kindness of the man, and how clear the tokens of it were in his face.

"Come now, old lad," said he, "for I deem that John Ball and Jack Straw have a word to say to us at the cross yet, since these men broke off the telling of the tale; there shall we know what we are to take in hand to-morrow. And afterwards thou shalt eat and drink in my house this once, if never again."

So we went through the orchard closes again; and others were about and anigh us, all turned towards the cross as we went over the dewy grass, whereon the moon was just beginning to throw shadows.

CHAPTER VII

MORE WORDS AT THE CROSS

I GOT into my old place again on the steps of the cross, Will Green beside me, and above me John Ball and Jack Straw again. The moon was half-way up the heavens now, and the short summer night had begun, calm and fragrant, with just so much noise outside our quiet circle as made one feel the world alive and happy.

We waited silently until we had heard John Ball and the story of what was to do; and presently he began to speak:

"Good people, it is begun, but not ended. Which of you is hardy enough to wend the road to London to-morrow?"

"All! All!" they shouted.

"Yea," said he, "even so I deemed of you. Yet forsooth hearken! London is a great and grievous city; and may-happen when ye come thither it shall seem to you overgreat to deal with, when ye remember the little townships and the cots ye came from.

"Moreover, when ye dwell here in Kent ye think forsooth of your brethren in Essex or Suffolk, and there belike an end. But from London ye may have an inkling of all the world, and over-burdensome maybe shall that seem to you, a few and a feeble people.

"Nevertheless I say to you, remember the Fellowship, in

the hope of which ye have this day conquered; and when ye come to London be wise and wary; and that is as much as to say, be bold and hardy; for in these days are ye building a house which shall not be overthrown, and the world shall not be too great or too little to hold it: for indeed it shall be the world itself, set free from evil-doers for friends to dwell in."

He ceased awhile, but they hearkened still, as if something more was coming. Then he said:

"To-morrow we shall take the road for Rochester; and most like it were well to see what Sir John Newton in the castle may say to us: for the man is no ill man, and hath a tongue well-shapen for words; and it were well that we had him out of the castle and away with us, and that we put a word in his mouth to say to the King. And wot ye well, good fellows, that by then we come to Rochester we shall be a goodly company, and ere we come to Blackheath a very great company; and at London Bridge who shall stay our host?

"Therefore there is nought that can undo us except our own selves and our hearkening to soft words from those who would slay us. They shall bid us go home and abide peacefully with our wives and children while they, the lords and councillors and lawyers, imagine counsel and remedy for us; and even so shall our own folly bid us; and if we hearken thereto we are undone indeed; for they shall fall upon our peace with war, and our wives and children they shall take from us, and some of us they shall hang, and some they shall scourge, and the others shall be their yoke-beasts—yea, and worse, for they shall lack meat more.

"To fools hearken not, whether they be yourselves or your foemen, for either shall lead you astray.

"With the lords parley not, for ye know already what they would say to you, and that is, 'Churl, let me bridle thee and saddle thee, and eat thy livelihood that thou winnest, and call thee hard names because I eat thee up; and for thee, speak not and do not, save as I bid thee.'

"All that is the end of their parleying.

"Therefore be ye bold, and again bold, and thrice bold! Grip the bow, handle the staff, draw the sword, and set on in the name of the Fellowship!"

He ended amid loud shouts; but straightway answering shouts were heard, and a great noise of the winding of horns, and I misdoubted a new onslaught; and some of those in the throng began to string their bows and handle their bills; but Will Green pulled me by the sleeve and said:

"Friends are these by the winding of their horns; thou art quit for this night, old lad." And then Jack Straw cried out from the cross: "Fair and softly, my masters! These be men of our Fellowship, and are for your guests this night; they are from the bents this side of Medway, and are with us here because of the pilgrimage road, and that is the best in these parts, and so the shortest to Rochester. And doubt ye nothing of our being taken unawares this night; for I have bidden and sent out watchers of the ways, and neither a man's son nor a mare's son may come in on us without espial. Now make we our friends welcome. Forsooth, I looked for them an hour later; and had they come an hour earlier yet, some heads would now lie on the cold grass which shall lie on a feather bed to-night. But let be, since all is well!

"Now get we home to our houses, and eat and drink and slumber this night, if never once again, amid the multitude of friends and fellows; and yet soberly and without riot, since so much work is to hand. Moreover the priest saith, bear ye the dead men, both friends and foes, into the chancel of the church, and there this night he will wake them: but after to-morrow let the dead abide to bury their dead!"

Therewith he leapt down from the cross, and Will and I bestirred ourselves and mingled with the new-comers. They were some three hundred strong, clad and armed in all ways like the people of our township, except some half-dozen whose armour shone cold like ice under the moon-beams. Will Green soon had a dozen of them by the sleeve to come home with him to board and bed, and then I lost him for some minutes, and turning about saw John Ball standing behind me, looking pensively on all the stir and merry humours of the joyous uplanders.

"Brother from Essex," said he, "shall I see thee again to-night? I were fain of speech with thee; for thou seemest like one that has seen more than most."

"Yea," said I, "if ye come to Will Green's house, for thither am I bidden."

"Thither shall I come," said he, smiling kindly, "or no man I know in field. Lo you, Will Green looking for something, and that is me. But in his house will be song and the talk of many friends; and forsooth I have words in me that crave to come out in a quiet place where they may have each one his own answer. If thou art not afraid of dead men who were alive and wicked this morning, come thou to the church when supper is done, and there we may talk all we will."

Will Green was standing beside us before he had done, with his hand laid on the priest's shoulder, waiting till he had spoken out; and as I nodded Yea to John Ball he said:

"Now, master priest, thou hast spoken enough this two or three hours, and this my new brother must tell and talk in my house; and there my maid will hear his wisdom which lay still under the hedge e'en now when the bolts were abroad. So come ye, and ye good fellows, come!"

So we turned away together into the little street. But while John Ball had been speaking to me I felt strangely, as though I had more things to say than the words I knew could make clear: as if I wanted to get from other people a new set of words. Moreover, as we passed up the street again I was once again smitten with the great beauty of the scene; the houses, the church with its new chancel and tower, snow-white in the moonbeams now; the dresses and arms of the people, men and women (for the latter were now mixed up with the men); their grave sonorous language, and the quaint and measured forms of speech, were again become a wonder to me and affected me almost to tears.

CHAPTER VIII

SUPPER AT WILL GREEN'S

I WALKED along with the others musing as if I did not belong to them, till we came to Will Green's house. He was one of the wealthier of the yeomen, and his house was one of those I told you of, the lower story of which was built of stone. It had not been built long, and was very trim and neat. The fit of wonder had worn off me again by then I reached it, or perhaps I should give you a closer description of it, for it was a handsome yeoman's dwelling of that day, which is as much as saying it was very beautiful. The house on the other side of it, the last house in the village, was old or even ancient; all built of stone, and except for a newer piece built on to it—a hall, it seemed—had round arches, some of them handsomely carved. I knew that this was the parson's house; but he was another sort of priest than John Ball, and what for fear, what for hatred, had gone back to his monastery with the two other chantrey priests who dwelt in that house; so that the men of the township, and more especially the women, were thinking gladly how John Ball should say mass in their new chancel on the morrow.

Will Green's daughter was waiting for him at the door and gave him a close and eager hug, and had a kiss to spare for each of us withal: a strong girl she was, as I have said, and sweet and wholesome also. She made merry with her father; yet it was easy to see that her heart was in her mouth all along. There was a younger girl some twelve summers old, and a lad of ten, who were easily to be known for his children; an old woman also, who had her livelihood there, and helped the household; and moreover three long young men, who came into the house after we had sat down, to whom Will nodded kindly. They were brisk lads and smart, but had been afield after the beasts that evening, and had not seen the fray.

The room we came into was indeed the house, for there was nothing but it on the ground floor, but a stair in the corner went up to the chamber or loft above. It was much like the room at the Rose, but bigger; the cupboard better wrought, and with more vessels on it, and handsomer. Also the walls, instead of being panelled, were hung with a coarse loosely-woven stuff of green worsted with birds and trees woven into it. There were flowers in plenty stuck about the room, mostly of the yellow blossoming flag or flower-de-luce, of which I had seen plenty in all the ditches, but in the window near the door was a pot full of those same white poppies I had seen when I first woke up; and the table was all set forth with meat and drink, a big salt-cellar of pewter in the middle, covered with a white cloth.

We sat down, the priest blessed the meat in the name of the Trinity, and we crossed ourselves and fell to. The victual was plentiful of broth and flesh meat, and bread and cherries, so we ate and drank, and talked lightly together when we were full.

Yet was not the feast so gay as might have been. Will Green had me to sit next to him, and on the other side sat John Ball, but the priest had grown somewhat distraught, and sat as one thinking of somewhat that was like to escape his thought. Will Green looked at his daughter from time to time, and whiles his eyes glanced round the fair chamber as one who loved it, and his kind face grew sad, yet never sullen. When the herdsmen came into the hall they fell straightway to asking questions concerning those of the Fellowship who had been slain in the fray, and of their wives and children; so that for a while thereafter no man cared to jest, for they were a neighbourly and kind folk, and were sorry both for the dead, and also for the living that should suffer from that day's work.

So then we sat silent awhile. The unseen moon was bright over the roof of the house, so that outside all was gleaming bright save the black shadows, though the moon came not into the room, and the white wall of the tower was the whitest and the brightest thing we could see.

Wide open were the windows, and the scents of the fragrant night floated in upon us, and the sounds of the men at their meat or making merry about the township; and whiles we heard the gibber of an owl from the trees westward of the church, and the sharp cry of a blackbird made fearful by the prowling stoat, or the far-off lowing of a cow from the upland pastures; or the hoofs of a horse trotting on the pilgrimage road (and one of our watchers would that be).

Thus we sat awhile, and once again came that feeling over me of wonder and pleasure at the strange and beautiful sights, mingled with the sights and sounds and scents beautiful indeed, yet not strange, but rather long familiar to me.

But now Will Green started in his seat where he sat with

his daughter hanging over his chair, her hand amidst his thick black curls, and she weeping softly, I thought; and his rough strong voice broke the silence.

"Why, lads and neighbours, what ails us? If the knights who fled from us this eve were to creep back hither and look in at the window, they would deem that they had slain us after all, and that we were but the ghosts of the men who fought them. Yet, forsooth, fair it is at whiles to sit with friends and let the summer night speak for us and tell us its tales. But now, sweetling, fetch the mazer and the wine."

"Forsooth," said John Ball, "if ye laugh not over-much now, ye shall laugh the more on the morrow of to-morrow, as ye draw nearer to the play of point and edge."

"That is sooth," said one of the upland guests. "So it was seen in France when we fought there; and the eve of fight was sober and the morn was merry."

"Yea," said another, "but there, forsooth, it was for nothing ye fought; and to-morrow it shall be for a fair reward."

"It was for life we fought," said the first.

"Yea," said the second, "for life; and leave to go home and find the lawyers at their fell game. Ho, Will Green, call a health over the cup!"

For now Will Green had a bowl of wine in his hand. He stood up and said: "Here, now, I call a health to the wrights of Kent who be turning our plough-shares into swords and our pruning-hooks into spears! Drink around, my masters!"

Then he drank, and his daughter filled the bowl brimming again and he passed it to me. As I took it I saw that it was of light polished wood curiously speckled, with a band of silver round it, on which was cut the legend, "*In the name of the Trinity fill the cup and drink to me.*" And before I drank, it came upon me to say, "To-morrow, and the fair days afterwards!"

Then I drank a great draught of the strong red wine, and passed it on; and every man said something over its as "The road to London Bridge!" "Hob Carter and his mate!" and so on, till last of all John Ball drank, saying:

"Ten years hence, and the freedom of the Fellowship!" Then he said to Will Green: "Now, Will, must I need, depart to go and wake the dead, both friend and foe in the church yonder; and whoso of you will be shriven let him come to me thither in the morn, nor spare for as little after sunrise as it may be. And this our friend and brother from over the water of Thames, he hath will to talk with me and I with him; so now will I take him by the hand: and so God keep you, fellows!"

I rose to meet him as he came round the head of the table, and took his hand. Will Green turned round to me and said:

"Thou wilt come back again timely, old lad; for betimes on the morrow must we rise if we shall dine at Rochester."

I stammered as I yea-said him; for John Ball was looking strangely at me with a half-smile, and my heart beat anxiously and fearfully: but we went quietly to the door and so out into the bright moonlight.

I lingered a little when we had passed the threshold, and looked back at the yellow-lighted window and the shapes of the men that I saw therein with a grief and longing that I could not give myself a reason for, since I was to come back so soon. John Ball did not press me to move forward, but held up his hand as if to bid me hearken. The folk and guests there had already shaken themselves down since our departure, and were gotten to be reasonably merry it seemed; for one of the guests, he who had spoken of France before, had fallen to singing a ballad of the war to a wild and melancholy tune. I remember the first rhymes of it, which I heard as I turned away my head and we moved on toward the church:

> "On a fair field of France
> We fought on a morning
> So lovely as it lieth
> Along by the water.
> There was many a lord there
> Mowed men in the medley,
> 'Midst the banners of the barons
> And bold men of the knighthood,
> And spearmen and sergeants
> And shooters of the shaft."

CHAPTER IX

BETWIXT THE LIVING AND
THE DEAD

WE entered the church through the south porch under
a round-arched door carved very richly, and with
a sculpture over the doorway and under the arch, which,
as far as I could see by the moonlight, figured St. Michael
and the Dragon. As I came into the rich gloom of the nave
I noticed for the first time that I had one of those white
poppies in my hand; I must have taken it out of the pot
by the window as I passed out of Will Green's house.

The nave was not very large, but it looked spacious too;
it was somewhat old, but well-built and handsome; the
roof of curved wooden rafters with great tie-beams going
from wall to wall. There was no light in it but that of the
moon streaming through the windows, which were by no
means large, and were glazed with white fretwork, with
here and there a little figure in very deep rich colours. Two
larger windows near the east end of each aisle had just been
made so that the church grew lighter toward the east, and
I could see all the work on the great screen between the nave
and chancel which glittered bright in new paint and gilding: a candle glimmered in the loft above it, before the huge
rood that filled up the whole space between the loft and the
chancel arch. There was an altar at the east end of each
aisle, the one on the south side standing against the outside
wall, the one on the north against a traceried gaily-painted
screen, for that aisle ran on along the chancel. There were a
few oak benches near this second altar, seemingly just made,
and well carved and moulded; otherwise the floor of the
nave, which was paved with a quaint pavement of glazed
tiles like the crocks I had seen outside as to ware, was quite
clear, and the shafts of the arches rose out of it white and
beautiful under the moon as though out of a sea, dark but
with gleams struck over it.

The priest let me linger and look round, when he had
crossed himself and give me the holy water; and then I saw

that the walls were figured all over with stories, a huge St. Christopher with his black beard looking like Will Green, being close to the porch by which we entered, and above the chancel arch the Doom of the last Day, in which the painter had not spared either kings or bishops, and in which a lawyer with his blue coif was one of the chief figures in the group which the Devil was hauling off to hell.

"Yea," said John Ball, "'tis a goodly church and fair as you may see 'twixt Canterbury and London as for its kind; and yet do I misdoubt me where those who are dead are housed, and where those shall house them after they are dead, who built this house for God to dwell in. God grant they be cleansed at last; forsooth one of them who is now alive is a foul swine and a cruel wolf. Art thou all so sure, scholar, that all such have souls? and if it be so, was it well done of God to make them? I speak to thee thus, for I think thou art no delator; and if thou be, why should I heed it, since I think not to come back from this journey."

I looked at him and, as it were, had some ado to answer him; but I said at last, "Friend, I never saw a soul, save in the body; I cannot tell."

He crossed himself and said, "Yet do I intend that ere many days are gone by my soul shall be in bliss among the fellowship of the saints, and merry shall it be, even before my body rises from the dead; for wisely I have wrought in the world, and I wot well of friends that are long ago gone from the world, as St. Martin, and St. Francis, and St. Thomas of Canterbury, who shall speak well of me to the heavenly Fellowship, and I shall in no wise lose my reward."

I looked shyly at him as he spoke; his face looked sweet and calm and happy, and I would have said no word to grieve him; and yet belike my eyes looked wonder on him: he seemed to note it and his face grew puzzled. "How deemest thou of these things?" said he: "why do men die else, if it be otherwise than this?"

I smiled: "Why then do they live?" said I.

Even in the white moonlight I saw his face flush, and he cried out in a great voice, "To do great deeds or to repent them that they ever were born."

"Yea," said I, "they live to live because the world liveth." He stretched out his hand to me and grasped mine, but said no more; and went on till we came to the door in the rood-screen; then he turned to me with his hand on the ring-latch, and said, "Hast thou seen many dead men?"

"Nay, but few," said I.

"And I a many," said he; "but come now and look on these, our friends first and then our foes, so that ye may not look to see them while we sit and talk of the days that are to be on the earth before the Day of Doom cometh."

So he opened the door, and we went into the chancel; a light burned on the high altar before the host, and looked red and strange in the moonlight that came through the wide traceried windows unstained by the pictures and beflowerings of the glazing; there were new stalls for the priests and vicars where we entered, carved more abundantly and beautifully than any of the woodwork I had yet seen, and everywhere was rich and fair colour and delicate and dainty form. Our dead lay just before the high altar on low biers, their faces all covered with linen cloths, for some of them had been sore smitten and hacked in the fray. We went up to them and John Ball took the cloth from the face of one; he had been shot to the heart with a shaft and his face was calm and smooth. He had been a young man fair and comely, with hair flaxen almost to whiteness; he lay there in his clothes as he had fallen, the hands crossed over his breast and holding a rush cross. His bow lay on one side of him, his quiver of shafts and his sword on the other.

John Ball spake to me while he held the corner of the sheet: "What sayest thou, scholar? feelest thou sorrow of heart when thou lookest on this, either for the man himself, or for thyself and the time when thou shalt be as he is?"

I said, "Nay, I feel no sorrow for this; for the man is not here: this is an empty house, and the master has gone from it. Forsooth, this to me is but as a waxen image of a man; nay, not even that, for if it were an image, it would be an image of the man as he was when he was alive. But here is no life nor semblance of life, and I am not moved by it; nay, I am more moved by the man's clothes and war-gear—there is more life in them than in him."

"Thou sayest sooth," said he; "but sorrowest thou not for thine own death when thou lookest on him?"

I said, "And how can I sorrow for that which I cannot so

much as think of? Bethink thee that while I am alive I cannot think that I shall die, or believe in death at all, although I know well that I shall die—I can but think of myself as living in some new way."

Again he looked on me as if puzzled; then his face cleared as he said, "Yea, forsooth, and that is what the Church meaneth by death, and even that I look for; and that hereafter I shall see all the deeds that I have done in the body, and what they really were, and what shall come of them; and ever shall I be a member of the Church, and that is the Fellowship; then, even as now."

I sighed as he spoke; then I said, "Yea, somewhat in this fashion have most of men thought, since no man that is can conceive of not being; and I mind me that in those stories of the old Danes, their common word for a man dying is to say, 'He changed his life.' "

"And so deemest thou?"

I shook my head and said nothing.

"What hast thou to say hereon?" said he, "for there seemeth something betwixt us twain as it were a wall that parteth us."

"This," said I, "that though I die and end, yet mankind yet liveth, therefore I end not, since I am a man; and even so thou deemest, good friend; or at the least even so thou doest, since now thou art ready to die in grief and torment rather than be unfaithful to the Fellowship, yea rather than fail to work thine utmost for it; whereas, as thou thyself saidst at the cross, with a few words spoken and a little huddling-up of the truth, with a few pennies paid, and a few masses sung, thou mightest have had a good place on this earth and in that heaven. And as thou doest, so now doth many a poor man unnamed and unknown, and shall do while the world lasteth: and they that do less than this, fail because of fear, and are ashamed of their cowardice, and make many tales to themselves to deceive themselves, lest they should grow too much ashamed to live. And trust me if this were not so, the world would not live, but would die, smothered by its own stink. Is the wall betwixt us gone, friend?"

He smiled as he looked at me, kindly, but sadly and shamefast, and shook his head.

Then in a while he said, "Now ye have seen the images of those who were our friends, come and see the images of those who were once our foes."

So he led the way through the side screen into the chancel aisle, and there on the pavement lay the bodies of the foemen, their weapons taken from them and they stripped of their armour, but not otherwise of their clothes, and their faces mostly, but not all, covered. At the east end of the aisle was another altar, covered with a rich cloth beautifully figured, and on the wall over it was a deal of tabernacle work, in the mid-most niche of it an image painted and gilt of a gay knight on horseback, cutting his own cloak in two with his sword to give a cantle of it to a half-naked beggar.

" Knowest thou any of these men ? " said I.

He said, "Some I should know, could I see their faces; but let them be."

"Were they evil men?" said I.

"Yea," he said, "some two or three. But I will not tell thee of them; let St. Martin, whose house this is, tell their story if he will. As for the rest they were hapless fools, or else men who must earn their bread somehow, and were driven to this bad way of earning it; God rest their souls! I will be no tale bearer, not even to God."

So we stood musing a little while, I gazing not on the dead men, but on the strange pictures on the wall, which were richer and deeper coloured than those in the nave; till at last John Ball turned to me and laid his hand on my shoulder. I started and said, "Yea, brother; now must I get me back to Will Green's house, as I promised to do so timely."

"Not yet, brother," said he; "I have still much to say to thee, and the night is yet young. Go we and sit in the stalls of the vicars, and let us ask and answer on matters concerning the fashion of this world of menfolk, and of this land wherein we dwell; for once more I deem of thee that thou hast seen things which I have not seen, and could not have seen." With that word he led me back into the chancel, and we sat down side by side in the stalls at the west end of it, facing the high altar and the great east window. By this time the chancel was getting dimmer as the moon wound round the heavens; but yet was there a twilight of the moon, so that I could still see the things about me for all the brightness of the window that faced us; and this moon twilight would last, I knew, until the short summer night should wane, and the twilight of the dawn begin to show us the colours of all things about us.

So we sat, and I gathered my thoughts to hear what he would say, and I myself was trying to think what I should ask of him; for I thought of him as he of me, that he had seen things which I could not have seen.

CHAPTER X

THOSE TWO TALK OF THE DAYS TO COME

"BROTHER," said John Ball, "how deemest thou of our adventure? I do not ask thee if thou thinkest we are right to play the play like men, but whether playing like men we shall fail like men?"

"Why dost thou ask me?" said I; "how much further than beyond this church can I see?"

"Far further," quoth he, "for I wot that thou art a scholar and hast read books; and withal, in some way that I cannot name, thou knowest more than we; as though with thee the world had lived longer than with us. Hide not, therefore, what thou hast in thine heart, for I think after this night I shall see thee no more, until we meet in the heavenly Fellowship."

"Friend," I said, "ask me what thou wilt; or rather ask thou the years to come to tell thee some little of their tale; and yet methinks thou thyself mayest have some deeming thereof."

He raised himself on the elbow of the stall and looked me full in the face, and said to me: "Is it so after all that thou art no man in the flesh, but art sent to me by the Master of the Fellowship, and the King's Son of Heaven, to tell me what shall be ? If that be so tell me straight out, since I had some deeming hereof before; whereas thy speech is like ours and yet unlike, and thy face hath something in it which is not after the fashion of our day. And yet take heed, if thou art such an one, I fear thee not, nay, nor him that sent thee; nor for thy bidding, nor for his, will I turn back from London Bridge but will press on, for I do what is meet and right."

"Nay," said I, "did I not tell thee e'en now that I knew life but not death? I am not dead; and as to who hath sent me, I say not that I am come by my own will; for I know not; yet also I know not the will that hath sent me hither. And this I say to thee, moreover, that if I know more than thou, I do far less; therefore thou art my captain and I thy minstrel."

He sighed as one from whom a weight had been lifted, and said: "Well, then, since thou art alive on the earth and a man like myself, tell me how deemest thou of our adventure: shall we come to London, and how shall we fare there?"

Said I, "What shall hinder you to come to London, and to fare there as ye will? For be sure that the Fellowship in Essex shall not fail you; nor shall the Londoners who hate the king's uncles withstand you; nor hath the Court any great force to meet you in the field; ye shall cast fear and trembling into their hearts."

"Even so, I thought," said he; "but afterwards what shall betide?"

Said I, "It grieves my heart to say that which I think. Yet hearken; many a man's son shall die who is now alive and happy, and if the soldiers be slain, and of them most not on the field, but by the lawyers, how shall the captains escape? Surely thou goest to thy death."

He smiled very sweetly, yet proudly, as he said: "Yea, the road is long, but the end cometh at last. Friend, many a day have I been dying; for my sister, with whom I have played and been merry in the autumn tide about the edges of the stubble-fields; and we gathered the nuts and bramble-berries there, and started thence the missel-thrush, and wondered at his voice and thought him big; and the sparrow-hawk wheeled and turned over the hedges and the weasel ran across the path, and the sound of the sheep-bells came to us from the downs as we sat happy on the grass; and she is dead and gone from the earth, for she pined from famine after the years of the great sickness; and my brother was slain in the French wars, and none thanked him for dying save he that stripped him of his gear; and my unwedded wife with whom I dwelt in love after I had taken the tonsure, and all men said she was good and fair, and true she was and lovely; she also is dead and gone from the earth; and why should I abide save for the deeds of the flesh which must be done? Truly, friend, this is but an old tale that men must die; and I will tell thee another, to wit, that they live: and I live now and shall live. Tell me then what shall befall?"

Somehow I could not heed him as a living man as much as I had done, and the voice that came from me seemed less of me as I answered:

"These men are strong and valiant as any that have been or shall be, and good fellows also and kindly; but they are simple, and see no great way before their own noses. The victory shall they have and shall not know what to do with it; they shall fight and overcome, because of their lack of knowledge, and because of their lack of knowledge shall they be cozened and betrayed when their captains are slain, and all shall come to nought by seeming; and the king's uncles shall prevail, that both they and the king may come to the shame that is appointed for them. And yet when the lords have vanquished, and all England lieth under them again, yet shall their victory be fruitless; for the free men that hold unfree lands shall they not bring under the collar again, and villeinage shall slip from their hands, till there be, and not long after ye are dead, but few unfree men in England; so that your lives and your deaths both shall bear fruit."

"Said I not," quoth John Ball, "that thou wert a sending from other times? Good is thy message, for the land shall be free. Tell on now."

He spoke eagerly, and I went on somewhat sadly: "The times shall better, though the king and lords shall worsen, the Gilds of Craft shall wax and become mightier; more recourse shall there be of foreign merchants. There shall be plenty in the land and not famine. Where a man now earneth two pennies he shall earn thrce."

"Yea," said he, "then shall those that labour become strong and stronger, and so soon shall it come about that all men shall work and none make to work, and so shall none be robbed, and at last shall all men labour and live and be happy, and have the goods of the earth without money and without price."

"Yea," said I, "that shall indeed come to pass, but not yet for a while, and belike a long while."

And I sat for long without speaking, and the church grew darker as the moon waned yet more.

Then I said: "Bethink thee that these men shall yet have masters over them who have at hand many a law and custom for the behoof of masters, and being masters can make yet more laws in the same behoof; and they shall suffer poor people to thrive just so long as their thriving shall profit the mastership and no longer; and so shall it be in those days I tell of; for there shall be king and lords and knights and squires still, with servants to do their bidding, and make honest men afraid; and all these will make nothing and eat much as aforetime, and the more that is made in the land the more shall they crave."

"Yea," said he, "that wot I well, that these are of the kin of the daughters of the horse-leech; but how shall they slake their greed, seeing that as thou sayest villeinage shall be gone? Belike their men shall pay them quit-rents and do them service, as freemen may, but all this according to law and not beyond it; so that though the workers shall be richer than they now be, the lords shall be no richer, and so all shall be on the road to being free and equal."

Said I, "Look you, friend; aforetime the lords, for the most part, held the land and all that was on it, and the men that were on it worked for them as their horses worked, and after they were fed and housed all was the lords'; but in the time to come the lords shall see their men thriving on the land and shall say once more, 'These men have more than they need, why have we not the surplus since we are their lords?' Moreover, in those days shall betide much chaffering for wares between man and man, and country and country; and the lords shall note that if there were less corn and less men on their lands there would be more sheep, that is to say more wool for chaffer, and that thereof they should have abundantly more than aforetime; since all the land they own, and it pays them quit-rent or service, save here and there a croft or a close of a yeoman; and all this might grow wool for them to sell to the Easterlings. Then shall England see a new thing, for whereas hitherto men have lived on the land and by it, the land shall no longer need them, but many sheep and a few shepherds shall make wool grow to be sold for money to the Easterlings, and that money shall the lords pouch: for, look you, they shall set the lawyers a-work and the strong hand moreover, and the land they shall take to themselves and their sheep; and except for these lords of land few shall be the free men that shall hold a rood of land whom the word of their lord may not turn adrift straightway."

"How mean you?" said John Ball: "shall all men be villeins again?"

"Nay," said I, "there shall be no villeins in England."

"Surely then," said he, "it shall be worse, and all men save a few shall be thralls to be bought and sold at the cross."

"Good friend," said I, "it shall not be so; all men shall be free even as ye would have it; yet, as I say, few indeed shall have so much land as they can stand upon save by buying such a grace of their masters."

"And now," said he, "I wot not what thou sayest. I know a thrall, and he is his master's every hour, and never his own; and a villein I know, and whiles he is his own and whiles his lord's; and I know a free man, and he is his own always; but how shall he be his own if he have nought whereby to make his livelihood? Or shall he be a thief and take from others? Then is he an outlaw. Wonderful is this thou tellest of a free man with nought whereby to live!"

"Yet so it shall be," said I, "and by such free men shall all wares be made."

"Nay, that cannot be; thou art talking riddles," said he; "for how shall a woodwright make a chest without the wood and the tools?"

Said I, "He must needs buy leave to labour of them that own all things except himself and such as himself."

"Yea, but wherewith shall he buy it?" said John Ball. "What hath he except himself?"

"With himself then shall he buy it," quoth I, "with his

body and the power of labour that lieth therein; with the price of his labour shall he buy leave to labour."

"Riddles again!" said he; "how can he sell his labour for aught else but his daily bread? He must win by his labour meat and drink and clothing and housing! Can he sell his labour twice over?"

"Not so," said I, "but this shall he do belike; he shall sell himself, that is the labour that is in him, to the master that suffers him to work, and that master shall give to him from out of the wares he maketh enough to keep him alive, and to beget children and nourish them till they be old enough to be sold like himself, and the residue shall the rich man keep to himself."

John Ball laughed aloud, and said: "Well, I perceive we are not yet out of the land of riddles. The man may well do what thou sayest and live, but he may not do it and live a free man."

"Thou sayest sooth," said I.

CHAPTER XI

HARD IT IS FOR THE OLD WORLD TO SEE THE NEW

HE held his peace awhile, and then he said: "But no man selleth himself and his children into thraldom uncompelled; nor is any fool so great a fool as willingly to take the name of freeman and the life of a thrall as payment for the very life of a freeman. Now would I ask thee somewhat else; and I am the readier to do so since I perceive that thou art a wondrous seer; for surely no man could of his own wit have imagined a tale of such follies as thou hast told me. Now well I wot that men having once shaken themselves clear of the burden of villeinage, as thou sayest we shall do (and I bless thee for the word), shall never bow down to this worser tyranny without sore strife in the world; and surely so sore shall it be, before our valiant sons give way, that maids and little lads shall take the sword and the spear, and in many a field men's blood and not water shall turn the grist-mills of England. But when all this is over, and the tyranny is established, because there are but few men in the land after the great war, how shall it be with you then? Will there not be many soldiers and sergeants and few workers? Surely in every parish ye shall have the constables to see that the men work; and they shall be saying every day, 'Such an one, hast thou yet sold thyself for this day or this week or this year? Go to now, and get thy bargain done, or it shall be the worse for thee.' And wheresoever work is going on there shall be constables again, and those that labour shall labour under the whip like the Hebrews in the land of Egypt. And every man that may, will steal as a dog snatches at a bone; and there again shall ye need more soldiers and more constables till the land is eaten up by them; nor shall the lords and the masters even be able to bear the burden of it; nor will their gains be so great, since that which each man may do in a day is not right great when all is said."

"Friend," said I, "from thine own valiancy and high heart thou speakest, when thou sayest that they who fall under this tyranny shall fight to the death against it. Wars indeed there shall be in the world, great and grievous, and yet few on this score; rather shall men fight as they have been fighting in France at the bidding of some lord of the manor, or some king, or at last at the bidding of some usurer and forestaller of the market. Valiant men, forsooth, shall arise in the beginning of these evil times, but though they shall die as ye shall, yet shall not their deaths be fruitful as yours shall be; because ye, forsooth, are fighting against villeinage which is waning, but they shall fight against usury which is waxing. And, moreover, I have been telling thee how it shall be when the measure of the time is full; and we, looking at these things from afar, can see them as they are indeed; but they who live at the beginning of those times and amidst them, shall not know what is doing around them; they shall indeed feel the plague and yet not know the remedy; by little and by little they shall fall from their better livelihood, and weak and helpless shall they grow, and have no might to withstand the evil of this tyranny; and then again when the times mend somewhat and they have but a little more ease, then shall it be to them like the kingdom of heaven, and they shall have no will to withstand any tyranny, but shall think themselves happy that they be pinched somewhat less. Also whereas thou sayest that there shall be for ever constables and sergeants going to and fro to drive men to work, and that they will not work save under the lash, thou art wrong and it shall not be so; for there shall ever be more workers than the masters may set to work, so that men shall strive eagerly for leave to work; and when one says, I will sell my hours at such and such a price, then another will say, and I for so much less; so that never shall the lords lack slaves willing to work, but often the slaves shall lack lords to buy them."

"Thou tellest marvels indeed," said he, "but how then? if all the churls work not, shall there not be famine and lack of wares?"

"Famine enough," said I, "yet not from lack of wares; it shall be clean contrary. What wilt thou say when I tell thee that in the latter days there shall be such traffic and such speedy travel across the seas that most wares shall be good cheap, and bread of all things the cheapest?"

Quoth he: "I should say that then there would be better livelihood for men, for in times of plenty it is well; for then men eat that which their own hands have harvested, and need not to spend of their substance in buying of others. Truly, it is well for honest men, but not so well for forestallers and regraters;[1] but who heeds what befalls such foul swine, who filch the money from people's purses, and do not one hair's turn of work to help them?"

"Yea, friend," I said, "but in those latter days all power shall be in the hands of these foul swine, and they shall be the rulers of all; therefore hearken, for I tell thee that times of plenty shall in those days be the times of famine, and all shall pray for the prices of wares to rise, so that the forestallers and regraters may thrive, and that some of their well-doing may overflow on to those on whom they live."

[1] Forestaller, one who buys up goods when they are cheap, and so raises the price for his own benefit; forestalls the due and real demand. Regrater, one who both buys and sells in the same market, or within five miles thereof; buys say a ton of cheese at 10 A.M. and sells it at 5 P.M. a penny a pound dearer without moving from his chair. The word "monopolist" will cover both species of thief.

"I am weary of thy riddles," he said. "Yet at least I hope that there may be fewer and fewer folk in the land; as may well be, if life is then so foul and wretched."

"Alas, poor man!" I said; "nor mayst thou imagine how foul and wretched it may be for many of the folk; and yet I tell thee that men shall increase and multiply, till where there is one man in the land now, there shall be twenty in those days—yea, in some places ten times twenty."

"I have but little heart to ask thee more questions," said he; "and when thou answerest, thy words are plain, but the things they tell of I may scarce understand. But tell me this: in those days will men deem that so it must be for ever, as great men even now tell us of our ills, or will they think of some remedy?"

I looked about me. There was but a glimmer of light in the church now, but what there was, was no longer the strange light of the moon, but the first coming of the kindly day.

"Yea," said John Ball, "'tis the twilight of the dawn. God and St. Christopher send us a good day!"

"John Ball," said I, "I have told thee that thy death will bring about that which thy life has striven for: thinkest thou that the thing which thou strivest for is worth the labour? or dost thou believe in the tale I have told thee of the days to come?"

He said: "I tell thee once again that I trust thee for a seer; because no man could make up such a tale as thou; the things which thou tellest are too wonderful for a minstrel, the tale too grievous. And whereas thou askest as to whether I count my labour lost, I say nay; if so be that in those latter times (and worser than ours they will be) men shall yet seek a remedy: therefore again I ask thee, is it so that they shall?"

"Yea," said I, "and their remedy shall be the same as thine, although the days be different: for if the folk be enthralled, what remedy save that they be set free? and if they have tried many roads towards freedom, and found that they led no-whither, then shall they try yet another. Yet in the days to come they shall be slothful to try it, because their masters shall be so much mightier than thine, that they shall not need to show the high hand, and until the days get to their evilest, men shall be cozened into thinking that it is of their own free will that they must needs buy leave to labour by pawning their labour that is to be. Moreover, your lords and masters seem very mighty to you, each one of them, and so they are, but they are few; and the masters of the days to come shall not each one of them seem very mighty to the men of those days, but they shall be very many, and they shall be of one intent in these matters without knowing it; like as one sees the oars of a galley when the rowers are hidden, that rise and fall as it were with one will."

"And yet," he said, "shall it not be the same with those that these men devour? shall not they also have one will?"

"Friend," I said, "they shall have the will to live, as the wretchedest thing living has: therefore shall they sell themselves that they may live, as I told thee; and their hard need shall be their lord's easy livelihood, and because of it he shall sleep without fear, since their need compelleth them not to loiter by the way to lament with friend or brother that they are pinched in their servitude, or to devise means for ending it. And yet indeed thou sayest it: they also shall have one will if they but knew it: but for a long while they shall have but a glimmer of knowledge of it: yet doubt it not that in the end they shall come to know it clearly, and then shall they bring about the remedy; and in those days shall it be seen that thou hast not wrought for nothing, because thou hast seen beforehand what the remedy should be, even as those of later days have seen it."

We both sat silent a little while. The twilight was gaining on the night, though slowly. I looked at the poppy which I still held in my hand, and bethought me of Will Green, and said.

"Lo, how the light is spreading: now must I get me back to Will Green's house as I promised."

"Go then," said he, "if thou wilt. Yet meseems before long he shall come to us; and then mayst thou sleep among the trees on the green grass till the sun is high, for the host shall not be on foot very early; and sweet it is to sleep in shadow by the sun in the full morning when one has been awake and troubled through the night-tide."

"Yet I will go now," said I; "I bid thee good-night, or rather good-morrow."

Therewith I half rose up; but as I did so the will to depart left me as though I had never had it, and I sat down again, and heard the voice of John Ball, at first as one speaking from far away, but little by little growing nearer and more familiar to me, and as if once more it were coming from the man himself whom I had got to know.

CHAPTER XII

ILL WOULD CHANGE BE AT WHILES WERE IT NOT FOR THE CHANGE BEYOND THE CHANGE

HE said: "Many strange things hast thou told me that I could not understand; yea, some my wit so failed to compass, that I cannot so much as ask thee questions concerning them; but of some matters would I ask thee, and I must hasten, for in very sooth the night is worn old and grey. Whereas thou sayest that in the days to come, when there shall be no labouring men who are not thralls after their new fashion, that their lords shall be many and very many, it seemeth to me that these same lords, if they be many, shall hardly be rich, or but very few of them, since they must verily feed and clothe and house their thralls, so that that which they take from them, since it will have to be dealt out amongst many, will not be enough to make many rich; since out of one man ye may get but one man's work; and pinch him never so sorely, still as aforesaid ye may not pinch him so sorely as not to feed him. Therefore, though the eyes of my mind may see a few lords and many slaves, yet can they not see many lords as well as many slaves; and if the slaves be many and the lords few, then some day shall the slaves make an end of that mastery by the force of their bodies. How then shall thy mastership of the latter days endure?"

"John Ball," said I, "mastership hath many shifts

K

whereby it striveth to keep itself alive in the world. And now hear a marvel: whereas thou sayest these two times that out of one man ye may get but one man's work, in days to come one man shall do the work of a hundred men—yea, of a thousand or more: and this is the shift of mastership that shall make many masters and many rich men."

John Ball laughed. "Great is my harvest of riddles to-night," said he; "for even if a man sleep not, and eat and drink while he is a-working, ye shall but make two men, or three at the most, out of him."

Said I: "Sawest thou ever a weaver at his loom?"

"Yea," said he, "many a time."

He was silent a little, and then said: "Yet I marvelled not at it; but now I marvel, because I know what thou wouldst say. Time was when the shuttle was thrust in and out of all the thousand threads of the warp, and it was long to do; but now the spring-staves go up and down as the man's feet move, and this and that leaf of the warp cometh forward and the shuttle goeth in one shot through all the thousand warps. Yea, so it is that this multiplieth a man many times. But look you, he is so multiplied already; and so hath he been, meseemeth, for many hundred years."

"Yea," said I, "but what hitherto needed the masters to multiply him more? For many hundred years the work-man was a thrall bought and sold at the cross; and for other hundreds of years he hath been a villein—that is, a working-beast and a part of the stock of the manor on which he liveth; but then thou and the like of thee shall free him, and then is mastership put to its shifts; for what should avail the mastery then, when the master no longer owneth the man by law as his chattel, nor any longer by law owneth him as stock of his land, if the master hath not that which he on whom he liveth may not lack and live withal, and cannot have without selling himself?"

He said nothing, but I saw his brow knitted and his lips pressed together as though in anger; and again I said:

"Thou hast seen the weaver at his loom: think how it should be if he sit no longer before the web and cast the shuttle and draw home the sley, but if the shed open of itself and the shuttle of itself speed through it as swift as the eye can follow, and the sley come home of itself; and

the weaver standing by and whistling *The Hunt's Up!* the
while, or looking to half-a-dozen looms and bidding them
what to do. And as with the weaver so with the potter,
and the smith, and every worker in metals, and all other
crafts, that it shall be for them looking on and tending, as
with the man that sitteth in the cart while the horse draws.
Yea, at last so shall it be even with those who are mere
husbandmen; and no longer shall the reaper fare afield in
the morning with his hook over his shoulder, and smite
and bind and smite again till the sun is down and the moon
is up; but he shall draw a thing made by men into the field
with one or two horses, and shall say the word and the
horses shall go up and down, and the thing shall reap and
gather and bind, and do the work of many men. Imagine
all this in thy mind if thou canst, at least as ye may imagine
a tale of enchantment told by a minstrel, and then tell me
what shouldst thou deem that the life of men would be
amidst all this, men such as these men of the township here,
or the men of the Canterbury gilds."

"Yea," said he; "but before I tell thee my thoughts of
thy tale of wonder, I would ask thee this: In those days
when men work so easily, surely they shall make more wares
than they can use in one country-side, or one good town,
whereas in another, where things have not gone as well,
they shall have less than they need; and even so it is with
us now, and thereof cometh scarcity and famine; and if
people may not come at each other's goods, it availeth the
whole land little that one country-side hath more than
enough while another hath less; for the goods shall abide
there in the storehouses of the rich place till they perish.
So if that be so in the days of wonder ye tell of (and I see
not how it can be otherwise), then shall men be but little
holpen by making all their wares so easily and with so little
labour."

I smiled again and said: "Yea, but it shall not be so; not
only shall men be multiplied a hundred and a thousand
fold, but the distance of one place from another shall be as
nothing; so that the wares which lie ready for market in
Durham in the evening may be in London on the morrow
morning; and the men of Wales may eat corn of Essex and
the men of Essex wear wool of Wales; so that, so far as the

flitting of goods to market goes, all the land shall be as one
parish. Nay, what say I? Not as to this land only shall it
be so, but even the Indies, and far countries of which thou
knowest not, shall be, so to say, at every man's door, and
wares which now ye account precious and dear-bought,
shall then be common things bought and sold for little price
at every huckster's stall. Say then, John, shall not those
days be merry, and plentiful of ease and contentment for
all men?"

"Brother," said he, "meseemeth some doleful mockery
lieth under these joyful tidings of thine; since thou hast
already partly told me to my sad bewilderment what the
life of man shall be in those days. Yet will I now for a little
set all that aside to consider thy strange tale as of a minstrel
from over sea, even as thou biddest me. Therefore I say,
that if men still abide men as I have known them, and
unless these folk of England change as the land changeth—
and forsooth of the men, for good and for evil, I can think
no other than I think now, or behold them other than I
have known them and loved them—I say if the men be still
men, what will happen except that there should be all plenty
in the land, and not one poor man therein, unless of his
own free will he choose to lack and be poor, as a man in
religion or such like; for there would then be such abundance of all good things, that, as greedy as the lords might
be, there would be enough to satisfy their greed and yet
leave good living for all who laboured with their hands; so
that these should labour far less than now, and they would
have time to learn knowledge, so that there should be no
learned or unlearned, for all should be learned; and they
would have time also to learn how to order the matters of
the parish and the hundred, and of the parliament of the
realm, so that the king should take no more than his own;
and to order the rule of the realm, so that all men, rich
and unrich, should have part therein; and so by undoing of
evil laws and making of good ones, that fashion would come
to an end whereof thou speakest, that rich men make laws
for their own behoof; for they should no longer be able to
do thus when all had part in making the laws; whereby it
would soon come about that there would be no men rich
and tyrannous, but all should have enough and to spare of

the increase of the earth and the work of their own hands. Yea surely, brother, if ever it cometh about that men shall be able to make things, and not men, work for their superfluities, and that the length of travel from one place to another be made of no account, and all the world be a market for all the world, then all shall live in health and wealth; and envy and grudging shall perish. For then shall we have conquered the earth and it shall be enough; and then shall the kingdom of heaven be come down to the earth in very deed. Why lookest thou so sad and sorry? what sayest thou?"

I said: "Hast thou forgotten already what I told thee, that in those latter days a man who hath nought save his own body (and such men shall be far the most of men) must needs pawn his labour for leave to labour? Can such a man be wealthy? Hast thou not called him a thrall?"

"Yea," he said; "but how could I deem that such things could be when those days should be come wherein men could make things work for them?"

"Poor man!" said I. "Learn that in those very days, when it shall be with the making of things as with the carter in the cart, that there he sitteth and shaketh the reins and the horse draweth and the cart goeth; in those days, I tell thee, many men shall be as poor and wretched always, year by year, as they are with thee when there is famine in the land; nor shall any have plenty and surety of livelihood save those that shall sit by and look on while others labour; and these, I tell thee, shall be a many, so that they shall see to the making of all laws, and in their hands shall be all power, and the labourers shall think that they cannot do without these men that live by robbing them, and shall praise them and wellnigh pray to them as ye pray to the saints, and the best worshipped man in the land shall be he who by forestalling and regrating hath gotten to him the most money."

"Yea," said he, "and shall they who see themselves robbed worship the robber? Then indeed shall men be changed from what they are now, and they shall be sluggards, dolts, and cowards beyond all the earth hath yet borne. Such are not the men I have known in my life-days, and that now I love in my death."

"Nay," I said, "but the robbery shall they not see; for

have I not told thee that they shall hold themselves to be free men? And for why? I will tell thee: but first tell me how it fares with men now; may the labouring man become a lord?"

He said: "The thing hath been seen that churls have risen from the dortoir of the monastery to the abbot's chair and the bishop's throne; yet not often; and whiles hath a bold sergeant become a wise captain, and they have made him squire and knight; and yet but very seldom. And now I suppose thou wilt tell me that the Church will open her arms wider to this poor people, and that many through her shall rise into lordship. But what availeth that? Nought were it to me if the Abbot of St. Alban's with his golden mitre sitting guarded by his knights and sergeants, or the Prior of Merton with his hawks and his hounds, had once been poor men, if they were now tyrants of poor men; nor would it better the matter if there were ten times as many Houses of Religion in the land as now are, and each with a churl's son for abbot or prior over it."

I smiled and said: "Comfort thyself; for in those days shall there be neither abbey nor priory in the land, nor monks nor friars, nor any religious." (He started as I spoke.) "But thou hast told me that hardly in these days may a poor man rise to be a lord: now I tell thee that in the days to come poor men shall be able to become lords and masters and do-nothings; and oft will it be seen that they shall do so; and it shall be even for that cause that their eyes shall be blinded to the robbing of themselves by others, because they shall hope in their souls that they may each live to rob others: and this shall be the very safeguard of all rule and law in those days."

"Now am I sorrier than thou hast yet made me," said he; "for when once this is established, how then can it be changed? Strong shall be the tyranny of the latter days. And now meseems, if thou sayest sooth, this time of the conquest of the earth shall not bring heaven down to the earth, as erst I deemed it would, but rather that it shall bring hell up on to the earth. Woe's me, brother, for thy sad and weary foretelling! And yet saidst thou that the men of those days would seek a remedy. Canst thou yet tell me, brother, what that remedy shall be, lest the sun

rise upon me made hopeless by thy tale of what is to be?
And, lo you, soon shall she rise upon the earth."

In truth the dawn was widening now, and the colours
coming into the pictures on wall and in window; and as
well as I could see through the varied glazing of these last
(and one window before me had as yet nothing but white
glass in it), the ruddy glow, which had but so little a while
quite died out in the west, was now beginning to gather in
the east—the new day was beginning. I looked at the poppy
that I still carried in my hand, and it seemed to me to have
withered and dwindled. I felt anxious to speak to my companion and tell him much, and withal I felt that I must
hasten, or for some reason or other I should be too late; so
I spoke at last loud and hurriedly:

"John Ball, be of good cheer; for once more thou knowest,
as I know, that the Fellowship of Men shall endure, however
many tribulations it may have to wear through. Look you,
a while ago was the light bright about us; but it was because
of the moon, and the night was deep notwithstanding, and
when the moonlight waned and died, and there was but
a little glimmer in place of the bright light, yet was the
world glad because all things knew that the glimmer was of
day and not of night. Lo you, an image of the times to
betide the hope of the Fellowship of Men. Yet forsooth, it
may well be that this bright day of summer which is now
dawning upon us is no image of the beginning of the day
that shall be; but rather shall that day-dawn be cold and
grey and surly; and yet by its light shall men see things as
they verily are, and no longer enchanted by the gleam of
the moon and the glamour of the dream-tide. By such grey
light shall wise men and valiant souls see the remedy, and
deal with it, a real thing that may be touched and handled,
and no glory of the heavens to be worshipped from afar off.
And what shall it be, as I told thee before, save that men
shall be determined to be free; yea, free as thou wouldst
have them, when thine hope rises the highest, and thou art
thinking not of the king's uncles, and poll-groat bailiffs, and
the villeinage of Essex, but of the end of all, when men shall
have the fruits of the earth and the fruits of their toil thereon, without money and without price. The time shall come,
John Ball, when that dream of thine that this shall one day

be, shall be a thing that men shall talk of soberly, and as a thing soon to come about, as even with thee they talk of the villeins becoming tenants paying their lord quit-rent; therefore, hast thou done well to hope it; and, if thou heedest this also, as I suppose thou heedest it little, thy name shall abide by thy hope in those days to come, and thou shalt not be forgotten."

I heard his voice come out of the twilight, scarcely seeing him, though now the light was growing fast, as he said:

"Brother, thou givest me heart again; yet since now I wot well that thou art a sending from far-off times and far-off things: tell thou, if thou mayest, to a man who is going to his death how this shall come about."

"Only this may I tell thee," said I; "to thee, when thou didst try to conceive of them, the ways of the days to come seemed follies scarce to be thought of; yet shall they come to be familiar things, and an order by which every man liveth, ill as he liveth, so that men shall deem of them, that thus it hath been since the beginning of the world, and that thus it shall be while the world endureth; and in this wise so shall they be thought of a long while; and the complaint of the poor the rich man shall heed, even as much and no more as he who lieth in pleasure under the lime-trees in the summer heedeth the murmur of his toiling bees. Yet in time shall this also grow old, and doubt shall creep in, because men shall scarce be able to live by that order, and the complaint of the poor shall be hearkened, no longer as a tale not utterly grievous, but as a threat of ruin, and a fear. Then shall these things, which to thee seem follies, and to the men between thee and me mere wisdom and the bond of stability, seem follies once again; yet, whereas men have so long lived by them, they shall cling to them yet from blindness and from fear; and those that see, and that have thus much conquered fear that they are furthering the real time that cometh and not the dream that faileth, these men shall the blind and the fearful mock and missay, and torment and murder: and great and grievous shall be the strife in those days, and many the failures of the wise, and too oft sore shall be the despair of the valiant; and back-sliding, and doubt, and contest between friends and fellows lacking time in the hubbub to understand each other, shall grieve many hearts and hinder the Host of the Fellowship: yet shall all bring about the end, till thy deeming of folly and ours shall be one, and thy hope and our hope; and then—the Day will have come."

Once more I heard the voice of John Ball: "Now, brother, I say farewell; for now verily hath the Day of the Earth come, and thou and I are lonely of each other again; thou hast been a dream to me as I to thee, and sorry and glad have we made each other, as tales of old time and the longing of times to come shall ever make men to be. I go to life and to death, and leave thee; and scarce do I know whether to wish thee some dream of the days beyond thine to tell what shall be, as thou hast told me, for I know not if that shall help or hinder thee; but since we have been kind and very friends, I will not leave thee without a wish of goodwill, so at least I wish thee what thou thyself wishest for thyself, and that is hopeful strife and blameless peace, which is to say in one word, life. Farewell, friend."

For some little time, although I had known that the daylight was growing and what was around me, I had scarce seen the things I had before noted so keenly; but now in a flash I saw all—the east crimson with sunrise through the white window on my right hand; the richly-carved stalls and gilded screen work, the pictures on the walls, the loveliness of the faultless colour of the mosaic window lights, the altar and the red light over it looking strange in the daylight, and the biers with the hidden dead men upon them that lay before the high altar. A great pain filled my heart at the sight of all that beauty, and withal I heard quick steps coming up the paved church-path to the porch, and the loud whistle of a sweet old tune therewith; then the footsteps stopped at the door; I heard the latch rattle, and knew that Will Green's hand was on the ring of it.

Then I strove to rise up, but fell back again; a white light, empty of all sights, broke upon me for a moment, and lo! behold, I was lying in my familiar bed, the south-westerly gale rattling the Venetian blinds and making their hold-fasts squeak.

I got up presently, and going to the window looked out on the winter morning; the river was before me broad between outer bank and bank, but it was nearly dead ebb, and there was a wide space of mud on each side of the hurrying stream, driven on the faster as it seemed by the push of the south-west wind. On the other side of the water the few willow-trees left us by the Thames Conservancy looked doubtfully alive against the bleak sky and the row of wretched-looking blue-slated houses, although, by the way, the latter were the backs of a sort of street of " villas " and not a slum; the road in front of the house was sooty and muddy at once, and in the air was that sense of dirty discomfort which one is never quit of in London. The morning was harsh, too, and though the wind was from the south-west it was as cold as a north wind; and yet amidst it all, I thought of the corner of the next bight of the river which I could not quite see from where I was, but over which one can see clear of houses and into Richmond Park, looking like the open country; and dirty as the river was, and harsh as was the January wind, they seemed to woo me toward the country-side, where away from the miseries of the "Great Wen" I might of my own will carry on a day-dream of the friends I had made in the dream of the night and against my will.

But as I turned away shivering and downhearted, on a sudden came the frightful noise of the "hooters," one after the other, that call the workmen to the factories, this one the after-breakfast one, more by token. So I grinned surlily, and dressed and got ready for my day's "work" as I call it, but which many a man besides John Ruskin (though not many in his position) would call "play."

A KING'S LESSON

IT is told of Matthias Corvinus, king of Hungary—the Alfred the Great of his time and people—that he once heard (once *only*?) that some (only *some*, my lad?) of his peasants were over-worked and under-fed. So he sent for his Council, and bade come thereto also some of the mayors of the good towns, and some of the lords of land and their bailiffs, and asked them of the truth thereof; and in diverse ways they all told one and the same tale, how the peasant carles were stout and well able to work and had enough and to spare of meat and drink, seeing that they were but churls; and how if they worked not at the least as hard as they did, it would be ill for them and ill for their lords; for that the more the churl hath the more he asketh; and that when he knoweth wealth, he knoweth the lack of it also, as it fared with our first parents in the Garden of God. The King sat and said but little while they spake, but he mis-doubted them that they were liars. So the Council brake up with nothing done; but the King took the matter to heart, being, as kings go, a just man, besides being more valiant than they mostly were, even in the old feudal time. So within two or three days, says the tale, he called together such lords and councillors as he deemed fittest, and bade busk them for a ride; and when they were ready he and they set out, over rough and smooth, decked out in all the glory of attire which was the wont of those days. Thus they rode till they came to some village or thorpe of the peasant folk, and through it to the vineyards where men were working on the sunny southern slopes that went up from the river: my tale does not say whether that were Theiss, or Donau, or what river. Well, I judge it was late spring or early summer, and the vines but just beginning to show their grapes; for the vintage is late in those lands, and some of the grapes are not gathered till the first frosts have touched them, whereby the wine made from them is the stronger and sweeter.

Anyhow there were the peasants, men and women, boys and young maidens, toiling and swinking; some hoeing between the vine-rows, some bearing baskets of dung up the steep slopes, some in one way, some in another, labouring for the fruit they should never eat, and the wine they should never drink. Thereto turned the King and got off his horse and began to climb up the stony ridges of the vineyard, and his lords in like manner followed him, wondering in their hearts what was toward; but to the one who was following next after him he turned about and said with a smile, "Yea, lords, this is a new game we are playing to-day, and a new knowledge will come from it." And the lord smiled, but somewhat sourly.

As for the peasants, great was their fear of those gay and golden lords. I judge that they did not know the King, since it was little likely that any one of them had seen his face; and they knew of him but as the Great Father, the mighty warrior who kept the Turk from harrying their thorpe. Though, forsooth, little matter was it to any man there whether Turk or Magyar was their over-lord, since to one master or another they had to pay the due tale of labouring days in the year, and hard was the livelihood that they earned for themselves on the days when they worked for themselves and their wives and children.

Well, belike they knew not the King; but amidst those rich lords they saw and knew their own lord, and of him they were sore afraid. But nought it availed them to flee away from those strong men and strong horses—they who had been toiling from before the rising of the sun, and now it wanted little more than an hour of noon: besides, with the King and lords was a guard of crossbowmen, who were left the other side of the vineyard wall—keen-eyed Italians of the mountains, straight shooters of the bolt. So the poor folk fled not; nay they made as if all this were none of their business, and went on with their work. For indeed each man said to himself, "If I be the one that is not slain, to-morrow I shall lack bread if I do not work my hardest to-day; and maybe I shall be headman if some of these be slain and I live."

Now comes the King amongst them and says: "Good fellows, which of you is the headman?"

Spake a man, sturdy and sunburnt, well on in years and grizzled: "I am the headman, lord."

"Give me thy hoe, then," says the King; "for now shall I order this matter myself, since these lords desire a new game, and are fain to work under me at vine-dressing. But do thou stand by me and set me right if I order them wrong: but the rest of you go play!"

The carle knew not what to think, and let the King stand with his hand stretched out, while he looked askance at his own lord and baron, who wagged his head at him grimly as one who says, "Do it, dog!"

Then the carle lets the hoe come into the King's hand; and the King falls to, and orders his lords for vine-dressing, to each his due share of the work; and whiles the carle said yea and whiles nay to his ordering. And then ye should have seen velvet cloaks cast off, and mantles of fine Flemish scarlet go to the dusty earth; as the lords and knights busked them to the work.

So they buckled to; and to most of them it seemed good game to play at vine-dressing. But one there was who, when his scarlet cloak was off, stood up in a doublet of glorious Persian web of gold and silk, such as men make not now, worth a hundred florins the Bremen ell. Unto him the King with no smile on his face gave the job of toing and froing up and down the hill with the biggest and the frailest dung-basket that there was; and thereat the silken lord screwed up a grin, that was sport to see, and all the lords laughed; and as he turned away he said, yet so that none heard him, "Do I serve this son's son of a whore that he should bid me carry dung?" For you must know that the King's father, John Hunyad, one of the great warriors of the world, the Hammer of the Turks, was not gotten in wedlock, though he were a king's son.

Well, they sped the work bravely for a while, and loud was the laughter as the hoes smote the earth and the flint stones tinkled and the cloud of dust rose up; the brocaded dung-bearer went up and down, cursing and swearing by the White God and the Black; and one would say to another, "See ye how gentle blood outgoes churls' blood, even when the gentle does the churl's work: these lazy loons smote but one stroke to our three." But the King, who worked no worse than any, laughed not at all; and meanwhile the poor folk stood by, not daring to speak a word one to the other; for they were still sore afraid, not now of being slain on the spot, but this rather was in their hearts: "These great and strong lords and knights have come to see what work a man may do without dying: if we are to have yet more days added to our year's tale of lords' labour, then are we lost without remedy." And their hearts sank within them.

So sped the work; and the sun rose yet higher in the heavens, and it was noon and more. And now there was no more laughter among those toiling lords, and the strokes of the hoe and mattock came far slower, while the dung-bearer sat down at the bottom of the hill and looked out on the river; but the King yet worked on doggedly, so for shame the other lords yet kept at it. Till at last the next man to the King let his hoe drop with a clatter, and swore a great oath. Now he was a strong black-bearded man in the prime of life, a valiant captain of that famous Black Band that had so often rent the Turkish array; and the King loved him for his sturdy valour; so he says to him, "Is aught wrong, Captain?"

"Nay, lord," says he, "ask the headman carle yonder what ails us."

"Headman," says the King, "what ails these strong knights? Have I ordered them wrongly?"

"Nay, but shirking ails them, lord," says he, "for they are weary; and no wonder, for they have been playing hard, and are of gentle blood."

"Is that so, lord," says the King, "that ye are weary already?"

Then the rest hung their heads and said nought, all save that captain of war; and he said, being a bold man and no liar: "King, I see what thou wouldst be at; thou hast brought us here to preach us a sermon from that Plato of thine; and to say sooth, so that I may swink no more, and go eat my dinner, now preach thy worst! Nay, if thou wilt be priest I will be thy deacon. Wilt thou that I ask this labouring carle a thing or two?"

"Yea," said the King. And there came, as it were, a cloud of thought over his face.

Then the captain straddled his legs and looked big,

and said to the carle: "Good fellow, how long have we been working here?"

"Two hours or thereabout, judging by the sun above us," says he.

"And how much of thy work have we done in that while?" says the captain, and winks his eye at him withal.

"Lord," says the carle, grinning a little despite himself. "be not wroth with my word. In the first half-hour ye did five-and-forty minutes' work of ours, and in the next half-hour scant a thirty minutes' work, and the third half-hour a fifteen minutes' work, and in the fourth half-hour two minutes' work." The grin now had faded from his face, but a gleam came into his eyes as he said: "And now, as I suppose, your day's work is done, and ye will go to your dinner, and eat the sweet and drink. the strong; and we shall eat a little rye-bread, and then be working here till after the sun has set and the moon has begun to cast shadows. Now for you, I wot not how ye shall sleep nor where, nor what white body ye shall hold in your arms while the night flits and the stars shine; but for us, while the stars yet shine, shall we be at it again, and bethink ye for what! I know not what game and play ye shall be devising for to-morrow as ye ride back home; but for us when we come back here to-morrow, it shall be as if there had been no yester-day and nothing done therein, and that work of that to-day shall be nought to us also, for we shall win no respite from our toil thereby, and the morrow of to-morrow will all be to begin again once more, and so on and on till no to-morrow abideth us. Therefore, if ye are thinking to lay some new tax or tale upon us, think twice of it, for we may not bear it. And all this I say with the less fear, because I perceive this man here beside me, in the black velvet jerkin and the gold chain on his neck, is the King; nor do I think he will slay me for my word since he hath so many a Turk before him and his mighty sword!"

Then said the captain: "Shall I smite the man, O King? or hath he preached thy sermon for thee?"

"Smite not, for he hath preached it," said the King. "Hearken to the carle's sermon, lords and councillors of mine! Yet when another hath spoken our thought, other thoughts are born therefrom, and now have I another sermon to preach; but I will refrain me as now. Let us down and to our dinner."

So they went, the King and his gentles, and sat down by the river under the rustle of the poplars, and they ate and drank and were merry. And the King bade bear up the broken meats to the vine-dressers, and a good draught of the archers' wine, and to the headman he gave a broad gold piece, and to each man three silver pennies. But when the poor folk had all that under their hands, it was to them as though the kingdom of heaven had come down to earth.

In the cool of the evening home rode the King and his lords. The King was distraught and silent; but at last the captain, who rode beside him, said to him: "Preach me now thine after-sermon, O King!"

"I think thou knowest it already," said the King, "else hadst thou not spoken in such wise to the carle; but tell me what is thy craft and the craft of all these, whereby ye live as the potter by making pots, and so forth?"

Said the captain: "As the potter lives by making pots, so we live by robbing the poor."

Again said the King: "And my trade?"

Said he, "Thy trade is to be a king of such thieves, yet no worser than the rest."

The King laughed.

"Bear that in mind," said he, "and then shall I tell thee my thought while yonder carle spake. 'Carle,' I thought, 'were I thou or such as thou, then would I take in my hand a sword or a spear, or were it only a hedge-stake, and bid others do the like, and forth would we go; and since we would be so many, and with nought to lose save a miserable life, we would do battle and prevail, and make an end of the craft of kings and of lords and of usurers, and there should be but one craft in the world, to wit, to work merrily for ourselves and to live merrily thereby.' "

Said the captain: "This then is thy sermon. Who will heed it if thou preach it?"

Said the King: "They who will take the mad king and put him in a king's madhouse, therefore do I forbear to preach it. Yet it *shall* be preached."

"And not heeded," said the captain, "save by those who head and hang the setters forth of new things that are good for the world. Our trade is safe for many and many a generation."

And therewith they came to the King's palace, and they ate and drank and slept and the world went on its ways.

THE STORY OF
THE UNKNOWN CHURCH

I WAS the master-mason of a church that was built more than six hundred years ago; it is now two hundred years since that church vanished from the face of the earth; it was destroyed utterly,—no fragment of it was left; not even the great pillars that bore up the tower at the cross, where the choir used to join the nave. No one knows now even where it stood, only in this very autumn-tide, if you knew the place, you would see the heaps made by the earth-covered ruins heaving the yellow corn into glorious waves, so that the place where my church used to be is as beautiful now as when it stood in all its splendour. I do not remember very much about the land where my church was; I have quite forgotten the name of it, but I know it was very beautiful, and even now, while I am thinking of it, comes a flood of old memories, and I almost seem to see it again,— that old beautiful land! only dimly do I see it in spring and summer and winter, but I see it in autumn-tide clearly now; yes, clearer, clearer, oh! so bright and glorious! yet it was beautiful too in spring, when the brown earth began to grow green: beautiful in summer, when the blue sky looked so much bluer, if you could hem a piece of it in between the new white carving; beautiful in the solemn starry nights, so solemn that it almost reached agony—the awe and joy one had in their great beauty. But of all these beautiful times, I remember the whole only of autumn-tide; the others come in bits to me; I can think only of parts of them, but all of autumn; and of all days and nights in autumn, I remember one more particularly. That autumn day the church was nearly finished, and the monks, for whom we were building the church, and the people, who lived in the town hard by, crowded round us oftentimes to watch us carving.

Now the great Church, and the buildings of the Abbey where the monks lived, were about three miles from the town, and the town stood on a hill overlooking the rich autumn country: it was girt about with great walls that had overhanging battlements, and towers at certain places all along the walls, and often we could see from the churchyard or the Abbey garden, the flash of helmets and spears, and the dim shadowy waving of banners, as the knights and lords and men-at-arms passed to an fro along the battlements; and we could see too in the town the three spires of the three churches; and the spire of the Cathedral, which was the tallest of the three, was gilt all over with gold, and always at night-time a great lamp shone from it that hung in the spire midway between the roof of the church and the cross at the top of the spire. The Abbey where we built the Church was not girt by stone walls, but by a circle of poplar trees, and whenever a wind passed over them, were it ever so little a breath, it set them all a-ripple; and when the wind was high, they bowed and swayed very low, and the wind, as it lifted the leaves, and showed their silvery white sides, or as again in the lulls of it, it let them drop, kept on changing the trees from green to white, and white to green; moreover, through the boughs and trunks of the poplars, we caught glimpses of the great golden corn sea, waving, waving, waving for leagues and leagues; and among the corn grew burning scarlet poppies, and blue corn-flowers; and the corn-flowers were so blue, that they gleamed, and seemed to burn with a steady light, as they grew beside the poppies among the gold of the wheat. Through the corn sea ran a blue river, and always green meadows and lines of tall poplars followed its windings. The old Church had been burned, and that was the reason why the monks caused me to build the new one; the buildings of the Abbey were built at the same time as the burned-down Church, more than a hundred years before I was born, and they were on the north side of the Church, and joined to it by a cloister of round arches, and in the midst of the cloister was a lawn, and in the midst of that lawn, a fountain of marble, carved round about with flowers and strange beasts; and at the edge of the lawn, near the round arches, were a great many sun-flowers that were all in blossom on that autumn day; and up many of the pillars of the cloister crept passion-flowers and roses. Then, farther from the Church, and past the cloister and its buildings, were many detached buildings, and a great garden round them, all within the circle of the poplar trees; in the garden were trellises covered over with roses, and convolvulus, and the great-leaved fiery nastur-tium; and specially all along by the poplar trees were there trellises, but on these grew nothing but deep crimson roses; the hollyhocks too were all out in blossom at that time, great spires of pink, and orange, and red, and white, with their soft, downy leaves. I said that nothing grew on the trellises by the poplars but crimson roses, but I was not quite right, for in many places the wild flowers had crept into the garden from without; lush green briony, with green-white blossoms, that grows so fast, one could almost think that we see it grow, and deadly nightshade, La bella donna, O! so beautiful; red berry, and purple, yellow-spiked flower, and deadly, cruel-looking, dark green leaf, all growing together in the glorious days of early autumn. And in the midst of the great garden was a conduit, with its sides carved with histories from the Bible, and there was on it too, as on the fountain in the cloister, much carving of flowers and strange beasts. Now the Church itself was surrounded on every side but the north by the cemetery, and there were many graves there, both of monks and of laymen, and often the friends of those, whose bodies lay there, had planted flowers about the graves of those they loved. I remember one such particularly, for at the head of it was a cross of carved wood, and at the foot of it, facing the cross, three tall sun-flowers; then in the midst of the cemetery was a cross of stone, carved on one side with the Crucifixion of our Lord Jesus Christ, and on the other with Our Lady holding the Divine Child. So that day, that I specially remember, in Autumn-tide, when the church was nearly finished, I was carving in the central porch of the west front; (for I carved all those bas-reliefs in the west front with my own hand;) beneath me my sister Margaret was carving at the flower-work, and the little quatrefoils that carry the signs of the zodiac and emblems of the months: now my sister Margaret was rather more than twenty years old at that time, and she was very beautiful, with dark brown hair and deep calm violet eyes. I had lived with her all my life, lived with her almost alone latterly, for our father and mother died when she was quite young, and I loved her very much, though I was not thinking of her just then, as she stood beneath me carving. Now the central porch was carved with a bas-relief of the Last Judgement, and it was divided into three parts by horizontal bands of deep flower-work. In the lowest divison, just over the doors, was carved The Rising of the Dead; above were angels blowing long trumpets, and Michael the Archangel weighing the souls, and the blessed led into heaven by angels, and the lost into hell by the devil; and in the topmost division was the Judge of the world.

All the figures in the porch were finished except one, and I remember when I woke that morning my exultation at the thought of my Church being so nearly finished; I remember, too, how a kind of misgiving mingled with the exultation, which, try all I could, I was unable to shake off; I thought then it was a rebuke for my pride, well, perhaps it was. The figure I had to carve was Abraham, sitting with a blossoming tree on each side of him, holding in his two hands the corners of his great robe, so that it made a mighty fold, wherein, with their hands crossed over their breasts, were the souls of the faithful, of whom he was called Father: I stood on the scaffolding for some time, while Margaret's chisel worked on bravely down below. I took mine in my hand, and stood so, listening to the noise of the masons inside, and two monks of the Abbey came and stood below me, and a knight, holding his little daughter by the hand, who every now and then looked up at him, and asked him strange questions. I did not think of these long, but began to think of Abraham, yet I could not think of him sitting there, quiet and solemn, while the Judgement-Trumpet was being blown; I rather thought of him as he looked when he chased those kings so far: riding far ahead of any of his company, with his mail-hood off his head, and lying in grim folds down his back, with the strong west wind blowing his wild black hair far out behind him, with the wind rippling the long scarlet pennon of his lance; riding there amid the rocks and the sands alone; with the last gleam of the armour

of the beaten kings disappearing behind the winding of the
pass; with his company a long, long way behind, quite out
of sight, though their trumpets sounded faintly among the
clefts of the rocks; and so I thought I saw him, till in his
fierce chase he leapt, horse and man, into a deep river,
quiet, swift, and smooth; and there was something in the
moving of the water-lilies as the breast of the horse swept
them aside, that suddenly took away the thought of
Abraham and brought a strange dream of lands I had never
seen; and the first was of a place where I was quite alone,
standing by the side of a river, and there was the sound of
singing a very long way off, but no living thing of any kind
could be seen, and the land was quite flat, quite without
hills, and quite without trees too, and the river wound very
much, making all kinds of quaint curves, and on the side
where I stood there grew nothing but long grass, but on the
other side grew, quite on to the horizon, a great sea of red
corn-poppies, only paths of white lilies wound all among
them, with here and there a great golden sun-flower. So I
looked down at the river by my feet, and saw how blue it
was, and how, as the stream went swiftly by, it swayed to
and fro the long green weeds, and I stood and looked at the
river for long, till at last I felt some one touch me on the
shoulder, and, looking round, I saw standing by me my
friend Amyot, whom I love better than any one else in the
world, but I thought in my dream that I was frightened
when I saw him, for his face had changed so, it was so
bright and almost transparent, and his eyes gleamed and
shone as I had never seen them do before. Oh! he was so
wondrously beautiful, so fearfully beautiful! and as I looked
at him the distant music swelled, and seemed to come close
up to me, and then swept by us, and fainted away, at last
died off entirely; and then I felt sick at heart, and faint,
and parched, and I stooped to drink of the water of the
river, and as soon as the water touched my lips, lo! the river
vanished, and the flat country with its poppies and lilies,
and I dreamed that I was in a boat by myself again, floating
in an almost land-locked bay of the northern sea, under a
cliff of dark basalt. I was lying on my back in the boat,
looking up at the intensely blue sky, and a long low swell
from the outer sea lifted the boat up and let it fall again

and carried it gradually nearer and nearer towards the dark cliff; and as I moved on, I saw at last, on the top of the cliff, a castle, with many towers, and on the highest tower of the castle there was a great white banner floating, with a red chevron on it, and three golden stars on the chevron; presently I saw too on one of the towers, growing in a cranny of the worn stones, a great bunch of golden and blood-red wall-flowers, and I watched the wall-flowers and banner for long; when suddenly I heard a trumpet blow from the castle, and saw a rush of armed men on to the battlements, and there was a fierce fight, till at last it was ended, and one went to the banner and pulled it down, and cast it over the cliff into the sea, and it came down in long sweeps, with the wind making little ripples in it;—slowly, slowly it came, till at last it fell over me and covered me from my feet till over my breast, and I let it stay there and looked again at the castle, and then I saw that there was an amber-coloured banner floating over the castle in place of the red chevron, and it was much larger than the other: also now, a man stood on the battlements, looking towards me; he had a tilting helmet on, with the visor down, and an amber-coloured surcoat over his armour: his right hand was ungauntleted, and he held it high above his head, and in his hand was the bunch of wall-flowers that I had seen growing on the wall; and his hand was white and small, like a woman's, for in my dream I could see even very far off things much clearer than we see real material things on the earth: presently he threw the wall-flowers over the cliff, and they fell in the boat just behind my head, and then I saw, looking down from the battlements of the castle, Amyot. He looked down towards me very sorrowfully, I thought, but, even as in the other dream, said nothing; so I thought in my dream that I wept for very pity, and for love of him, for he looked as a man just risen from a long illness, and who will carry till he dies a dull pain about with him. He was very thin, and his long black hair drooped all about his face, as he leaned over the battlements looking at me: he was quite pale, and his cheeks were hollow, but his eyes large, and soft, and sad. So I reached out my arms to him, and suddenly I was walking with him in a lovely garden, and we said nothing, for the music which I had heard at first was sounding close to us now, and there were many birds in the boughs of the trees: oh, such birds! gold and ruby, and emerald, but they sung not at all, but were quite silent, as though they too were listening to the music. Now all this time Amyot and I had been looking at each other, but just then I turned my head away from him, and as soon as I did so, the music ended with a long wail, and when I turned again Amyot was gone; then I felt even more sad and sick at heart than I had before when I was by the river, and I leaned against a tree, and put my hands before my eyes. When I looked again the garden was gone, and I knew not where I was, and presently all my dreams were gone. The chips were flying bravely from the stone under my chisel at last, and all my thoughts now were in my carving, when I heard my name, "Walter," called, and when I looked down I saw one standing below me, whom I had seen in my dreams just before—Amyot. I had no hopes of seeing him for a long time, perhaps I might never see him again, I thought, for he was away (as I thought) fighting in the holy wars, and it made me almost beside myself to see him standing close by me in the flesh. I got down from my scaffolding as soon as I could, and all thoughts else were soon drowned in the joy of having him by me; Margaret, too, how glad she must have been, for she had been betrothed to him for some time before he went to the wars, and he had been five years away; five years! and how we had thought of him through those many weary days! how often his face had come before me! his brave, honest face, the most beautiful among all the faces of men and women I have ever seen. Yes, I remember how five years ago I held his hand as we came together out of the cathedral of that great, far-off city, whose name I forget now; and then I remember the stamping of the horses' feet; I remember how his hand left mine at last, and then, some one looking back at me earnestly as they all rode on together—looking back, with his hand on the saddle behind him, while the trumpets sang in long solemn peals as they all rode on together, with the glimmer of arms and the fluttering of banners, and the clinking of the rings of the mail, that sounded like the falling of many drops of water into the deep, still waters of some pool that the rocks nearly meet over; and the gleam and flash of the

swords, and the glimmer of the lance-heads and the flutter
of the rippled banners, that streamed out from them, swept
past me, and were gone, and they seemed like a pageant in
a dream, whose meaning we know not; and those sounds
too, the trumpets, and the clink of the mail, and the thunder
of the horse-hoofs, they seemed dream-like too—and it was
all like a dream that he should leave me, for we had said
that we should always be together; but he went away, and
now he is come back again.

We were by his bed-side, Margaret and I; I stood and
leaned over him, and my hair fell sideways over my face
and touched his face: Margaret kneeled beside me, quivering in every limb, not with pain, I think, but rather shaken
by a passion of earnest prayer. After some time (I know not
how long), I looked up from his face to the window underneath which he lay; I do not know what time of the day it
was, but I know that it was a glorious autumn day, a day
soft with melting golden haze: a vine and a rose grew
together, and trailed half across the window, so that I could
not see much of the beautiful blue sky, and nothing of town
or country beyond; the vine leaves were touched with red
here and there, and three over-blown roses, light pink roses,
hung amongst them. I remember dwelling on the strange
lines the autumn had made in red on one of the gold-green
vine leaves, and watching one leaf of one of the over-blown
roses, expecting it to fall every minute; but as I gazed, and
felt disappointed that the rose leaf had not fallen yet, I felt
my pain suddenly shoot through me, and I remembered
what I had lost; and then came bitter, bitter dreams,—
dreams which had once made me happy,—dreams of the
things I had hoped would be, of the things that would never
be now; they came between the fair vine leaves and rose
blossoms, and that which lay before the window; they came
as before, perfect in colour and form, sweet sounds and
shapes. But now in every one was something unutterably
miserable; they would not go away, they put out the steady
glow of the golden haze, the sweet light of the sun through
the vine leaves, the soft leaning of the full blown roses. I
wandered in them for a long time; at last I felt a hand put
me aside gently, for I was standing at the head of—of the
bed; then some one kissed my forehead, and words were

spoken—I know not what words. The bitter dreams left
me for the bitterer reality at last; for I had found him that
morning lying dead, only the morning after I had seen him
when he had come back from his long absence—I had found
him lying dead, with his hands crossed downwards, with
his eyes closed, as though the angels had done that for him;
and now when I looked at him he still lay there, and
Margaret knelt by him with her face touching his: she was
not quivering now, her lips moved not at all as they had done
just before; and so, suddenly those words came to my mind
which she had spoken when she kissed me, and which at the
time I had only heard with my outward hearing, for she had
said, "Walter, farewell, and Christ keep you; but for me, I
must be with him, for so I promised him last night that I would
never leave him any more, and God will let me go." And verily
Margaret and Amyot did go, and left me very lonely and sad.

It was just beneath the westernmost arch of the nave,
there I carved their tomb. I was a long time carving it; I
did not think I should be so long at first, and I said, "I shall
die when I have finished carving it," thinking that would be
a very short time. But so it happened after I had carved
those two whom I loved, lying with clasped hands like husband and wife above their tomb, that I could not yet leave
carving it; and so that I might be near them I became a
monk, and used to sit in the choir and sing, thinking of the
time when we should all be together again. And as I had
time I used to go to the westernmost arch of the nave and
work at the tomb that was there under the great, sweeping
arch; and in process of time I raised a marble canopy that
reached quite up to the top of the arch, and I painted it too
as fair as I could, and carved it all about with many flowers
and histories, and in them I carved the faces of those I had
known on earth (for I was not as one on earth now, but
seemed quite away out of the world). And as I carved,
sometimes the monks and other people too would come and
gaze, and watch how the flowers grew; and sometimes too
as they gazed, they would weep for pity, knowing how all had
been. So my life passed, and I lived in that abbey for twenty
years after he died, till one morning, quite early, when they
came into the church for matins, they found me lying dead,
with my chisel in my hand, underneath the last lily of the tomb.

STORIES IN VERSE

The Wanderers : P. 284

The Pilgrims of Hope : P. 355

THE WANDERERS *forms the Prologue to* The Earthly Paradise. *The first volume of* The Earthly Paradise, *including this story, was published by F. S. Ellis in 1868.*[1] *This volume was divided into two in the large-paper edition, and has been so divided in some subsequent editions. Two further volumes appeared from the same publisher in 1870.*

[1] 676 pp. Crown 8vo. Large-paper edition, in 2 volumes, demy 8vo.

THE PILGRIMS OF HOPE *first appeared in* The Commonweal *between April 1885 and July 1886. Three sections,* The Message of the March Wind, Mother and Son, *and* The Half of Life Gone, *were reprinted at the Kelmscott Press in* Poems by the Way *in 1891.*[1] *There was an ordinary edition of* Poems by the Way *by Reeves and Turner the same year.*[2] *The* Pilgrims of Hope *was reprinted complete in a private edition by H. Buxton Forman in 1886,*[3] *and in an unauthorised American edition by T. B. Mosher, of Portland, Maine, in 1901.*[4] *The first published English edition in book form appeared in Messrs. Longmans' Pocket Library in 1915, with* Chants for Socialists *added.*[5]

[1] pp. 197. Quarto (crown 8vo. size), bound in vellum.
[2] pp. iv. + 196 Imperial 16mo. Large-paper edition, post 4to.
[3] pp. viii + 61. Square crown 8vo. Wrappers.
[4] pp. viii + 53. Paper boards.
[5] pp. viii + 81.

THE WANDERERS

ARGUMENT

Certain gentlemen and mariners of Norway, having considered
all that they had heard of the Earthly Paradise, set sail to find
it, and after many troubles and the lapse of many years came
old men to some Western land, of which they had never before
heard: there they died, when they had dwelt there certain years,
much honoured of the strange people.

Forget six counties overhung with smoke,
Forget the snorting steam and piston stroke,
Forget the spreading of the hideous town;
Think rather of the pack-horse on the down,
And dream of London, small, and white, and clean,
The clear Thames bordered by its gardens green;
Think, that below bridge the green lapping waves
Smite some few keels that bear Levantine staves,
Cut from the yew wood on the burnt-up hill,
And pointed jars that Greek hands toiled to fill,
And treasured scanty spice from some far sea,
Florence gold cloth, and Ypres napery,
And cloth of Bruges, and hogsheads of Guienne;
While nigh the thronged wharf Geoffrey Chaucer's
        pen
Moves over bills of lading—mid such times
Shall dwell the hollow puppets of my rhymes.

A nameless city in a distant sea,
White as the changing walls of faërie,
Thronged with much people clad in ancient guise
I now am fain to set before your eyes;
There, leave the clear green water and the quays,
And pass betwixt its marble palaces,
Until ye come unto the chiefest square;
A bubbling conduit is set midmost there,
And round about it now the maidens throng,

With jest and laughter, and sweet broken song,
Making but light of labour new begun
While in their vessels gleams the morning sun.
　On one side of the square a temple stands
Wherein the gods worshipped in ancient lands
Still have their altars; a great market-place
Upon two other sides fills all the space,
And thence the busy hum of men comes forth;
But on the cold side looking toward the north
A pillared council-house may you behold,
Within whose porch are images of gold,
Gods of the nations who dwelt anciently
About the borders of the Grecian sea.

　Pass now between them, push the brazen door,
And standing on the polished marble floor
Leave all the noises of the square behind;
Most calm that reverent chamber shall ye find,
Silent at first, but for the noise you made
When on the brazen door your hand you laid
To shut it after you—but now behold
The city rulers on their thrones of gold,
Clad in most fair attire, and in their hands
Long carven silver-banded ebony wands;
Then from the daïs drop your eyes and see
Soldiers and peasants standing reverently
Before those elders, round a little band
Who bear such arms as guard the English land,
But battered, rent, and rusted sore, and they,
The men themselves, are shrivelled, bent, and grey;
And as they lean with pain upon their spears
Their brows seem furrowed deep with more than years;
For sorrow dulls their heavy sunken eyes;
Bent are they less with time than miseries.

　Pondering on them the city grey-beards gaze
Through kindly eyes, midst thoughts of other days,
And pity for poor souls, and vague regret
For all the things that might have happened yet,
Until, their wonder gathering to a head,
The wisest man, who long that land has led,

Breaks the deep silence, unto whom again
A wanderer answers. Slowly as in pain,
And with a hollow voice as from a tomb
At first he tells the story of his doom,
But as it grows and once more hopes and fears,
Both measureless, are ringing round his ears,
His eyes grow bright, his seeming days decrease,
For grief once told brings somewhat back of peace.

THE ELDER OF THE CITY:

From what unheard-of world, in what strange keel,
Have ye come hither to our commonweal?
No barbarous folk, as these our peasants say,
But learned in memories of a long-past day,
Speaking, some few at least, the ancient tongue
That through the lapse of ages still has clung
To us, the seed of the Ionian race.
Speak out and fear not; if ye need a place
Wherein to pass the end of life away,
That shall ye gain from us from this same day,
Unless the enemies of God ye are;
We fear not you and yours to bear us war,
And scarce can think that ye will try again
Across the perils of the shifting plain
To seek your own land, whereso that may be:
For folk of ours bearing the memory
Of our old land, in days past oft have striven
To reach it, unto none of whom was given
To come again and tell us of the tale,
Therefore our ships are now content to sail,
About these happy islands that we know.

THE WANDERER:

Masters, I have to tell a tale of woe,
A tale of folly and of wasted life,
Hope against hope, the bitter dregs of strife,
Ending, where all things end, in death at last:
So if I tell the story of the past,
Let it be worth some little rest, I pray,
A little slumber ere the end of day.

No wonder if the Grecian tongue I know,
Since at Byzantium many a year ago
My father bore the twibil valiantly;
There did he marry, and get me, and die,
And I went back to Norway to my kin,
Long ere this beard ye see did first begin
To shade my mouth, but nathless not before
Among the Greeks I gathered some small lore,
And standing midst the Væring warriors heard
From this or that man many a wondrous word;
For ye shall know that though we worshipped God,
And heard mass duly, still of Swithiod
The Greater, Odin and his house of gold,
The noble stories ceased not to be told ;
These moved me more than words of mine can say
E'en while at Micklegarth my folk did stay;
But when I reached one dying autumn-tide
My uncle's dwelling near the forest side,
And saw the land so scanty and so bare,
And all the hard things men contend with there,
A little and unworthy land it seemed,
And all the more of Asgard's days I dreamed,
And worthier seemed the ancient faith of praise.

But now, but now—when one of all those days
Like Lazarus' finger on my heart should be
Breaking the fiery fixed eternity,
But for one moment—could I see once more
The grey-roofed sea-port sloping towards the shore
Or note the brown boats standing in from sea,
Or the great dromond swinging from the quay,
Or in the beech-woods watch the screaming jay
Shoot up betwixt the tall trunks, smooth and grey.
Yea, could I see the days before distress
When very longing was but happiness!

Within our house there was a Breton squire
Well learned, who fail'd not to blow up the fire
That evermore unholpen burned in me
Strange lands and things beyond belief to see;
Much lore of many lands this Breton knew;

And for one tale I told, he told me two.
He, counting Asgard but a new-told thing,
Yet spoke of gardens ever blossoming
Across the western sea where none grew old,
E'en as the books at Micklegarth had told,
And said moreover that an English knight
Had had the Earthly Paradise in sight,
And heard the songs of those that dwelt therein,
But entered not, being hindered by his sin.
Shortly, so much of this and that he said
That in my heart the sharp barb enteréd,
And like real life would empty stories seem,
And life from day to day an empty dream.

Another man there was, a Swabian priest,
Who knew the maladies of man and beast,
And what things helped them; he the stone still sought
Whereby base metal into gold is brought,
And strove to gain the precious draught, whereby
Men live midst mortal men, yet never die;
Tales of the Kaiser Redbeard could he tell
Who neither went to Heaven nor yet to Hell,
When from that fight upon the Asian plain
He vanished, but still lives to come again
Men know not how or when; but I listening
Unto this tale thought it a certain thing
That in some hidden vale of Swithiod
Across the golden pavement still he trod.

But while our longing for such things so grew,
And ever more and more we deemed them true,
Upon the land a pestilence there fell
Unheard of yet in any chronicle,
And, as the people died full fast of it,
With these two men it chanced me once to sit,
This learned squire whose name was Nicholas,
And Swabian Laurence, as our manner was;
For, could we help it, scarcely did we part
From dawn to dusk: so heavy, sad at heart,

We from the castle-yard beheld the bay
Upon that ne'er-to-be-forgotten day,
Little we said amidst that dreary mood,
And certes nought that we could say was good.

It was a bright September afternoon,
The parched-up beech-trees would be yellowing soon;
The yellow flowers grown deeper with the sun
Were letting fall their petals one by one;
No wind there was, a haze was gathering o'er
The furthest bound of the faint yellow shore;
And in the oily waters of the bay
Scarce moving aught some fisher-cobbles lay,
And all seemed peace; and had been peace indeed
But that we young men of our life had need,
And to our listening ears a sound was borne
That made the sunlight wretched and forlorn—
The heavy tolling of the minster bell;
And nigher yet a tinkling sound did tell
That through the streets they bore our Saviour Christ
By dying lips in anguish to be kissed.

At last spoke Nicholas, "How long shall we
Abide here, looking forth into the sea
Expecting when our turn shall come to die?
Fair fellows, will ye come with me and try
Now at our worst that long-desired quest,
Now—when our worst is death, and life our best?"
"Nay, but thou know'st," I said, "that I but wait
The coming of some man, the turn of fate,
To make this voyage—but I die meanwhile,
For I am poor, though my blood be not vile,
Nor yet for all his lore doth Laurence hold
Within his crucibles aught like to gold;
And what hast thou, whose father driven forth
By Charles of Blois, found shelter in the North?
But little riches as I needs must deem."
"Well," said he, "things are better than they seem,
For 'neath my bed an iron chest I have
That holdeth things I have made shift to save
E'en for this end; moreover, hark to this.

L

In the next firth a fair long-ship there is
Well victualled, ready even now for sea,
And I may say it 'longeth unto me;
Since Marcus Erling, late its owner, lies
Dead at the end of many miseries,
And little Kirstin, as thou well mayst know,
Would be content throughout the world to go
If I but took her hand, and now still more
Hath heart to leave this poor death-stricken shore.
Therefore my gold shall buy us Bordeaux swords
And Bordeaux wine as we go oceanwards.
    "What say ye, will ye go with me to-night,
Setting your faces to undreamed delight,
Turning your backs unto this troublous hell,
Or is the time too short to say farewell?"

    "Not so," I said, "rather would I depart
Now while thou speakest; never has my heart
Been set on anything within this land."
    Then said the Swabian, "Let us now take hand
And swear to follow evermore this quest
Till death or life have set our hearts at rest."
    So with joined hands we swore, and Nicholas said.
"To-night, fair friends, be ye apparelléd
To leave this land, bring all the arms ye can
And such men as ye trust; my own good man
Guards the small postern looking towards St. Bride,
And good it were ye should not be espied,
Since mayhap freely ye should not go hence,
Thou Rolf in special; for this pestilence
Makes all men hard and cruel, nor are they
Willing that folk should 'scape if they must stay:
Be wise; I bid you for a while farewell,
Leave ye this stronghold when St. Peter's bell
Strikes midnight, all will surely then be still,
And I will bide you at King Tryggvi's hill
Outside the city gates."
                              Each went his way
Therewith, and I the remnant of that day
Gained for the quest three men that I deemed true,
And did such other things as I must do,

And still was ever listening for the chime,
Half maddened by the lazy lapse of time;
Yea, scarce I thought indeed that I should live
Till the great tower the joyful sound should give
That set us free. And so the hours went past,
Till startled by the echoing clang at last
That told of midnight, armed from head to heel
Down to the open postern did I steal,
Bearing small wealth—this sword that yet hangs here
Worn thin and narrow with so many a year,
My father's axe that from Byzantium,
With some few gems my pouch yet held, had come,
Nought else that shone with silver or with gold.

But by the postern gate could I behold
Laurence the priest all armed as if for war,
And my three men were standing not right far
From off the town-wall, having some small store
Of arms and furs and raiment: then once more
I turned, and saw the autumn moonlight fall
Upon the new-built bastions of the wall,
Strange with black shadow and grey flood of light,
And further off I saw the lead shine bright
On tower and turret-roof against the sky,
And looking down I saw the old town lie
Black in the shade of the o'er-hanging hill,
Stricken with death, and dreary, but all still
Until it reached the water of the bay,
That in the dead night smote against the quay
Not all unheard, though there was little wind.
But as I turned to leave the place behind,
The wind's light sound, the slowly falling swell,
Were hushed at once by that shrill-tinkling bell,
That in that stillness jarring on mine ears,
With sudden jangle checked the rising tears,
And now the freshness of the open sea
Seemed ease and joy and very life to me.

So greeting my new mates with little sound,
We made good haste to reach King Tryggvi's mound,
And there the Breton Nicholas beheld,
Who by the hand fair Kirstin Erling held,
And round about them twenty men there stood,

Of whom the more part on the holy rood
Were sworn till death to follow up the quest,
And Kirstin was the mistress of the rest.

Again betwixt us was there little speech,
But swiftly did we set on toward the beach,
And coming there our keel, the Fighting Man,
We boarded, and the long oars out we ran,
And swept from out the firth, and sped so well
That scarcely could we hear St. Peter's bell
Toll one, although the light wind blew from land;
Then hoisting sail southward we 'gan to stand,
And much I joyed beneath the moon to see
The lessening land that might have been to me
A kindly giver of wife, child, and friend,
And happy life, or at the worser end
A quiet grave till doomsday rend the earth.

Night passed, day dawned, and we grew full of mirth
As with the ever-rising morning wind
Still further lay our threatened death behind,
Or so we thought: some eighty men we were,
Of whom but fifty knew the shipman's gear,
The rest were uplanders; midst such of these
As knew not of our quest, with promises
Went Nicholas dealing florins round about,
With still a fresh tale for each new man's doubt,
Till all were fairly won or seemed to be
To that strange desperate voyage o'er the sea.

Now if ye ask me from what land I come
With all my folly,—Wick was once my home,
Where Tryggvi Olaf's son and Olaf's sire
Lit to the ancient Gods the sacred fire,
Unto whose line am I myself akin,
Through him who Astrid in old time did win,
King Olaf's widow: let all that go by,
Since I was born at least to misery.

Now Nicholas came to Laurence and to me
To talk of what he deemed our course should be,
To whom agape I listened, since I knew
Nought but old tales, nor aught of false and true
Midst these, for all of one kind seemed to be
The Vineland voyage o'er the unknown sea
And Swegdir's search for Godhome, when he found
The entrance to a new world underground;
But Nicholas o'er many books had pored
And this and that thing in his mind had stored,
And idle tales from true report he knew.
—Would he were living now, to tell to you
This story that my feeble lips must tell!
    Now he indeed of Vineland knew full well,
Both from my tales where truth perchance touched lies,
And from the ancient written histories;
But now he said, "The land was good enow
That Leif the son of Eric came unto,
But this was not our world, nay scarce could be
The door into a place so heavenly
As that we seek, therefore my rede is this,
That we to gain that sure abode of bliss
Risk dying in an unknown landless sea;
Although full certainly it seems to me
All that we long for there we needs must find.

    "Therefore, O friends, if ye are of my mind,
When we are passed the French and English strait
Let us seek news of that desired gate
To immortality and blessed rest
Within the landless waters of the west,
But still a little to the southward steer.
Certes no Greenland winter waits us there,
No year-long night, but rather we shall find
Spice-trees set waving by the western wind,
And gentle folk who know no guile at least,
And many a bright-winged bird and soft-skinned beast,
For gently must the year upon them fall.
    "Now since the Fighting Man is over small
To hold the mighty stores that we shall need,
To turn as now to Bremen is my rede,

And there to buy a new keel with my gold,
And fill her with such things as she may hold;
And thou henceforward, Rolf, her lord shalt be,
Since thou art not unskilled upon the sea."

But unto me most fair his saying seemed,
For a land unknown to all I dreamed,
And certainly by some warm sea I thought
That we the soonest thereto should be brought.
Therefore with mirth enow passed every day
Till in the Weser stream at last we lay
Hearkening the bells of Bremen ring to mass,
For on a Sunday morn our coming was.
There in a while to chaffer did we fall,
And of the merchants bought a dromond tall
They called the Rose-Garland, and her we stored
With such-like victuals as we well might hoard,
And arms and raiment; also there we gained
Some few men more by stories true and feigned,
And by that time, now needing nought at all,
We weighed, well armed, with good hope not to fall
Into the hands of rovers of the sea,
Since at that time had we heard certainly
Edward of England drew all men to him,
And that his fleet held whatso keel could swim
From Jutland to Land's End; for all that, we
Thought it but wise to keep the open sea
And give to warring lands a full wide berth;
Since unto all of us our lives seemed worth
A better purchase than they erst had been.

So it befell that we no sail had seen
Till the sixth day at morn, when we drew near
The land at last and saw the French coast clear,—
The high land over Guines our pilot said.
There at the day-break, we, apparelléd
Like merchant ships in seeming, now perforce
Must meet a navy drawing thwart our course,
Whose sails and painted hulls not far away
Rolled slowly o'er the leaden sea and grey,
Beneath the night-clouds by no sun yet cleared;
But we with anxious hearts this navy neared,

For we sailed deep and heavy, and to fly
Would nought avail since we were drawn so nigh,
And fighting, must we meet but certain death.

Soon with amazement did I hold my breath
As from the wide bows of the Rose-Garland,
I saw the sun, new risen o'er the land,
Light up the shield-hung side of keel on keel,
Their sails like knights' coats, and the points of steel
Glittering from waist and castle and high top.
And well indeed awhile my heart might stop
As heading all the crowded van I saw,
Huge, swelling out without a crease or flaw,
A sail where, on the quartered blue and red,
In silk and gold right well aparelléd,
The lilies gleamed, the thin gaunt leopards glared
Out toward the land where even now there flared
The dying beacons. Ah, with such an one
Could I from town to town of France have run
To end my life upon some glorious day
Where stand the banners brighter than the May
Above the deeds of men, as certainly
This king himself has full oft wished to die.

And who knows now beneath what field he lies,
Amidst what mighty bones of enemies?
Ah, surely it had been a glorious thing
From such a field to lead forth such a king,
That he might live again with happy days,
And more than ever win the people's praise,
Nor had it been an evil lot to stand
On the worse side, with people of the land
'Gainst such a man, when even this might fall,
That it might be my luck some day to call
My battle-cry o'er his low-lying head,
And I be evermore rememberéd.

Well as we neared and neared, such thoughts I had
Whereby perchance I was the less a-drad
Of what might come, and at the worst we deemed
They would not scorn our swords; but as I dreamed
Of fair towns won and desperate feats of war,
And my old follies now were driven afar
By that most glorious sight, a loud halloo

Came down the wind, and one by me who knew
The English tongue cried that they bade us run
Close up and board, nor was there any one
Who durst say nay to that, so presently
Both keels were underneath the big ship's lee;
While Nicholas and I together passed
Betwixt the crowd of archers by the mast
Unto the poop, where, 'neath his canopy
The king sat, eyeing us as we drew nigh.

Broad-browed he was, hook-nosed, with wide grey eyes
No longer eager for the coming prize,
But keen and steadfast, many an ageing line,
Half hidden by his sweeping beard and fine,
Ploughed his thin cheeks, his hair was more than grey,
And like to one he seemed whose better day
Is over to himself, though foolish fame
Shouts louder year by year his empty name.
Unarmed he was, nor clad upon that morn
Much like a king, an ivory hunting-horn
Was slung about him, rich with gems and gold,
And a great white ger-falcon did he hold
Upon his fist; before his feet there sat
A scrivener making notes of this or that
As the king bade him, and behind his chair
His captains stood in armour rich and fair;
And by his side unhelmed, but armed, stood one
I deemed none other than the prince his son;
For in a coat of England was he clad,
And on his head a coronel he had.
Tall was he, slim, made apt for feats of war;
A splendid lord, yea, he seemed prouder far
Than was his sire, yet his eyes therewithal
With languid careless glance seemed wont to fall
On things about, as though he deemed that nought
Could fail unbidden to do all his thought.
But close by him stood a war-beaten knight,
Whose coat of war bore on a field of white
A sharp red pile, and he of all men there
Methought would be the one that I should fear
If I led men.

                    But midst my thoughts I heard
The king's voice as the high-seat now we neared,
And knew his speech, because in French it was,
That erewhile I had learnt of Nicholas.
"Fair sirs, what are ye? for on this one day,
I rule the narrow seas mine ancient way.
Me seemeth in the highest bark I know
The Flemish handiwork, but yet ye show
Unlike to merchants, though your ships are deep
And slowly through the water do ye creep;
And thou, fair sir, seem'st journeying from the north
With peltries Bordeaux-ward? Nay then go forth,
Thou wilt not harm us; yet if ye be men
Well-born and warlike, these are fair days, when
The good heart wins more than the merchant keeps,
And safest still in steel the young head sleeps;
And here are banners thou mayest stand beneath
And not be shamed either in life or death—
What, man, thou reddenest, wouldst thou say me no,
If underneath my banner thou shouldst go?
Nay, thou mayst speak, or let thy fellow say
What he is stuffed with, be it yea or nay."
    For as he spoke my fellow gazed on me
With something like to fear, and hurriedly
As I bent forward, thrust me on one side,
And scarce the king's last word would he abide
But 'gan to say, "Sire, from the north we come,
Though as for me far nigher is my home.
Thy foes, my Lord, drove out my kin and me,
Ere yet thine armed hand was upon the sea;
Chandos shall surely know my father's name,
Loys of Dinan, which ill-luck, sword, and flame,
Lord Charles of Blois, the French king, and the pest
In this and that land now have laid to rest,
Except for me alone. And now, my Lord,
If I shall seem to speak an idle word
To such as thou art, pardon me therefore;
But we, part taught by ancient books and lore,
And part by what, nor yet so long ago,
This man's own countrymen have come to do,
Have gathered hope to find across the sea

A land where we shall gain felicity
Past tongue of man to tell of; and our life
Is not so sweet here, or so free from strife,
Or glorious deeds so common, that, if we
Should think a certain path at last to see
To such a place, men then could think us wise
To turn away therefrom, and shut our eyes,
Because at many a turning here and there
Swift death might lurk, or unaccustomed fear.
O King, I pray thee in this young man's face
Flash not thy banner, nor with thy frank grace
Tear him from life; but go thy way, let us
Find hidden death, or life more glorious
Than thou durst think of, knowing not the gate
Whereby to flee from that all-shadowing fate.

"O King, since I could walk a yard or twain,
Or utter anything but cries of pain,
Death was before me; yea, on the first morn
That I remember aught, among the corn
I wandered with my nurse, behind us lay
The walls of Vannes, white in the summer day,
The reapers whistled, the brown maidens sung,
As on the wain the topmost sheaf they hung,
The swallow wheeled above high up in air,
And midst the labour all was sweet and fair;
When on the winding road between the fields
I saw a glittering line of spears and shields,
And pleased therewith called out to some one by
E'en as I could; he scarce for fear could cry
'The French, the French!' and turned and ran his best
Toward the town gates, and we ran with the rest,
I wailing loud who knew not why at all;
But ere we reached the gates my nurse did fall,
I with her, and I wondered much that she
Just as she fell should still lie quietly;
Nor did the coloured feathers that I found
Stuck in her side, as frightened I crawled round,
Tell me the tale, though I was sore afeard
At all the cries and wailing that I heard.

"I say, my Lord, that arrow-flight now seems
The first thing rising clear from feeble dreams,

And that was death; and the next thing was death,
For through our house all spoke with bated breath
And wore black clothes; withal they came to me
A little child, and did off hastily
My shoon and hosen, and with that I heard
The sound of doleful singing, and afeard
Forbore to question, when I saw the feet
Of all were bare, like mine, as toward the street
We passed, and joined a crowd in such-like guise
Who through the town sang woeful litanies,
Pressing the stones with feet unused and soft,
And bearing images of saints aloft,
In hope 'gainst hope to save us from the rage
Of that fell pest, that as an unseen cage
Hemmed France about, and me and such as me
They made partakers of their misery.
    "Lo death again, and if the time served now
Full many another picture could I show
Of death and death, and men who ever strive
Through every misery at least to live.
The priest within the minster preaches it,
And brooding o'er it doth the wise man sit
Letting life's joys go by. Well, blame me then,
If I who love this changing life of men,
And every minute of whose life were bliss
Too great to long for greater, but for this—
Mock me, who take this death-bound life in hand
And risk the rag to find a happy land,
Where at the worst death is so far away
No man need think of him from day to day—
Mock me, but let us go, for I am fain
Our restless road, the landless sea, to gain."

His words nigh made me weep, but while he spoke
I noted how a mocking smile just broke
The thin line of the Prince's lips, and he
Who carried the afore-named armoury
Puffed out his wind-beat cheeks and whistled low:
But the king smiled, and said, "Can it be so?
I know not, and ye twain are such as find
The things whereto old kings must needs be blind.

For you the world is wide—but not for me,
Who once had dreams of one great victory
Wherein that world lay vanquished by my throne,
And now, the victor in so many an one,
Find that in Asia Alexander died
And will not live again; the world is wide
For you I say,—for me a narrow space
Betwixt the four walls of a fighting place.

"Poor man, why should I stay thee? live thy fill
Of that fair life, wherein thou seest no ill
But fear of that fair rest I hope to win
One day, when I have purged me of my sin.

"Farewell, it yet may hap that I a king
Shall be remembered but by this one thing,
That on the morn before ye crossed the sea
Ye gave and took in common talk with me;
But with this ring keep memory of the morn,
O Breton, and thou Northman, by this horn
Remember me, who am of Odin's blood,
As heralds say: moreover it were good
Ye had some lines of writing 'neath my seal,
Or ye might find it somewhat hard to deal
With some of mine, who pass not for a word
Whate'er they deem may hold a hostile sword."

So as we kneeled this royal man to thank,
A clerk brought forth two passes sealed and blank,
And when we had them, with the horn and ring,
With few words did we leave the noble King,
And as adown the gangway steps we passed,
We saw the yards swing creaking round the mast,
And heard the shipman's ho, for one by one
The van outsailed before, by him had run
E'en as he stayed for us, and now indeed
Of his main battle must he take good heed:
But as from off the mighty side we pushed,
And in between us the green water rushed,
I heard his scalds strike up triumphantly
Some song that told not of the weary sea,
But rather of the mead and fair green-wood,
And as we leaned o'er to the wind, I stood

And saw the bright sails leave us, and soon lost
The pensive music by the strong wind tossed
From wave to wave; then turning I espied
Glittering and white upon the weather side
The land he came from, o'er the bright green sea,
Scarce duller than the land upon our lea;
For now the clouds had fled before the sun
And the bright autumn day was well begun.
Then I cried out for music too, and heard
The minstrels sing some well-remembered word,
And while they sung, before me still I gazed,
Silent with thought of many things, and mazed
With many longings; when I looked again
To see those lands, nought but the restless plain
With some far-off small fisher-boat was left.
A little hour for evermore had reft
The sight of Europe from my helpless eyes,
And crowned my store of hapless memories.

THE ELDER OF THE CITY:

Sit, friends, and tell your tale which seems to us
Shall be a strange tale and a piteous,
Nor shall it lack our pity for its woe,
Nor ye due thanks for all the things ye show
Of kingdoms nigh forgot that once were great,
And small lands come to glorious estate.
But, sirs, ye faint: behold these maidens stand
Bearing the blood of this our sunburnt land
In well-wrought cups,—drink now of this, that while
Ye poor folk wandered, hid from fortune's smile
Abode your coming, hidden none the less
Below the earth from summer's happiness.

THE WANDERERS:

Fair sirs, we thank you, hoping we have come
Through many wanderings to a quiet home
Befitting dying men—Good health and peace
To you and to this land, and fair increase
Of everything that ye can wish to have!

But to my tale: A fair south-east wind drave
Our ships for ten days more, and ever we
Sailed mile for mile together steadily,
But the tenth day I saw the Fighting Man
Brought up to wait me, and when nigh I ran
Her captain hailed me, saying that he thought
That we too far to northward had been brought,
And we must do our southing while we could;
So, as his will to me was ever good
In such-like things, we changed our course straight-
    way,
And as we might till the eleventh day
Stretched somewhat south; then baffling grew the
    wind,
But as we still were ignorant and blind
Nor knew our port, we sailed on helplessly
O'er a smooth sea, beneath a lovely sky,
And westward ever, but no signs of land
All through these days we saw on either hand,
Nor indeed hoped to see, because we knew
Some watery desert we must journey through,
That had been huge enough to keep all men
From gaining that we sought for until then.

Yet when I grew downcast, I did not fail
To call to mind, how from our land set sail
A certain man, and, after he had passed
Through many unknown seas, did reach at last
A rocky island's shore one foggy day,
And while a little off the land he lay
As in a dream he heard the folk call out
In his own tongue, but mazed and all in doubt
He turned therefrom, and afterwards in strife
With winds and waters, much of precious life
He wasted utterly, for when again
He reached his port after long months of pain,
Unto Biarmeland he chanced to go,
And there the isle he left so long ago
He knew at once, where many Northmen were.
    And such a fate I could not choose but fear
For us sometimes; and sometimes when at night

Beneath the moon I watched the foam fly white
From off our bows, and thought how weak and small
Showed the Rose-Garland's mast that looked so tall
Beside the quays of Bremen; when I saw
With measured steps the watch on toward me draw,
And in the moon the helmsman's peering face,
And 'twixt the cordage strained across my place
Beheld the white sail of the Fighting Man
Lead down the pathway of the moonlight wan—
Then when the ocean seemed so measureless
The very sky itself might well be less,
When midst the changeless piping of the wind
The intertwined slow waves pressed on behind
Rolled o'er our wake and made it nought again,
Then would it seem an ill thing and a vain
To leave the hopeful world that we had known,
When all was o'er, hopeless to die alone
Within this changeless world of waters grey.

But hope would come back to me with the day,
The talk of men, the viol's quivering strings,
Would bring my heart to think of better things.
Nor were our folk down-hearted through all this;
For partly with the hope of that vague bliss
Were they made happy, partly the soft air
And idle days wherethrough we then did fare
Were joy enow to rude sea-faring folk.

But this our ease at last a tempest broke
And we must scud before it helplessly,
Fearing each moment lest some climbing sea
Should topple o'er our poop and end us there;
Nathless we 'scaped, and still the wind blew fair
For what we deemed was our right course; but when
On the third eve, we, as delivered men,
Took breath because the gale was now blown out,
And from our rolling deck we looked about
Over the ridges of the dark grey seas,
And saw the sun, setting in golden ease,
Smile out at last from out the just-cleared sky
Over the ocean's weltering misery,

Still nothing of the Fighting Man we saw,
Which last was seen when the first gusty flaw
Smote them and us; but nothing would avail
To mend the thing, so onward did we sail,
But slowly, through the moonlit night and fair,
With all sails set that we could hoist in air,
And rolling heavily at first; for still
Each wave came on a glittering rippled hill,
And lifting us aloft, showed from its height
The waste of waves, and then to lightless night
Dropped us adown, and much ado had we
To ride unspilt the wallow of the sea.

But the sun rose up in a cloudless sky,
And from the east the wind blew cheerily,
And southwest still we steered; till on a day
As nigh the mast deep in dull thoughts I lay,
I heard a shout, and turning could I see
One of the shipmen hurrying fast to me
With something in his hand, who cast adown
Close to my hand a mass of sea-weed brown
Without more words, then knew I certainly
The wrack, that oft before I had seen lie
In sandy bights of Norway, and that eve
Just as the sun the ridgy sea would leave,
Shore birds we saw, that flew so nigh, we heard
Their hoarse loud voice that seemed a heavenly word

Then all were glad, but I a fool and young
Slept not that night, but walked the deck and sung
Snatches of songs, and verily I think
I thought next morn of some fresh stream to drink.
What say I? next morn did I think to be
Set in my godless fair eternity.

Sirs, ye are old, and ye have seen perchance
Some little child for very gladness dance
Over a scarcely-noticed worthless thing,
Worth more to him than ransom of a king;
Did not a pang of more than pity take
Your heart thereat, not for the youngling's sake,
But for your own, for man that passes by,
So like to God, so like the beasts that die?

Lo, sirs, my pity for myself is such,
When like an image that my hand can touch
My old self grows unto myself grown old,
—Sirs, I forget, my story is not told.

Next morn more wrack we saw, more birds, but still
No land as yet either for good or ill,
But with the light increased the favouring breeze,
And smoothly did we mount the ridgy seas.
Then as anigh the good ship's stern I stood
Gazing adown, a piece of rough-hewn wood
On a wave's crest I saw, and loud I cried:
"Drift-wood! drift-wood!" and one from by my side,
Maddened with joy, made for the shrouds, and clomb
Up to the top to look on his new home,
For sure he thought the green earth soon to see;
But gazing thence about him, presently
He shouted out, "A sail astern, a sail!"
Freshening the hope that now had 'gun to fail
Of seeing our fellows with the earth new found;
Wherefore we shortened sail, and sweeping round
The hazy edges of the sea and sky,
Soon from the deck could see that sail draw nigh,
Half fearful lest she yet might chance to be
The floating house of some strange enemy,
Till on her sail we could at last behold
The ruddy lion with the axe of gold,
And Marcus Erling's sign set corner-wise,
The green, gold-fruited tree of Paradise.
—Ah, what a meeting as she drew anigh,
Greeted with ringing shouts and minstrelsy!
Alas, the joyful fever of that day,
When all we met still told of land that lay
Not far ahead! Yet at our joyous feast
A word of warning spoke the Swabian priest
To me and Nicholas, for, "O friends," he said,
"Right welcome is the land that lies ahead
To us who cannot turn, and in this air,
Washed by this sea, it cannot but be fair,
And good for us poor men I make no doubt;
Yet, fellows, must I warn you not to shout

Ere we have left the troublous wood behind
Wherein we wander desperate and blind:
Think what may dwell there! Call to mind the tale
We heard last winter o'er the yule-tide ale,
When that small, withered, black-eyed Genoese
Told of the island in the outer seas
He and his fellows reached upon a tide,
And how, as lying by a streamlet's side,
With ripe fruits ready unto every hand,
And lacking not for women of the land,
The devils came and slew them, all but him,
Who, how he scarce knew, made a shift to swim
Off to his ship: nor must ye, fellows, fear
Such things alone, for mayhap men dwell here
Who worship dreadful gods, and sacrifice
Poor travellers to them in such horrid wise
As I have heard of; or let this go by,
Yet we may chance to come to slavery,
Or all our strength and weapons be too poor
To conquer such beasts as the unknown shore
May breed; or set all these ill things aside,
It yet may be our lot to wander wide
Through many lands before at last we come
Unto the gates of our enduring home."

But what availed such warning unto us,
Who by this change made nigh delirious,
Spake wisdom outward from the teeth, but thought
That in a little hour we should be brought
Unto that bliss our hearts were set upon,
That more than very heaven we now had won.

Well, the next morn unto our land we came,
And even now my cheeks grow red with shame,
To think what words I said to Nicholas,
(Since on that night in the great ship I was,)
Asking him questions, as if he were God,
Or at the least in that fair land had trod,
And knew it well, and still he answered me
As some great doctor in theology
Might his poor scholar, asking him of heaven.
But unto me next morn the grace was given

To see land first, and when men certainly
That blessed sight of all sights could descry,
All hearts were melted, and with happy tears,
Born of the death of all our doubts and fears,
Yea, with loud weeping, each did each embrace
For joy that we had gained the glorious place.
Then must the minstrels sing, then must they play
Some joyous strain to welcome in the day,
But for hot tears could see nor bow nor string,
Nor for the rising sobs make shift to sing;
Yea, some of us in that first ecstasy
For joy of 'scaping death went near to die.

Then might be seen how hard is this world's lot
When such a marvel was our grief forgot,
And what a thing the world's joy is to bear,
When on our hearts the broken bonds of care
Had left such scars, no man of us could say
The burning words upon his lips that lay;
Since, trained to hide the depths of misery,
Amidst that joy no more our tongues were free.
Ah, then it was indeed when first I knew,
When all our wildest dreams seemed coming true,
And we had reached the gates of Paradise
And endless bliss, at what unmeasured price
Man sets his life, and drawing happy breath,
I shuddered at the once familiar death.

Alas, the happy day! the foolish day!
Alas, the sweet time, too soon passed away!

Well, in a while I gained the Rose-Garland,
And as toward shore we steadily did stand
With all sail set, the wind, which had been light
Since the beginning of the just past night,
Failed utterly, and the sharp ripple slept,
Then toiling hard forward our keels we swept,
Making small way, until night fell again,
And then, although of landing we were fain,
Needs must we wait; but when the sun was set
Then the cool night a light air did beget,
And 'neath the stars slowly we moved along,
And found ourselves within a current strong

At daybreak, and the land beneath our lee.
There a long line of breakers could we see,
That on a yellow sandy beach did fall,
And then a belt of grass, and then a wall
Of green trees, rising dark against the sky.
Not long we looked, but anchored presently
A furlong from the shore, and then, all armed,
Into the boats the most part of us swarmed,
And pulled with eager hands unto the beach;
But when the seething surf our prow did reach,
From off the bows I leapt into the sea
Waist deep, and, wading, was the first to be
Upon that land; then to the flowers I ran,
And cried aloud like to a drunken man
Words without meaning, whereof none took heed,
For all across the yellow beach made speed
To roll among the fair flowers and the grass.

But when our folly somewhat tempered was,
And we could talk like men, we thought it good
To try if we could pierce the thick black wood,
And see what men might dwell in that new land;
But when we entered it, on either hand
Uprose the trunks, with underwood entwined
Making one thicket, thorny, dense, and blind;
Where with our axes, labouring half the day,
We scarcely made some half a rod of way;

Therefore, we left that place and tried again,
Yea, many times, but yet was all in vain;
So to the ships we went, when we had been
A long way in our arms, nor yet had seen
A sign of man, but as for living things,
Gay birds with many-coloured crests and wings,
Conies anigh the beach, and while we hacked
Within the wood, grey serpents, yellow-backed,
And monstrous lizards; yea, and one man said
That 'midst the thorns he saw a dragon's head;
And keeping still his eyes on it he felt
For a stout shaft he had within his belt;
But just as he had got it to the string
And drawn his hand aback, the loathly thing
Vanished away, and how he could not tell.

Now spite of all, little our courage fell,
For this day's work, nay rather, all things seemed
To show that we no foolish dream had dreamed—
The pathless, fearful sea, the land that lay
So strange, so hard to find, so far away,
The lovely summer air, the while we knew
That unto winter now at home it grew,
The flowery shore, the dragon-guarded wood,
So hard to pierce—each one of these made good
The foolish hope that led us from our home,
That we to utter misery might come.

Now next morn when the tide began to flow
We weighed, and somewhat northward did we go
Coasting that land, and every now and then
We went ashore to try the woods again,
But little change we found in them, until
Inland we saw a bare and scarped white hill
Rise o'er their tops, and going further on
Unto a broad green river's mouth we won,
And entering there, ran up it with the flood,
For it was deep, although 'twixt walls of wood
Darkly enough its shaded stream did flow,
And high trees hid the hill we saw just now.
So as we peered about from side to side
A path upon the right bank we espied
Through the thick wood, and mooring hastily
Our ships unto the trunks of trees thereby,
Laurence and I with sixty men took land
With bow or cutting sword or bill in hand,
And bearing food to last till the third day;
But with the others there did Nicholas stay
To guard the ships, with whom was Kirstin still,
Who now seemed pining for old things, and ill,
Spite of the sea-breeze and the lovely air.
But as for us, we followed up with care
A winding path, looking from left to right
Lest any deadly thing should come in sight;
And certainly our path a dragon crossed
That in the thicket presently we lost;
And some men said a leopard they espied,

And further on we heard a beast that cried;
Serpents we saw, like those we erst had seen,
And many-coloured birds, and lizards green,
And apes that chattered from amidst the trees.
   So on we went until a dying breeze
We felt upon our faces, and soon grew
The forest thinner, till at last we knew
The great scarped hill, which if we now could scale,
For sight of much far country would avail;
But coming there we climbed it easily,
For though escarped and rough toward the sea,
The beaten path we followed led us round
To where a soft and grassy slope we found,
And there it forked; one arm led up the hill,
Another through the forest wound on still;
Which last we left, in good hope soon to see
Some signs of man, which happened presently;
For two-thirds up the hill we reached a space
Levelled by man's hand in the mountain's face,
And there a rude shrine stood, of unhewn stones
Both walls and roof, with a great heap of bones
Piled up outside it: there awhile we stood
In doubt, for something there made cold our blood,
Till brother Laurence, with a whispered word,
Crossed himself thrice, and drawing forth his sword
Entered alone, but therewith presently
From the inside called out aloud to me
To follow, so I trembling, yet went in
To that abode of unknown monstrous sin,
And others followed: therein could we see,
Amidst the gloom by peering steadily,
An altar of rough stones, and over it
We saw a god of yellow metal sit,
A cubit long, which Laurence with his tongue
Had touched and found pure gold; withal there hung
Against the wall men's bodies brown and dry,
Which gaudy rags of raiment wretchedly
Did wrap about, and all their heads were wreathed
With golden chaplets; and meanwhile we breathed
A heavy, faint, and sweet spice-laden air,
As though that incense late were scattered there.

But from that house of devils soon we passed
Trembling and pale, Laurence the priest, the last,
And got away in haste, nor durst we take
Those golden chaplets for their wearers' sake,
Or that grim golden devil whose they were;
Yet for the rest, although they brought us fear
They did but seem to show our heaven anigh
Because we deemed these might have come to die
In seeking it, being slain for fatal sin.

And now we set ourselves in haste to win
Up to that mountain's top, and on the way
Looked backward oft upon the land that lay
Beneath the hill, and still on every hand
The forest seemed to cover all the land,
But that some four leagues off we saw a space
Cleared of the trees, and in that open place
Houses we seemed to see, and rising smoke
That told where dwelt the unknown, unseen folk.

But when at last the utmost top we won
A dismal sight our eyes must look upon;
The mountain's summit, levelled by man's art,
Was hedged by high stones set some yard apart
All round a smooth paved space, and midst of these
We saw a group of well-wrought images,
Or so they seemed at first, who stood around
An old hoar man laid on the rocky ground
Who seemed to live as yet; now drawing near
We saw indeed what things these figures were;
Dead corpses, by some deft embalmer dried,
And on this mountain after they had died
Set up like players at a yule-tide feast;
Here stood a hunter, with a spotted beast
Most like a leopard, writhing up his spear;
Nigh the old man stood one as if drawn near
To give him drink, and on each side his head
Two damsels daintily apparelled;
And then again, nigh him who bore the cup,
Were two who 'twixt them bore a litter up
As though upon a journey he should go,
And round about stood men with spear and bow,
And painted targets as the guard to all,

Headed by one beyond man's stature tall,
Who, half turned round, as though he gave the word,
Seemed as he once had been a mighty lord.
   But the live man amid the corpses laid,
Turning from side to side, some faint word said
Now and again, but kept his eyes shut fast;
And we when from the green slope we had passed
On to this dreadful stage, awe-struck and scared,
Awhile upon the ghastly puppets stared,
Then trembling, with drawn swords, came close anigh
To where the hapless ancient man did lie,
Who at the noise we made now oped his eyes
And fixing them upon us did uprise,
And with a fearful scream stretched out his hand,
While upright on his head his hair did stand
For very terror, while we none the less
Were rooted to the ground for fearfulness,
And scarce our weapons could make shift to hold.
But as we stood and gazed, over he rolled
Like a death-stricken bull, and there he lay,
With his long-hoarded life quite past away.
   Then in our hearts did wonder conquer fear,
And to the dead men did we draw anear
And found them such-like things as I have said,
But he, their master, was apparelled
Like to those others that we saw e'en now
Hung up within the dreary house below.

   Right little courage had we there to stay,
So down the hill again we took our way,
When looking landward thence we had but seen,
All round about, the forest dull and green,
Pierced by the river where our ships we left,
And bounded by far-off blue mountains, cleft
By passes here and there; but we went by
The chapel of the gold god silently,
For doubts had risen in our hearts at last
If yet the bitterness of death were past.
   But having come again into the wood,
We there took counsel whether it were good
To turn back to the ships, or push on still

Till we had reached the place that from the hill
We had beheld, and since the last seemed best
Onward we marched, scarce staying to take rest
And eat some food, for feverish did we grow
For haste the best or worst of all to know.
  Along the path that, as I said before,
Led from the hill, we went, and laboured sore
To gain the open ere the night should fall,
But yet in vain, for like a dreary pall
Cast o'er the world, the darkness hemmed us in.
And though we struggled desperately to win
From out the forest through the very night,
Yet did that labour so abate our might,
We thought it good to rest among the trees,
Nor come on those who might be enemies
In the thick darkness, neither did we dare
To light a fire lest folk should slay us there
Mazed and defenceless; so the one half slept
As they might do, the while the others kept
Good guard in turn; and as we watched we heard
Sounds that might well have made bold men afeard
And cowards die of fear, but we, alone,
Apart from all, such desperate men were grown,
If we should fail to win our Paradise,
That common life we now might well despise.
  So by the day-break on our way we were
When we had seen to all our fighting gear;
And soon we came unto that open space,
And here and there about a grassy place
Saw houses scattered, neither great nor fair,
For they were framed of trees as they grew there,
And walled with wattle-work from tree to tree;
And thereabout beasts unknown did we see,
Four-footed, tame; and soon a man came out
From the first house, and with a startled shout
Took to his heels, and soon from far and near,
The folk swarmed out, and still as in great fear
Gave us no second look, but ran their best,
And they being clad but lightly for the rest,
To follow them seemed little mastery.
So to their houses gat we speedily

To see if we might take some loiterer;
And some few feeble folk did we find there,
Though most had fled, and unto these with pain
We made some little of our meaning plain,
And sent an old man forth into the wood
To show his fellows that our will was good.
Who going from us came back presently
His message done, and with him two or three
The boldest of his folk, and they in turn
A little of us by our signs did learn,
Then went their way: and so at last all fear
Was laid aside, and thronging they drew near
To look upon us; and at last came one
Who had upon his breast a golden sun,
And in strange glittering gay attire was clad;
He let us know our coming made him glad,
And bade us come with him; so thereon we,
Thinking him some one in authority,
Rose up and followed him, who with glad face
Led us through closer streets of that strange place,
And brought us lastly to a shapely hall
Round and high-roofed, held up with tree-trunks tall,
And midst his lords the barbarous king sat there,
Gold-crowned, in strange apparel rich and fair,
Whereat we shuddered, for we saw that he
Was clad like him that erewhile we did see
Upon the hill, and like those other ones
Hung in the dismal shrine of unhewn stones.

Yet nought of evil did he seem to think,
But bade us sit by him and eat and drink,
So eating did we speak by signs meanwhile
Each unto each, and they would laugh and smile
As folk well pleased; and with them all that day
Well feasted, learning some things did we stay.
And sure of all the folk I ever saw
These were the gentlest: if they had a law
We knew not then, but still they seemed to be
Like the gold people of antiquity.

Now when we tried to ask for that good land,
Eastward and seaward did they point the hand;
Yet if they knew what thing we meant thereby

We knew not; but when we for our reply
Said that we came thence, they made signs to say
They knew it well, and kneeling down they lay
Before our feet, as people worshipping.

But we, though somewhat troubled at this thing,
Failed not to hope, because it seemed to us
That this so simple folk and virtuous,
So happy midst their dreary forest bowers,
Showed at the least a better land than ours,
And some yet better thing far onward lay.

Amidst all this we made a shift to pray
That some of them would go with us, to be
Our fellows on the perilous green sea,
And much did they rejoice when this they knew,
And straightway midst their young men lots they drew,
And the next morn of these they gave us ten,
And wept at our departing.

Now these men,
Though brown indeed through dint of that hot sun,
Were comely and well knit, as any one
I saw in Greece, and fit for deeds of war,
Though as I said of all men gentlest far;
Their arms were axe and spear, and shield and bow,
But nought of iron did they seem to know,
For all their cutting tools were edged with flint,
Or with soft copper, that soon turned and bent;
With cloths of cotton were their bodies clad,
But other raiment for delight they had
Most fairly woven of some unknown thing;
And all of them from little child to king
Had many ornaments of beaten gold:
Certes, we might have gathered wealth untold
Amongst them, if thereto had turned our thought.
But none the glittering evil valued aught.

Now of these foresters, we learned, that they,
Hemmed by the woods, went seldom a long way
From where we saw them, and no boat they had,
Nor much of other people good or bad
They knew, and ever had they little war:
But now and then a folk would come from far
In ships unlike to ours, and for their gold

Would give them goods; and some men over bold,
Who dwelt beyond the great hill we had seen,
Had waged them war, but these all slain had been
Among the tangled woods by men who knew
What tracks of beasts the thicket might pierce through.

Such things they told us whom we brought away,
But after this; for certes on that day
Not much we gathered of their way of life.

So to the ships we came at last, and rife
With many things new learned, we told them all,
And though our courage might begin to fall
A little now, yet each to other we
Made countenance of great felicity,
And spoke as if the prize were well-nigh won.

Behold then, sirs, how fortune led us on,
Little by little till we reached the worst,
And still our lives grew more and more accurst.

THE ELDER OF THE CITY:

Nay, friends, believe your worser life now past,
And that a little bliss is reached at last;
Take heart, therefore, for like a tale so told
Is each man's life: and ye, who have been bold
To see and suffer such unheard-of things,
Henceforth shall be more worshipped than the kings
We hear you name; since then ye reach this day,
How are ye worse for what has passed away?

THE WANDERER:

Kind folk, what words of ours can give you praise
That fits your kindness; yet for those past days,
If we bemoan our lot, think this at least:
We are as men who cast aside a feast
Amidst their lowly fellows, that they may
Eat with the king, and who at end of day,
Bearing sore stripes, with great humility
Must pray the bedesmen of those men to be,
They scorned that day while yet the sun was high.

Not long within the river did we lie,
But put to sea intending as before

To coast with watchful eyes the unknown shore,
And strive to pierce the woods: three days we sailed,
And little all our watchfulness availed,
Though all that time the wind was fair enow;
But on the fourth day it began to blow
From off the land, and still increased on us
Until the storm, grown wild and furious,
Although at anchor still we strove to ride,
Had blown us out into the ocean wide,
Far out of sight of land; and when at last,
After three days, its fury was o'erpast,
Of all our counsels this one was the best,
To beat back blindly to the longed-for west.
Baffling the wind was, toilsome was the way,
Nor did we make land till the thirtieth day,
When both flesh-meat and water were nigh spent;
But anchoring at last, ashore we went,
And found the land far better than the first,
For this with no thick forest was accurst,
Though here and there were scattered clumps of wood.
The air was cooler, too, but soft and good;
Fair streams we saw, and herds of goats and deer,
But nothing noisome for a man to fear.
    So since at anchor safe our good ships lay
Within the long horns of a sandy bay,
We thought it good ashore to take our ease,
And pitched our tents anigh some maple-trees
Not far from shore, and there with little pain
Enough of venison quickly did we gain
To feast us all, and high feast did we hold,
Lighting great fires, for now the nights were cold,
And we were fain a noble roast to eat;
Nor did we lack for drink to better meat,
For from the dark hold of the Rose-Garland
A well-hooped cask our shipmen brought a-land,
That knew some white-walled city of the Rhine.
    There crowned with flowers, and flushed with noble wine,
Hearkening the distant murmur of the main,
And safe upon our promised land again,
What wonder if our vain hopes rose once more
And Heaven seemed dull beside that twice-won shore.

By midnight in our tents were we asleep,
And little watch that night did any keep,
For as our garden that fair land we deemed.
But in my sleep of lovely things I dreamed,
For I was back at Micklegarth once more,
But not a court-man's son there as of yore,
But the Greek king, or so I seemed to be,
Set on the throne whose awe and majesty
Gold lions guard; before whose moveless feet
A damsel knelt, praying in words so sweet
For what I know not now, that both mine eyes
Grew full of tears, and I must bid her rise
And sit beside me; step by step she came
Up the gold stair, setting my heart a-flame
With all her beauty, till she reached the throne
And there sat down, but as with her alone
In that vast hall, my hand her hand did seek,
And on my face I felt her balmy cheek,
Throughout my heart there shot a dreadful pang,
And down below us, with a sudden clang
The golden lions rose, and roared aloud,
And in at every door did armed men crowd,
Shouting out death and curses, and I fell
Dreaming indeed that this at last was hell.

But therewithal I woke, and through the night
Heard shrieks and shouts and clamour of the fight,
And snatching up my axe, unarmed beside
Nor scarce awaked, my rallying cry I cried,
And with good haste unto the hubbub went;
But even in the entry of the tent
Some dark mass hid the star-besprinkled sky,
And whistling past my head a spear did fly,
And striking out I saw a naked man
Fall 'neath my blow, nor heeded him, but ran
Unto the captain's tent, for there indeed
I saw my fellows stand at desperate need,
Beset with foes, nor yet armed more than I,
Though on the way I rallied hastily
Some better armed, with whom I straightway fell
Upon the foe, who with a hideous yell

Turned round upon us; but we desperate
And fresh, and dangerous for our axes' weight,
Fought so that they must needs give back a pace
And yield our fellows some small breathing space.
Then gathering all together, side by side
We laid our weapons, and our cries we cried
And rushed upon them, who abode no more
Our levelled points, but scattering from the shore
Ran here and there, but when some two or three
We in the chase had slain right easily,
We held our hands, nor followed more their flight,
Fearing the many chances of the night.

Then did we light our watch-fires up again
And armed us all, and found three good men slain;
Ten wounded, among whom was Nicholas,
Though little heedful of these things he was,
For in his tent he sat upon the ground,
Holding fair Kirstin's hand, whom he had found
Dead, with a feathered javelin in her breast.

But taking counsel now, we thought it best
To gather up our goods and get away
Unto the ships, and there to wait the day;
Nor did we loiter, fearful lest the foe,
Who somewhat now our feebleness must know,
Should come on us with force made manifold,
And all our story quickly should be told.
So to our boats in haste the others gat,
But in his tent, not speaking, Nicholas sat,
Nor moved when o'er his head we struck the tent.
But when all things were ready, then I went
And raised the body up, and silently
Bore it adown the beach unto the sea;
Then he arose and followed me, and when
He reached at last the now embarking men,
And in a boat my burden I had laid,
He sat beside; but no word had he said
Since first he knew her slain. Such ending had
The night at whose beginning all were glad.

One wounded man of theirs we brought with us,
Hoping for news, but he grew furious

When he awoke aboard from out his swoon,
And tore his wounds, and smote himself, and soon
Died outright, though his hurts were slight enow,
So nought from him of that land could we know.
But now as we that luckless country scanned,
Just at the daybreak did we see a band
Of these barbarians come with shout and yell
Across the place where all these things befell,
Down to the very edges of the sea;
But though armed now, by day, we easily
Had made a shift no few of them to slay,
It seemed to us the better course to weigh
And try another entry to that land;
So southward with a light wind did we stand,
Not losing sight of shore, and now and then
I led ashore the more part of our men
Well armed, by daylight, and the barbarous folk
Once and again from bushments on us broke,
Whom without loss of men we brushed away.
But in our turn it happed to us one day
Upon a knot of them unwares to come;
These we bore back with us, the most of whom
Would neither eat nor drink, but sullenly
Sat in a corner of the ship to die;
But 'mongst them was a woman, who at last,
Won by the glitter of some toy we cast
About her neck, by soft words and by wine,
Began to answer us by sign to sign;
Of whom we learned not much indeed, but when
We set on shore those tameless savage men,
And would have left her too, she seemed to pray,
For terror of her folk, with us to stay:
Therefore we took her back with us, and she,
Though learning not our tongue too easily,
Unto the forest-folk began to speak.

Now midst all this passed many a weary week,
And we no nigher all the time had come
Unto the portal of our blissful home,
And needs our bright hope somewhat must decay;
Yet none the less as dull day passed by day,

Still onward by our folly were we led,
And still with lies our wavering hearts we fed.

Happy we were in this, that still the wind
Blew as we wished, and still the air was kind;
Nor failed we of fresh water as we went
Along the coast, and oft our bows we bent
On beast and fowl, and had no lack of food.

Upon a day it chanced, that as we stood
Somewhat off shore to fetch about a ness,
Although the wind was blowing less and less,
We were entrapped into a fearful sea,
And carried by a current furiously
Away from shore, and there were we so tost
That for awhile we deemed ourselves but lost
Amid those tumbling waves; but now at last,
When out of sight of land we long had passed,
The sea fell, and again toward land we stood,
Which, reached upon the tenth day, seemed right good
But yet untilled, and mountains rose up high
Far inland, mingling with the cloudy sky.

Once more we took the land, and since we found
That, more than ever, beasts did there abound,
We pitched our camp beside a little stream,
But scarcely there of Paradise did dream
As heretofore. Our camp we fortified
With wall and dyke, and then the land we tried,
And found the people most untaught and wild,
Nigh void of arts, but harmless, good and mild,
Nor fearing us: with some of these we went
Back to our camp and people, with intent
To question them by her we last had got.
But when she heard their tongue she knew it not,
Nor they her tongue; howbeit they seemed to say,
That o'er the mountains other lands there lay
Where folk dwelt, clothed and armed like unto us,
But made withal as they were timorous
And feared them much. Then we made signs that we,
So little feared by all that tumbling sea,
Would go to seek them; but they still would stay
Our journey; nathless what they meant to say
We scarce knew yet: howbeit, since these men

M

Were friendly, and the weather, which till then
Had been most fair, now grew to storm and rain,
And the wind blew on land, and not in vain
To us poor fools, that tale, half understood
Those folk had told: midst all, we thought it good
To haul our ships ashore, and build us there
A place where we might dwell, till we could fare
Along the coast, or inland it might be,
That fertile realm, those goodly men to see.

Right foul the weather was a dreary space
While we abode with people of that place,
And built them huts, as well we could, for we
Who dwell in Norway have great mastery
In woodwright's craft; but they in turn would bring
Wild fruits to us, and many a woodland thing,
And catch us fish, and show us how to take
The smaller beasts, and meanwhile for our sake
They learned our tongue, and we too somewhat learned
Of words of theirs; but day by day we yearned
To cross those mountains, and I woke no morn,
To find myself lost, wretched and forlorn,
But those far-off white summits gave me heart;
Now too those folk their story could impart
Concerning them, and that in short was this:
Beyond them lay a fair abode of bliss
Where dwelt men like the Gods, and clad as we,
Who doubtless lived on through eternity
Unless the very world should come to nought;
But never had they had the impious thought
To scale those mountains; since most surely, none
Of men they knew could follow up the sun,
The fearful sun, and live; but as for us
They said, who were so wise and glorious,
It might not be so.

                            Thus they spoke one eve
When the black rain-clouds for a while did leave
Upon the fresh and teeming earth to frown,
And we they spoke to had just set us down
Midmost their village: from the resting earth
Sweet odours rose, and in their noisy mirth
The women played, as rising from the brook

Off their long locks the glittering drops they shook;
Betwixt the huts the children raced along;
Some man was singing a wild barbarous song
Anigh us, and these folk possessing nought,
And lacking nought, lived happy, free from thought,
Or so it seemed: but we, what thing could pay
For all that we had left so far away?

Such thoughts as these I uttered murmuringly,
But lifting up mine eyes, against the sky
Beheld the snowy peaks brought near to us
By a strange sunset, red and glorious,
That seemed as though the much-praised land it lit,
And would do, long hours after we must sit
Beneath the twinkling stars with none to heed:
And though I knew it was not so indeed,
Yet did it seem to answer me, as though
It called us once more on our quest to go.

Then springing up I raised my voice and said:
"What is it, fellows? fear ye to be dead
Upon those peaks, when, if ye loiter here
Half dead, with very death still drawing near,
Your lives are wasted all the more for this,
That ye in this world thought to garner bliss?
Unless indeed ye chance to think it well
With this unclad and barbarous folk to dwell,
Deedless and hopeless; ye, to whom the land
That o'er the world has sent so many a band
Of conquering men, was yet not good enough.
Did ye then deem the way would not be rough
Unto the lovely land ye so desire?
Did ye not rather swear through blood and fire,
And all ill things to follow up this quest
Till life or death your longing laid to rest?
Let us not linger here then, until fate
Make longing unavailing, hope too late,
And turn to lamentations all our prayers!
But with to-morrow cast aside your cares,
And stout of heart make ready for the strife
'Twixt this short time of dreaming and real life.

Lo now, if but the half will come with me,
The summit of those mountains will I see,

Or else die first; yea, if but twenty men
Will follow me; nor will I stay if ten
Will share my trouble or felicity—
What do I say? alone, O friends, will I
Seek for my life, for no man can die twice,
And death or life may give me Paradise!"

Then Nicholas said: "Rolf, I will go with thee,
For desperate do I think the quest to be,
And I shall die, and that to me is well,
Or else I may forget, I cannot tell—
Still I will go."

                Then Laurence said: " I too
Will go, remembering what I said to you,
When any land, the first to which we came
Seemed that we sought, and set your hearts aflame,
And all seemed won to you: but still I think,
Perchance years hence, the fount of life to drink,
Unless by some ill chance I first am slain.
But boundless risk must pay for boundless gain."

So most men said, but yet a few there were
Who said: "Nay, soothly let us live on here,
We have been fools and we must pay therefore
With this dull life, and labour very sore
Until we die; yet are we grown too wise
Upon this earth to seek for Paradise;
Leave us, but ye may yet come back again
When ye have found your trouble nought and vain."

Well, in three days we left those men behind,
To dwell among the simple folk and kind
Who were our guides at first, until that we
Reached the green hills clustered confusedly
About the mountains; then they turned, right glad
That till that time no horrors they had had;
But we still hopeful, making nought of time,
The rugged rocks now set ourselves to climb,
And lonely there for days and days and days
We stumbled through the blind and bitter ways,
Now rising to the never-melting snow,
Now beaten thence, and fain to try below
Another kingdom of that world of stone.

At last when all our means of life were gone,
And some of us had fallen in the fight
With cold and weariness, we came in sight
Of what we hungered for—what then—what then?
A savage land, a land untilled again,
No lack of food while lasted shaft or bow,
But folk the worst of all we came to know;
Scarce like to men, yea, worse than most of beasts,
For of men slain they made their impious feasts;
These, as I deem for our fresh blood athirst,
From out the thick wood often on us burst,
Not heeding death, and in confuséd fight
We spent full many a wretched day and night,
That yet were happiest of the times we knew,
For with our grief such fearful foes we grew,
That Odin's gods had hardly scared men more
As fearless through the naked press we bore.

At first indeed some prisoners did we take,
Asking them questions for our fâir land's sake,
Hoping 'gainst hope; but when in vain had been
Our questioning, and we one day had seen
Their way of banqueting, then axe and spear
Ended the wretched life and sullen fear
Of any wild man wounded in the fight.

So with the failing of our hoped delight
We grew to be like devils: then I knew
At my own cost, what each man cometh to
When every pleasure from his life is gone,
And hunger and desire of life alone,
That still beget dull rage and bestial fears,
Like gnawing serpents through the world he bears.

What time we spent there? nay, I do not know:
For happy folk no time can pass too slow
Because they die. Because at last they die
And are at rest, no time too fast can fly
For wretches: but eternity of woe
Had hemmed us in, and neither fast nor slow
Passed the dull time as we held reckoning.

Yet midst so many a wretched, hopeless thing
One hope there was, if it was still a hope,
At least, at last, to turn, and scale the cope

Of those dread mountains we had clambered o'er.
And we did turn, and with what labour sore,
What thirst, what hunger, and what wretchedness
We struggled daily, how can words express?
Yet amidst all, the kind God led us on
Until at last a high raised pass we won
And like grey clouds afar beheld the sea,
And weakened with our toil and misery
Wept at that sight, that like a friend did seem
Forgotten long, beheld but in a dream
When we know not if we be still alive.

But thence descending, we with rocks did strive,
Till dwindled, worn, at last we reached the plain
And came unto our untaught friends again,
And those we left, who yet alive and well,
Wedded to brown wives, fain would have us tell
The story of our woes, which when they heard,
The country people wondered at our word,
But not our fellows; and so all being said
A little there we gathered lustihead,
Still talking over what was best to do.
And we the leaders yet were fain to go
From sea to sea and take what God might send,
Who at the worst our hopes and griefs would end
With that same death we once had hoped to stay,
Or even yet might send us such a day,
That our past troubles should but make us glad
As men rejoice in pensive songs and sad.
This was our counsel; those that we had left
Said, that they once before had been bereft
Of friends and country by a sick man's dream,
That this their life not evil did they deem
Nor would they rashly cast it down the wind;
But whoso wandered, they would stay behind.
Others there were who said, whate'er might come,
They would at least seek for the happy home
They had forgotten once, and there at last
In penitence for sins and follies past
Wait for the death that they in vain had fled.

Well, when all things by all sides had been said

We drew the ships again unto the sea,
Which those who went not with us, carefully
Had tended for those years we were away
(Which still they said was ten months and a day);
And these we rigged, and in a little while
The Fighting Man looked o'er the false sea's smile
Unto the land of Norway, and our band
Across the bulwarks of the Rose-Garland,
Amidst of tears and doubt and misery
Sent after them a feeble farewell cry,
And they returned a tremulous faint cheer,
While from the sandy shell-strewn beach anear
The soft west wind across the waves bore out
A strange confuséd noise of wail and shout,
For there the dark line of the outland folk
A few familiar grey-eyed faces broke,
That minded us of Norway left astern,
Ere we began our heavy task to learn.

THE ELDER OF THE CITY:

Sirs, by my deeming had ye still gone on
When ye had crossed the mountains, ye had won
Unto another sea at last, and there
Had found clad folk, and cities great and fair,
Though not the deathless country of your thought.

THE WANDERER:

Yea, sirs, and short of that we had deemed nought,
Ere yet our hope of life had fully died;
And for those cities scarce should we have tried,
E'en had we known of them, and certainly
Nought but those bestial people did we see.
But let me hasten now unto the end.

Fair wind and lovely weather God did send
To us deserted men, who but two score
Now mustered: so we stood off from the shore
Still stretching south till we lost land again,
Because we deemed the labour would be vain
To try the shore too near where we had been,
Where none of us as yet a sign had seen.

Of that which we desired. And now we few,
Thus left alone, each unto other grew
The dearer friends, and less accursed we seemed
As still the less of 'scaping death we dreamed,
And knew the lot of all men should be ours,
A chequered day of sunshine and of showers
Fading to twilight and dark night at last.

Those forest folk with ours their lot had cast,
And ever unto us were leal and true,
And now when all our tongue at last they knew
They told us tales, too long to tell as now;
Yet this one thing I fain to you would show
About the dying man our sight did kill
Amidst the corpses on that dreary hill:
Namely, that when their King drew nigh to death,
But still had left in him some little breath,
They bore him to that hill, when they had slain,
By a wild root that killed with little pain,
His servants and his wives like as we saw,
Thinking that thence the gods his soul would draw
To heaven; but the King being dead at last,
The servants dead being taken down, they cast
Into the river, but the King they hung
Embalmed within that chapel, where they sung
Some office over him in solemn wise,
Amidst the smoke of plenteous sacrifice.

Well, though wild hope no longer in us burned,
Unto the land within a while we turned,
And found it much the same, and still untilled,
And still its people of all arts unskilled;
And some were dangerous and some were kind;
But midst them no more tidings did we find
Of what we once had deemed well won, but now
Was like the dream of some past kingly show.
What shall I say of all these savages,
Of these wide plains beset with unsown trees,
Through which untamed man-fearing beasts did range?
To us at least there seemed but little change,
For we were growing weary of the world.
Whiles did we dwell ashore, whiles were we hurled

Out to the landless ocean, whiles we lay
Long time within some river or deep bay;
And so the months went by, until at last,
When now three years were fully overpast
Since we had left our fellows, and grown old
Our leaky ship along the water rolled,
Upon a day unto a land we came
Whose people spoke a tongue well-nigh the same
As that our forest people used, and who
A little of the arts of mankind knew,
And tilled the kind earth, certes not in vain;
For wealth of melons we saw there, and grain
Strange unto us. Now battered as we were,
Grown old before our time, in worn-out gear,
These people, when we first set foot ashore,
Garlands of flowers and fruits unto us bore,
And worshipped us as gods, and for no words
That we could say would cease to call us lords,
And pray our help to give them bliss and peace,
And fruitful seasons of the earth's increase.

Withal at last, they, when in talk they fell
With our good forest-folk, to them did tell
That they were subject to a mighty king,
Who, as they said, ruled over everything,
And, dwelling in a glorious city, had
All things that men desire to make them glad.
"He," said they, "none the less shall be but slave
Unto your lords, and all that he may have
Will he but take as free gifts at their hands,
If they will deign henceforth to bless his lands
With their most godlike presence."
                                    Ye can think
How we poor wretched souls outworn might shrink
From such strange worship, that like mocking seemed
To us, who of a godlike state had dreamed,
And missed it in such wise; yet none the less
An earthly haven to our wretchedness
This city seemed, therefore we 'gan to pray
That some of them would guide us on our way,
Which words of ours they heard most joyously,
And brought us to their houses nigh the sea,

And feasted us with such things as they might.
   But almost ere the ending of the night
We started on our journey, being up-borne
In litters, like to kings, who so forlorn
Had been erewhile; so in some ten days' space
They brought us nigh their king's abiding place;
And as we went the land seemed fair enough,
Though sometimes did we pass through forests rough,
Deserts and fens, yet for the most, the way
Through ordered villages and tilled land lay,
Which after all the squalid miseries
We had beheld, seemed heaven unto our eyes,
Though strange to us it was.

                But now when we
From a hill-side the city well could see,
Our guides there prayed us to abide awhile,
Wherefore we stayed, though eager to beguile
Our downcast hearts from brooding o'er our woe
By all the new things that abode might show;
So while we bided on that flowery down
The swiftest of them sped on toward the town
To bear them news of this unhoped-for bliss;
And we, who now some little happiness
Could find in that fair place and pleasant air,
Sat 'neath strange trees, on new flowers growing there
Of scent unlike to those we knew of old,
While unfamiliar tales the strange birds told.
But certes seemed that city fair enow
That spread out o'er the well-tilled vale below,
Though nowise built like such as we had seen;
Walled with white walls it was, and gardens green
Were set between the houses everywhere;
And now and then rose up a tower foursquare
Lessening in stage on stage: with many a hue
The house walls glowed, of red and green and blue,
And some with gold were well adorned, and one
From roofs of gold flashed back the noontide sun.
Had we but seen such things not long ago
We should have hastened us to come thereto,
In hope to find the very heaven we sought.
   But now while quietly we sat, and thought

Of many things, the gate wherein that road
Had end, was opened wide, and thereout flowed
A glittering throng of people, young and old,
And men and women, much adorned with gold;
Wherefore we rose to meet them, who stood still
When they beheld us winding down the hill,
And lined both sides of the grey road, but we
Now drawing nigh them, first of all could see
Old men in venerable raiment clad,
White-bearded, who sweet flowering branches had
In their right hands; then young men armed right
    well
After their way, which now were long to tell;
Then damsels clad in radiant gold array,
Who with sweet-smelling blossoms strewed the way
Before our feet; then men with gleaming swords
And glittering robes, and crowned like mighty lords;
And last of all, within the very gate
The King himself, round whom our guides did wait,
Kneeling with humble faces downward bent.

    What wonder if, as 'twixt these folk we went,
Hearkening their singing and sweet minstrelsy,
A little nigher now seemed our heaven to be—
Alas, a fair folk, a sweet spot of earth,
A land where many a lovely thing has birth,
But where all fair things come at last to die.

    Now when we three unto the King drew nigh
Before our fellows, he, adored of all,
Spared not before us on his knees to fall,
And as we deemed who knew his speech but ill,
Began to pray us to bide with him still,
Telling withal of some old prophecy
Which seemed to say that there we should not die.

    What could we do amidst these splendid lords?
No time it was to doubt or make long words,
Nor with a short but happy life at hand
Durst we to ask about the deathless land,
Though well we felt the life whereof he spoke,
Could never be among those mortal folk.
Therefore we way-worn, disappointed men,
So richly dowered with three-score years and ten,

Vouchsafed to grant the King his whole request;
Thinking within that town awhile to rest,
And gather news about the hope that fled
Still on before us, risen from the dead,
From out its tomb of toil and misery,
That held it while we saw but sea and sky,
Or untilled lands and people void of bliss,
And our own faces heavy with distress.

But entering now that town, what huge delight
We had therein, how lovely to our sight
Was the well-ordered life of people there,
Who on that night within a palace fair
Made us a feast with great solemnity,
Till we forgot that we came there to die,
If we should leave our quest; for e'en as kings
They treated us, and whatsoever things
We asked for, or could think of, those were ours.

Houses we had, noble with walls and towers,
Lovely with gardens, cooled with running streams,
And rich with gold beyond a miser's dreams,
And men and women slaves, whose very lives
Were in our hands; and fair and princely wives
If so we would; and all things for delight,
Good to the taste or beautiful to sight
The land might yield.   They taught us of their law;
The muster of their men-at-arms we saw,
As men who owned them; in their judgment-place
Our lightest word made glad the pleader's face,
And the judge trembled at our faintest frown.

Think then, if we, late driven up and down
Upon the uncertain sea, or struggling sore
With barbarous men upon an untilled shore,
Or at the best, midst people ignorant
Of arts and letters, fighting against want
Of very food—think if we now were glad
From day to day, and as folk crazed and mad
Deemed our old selves, the wanderers on the sea.

And if at whiles midst our felicity
We yet remembered us of that past day
When in the long swell off the land we lay,
Weeping for joy at our accomplished dream,

And each to each a very god did seem,
For fear was dead—if we remembered this,
Yet after all, was this our life of bliss,
A little thing that we had gained at last?
And must we sorrow for the idle past,
Or think it ill that thither we were led?
Thus seemed our old desire quite quenched and dead.
    You must remember that we yet were young.
Five years had passed since the grey fieldfare sung
To me a dreaming youth laid 'neath the thorn;
And though while we were wandering and forlorn
I seemed grown old and withered suddenly,
But twenty summers had I seen go by
When I left Wickland on that desperate cruise.
But now again our wrinkles did we lose
With memory of our ills, and like a dream
Our fevered quest with its bad days did seem,
And many things grew fresh again, forgot
While in our hearts that wild desire was hot:
Yea, though at thought of Norway we might sigh,
Small was the pain which that sweet memory
Brought with its images seen fresh and clear,
And many an old familiar thing grown dear,
But little loved the while we lived with it.

    So smoothly o'er our heads the days did flit,
Yet not eventless either, for we taught
Such lore as we from our own land had brought
Unto this folk, who when they wrote must draw
Such draughts as erst at Micklegarth I saw,
Writ for the evil Pharaoh-kings of old;
Their arms were edged with copper or with gold,
Whereof they had great plenty, or with flint;
No armour had they fit to bear the dint
Of tools like ours, and little could avail
Their archer craft; their boats knew nought of sail,
And many a feat of building could we show,
Which midst their splendour still they did not know.
    And midst of all, war fell upon the land,
And in forefront of battle must we stand,
To do our best, though little mastery

We thought it then to make such foemen flee
As there we met; but when again we came
Into the town, with something like to shame
We took the worship of that simple folk
Rejoicing for their freedom from the yoke
That round about their necks had hung so long.

For thus that war began: some monarch strong
Conquered their land of old, and thereon laid
A dreadful tribute, which they still had paid
With tears and curses; for as each fifth year
Came round, this heavy shame they needs must bear:
Ten youths, ten maidens must they choose by lot
Among the fairest that they then had got,
Who a long journey o'er the hills must go
Unto the tyrant, nor with signs of woe
Enter his city, but in bright array,
And harbingered by songs and carols gay,
Betake them to the temple of his god;
But when the streets their weary feet had trod
Their wails must crown the long festivity,
For on the golden altar must they die.

Such was the sentence till the year we came,
And counselled them to put away this shame
If they must die therefor; so on that year
Barren of blood the devil's altars were,
Wherefore a herald clad in strange attire
The tyrant sent them, and but blood and fire
His best words were; him they sent back again
Defied by us, who made his threats but vain,
When face to face with those ill folk we stood
Ready to seal our counsel with our blood.

Past all belief they loved us for all this,
And if it would have added to our bliss
That they should die, this surely they had done.
So smoothly slipped the years past one by one,
And we had lived and died as happy there
As any men the labouring earth may bear,
But for the poison of that wickedness
That led us on God's edicts to redress.
At first indeed death seemed so far away,
So sweet in our new home was every day,

That we forgot death like the most of men
Who cannot count the threescore years and ten;
Yet we grew fearful as the time drew on,
And needs must think of all we might have won,
Yea, by so much the happier that we were
By just so much increased on us our fear,
And those old times of our past misery
Seemed not so evil as the days went by
Faster and faster with the years' increase,
For loss of youth to us was loss of peace.

Two gates unto the road of life there are,
And to the happy youth both seem afar,
Both seem afar; so far the past one seems,
The gate of birth, made dim with many dreams,
Bright with remembered hopes, beset with flowers;
So far it seems he cannot count the hours
That to this midway path have led him on
Where every joy of life now seemeth won—
So far, he thinks not of the other gate,
Within whose shade the ghosts of dead hopes wait
To call upon him as he draws anear,
Despoiled, alone, and dull with many a fear:
"Where is thy work? how little thou hast done,
Where are thy friends, why art thou so alone?"
How shall he weigh his life? slow goes the time
The while the fresh dew-sprinkled hill we climb,
Thinking of what shall be the other side;
Slow pass perchance the minutes we abide
On the gained summit, blinking at the sun;
But when the downward journey is begun
No more our feet may loiter; past our ears
Shrieks the harsh wind scarce noted midst our fears,
And battling with the hostile things we meet
Till, ere we know it, our weak shrinking feet
Have brought us to the end and all is done.

And so with us it was, when youth twice won
Now for the second time had passed away,
And we unwitting were grown old and grey,
And one by one, the death of some dear friend,
Some cherished hope, brought to a troublous end

Our joyous life; as in a dawn of June
The lover, dreaming of the brown bird's tune
And longing lips unto his own brought near,
Wakes up the crashing thunder-peal to hear.
So, sirs, when this world's pleasures came to nought,
Not upon God we set our wayward thought,
But on the folly our own hearts had made;
Once more the stories of the past we weighed
With what we hitherto had found; once more
We longed to be by some unknown far shore;
Once more our life seemed trivial, poor and vain,
Till we our lost fool's paradise might gain.
Yea, we were like the felon doomed to die,
Who when unto the sword he draws anigh
Struggles and cries, though erewhile in his cell
He heard the priest of heaven and pardon tell,
Weeping and half contented to be slain.

Was I the first who thought of this again?
Perchance I was; but howsoe'er that be,
Long time I thought of these things certainly
Ere I durst stir my fellows to the quest,
Though secretly myself, with little rest
For tidings of our lovely land I sought.
Should prisoners from another folk be brought
Unto our town, I questioned them of this;
I asked the wandering merchants of a bliss
They dreamed not of, in chaffering for their goods;
The hunter in the far-off lonely woods,
The fisher in the rivers nigh the sea,
Must tell their wild strange stories unto me.
Within the temples books of records lay
Such as I told of, thereon day by day
I pored, and got long stories from the priests
Of many-handed gods with heads of beasts,
And such-like dreariness; and still, midst all
Sometimes a glimmering light would seem to fall
Upon my ignorance, and less content
As time went on I grew, and ever went
About my daily life distractedly,
Until at last I felt that I must die

Nor dealeth time with men so marvellously
That he should seem like twenty, I fourscore:
Thou art my nephew, let the jest pass o'er."
　"Nay," said he, "but it is not good to talk
Here in the crowded street, so let us walk
Unto thine habitation; dost thou mind,
When we were boys, how once we chanced to find
That crock of copper money hid away
Up in the loft, and how on that same day
We bought this toy and that, thou a short sword
And I a brazen boat." 　But at that word
The old man wildly on him 'gan to stare
And said no more, the while we three did fare
Unto his house, but there we being alone,
Many undoubted signs the younger one
Gave to his brother, saying withal that he
Had gained the land of all felicity,
Where, after trials too long then to tell,
The slough of grisly eld from off him fell,
And left him strong and fair and young again;
Neither from that time had he suffered pain
Greater or less, or feared at all to die:
And though, he said, he knew not certainly
If he should live for ever, this he knew
His days should not be full of pain and few
As most men's lives were.　Now when asked why he
Had left his home, a deadly land to see,
He said that people's chiefs had sent him there,
Moved by report that tall men, white and fair,
Like to the Gods, had come across the sea,
Of whom old seers had told that they should be
Lords of that land; therefore his charge was this,
To lead us forth to that abode of bliss,
But secretly, since for the other folk
They were as beasts to toil beneath the yoke.
"But," said he, "brother, thou shalt go with me,
If now at last no doubt be left in thee
Of who I am." 　At that, to end it all
The weak old man upon his neck did fall,
Rejoicing for his lot with many tears:

But I, rejoicing too, yet felt vague fears
Within my heart, for now almost too nigh
We seemed to that long-sought felicity.
What should I do though? What could it avail
Unto these men, to make a feignéd tale?
Besides in all no faltering could I find,
Nor did they go beyond, or fall behind,
What in such cases such-like men would do,
Therefore I needs must think their story true.

So now unto my fellows did I go
And all things in due order straight did show,
And had the man who told·the tale at hand;
Of whom some made great question of the land,
And where it was, and how he found it first;
And still he answered boldly to the worst
Of all their questions: then from out the place
He went, and we were left there face to face.

And joy it was to see the dark cheeks, tanned
By many a summer of that fervent land,
Flush up with joy, and see the grey eyes gleam
Through the dull film of years, as that sweet dream
Flickered before them, now grown real and true.

But when the certainty of all we knew,
Deeming for sure our quest would not be vain,
We got us ready for the sea again.
But to the city's folk we told no more
Than that we needs must make for some far shore,
Whence we would come again to them, and bring
For them and us full many a wished-for thing
To make them glad.
                        Then answered they indeed
That our departing made their hearts to bleed,
But with no long words did they bid us stay,
And I remembered me of that past day,
And somewhat grieved I felt, that so it was:
Not thinking how the deeds of men must pass,
And their remembrance as their bodies die;
Or, if their memories fade not utterly,
Like curious pictures shall they be at best,
For men to gaze at while they sit at rest,
Talking of alien things and feasting well.

Ah me! I loiter, being right loth to tell
The things that happened to us in the end.
Down to the noble river did we wend
Where lay the ships we taught these folk to make,
And there the fairest of them did we take
And so began our voyage; thirty-three
Were left of us, who erst had crossed the sea,
Five of the forest people, and beside
None but the fair young man, our new-found guide,
And his old brother; setting sail with these
We left astern our gilded palaces
And all the good things God had given us there
With small regret, however good they were.

Well, in twelve days our vessel reached the sea,
When turning round we ran on northerly
In sight of land at whiles; what need to say
How the time past from hopeful day to day?
Suffice it that the wind was fair and good,
And we most joyful, as still north we stood;
Until when we a month at sea had been,
And for six days no land at all had seen,
We sighted it once more, whereon our guide
Shouted: "O fellows, lay all fear aside,
This is the land whereof I spake to you."
But when the happy tidings all men knew,
Trembling and pale we watched the land grow great,
And when above the waves the noontide heat
Had raised a vapour 'twixt us and the land
That afternoon, we saw a high ness stand
Out in the sea, and nigher when we came,
And all the sky with sunset was a-flame,
'Neath the dark hill we saw a city lie,
Washed by the waves, girt round with ramparts high.

A little nigher yet, and then our guide
Bade us to anchor, lowering from our side
The sailless keel wherein he erst had come,
Through many risks, to bring us to his home.
But when our eager hands this thing had done,
He and his brother gat therein alone.
But first he said: "Abide here till the morn,
And when ye hear the sound of harp and horn,

And varied music, run out every oar,
Up anchor, and make boldly for the shore.
O happy men! well-nigh do I regret
That I am not as you, to whom as yet
That moment past all moments is unknown,
When first unending life to you is shown.
But now I go, that all in readiness
May be, your souls with this delight to bless."

    He waved farewell to us and went, but we,
As the night grew, beheld across the sea
Lights moving on the quays, and now and then
We heard the chanting of the outland men.
How can I tell of that strange troublous night?
Troublous and strange, though 'neath the moonshine
        white,
Peace seemed upon the sea, the glimmering town,
The shadows of the tree-besprinkled down,
The moveless dewy folds of our loose sail;
But how could these for peace to us avail?

    Weary with longing, blind with great amaze,
We struggled now with past and future days;
And not in vain our former joy we thought,
Since thirty years our wandering feet had brought
To this at last—and yet, what will you have?
Can man be made content? We wished to save
The bygone years; our hope, our painted toy,
We feared to miss, drowned in that sea of joy.
Old faces still reproached us: "We are gone,
And ye are entering into bliss alone;
And can ye now forget? Year passes year,
And still ye live on joyous, free from fear;
But where are we; where is the memory
Of us, to whom ye once were drawn so nigh?
Forgetting and alone ye enter in;
Remembering all, alone we wail our sin,
And cannot touch you." Ah, the blessed pain!
When heaven just gained was scarcely all a gain.
How could we weigh that boundless treasure then,
Or count the sorrows of the sons of men?
Ah, woe is me to think upon that night!

Day came, and with the dawning of the light
We were astir, and from our deck espied
The people clustering by the water-side,
As if to meet us; then across the sea
We heard great horns strike up triumphantly,
And then scarce knowing what we did, we weighed,
And running out the oars for shore we made,
With banners fluttering out from yard and mast.
We reached the well-built marble quays at last,
Crowded with folk, and in the front of these
There stood our guide, decked out with braveries,
Holding his feeble brother by the hand;
Then speechless, trembling, did we now take land,
Leaving all woes behind; but when our feet
The happy soil of that blest land did meet,
Fast fell our tears, as on a July day
The thunder-shower falls pattering on the way,
And certes some one we desired to bless,
But scarce knew whom midst all our thankfulness.

Now the crowd opened, and an ordered band
Of youths and damsels, flowering boughs in hand,
Came forth to meet us, just as long ago,
When first we won some rest from pain and woe,
Except that now eld chained not any one,
No man was wrinkled but ourselves alone,
But smooth and beautiful, bright-eyed and glad,
Were all we saw, in fair thin raiment clad
Fit for the sunny place.

                But now our friend,
Our guide, who brought us to this glorious end,
Led us amidst that band, who 'gan to sing
Some hymn of welcome, midst whose carolling
Faint-hearted men we must have been indeed
To doubt that all was won; nor did we heed
That, when we well were gotten from the quay,
Armed men went past us, by the very way
That we had come, nor thought of their intent,
For armour unto us was ornament,
And had been now, for many peaceful years,
Since bow and axe had dried the people's tears.

Let all that pass. With song and minstrelsy

Through many streets they led us, fair to see,
For nowhere did we meet maimed, poor or old,
But all were young and clad in silk and gold.
Like a king's court the common ways did seem
On that fair morn of our accomplished dream.

Far did we go, through market-place and square,
Past fane and palace, till a temple fair
We came to, set aback midst towering trees,
But raised above the tallest of all these.
So there we entered through a brazen gate,
And all the thronging folk without did wait,
Except the golden-clad melodious band.
But when within the precinct we did stand,
Another rampart girdled round the fane,
And that being past, another one again,
And small space was betwixt them, all these three
Of white stones laid in wondrous masonry
Were builded, but the fourth we now passed through
Was half of white and half of ruddy hue;
Nor did we reach the temple through this one,
For now a fifth wall came, of dark red stone
With golden coping and wide doors of gold;
And this being past, our eyes could then behold
The marvellous temple, foursquare, rising high
In stage on stage up toward the summer sky,
Like the unfinished tower that Nimrod built
Before the concord of the world was spilt.

So now we came into the lowest hall,
A mighty way across from wall to wall,
Where carven pillars held a gold roof up,
And silver walls fine as an Indian cup,
With figures monstrous as a dream were wrought;
And under foot the floor beyond all thought
Was wonderful, for like the tumbling sea
Beset with monsters did it seem to be;
But in the midst a pool of ruddy gold
Caught in its waves a glittering fountain cold,
And through the bright shower of its silver spray
Dimly we saw the high-raised daïs, gay
With wondrous hangings, for high up and small
The windows were within the dreamlike hall;

Betwixt the pillars wandered damsels fair
Crooning low songs, or filling all the air
With incense wafted to strange images
That made us tremble, since we saw in these
The devils unto whom we now must cry
Ere we begin our new felicity:
Nathless no altars did we see but one
Which dimly from before the daïs shone
Built of green stone, with horns of copper bright.

Now when we entered from the outer light
And all the scents of the fresh day were past,
With its sweet breezes, a dull shade seemed cast
Over our joy; what then? not if we would
Could we turn back—and surely all was good.

But now they brought us vestments rich and fair,
And bade us our own raiment put off there,
Which straight we did, and with a hollow sound
Like mournful bells our armour smote the ground,
And damsels took the weapons from our hands
That might have gleamed with death in other lands,
And won us praise; at last when all was done,
And brighter than the Kaiser each man shone,
Us unarmed helpless men the music led
Up to the daïs, and there our old guide said:
"Rest, happy men, the time will not be long
Ere they will bring with incense, dance and song
The sacred cup, your life and happiness,
And many a time this fair hour shall ye bless."

Alas, sirs! words are weak to tell of it,
I seemed to see a smile of mockery flit
Across his face as from our thrones he turned,
And in my heart a sudden fear there burned,
The last, I said, for ever and a day;
But even then with harsh and ominous bray
A trumpet through the monstrous pillars rung,
And to our feet with sudden fear we sprung—
Too late, too late! for through all doors did stream
Armed men, that filled the place with clash and gleam,
And when the dull sound of their moving feet
Was still, a fearful sight our eyes did meet,

A fearful sight to us: *old men and grey*
Betwixt the bands of soldiers took their way,
And at their head in wonderful attire,
Holding within his hand a pot of fire,
Moved the false brother of the traitorous guide,
Who with bowed head walked ever by his side;
But as anigh the elders 'gan to draw,
We, almost turned to stone by what we saw,
Heard the old man say to the younger one:
"Speak to them that thou knowest, O fair *Son !*"

Then the wretch said, "O ye, who sought to find
Unending life against the law of kind,
Within this land, fear ye not now too much,
For no man's hand your bodies here shall touch,
But rather with all reverence folk shall tend
Your daily lives, until at last they end
By slow decay: and ye shall pardon us
The trap whereby beings made so glorious
As ye are made, we drew unto this place.
Rest ye content then! for although your race
Comes from the Gods, yet are ye conquered here,
As we would conquer them, if we knew where
They dwell from day to day, and with what arms
We, overcoming them, might win such charms
That we might make the world what ye desire.

"Rest then at ease, and if ye e'er shall tire
Of this abode, remember at the worst
Life flitteth, whether it be blest or cursed.
But will ye tire? ye are our gods on earth
Whiles that ye live, nor shall your lives lack mirth,
For song, fair women and heart-cheering wine
The chain of solemn days shall here entwine
With odorous flowers; ah, surely ye are come,
When all is said, unto an envied home."

Like an old dream, dreamed in another dream,
I hear his voice now, see the hopeless gleam,
Through the dark place of that thick wood of spears.
That fountain's splash rings yet within mine ears
I thought the fountain of eternal youth—
Yet I can scarce remember in good truth

What then I felt: I should have felt as he
Who, waking after some festivity,
Sees a dim land, and things unspeakable,
And comes to know at last that it is hell—
I cannot tell you, nor can tell you why,
Driven by what hope, I cried my battle-cry
And rushed upon him; this I know indeed,
My naked hands were good to me at need,
That sent the traitor to his due reward,
Ere I was dragged off by the hurrying guard,
Who spite of all used neither sword nor spear,
Nay as it seemed, touched us with awe and fear.
Though at the last, grown all too weak to strive,
They brought us to the daïs scarce alive,
And changed our tattered robes again, and there
Bound did we sit, each in his golden chair,
Beholding many mummeries that they wrought
About the altar; till at last they brought,
Crowned with fair flowers, and clad in robes of gold,
The folk that from the wood we won of old—
Why make long words? before our very eyes
Our friends they slew, a fitting sacrifice
To us their new-gained gods, who sought to find
Within that land, a people just and kind
That could not die, or take away the breath
From living men.
                    What thing but that same death
Had we left now to hope for? death must come
And find us somewhere an enduring home.
Will grief kill men, as some folk think it will?
Then are we of all men most hard to kill.
The time went past, the dreary days went by
In dull unvarying round of misery,
Nor can I tell if it went fast or slow,
What would it profit you the time to know
That we spent there; all I can say to you
Is, that no hope our prison wall shone through,
That ever we were guarded carefully,
While day and dark and dark and day went by
Like such a dream, as in the early night
The sleeper wakes from in such sore affright,

Such panting horror, that to sleep again
He will not turn, to meet such shameful pain.

Lo such were we, but as we hoped before
Where no hope was, so now, when all seemed o'er
But sorrow for our lives so cast away,
Again the bright sun brought about the day.
    At last the temple's dull monotony
Was broke by noise of armed men hurrying by
Within the precinct, and we seemed to hear
Shouts from without of anger and of fear,
And noises as of battle; and red blaze
The night sky showed; this lasted through two days.
But on the third our guards were whispering
Pale-faced, as though they feared some coming thing,
And when the din increased about noontide,
No longer there with us would they abide,
But left us free; judge then if our hearts beat,
When any pain, or death itself was sweet
To hideous life within that wicked place,
Where every day brought on its own disgrace.
    Few words betwixt us passed; we knew indeed
Where our old armour once so good at need
Hung up as relics nigh the altar-stead;
Thither we hurried, and from heel to head
Soon were we armed, and our old spears and swords
Clashing 'gainst steel and stone, spoke hopeful words
To us, the children of a warrior race.
But round unto the hubbub did we face
And through the precinct strove to make our way
Set close together; in besmirched array
Some met us, and some wounded very sore,
And some who wounded men to harbour bore;
But these too busy with their pain or woe
To note us much, unchallenged let us go:
Then here and there we passed some shrinking maid
In a dark corner trembling and afraid,
But eager for the news about the fight.
Through trodden gardens then we came in sight
Of the third rampart that begirt the fane,
Which now the foemen seemed at point to gain,

For o'er the wall the ladders 'gan to show,
And huge confusion was there down below
'Twixt wall and wall; but as the gate we passed
A man from out the crowd came hurrying fast,
But, drawing nigh us, stopped short suddenly,
And cried, "O masters, help us or we die!
This impious people 'gainst their ancient lords
Have turned, and in their madness drawn their swords
Yea, and they now prevail, and fearing not
The dreadful gods, still grows their wrath more hot.
Wherefore to bring you here was my intent,
But the kind gods themselves your hands have sent
To save us all, and this fair holy house
With your strange arms, and hearts most valorous."
    No word we said, for even as he spoke
A frightful clamour from the wall outbroke,
As the thin line of soldiers thereupon
Crushed back and broken, left the rampart won,
And leapt and tumbled therefrom as they could,
While in their place the conquering foemen stood:
Then the weak, wavering, huddled crowd below
Their weight upon the inner wall 'gan throw,
And at the narrow gates by hundreds died;
For not long did the enemy abide
On the gained rampart, but by every way
Got to the ground and 'gan all round to slay,
Till great and grim the slaughter grew to be.
But we well pleased our tyrants' end to see
Still firm against the inner wall did stand,
While round us surged the press on either hand.
Nor did we fear, for what was left of life
For us to fear for? so at last the strife
Drawn inward, in that place did much abate,
And we began to move unto the gate
Betwixt the dead and living; and these last
Ever with fearful glances by us passed
Nor hindered aught; but mindful of the lore
Our fathers gained on many a bloody shore,
We, when unto the street we made our way,
Moved as in fight nor broke our close array,
Though no man harmed us of the troubled crowd

That thronged the streets with shouts and curses loud;
But rather when our clashing arms they heard
Their hubbub lulled, and they as men afeard
Drew back before us.

              Well, as nigh we drew
Unto the sea, the men showed sparse and few,
Though frightened women standing in the street
Before their doors we did not fail to meet,
And passed by folk who at their doors laid down
Men wounded in the fight; so through the town
We reached the unguarded water-gate at last,
And there, nigh weeping, saw the green waves cast
Against the quays, whereby five tall ships lay:
For in that devil's house, right many a day
Had passed with all its dull obscenity
Uncounted by us while we longed to die,
And while of all men we were out of sight,
Except those priests, the people as they might
Made ships like ours; in whose new handiwork
Few mariners and fearful now did lurk,
And these soon fled before us: therefore we
Stayed not to think, but running hastily
Down the lone quay, seized on the nighest ship,
Nor yet till we had let the hawser slip
Dared we be glad, and then indeed once more,
Though we no longer hoped for our fair shore,
Our past disgrace, worse than the very hell,
Though hope was dead, made things seem more than
    well;
For if we died that night, yet were we free.

  Ah! with what joy we sniffed the fresh salt sea
After the musky odours of that place;
With what delight each felt upon his face
The careless wind, our master and our slave,
As through the green seas fast from shore we drave,
Scarce witting where we went.

                    But now when we
Beheld that city, far across the sea,
A thing gone past, nor any more could hear
The mingled shouts of victory and of fear,
From out the midst thereof shot up a fire,

In a long, wavering, murky, smoke-capped spire
That still with every minute wider grew,
So that the ending of the place we knew
Where we had passed such days of misery,
And still more glad turned round unto the sea.

My tale grows near its ending, for we stood
Southward to our kind folk e'en as we could,
But made slow way, for ever heavily
Our ship sailed, and she often needs must lie
At anchor in some bay, the while with fear
Ourselves, we followed up the fearful deer,
Or filled our water-vessels; for indeed,
Of meat and drink were we in bitter need,
As well might be, for scarcely could we choose
What ship from off that harbour to cast loose.
Midst this there died the captain, Nicholas,
Whom, though he brought us even to this pass,
I loved the most of all men; even now
When that seems long past, I can scarce tell how
I bear to live, since he could live no more.
Certes he took our failure very sore,
And often do I think he fain had died,
But yet for very love must needs abide
A little while, and yet a while again,
As though to share the utmost of our pain,
And miss the ray of comfort and sweet rest
Wherewith ye end our long disastrous quest
A drearier place than ever heretofore
The world seemed, as from that far nameless shore
We turned and left him 'neath the trees to bide;
For midst our rest worn out at last he died.
And such seemed like to hap to us as well,
If any harder thing to us befell
Than was our common life; and still we talked
How our old friends would meet men foiled, and
    balked
Of all the things that were to make them glad.
Ah, sirs! no sight of them henceforth we had;
A wind arose, which blowing furiously
Drove us out helpless to the open sea;

Eight days it blew, and when it fell, we lay
Leaky, dismasted, a most helpless prey
To winds and waves and with but little food.
Then with hard toil a feeble sail and rude
We rigged up somehow, and nigh hopelessly,
Expecting death, we staggered o'er the sea
For ten days more, but when all food and drink
Were gone for three days, and we needs must think
That in mid ocean we were doomed to die,
One morn again did land before us lie:
And we rejoiced; as much as least as he,
Who tossing on his bed deliriously,
Tortured with pain, hears the physician say
That he shall have one quiet painless day
Before he dies. What more? we soon did stand
In this your peaceful and delicious land
Amongst the simple kindly country folk;
But when I heard the language that they spoke,
From out my heart a joyous cry there burst,
So sore for friendly words was I athirst,
And I must fall a-weeping, to have come
To such a place that seemed a blissful home,
After the tossing from rough sea to sea;
So weak at last, so beaten down were we.

What shall I say in these kind people's praise
Who treated us like brothers for ten days,
Till with their tending we grew strong again,
And then withal in country cart and wain
Brought us unto this city where we are;
May God be good to them for all their care.

And now, sirs, all our wanderings have ye heard,
And all our story to the utmost word;
And here hath ending all our foolish quest,
Not at the worst if hardly at the best,
Since ye are good—Sirs, we are old and grey
Before our time; in what coin shall we pay
For this your goodness? take it not amiss
That we, poor souls, must pay you back for this
As good men pay back God, Who, raised above
The heavens and earth, yet needeth earthly love.

THE ELDER OF THE CITY:

Oh, friends, content you! this is much indeed,
And we are paid, thus garnering for our need
Your blessings only, bringing in their train
God's blessings as the south wind brings the rain.
And for the rest, no little thing shall be
(Since ye through all yet keep your memory)
The gentle music of the bygone years,
Long past to us with all their hopes and fears.
Think, if the gods, who mayhap love us well,
Sent to our gates some ancient chronicle
Of that sweet unforgotten land long left,
Of all the lands wherefrom we now are reft—.
—Think, with what joyous hearts, what reverence,
What songs, what sweet flowers we should bring it
        thence,
What images would guard it, what a shrine
Above its well-loved black and white should shine!
How should it pay our labour day by day
To look upon the fair place where it lay;
With what rejoicings even should we take
Each well-writ copy that the scribes might make,
And bear them forth to hear the people's shout,
E'en as good rulers' children are borne out
To take the people's blessing on their birth,
When all the city falls to joy and mirth.

Such, sirs, are ye, our living chronicle,
And scarce can we be grieved at what befell
Your lives in that too hopeless quest of yours,
Since it shall bring us wealth of happy hours
Whiles that we live, and to our sons, delight,
And their sons' sons.
                    But now, sirs, let us go,
That we your new abodes with us may show,
And tell you what your life henceforth may be,
But poor, alas, to that ye hoped to see.

N

Think, listener, that I had the luck to stand,
Awhile ago within a flowery land,
Fair beyond words; that thence I brought away
Some blossoms that before my footsteps lay,
Not plucked by me, not over-fresh or bright;
Yet, since they minded me of that delight,
Within the pages of this book I laid
Their tender petals, there in peace to fade.
Dry are they now, and void of all their scent
And lovely colour, yet what once was meant
By these dull stains, some men may yet descry
As dead upon the quivering leaves they lie.

Behold them here, and mock me if you will,
But yet believe no scorn of men can kill
My love of that fair land wherefrom they came,
Where midst the grass their petals once did flame.

Moreover, since that land as ye should know,
Bears not alone the gems for summer's show,
Or gold and pearls for fresh green-coated spring,
Or rich adornment for the flickering wing
Of fleeting autumn, but hath little fear
For the white conqueror of the fruitful year;
So in these pages month by month I show
Some portion of the flowers that erst did blow
In lovely meadows of the varying land,
Wherein erewhile I had the luck to stand.

THE PILGRIMS OF HOPE

I

THE MESSAGE OF THE MARCH WIND

Fair now is the springtide, now earth lies beholding
　　With the eyes of a lover the face of the sun;
Long lasteth the daylight, and hope is enfolding
　　The green-growing acres with increase begun.

Now sweet, sweet it is through the land to be straying
　　Mid the birds and the blossoms and the beasts of the field;
Love mingles with love, and no evil is weighing
　　On thy heart or mine, where all sorrow is healed.

From township to township, o'er down and by tillage
　　Far, far have we wandered and long was the day,
But now cometh eve at the end of the village,
　　Where over the grey wall the church riseth grey.

There is wind in the twilight; in the white road before us
　　The straw from the ox-yard is blowing about;
The moon's rim is rising, a star glitters o'er us,
　　And the vane on the spire-top is swinging in doubt.

Down there dips the highway, toward the bridge crossing
　　over
　　The brook that runs on to the Thames and the sea.
Draw closer, my sweet, we are lover and lover;
　　This eve art thou given to gladness and me.

Shall we be glad always? Come closer and hearken:
    Three fields further on, as they told me down there,
When the young moon has set, if the March sky should
      darken,
    We might see from the hill-top the great city's glare.

Hark, the wind in the elm-boughs! From London it
      bloweth,
    And telling of gold, and of hope and unrest;
Of power that helps not; of wisdom that knoweth,
    But teacheth not aught of the worst and the best.

Of the rich men it telleth, and strange is the story
    How they have, and they hanker, and grip far and wide;
And they live and they die, and the earth and its glory
    Has been but a burden they scarce might abide.

Hark! the March wind again of a people is telling;
    Of the life that they live there, so haggard and grim,
That if we and our love amidst them had been dwelling
    My fondness had faltered, thy beauty grown dim.

This land we have loved in our love and our leisure
    For them hangs in heaven, high out of their reach;
The wide hills o'er the sea-plain for them have no pleasure,
    The grey homes of their fathers no story to teach.

The singers have sung and the builders have builded,
    The painters have fashioned their tales of delight;
For what and for whom hath the world's book been gilded,
    When all is for these but the blackness of night?

How long and for what is their patience abiding?
    How oft and how oft shall their story be told,
While the hope that none seeketh in darkness is hiding
    And in grief and in sorrow the world groweth old?

Come back to the inn, love, and the lights and the fire,
    And the fiddler's old tune and the shuffling of feet;
For there in a while shall be rest and desire,
    And there shall the morrow's uprising be sweet.

Yet, love, as we wend the wind bloweth behind us
  And beareth the last tale it telleth to-night,
How here in the springtide the message shall find us;
  For the hope that none seeketh is coming to light.

Like the seed of midwinter, unheeded, unperished,
  Like the autumn-sown wheat 'neath the snow lying green,
Like the love that o'ertook us, unawares and uncherished,
  Like the babe 'neath thy girdle that groweth unseen,

So the hope of the people now buddeth and groweth—
  Rest fadeth before it, and blindness and fear;
It biddeth us learn all the wisdom it knoweth;
  It hath found us and held us, and biddeth us hear:

For it beareth the message: "Rise up on the morrow
  And go on your ways toward the doubt and the strife;
Join hope to our hope and blend sorrow with sorrow,
  And seek for men's love in the short days of life."

But lo, the old inn, and the lights and the fire,
  And the fiddler's old tune and the shuffling of feet;
Soon for us shall be quiet and rest and desire,
  And to-morrow's uprising to deeds shall be sweet.

II

THE BRIDGE AND THE STREET

In the midst of the bridge there we stopped and we
      wondered
  In London at last, and the moon going down,
All sullied and red where the mast-wood was sundered
  By the void of the night-mist, the breath of the town.

On each side lay the City, and Thames ran between it
  Dark, struggling, unheard 'neath the wheels and the
  ·feet.
A strange dream it was that we ever had seen it,
  And strange was the hope we had wandered to meet.

Was all nought but confusion? What man and what
    master
Had each of these people that hastened along?
Like a flood flowed the faces, and faster and faster
    Went the drift of the feet of the hurrying throng.

Till all these seemed but one thing, and we twain another,
    A thing frail and feeble and young and unknown;
What sign mid all these to tell foeman from brother?
    What sign of the hope in our hearts that had grown?

We went to our lodging afar from the river,
    And slept and forgot—and remembered in dreams;
And friends that I knew not I strove to deliver
    From a crowd that swept o'er us in measureless
        streams,

Wending whither I knew not: till meseemed I was waking
    To the first night in London, and lay by my love,
And she worn and changed, and my very heart aching
    With a terror of soul that forbade me to move.

Till I woke, in good sooth, and she lay there beside me,
    Fresh, lovely in sleep; but awhile yet I lay,
For the fear of the dream-tide yet seemed to abide me
    In the cold and sad time ere the dawn of the day.

Then I went to the window, and saw down below me
    The market-wains wending adown the dim street,
And the scent of the hay and the herbs seemed to know
        me,
    And seek out my heart the dawn's sorrow to meet.

They passed, and day grew, and with pitiless faces
    The dull houses stared on the prey they had trapped;
'Twas as though they had slain all the fair morning places
    Where in love and in leisure our joyance had happed.

My heart sank; I murmured, "What's this we are doing
  In this grim net of London, this prison built stark
With the greed of the ages, our young lives pursuing
  A phantom that leads but to death in the dark?"

Day grew, and no longer was dusk with it striving,
  And now here and there a few people went by.
As an image of what was once eager and living
  Seemed the hope that had led us to live or to die.

Yet nought else seemed happy; the past and its pleasure
  Was light, and unworthy, had been and was gone;
If hope had deceived us, if hid were its treasure,
  Nought now would be left us of all life had won.

O love, stand beside me; the sun is uprisen
  On the first day of London; and shame hath been here.
For I saw our new life like the bars of a prison,
  And hope grew a-cold, and I parleyed with fear.

Ah! I sadden thy face, and thy grey eyes are chiding!
  Yea, but life is no longer as stories of yore;
From us from henceforth no fair words shall be hiding
  The nights of the wretched, the days of the poor.

Time was we have grieved, we have feared, we have
    faltered,
  For ourselves, for each other, while yet we were twain;
And no whit of the world by our sorrow was altered,
  Our faintness grieved nothing, our fear was in vain.

Now our fear and our faintness, our sorrow, our passion,
  We shall feel all henceforth as we felt it erewhile;
But now from all this the due deeds we shall fashion
  Of the eyes without blindness, the heart without guile.

Let us grieve then—and help every soul in our sorrow;
  Let us fear—and press forward where few dare to go;
Let us falter in hope—and plan deeds for the morrow,
  The world crowned with freedom, the fall of the foe.

As the soldier who goes from his homestead a-weeping,
    And whose mouth yet remembers his sweetheart's
        embrace,
While all round about him the bullets are sweeping,
    But stern and stout-hearted dies there in his place;

Yea, so let our lives be! e'en such that hereafter,
    When the battle is won and the story is told,
Our pain shall be hid, and remembered our laughter,
    And our names shall be those of the bright and the bold.

NOTE.—This section had the following note in *The Commonweal:*
"It is the intention of the author to follow the fortunes of the
lovers who in the 'Message of the March Wind' were already
touched by sympathy with the cause of the people."

III

SENDING TO THE WAR

It was down in our far-off village that we heard of the
    war begun,
But none of the neighbours were in it save the squire's thick-
    lipped son,
A youth and a fool and a captain, who came and went away,
And left me glad of his going. There was little for us to say
Of the war and its why and wherefore—and we said it often
    enough;
The papers gave us our wisdom, and we used it up in the
    rough.
But I held my peace and wondered; for I thought of the
    folly of men,
The fair lives ruined and broken that ne'er could be mended
    again;
And the tale by lies bewildered, and no cause for a man to
    choose;
Nothing to curse or to bless—just a game to win or to lose.

But here were the streets of London—strife stalking wide in
    the world;
And the flag of an ancient people to the battle-breeze
    unfurled.
And who was helping or heeding? The gaudy shops dis-
    played
The toys of rich men's folly, by blinded labour made;
And still from nought to nothing the bright-skinned horses
    drew
Dull men and sleek-faced women with never a deed to do;
While all about and around them the street-flood ebbed and
    flowed,
Worn feet, grey anxious faces, grey backs bowed 'neath the
    load.
Lo the sons of an ancient people! And for this they fought
    and fell
In the days by fame made glorious, in the tale that singers
    tell.

We two we stood in the street in the midst of a mighty crowd,
The sound of its mingled murmur in the heavens above was
    loud,
And earth was foul with its squalor—that stream of every
    day,
The hurrying feet of labour, the faces worn and grey,
Were a sore and grievous sight, and enough and to spare
    had I seen
Of hard and pinching want midst our quiet fields and green;
But all was nothing to this, the London holiday throng.
Dull and with hang-dog gait they stood or shuffled along,
While the stench from the lairs they had lain in last night
    went up in the wind,
And poisoned the sun-lit spring: no story men can find
Is fit for the tale of their lives; no word that man hath made
Can tell the hue of their faces, or their rags by filth o'er-laid:
For this hath our age invented—these are the sons of the free,
Who shall bear our name triumphant o'er every land and
    sea.
Read ye their souls in their faces, and what shall help you
    there?

Joyless, hopeless, shameless, angerless, set is their stare:
This is the thing we have made, and what shall help us now,
For the field hath been laboured and tilled and the teeth of
    the dragon shall grow.

But why are they gathered together? what is this crowd in
    the street?
This is a holiday morning, though here and there we meet
The hurrying tradesman's broadcloth, or the workman's
    basket of tools.
Men say that at last we are rending the snares of knaves
    and fools;
That a cry from the heart of the nation against the foe is
    hurled,
And the flag of an ancient people to the battle-breeze
    unfurled.
The soldiers are off to the war, we are here to see the sight,
And all our griefs shall be hidden by the thought of our
    country's might.
'Tis the ordered anger of England and her hope for the
    good of the Earth
That we to-day are speeding, and many a gift of worth
Shall follow the brand and the bullet, and our wrath shall
    be no curse,
But a blessing of life to the helpless—unless we are liars and
    worse—
And these that we see are the senders; these are they that
    speed
The dread and the blessing of England to help the world at
    its need.

Sick unto death was my hope, and I turned and looked on
    my dear,
And beheld her frightened wonder, and her grief without
    a tear,
And knew how her thought was mine—when, hark! o'er the
    hubbub and noise,
Faint and a long way off, the music's measured voice,
And the crowd was swaying and swaying, and somehow, I
    knew not why,
A dream came into my heart of deliverance drawing anigh.

Then with roll and thunder of drums grew the music louder
and loud,
And the whole street tumbled and surged, and cleft was the
holiday crowd,
Till two walls of faces and rags lined either side of the way.
Then clamour of shouts rose upward, as bright and glittering
gay
Came the voiceful brass of the band, and my heart beat fast
and fast,
For the river of steel came on, and the wrath of England
passed
Through the want and the woe of the town, and strange
and wild was my thought,
And my clenched hands wandered about as though a
weapon they sought.

Hubbub and din was behind them, and the shuffling hag-
gard throng,
Wandering aimless about, tangled the street for long;
But the shouts and the rhythmic noise we still heard far
away,
And my dream was become a picture of the deeds of an-
other day.
Far and far was I borne, away o'er the years to come,
And again was the ordered march, and the thunder of the
drum,
And the bickering points of steel, and the horses shifting
about
'Neath the flashing swords of the captains—then the silence
after the shout—

Sun and wind in the street, familiar things made clear,
Made strange by the breathless waiting for the deeds that
are drawing anear.
For woe had grown into will, and wrath was bared of its
sheath,
And stark in the streets of London stood the crop of the
dragon's teeth.
Where then in my dream were the poor and the wall of
faces wan ?
Here and here by my side, shoulder to shoulder of man,

Hope in the simple folk, hope in the hearts of the wise,
For the happy life to follow, or death and the ending of lies,
Hope is awake in the faces angerless now no more,
Till the new peace dawn on the world, the fruit of the
people's war.

War in the world abroad a thousand leagues away,
While custom's wheel goes round and day devoureth day.
Peace at home!—what peace, while the rich man's mill is
strife,
And the poor is the grist that he grindeth, and life devoureth
life?

IV

MOTHER AND SON

Now sleeps the land of houses, and dead night holds the
street,
And there thou liest, my baby, and sleepest soft and sweet;
My man is away for awhile, but safe and alone we lie;
And none heareth thy breath but thy mother, and the moon
looking down from the sky
On the weary waste of the town, as it looked on the grass-
edged road
Still warm with yesterday's sun, when I left my old abode,
Hand in hand with my love, that night of all nights in the
year;
When the river of love o'erflowed and drowned all doubt
and fear,
And we two were alone in the world, and once, if never
again,
We knew of the secret of earth and the tale of its labour
and pain.

Lo amidst London I lift thee, and how little and light thou
art,
And thou without hope or fear, thou fear and hope of my
heart !
Lo here thy body beginning, O son, and thy soul and thy
life;

But how will it be if thou livest, and enterest into the strife,
And in love we dwell together when the man is grown in
thee,
When thy sweet speech I shall hearken, and yet 'twixt thee
and me
Shall rise that wall of distance, that round each one doth
grow,
And maketh it hard and bitter each other's thought to
know?
Now, therefore, while yet thou art little and hast no thought
of thine own,
I will tell thee a word of the world, of the hope whence thou
has grown,
Of the love that once begat thee, of the sorrow that hath
made
Thy little heart of hunger, and thy hands on my bosom laid.
Then mayst thou remember hereafter, as whiles when
people say
All this hath happened before in the life of another day;
So mayst thou dimly remember this tale of thy mother's
voice,
As oft in the calm of dawning I have heard the birds rejoice,
As oft I have heard the storm-wind go moaning through the
wood,
And I knew that earth was speaking, and the mother's voice
was good.

Now, to thee alone will I tell it that thy mother's body is fair,
In the guise of the country maidens who play with the sun
and the air,
Who have stood in the row of the reapers in the August
afternoon,
Who have sat by the frozen water in the highday of the
moon,
When the lights of the Christmas feasting were dead in the
house on the hill,
And the wild geese gone to the salt marsh had left the winter
still.
Yea, I am fair, my firstling; if thou couldst but remember
me!

The hair that thy small hand clutcheth is a goodly sight to
  see;
I am true, but my face is a snare; soft and deep are my eyes,
And they seem for men's beguiling fulfilled with the dreams
  of the wise.
Kind are my lips, and they look as though my soul had
  learned
Deep things I have never heard of. My face and my hands
  are burned
By the lovely sun of the acres; three months of London-town
And thy birth-bed have bleached them indeed—"But lo,
  where the edge of the gown"
(So said thy father one day) "parteth the wrist white as curd
From the brown of the hands that I love, bright as the wing
  of a bird."

Such is thy mother, O firstling, yet strong as the maidens
  of old,
Whose spears and whose swords were the warders of home-
  stead, of field and of fold.
Oft were my feet on the highway, often they wearied the
  grass;
From dusk unto dusk of the summer three times in a week
  would I pass
To the downs from the house on the river through the waves
  of the blossoming corn.
Fair then I lay down in the even, and fresh I arose on the
  morn,
And scarce in the noon was I weary. Ah, son, in the days
  of thy strife,
If thy soul could harbour a dream of the blossom of my life!
It would be as sunlit meadows beheld from a tossing sea,
And thy soul should look on a vision of the peace that is to
  be.

Yet, yet the tears on my cheek! And what is this doth move
My heart to thy heart, beloved, save the flood of yearning
  love?
For fair and fierce is thy father, and soft and strange are
  his eyes

That look on the days that shall be with the hope of the
    brave and the wise.
It was many a day that we laughed as over the meadows
    we walked,
And many a day I hearkened and the pictures came as he
    talked;
It was many a day that we longed, and we lingered late at
    eve
Ere speech from speech was sundered, and my hand his
    hand could leave.
Then I wept when I was alone, and I longed till the day-
    light came;
And down the stairs I stole, and there was our housekeeping
    dame
(No mother of me, the foundling) kindling the fire betimes
Ere the haymaking folk went forth to the meadows down
    by the limes;
All things I saw at a glance; the quickening fire-tongues
    leapt
Through the crackling heap of sticks, and the sweet smoke
    up from it crept,
And close to the very hearth the low sun flooded the floor,
And the cat and her kittens played in the sun by the open
    door.
The garden was fair in the morning, and there in the road
    he stood
Beyond the crimson daisies and the bush of southernwood.
Then side by side together through the grey-walled place
    we went,
And O the fear departed, and the rest and sweet content!

Son, sorrow and wisdom he taught me, and sore I grieved
    and learned
As we twain grew into one; and the heart within me burned
With the very hopes of his heart. Ah, son, it is piteous,
But never again in my life shall I dare to speak to thee
    thus;
So may these lonely words about thee creep and cling,
These words of the lonely night in the days of our wayfaring.

Many a child of woman to-night is born in the town,
The desert of folly and wrong; and of what and whence
    are they grown?
Many and many an one of wont and use is born;
For a husband is taken to bed as a hat or a ribbon is worn.
Prudence begets her thousands: "Good is a housekeeper's
    life,
So shall I sell my body that I may be matron and wife."
"And I shall endure foul wedlock and bear the children of
    need."
Some are there born of hate—many the children of greed.
"I, I too can be wedded, though thou my love hast got."
"I am fair and hard of heart, and riches shall be my lot."
And all these are the good and the happy, on whom the
    world dawns fair.
O son, when wilt thou learn of those that are born of
    despair,
As the fabled mud of the Nile that quickens under the sun
With a growth of creeping things, half dead when just
    begun?
E'en such is the care of Nature that man should never die,
Though she breed of the fools of the earth, and the dregs
    of the city sty.
But thou, O son, O son, of very love wert born,
When our hope fulfilled bred hope, and fear was a folly
    outworn;
On the eve of the toil and the battle all sorrow and grief
    we weighed,
We hoped and we were not ashamed, we knew and we were
    not afraid.

Now waneth the night and the moon—ah, son, it is piteous
That never again in my life shall I dare to speak to thee
    thus.
But sure from the wise and the simple shall the mighty
    come to birth;
And fair were my fate, beloved, if I be yet on the earth
When the world is awaken at last, and from mouth to mouth
    they tell
Of thy love and thy deeds and thy valour, and thy hope
    that nought can quell.

V

NEW BIRTH

It was twenty-five years ago that I lay in my mother's lap
New born to life, nor knowing one whit of all that should
hap:
That day was I won from nothing to the world of struggle
and pain,
Twenty-five years ago—and to-night am I born again.

I look and behold the days of the years that are passed
away,
And my soul is full of their wealth, for oft were they blithe
and gay
As the hours of bird and of beast: they have made me calm
and strong
To wade the stream of confusion, the river of grief and
wrong.

A rich man was my father, but he skulked ere I was born,
And gave my mother money, but left her life to scorn;
And we dwelt alone in our village: I knew not my mother's
"shame,"
But her love and her wisdom I knew till death and the
parting came.
Then a lawyer paid me money, and I lived awhile at a
school,
And learned the lore of the ancients, and how the knave
and the fool
Have been mostly the masters of earth: yet the earth seemed
fair and good
With the wealth of field and homestead, and garden and
river and wood;
And I was glad amidst it, and little of evil I knew
As I did in sport and pastime such deeds as a youth might
do,
Who deems he shall live for ever. Till at last it befel on a
day
That I came across our Frenchman at the edge of the new-
mown hay,

A-fishing as he was wont, alone as he always was;
So I helped the dark old man to bring a chub to grass,
And somehow he knew of my birth, and somehow we came
    to be friends,
Till he got to telling me chapters of the tale that never ends;
The battle of grief and hope with riches and folly and wrong.
He told how the weak conspire, he told of the fear of the
    strong;
He told of dreams grown deeds, deeds done ere time was
    ripe,
Of hope that melted in air like the smoke of his evening
    pipe;
Of the fight long after hope in the teeth of all despair;
Of battle and prison and death, of life stripped naked and
    bare.
But to me it all seemed happy, for I gilded all with the gold
Of youth that believes not in death, nor knoweth of hope
    grown cold.
I hearkened and learned, and longed with a longing that
    had no name,
Till I went my ways to our village and again departure
    came.

Wide now the world was grown, and I saw things clear
    and grim,
That awhile agone smiled on me from the dream-mist
    doubtful and dim.
I knew that the poor were poor, and had no heart or hope;
And I knew that I was nothing with the least of evils to cope;
So I thought the thoughts of a man, and I fell into bitter
    mood,
Wherein, except as a picture, there was nought on the earth
    that was good;
Till I met the woman I love, and she asked, as folk ask of
    the wise,
Of the root and meaning of things that she saw in the world
    of lies.
I told her all I knew, and the tale told lifted the load
That made me less than a man; and she set my feet on the
    road.

So we left our pleasure behind to seek for hope and for life,
And to London we came, if perchance there smouldered
the embers of strife
Such as our Frenchman had told of; and I wrote to him to
ask
If he would be our master, and set the learners their task.
But "dead" was the word on the letter when it came back
to me,
And all that we saw henceforward with our own eyes must
we see.
So we looked and wondered and sickened; not for ourselves
indeed:
My father by now had died, but he left enough for my need;
And besides, away in our village the joiner's craft had I
learned,
And I worked as other men work, and money and wisdom
I earned.
Yet little from day to day in street or workshop I met
To nourish the plant of hope that deep in my heart had
been set.
The life of the poor we learned, and to me there was nothing
new
In their day of little deeds that ever deathward drew.
But new was the horror of London that went on all the
while
That rich men played at their ease for name and fame to
beguile
The days of their empty lives, and praised the deeds they
did,
As though they had fashioned the earth and found out the
sun long hid ;
Though some of them busied themselves from hopeless day
to day
With the lives of the slaves of the rich and the hell wherein
they lay.
They wrought meseems as those who should make a bar-
gain with hell,
That it grow a little cooler, and thus for ever to dwell.

So passed the world on its ways, and weary with waiting
    we were.
Men ate and drank and married; no wild cry smote the air,
No great crowd ran together to greet the day of doom;
And ever more and more seemed the town like a monstrous
    tomb
To us, the Pilgrims of Hope, until to-night it came,
And Hope on the stones of the street is written in letters of
    flame.

This is how it befel: a workmate of mine had heard
Some bitter speech in my mouth, and he took me up at the
    word,
And said: "Come over to-morrow to our Radical spouting-
    place;
For there, if we hear nothing new, at least we shall see a
    new face;
He is one of those Communist chaps, and 'tis like that you
    two may agree."
So we went, and the street was as dull and as common as
    aught you could see;
Dull and dirty the room. Just over the chairman's chair
Was a bust, a Quaker's face with nose cocked up in the air;
There were common prints on the wall of the heads of the
    party fray,
And Mazzini dark and lean amidst them gone astray.
Some thirty men we were of the kind that I knew full well,
Listless, rubbed down to the type of our easy-going hell.
My heart sank down as I entered, and wearily there I sat
While the chairman strove to end his maunder of this and
    of that.
And partly shy he seemed, and partly indeed ashamed
Of the grizzled man beside him as his name to us he named.
He rose, thickset and short, and dressed in shabby blue,
And even as he began it seemed as though I knew
The thing he was going to say, though I never heard it
    before.
He spoke, were it well, were it ill, as though a message he
    bore,
A word that he could not refrain from many a million of
    men.

Nor aught seemed the sordid room and the few that were
    listening then
Save the hall of the labouring earth and the world which
    was to be.
Bitter to many the message, but sweet indeed unto me,
Of man without a master, and earth without a strife,
And every soul rejoicing in the sweet and bitter of life:
Of peace and good-will he told, and I knew that in faith he
    spake,
But his words were my very thoughts, and I saw the battle
    awake,
And I followed from end to end; and triumph grew in my
    heart
As he called on each that heard him to arise and play his
    part
In the tale of the new-told gospel, lest as slaves they should
    live and die.

He ceased, and I thought the hearers would rise up with
    one cry,
And bid him straight enrol them; but they, they applauded
    indeed,
For the man was grown full eager, and had made them
    hearken and heed:
But they sat and made no sign, and two of the glibber kind
Stood up to jeer and to carp, his fiery words to blind.
I did not listen to them, but failed not his voice to hear
When he rose to answer the carpers, striving to make more
    clear
That which was clear already; not overwell, I knew,
He answered the sneers and the silence, so hot and eager
    he grew;
But my hope full well he answered, and when he called again
On men to band together lest they live and die in vain,
In fear lest he should escape me, I rose ere the meeting
    was done,
And gave him my name and my faith—and I was the only one.
He smiled as he heard the jeers, and there was a shake of
    the hand,
He spoke like a friend long known; and lo! I was one of the
    band.

And now the streets seem gay and the high stars glittering
　　bright;
And for me, I sing amongst them, for my heart is full and
　　light.
I see the deeds to be done and the day to come on the earth,
And riches vanished away and sorrow turned to mirth;
I see the city squalor and the country stupor gone.
And we a part of it all—we twain no longer alone
In the days to come of the pleasure, in the days that are of
　　the fight—
I was born once long ago: I am born again to-night.

VI

THE NEW PROLETARIAN

How near to the goal are we now, and what shall we live
　　to behold?
Will it come a day of surprise to the best of the hopeful
　　and bold?
Shall the sun arise some morning and see men falling to
　　work,
Smiling and loving their lives, not fearing the ill that may
　　lurk
In every house on their road, in the very ground that they
　　tread?
Shall the sun see famine slain, and the fear of children dead?
Shall he look adown on men set free from the burden of
　　care,
And the earth grown like to himself, so comely, clean and
　　fair?
Or else will it linger and loiter, till hope deferred hath
　　spoiled
All bloom of the life of man—yea, the day for which we
　　have toiled?
Till our hearts be turned to stone by the griefs that we have
　　borne,
And our loving kindness seared by love from our anguish
　　torn.

Till our hope grow a wrathful fire, and the light of the
    second birth
Be a flame to burn up the weeds from the lean impoverished
    earth.

What's this? Meseems it was but a little while ago
When the merest sparkle of hope set all my heart aglow!
The hope of the day was enough; but now 'tis the very day
That wearies my hope with longing. What's changed or
    gone away?
Or what is it drags at my heart-strings?—is it aught save
    the coward's fear?
In this little room where I sit is all that I hold most dear—
My love, and the love we have fashioned, my wife and the
    little lad.
Yet the four walls look upon us with other eyes than they
    had,
For indeed a thing hath happened. Last week at my craft
    I worked,
Lest oft in the grey of the morning my heart should tell me
    I shirked;
But to-day I work for us three, lest he and she and I
In the mud of the street should draggle till we come to the
    workhouse or die.

Not long to tell is the story, for, as I told you before,
A lawyer paid me the money which came from my father's
    store.
Well, now the lawyer is dead, and a curious tangle of theft,
It seems, is what he has lived by, and none of my money is
    left.
So I who have worked for my pleasure now work for utter
    need:
In "the noble army of labour" I now am a soldier indeed.

"You are young, you belong to the class that you love,"
    saith the rich man's sneer;
"Work on with your class and be thankful." All that I
    hearken to hear,
Nor heed the laughter much; have patience a little while,
I will tell you what's in my heart, nor hide a jot by guile.

When I worked pretty much for my pleasure I really
    worked with a will,
It was well and workmanlike done, and my fellows knew
    my skill,
And deemed me one of themselves though they called me
    gentleman Dick,
Since they knew I had some money; but now that to work
    I must stick,
Or fall into utter ruin, there's something gone, I find;
The work goes, cleared is the job, but there's something left
    behind;
I take up fear with my chisel, fear lies 'twixt me and my plane,
And I wake in the merry morning to a new unwonted pain.
That's fear: I shall live it down—and many a thing besides
Till I win the poor dulled heart which the workman's
    jacket hides.
Were it not for the Hope of Hopes I know my journey's end
And would wish I had ne'er been born the weary way to
    wend.
Now further, well you may think we have lived no gentle-
    man's life,
My wife is my servant, and I am the servant of my wife,
And we make no work for each other; but country folk we
    were,
And she sickened sore for the grass and the breath of the
    fragrant air
That had made her lovely and strong; and so up here we
    came
To the northern slopes of the town to live with a country
    dame,
Who can talk of the field-folks' ways: not one of the newest
    the house,
The woodwork worn to the bone, its panels the land of the
    mouse,
Its windows rattling and loose, its floors all up and down;
But this at least it was, just a cottage left in the town.
There might you sit in our parlour in the Sunday afternoon
And watch the sun through the vine-leaves and fall to
    dreaming that soon
You would see the grey team passing, their fetlocks wet with
    the brook.

Or the shining mountainous straw-load: there the summer
    moon would look
Through the leaves on the lampless room, wherein we sat
    we twain,
All London vanished away; and the morn of the summer
    rain
Would waft us the scent of the hay; or the first faint yellow
    leaves
Would flutter adown before us and tell of the acres of
    sheaves.

All this hath our lawyer eaten, and to-morrow must we go
To a room near my master's shop, in the purlieus of Soho.
No words of its shabby meanness! But that is our prison-cell
In the jail of weary London. Therein for us must dwell
The hope of the world that shall be, that rose a glimmering
    spark
As the last thin flame of our pleasure sank quavering in the
    dark.

Again the rich man jeereth: "The man is a coward, or
    worse—
He bewails his feeble pleasure; he quails before the curse
Which many a man endureth with calm and smiling face."
Nay, the man is a man, by your leave! Or put yourself in
    his place,
And see if the tale reads better. The haven of rest destroyed,
And nothing left of the life that was once so well enjoyed
But leave to live and labour, and the glimmer of hope
    deferred.
Now know I the cry of the poor no more as a story heard,
But rather a wordless wail forced forth from the weary heart.
Now, now when hope ariseth I shall surely know my part.

There's a little more to tell. When those last words were
    said,
At least I was yet a-working, and earning daily bread.
But now all that is changed, and meseems adown the stair
That leads to the nethermost pit, man, wife and child must
    fare.

When I joined the Communist folk, I did what in me lay
To learn the grounds of their faith. I read day after day
Whatever books I could handle, and heard about and about
What talk was going amongst them; and I burned up doubt
    after doubt,
Until it befel at last that to others I needs must speak
(Indeed, they pressed me to that while yet I was weaker
    than weak).
So I began the business, and in street-corners I spake
To knots of men. Indeed, that made my very heart ache,
So hopeless it seemed; for some stood by like men of wood;
And some, though fain to listen, but a few words understood;
And some but hooted and jeered: but whiles across some I
    came
Who were keen and eager to hear; as in dry flax the flame
So the quick thought flickered amongst them: and that
    indeed was a feast.
So about the streets I went, and the work on my hands
    increased;
And to say the very truth betwixt the smooth and the rough
It was work and hope went with it, and I liked it well
    enough:
Nor made I any secret of all that I was at
But daily talked in our shop and spoke of this and of that.
Then vanished my money away, and like a fool I told
Some one or two of the loss. Did that make the master
    bold?
Before I was one of his lot, and as queer as my head might be
I might do pretty much as I liked. Well now he sent for me
And spoke out in very words my thought of the rich man's
    jeer:
"Well, sir, you have got your wish, as far as I can hear,
And are now no thief of labour, but an honest working
    man:
Now I'll give you a word of warning: stay in it as long as
    you can,
This working lot that you like so: you're pretty well off as
    you are.
So take another warning: I have thought you went too far,
And now I am quite sure of it; so make an end of your talk
At once and for ever henceforth, or out of my shop you walk;

There are plenty of men to be had who are quite as good as
    you.
And mind you, anywhere else you'll scarce get work to do,
Unless you rule your tongue;—good morning; stick to your
    work."

The hot blood rose to my eyes, somewhere a thought did
    lurk
To finish both him and the job: but I knew now what I was,
And out of the little office in helpless rage did I pass
And went to my work, a *slave*, for the sake of my child and
    my sweet.
Did men look for the brand on my forehead that eve as I
    went through the street?
And what was the end after all? Why, one of my shop-
    mates heard
My next night's speech in the street, and passed on some
    bitter word,
And that week came a word with my money: "You needn't
    come again."
And the shame of my four days' silence had been but grief
    in vain.

Well I see the days before me: this time we shall not die
Nor go to the workhouse at once: I shall get work by-and-by,
And shall work in fear at first, and at last forget my fear,
And drudge on from day to day, since it seems that I hold
    life dear.
'Tis the lot of many millions! Yet if half of those millions
    knew
The hope that my heart hath learned, we should find a
    deed to do,
And who or what should withstand us? And I, e'en I
    might live
To know the love of my fellows and the gifts that earth can
    give.

VII

IN PRISON—AND AT HOME

The first of the nights is this, and I cannot go to bed;
I long for the dawning sorely, although when the night
    shall be dead,
Scarce to me shall the day be alive. Twice twenty-eight
    nights more,
Twice twenty-eight long days till the evil dream be o'er!
And he, does he count the hours as he lies in his prison-cell?
Does he nurse and cherish his pain? Nay, I know his strong
    heart well,
Swift shall his soul fare forth; he is here, and bears me away,
Till hand in hand we depart toward the hope of the earlier
    day.
Yea, here or there he sees it: in the street, in the cell, he sees
The vision he made me behold mid the stems of the blossom-
    ing trees,
When spring lay light on the earth, and first and at last I
    knew
How sweet was his clinging hand, how fair were the deeds
    he would do.

Nay, how wilt thou weep and be soft and cherish a pleasure
    in pain,
When the days and their task are before thee and awhile
    thou must work for twain?
O face, thou shalt lose yet more of thy fairness, be thinner
    no doubt,
And be waxen white and worn by the day that he cometh
    out!
Hand, how pale thou shalt be! how changed from the sun-
    burnt hand
That he kissed as it handled the rake in the noon of the
    summer land!

Let me think then it is but a trifle: the neighbours have told
    me so;
"Two months! why that is nothing and the time will
    speedily go."
'Tis nothing—O empty bed, let me work then for his sake!
I will copy out the paper which he thought the *News* might
    take,
If my eyes may see the letters; 'tis a picture of our life
And the little deeds of our days ere we thought of prison
    and strife.

Yes, neighbour, yes I am early—and I was late last night;
Bedless I wore through the hours and made a shift to write.
It was kind of you to come, nor will it grieve me at all
To tell you why he's in prison and how the thing did befal;
For I know you are with us at heart, and belike will join
    us soon.
It was thus—we went to a meeting on Saturday afternoon,
At a new place down in the West, a wretched quarter
    enough,
Where the rich men's houses are elbowed by ragged streets
    and rough,
Which are worse than they seem to be. (Poor thing! you
    know too well
How pass the days and the nights within that bricken hell!)
There, then, on a bit of waste we stood 'twixt the rich and
    the poor;
And Jack was the first to speak; that was he that you met
    at the door
Last week. It was quiet at first; and dull they most of them
    stood
As though they heeded nothing, nor thought of bad or of
    good,
Not even that they were poor, and haggard and dirty and
    dull:
Nay, some were so rich indeed that they with liquor were
    full,
And dull wrath rose in their souls as the hot words went by
    their ears,
For they deemed they were mocked and rated by men that
    were more than their peers.

But for some, they seemed to think that a prelude was all
    this
To the preachment of saving of souls, and hell, and endless
    bliss;
While some (O the hearts of slaves!) although they might
    understand,
When they heard their masters and feeders called thieves
    of wealth and of land,
Were as angry as though *they* were cursed. Withal there
    were some that heard,
And stood and pondered it all, and garnered a hope and a
    word.
Ah! heavy my heart was grown as I gazed on the terrible
    throng.
Lo! these that should have been the glad and the deft and
    the strong,
How were they dull and abased as the very filth of the road!
And who should waken their souls or clear their hearts of
    the load?

The crowd was growing and growing, and therewith the
    jeering grew;
And now that the time was come for an ugly brawl I knew,
When I saw how midst of the workmen some well-dressed
    men there came,
Of the scum of the well-to-do, brutes void of pity or shame;
The thief is a saint beside them. These raised a jeering noise,
And our speaker quailed before it, and the hubbub drowned
    his voice.
Then Richard put him aside and rose at once in his place,
And over the rags and the squalor beamed out his beautiful
    face,
And his sweet voice rang through the tumult, and I think
    the crowd would have hushed
And hearkened his manly words; but a well-dressed reptile
    pushed
Right into the ring about us and screeched out infamies
That sickened the soul to hearken; till he caught my angry
    eyes
And my voice that cried out at him, and straight on me
    he turned,

A foul word smote my heart and his cane on my shoulders
burned.
But e'en as a kestrel stoops down Richard leapt from his
stool
And drave his strong right hand amidst the mouth of the
fool.
Then all was mingled together, and away from him was I
torn,
And, hustled hither and thither, on the surging crowd was
borne;
But at last I felt my feet, for the crowd began to thin,
And I looked about for Richard that away from thence we
might win;
When lo, the police amidst us, and Richard hustled along
Betwixt a pair of blue-coats as the doer of all the wrong!

Little longer, friend, is the story; I scarce have seen him
again;
I could not get him bail despite my trouble and pain;
And this morning he stood in the dock: for all that that
might avail,
They might just as well have dragged him at once to the
destined jail.
The police had got their man and they meant to keep him
there,
And whatever tale was needful they had no trouble to swear.

Well, the white-haired fool on the bench was busy it seems
that day,
And so with the words "Two months," he swept the case
away;
Yet he lectured my man ere he went, but not for the riot
indeed,
For which he was sent to prison, but for holding a dangerous
creed.
"What have you got to do to preach such perilous stuff?
To take some care of yourself should find you work enough.
If you needs must preach or lecture, then hire a chapel or
hall;
Though indeed if you take my advice you'll just preach
nothing at all,

But stick to your work: you seem clever; who knows but
    you might rise,
And become a little builder should you condescend to be
    wise?
For in spite of your silly sedition, the land that we live in
    is free,
And opens a pathway to merit for you as well as for me."

Ah, friend, am I grown light-headed with the lonely grief
    of the night,
That I babble of this babble? Woe's me, how little and light
Is this beginning of trouble to all that yet shall be borne—
At worst but as the shower that lays but a yard of the corn
Before the hailstorm cometh and flattens the field to the
    earth.

O for a word from my love of the hope of the second birth!
Could he clear my vision to see the sword creeping out of
    the sheath
Inch by inch as we writhe in the toils of our living death!
Could he but strengthen my heart to know that we cannot
    fail;
For alas, I am lonely here—helpless and feeble and frail;
I am e'en as the poor of the earth, e'en they that are now
    alive;
And where is their might and their cunning with the mighty
    of men to strive?
Though they that come after be strong to win the day and
    the crown,
Ah, ever must we the deedless to the deedless dark go down,
Still crying, "To-morrow, to-morrow, to-morrow yet shall be
The new-born sun's arising o'er happy earth and sea"—
And we not there to greet it—for to-day and its life we yearn,
And where is the end of toiling and whitherward now shall
    we turn
But to patience, ever patience, and yet and yet to bear;
And yet, forlorn, unanswered as oft before to hear,
Through the tales of the ancient fathers and the dreams that
    mock our wrong.
That cry to the naked heavens, "How long, O Lord! how
    long?"

VIII

THE HALF OF LIFE GONE

The days have slain the days, and the seasons have gone by
And brought me the summer again; and here on the grass
      I lie
As erst I lay and was glad ere I meddled with right and
      with wrong.
Wide lies the mead as of old, and the river is creeping along
By the side of the elm-clad bank that turns its weedy stream,
And grey o'er its hither lip the quivering rushes gleam.
There is work in the mead as of old; they are eager at win-
      ning the hay,
While every sun sets bright and begets a fairer day.
The forks shine white in the sun round the yellow red-
      wheeled wain,
Where the mountain of hay grows fast; and now from out
      of the lane
Comes the ox-team drawing another, comes the bailiff and
      the beer,
And thump, thump, goes the farmer's nag o'er the narrow
      bridge of the weir.
High up and light are the clouds, and though the swallows
      flit
So high o'er the sunlit earth, they are well a part of it,
And so, though high over them, are the wings of the wander-
      ing herne;
In measureless depths above him doth the fair sky quiver
      and burn;
The dear sun floods the land as the morning falls toward
      noon,
And a little wind is awake in the best of the latter June.

They are busy winning the hay, and the life and the picture
      they make,
If I were as once I was, I should deem it made for my sake;
For here if one need not work is a place for happy rest,
While one's thought wends over the world, north, south,
      and east and west.

      O

There are the men and the maids, and the wives and the
gaffers grey
Of the fields I know so well, and but little changed are they
Since I was a lad amongst them; and yet how great is the
change!
Strange are they grown unto me; yea, I to myself am
strange.
Their talk and their laughter mingling with the music of
the meads
Has now no meaning to me to help or to hinder my needs,
So far from them have I drifted. And yet amidst them goes
A part of myself, my boy, and of pleasure and pain he knows,
And deems it something strange when he is other than glad.
Lo now! the woman that stoops and kisses the face of the lad,
And puts a rake in his hand and laughs in his laughing
face—
Whose is the voice that laughs in the old familiar place?
Whose should it be but my love's, if my love were yet on the
earth?
Could she refrain from the fields where my joy and her joy
had birth,
When I was there and her child, on the grass that knew her
feet
Mid the flowers that led her on when the summer eve was
sweet?

No, no, it is she no longer; never again can she come
And behold the hay-wains creeping o'er the meadows of
her home;
No more can she kiss her son or put the rake in his hand
That she handled a while agone in the midst of the hay-
making band.
Her laughter is gone and her life; there is no such thing on
the earth,
No share for me then in the stir, no share in the hurry and
mirth.

Nay, let me look and believe that all these will vanish away,
At least when the night has fallen, and that she will be there
    mid the hay,
Happy and weary with work, waiting and longing for love.
There will she be, as of old, when the great moon hung
    above,
And lightless and dead was the village, and nought but the
    weir was awake;
There will she rise to meet me, and my hands will she hasten
    to take,
And thence shall we wander away, and over the ancient
    bridge
By many a rose-hung hedgerow, till we reach the sun-burnt
    ridge
And the great trench digged by the Romans: there then
    awhile shall we stand,
To watch the dawn come creeping o'er the fragrant lovely
    land,
Till all the world awaketh, and draws us down, we twain,
To the deeds of the field and the fold and the merry
    summer's gain.
Ah thus, only thus shall I see her, in dreams of the day or
    the night,
When my soul is beguiled of its sorrow to remember past
    delight.
She is gone. She was and she is not; there is no such thing
    on the earth
But e'en as a picture painted; and for me there is void and
    dearth
That I cannot name or measure.
                      Yet for me and all these she died,
E'en as she lived for awhile, that the better day might
    betide.
Therefore I live, and I shall live till the last day's work
    shall fail.
Have patience now but a little and I will tell you the tale
Of how and why she died, and why I am weak and worn,
And have wandered away to the meadows and the place
    where I was born:
But here and to-day I cannot; for ever my thought will
    stray

To that hope fulfilled for a little and the bliss of the earlier
    day.
Of the great world's hope and anguish to-day I scarce can
    think:
Like a ghost from the lives of the living and their earthly
    deeds I shrink.
I will go adown by the water and over the ancient bridge,
And wend in our footsteps of old till I come to the sun-burnt
    ridge,
And the great trench digged by the Romans; and thence
    awhile will I gaze,
And see three teeming counties stretch out till they fade in
    the haze;
And in all the dwellings of man that thence mine eyes shall
    see,
What man as hapless as I am beneath the sun shall be?

O fool, what words are these? Thou hast a sorrow to nurse,
And thou hast been bold and happy; but these, if they
    utter a curse,
No sting it has and no meaning—it is empty sound on the
    air.
Thy life is full of mourning, and theirs so empty and bare
That they have no words of complaining; nor so happy
    have they been
That they may measure sorrow or tell what grief may mean.
And thou, thou hast deeds to do, and toil to meet thee soon;
Depart and ponder on these through the sun-worn after-
    noon.

IX

A NEW FRIEND

I have promised to tell you the story of how I was left
    alone
Sick and wounded and sore, and why the woman is gone
That I deemed a part of my life. Tell me when all is told,
If you deem it fit that the earth, that the world of men
    should hold
My work and my weariness still; yet think of that other life,
The child of me and of her, and the years and the coming
    strife.

After I came out of prison our living was hard to earn
By the work of my hands, and of hers; to shifts we had to
    turn,
Such as the poor know well, and the rich cannot understand,
And just out of the gutter we stood, still loving and hand in
    hand.

Do you ask me if still amidst all I held the hunt in view,
And the hope of the morning of life, all the things I should
    do and undo?
Be easy, I am not a coward: nay little prudence I learned,
I spoke and I suffered for speaking, and my meat by my
    manhood was burned.
When the poor man thinks—and rebels, the whip lies ready
    anear;
But he who is rebel and rich may live safe for many a year,
While he warms his heart with pictures of all the glory to
    come.
There's the storm of the press and the critics maybe, but
    sweet is his home,
There is meat in the morn and the even, and rest when the
    day is done,
All is fair and orderly there as the rising and setting sun—
And I know both the rich and the poor.
               Well, I grew bitter they said;
'Tis not unlike that I did, for bitter indeed was my bread,
And surely the nursling plant shall smack of its nourishing
    soil.

And here was our life in short, pinching and worry and toil,
One petty fear thrust out by another come in its place,
Each scrap of life but a fear, and the sum of it wretched and
   base.

E'en so fare millions of men, where men for money are
   made,
Where the poor are dumb and deedless, where the rich are
   not afraid.

Ah, am I bitter again? Well, these are our breeding-stock,
The very base of order, and the state's foundation rock;
Is it so good and so safe that their manhood should be
   outworn
By the struggle for anxious life, the dull pain dismally borne,
Till all that was man within them is dead and vanished
   away?

Were it not even better that all these should think on a day
As they look on each other's sad faces, and see how many
   they are:
"What are these tales of old time of men who were mighty
   in war?
They fought for some city's dominion, for the name of a
   forest or field;
They fell that no alien's token should be blazoned on their
   shield;
And for this is their valour praised and dear is their renown,
And their names are beloved for ever and they wear the
   patriot's crown;
And shall we then wait in the streets and this heap of misery,
Till their stones rise up to help us or the far heavens set us
   free?
For we, we shall fight for no name, no blazon on banner or
   shield;
But that man to man may hearken and the earth her
   increase yield;
That never again in the world may be sights like we have
   seen;
That never again in the world may be men like we have
   been,
That never again like ours may be manhood spoilt and
   blurred."

Yea even so was I bitter, and this was my evilest word:

"Spend and be spent for our hope, and you at least shall be
    free,

Though you be rugged and coarse, as wasted and worn as
    you be."

Well, "bitter" I was, and denounced, and scarcely at last
    might we stand

From out of the very gutter, as we wended hand in hand.

I had written before for the papers, but so "bitter" was I
    grown,

That none of them now would have me that could pay me
    half-a-crown,

And the worst seemed closing around us; when as it needs
    must chance,

I spoke at some Radical Club of the Great Revolution in
    France.

Indeed I said nothing new to those who had learned it all,

And yet as something strange on some of the folk did it fall,

It was late in the terrible war, and France to the end drew
    nigh,

And some of us stood agape to see how the war would
    die,

And what would spring from its ashes. So when the talk
    was o'er

And after the stir and excitement I felt the burden I bore

Heavier yet for it all, there came to speak to me

A serious well-dressed man, a "gentleman," young I could see,

And we fell to talk together, and he shyly gave me praise,

And asked, though scarcely in words, of my past and my
    "better days."

Well, there,—I let it all out, and I flushed as I strode along,

(For we were walking by now) and bitterly spoke of the
    wrong.

Maybe I taught him something, but ready he was to learn,

And had come to our workmen meetings some knowledge
    of men to learn.

He kindled afresh at my words, although to try him I spake

More roughly than I was wont; but every word did he take

For what it was really worth, nor even laughter he spared,

As though he would look on life of its rags of habit bared.

Well, why should I be ashamed that he helped me at my
    need?

My wife and my child, must I kill them? And the man was
    a friend indeed,

And the work that he got me I did (it was writing, you
    understand)

As well as another might do it.   To be short, he joined our
    band

Before many days were over, and we saw him everywhere

That we workmen met together, though I brought him not
    to my lair.

Eager he grew for the Cause, and we twain grew friend and
    friend:

He was dainty of mind and of body; most brave, as he
    showed in the end;

Merry despite of his sadness, quick-witted and speedy to see:

Like a perfect knight of old time as the poets would have
    them to be.

That was the friend that I won by my bitter speech at last.

He loved me; he grieved my soul: now the love and the
    grief are past;

He is gone with his eager learning, his sadness and his mirth,

His hope and his fond desire.   There is no such thing on the
    earth.

He died not unbefriended—nor unbeloved maybe.

Betwixt my life and his longing there rolls a boundless sea.

And what are those memories now to all that I have to do,

The deeds to be done so many, the days of my life so few?

X

READY TO DEPART

I said of my friend new-found that at first he saw not my
    lair;
Yet he and I and my wife were together here and there;
And at last as my work increased and my den to a dwelling
    grew,
He came there often enough, and yet more together we drew.
Then came a change in the man; for a month he kept away,
Then came again and was with us for a fortnight every day,
But often he sat there silent, which was little his wont with
    us.
And at first I had no inkling of what constrained him thus;
I might have thought that he faltered, but now and again
    there came,
When we spoke of the Cause and its doings, a flash of his
    eager flame,
And he seemed himself for a while; then the brightness
    would fade away,
And he gloomed and shrank from my eyes.
                        Thus passed day after day,
And grieved I grew, and I pondered: till at last one eve we
    sat
In the fire-lit room together, and talked of this and that,
But chiefly indeed of the war and what would come of it;
For Paris drew near to its fall, and wild hopes 'gan to flit
Amidst us Communist folk; and we talked of what might
    be done
When the Germans had gone their ways and the two were
    left alone,
Betrayers and betrayed in war-worn wasted France.

As I spoke the word "betrayed," my eyes met his in a glance,
And swiftly he turned away; then back with a steady gaze
He turned on me; and it seemed as when a sword-point
    plays
Round the sword in a battle's beginning and the coming on
    of strife.
For I knew though he looked on me, he saw not me, but
    my wife:
And he reddened up to the brow, and the tumult of the
    blood
Nigh blinded my eyes for a while, that I scarce saw bad or
    good,
Till I knew that he was arisen and had gone without a word.
Then I turned about unto her, and a quivering voice I heard
Like music without a meaning, and twice I heard my name.
"O Richard, Richard!" she said, and her arms about me
    came,
And her tears and the lips that I loved were on my face
    once more.
A while I clung to her body, and longing sweet and sore
Beguiled my heart of its sorrow; then we sundered and sore
    she wept,
While fair pictures of days departed about my sad heart
    crept,
And mazed I felt and weary.   But we sat apart again,
Not speaking, while between us was the sharp and bitter
    pain
As the sword 'twixt the lovers bewildered in the fruitless
    marriage bed.
Yet a while, and we spoke together, and I scarce knew what
    I said,
But it was not wrath or reproaching, or the chill of love-born
    hate;
For belike around and about.us, we felt the brooding fate.
We were gentle and kind together, and if any had seen us so,
They had said, "These two are one in the face of all trouble
    and woe."
But indeed as a wedded couple we shrank from the eyes of
    men,
As we dwelt together and pondered on the days that come
    not again.

Days passed and we dwelt together; nor Arthur came for
 awhile;
Gravely it was and sadly, and with no greeting smile,
That we twain met at our meetings: but no growth of hate
 was yet,
Though my heart at first would be sinking as our thoughts
 and our eyes they met:
And when he spake amidst us and as one we two agreed,
And I knew of his faith and his wisdom, then sore was my
 heart indeed.
We shrank from meeting alone: for the words we had to say
Our thoughts would nowise fashion—not yet for many a day.

Unhappy days of all days! Yet O might they come again!
So sore as my longing returneth to their trouble and sorrow
 and pain!

But time passed, and once we were sitting, my wife and I
 in our room,
And it was in the London twilight and the February gloom,
When there came a knock, and he entered all pale, though
 bright were his eyes,
And I knew that something had happened, and my heart
 to my mouth did arise.
"It is over," he said "—and beginning; for Paris has fallen
 at last,
And who knows what next shall happen after all that has
 happened and passed?
There now may we all be wanted."
                                    I took up the word: "Well then
Let us go, we three together, and there to die like men."

"Nay," he said, "to live and be happy like men." Then he
 flushed up red,
And she no less as she hearkened, as one thought through
 their bodies had sped.
Then I reached out my hand unto him, and I kissed her
 once on the brow,
But no word craving forgiveness, and no word of pardon
 e'en now,
Our minds for our mouths might fashion.

In the February gloom
And into the dark we sat planning, and there was I in the
      room,
And in speech I gave and I took; but yet alone and apart
In the fields where I once was a youngling whiles wandered
      the thoughts of my heart,
And whiles in the unseen Paris, and the streets made ready
      for war.
Night grew and we lit the candles, and we drew together
      more,
And whiles we differed a little as we settled what to do,
And my soul was cleared of confusion as nigher the deed-
      time drew.

Well, I took my child into the country, as we had settled there,
And gave him o'er to be cherished by a kindly woman's care,
A friend of my mother's, but younger: and for Arthur, I let
      him give
His money, as mine was but little, that the boy might
      flourish and live.
Lest we three, or I and Arthur, should perish in tumult and
      war,
And at least the face of his father he should look on never
      more.
You cry out shame on my honour? But yet remember again
That a man in my boy was growing; must my passing pride
      and pain
Undo the manhood within him and his days and their
      doings blight?
So I thrust my pride away, and I did what I deemed was right,
And left him down in our country.
                              And well may you think indeed
How my sad heart swelled at departing from the peace of
      river and mead,
But I held all sternly aback and again to the town did I pass.
And as alone I journeyed, this was ever in my heart:
"They may die; they may live and be happy; but for me I
      know my part,
In Paris to do my utmost, and there in Paris to die!"
And I said, "The day of the deeds and the day of deliver-
      ance is nigh."

XI

A GLIMPSE OF THE COMING DAY

It was strange indeed, that journey! Never yet had I
    crossed the sea
Or looked on another people than the folk that had fostered
    me,
And my heart rose up and fluttered as in the misty night
We came on the fleet of the fishers slow rolling in the light
Of the hidden moon, as the sea dim under the false dawn
    lay;
And so like shadows of ships through the night they faded
    away,
And Calais pier was upon us. Dreamlike it was indeed
As we sat in the train together, and toward the end made
    speed.
But a dull sleep came upon me, and through the sleep a
    dream
Of the Frenchman who once was my master by the side of
    the willowy stream;
And he talked and told me tales of the war unwaged as yet,
And the victory never won, and bade me never forget,
While I walked on, still unhappy, by the home of the dark-
    striped perch.
Till at last, with a flash of light and a rattle and side-long
    lurch,
I woke up dazed and witless, till my sorrow awoke again,
And the grey of the morn was upon us as we sped through
    the poplar plain,
By the brimming streams and the houses with their grey
    roofs warped and bent,
And the horseless plough in the furrow, and things fair and
    innocent.
And there sat my wife before me, and she, too, dreamed as
    she slept;
For the slow tears fell from her eyelids as in her sleep she
    wept.

But Arthur sat by my side and waked; and flushed was his
    face,

And his eyes were quick to behold the picture of each fair
    place

That we flashed by as on we hurried; and I knew that the
    joy of life

Was strongly stirred within him by the thought of the
    coming strife.

Then I too thought for a little, It is good in grief's despite,

It is good to see earth's pictures, and so live in the day and
    the light.

Yea, we deemed that to death we were hastening, and it
    made our vision clear,

And we knew the delight of our life-days, and held their
    sorrow dear.

But now when we came unto Paris and were out in the sun
    and the street,

It was strange to see the faces that our wondering eyes did
    meet;

Such joy and peace and pleasure! That folk were glad we
    knew,

But knew not the why and the wherefore; and we who had
    just come through

The vanquished land and down-cast and there at St. Denis
    e'en now

Had seen the German soldiers, and heard their bugles blow,

And the drum and fife go rattling through the freshness of
    the morn—

Yet here we beheld all joyous the folk they had made
    forlorn!

So at last from a grey stone building we saw a great flag fly,.

One colour, red and solemn 'gainst the blue of the spring-
    tide sky,

And we stopped and turned to each other, and as each at
    each did we gaze,

The city's hope enwrapped us with joy and great amaze.

As folk in a dream we washed and we ate, and in all detail,
Oft told and in many a fashion, did we have all yesterday's
        tale:
How while we were threading our tangle of trouble in
        London there,
And I for my part, let me say it, within but a step of despair,
In Paris the day of days had betid; for the vile dwarf's
        stroke,   .
To madden Paris and crush her, had been struck and the
        dull sword broke;
There was now no foe and no fool in the city, and Paris was
        free;
And e'en as she is this morning, to-morrow all France
        will be.
We heard, and our hearts were saying, "In a little while all
        the earth—"
And that day at last of all days I knew what life was worth;
For I saw what few have beheld, a folk with all hearts gay.
Then at last I knew indeed that our word of the coming day,
That so oft in grief and in sorrow I had preached, and
        scarcely knew
If it was but despair of the present or the hope of the day
        that was due—
I say that I saw it now, real, solid and at hand.

And strange how my heart went back to our little nook of
        the land,
And how plain and clear I saw it, as though I longed indeed
To give it a share of the joy and the satisfaction of need
That here in the folk I beheld. For this in our country spring
Did the starlings bechatter the gables, and the thrush in the
        thorn-bush sing,
And the green cloud spread o'er the willows, and the little
        children rejoice
And shouts midst a nameless longing to the morning's min-
        gled voice;
For this was the promise of spring-tide, and the new leaves
        longing to burst,
And the white roads threading the acres, and the sun-
        warmed meadows athirst.
Once all was the work of sorrow and the life without reward,

And the toil that fear hath bidden, and the folly of master
    and lord;
But now are all things changing, and hope without a fear
Shall speed us on through the story of the changes of the
    year.
Now spring shall pluck the garland that summer weaves for
    all,
And autumn spread the banquet and winter fill the hall.
O earth, thou kind bestower, thou ancient fruitful place,
How lovely and beloved now gleams thy happy face!

And O mother, mother, I said, hadst thou known as I lay
    in thy lap,
And for me thou hopedst and fearedst, on what days my
    life should hap,
Hadst thou known of the death that I look for, and the
    deeds wherein I should deal,
How calm had been thy gladness! How sweet hadst thou
    smiled on my weal!
As some woman of old hadst thou wondered, who hath
    brought forth a god of the earth,
And in joy that knoweth no speech she dreams of the happy
    birth.

Yea, fair were those hours indeed, whatever hereafter might
    come,
And they swept over all my sorrow, and all thought of my
    wildered home.
But not for dreams of rejoicing had we come across the
    sea:
That day we delivered the letters that our friends had given
    to me,
And we craved for some work for the cause. And what work
    was there indeed,
But to learn the business of battle and the manner of dying
    at need?
We three could think of none other, and we wrought our
    best therein;
And both of us made a shift the sergeant's stripes to win,
For diligent were we indeed: and he, as in all he did,
Showed a cheerful ready talent that nowise might be hid,

And yet hurt the pride of no man that he needs must step
  before.

But as for my wife, the *brancard* of the ambulance-women
  she wore,

And gently and bravely would serve us; and to all as a sister
  to be—

A sister amidst of the strangers—and, alas! a sister to me.

XII

MEETING THE WAR-MACHINE

So we dwelt in the war-girdled city as a very part of its
  life.

Looking back at it all from England, I an atom of the strife,

I can see that I might have seen what the end would be
  from the first,

The hope of man devoured in the day when the Gods are
  athirst.

But those days we lived, as I tell you, a life that was not
  our own;

And we saw but the hope of the world, and the seed that
  the ages had sown,

Spring up now a fair-blossomed tree from the earth lying
  over the dead;

Earth quickened, earth kindled to spring-tide with the blood
  that her lovers have shed,

With the happy days cast off for the sake of her happy day,

With the love of women foregone, and the bright youth
  worn away,

With the gentleness stripped from the lives thrust into the
  jostle of war,

With the hope of the hardy heart forever dwindling afar.

O Earth, Earth, look on thy lovers, who knew all thy gifts
  and thy gain,

But cast them aside for thy sake, and caught up barren pain!

Indeed of some art thou mindful, and ne'er shalt forget
  their tale,

Till shrunk are the floods of thine ocean and thy sun is
    waxen pale.
But rather I bid thee remember e'en these of the latter
    days,
Who were fed by no fair promise and made drunken by no
    praise.
For them no opening heaven reached out the martyr's
    crown;
No folk delivered wept them, and no harvest of renown
They reaped with the scythe of battle; nor round their dying
    bed
Did kindly friendly farewell the dew of blessing shed;
In the sordid streets of the city mid a folk that knew them
    not,
In the living death of the prison didst thou deal them out
    their lot,
Yet foundest them deeds to be doing; and no feeble folk
    were they
To scowl on their own undoing and wail their lives away;
But oft were they blithe and merry and deft from the strife
    to wring
Some joy that others gained not midst their peaceful way-
    faring.
So fared they, giftless ever, and no help of fortune sought.
Their life was thy deliverance, O Earth, and for thee they
    fought;
Mid the jeers of the happy and deedless, mid failing friends
    they went
To their foredoomed fruitful ending on the love of thee
    intent.

Yea and we were a part of it all, the beginning of the end,
That first fight of the uttermost battle whither all the nations
    wend;
And yet could I tell you its story, you might think it little
    and mean.
For few of you now will be thinking of the day that might
    have been,
And fewer still meseemeth of the day that yet shall be,
That shall light up that first beginning and its tangled
    misery.

For indeed a very machine is the war that now men wage;
Nor have we hold of its handle, we gulled of our heritage,
We workmen slaves of machines. Well, it ground us small
    enough
This machine of the beaten Bourgeois; though oft the work
    was rough
That it turned out for its money. Like other young soldiers
    at first
I scarcely knew the wherefore why our side had had the
    worst;
For man to man and in knots we faced the matter well;
And I thought, well to-morrow or next day a new tale will
    be to tell.
I was fierce and not afraid; yet O were the wood-sides
    fair,
And the crofts and the sunny gardens, though death they
    harboured there!
And few but fools are fain of leaving the world outright,
And the story over and done, and an end of the life and the
    light.
No hatred of life, thou knowest, O Earth, mid the bullets
    I bore,
Though pain and grief oppressed me that I never may suffer
    more.
But in those days past over did life and death seem one;
Yea the life had we attained to which could never be
    undone.

You would have me tell of the fighting? Well, you know it
    was new to me,
Yet it soon seemed as if it had been for ever, and ever would
    be.
The morn when we made that sally, some thought (and yet
    not I)
That a few days and all would be over: just a few had got
    to die,
And the rest would be happy thenceforward. But my stub-
    born country blood
Was bidding me hold my halloo till we were out of the wood.
And that was the reason perhaps why little disheartened I
    was,

As we stood all huddled together that night in a helpless
    mass,
As beaten men are wont: and I knew enough of war
To know midst its unskilled labour what slips full often are.

There was Arthur unhurt beside me, and my wife come
    back again,
And surely that eve between us there was love though no
    lack of pain
As we talked all the matter over, and our hearts spake more
    than our lips;
And we said, "We shall learn, we shall learn—yea, e'en from
    disasters and slips."

Well, many a thing we learned, but we learned not how to
    prevail
O'er the brutal war-machine, the ruthless grinder of bale;
By the bourgeois world it was made, for the bourgeois world;
    and we,
We were e'en as the village weaver 'gainst the power-loom,
    maybe.
It drew on nearer and nearer, and we 'gan to look to the
    end—
We three, at least—and our lives began with death to blend;
Though we were long a-dying—though I dwell on yet as a
    ghost
In the land where we once were happy, to look on the loved
    and the lost.

XIII

THE STORY'S ENDING

How can I tell you the story of the Hope and its defence?

We wrought in a narrow circle; it was hither and thither
and thence;

To the walls, and back for a little; to the fort and there to
abide,

Grey-beards and boys and women; they lived there—and
they died;

Nor counted much in the story. I have heard it told since
then,

And mere lies our deeds have turned to in the mouths of
happy men,

And e'en those will be soon forgotten as the world wends
on its way,

Too busy for truth or kindness. Yet my soul is seeing the
day

When those who are now but children the new generation
shall be,

And e'en in our land of commerce and the workshop over
the sea,

Amid them shall spring up the story; yea the very breath of
the air

To the yearning hearts of the workers true tale of it all shall
bear.

Year after year shall men meet with the red flag over head,

And shall call on the help of the vanquished and the kindness of the dead.

And time that weareth most things, and the years that
overgrow

The tale of the fools triumphant, yet clearer and clearer
shall show

The deeds of the helpers of menfolk to every age and clime,

The deeds of the cursed and the conquered that were wise
before their time.

Of these were my wife and my friend; there they ended their
    wayfaring
Like the generations before them thick thronging as leaves
    of the spring,
Fast falling as leaves of the autumn as the ancient singer
    hath said,
And each one with a love and a story. Ah the grief of the
    early dead!
"What is all this talk?" you are saying; "why all this long
    delay?"
Yes, indeed, it is hard in the telling. Of things too grievous
    to say
I would be, but cannot be, silent. Well, I hurry on to the
    end—
For it drew to the latter ending of the hope that we helped
    to defend.
The forts were gone and the foemen drew near to the thin-
    manned wall,
And it wanted not many hours to the last hour and the fall,
And we lived amid the bullets and seldom went away.
To what as yet were the streets by night-tide or by day.
We three, we fought together, and I did the best I could,
Too busy to think of the ending; but Arthur was better
    than good;
Resourceful, keen and eager, from post to post he ran,
To thrust out aught that was moving and bring up the
    uttermost man,
He was gone on some such errand, and was absent a little
    space,
When I turned about for a moment and saw my wife's fair
    face,
And her foot set firm on the rampart, as she hastened here
    and there,
To some of our wounded comrades such help as she could
    to bear.
Then straight she looked upon me with such lovely, friendly
    eyes
Of the days gone by and remembered, that up from my
    heart 'gan rise
The choking sobbing passion; but I kept it aback, and
    smiled,

And waved my hand aloft—But therewith her face turned
    wild
In a moment of time, and she stared along the length of the
    wall,
And I saw a man who was running and crouching, stagger
    and fall,
And knew it for Arthur at once; but voiceless toward him
    she ran,
I with her, crying aloud. But or ever we reached the man,
Lo! a roar and a crash around us and my sick brain whirling
    around,
And a white light turning to black, and no sky and no air
    and no ground,
And then what I needs must tell of as a great blank; but
    indeed
No words to tell of its horror hath language for my need:
As a map is to a picture, so is all that my words can say.

But when I came to myself, in a friend's house sick I lay
Amid strange blended noises, and my own mind wandering
    there;
Delirium in me indeed and around me everywhere.
That passed, and all things grew calmer, I with them: all
    the stress
That the last three months had been on me now sank to
    helplessness.
I bettered, and then they told me the tale of what had
    betid;
And first, that under the name of a friend of theirs I was
    hid,
Who was slain by mere misadventure, and was English as
    was I,
And no rebel, and had due papers wherewith I might well
    slip by
When I was somewhat better. Then I knew, though they
    had not told,
How all was fallen together, and my heart grew sick and cold.
And yet indeed thenceforward I strove my life to live,
That e'en as I was and so hapless I yet might live to strive.
It was but few words they told me of that murder great and
    grim,

And how with the blood of the guiltless the city's streets did
swim,
And of other horrors they told not, except in a word or two,
When they told of their scheme to save me from the hands
of the villainous crew,
Whereby I guessed what was happening in the main with-
out detail.
And so at last it came to their telling the other tale
Of my wife and my friend; though that also methought I
knew too well.
Well, they said that I had been wounded by the fragment
of a shell,
Another of which had slain her outright, as forth she ran
Toward Arthur struck by a bullet. She never touched the
man
Alive and she also alive; but thereafter as they lay
Both dead on one litter together, then folk who knew not us,
But were moved by seeing the twain so fair and so piteous,
Took them for husband and wife who were fated there to
die,
Or, it may be lover and lover indeed—but what know I?

Well, you know that I 'scaped from Paris, and crossed the
narrow sea,
And made my way to the country where we twain were
wont to be,
And that is the last and the latest of the tale I have to tell.
I came not here to be bidding my happiness farewell,
And to nurse my grief and to win me the gain of a wounded
life,
That because of the bygone sorrow may hide away from the
strife.
I came to look to my son, and myself to get stout and strong,
That two men there might he hereafter to battle against the
wrong;
And I cling to the love of the past and the love of the day
to be,
And the present, it is but the building of the man to be
strong in me.

SHORTER POEMS

THE DEFENCE OF GUENEVERE AND OTHER POEMS *was published by Bell and Daldy in 1858, and dedicated to Dante Gabriel Rossetti.*[1] *It was Morris's second work in volume form,* Sir Galahad, a Christmas Mystery *having been published earlier in the same year. In the present selection, the following poems are taken from the* Defence :— The Defence of Guenevere, Old Love, Shameful Death, Golden Wings, The Haystack in the Floods, Summer Dawn, In Prison.

[1] pp. iv + 248. Foolscap 8vo.

THE EARTHLY PARADISE. *See under* The Wanderers, *in the section,* Stories in Verse. *Here are selected the opening poem, and the twelve short lyrics interspersed between the stories for each month in the year.*

CHANTS FOR SOCIALISTS *chiefly appeared in the first instance in Socialist journals or in pamphlet form.* Chants for Socialists, No. I, The Day is Coming[1] *was published as a pamphlet for the Democratic Federation (later the Social Democratic Federation) in 1884 by Reeves.* Numbers 2 (The Voice of Toil), 3 (All for the Cause), *and* 4 (No Master) *appeared in* Justice, *the organ of the S.D.F., in 1884, and the two former were reprinted together as a pamphlet the same year.*[2] *In 1885, after Morris's break with the S.D.F., the Socialist League issued a pamphlet containing these four chants, with two more* (The Message of the March Wind *and* The March of the Workers) *under the collective title,* Chants for Socialists.[3] *In a further edition, also of 1885,* Down among the Dead Men *was added.*[4] *In 1888 the* Chants *were re-issued, in one pamphlet with a Socialist League* Manifesto *and a series of tracts in* The Socialist Platform.[5] *Later the* Chants *were included in one bound volume with* The Pilgrims of Hope (*q.v.*) *in 1915. The* Death Song *was issued separately as a pamphlet, with a "Memorial Design" by Walter Crane, in 1887.*[6]

[1] pp. 8. Trimmed 8vo.
[2] pp. 8. Untrimmed crown 8vo.
[3] pp. 16. Uncut demy 8vo.
[4] pp. 16 Crown 8vo.
[5] Simply 4 bound up with other pamphlets.
[6] pp. 8. Royal 8vo.

POEMS BY THE WAY. *See under* The Pilgrims of Hope.

From *THE DEFENCE OF GUENEVERE AND OTHER POEMS*

THE DEFENCE OF GUENEVERE

But, knowing now that they would have her speak,
She threw her wet hair backward from her brow,
Her hand close to her mouth touching her cheek,

As though she had had there a shameful blow,
And feeling it shameful to feel ought but shame
All through her heart, yet felt her cheek burned so,

She must a little touch it; like one lame
She walked away from Gauwaine, with her head
Still lifted up; and on her cheek of flame

The tears dried quick; she stopped at last and said:
"O knights and lords, it seems but little skill
To talk of well-known things past now and dead.

"God wot I ought to say, I have done ill,
And pray you all forgiveness heartily!
Because you must be right such great lords—still

"Listen, suppose your time were come to die,
And you were quite alone and very weak;
Yea, laid a dying while very mightily

"The wind was ruffling up the narrow streak
Of river through your broad lands running well:
Suppose a hush should come, then some one speak:

" 'One of these cloths is heaven, and one is hell,
Now choose one cloth for ever, which they be,
I will not tell you, you must somehow tell

" 'Of your own strength and mightiness; here, see!'
Yea, yea, my lord, and you to ope your eyes,
At foot of your familiar bed to see

"A great God's angel standing, with such dyes,
Not known on earth, on his great wings, and hands,
Held out two ways, light from the inner skies

"Showing him well, and making his commands
Seem to be God's commands, moreover, too,
Holding within his hands the cloths on wands;

"And one of these strange choosing cloths was blue,
Wavy and long and one cut short and red;
No man could tell the better of the two.

"After a shivering half-hour you said,
'God help! heaven's colour, the blue'; and he said,
            'hell.'
Perhaps you then would roll upon your bed,

"And cry to all good men that loved you well,
'Ah Christ! if only I had known, known, known';
Launcelot went away, then I could tell,

"Like wisest man how all things would be, moan,
And roll and hurt myself, and long to die,
And yet fear much to die for what was sown.

"Nevertheless you, O Sir Gauwaine, lie,
Whatever may have happened through these years,
God knows I speak truth, saying that you lie."

Her voice was low at first, being full of tears,
But as it cleared, it grew full loud and shrill,
Growing a windy shriek in all men's ears,

A ringing in their startled brains, until
She said that Gauwaine lied, then her voice sunk,
And her great eyes began again to fill,

Though still she stood right up, and never shrunk,
But spoke on bravely, glorious lady fair!
Whatever tears her full lips may have drunk,

She stood, and seemed to think, and wrung her hair,
Spoke out at last with no more trace of shame,
With passionate twisting of her body there:

"It chanced upon a day that Launcelot came
To dwell at Arthur's court: at Christmas-time
This happened; when the heralds sung his name,

" 'Son of King Ban of Benwick,' seemed to chime
Along with all the bells that rang that day,
O'er the white roofs, with little change of rhyme.

"Christmas and whitened winter passed away,
And over me the April sunshine came,
Made very awful with black hail-clouds, yea

"And in the Summer I grew white with flame,
And bowed my head down—Autumn, and the sick
Sure knowledge things would never be the same,

"However often Spring might be most thick
Of blossoms and buds, smote on me, and I grew
Careless of most things, let the clock tick, tick,

"To my unhappy pulse, that beat right through
My eager body; while I laughed out loud,
And let my lips curl up at false or true,

"Seemed cold and shallow without any cloud.
Behold my judges, then the cloths were brought:
While I was dizzied thus, old thoughts would crowd,

"Belonging to the time ere I was bought
By Arthur's great name and his little love,
Must I give up for ever then, I thought,

"That which I deemed would ever round me move
Glorifying all things; for a little word,
Scarce ever meant at all, must I now prove

"Stone-cold for ever? Pray you, does the Lord
Will that all folks should be quite happy and good?
I love God now a little, if this cord

"Were broken, once for all what striving could
Make me love anything in earth or heaven.
So day by day it grew, as if one should

"Slip slowly down some path worn smooth and even,
Down to a cool sea on a summer day;
Yet still in slipping was there some small leaven

"Of stretched hands catching small stones by the way,
Until one surely reached the sea at last,
And felt strange new joy as the worn head lay

"Back, with the hair like sea-weed; yea all past
Sweat of the forehead, dryness of the lips,
Washed utterly out by the dear waves o'ercast

"In the lone sea, far off from any ships!
Do I not know now of a day in Spring?
No minute of that wild day ever slips

"From out my memory; I hear thrushes sing,
And wheresoever I may be, straightway
Thoughts of it all come up with most fresh sting;

"I was half mad with beauty on that day,
And went without my ladies all alone,
In a quiet garden walled round every way;

"I was right joyful of that wall of stone,
That shut the flowers and trees up with the sky,
And trebled all the beauty: to the bone,

"Yea right through to my heart, grown very shy
With weary thoughts, it pierced, and made me glad;
Exceedingly glad, and I knew verily,

"A little thing just then had made me mad;
I dared not think, as I was wont to do,
Sometimes, upon my beauty; if I had

"Held out my long hand up against the blue,
And, looking on the tenderly darken'd fingers,
Thought that by rights one ought to see quite through,

"There, see you, where the soft still light yet lingers,
Round by the edges; what should I have done,
If this had joined with yellow spotted singers,

"And startling green drawn upward by the sun?
But shouting, loosed out, see now! all my hair,
And trancedly stood watching the west wind run

"With faintest half-heard breathing sound—why there
I lose my head e'en now in doing this;
But shortly listen—In that garden fair

"Came Launcelot walking; this is true, the kiss
Wherewith we kissed in meeting that spring day,
I scarce dare talk of the remember'd bliss,

"When both our mouths went wandering in one way,
And aching sorely, met among the leaves;
Our hands being left behind strained far away.

"Never within a yard of my bright sleeves
Had Launcelot come before—and now, so nigh!
After that day why is it Guenevere grieves?

"Nevertheless you, O Sir Gauwaine, lie,
Whatever happened on through all those years,
God knows I speak truth, saying that you lie.

"Being such a lady could I weep these tears
If this were true? A great queen such as I
Having sinn'd this way, straight her conscience sears;

"And afterwards she liveth hatefully,
Slaying and poisoning, certes never weeps,—
Gauwaine be friends now, speak me lovingly.

"Do I not see how God's dear pity creeps
All through your frame, and trembles in your mouth?
Remember in what grave your mother sleeps,

"Buried in some place far down in the south,
Men are forgetting as I speak to you;
By her head sever'd in that awful drouth

"Of pity that drew Agravaine's fell blow,
I pray your pity! let me not scream out
For ever after, when the shrill winds blow

"Through half your castle-locks! let me not shout
For ever after in the winter night
When you ride out alone! in battle-rout

"Let not my rusting tears make your sword light!
Ah! God of mercy how he turns away!
So, ever must I dress me to the fight,

"So—let God's justice work! Gauwaine, I say,
See me hew down your proofs: yea all men know
Even as you said how Mellyagraunce one day,

"One bitter day in *la Fausse Garde*, for so
All good knights held it after, saw—
Yea, sirs, by cursed unknightly outrage; though

"You, Gauwaine, held his word without a flaw,
This Mellyagraunce saw blood upon my bed—
Whose blood then pray you? is there any law

"To make a queen say why some spots of red
Lie on her coverlet? or will you say,
'Your hands are white, lady, as when you wed,

" 'Where did you bleed?' and must I stammer out—
    'Nay,
I blush indeed, fair lord, only to rend
My sleeve up to my shoulder, where there lay

" 'A knife-point last night': so must I defend
The honour of the lady Guenevere?
Not so, fair lords, even if the world should end

"This very day, and you were judges here
Instead of God. Did you see Mellyagraunce
When Launcelot stood by him? what white fear

"Curdled his blood, and how his teeth did dance,
His side sink in? as my knight cried and said,
'Slayer of unarm'd men, here is a chance!

" 'Setter of traps, I pray you guard your head,
By God I am so glad to fight with you,
Stripper of ladies, that my hand feels lead

" 'For driving weight; hurrah now! draw and do,
For all my wounds are moving in my breast,
And I am getting mad with waiting so.'

"He struck his hands together o'er the beast,
Who fell down flat, and grovell'd at his feet,
And groan'd at being slain so young—'at least.'

"My knight said, 'Rise you, sir, who are so fleet
At catching ladies, half-arm'd will I fight,
My left side all uncovered!' then I weet,

"Up sprang Sir Mellyagraunce with great delight
Upon his knave's face; not until just then
Did I quite hate him, as I saw my knight

"Along the lists look to my stake and pen
With such a joyous smile, it made me sigh
From agony beneath my waist-chain, when

"The fight began, and to me they drew nigh;
Ever Sir Launcelot kept him on the right,
And traversed warily, and ever high

"And fast leapt caitiff's sword, until my knight
Sudden threw up his sword to his left hand,
Caught it, and swung it; that was all the fight.

"Except a spout of blood on the hot land;
For it was hottest summer; and I know
I wonder'd how the fire, while I should stand,

"And burn, against the heat, would quiver so,
Yards above my head; thus these matters went;
Which things were only warnings of the woe

P

"That fell on me. Yet Mellyagraunce was shent,
For Mellyagraunce had fought against the Lord;
Therefore, my lords, take heed lest you be blent

"With all this wickedness; say no rash word
Against me, being so beautiful; my eyes,
Wept all away to grey, may bring some sword

"To drown you in your blood; see my breast rise,
Like waves of purple sea, as here I stand;
And how my arms are moved in wonderful wise,

"Yea also at my full heart's strong command,
See through my long throat how the words go up
In ripples to my mouth; how in my hand

"The shadow lies like wine within a cup
Of marvellously colour'd gold; yea now
This little wind is rising, look you up,

"And wonder how the light is falling so
Within my moving tresses: will you dare,
When you have looked a little on my brow,

"To say this thing is vile? or will you care
For any plausible lies of cunning woof,
When you can see my face with no lie there

"For ever? am I not a gracious proof—
'But in your chamber Launcelot was found'—
Is there a good knight then would stand aloof,

"When a queen says with gentle queenly sound:
'O true as steel come now and talk with me,
I love to see your step upon the ground

" 'Unwavering, also well I love to see
That gracious smile light up your face, and hear
Your wonderful words, that all mean verily

" 'The thing they seem to mean: good friend, so dear
To me in everything, come here to-night,
Or else the hours will pass most dull and drear;

" 'If you come not, I fear this time I might
Get thinking over much of times gone by,
When I was young, and green hope was in sight;

" 'For no man cares now to know why I sigh;
And no man comes to sing me pleasant songs,
Nor any brings me the sweet flowers that lie

" 'So thick in the gardens; therefore one so longs
To see you, Launcelot; that we may be
Like children once again, free from all wrongs

" 'Just for one night.' Did he not come to me?
What thing could keep true Launcelot away
If I said 'come'? there was one less than three

"In my quiet room that night, and we were gay;
Till sudden I rose up, weak, pale, and sick,
Because a bawling broke our dream up, yea

"I looked at Launcelot's face and could not speak,
For he looked helpless too, for a little while;
Then I remember how I tried to shriek,

"And could not, but fell down; from tile to tile
The stones they threw up rattled o'er my head,
And made me dizzier; till within a while

"My maids were all about me, and my head
On Launcelot's breast was being soothed away
From its white chattering, until Launcelot said—

"By God! I will not tell you more to-day,
Judge any way you will—what matters it?
You know quite well the story of that fray,

"How Launcelot still'd their bawling, the mad fit
That caught up Gauwaine—all, all, verily,
But just that which would save me; these things flit.

"Nevertheless you, O Sir Gauwaine, lie,
Whatever may have happen'd these long years,
God knows I speak truth, saying that you lie!

"All I have said is truth, by Christ's dear tears."
She would not speak another word, but stood
Turn'd sideways; listening, like a man who hears

His brother's trumpet sounding through the wood
Of his foes' lances. She lean'd eagerly,
And gave a slight spring sometimes, as she could

At last hear something really; joyfully
Her cheek grew crimson, as the headlong speed
Of the roan charger drew all men to see,
The knight who came was Launcelot at good need.

OLD LOVE

"You must be very old, Sir Giles,"
    I said; he said: "Yea, very old":
Whereat the mournfullest of smiles
    Creased his dry skin with many a fold.

"They hammer'd out my basnet point
    Into a round salade," he said,
"The basnet being quite out of joint,
    Natheless the salade rasps my head."

He gazed at the great fire awhile:
    "And you are getting old, Sir John";
(He said this with that cunning smile
    That was most sad;) "we both wear on,

"Knights come to court and look at me,
    With eyebrows up, except my lord,
And my dear lady, none I see
    That know the ways of my old sword."

(My lady! at that word no pang
    Stopp'd all my blood.) "But tell me, John,
Is it quite true that pagans hang
    So thick about the east, that on

"The eastern sea no Venice flag
  Can fly unpaid for?" "True," I said,
"And in such way the miscreants drag
  Christ's cross upon the ground, I dread

"That Constantine must fall this year."
  Within my heart; "These things are small;
This is not small, that things outwear
  I thought were made for ever, yea, all,

"All things go soon or late"; I said—
  I saw the duke in court next day;
Just as before, his grand great head
  Above his gold robes dreaming lay,

Only his face was paler; there
  I saw his duchess sit by him;
And she—she was changed more; her hair
  Before my eyes that used to swim,

And make me dizzy with great bliss
  Once, when I used to watch her sit—
Her hair is bright still, yet it is
  As though some dust were thrown on it.

Her eyes are shallower, as though
  Some grey glass were behind; her brow
And cheeks the straining bones show through,
  Are not so good for kissing now.

Her lips are drier now she is
  A great duke's wife these many years,
They will not shudder with a kiss
  As once they did, being moist with tears.

Also her hands have lost that way
  Of clinging that they used to have;
They look'd quite easy, as they lay
  Upon the silken cushions brave

With broidery of the apples green
  My Lord Duke bears upon his shield.
Her face, alas! that I have seen
  Look fresher than an April field,

This is all gone now; gone also
  Her tender walking; when she walks
She is most queenly I well know,
  And she is fair still:—as the stalks

Of faded summer-lilies are,
  So is she grown now unto me
This spring-time, when the flowers star
  The meadows, birds sing wonderfully.

I warrant once she used to cling
  About his neck, and kiss'd him so,
And then his coming step would ring
  Joy-bells for her,—some time ago.

Ah! sometimes like an idle dream
  That hinders true life overmuch,
Sometimes like a lost heaven, these seem.—
  This love is not so hard to smutch.

SHAMEFUL DEATH

There were four of us about that bed;
  The mass-priest knelt at the side,
I and his mother stood at the head,
  Over his feet lay the bride;
We were quite sure that he was dead,
  Though his eyes were open wide.

He did not die in the night,
  He did not die in the day,
But in the morning twilight
  His spirit pass'd away,
When neither sun nor moon was bright,
  And the trees were merely grey.

He was not slain with the sword,
  Knight's axe, or the knightly spear,
Yet spoke he never a word
  After he came in here;
I cut away the cord
  From the neck of my brother dear.

He did not strike one blow,
  For the recreants came behind,
In a place where the hornbeams grow,
  A path right hard to find,
For the hornbeam boughs swing so,
  That the twilight makes it blind.

They lighted a great torch then
  When his arms were pinion'd fast,
Sir John the knight of the Fen,
  Sir Guy of the Dolorous Blast,
With knights threescore and ten,
  Hung brave Lord Hugh at last.

I am threescore and ten,
  And my hair is all turn'd grey,
But I met Sir John of the Fen
  Long ago on a summer day,
And am glad to think of the moment when
  I took his life away.

I am threescore and ten,
  And my strength is mostly pass'd,
But long ago I and my men,
  When the sky was overcast,
And the smoke roll'd over the reeds of the fen,
  Slew Guy of the Dolorous Blast.

And now, knights all of you,
  I pray you pray for Sir Hugh,
A good knight and a true,
  And for Alice, his wife, pray too.

GOLDEN WINGS

Midways of a walled garden,
    In the happy poplar land,
    Did an ancient castle stand,
With an old knight for a warden.

Many scarlet bricks there were
    In its walls, and old grey stone;
    Over which red apples shone
At the right time of the year.

On the bricks the green moss grew,
    Yellow lichen on the stone,
    Over which red apples shone;
Little war that castle knew.

Deep green water fill'd the moat,
    Each side had a red-brick lip,
    Green and mossy with the drip
Of dew and rain; there was a boat

Of carven wood, with hangings green
    About the stern; it was great bliss
    For lovers to sit there and kiss
In the hot summer noons, not seen.

Across the moat the fresh west wind
    In very little ripples went;
    The way the heavy aspens bent
Towards it, was a thing to mind.

The painted drawbridge over it
    Went up and down with gilded chains,
    'Twas pleasant in the summer rains
Within the bridge-house there to sit.

There were five swans that ne'er did eat
    The water-weeds, for ladies came
    Each day, and young knights did the same,
And gave them cakes and bread for meat.

They had a house of painted wood,
   A red roof gold-spiked over it,
   Wherein upon their eggs to sit
Week after week; no drop of blood,

Drawn from men's bodies by sword-blows,
   Came over there, or any tear;
   Most certainly from year to year
'Twas pleasant as a Provence rose.

The banners seem'd quite full of ease,
   That over the turret-roofs hung down;
   The battlements could get no frown
From the flower-moulded cornices.

Who walked in that garden there?
   Miles and Giles and Isabeau,
   Tall Jehane du Castel beau,
Alice of the golden hair,

Big Sir Gervaise, the good knight,
   Fair Ellayne le Violet,
   Mary, Constance fille de fay,
Many dames with footfall light.

Whosoever wander'd there,
   Whether it be dame or knight,
   Half of scarlet, half of white
Their raiment was; of roses fair

Each wore a garland on the head,
   At Ladies' Gard the way was so:
   Fair Jehane du Castel beau
Wore her wreath till it was dead.

Little joy she had of it,
   Of the raiment white and red,
   Or the garland on her head,
She had none with whom to sit

In the carven boat at noon;
  None the more did Jehane weep,
  She would only stand and keep
Saying, "He will be here soon."

Many times in the long day
  Miles and Giles and Gervaise past,
  Holding each some white hand fast,
Every time they heard her say:

"Summer cometh to an end,
  Undern cometh after noon;
  Golden wings will be here soon,
What if I some token send?"

Wherefore that night within the hall,
  With open mouth and open eyes,
  Like some one listening with surprise,
She sat before the sight of all.

Stoop'd down a little she sat there,
  With neck stretch'd out and chin thrown up,
  One hand around a golden cup;
And strangely with her fingers fair

She beat some tune upon the gold;
  The minstrels in the gallery
  Sung: "Arthur, who will never die,
In Avallon he groweth old."

And when the song was ended, she
  Rose and caught up her gown and ran;
  None stopp'd her eager face and wan
Of all that pleasant company.

Right so within her own chamber
  Upon her bed she sat; and drew
  Her breath in quick gasps; till she knew
That no man follow'd after her:

She took the garland from her nead,
   Loosed all her hair, and let it lie
   Upon the coverlit; thereby
She laid the gown of white and red;

And she took off her scarlet shoon,
   And bared her feet; still more and more
   Her sweet face redden'd; evermore
She murmur'd: "He will be here soon;

"Truly he cannot fail to know
   My tender body waits him here;
   And if he knows, I have no fear
For poor Jehane du Castel beau."

She took a sword within her hand,
   Whose hilts were silver, and she sung,
   Somehow like this, wild words that rung
A long way over the moonlit land:—

      Gold wings across the sea!
      Grey light from tree to tree,
      Gold hair beside my knee,
      I pray thee come to me,
      Gold wings!

         The water slips,
      The red-bill'd moorhen dips.
      Sweet kisses on red lips;
      Alas! the red rust grips,
      And the blood-red dagger rips,
      Yet, O knight, come to me!

      Are not my blue eyes sweet?
      The west wind from the wheat
      Blows cold across my feet;
      Is it not time to meet
      Gold wings across the sea?

      White swans on the green moat,
      Small feathers left afloat
      By the blue-painted boat;
      Swift running of the stoat;
      Sweet gurgling note by note
      Of sweet music.

O gold wings,
Listen how gold hair sings,
And the Ladies' Castle rings
Gold wings across the sea.

I sit on a purple bed,
Outside the wall is red,
Thereby the apple hangs,
And the wasp, caught by the fangs,

Dies in the autumn night.
And the bat flits till light,
And the love-crazed knight

Kisses the long wet grass:
The weary days pass,—
Gold wings across the sea!

Gold wings across the sea!
Moonlight from tree to tree,
Sweet hair laid on my knee,
O, sweet knight, come to me!

Gold wings, the short night slips,
The white swan's long neck drips,
I pray thee, kiss my lips,
Gold wings across the sea.

No answer through the moonlit night;
   No answer in the cold grey dawn;
   No answer when the shaven lawn
Grew green, and all the roses bright.

Her tired feet look'd cold and thin,
   Her lips were twitch'd, and wretched tears,
   Some, as she lay, roll'd past her ears,
Some fell from off her quivering chin.

Her long throat, stretch'd to its full length,
   Rose up and fell right brokenly;
   As though the unhappy heart was nigh
Striving to break with all its strength.

And when she slipp'd from off the bed,
   Her cramp'd feet would not hold her; she
   Sank down and crept on hand and knee,
On the window-sill she laid her head.

There, with crooked arm upon the sill,
   She look'd out, muttering dismally:
   "There is no sail upon the sea,
No pennon on the empty hill.

"I cannot stay here all alone,
   Or meet their happy faces here,
   And wretchedly I have no fear;
A little while, and I am gone."

Therewith she rose upon her feet,
   And totter'd; cold and misery
   Still made the deep sobs come, till she
At last stretch'd out her fingers sweet,

And caught the great sword in her hand;
   And, stealing down the silent stair,
   Barefooted in the morning air,
And only in her smock, did stand

Upright upon the green lawn grass;
   And hope grew in her as she said:
   "I have thrown off the white and red,
And pray God it may come to pass

"I meet him; if ten years go by
   Before I meet him; if, indeed,
   Meanwhile both soul and body bleed,
Yet there is end of misery,

"And I have hope. He could not come,
   But I can go to him and show
   These new things I have got to know,
And make him speak, who has been dumb."

O Jehane! the red morning sun
   Changed her white feet to glowing gold,
   Upon her smock, on crease and fold,
Changed that to gold which had been dun.

O Miles, and Giles, and Isabeau,
   Fair Ellayne le Violet,
   Mary, Constance fille de fay!
Where is Jehane du Castel beau?

O big Gervaise ride apace!
   Down to the hard yellow sand,
   Where the water meets the land.
This is Jehane by her face;

Why has she a broken sword?
   Mary! she is slain outright;
   Verily a piteous sight;
Take her up without a word!

Giles and Miles and Gervaise there,
   Ladies' Gard must meet the war:
   Whatsoever knights these are,
Man the walls withouten fear!

Axes to the apple trees,
   Axes to the aspens tall!
   Barriers without the wall
May be lightly made of these.

O poor shivering Isabeau;
   Poor Ellayne le Violet,
   Bent with fear! we miss to-day
Brave Jehane du Castel beau.

O poor Mary, weeping so!
   Wretched Constance fille de fay!
   Verily we miss to-day
Fair Jehane du Castel beau.

The apples now grow green and sour
 Upon the mouldering castle-wall,
 Before they ripen there they fall:
There are no banners on the tower.

The draggled swans most eagerly eat
 The green weeds trailing in the moat;
 Inside the rotting leaky boat
You see a slain man's stiffen'd feet.

THE HAYSTACK IN THE FLOODS

 Had she come all the way for this,
 To part at last without a kiss?
 Yea, had she borne the dirt and rain
 That her own eyes might see him slain
 Beside the haystack in the floods?

 Along the dripping leafless woods,
 The stirrup touching either shoe,
 She rode astride as troopers do;
 With kirtle kilted to her knee,
 To which the mud splash'd wretchedly;
 And the wet dripp'd from every tree
 Upon her head and heavy hair,
 And on her eyelids broad and fair;
 The tears and rain ran down her face.
 By fits and starts they rode apace,
 And very often was his place
 Far off from her; he had to ride
 Ahead, to see what might betide
 When the roads cross'd; and sometimes, when
 There rose a murmuring from his men,
 Had to turn back with promises;
 Ah me! she had but little ease;
 And often for pure doubt and dread
 She sobb'd, made giddy in the head
 By the swift riding; while, for cold,
 Her slender fingers scarce could hold

The wet reins; yea, and scarcely, too,
She felt the foot within her shoe
Against the stirrup: all for this,
To part at last without a kiss
Beside the haystack in the floods.

For when they near'd that old soak'd hay,
They saw across the only way
That Judas, Godmar, and the three
Red running lions dismally
Grinn'd from his pennon, under which,
In one straight line along the ditch,
They counted thirty heads.

                        So then,
While Robert turn'd round to his men,
She saw at once the wretched end,
And, stooping down, tried hard to rend
Her coif the wrong way from her head,
And hid her eyes; while Robert said:
"Nay, love, 'tis scarcely two to one,
At Poictiers where we made them run
So fast—why, sweet my love, good cheer.
The Gascon frontier is so near,
Nought after this."

                        But, "O," she said,
"My God! my God! I have to tread
The long way back without you; then
The court at Paris; those six men;
The gratings of the Chatelet;
The swift Seine on some rainy day
Like this, and people standing by,
And laughing, while my weak hands try
To recollect how strong men swim,
All this, or else a life with him,
For which I should be damned at last,
Would God that this next hour were past!"

He answer'd not, but cried his cry,
"St. George for Marny!" cheerily;
And laid his hand upon her rein.
Alas! no man of all his train
Gave back that cheery cry again;
And, while for rage his thumb beat fast
Upon his sword-hilts, some one cast
About his neck a kerchief long,
And bound him.

        Then they went along
To Godmar; who said: "Now, Jehane,
Your lover's life is on the wane
So fast, that, if this very hour
You yield not as my paramour,
He will not see the rain leave off—
Nay, keep your tongue from gibe and scoff,
Sir Robert, or I slay you now."

She laid her hand upon her brow,
Then gazed upon the palm, as though
She thought her forehead bled, and—"No,"
She said, and turn'd her head away,
As there were nothing else to say,
And everything were settled: red
Grew Godmar's face from chin to head:
"Jehane, on yonder hill there stands
My castle, guarding well my lands:
What hinders me from taking you,
And doing that I list to do
To your fair wilful body, while
Your knight lies dead?"

        A wicked smile
Wrinkled her face, her lips grew thin,
A long way out she thrust her chin:
"You know that I should strangle you
While you were sleeping; or bite through
Your throat, by God's help—ah!" she said,
"Lord Jesus, pity your poor maid!
For in such wise they hem me in,
I cannot choose but sin and sin,

Whatever happens: yet I think
They could not make me eat or drink,
And so should I just reach my rest."
"Nay, if you do not my behest,
O Jehane! though I love you well,"
Said Godmar, "would I fail to tell
All that I know." "Foul lies," she said.
"Eh? lies my Jehane? by God's head,
At Paris folks would deem them true!
Do you know, Jehane, they cry for you,
'Jehane the brown! Jehane the brown!
Give us Jehane to burn or drown!'—
Eh—gag me Robert!—sweet my friend,
This were indeed a piteous end
For those long fingers, and long feet,
And long neck, and smooth shoulders sweet;
An end that few men would forget
That saw it—So, an hour yet:
Consider, Jehane, which to take
Of life or death!"

         So, scarce awake,
Dismounting, did she leave that place,
And totter some yards: with her face
Turn'd upward to the sky she lay,
Her head on a wet heap of hay,
And fell asleep: and while she slept,
And did not dream, the minutes crept
Round to the twelve again; but she,
Being waked at last, sigh'd quietly,
And strangely childlike came, and said:
"I will not." Straightway Godmar's head,
As though it hung on strong wires, turn'd
Most sharply round, and his face burn'd.

For Robert—both his eyes were dry,
He could not weep, but gloomily
He seem'd to watch the rain; yea, too,
His lips were firm; he tried once more
To touch her lips; she reach'd out, sore
And vain desire so tortured them,
The poor grey lips, and now the hem
Of his sleeve brush'd them.

     With a start
Up Godmar rose, thrust them apart;
From Robert's throat he loosed the bands
Of silk and mail; with empty hands
Held out, she stood and gazed, and saw,
The long bright blade without a flaw
Glide out from Godmar's sheath, his hand
In Robert's hair; she saw him bend
Back Robert's head; she saw him send
The thin steel down; the blow told well,
Right backward the knight Robert fell,
And moan'd as dogs do, being half dead,
Unwitting, as I deem: so then
Godmar turn'd grinning to his men,
Who ran, some five or six, and beat
His head to pieces at their feet.

Then Godmar turn'd again, and said:
"So, Jehane, the first fitte is read!
Take note, my lady, that your way
Lies backward to the Chatelet!"
She shook her head and gazed awhile
At her cold hands with a rueful smile,
As though this thing had made her mad.

This was the parting that they had
Beside the haystack in the floods.

SUMMER DAWN

Pray but one prayer for me 'twixt thy closed lips,
  Think but one thought of me up in the stars.
The summer night waneth, the morning light slips,
  Faint and grey 'twixt the leaves of the aspen,
    betwixt the cloud-bars,
That are patiently waiting there for the dawn :
  Patient and colourless, though Heaven's gold
Waits to float through them along with the sun.
Far out in the meadows, above the young corn,
  The heavy elms wait, and restless and cold
The uneasy wind rises ; the roses are dun;
Through the long twilight they pray for the dawn,
Round the lone house in the midst of the corn.
  Speak but one word to me over the corn,
  Over the tender, bow'd locks of the corn.

IN PRISON

Wearily, drearily,
Half the day long,
Flap the great banners
High over the stone;
Strangely and eerily
Sounds the wind's song,
Bending the banner-poles.

While, all alone,
Watching the loophole's spark,
Lie I, with life all dark,
Feet tether'd, hands fetter'd
Fast to the stone,
The grim walls, square letter'd
With prison'd men's groan.

Still strain the banner-poles
Through the wind's song,
Westward the banner rolls
Over my wrong.

THE EARTHLY PARADISE

Of Heaven or Hell I have no power to sing,
I cannot ease the burden of your fears,
Or make quick-coming death a little thing,
Or bring again the pleasure of past years,
Nor for my words shall ye forget your tears,
Or hope again for aught that I can say,
The idle singer of an empty day.

But rather, when aweary of your mirth,
From full hearts still unsatisfied ye sigh,
And, feeling kindly unto all the earth,
Grudge every minute as it passes by,
Made the more mindful that the sweet days die—
Remember me a little then I pray,
The idle singer of an empty day.

The heavy trouble, the bewildering care
That weighs us down who live and earn our bread,
These idle verses have no power to bear;
So let me sing of names remembered,
Because they, living not, can ne'er be dead,
Or long time take their memory quite away
From us poor singers of an empty day.

Dreamer of dreams, born out of my due time,
Why should I strive to set the crooked straight?
Let it suffice me that my murmuring rhyme
Beats with light wing against the ivory gate,
Telling a tale not too importunate
To those who in the sleepy region stay,
Lulled by the singer of an empty day.

Folk say, a wizard to a northern king
At Christmas-tide such wondrous things did show,
That through one window men beheld the spring,
And through another saw the summer glow,

And through a third the fruited vines a-row,
While still, unheard, but in its wonted way,
Piped the drear wind of that December day.

So with this Earthly Paradise it is,
If ye will read aright, and pardon me,
Who strive to build a shadowy isle of bliss
Midmost the beating of the steely sea,
Where tossed about all hearts of men must be;
Whose ravening monsters mighty men shall slay,
Not the poor singer of an empty day.

·

MARCH

Slayer of the winter, art thou here again?
O welcome, thou that bring'st the summer nigh!
The bitter wind makes not thy victory vain,
Nor will we mock thee for thy faint blue sky.
Welcome, O March! whose kindly days and dry
Make April ready for the throstle's song,
Thou first redresser of the winter's wrong!

Yea, welcome March! and though I die ere June,
Yet for the hope of life I give thee praise,
Striving to swell the burden of the tune
That even now I hear thy brown birds raise,
Unmindful of the past or coming days;
Who sing: "O joy! a new year is begun:
What happiness to look upon the sun!"

Ah, what begetteth all this storm of bliss
But Death himself, who crying solemnly,
E'en from the heart of sweet Forgetfulness,
Bids us "Rejoice, lest pleasureless ye die.
Within a little time must ye go by.
Stretch forth your open hands, and while ye live
Take all the gifts that Death and Life may give."

Behold once more within a quiet land
The remnant of that once aspiring band,
With all hopes fallen away, but such as light
The sons of men to that unfailing night,
That death they needs must look on face to face.

   Time passed, and ever fell the days apace
From off the new-strung chaplet of their life;
Yet though the time with no bright deeds was rife,
Though no fulfilled desire now made them glad,
They were not quite unhappy, rest they had,
And with their hope their fear had passed away;
New things and strange they saw from day to day;
Honoured they were, and had no lack of things
For which men crouch before the feet of kings,
And, stripped of honour, yet may fail to have.

   Therefore their latter journey to the grave
Was like those days of later autumn-tide,
When he who in some town may chance to bide
Opens the window for the balmy air,
And seeing the golden hazy sky so fair,
And from some city garden hearing still
The wheeling rooks the air with music fill,
Sweet hopeful music, thinketh, Is this spring,
Surely the year can scarce be perishing?
But then he leaves the clamour of the town,
And sees the withered scanty leaves fall down,
The half-ploughed field, the flowerless garden--plot
The dark full stream by summer long forgot,
The tangled hedges where, relaxed and dead,
The twining plants their withered berries shed,
And feels therewith the treachery of the sun,
And knows the pleasant time is well-nigh done.

   In such St. Luke's short summer lived these men,
Nearing the goal of threescore years and ten;
The elders of the town their comrades were,
And they to them were waxen now as dear
As ancient men to ancient men can be;
Grave matters of belief and polity
They spoke of oft, but not alone of these;
For in their times of idleness and ease
They told of poets' vain imaginings,

And memories vague of half-forgotten things,
Not true nor false, but sweet to think upon.

For nigh the time when first that land they won,
When new-born March made fresh the hopeful air,
The wanderers sat within a chamber fair,
Guests of that city's rulers; when the day
Far from the sunny noon had fallen away;
The sky grew dark, and on the window-pane
They heard the beating of the sudden rain.
Then, all being satisfied with plenteous feast,
There spoke an ancient man, the land's chief priest,
Who said, "Dear guests, the year begins to-day,
And fain are we, before it pass away,
To hear some tales of that now altered world,
Wherefrom our fathers in old time were hurled
By the hard hands of fate and destiny.
Nor would ye hear perchance unwillingly
How we have dealt with stories of the land
Wherein the tombs of our forefathers stand:
Wherefore henceforth two solemn feasts shall be
In every month, at which some history
Shall crown our joyance; and this day, indeed,
I have a story ready for our need,
If ye will hear it; though perchance it is
That many things therein are writ amiss,
This part forgotten, that part grown too great;
For these things, too, are in the hands of fate."
They cried aloud for joy to hear him speak,
And as again the sinking sun did break
Through the dark clouds and blazed adown the hall,
His clear thin voice upon their ears did fall,
Telling a tale of times long passed away,
When men might cross a kingdom in a day,
And kings remembered they should one day die,
And all folk dwelt in great simplicity.

APRIL

O fair midspring, besung so oft and oft,
How can I praise thy loveliness enow?
Thy sun that burns not, and thy breezes soft
That o'er the blossoms of the orchard blow,
The thousand things that 'neath the young leaves
  grow,
The hopes and chances of the growing year,
Winter forgotten long, and summer near.

When Summer brings the lily and the rose,
She brings us fear; her very death she brings
Hid in her anxious heart, the forge of woes;
And, dull with fear, no more the mavis sings.
But thou! thou diest not, but thy fresh life clings
About the fainting autumn's sweet decay,
When in the earth the hopeful seed they lay.

Ah! life of all the year, why yet do I
Amid thy snowy blossoms' fragrant drift,
Still long for that which never draweth nigh,
Striving my pleasure from my pain to sift,
Some weight from off my fluttering mirth to lift?
—Now, when far bells are ringing, "Come again,
Come back, past years! why will ye pass in vain?"

And now the watery April sun lit up
Upon the fair board golden ewer and cup,
And over the bright silken tapestry
The fresh young boughs were gladdening every eye,
And round the board old faces you might see
Amidst the blossoms and their greenery.
So when the flutes were silent, and the birds,
Rejoicing in their flood of unknown words,
Were heard again, a silken-fastened book
A certain elder from his raiment took,
And said, "O friends, few words are best to—
And no new thing I bring you; yet ye may
Be pleased to hear an ancient tale again,
That, told so long ago, doth yet remain

Fresh e'en 'mongst us, far from the Argive land:
Which tale this book, writ wholly by mine hand,
Holds gathered up as I have heard it told.

"Surely I fear me, midst the ancient gold
Base metal ye will light on here and there,
Though I have noted everything with care,
And with good will have set down nothing new
Nor holds the land another book for you
That has the tale in full with nought beside,
So unto me let your good word betide;
Though, take it as ye may, no small delight
I had, herein this well-loved tale to write."

MAY

O love, this morn when the sweet nightingale
Had so long finished all he had to say,
That thou hadst slept, and sleep had told his tale;
And midst a peaceful dream had stolen away
In fragrant dawning of the first of May,
Didst thou see aught? didst thou hear voices sing
Ere to the risen sun the bells 'gan ring?

For then methought the Lord of Love went by
To take possession of his flowery throne,
Ringed round with maids, and youths, and min-
        strelsy;
A little while I sighed to find him gone,
A little while the dawning was alone,
And the light gathered; then I held my breath,
And shuddered at the sight of Eld and Death.

Alas! Love passed me in the twilight dun,
His music hushed the wakening ousel's song;
But on these twain shone out the golden sun,
And o'er their heads the brown bird's tune was strong,
As shivering, 'twixt the trees they stole along;
None noted aught their noiseless passing by,
The world had quite forgotten it must die.

Now must these men be glad a little while
That they had lived to see May once more smile
Upon the earth; wherefore, as men who know
How fast the bad days and the good days go,
They gathered at the feast: the fair abode
Wherein they sat, o'er looked, across the road
Unhedged green meads, which willowy streams
    passed through,

And on that morn, before the fresh May dew
Had dried upon the sunniest spot of grass,
From bush to bush did youths and maidens pass
In raiment meet for May apparelled,
Gathering the milk-white blossoms and the red;
And now, with noon long past, and that bright day
Growing aweary, on the sunny way
They wandered, crowned with flowers, and loitering,
And weary, yet were fresh enough to sing
The carols of the morn, and pensive, still
Had cast away their doubt of death and ill,
And flushed with love, no more grew red with shame.

So to the elders as they sat, there came,
With scent of flowers, the murmur of that folk
Wherethrough from time to time a song outbroke,
Till scarce they thought about the story due;
Yet, when anigh to sun-setting it grew,
A book upon the board an elder laid,
And turning from the open window said,
"Too fair a tale the lovely time doth ask,
For this of mine to be an easy task,
Yet in what words soever this is writ,
As for the matter, I dare say of it
That it is lovely as the lovely May;
Pass then the manner, since the learned say
No written record was there of the tale,
Ere we from our fair land of Greece set sail;
How this may be I know not, this I know
That such like tales the wind would seem to blow
From place to place, e'en as the feathery seed
Is borne across the sea to help the need
Of barren isles; so, sirs, from seed thus sown,
This flower, a gift from other lands has grown.

JUNE

O June, O June, that we desired so,
Wilt thou not make us happy on this day?
Across the river thy soft breezes blow
Sweet with the scent of beanfields far away,
Above our heads rustle the aspens grey,
Calm is the sky with harmless clouds beset,
No thought of storm the morning vexes yet.

See, we have left our hopes and fears behind
To give our very hearts up unto thee;
What better place than this then could we find
By this sweet stream that knows not of the sea,
That guesses not the city's misery,
This little stream whose hamlets scarce have
    names,
This far-off, lonely mother of the Thames?

Here then, O June, thy kindness will we take;
And if indeed but pensive men we seem,
What should we do? thou wouldst not have us
    wake
From out the arms of this rare happy dream
And wish to leave the murmur of the stream,
The rustling boughs, the twitter of the birds,
And all thy thousand peaceful happy words.

Now in the early June they deemed it good
That they should go unto a house that stood
On their chief river, so upon a day
With favouring wind and tide they took their way
Up the fair stream; most lovely was the time
Even amidst the days of that fair clime,
And still the wanderers thought about their lives,
And that desire that rippling water gives
To youthful hearts to wander anywhere.
    So midst sweet sights and sounds a house most
    fair

They came to, set upon the river side
Where kindly folk their coming did abide;
There they took land, and in the lime-trees' shade
Beneath the trees they found the fair feast laid,
And sat, well pleased; but when the water-hen
Had got at last to think them harmless men,
And they with rest, and pleasure, and old wine,
Began to feel immortal and divine,
An elder spoke, "O gentle friends, the day
Amid such calm delight now slips away,
And ye yourselves are grown so bright and glad
I care not if I tell you something sad;
Sad, though the life I tell you of passed by,
Unstained by sordid strife or misery;
Sad, because though a glorious end it tells,
Yet on the end of glorious life it dwells,
And striving through all things to reach the best
Upon no midway happiness will rest."

JULY

Fair was the morn to-day, the blossom's scent
Floated across the fresh grass, and the bees
With low vexed song from rose to lily went;
A gentle wind was in the heavy trees,
And thine eyes shone with joyous memories;
Fair was the early morn, and fair wert thou,
And I was happy—Ah, be happy now!

Peace and content without us, love within
That hour there was, now thunder and wild rain
Have wrapped the cowering world, and foolish sin,
And nameless pride, have made us wise in vain;
Ah, love! although the morn shall come again,
And on new rose-buds the new sun shall smile,
Can we regain what we have lost meanwhile?

E'en now the west grows clear of storm and threat,
But midst the lightning did the fair sun die—
Ah, he shall rise again for ages yet,
He cannot waste his life—but thou and I—
Who knows if next morn this felicity
My lips may feel, or if thou still shalt live
This seal of love renewed once more to give?

Within a lovely valley, watered well
With flowery streams, the July feast befell,
And there within the Chief-priest's fair abode
They cast aside their trouble's heavy load,
Scarce made aweary by the sultry day.
The earth no longer laboured; shaded lay
The sweet-breathed kine; across the sunny vale,
From hill to hill, the wandering rook did sail,
Lazily croaking, midst his dreams of spring;
Nor more awake the pink-foot dove did cling
Unto the beech-bough, murmuring now and then.
All rested but the restless sons of men
And the great sun that wrought this happiness,
And all the vale with fruitful hopes did bless.
　　So in a marble chamber bright with flowers,
The old men feasted through the fresher hours,
And at the hottest time of all the day
When now the sun was on his downward way,
Sat listening to a tale an elder told,
New to his fathers while they yet did hold
The cities of some far-off Grecian isle,
Though in the heavens the cloud of force and guile
Was gathering dark that sent them o'er the sea
To win new lands for their posterity.

AUGUST

Across the gap made by our English hinds,
Amidst the Roman's handiwork, behold
Far off the long-roofed church; the shepherd binds
The withy round the hurdles of his fold,
Down in the foss the river fed of old,
That through long lapse of time has grown to be
The little grassy valley that you see.

Rest here awhile, not yet the eve is still,
The bees are wandering yet, and you may hear
The barley mowers on the trenchéd hill,
The sheep-bells, and the restless changing weir,
All little sounds made musical and clear
Beneath the sky that burning August gives,
While yet the thought of glorious Summer lives.

Ah, love! such happy days, such days as these,
Must we still waste them, craving for the best,
Like lovers o'er the painted images
Of those who once their yearning hearts have blessed?
Have we been happy on our day of rest?
Thine eyes say "yes,"—but if it came again,
Perchance its ending would not seem so vain.

Now came fulfilment of the year's desire,
The tall wheat, coloured by the August fire
Grew heavy-headed, dreading its decay,
And blacker grew the elm-trees day by day.
About the edges of the yellow corn,
And o'er the gardens grown somewhat outworn
The bees went hurrying to fill up their store;
The apple-boughs bent over more and more;
With peach and apricot the garden wall
Was odorous, and the pears began to fall
From off the high tree with each freshening breeze.
So in a house bordered about with trees,
A little raised above the waving gold
The Wanderers heard this marvellous story told,
While 'twixt the gleaming flasks of ancient wine,
They watched the reapers' slow advancing line.

SEPTEMBER

O come at last, to whom the spring-tide's hope
Looked for through blossoms, what hast thou for
   me?
Green grows the grass upon the dewy slope
Beneath thy gold-hung, grey-leaved apple-tree
Moveless, e'en as the autumn fain would be
That shades its sad eyes from the rising sun
And weeps at eve because the day is done.

What vision wilt thou give me, autumn morn,
To make thy pensive sweetness more complete?
What tale, ne'er to be told, of folk unborn?
What images of grey-clad damsels sweet
Shall cross thy sward with dainty noiseless feet?
What nameless shamefast longings made alive,
Soft-eyed September, will thy sad heart give?

Look long, O longing eyes, and look in vain!
Strain idly, aching heart, and yet be wise,
And hope no more for things to come again
That thou beheldest once with careless eyes!
Like a new-wakened man thou art, who tries
To dream again the dream that made him glad
When in his arms his loving love he had.

Mid young September's fruit-trees next they met
With calm hearts, willing such things to forget
As men had best forget; and certainly
E'en such a day it was when this might be
If e'er it might be; fair, without a cloud,
Yet windless, so that a grey haze did shroud
The bright blue; neither burning overmuch,
Nor chill, the blood of those old folk to touch
With fretful, restless memory of despair.
Withal no promise of the fruitful year
Seemed unfulfilled in that fair autumn-tide;
The level ground along the river-side

Was merry through the day with sounds of those
Who gathered apples; o'er the stream arose
The northward-looking slopes where the swine
    ranged
Over the fields that hook and scythe had changed
Since the last month; but 'twixt the tree-boles grey
Above them did they see the terraced way,
And over that the vine-stocks, row on row,
Whose dusty leaves, well thinned and yellowing now,
But little hid the bright-bloomed vine-bunches.

    There day-long 'neath the shadows of the trees
Those elders sat; chary of speech they were,
For good it seemed to watch the young folk there,
Not so much busied with their harvesting,
But o'er their baskets they might stop to sing;
Nor for the end of labour all so fain
But eyes of men from eyes of maids might gain
Some look desired.
              So at the midday those
Who played with labour in the deep green close
Stinted their gathering for awhile to eat;
Then to the elders did it seem most meet
Amidst of these to set forth what they might
Of lore remembered, and to let the night
Bury its own dead thoughts with wine and sleep;
So while the loitering autumn sun did creep
O'er flower-crowned heads, and past sweet eyes of
    grey,
And eager lips, and fresh round limbs that lay
Amid the golden fruit—fruit sweet and fair
Themselves, that happy days and love did bear
And life unburdened—while the failing sun
Drew up the light clouds, was this tale begun,
Sad, but not sad enow to load the yoke,
E'en by a feather's weight, of those old folk.
Sad, and believed but for its sweetness' sake
By the young folk, desiring not to break
The spell that sorrow's image cast on them,
As dreamlike she went past with fluttering hem.

Q

OCTOBER

O love, turn from the unchanging sea, and gaze
Down these grey slopes upon the year grown old,
A-dying mid the autumn-scented haze,
That hangeth o'er the hollow in the wold,
Where the wind-bitten ancient elms enfold
Grey church, long barn, orchard, and red-roofed
    stead,
Wrought in dead days for men a long while dead.

Come down, O love; may not our hands still meet,
Since still we live to-day, forgetting June,
Forgetting May, deeming October sweet—
—O hearken, hearken! through the afternoon,
The grey tower sings a strange old tinkling tune!
Sweet, sweet, and sad, the toiling year's last breath,
Too satiate of life to strive with death.

And we too—will it not be soft and kind,
That rest from life, from patience and from pain;
That rest from bliss we know not when we find;
That rest from Love which ne'er the end can gain?—
Hark, how the tune swells, that erewhile did wane!
Look up, love!—ah, cling close and never move!
How can I have enough of life and love?

October drew our elders to a house,
That mid the tangled vines, and clamorous
Glad vintagers, stood calm, slim-pillared, white,
As though it fain would hide away from sight
The joy that through the sad lost autumn rung.
As hot the day was, as when summer hung,
With worn feet, on the last step of July,
Ashamed to cast its flowery raiment by:
Round the old men the white porch-pillars stood,
Gold-stained, as with the sun, streaked as with blood,
Blood of the earth, at least; and to and fro
Before them did the high-girt maidens go,

Eager, bright-eyed, and careless of to-morn;
And young men with them, nowise made forlorn
By love and autumn-tide; and in nowise
Content to pray for love with hopeless eyes,
Close lips, and timid hands; rather, indeed,
Lest youth and life should fail them at their need,
At what light joyous semblance of him ran
Amidst the vines, 'twixt eyes of maid and man,
Wilfully blind they caught.

              But now at last,
As in the apple-gathering tide late past,
So would the elders do now; in a while,
He who should tell the tale, with a grave smile,
And eyes fixed on the fairest damsel there,
Began to say: "Ye blithe folk well might bear
To hearken to a sad tale; yet to-day
No heart I have to cast all hope away
From out my history: so be warned hereby,
Nor wait unto the end, deliciously
To nurse your pity; for the end is good
And peaceful, howso buffeting and rude
Winds, waves, and men were, ere the end was done."

The sweet eyes that his eyes were set upon
Were hid by shamefast lids as he did speak,
And redder colour burned on her fresh cheek,
And her lips smiled, as, with a half-sad sigh,
He 'gan to tell this lovesome history.

NOVEMBER

Are thine eyes weary? is thy heart too sick
To struggle any more with doubt and thought,
Whose formless veil draws darkening now and thick
Across thee, e'en as smoke-tinged mist-wreaths brought
Down a fair dale to make it blind and nought?
Art thou so weary that no world there seems
Beyond these four walls, hung with pain and dreams?

Look out upon the real world, where the moon,
Half-way 'twixt root and crown of these high trees,
Turns the dead midnight into dreamy noon,
Silent and full of wonders, for the breeze
Died at the sunset, and no images,
No hopes of day, are left in sky or earth—
Is it not fair, and of most wondrous worth?

Yea, I have looked, and seen November there;
The changeless seal of change it seemed to be,
Fair death of things that, living once, were fair;
Bright sign of loneliness too great for me,
Strange image of the dread eternity,
In whose void patience how can these have part,
These outstretched feverish hands, this restless heart?

On a clear eve, when the November sky
Grew red with promise of the hoar-frost nigh,
These ancient men turned from the outside cold,
With something like content that they, grown old,
Needed but little now to help the ease
Of those last days before the final peace.
The empty month for them left no regret
For sweet things gained and lost, and longed for yet,
'Twixt spring-tide and this dying of the year.
Few things of small account the whole did bear,
Nor like a long lifetime of misery
Those few days seemed, as oft to such may be
As, seeing the patience of the world, whereby
Midst all its strife it falls not utterly

Into a wild, confused mass of pain,
Yet note it not, and have no will to gain,
Since they are young, a little time of rest,
Midst their vain raging for the hopeless best.

Such thought, perchance, was in his heart, who broke
The silence of the fireside now, and spoke;
"This eve my tale tells of a fair maid born
Within a peaceful land, that peace to scorn,
In turn to scorn the deeds of mighty kings,
The counsel of the wise, and far-famed things,
And envied lives; so, born for discontent,
She through the eager world of base folk went,
Still gaining nought but heavier weariness.
God grant that somewhere now content may bless
Her yearning heart; that she may look and smile
On the strange earth that wearied her awhile,
And now forgets her! Yet so do not we,
Though some of us have lived full happily!"

DECEMBER

Dead lonely night and all streets quiet now,
Thin o'er the moon the hindmost cloud swims past
Of that great rack that brought us up the snow;
On earth strange shadows o'er the snow are cast;
Pale stars, bright moon, swift cloud make heaven so
    vast
That earth left silent by the wind of night
Seems shrunken 'neath the grey unmeasured height.

Ah! through the hush the looked-for midnight
    clangs!
And then, e'en while its last stroke's solemn drone
In the cold air by unlit windows hangs,
Out break the bells above the year foredone,
Change, kindness lost, love left unloved alone;
Till their despairing sweetness makes thee deem
Thou once wert loved, if but amidst a dream.

O thou who clingest still to life and love,
Though nought of good, no God thou mayst discern,
Though nought that is, thine utmost woe can move,
Though no soul knows wherewith thine heart doth yearn,
Yet, since thy weary lips no curse can learn,
Cast no least thing thou lovedst once away,
Since yet perchance thine eyes shall see the day.

December came, with mirth men needs must make
E'en for the empty days and leisure's sake
That earth's cold leaden sleep doth bring; so there
Our elders sat within the guest-hall fair,
Not looking older for the snow without;
Cheery enough; remembering not old doubt,
A gnawing pain once, grown too hard to bear,
And so cast by; not thinking of old fear,
That conquering once, e'en with its victory
Must fade away, and, like all things else, die.
Not thinking of much else than that they had
Enough of life to make them somewhat glad
When all went well with them. Now so it fell
That mariners were there, who 'gan to tell
Mishaps betid upon the winter seas,
Which set some younger men amidst of these
To ask the Wanderers of their voyage vain,
As knowing scarce the tale thereof. Small pain
It gave them now to answer: yet belike
On the old men, their hosts, the thing did strike
In jarring wise, this turning o'er and o'er
Of memories once so bitter sharp and sore.
Wherefore at last an elder said, "Let be,
My masters! if about the troublous sea
Ye needs must hear, hearken a tale once told
By kin of ours in the dim days of old,
Whose thoughts when turning to a peaceful home
Unto this very west of ours must come—
Scarce causelessly meseems when all is said,
And I remember that years bow my head,
And not the trouble of those days of war,
Of loss and wrong that in old stories are."

JANUARY

From this dull rainy undersky and low,
This murky ending of a leaden day,   ·
That never knew the sun, this half-thawed snow,
These tossing black boughs faint against the grey
Of gathering night, thou turnest, dear, away
Silent, but with thy scarce-seen kindly smile
Sent through the dusk my longing to beguile.

There, the lights gleam, and all is dark without!
And in the sudden change our eyes meet dazed—
O look, love, look again! the veil of doubt
Just for one flash, past counting, then was raised!
O eyes of heaven, as clear thy sweet soul blazed
On mine a moment! O come back again
Strange rest and dear amid the long dull pain!

Nay, nay, gone by! though there she sitteth still,
With wide grey eyes so frank and fathomless—
Be patient, heart, thy days they yet shall fill
With utter rest—Yea, now thy pain they bless,
And feed thy last hope of the world's redress—
O unseen hurrying rack! O wailing wind!
What rest and where go ye this night to find?

The year has changed its name since that last tale;
Yet nought the prisoned spring doth that avail.
Deep buried under snow the country lies;
Made dim by whirling flakes the rook still flies
South-west before the wind; noon is as still
As midnight on the southward-looking hill,
Whose slopes have heard so many words and loud
Since on the vine the woolly buds first showed,
The raven hanging o'er the farmstead gate,
While for another death his eye doth wait,
Hears but the muffled sound of crowded byre
And winds' moan round the wall. Up in the spire
The watcher set high o'er the half-hid town

Hearkens the sound of chiming bells fall down
Below him; and so dull and dead they seem
That he might well-nigh be amidst a dream
Wherein folk hear and hear not.

                     Such a tide,
With all work gone from the hushed world outside,
Still finds our old folk living, and they sit
Watching the snow-flakes by the window flit
Midmost the time 'twixt noon and dusk; till now
One of the elders clears his knitted brow,
And says:

            "Well, hearken of a man who first
In every place seemed doomed to be accursed;
To tell about his ill hap lies on me;
Before the winter is quite o'er, maybe
Some other mouth of his good hap may tell;
But no third tale there is, of what befell
His fated life, when he had won his place;
And that perchance is not so ill a case
For him and us; for we may rise up, glad
At all the rest and triumph that he had
Before he died; while he, forgetting clean
The sorrow and the joy his eyes had seen,
Lies quiet and well-famed—and serves to-day
To wear a space of winter-tide away."

FEBRUARY

Noon—and the north-west sweeps the empty road,
The rain-washed fields from hedge to hedge are bare;
Beneath the leafless elms some hind's abode
Looks small and void, and no smoke meets the air
From its poor hearth: one lonely rook doth dare
The gale, and beats above the unseen corn,
Then turns, and whirling down the wind is borne.

Shall it not hap that on some dawn of May
Thou shalt awake, and, thinking of days dead,
See nothing clear but this same dreary day,
Of all the days that have passed o'er thine head?
Shalt thou not wonder, looking from thy bed,
Through green leaves on the windless east a-fire,
That this day too thine heart doth still desire?

Shalt thou not wonder that it liveth yet,
The useless hope, the useless craving pain,
That made thy face, that lonely noontide, wet
With more than beating of the chilly rain?
Shalt thou not hope for joy new born again,
Since no grief ever born can ever die
Through changeless change of seasons passing by?

The change has come at last, and from the west
Drives on the wind, and gives the clouds no rest,
And ruffles up the water thin that lies
Over the surface of the thawing ice;
Sunrise and sunset with no glorious show
Are seen, as late they were across the snow;
The wet-lipped west wind chilleth to the bone
More than the light and flickering east hath done.
Full soberly the earth's fresh hope begins,
Nor stays to think of what each new day wins:
And still it seems to bid us turn away
From this chill thaw to dream of blossomed May:
E'en as some hapless lover's dull shame sinks

Away sometimes in day-dreams, and he thinks
No more of yesterday's disgrace and foil,
No more he thinks of all the sickening toil
Of piling straw on straw to reach the sky;
But rather now a pitying face draws nigh,
Mid tears and prayers for pardon; and a tale
To make love tenderer now is all the bale
Love brought him erst.
                    But on this chill dank tide
Still are the old men by the fireside,
And all things cheerful round the day just done
Shut out the memory of the cloud-drowned sun,
And dripping bough and blotched and snow-soaked
        earth;
And little as the tide seemed made for mirth,
Scarcely they lacked it less than months agone,
When on their wrinkles bright the great sun shone;
Rather, perchance, less pensive now they were,
And meeter for that cause old tales to hear
Of stirring deeds long dead:
                    So, as it fell,
Preluding nought, an elder 'gan to tell
The story promised in mid-winter days
Of all that latter end of bliss and praise
That erst befell Bellerophon the bright,
Ere all except his name sank into night.

From *CHANTS FOR SOCIALISTS*

THE VOICE OF TOIL

I heard men saying, Leave hope and praying,
  All days shall be as all have been;
To-day and to-morrow bring fear and sorrow,
  The never-ending toil between.

When Earth was younger mid toil and hunger,
  In hope we strove, and our hands were strong;
Then great men led us, with words they fed us,
  And bade us right the earthly wrong.

Go read in story their deeds and glory,
  Their names amidst the nameless dead;
Turn then from lying to us slow-dying
  In that good world to which they led;

Where fast and faster our iron master,
  The thing we made, for ever drives,
Bids us grind treasure and fashion pleasure
  For other hopes and other lives.

Where home is a hovel and dull we grovel,
  Forgetting that the world is fair;
Where no babe we cherish, lest its very soul perish;
  Where our mirth is crime, our love a snare.

Who now shall lead us, what god shall heed us
  As we lie in the hell our hands have won?
For us are no rulers but fools and befoolers,
  The great are fallen, the wise men gone.

I heard men saying, Leave tears and praying,
  The sharp knife heedeth not the sheep;
Are we not stronger than the rich and the wronger,
  When day breaks over dreams and sleep?

Come, shoulder to shoulder ere the world grows older!
  Help lies in nought but thee and me;
Hope is before us, the long years that bore us
  Bore leaders more than men may be.

Let dead hearts tarry and trade and marry,
  And trembling nurse their dreams of mirth,
While we the living our lifes are giving
  To bring the bright new world to birth.

Come, shoulder to shoulder ere earth grows older
  The Cause spreads over land and sea;
Now the world shaketh, and fear awaketh
  And joy at last for thee and me.

NO MASTER

Saith man to man, We've heard and known
  That we no master need
To live upon this earth, our own,
  In fair and manly deed.
The grief of slaves long passed away
  For us hath forged the chain,
Till now each worker's patient day
  Builds up the House of Pain.

And we, shall we too, crouch and quail,
  Ashamed, afraid of strife,
And lest our lives untimely fail
  Embrace the Death in Life?
Nay, cry aloud, and have no fear,
  We few against the world;
Awake, arise! the hope we bear
  Against the curse is hurled.

It grows and grows—are we the same,
  The feeble band, the few?
Or what are these with eyes aflame,
  And hands to deal and do?
This is the host that bears the word,
  No MASTER HIGH OR LOW—
A lightning flame, a shearing sword,
  A storm to overthrow.

ALL FOR THE CAUSE

Hear a word, a word in season, for the day is drawing
   nigh,
When the Cause shall call upon us, some to live, and some
   to die!

He that dies shall not die lonely, many an one hath gone
   before;
He that lives shall bear no burden heavier than the life they
   bore.

Nothing ancient is their story, e'en but yesterday they bled,
Youngest they of earth's beloved, last of all the valiant dead.

E'en the tidings we are telling was the tale they had to tell,
E'en the hope that our hearts cherish, was the hope for
   which they fell.

In the grave where tyrants thrust them, lies their labour
   and their pain,
But undying from their sorrow springeth up the hope again.

Mourn not therefore, nor lament it, that the world outlives
   their life;
Voice and vision yet they give us, making strong our hands
   for strife.

Some had name, and fame, and honour, learn'd they were,
   and wise and strong;
Some were nameless, poor, unlettered, weak in all but grief
   and wrong.

Named and nameless all live in us; one and all they lead
   us yet
Every pain to count for nothing, every sorrow to forget.

Hearken how they cry, "O happy, happy ye that ye were
   born
In the sad slow night's departing, in the rising of the morn.

"Fair the crown the Cause hath for you, well to die or well
    to live
Through the battle, through the tangle, peace to gain or
    peace to give."

Ah, it may be! Oft meseemeth, in the days that yet shall be,
When no slave of gold abideth 'twixt the breadth of sea to
    sea.

Oft, when men and maids are merry, ere the sunlight leaves
    the earth,
And they bless the day beloved, all too short for all their
    mirth,

Some shall pause awhile and ponder on the bitter days of
    old,
Ere the toil of strife and battle overthrew the curse of gold;

Then 'twixt lips of loved and lover solemn thoughts of us
    shall rise;
We who once were fools and dreamers, then shall be the
    brave and wise.

There amidst the world new-builded shall our earthly deeds
    abide,
Though our names be all forgotten, and the tale of how we
    died.

Life or death then, who shall heed it, what we gain or what
    we lose?
Fair flies life amid the struggle, and the Cause for each shall
    choose.

Hear a word, a word in season, for the day is drawing nigh,
When the Cause shall call upon us, some to live, and some
    to die!

THE MARCH OF THE WORKERS

What is this, the sound and rumour? What is this that
    all men hear,
Like the wind in hollow valleys when the storm is drawing
    near,
Like the rolling on of ocean in the eventide of fear?
                  'Tis the people marching on.

Whither go they, and whence come they? What are these
    of whom ye tell?
In what country are they dwelling 'twixt the gates of heaven
    and hell?
Are they mine or thine for money? Will they serve a
    master well?
                  Still the rumour's marching on.

        Hark the rolling of the thunder!
        Lo the sun! and lo thereunder
        Riseth wrath, and hope, and wonder,
             And the host comes marching on.

Forth they come from grief and torment; on they wend
    toward health and mirth,
All the wide world is their dwelling, every corner of the earth.
Buy them, sell them for thy service! Try the bargain what
    'tis worth,
                  For the days are marching on.

These are they who build thy houses, weave thy raiment,
    win thy wheat,
Smooth the rugged, fill the barren, turn the bitter into sweet,
All for thee this day—and ever. What reward for them is
    meet
                  Till the host comes marching on?

        Hark the rolling of the thunder!
        Lo the sun! and lo thereunder
        Riseth wrath, and hope, and wonder,
             And the host comes marching on.

Many a hundred years passed over have they laboured deaf
    and blind;
Never tidings reached their sorrow, never hope their toil
    might find.
Now at last they've heard and hear it, and the cry comes
    down the wind,
                And their feet are marching on.

O ye rich men hear and tremble! for with words the sound
    is rife:
"Once for you and death we laboured; changed hence-
    forward is the strife.
We are men, and we shall battle for the world of men and
    life;
                And our host is marching on."

        Hark the rolling of the thunder!
        Lo the sun! and lo thereunder
        Riseth wrath, and hope, and wonder,
              And the host comes marching on.

"Is it war, then? Will ye perish as the dry wood in the fire?
Is it peace? Then be ye of us, let your hope be our desire.
Come and live! for life awaketh, and the world shall never
    tire;
                And hope is marching on.

"On we march then, we the workers, and the rumour that
    ye hear
Is the blended sound of battle and deliv'rance drawing near;
For the hope of every creature is the banner that we bear,
              And the world is marching on."

        Hark the rolling of the thunder!
        Lo the sun! and lo thereunder
        Riseth wrath, and hope, and wonder,
              And the host comes marching on.

A DEATH SONG

What cometh here from west to east awending?
And who are these, the marchers stern and slow?
We bear the message that the rich are sending
Aback to those who bade them wake and know.
Not one, not one, nor thousands must they slay,
But one and all if they would dusk the day.

We asked them for a life of toilsome earning,
They bade us bide their leisure for our bread;
We craved to speak to tell our woeful learning:
We come back speechless, bearing back our dead.
Not one, not one, nor thousands must they slay,
But one and all if they would dusk the day.

They will not learn; they have no ears to hearken.
They turn their faces from the eyes of fate;
Their gay-lit halls shut out the skies that darken.
But, lo! this dead man knocking at the gate.
Not one, not one, nor thousands must they slay,
But one and all if they would dusk the day.

Here lies the sign that we shall break our prison;
Amidst the storm he won a prisoner's rest;
But in the cloudy dawn the sun arisen
Brings us our day of work to win the best.
Not one, not one, nor thousands must they slay,
But one and all if they would dusk the day.

FROM THE UPLAND
TO THE SEA

Shall we wake one morn of spring,
Glad at heart of everything,
Yet pensive with the thought of eve?
Then the white house shall we leave,
Pass the wind-flowers and the bays,
Through the garth, and go our ways,
Wandering down among the meads
Till our very joyance needs
Rest at last; till we shall come
To that Sun-god's lonely home,
Lonely on the hillside grey,
Whence the sheep have gone away;
Lonely till the feast-time is,
When with prayer and praise of bliss,
Thither comes the country side.
There awhile shall we abide,
Sitting low down in the porch
By that image with the torch:
Thy one white hand laid upon
The black pillar that was won
From the far-off Indian mine;
And my hand nigh touching thine.
But not touching; and thy gown
Fair with spring-flowers cast adown
From thy bosom and thy brow.
There the south-west wind shall blow
Through thine hair to reach my cheek,
As thou sittest, nor mayst speak,
Nor mayst move the hand I kiss
For the very depth of bliss;
Nay, nor turn thine eyes to me.
Then desire of the great sea
Nigh enow, but all unheard,
In the hearts of us is stirred,

And we rise, we twain at last,
And the daffodils downcast,
Feel thy feet and we are gone
From the lonely Sun-Crowned one.
Then the meads fade at our back,
And the spring day 'gins to lack
That fresh hope that once it had;
But we twain grow yet more glad,
And apart no more may go
When the grassy slope and low
Dieth in the shingly sand:
Then we wander hand in hand
By the edges of the sea,
And I weary more for thee
Than if far apart we were,
With a space of desert drear
'Twixt thy lips and mine, O love!
Ah, my joy, my joy thereof!

ICELAND FIRST SEEN

Lo from our loitering ship
a new land at last to be seen;
Toothed rocks down the side of the firth
on the east guard a weary wide lea,
And black slope the hillsides above,
striped adown with their desolate green:
And a peak rises up on the west
from the meeting of cloud and of sea,
Foursquare from base unto point
like the building of Gods that have been,
The last of that waste of the mountains
all cloud-wreathed and snow-flecked and grey,
And bright with the dawn that began
just now at the ending of day.

Ah! what came we forth for to see
that our hearts are so hot with desire?
Is it enough for our rest,
the sight of this desolate strand,

And the mountain-waste voiceless as death
but for winds that may sleep not nor tire?
Why do we long to wend forth
through the length and breadth of a land,
Dreadful with grinding of ice,
and record of scarce hidden fire,
But that there 'mid the grey grassy dales
sore scarred by the ruining streams
Lives the tale of the Northland of old
and the undying glory of dreams?

O land, as some cave by the sea
where the treasures of old have been laid,
The sword it may be of a king
whose name was the turning of fight:
Or the staff of some wise of the world
that many things made and unmade.
Or the ring of a woman maybe
whose woe is grown wealth and delight.
No wheat and no wine grows above it,
no orchard for blossom and shade;
The few ships that sail by its blackness
but deem it the mouth of a grave;
Yet sure when the world shall awaken,
this too shall be mighty to save.

Or rather, O land, if a marvel
it seemeth that men ever sought
Thy wastes for a field and a garden
fulfilled of all wonder and doubt,
And feasted amidst of the winter
when the fight of the year had been fought,
Whose plunder all gathered together
was little to babble about;
Cry aloud from thy wastes, O thou land,
"Not for this nor for that was I wrought
Amid waning of realms and of riches
and death of things worshipped and sure,
I abide here the spouse of a God,
and I made and I make and endure."

O Queen of the grief without knowledge,
of the courage that may not avail,
Of the longing that may not attain,
of the love that shall never forget,
More joy than the gladness of laughter
thy voice hath amidst of its wail:
More hope than of pleasure fulfilled
amidst of thy blindness is set;
More glorious than gaining of all
thine unfaltering hand that shall fail:
For what is the mark on thy brow
but the brand that thy Brynhild doth bear?
Lone once, and loved and undone
by a love that no ages outwear.

Ah! when thy Balder comes back,
and bears from the heart of the Sun
Peace and the healing of pain,
and the wisdom that waiteth no more;
And the lilies are laid on thy brow
'mid the crown of the deeds thou hast done;
And the roses spring up by thy feet
that the rocks of the wilderness wore.
Ah! when thy Balder comes back
and we gather the gains he hath won,
Shall we not linger a little
to talk of thy sweetness of old,
Yea, turn back awhile to thy travail
whence the Gods stood aloof to behold?

A GARDEN BY THE SEA

I know a little garden-close,
Set thick with lily and red rose,
Where I would wander if I might
From dewy morn to dewy night,
And have one with me wandering.

And though within it no birds sing,
And though no pillared house is there,
And though the apple-boughs are bare
Of fruit and blossom, would to God
Her feet upon the green grass trod,
And I beheld them as before.

There comes a murmur from the shore,
And in the close two fair streams are,
Drawn from the purple hills afar,
Drawn down unto the restless sea:
Dark hills whose heath-bloom feeds no bee,
Dark shore no ship has ever seen,
Tormented by the billows green
Whose murmur comes unceasingly
Unto the place for which I cry.
For which I cry both day and night,
For which I let slip all delight,
Whereby I grow both deaf and blind,
Careless to win, unskilled to find,
And quick to lose what all men seek.

Yet tottering as I am and weak,
Still have I left a little breath
To seek within the jaws of death
An entrance to that happy place,
To seek the unforgotten face,
Once seen, once kissed, once reft from me
Anigh the murmuring of the sea.

LECTURES AND ESSAYS

GOTHIC ARCHITECTURE, *first spoken as a lecture to the Arts and Crafts Exhibition Society in 1889, was printed at the Kelmscott Press in 1893 in the "Golden" type.*[1]

[1] pp. ii + 68. 16mo. Paper boards. Also an edition printed on vellum.

HOPES AND FEARS FOR ART *was first published in volume form in 1882, by Ellis and White.*[1] *Of the essays here selected,* The Lesser Arts *first appeared in 1878 as a pamphlet, under the title* The Decorative Arts.[2] The Art of the People *was published as a pamphlet in 1879, as* An Address delivered in the Town Hall, Birmingham[3]; The Beauty of Life *appeared similarly in 1880, as* Labour and Pleasure versus Labour and Sorrow.[4]

[1] pp. ii + 217. Crown 8vo.
[2] pp. 32. Crown 8vo. Published by Ellis and White.
[3] pp. 23. 8vo. Published by Osborne, Birmingham.
[4] pp. 31. 8vo. Published by Cund Bros., Birmingham.

SIGNS OF CHANGE *appeared in volume form in 1888, by Reeves and Turner.*[1] *Of the selected lectures,* How We Live and How We Might Live *appeared first in* The Commonweal. The Aims of Art *was published as a pamphlet in 1887, at the* Commonweal *office.*[2] Useful Work versus Useless Toil *also appeared as a pamphlet, issued in 1885 by the Socialist League.*[3]

[1] pp. xii + 204. Crown 8vo.
[2] pp. 40. Demy 16mo.
[3] pp. 24. Crown 8vo.

ART AND SOCIALISM *was first published in 1884, as No. VII of the Leek Bijou Reprints.*[1] *Its first appearance in volume form was in* Architecture, Industry and Wealth, *published by Longmans, Green, in 1902, and printed in the "Golden" type.*[2]

[1] pp. 72. Crown 16mo. [2] pp. 163. Quarto.

A FACTORY AS IT MIGHT BE *appeared first in* Justice, *the organ of the Social Democratic Federation, in 1884 (No. 18). It was published as a pamphlet in 1907, at the Twentieth Century Press.*[1] *It is not included in Morris's Collected Works.*

[1] pp. 16. Demy 8vo.

HOW I BECAME A SOCIALIST *first appeared in* Justice, *June 16, 1894. It was re-issued as a pamphlet in 1896, in commemoration of Morris's death, with two other short articles, and an introduction by H. M. Hyndman, at the Twentieth Century Press.*[1] *It is included in Vol. 23 of the* Collected Works.

[1] pp. 16. Crown 8vo.

COMMUNISM *was published as Fabian Tract 113, with a preface by Bernard Shaw, in 1903.*[1] *It appears in the bound volume of* Fabian Tracts, *and in Vol. 23 of the* Collected Works.

[1] pp. 16. Demy 8vo.

GOTHIC ARCHITECTURE

BY the word Architecture is, I suppose, commonly understood the art of ornamental building, and in this sense I shall often have to use it here. Yet I would not like you to think of its productions merely as well-constructed and well-proportioned buildings, each one of which is handed over by the architect to other artists to finish, after his designs have been carried out (as we say) by a number of mechanical workers, who are not artists. A true architectural work rather is a building duly provided with all necessary furniture, decorated with all due ornament, according to the use, quality, and dignity of the building, from mere mouldings or abstract lines, to the great epical works of sculpture and painting, which, except as decorations of the nobler form of such buildings, cannot be produced at all. So looked on, a work of architecture is a harmonious co-operative work of art, inclusive of all the serious arts, all those which are not engaged in the production of mere toys, or of ephemeral prettinesses.

Now these works of art are man's expression of the value of life, and also the production of them makes his life of value: and since they can only be produced by the general good-will and help of the public, their continuous production, or the existence of the true Art of Architecture, betokens a society which, whatever elements of change it may bear within it, may be called stable, since it is founded on the happy exercise of the energies of the most useful part of its population.

What the absence of this Art of Architecture may betoken in the long run it is not easy for us to say: because that lack belongs only to these later times of the world's history, which as yet we cannot fairly see, because they are too near to us; but clearly in the present it indicates a transference of the interest of civilised men from the development of the human and intellectual energies of the race to the development of its mechanical energies. If this tendency is to go along the logical road of development, it must be said that it will destroy the arts of design and all that is analogous to them in literature; but the logical outcome of obvious tendencies is often thwarted by the historical development; that is, by what I can call by no better name than the collective will of mankind; and unless my hopes deceive me, I should say that this process has already begun, that there is a revolt on foot against the utilitarianism which threatens to destroy the Arts; and that it is deeper rooted than a mere passing fashion. For myself I do not indeed believe that this revolt can effect much, so long as the present state of society lasts; but as I am sure that great changes which will bring about a new state of society are rapidly advancing upon us, I think it a matter of much importance that these two revolts should join hands, or at least should learn to understand one another. If the New society when it comes (itself the result of the ceaseless evolution of countless years of tradition) should find the world cut off from all tradition of art, all aspiration towards the beauty which man has proved that he can create, much time will be lost in running hither and thither after the new thread of art; many lives will be barren of a manly pleasure which the world can ill afford to lose even for a short time. I ask you, therefore, to accept what follows as a contribution toward the revolt against utilitarianism, toward the attempt at catching-up the slender thread of tradition before it be too late.

Now, that Harmonious Architectural unit, inclusive of the arts in general, is no mere dream. I have said that it is only in these later times that it has become extinct: until the rise of modern society, no Civilisation, no Barbarism has been without it in some form; but it reached its fullest development in the Middle Ages, an epoch really more remote from our modern habits of life and thought than the older civilisations were, though an important part of its life was carried on in our own country by men of our own blood. Nevertheless, remote as those times are from ours, if we are ever to have architecture at all, we must take up the thread of tradition there and nowhere else, because that Gothic Architecture is the most completely organic form of the Art which the world has seen; the break in the thread

of tradition could only occur there: all the former developments tended thitherward, and to ignore this fact and
attempt to catch up the thread before that point was
reached, would be a mere piece of artificiality, betokening,
not new birth, but a corruption into mere whim of the
ancient traditions.

In order to illustrate this position of mine, I must ask
you to allow me to run very briefly over the historical
sequence of events which led to Gothic Architecture and
its fall, and to pardon me for stating familiar and elementary facts which are necessary for my purpose. I must
admit also that in doing this I must mostly take my illus-
trations from works that appear on the face of them to
belong to the category of ornamental building, rather than
that of those complete and inclusive works of which I have
spoken. But this incompleteness is only on the surface ; to
those who study them they appear as belonging to the class
of complete architectural works; they are lacking in completeness only through the consequences of the lapse of
time and the folly of men, who did not know what they
were, who, pretending to use them, marred their real use
as works of art; or in a similar spirit abused them by making them serve their turn as instruments to express their
passing passion and spite of the hour.

We may divide the history of the Art of Architecture into
two periods, the Ancient and the Mediæval: the Ancient
again may be divided into two styles, the barbarian (in the
Greek sense) and the classical. We have, then, three great
styles to consider: the Barbarian, the Classical, and the
Mediæval. The two former, however, were partly syn-
chronous, and at least overlapped somewhat. When the
curtain of the stage of definite history first draws up, we
find the small exclusive circle of the highest civilisation,
which was dominated by Hellenic thought and science,
fitted with a very distinctive and orderly architectural
style. That style appears to us to be, within its limits, one
of extreme refinement, and perhaps seemed so to those who
originally practised it. Moreover, it is ornamented with
figure-sculpture far advanced towards perfection even at an
early period of its existence, and swiftly growing in technical excellence; yet for all that, it is, after all, a part of the

general style of architecture of the Barbarian world, and only outgoes it in the excellence of its figure-sculpture and its refinement. The bones of it, its merely architectural part, are little changed from the Barbarian or primal building, which is a mere piling or jointing together of material, giving one no sense of growth in the building itself and no sense of the possibility of growth in the style.

The one Greek form of building with which we are really familiar, the columnar temple, though always built with blocks of stone, is clearly a deduction from the wooden god's-house or shrine, which was a necessary part of the equipment of the not very remote ancestors of the Periclean Greeks; nor had this god's-house changed so much as the city had changed from the Tribe, or the Worship of the City (the true religion of the Greeks) from the Worship of the Ancestors of the Tribe. In fact, rigid conservatism of form is an essential part of Greek architecture as we know it. From this conservatism of form there resulted a jostling between the building and its higher ornament. In early days, indeed, when some healthy barbarism yet clung to the sculpture, the discrepancy is not felt; but as increasing civilisation demands from the sculptors more naturalism and less restraint, it becomes more and more obvious, and more and more painful; till at last it becomes clear that sculpture has ceased to be a part of architecture and has become an extraneous art bound to the building by habit or superstition. The form of the ornamental building of the Greeks, then, was very limited, had no capacity in it for development, and tended to divorce from its higher or epical ornament. What is to be said about the spirit of it which ruled that form? This I think; that the narrow superstition of the form of the Greek temple was not a matter of accident, but was the due expression of the exclusiveness and aristocratic arrogance of the ancient Greek mind, a natural result of which was a demand for pedantic perfection in all the parts and details of a building; so that the inferior parts of the ornament are so slavishly subordinated to the superior, that no invention or individuality is possible in them, whence comes a kind of bareness and blankness, a rejection in short of all romance, which does not indeed destroy their interest as relics of past history, but which puts

the style of them aside as any possible foundation for the
style of the future architecture of the world. It must be
remembered also that this attempt at absolute perfection
soon proved a snare to Greek architecture; for it could not
be kept up long. It was easy indeed to ensure the perfect
execution of a fret or a dentil; not so easy to ensure the perfection of the higher ornament: so that as Greek energy
began to fall back from its high-water mark, the demand for
absolute perfection became rather a demand for absolute
plausibility, which speedily dragged the architectural arts
into mere Academicism.

But long before classical art reached the last depths of
that degradation, it had brought to birth another style of
architecture, the Roman style, which to start with was
differentiated from the Greek by having the habitual use of
the arch forced upon it. To my mind, organic Architecture, Architecture which must necessarily grow, dates from
the habitual use of the arch, which, taking into consideration its combined utility and beauty, must be pronounced
to be the greatest invention of the human race. Until the
time when man not only had invented the arch, but had
gathered boldness to use it habitually, architecture was
necessarily so limited, that strong growth was impossible to
it. It was quite natural that a people should crystallize the
first convenient form of building they might happen upon,
or, like the Greeks, accept a traditional form without aspiration towards anything more complex or interesting. Till
the arch came into use, building men were the slaves of
conditions of climate, materials, kind of labour available,
and so forth. But once furnished with the arch, man has
conquered Nature in the matter of building; he can defy
the rigours of all climates under which men can live with
fair comfort: splendid materials are not necessary to him;
he can attain a good result from shabby and scrappy
materials. When he wants size and span he does not need
a horde of war-captured slaves to work for him; the free
citizens (if there be any such) can do all that is needed without grinding their lives out before their time. The arch can
do all that architecture needs, and in turn from the time
when the Arch comes into habitual use, the main artistic
business of architecture is the decoration of the Arch; the

only satisfactory style is that which never disguises its office, but adorns and glorifies it. This the Roman architecture, the first style that used the arch, did not do. It used the arch frankly and simply indeed, in one part of its work, but did not adorn it; this part of the Roman building must, however, be called engineering rather than architecture, though its massive and simple dignity is a wonderful contrast to the horrible and restless nightmare of modern engineering. In the other side of its work, the ornamental side, Roman building used the arch and adorned it, but disguised its office, and pretended that the structure of its buildings was still that of the lintel, and that the arch bore no weight worth speaking of. For the Romans had no ornamental building of their own (perhaps we should say no art of their own) and therefore fitted their ideas of the ideas of the Greek sculpture-architect on to their own massive building; and as the Greek plastered his energetic and capable civilised sculpture on to the magnified shrine of his forefathers, so the Roman plastered sculpture, shrine, and all, on to his magnificent engineer's work. In fact, this kind of front-building or veneering was the main resource of Roman ornament; the construction and ornament did not interpenetrate; and to us at this date its seems doubtful if he gained by hiding with marble veneer the solid and beautiful construction of his wall of brick or concrete; since others have used marble far better than he did, but none have built a wall or turned an arch better. As to the Roman ornament, it is not in itself worth much sacrifice of interest in the construction: the Greek ornament was cruelly limited and conventional; but everything about it was in its place, and there was a reason for everything, even though that reason were founded on superstition. But the Roman ornament has no more freedom than the Greek, while it has lost the logic of the latter: it is rich and handsome, and that is all the reason it can give for its existence; nor does its execution and its design interpenetrate. One cannot conceive of the Greek ornament existing apart from the precision of its execution; but well as the Roman ornament is executed in all important works, one almost wishes it were less well executed, so that some mystery might be added to its florid handsomeness. Once again, it is a piece of necessary history, and to criticize it from the point of view of work of to-day would be like finding fault with a geological epoch: and who can help feeling touched by its remnants which show crumbling and battered amidst the incongruous mass of modern houses, amidst the disorder, vulgarity and squalor of some modern town? If I have ventured to call your attention to what it was as architecture, it is because of the abuse of it which took place in later times and has even lasted into our own anti-architectural days; and because it is necessary to point out that it has not got the qualities essential to making it a foundation for any possible new-birth of the arts. In its own time it was for centuries the only thing that redeemed the academical period of classical art from mere nothingness, and though it may almost be said to have perished before the change came, yet in perishing it gave some token of the coming change, which indeed was as slow as the decay of imperial Rome herself. It was in the height of the taxgathering period of the Roman Peace, in the last days of Diocletian (died 313) in the palace of Spalato which he built himself to rest in after he was satiated with rule, that the rebel, Change, first showed in Roman art, and that the builders admitted that their false lintel was false, and that the arch could do without it.

This was the first obscure beginning of Gothic or organic Architecture; henceforth till the beginning of the modern epoch all is growth uninterrupted, however slow. Indeed, it is slow enough at first: Organic Architecture took two centuries to free itself from the fetters which the Academical ages had cast over it, and the Peace of Rome had vanished before it was free. But the full change came at last, and the architecture was born which logically should have supplanted the primitive lintel-architecture, of which the civilized style of Greece was the last development. Architecture was become organic; henceforth no academical period was possible to it, nothing but death could stop its growth.

The first expression of this freedom is called Byzantine Art, and there is nothing to object to in the name. For centuries Byzantium was the centre of it, and its first great work in that city (the Church of the Holy Wisdom, built by

R

Justinian in the year 540) remains its greatest work. The style leaps into sudden completeness in this most lovely building: for there are few works extant of much importance of earlier date. As to its origin, of course buildings were raised all through the sickness of classical art, and traditional forms and ways of work were still in use, and these traditions, which by this time included the forms of Roman building, were now in the hands of the Greeks. This Romano-Greek building in Greek hands met with traditions drawn from many sources. In Syria, the borderland of so many races and customs, the East mingled with the West, and Byzantine art was born. Its characteristics are simplicity of structure and outline of mass; amazing delicacy of ornament combined with abhorrence of vagueness: it is bright and clear in colour, pure in line, hating barrenness as much as vagueness; redundant, but not florid, the very opposite of Roman architecture in spirit, though it took so many of its forms and revivified them. Nothing more beautiful than its best works has ever been produced by man, but in spite of its stately loveliness and quietude, it was the mother of fierce vigour in the days to come, for from its first days in St. Sophia, Gothic architecture has still one thousand years of life before it. East and West it overran the world wherever men built with history behind them. In the East it mingled with the traditions of the native populations, especially with Persia of the Sassanian period, and produced the whole body of what we, very erroneously, call Arab Art (for the Arabs never had any art) from Isphahan to Granada. In the West it settled itself in the parts of Italy that Justinian had conquered, notably Ravenna, and thence came to Venice. From Italy, or perhaps even from Byzantium itself, it was carried into Germany and pre-Norman England, touching even Ireland and Scandinavia. Rome adopted it, and sent it another road through the south of France, where it fell under the influence of provincial Roman architecture, and produced a very strong orderly and logical substyle, just what one imagines the ancient Romans might have built, if they had been able to resist the conquered Greeks who took them captive. Thence it spread all over France, the first development of the architecture of the most architectural of peoples, and in the north of that country fell under the influence of the Scandinavian and Teutonic tribes, and produced the last of the round arched Gothic styles, (named by us Norman) which those energetic warriors carried into Sicily, where it mingled with the Saracenic Byzantine and produced lovely works. But we know it best in our own country; for Duke William's intrusive monks used it everywhere, and it drove out the native English style derived from Byzantium through Germany.

Here on the verge of a new change, a change of form important enough (though not a change of essence), we may pause to consider once more what its essential qualities were. It was the first style since the invention of the arch that did due honour to it, and instead of concealing it decorated it in a logical manner. This was much; but the complete freedom that it had won, which indeed was the source of its ingenuousness, was more. It had shaken off the fetters of Greek superstition and aristocracy, and Roman pedantry, and though it must needs have had laws to be a style at all, it followed them of free will, and yet unconsciously. The cant of the beauty of simplicity (i.e., bareness and barrenness) did not afflict it: it was not ashamed of redundancy of material, or superabundance of ornament, any more than nature is. Slim elegance it could produce, or sturdy solidity, as its moods went. Material was not its master, but its servant: marble was not necessary to its beauty; stone would do, or brick, or timber. In default of carving it would set together cubes of glass or whatsoever was shining and fair-hued, and cover every portion of its interiors with a fairy coat of splendour; or would mould mere plaster into intricacy of work scarce to be followed, but never wearying the eyes with its delicacy and expressiveness of line. Smoothness it loves, the utmost finish that the hand can give; but if material or skill fail, the rougher work shall so be wrought that it also shall please us with its inventive suggestion. For the iron rule of the classical period, the acknowledged slavery of every one but the great man, was gone, and freedom had taken its place: but harmonious freedom. Subordination there is, but subordination of effect, not uniformity of detail; true and necessary subordination, not pedantic.

The full measure of this freedom Gothic Architecture did

not gain until it was in the hands of the workmen of Europe, the gildsmen of the Free Cities, who on many a bloody field proved how dearly they valued their corporate life by the generous valour with which they risked their individual lives in its defence. But from the first, the tendency was towards this freedom of hand and mind subordinated to the co-operative harmony which made the freedom possible. That is the spirit of Gothic Architecture.

Let us go on a while with our history: Up to this point the progress had always been from East to West, i.e., the East carried the West with it; the West must now go to the East to fetch new gain thence. A revival of religion was one of the moving causes of energy in the early Middle Ages in Europe, and this religion (with its enthusiasm for visible tokens of the objects of worship) impelled people to visit the East, which held the centre of that worship. Thence arose the warlike pilgrimages of the Crusades amongst races by no means prepared to turn their cheeks to the smiter. True it is that the tendency of the extreme West to seek East did not begin with the days just before the Crusades. There was a thin stream of pilgrims setting eastward long before, and the Scandinavians had found their way to Byzantium, not as pilgrims but as soldiers, and under the name of Vœrings a body-guard of their blood upheld the throne of the Greek Kaiser, and many of them, returning home, bore with them ideas of art which were not lost on their scanty but energetic populations. But the crusades brought gain from the East in a far more wholesale manner; and I think it is clear that part of that gain was the idea of art that brought about the change from round-arched to pointed Gothic. In those days (perhaps in ours also) it was the rule for conquerors settling in any country to assume that there could be no other system of society save that into which they had been born; and accordingly conquered Syria received a due feudal government, with the King of Jerusalem for Suzerain, the one person allowed by the heralds to bear metal on metal in his coat-armour. Nevertheless, the Westerners who settled in this new realm, few in number as they were, readily received impressions from the art which they saw around them, the Saracenic Byzantine Art, which was, after all, sympathetic with their own minds: and these impressions produced the change. For it is not to be thought that there was any direct borrowing of forms from the East in the gradual change from the round-arched to the pointed Gothic: there was nothing more obvious at work than the influence of a kindred style, whose superior lightness and elegance gave a hint of the road which development might take.

Certainly this change in form, when it came, was a startling one: the pointed-arched Gothic when it had grown out of its brief and most beautiful transition, was a vigorous youth indeed. It carried combined strength and elegance almost as far as it could be carried: indeed, sometimes one might think it overdid the lightness of effect, as e.g., in the interior of Salisbury Cathedral. If some abbot or monk of the eleventh century could have been brought back to his rebuilt church of the thirteenth, he might almost have thought that some miracle had taken place: the huge cylindrical or square piers transformed into clusters of slim, elegant shafts; the narrow round-headed windows supplanted by tall wide lancets showing the germs of the elaborate traceries of the next century, and elegantly glazed with pattern and subject. The bold vault spanning the wide nave instead of the flat wooden ceiling of past days; the extreme richness of the mouldings with which every member is treated; the elegance and order of the floral sculpture, the grace and good drawing of the imagery: in short, a complete and logical style with no longer anything to apologise for, claiming homage from the intellect, as well as the imagination of men; the developed Gothic Architecture which has shaken off the trammels of Byzantium as well as of Rome, but which has, nevertheless, reached its glorious position step by step with no break and no conscious effort after novelty from the wall of Tiryns and the Treasury of Mycenæ.

This point of development was attained amidst a period of social conflict, the facts and tendencies of which, ignored by the historians of the eighteenth century, have been laid open to our view by our modern school of evolutionary historians. In the twelfth century the actual handicraftsmen found themselves at last face to face with the development of the earlier associations of freemen which were the survivals from the tribal society of Europe: in the teeth of these exclusive and aristocratic municipalities the handi-craftsmen had associated themselves into guilds of craft, and were claiming their freedom from legal and arbitrary oppression, and a share in the government of the towns; by the end of the thirteenth century they had conquered the position everywhere and within the next fifty or sixty years the governors of the free towns were the delegates of the craft guilds, and all handicraft was included in their associations. This period of their triumph, marked amidst other events by the Battle of Courtray, where the chivalry of France turned their backs in flight before the Flemish weavers, was the period during which Gothic Architecture reached its zenith. It must be admitted, I think, that during this epoch, as far as the art of beautiful building is con-cerned, France and England were the architectural countries par excellence; but all over the intelligent world was spread this bright, glittering, joyous art, which had now reached its acme of elegance and beauty: and moreover in its furniture, of which I have spoken above, the excellence was shared in various measure betwixt the countries of Europe. And let me note in passing that the necessarily ordinary conception of a Gothic interior as being a colourless whitey-grey place dependent on nothing but the architec-tural forms, is about as far from the fact as the correspond-ing idea of a Greek temple standing in all the chastity of white marble. We must remember, on the contrary, that both buildings were clad, and that the noblest part of their raiment was their share of a great epic, a story appealing to the hearts and minds of men. And in the Gothic building, especially in the half century we now have before us, every part of it, walls, windows, floor, was all looked on as space for the representation of incidents of the great story of mankind, as it had presented itself to the minds of men then living; and this space was used with the greatest frankness of prodigality, and one may fairly say that wherever a picture could be painted there it was painted.

For now Gothic Architecture had completed its furniture: Dante, Chaucer, Petrarch; the German hero ballad-epics, the French Romances, the English Forest-ballads, that epic of revolt, as it has been called, the Icelandic Sagas, Froissart and the Chroniclers, represent its literature. Its painting embraces a host of names (of Italy and Flanders chiefly), the two great realists Giotto and Van Eyk at their head: but every village has its painter, its carvers, its actors even; every man who produces works of handicraft is an artist. The few pieces of household goods left of its wreckage are marvels of beauty; its woven cloths and embroideries are worthy of its loveliest building, its pictured and ornamented books would be enough in themselves to make a great period of art, so excellent as they are in epic intention, in completeness of unerring decoration, and in marvellous skill of hand. In short, those masterpieces of noble building, those specimens of architecture, as we call them, the sight of which makes the holiday of our lives to-day, are the standard of the whole art of those times, and tell the story of all the completeness of art in the heyday of life, as well as that of the sad story which follows. For when anything human has arrived at quasi-completion there remains for it decay and death, in order that the new thing may be born from it: and this wonderful, joyous art of the Middle-ages could by no means escape its fate.

In the middle of the fourteenth century Europe was scourged by that mysterious terror the Black Death (a similar terror to which perhaps waylays the modern world), and, along with it, the no less mysterious pests of Commercialism and Bureaucracy attacked us. This misfortune was the turning-point of the Middle Ages ; once again a great change was at hand.

The birth and growth of the coming change was marked by art with all fidelity. Gothic Architecture began to alter its character in the years that immediately followed on the Great Pest; it began to lose its exaltation of style and to suffer a diminution in the generous wealth of beauty which it gave us in its heyday. In some places, e.g., England, it grew more crabbed, and even sometimes more common-place; in others, as in France, it lost order, virility, and purity of line. But for a long time yet it was alive and vigorous, and showed even greater capacity than before for adapting itself to the needs of a developing society: nor did the change of style affect all its furniture injuriously; some of the subsidiary arts as, e.g., Flemish tapestry and English wood-carving, rather gained than lost for many years.

At last, with the close of the Fifteenth century, the Great Change became obvious; and we must remember that it was no superficial change of form, but a change of spirit affecting every form inevitably. This change we have some-what boastfully, and as regards the arts quite untruthfully, called the New Birth. But let us see what it means.

Society was preparing for a complete recasting of its elements: the Mediæval Society of Status was in process of transition into the modern Society of Contract. New classes were being formed to fit the new system of production which was at the bottom of this; political life began again with the new birth of bureaucracy ; and political, as distinguished from natural, nationalities were being hammered together for the use of that bureaucracy, which was itself a necessity to the new system. And withal a new religion was being fashioned to fit the new theory of life: in short, the Age of Commercialism was being born.

Now some of us think that all this was a source of misery and degradation to the world at the time, that it is still causing misery and degradation, and that as a system it is bound to give place to a better one. Yet we admit that it had a beneficent function to perform; that amidst all the ugliness and confusion which it brought with it, it was a necessary instrument for the development of freedom of thought and the capacities of man; for the subjugation of nature to his material needs. This Great Change, I say, was necessary and inevitable, and on this side, the side of commerce and commercial science and politics, was a genuine new birth. On this side it did not look backward but forward: there had been nothing like it in past history; it was founded on no pedantic model; necessity, not whim, was its craftsmaster.

But, strange to say, to this living body of social, political, religious, scientific New Birth was bound the dead corpse of a past art. On every other side it bade men look forward to some change or other, were it good or bad: on the side of art, with the sternest pedagogic utterance, it bade men look backward across the days of the "Fathers and famous men that begat them," and in scorn of them, to an art that had been dead a thousand years before. Hitherto from the very beginning the past was past, all of it that was not alive in the present, unconsciously to the men of the present. Henceforth the past was to be our present, and the blankness of its dead wall was to shut out the future from us. There are many artists at present who do not sufficiently estimate the enormity, the portentousness of this change, and how closely it is connected with the Victorian Architecture of the brick box and the slate lid, which helps to make us the dullards that we are. How on earth could people's ideas of beauty change so? you may say. Well, was it their ideas of beauty that changed? Was it not rather that beauty, however unconsciously, was no longer an object of attainment with the men of that epoch?

This used once to puzzle me in the presence of one of the so-called masterpieces of the New Birth, the revived classical style, such a building as St. Paul's in London, for example. I have found it difficult to put myself in the frame of mind which could accept such a work as a substitute for even the latest and worst Gothic building. Such taste seemed to me like the taste of a man who should prefer his lady-love bald. But now I know that it was not a matter of choice on the part of any one then alive who had an eye for beauty: if the change had been made on the grounds of beauty it would be wholly inexplicable; but it was not so. In the early days of the Renaissance there were artists possessed of the highest qualities; but those great men (whose greatness, mind you, was only in work not carried out by co-operation, painting and sculpture for the most part) were really but the fruit of the blossoming-time, the Gothic period; as was abundantly proved by the succeeding periods of the Renaissance, which produced nothing but inanity and plausibility in all the arts. A few individual artists were great truly; but artists were no longer the masters of art, because the people had ceased to be artists: its masters were pedants. St. Peter's in Rome, St. Paul's in London, were not built to be beautiful, or to be beautiful and convenient. They were not built to be homes of the citizens in their moments of exaltation, their supreme grief or supreme hope, but to be proper, respectable, and therefore to show the due amount of cultivation, and knowledge of the only peoples and times that in the minds of their ignorant builders were not ignorant barbarians. They were built to be the homes of a decent unenthusiastic ecclesiasticism, of those whom we sometimes call Dons now-a-days. Beauty and romance were outside the aspirations of their builders. Nor could it have been otherwise in those days; for, once again, architectural beauty is the result of the harmonious and intelligent co-operation of the whole body of people engaged in producing the work of the workman; and by the time that the changeling New Birth was grown to be a vigorous imp, such workmen no longer existed. By that time Europe had begun to transform the great army of artist-craftsmen, who had produced the beauty of her cities, her churches, manor-houses and cottages, into an enormous stock of human machines, who had little chance of earning a bare livelihood if they lingered over their toil to think of what they were doing: who were not asked to think, paid to think, or allowed to think. That invention we have, I should hope, about perfected by this time, and it must soon give place to a new one. Which is happy; for as long as the invention is in use you need not trouble yourselves about architecture, since you will not get it, as the common expression of our life, that is as a genuine thing.

But at present I am not going to say anything about direct remedies for the miseries of the New Birth; I can only tell you what you ought to do if you can.   I want you to see that from the brief historic review of the progress of the Arts it results that to-day there is only one style of Architecture on which it is possible to found a true living art, which is free to adapt itself to the varying conditions of social life, climate, and so forth, and that that style is Gothic architecture. The greater part of what we now call architecture is but an imitation of an imitation of an imitation, the result of a tradition of dull respectability, or of foolish whims without root or growth in them.

Let us look at an instance of pedantic retrospection employed in the service of art. A Greek columnar temple, when it was a real thing, was a kind of holy railing built round a shrine: these things the people of that day wanted, and they naturally took the form of a Greek Temple under the climate of Greece and given the mood of its people.

But do we want those things? If so, I should like to know what for. And if we pretend we do and so force a Greek Temple on a modern city, we produce such a gross piece of ugly absurdity as you may see spanning the Lochs at Edinburgh. In these islands we want a roof and walls with windows cut in them; and these things a Greek Temple does not pretend to give us.

Will a Roman building allow us to have these necessaries? Well, only on the terms that we are to be ashamed of wall, roof, and windows, and pretend that we haven't got either of them, but rather a whimsical attempt at the imitation of a Greek Temple.

Will a neo-classical building allow us these necessities? Pretty much on the same terms as the Roman one; except when it is rather more than half Gothic. It will force us to pretend that we have neither roof, walls, nor windows, nothing but an imitation of the Roman travesty of a Greek Temple.

Now a Gothic building has walls that it is not ashamed of; and in those walls you may cut windows wherever you please; and, if you please may decorate them to show that you are not ashamed of them; your windows, which you must have, become one of the great beauties of your house, and you have no longer to make a lesion in logic in order not to sit in pitchy darkness in your own house, as in the sham sham-Roman style; your window, I say, is no longer a concession to human weakness, an ugly necessity (generally ugly enough in all conscience) but a glory of the art of Building. As for the roof in the sham style: unless the building is infected with Gothic common sense, you must pretend that you are living in a hot country which needs nothing but an awning, and that it never rains or snows in these islands. Whereas in a Gothic building the roof both within and without (especially within, as is most meet) is the crown of its beauties, the abiding place of its brain.

Again, consider the exterior of our buildings, that part of them that is common to all passersby, and that no man can turn into private property unless he builds amidst an inaccessible park. The original of our neo-classic architecture was designed for marble in a bright dry climate, which only weathers it to a golden tone. Do we really like a neo-classic

building weather-beaten by the roughness of hundreds of
English winters from October to June? And on the other
hand, can any of us fail to be touched by the weathered
surface of a Gothic building which has escaped the restorers'
hands? Do we not clearly know the latter to be a piece of
nature, that more excellent mood of nature that uses the
hands and wills of men as instruments of creation?

Indeed time would fail me to go into the many sides of
the contrast between the Architecture which is a mere
pedantic imitation of what was once alive, and that which
after a development of long centuries has still in it, as I
think, capacities for fresh developments, since its life was
cut short by an arbitrary recurrence to a style which
had long lost all elements of life and growth. Once for
all, then, when the modern world finds that the eclecti-
cism of the present is barren and fruitless, and that it needs
and will have a style of architecture which, I must tell
you once more, can only be as part of a change as wide
and deep as that which destroyed Feudalism; when it
has come to that conclusion, the style of architecture
will have to be historic in the true sense; it will not be
able to dispense with tradition; it cannot begin at least
with doing something quite different from anything that has
been done before; yet whatever the form of it may be, the
spirit of it will be sympathy with the needs and aspirations
of its own time, not simulation of needs and aspirations
passed away. Thus it will remember the history of the
past, make history in the present, and teach history in the
future. As to the form of it, I see nothing for it but that the
form, as well as the spirit, must be Gothic; an organic style
cannot spring out of an eclectic one, but only from an
organic one. In the future, therefore, our style of architecture must be Gothic Architecture.

And meanwhile of the world demanding architecture,
what are we to do? Meanwhile? After all, is there any
meanwhile? Are we not now demanding Gothic Architecture and crying for the fresh New Birth? To me it seems
so. It is true that the world is uglier now than it was fifty
years ago; but then people thought that ugliness a desirable
thing, and looked at it with complacency as a sign of civilisation, which no doubt it is. Now we are no longer

complacent, but are grumbling in a dim unorganised manner. We feel a loss, and unless we are very unreal and helpless we shall presently begin to try to supply that loss. Art cannot be dead so long as we feel the lack of it, I say: and though we shall probably try many roundabout ways for filling up the lack; yet we shall at last be driven into the one right way of concluding that in spite of all risks, and all losses, unhappy and slavish work must come to an end. In that day we shall take Gothic Architecture by the hand, and know it for what it was and what it is.

THE LESSER ARTS

HEREAFTER I hope in another lecture to have the pleasure of laying before you an historical survey of the lesser, or as they are called the Decorative Arts, and I must confess it would have been pleasanter to me to have begun my talk with you by entering at once upon the subject of the history of this great industry; but, as I have something to say in a third lecture about various matters connected with the practice of Decoration among ourselves in these days, I feel that I should be in a false position before you, and one that might lead to confusion, or overmuch explanation, if I did not let you know what I think on the nature and scope of these arts, on their condition at the present time, and their outlook in times to come. In doing this it is like enough that I shall say things with which you will very much disagree; I must ask you therefore from the outset to believe that whatever I may blame or whatever I may praise, I neither, when I think of what history has been, am inclined to lament the past, to despise the present, or despair of the future; that I believe all the change and stir about us is a sign of the world's life, and that it will lead —by ways, indeed, of which we have no guess—to the bettering of all mankind.

Now as to the scope and nature of these Arts I have to say, that though when I come more into the details of my subject I shall not meddle much with the great art of Architecture, and less still with the great arts commonly called Sculpture and Painting, yet I cannot in my own mind quite sever them from those lesser so-called Decorative Arts, which I have to speak about: it is only in latter times, and under the most intricate conditions of life, that they have fallen apart from one another; and I hold that, when they are so parted, it is ill for the Arts altogether: the lesser ones become trivial, mechanical, unintelligent, incapable of resisting the changes pressed upon them by fashion or

494

dishonesty; while the greater, however they may be practised for a while by men of great minds and wonder-working hands, unhelped by the lesser, unhelped by each other, are sure to lose their dignity of popular arts, and become nothing but dull adjuncts to unmeaning pomp, or ingenious toys for a few rich and idle men.

However, I have not undertaken to talk to you of Architecture, Sculpture, and Painting, in the narrower sense of those words, since, most unhappily as I think, these master-arts, these arts more specially of the intellect, are at the present day divorced from decoration in its narrower sense. Our subject is that great body of art, by means of which men have at all times more or less striven to beautify the familiar matters of everyday life: a wide subject, a great industry; both a great part of the history of the world, and a most helpful instrument to the study of that history.

A very great industry indeed, comprising the crafts of house-building, painting, joinery and carpentry, smiths' work, pottery and glass-making, weaving, and many others: a body of art most important to the public in general, but still more so to us handicraftsmen; since there is scarce anything that they use, and that we fashion, but it has always been thought to be unfinished till it has had some touch or other of decoration about it. True it is that in many or most cases we have got so used to this ornament, that we look upon it as if it had grown of itself, and note it no more than the mosses on the dry sticks with which we light our fires. So much the worse! for there *is* the decoration, or some pretence of it, and it has, or ought to have, a use and a meaning. For, and this is at the root of the whole matter, everything made by man's hands has a form, which must be either beautiful or ugly; beautiful if it is in accord with Nature, and helps her; ugly if it is discordant with Nature, and thwarts her; it cannot be indifferent: we, for our parts, are busy or sluggish, eager or unhappy, and our eyes are apt to get dulled to this eventfulness of form in those things which we are always looking at. Now it is one of the chief uses of decoration, the chief part of its alliance with nature, that it has to sharpen our dulled senses in this matter: for this end are those wonders of intricate patterns interwoven, those strange forms invented, which men have so long delighted in: forms and intricacies that do not necessarily imitate nature, but in which the hand of the craftsman is guided to work in the way that she does, till the web, the cup, or the knife, look as natural, nay as lovely, as the green field, the river bank, or the mountain flint.

To give people pleasure in the things they must perforce *use*, that is one great office of decoration; to give people pleasure in the things they must perforce *make*, that is the other use of it.

Does not our subject look important enough now? I say that without these arts, our rest would be vacant and uninteresting, our labour mere endurance, mere wearing away of body and mind.

As for that last use of these arts, the giving us pleasure in our work, I scarcely know how to speak strongly enough of it; and yet if I did not know the value of repeating a truth again and again, I should have to excuse myself to you for saying any more about this, when I remember how a great man now living has spoken of it: I mean my friend Professor John Ruskin: if you read the chapter in the 2nd vol. of his *Stones of Venice* entitled, "On the Nature of Gothic, and the Office of the Workman therein," you will read at once the truest and the most eloquent words that can possibly be said on the subject. What I have to say upon it can scarcely be more than an echo of his words, yet I repeat there is some use in reiterating a truth, lest it be forgotten; so I will say this much further: we all know what people have said about the curse of labour, and what heavy and grievous nonsense are the more part of their words thereupon; whereas indeed the real curses of craftsmen have been the curse of stupidity, and the curse of injustice from within and from without: no, I cannot suppose there is anybody here who would think it either a good life, or an amusing one, to sit with one's hands before one doing nothing—to live like a gentleman, as fools call it.

Nevertheless there *is* dull work to be done, and a weary business it is setting men about such work, and seeing them through it, and I would rather do the work twice over with my own hands than have such a job: but now only let the arts which we are talking of beautify our labour, and be widely spread, intelligent, well understood both by the

maker and the user, let them grow in one word *popular*, and
there will be pretty much an end of dull work and its wearing slavery; and no man will any longer have an excuse for
talking about the curse of labour, no man will any longer
have an excuse for evading the blessing of labour. I believe
there is nothing that will aid the world's progress so much
as the attainment of this; I protest there is nothing in the
world that I desire so much as this, wrapped up, as I am
sure it is, with changes political and social, that in one way
or another we all desire.

Now if the objection be made, that these arts have been
the handmaids of luxury, of tyranny and of superstition,
I must needs say that it is true in a sense; they have been so
used, as many other excellent things have been. But it is
also true that, among some nations, their most vigorous and
freest times have been the very blossoming times of art:
while at the same time, I must allow that these decorative
arts have flourished among oppressed peoples, who have
seemed to have no hope of freedom: yet I do not think that
we shall be wrong in thinking that at such times, among such
peoples, art, at least, was free; when it has not been, when
it has really been gripped by superstition, or by luxury, it
has straightway begun to sicken under that grip. Nor must
you forget that when men say popes, kings, and emperors
built such and such buildings, it is a mere way of speaking.
You look in your history-books to see who built Westminster
Abbey, who built St. Sophia at Constantinople, and they
tell you Henry III., Justinian the Emperor. Did they? or,
rather, men like you and me, handicraftsmen, who have left
no names behind them, nothing but their work?

Now as these arts call people's attention and interest to
the matters of every-day life in the present, so also, and that
I think is no little matter, they call our attention at every
step to that history, of which, I said before, they are so great
a part; for no nation, no state of society, however rude, has
been wholly without them: nay, there are peoples not a
few, of whom we know scarce anything, save that they
thought such and such forms beautiful. So strong is the
bond between history and decoration, that in the practice
of the latter we cannot, if we would, wholly shake off the
influence of past times over what we do at present. I do

not think it is too much to say that no man, however original he may be, can sit down to-day and draw the ornament of a cloth, or the form of an ordinary vessel or piece of furniture, that will be other than a development or a degradation of forms used hundreds of years ago; and these, too, very often, forms that once had a serious meaning, though they are now become little more than a habit of the hand; forms that were once perhaps the mysterious symbols of worships and beliefs now little remembered or wholly forgotten. Those who have diligently followed the delightful study of these arts are able as if through windows to look upon the life of the past:—the very first beginnings of thought among nations whom we cannot even name; the terrible empires of the ancient East; the free vigour and glory of Greece; the heavy weight, the firm grasp of Rome; the fall of her temporal Empire which spread so wide about the world all that good and evil which men can never forget, and never cease to feel; the clashing of East and West, South and North, about her rich and fruitful daughter Byzantium; the rise, the dissensions, and the waning of Islam; the wanderings of Scandinavia; the Crusades; the foundation of the States of modern Europe; the struggles of free thought with ancient dying system—with all these events and their meaning is the history of popular art interwoven; with all this, I say, the careful student of decoration as an historical industry must be familiar. When I think of this, and the usefulness of all this knowledge, at a time when history has become so earnest a study amongst us as to have given us, as it were, a new sense: at a time when we so long to know the reality of all that has happened, and are to be put off no longer with the dull records of the battles and intrigues of kings and scoundrels,—I say when I think of all this, I hardly know how to say that this interweaving of the Decorative Arts with the history of the past is of less importance than their dealings with the life of the present: for should not these memories also be a part of our daily life?

And now let me recapitulate a little before I go further, before we begin to look into the condition of the arts at the present day. These arts, I have said, are part of a great system invented for the expression of a man's delight in beauty: all peoples and times have used them; they have been the joy of free nations, and the solace of oppressed nations; religion has used and elevated them, has abused and degraded them; they are connected with all history, and are clear teachers of it; and, best of all, they are the sweeteners of human labour, both to the handicraftsman, whose life is spent in working in them, and to people in general who are influenced by the sight of them at every turn of the day's work: they make our toil happy, our rest fruitful.

And now if all I have said seems to you but mere openmouthed praise of these arts, I must say that it is not for nothing that what I have hitherto put before you has taken that form.

It is because I must now ask you this question: All these good things—will you have them? will you cast them from you?

Are you surprised at my question—you, most of whom, like myself, are engaged in the actual practice of the arts that are, or ought to be, popular?

In explanation, I must somewhat repeat what I have already said. Time was when the mystery and wonder of handicrafts were well acknowledged by the world, when imagination and fancy mingled with all things made by man; and in those days all handicraftsmen were *artists*, as we should now call them. But the thought of man became more intricate, more difficult to express; art grew a heavier thing to deal with, and its labour was more divided among great men, lesser men, and little men; till that art, which was once scarce more than a rest of body and soul, as the hand cast the shuttle or swung the hammer, became to some men so serious a labour, that their working lives have been one long tragedy of hope and fear, joy and trouble. This was the growth of art: like all growth, it was good and fruitful for awhile; like all fruitful growth, it grew into decay; like all decay of what was once fruitful, it will grow into something new.

Into decay; for as the arts sundered into the greater and the lesser, contempt on one side, carelessness on the other arose, both begotten of ignorance of that *philosophy* of the Decorative Arts, a hint of which I have tried just now to put before you. The artist came out from the handicraftsmen, and left them without hope of elevation, while he himself was left without the help of intelligent, industrious sympathy. Both have suffered; the artist no less than the workman. It is with art as it fares with a company of soldiers before a redoubt, when the captain runs forward full of hope and energy, but looks not behind him to see if his men are following, and they hang back, not knowing why they are brought there to die. The captain's life is spent for nothing, and his men are sullen prisoners in the redoubt of Unhappiness and Brutality.

I must in plain words say of the Decorative Arts, of all the arts, that it is not so much that we are inferior in them to all who have gone before us, but rather that they are in a state of anarchy and disorganisation, which makes a sweeping change necessary and certain.

So that again I ask my question, All that good fruit which the arts should bear, will you have it? will you cast it from you? Shall that sweeping change that must come, be the change of loss or of gain?

We who believe in the continuous life of the world, surely we are bound to hope that the change will bring us gain and not loss, and to strive to bring that gain about.

Yet how the world may answer my question, who can say? A man in his short life can see but a little way ahead, and even in mine, wonderful and unexpected things have come to pass. I must needs say that therein lies my hope rather than in all I see going on round about us. Without disputing that if the imaginative arts perish, some new thing, at present unguessed of, *may* be put forward to supply their loss in men's lives, I cannot feel happy in that prospect, nor can I believe that mankind will endure such a loss for ever: but in the meantime the present state of the arts and their dealings with modern life and progress seem to me to point, in appearance at least, to this immediate future; that the world, which has for a long time busied itself about other matters than the arts, and has carelessly let them sink lower and lower, till many not uncultivated men, ignorant of what they once were, and hopeless of what they might yet be, look upon them with mere contempt; that the world, I say, thus busied and hurried, will one day wipe the slate, and be clean rid in her impatience of the whole matter with all this tangle and trouble.

And then—what then?

Even now amid the squalor of London it is hard to imagine what it will be. Architecture, Sculpture, Painting, with the crowd of lesser arts that belong to them, these, together with Music and Poetry, will be dead and forgotten, will no longer excite or amuse people in the least: for, once more, we must not deceive ourselves; the death of one art means the death of all; the only difference in their fate will be that the luckiest will be eaten the last—the luckiest, or the unluckiest: in all that has to do with beauty the invention and ingenuity of man will have come to a dead stop; and all the while Nature will go on with her eternal recurrence of lovely changes—spring, summer, autumn, and winter; sunshine, rain, and snow; storm and fair weather; dawn, noon, and sunset; day and night—ever bearing witness against man that he has deliberately chosen ugliness instead of beauty, and to live where he is strongest amidst squalor or blank emptiness.

You see, sirs, we cannot quite imagine it; any more, perhaps, than our forefathers of ancient London, living in the pretty, carefully whitened houses, with the famous church and its huge spire rising above them,—than they, passing about the fair gardens running down to the broad river, could have imagined a whole county or more covered over with hideous hovels, big, middle-sized, and little, which should one day be called London.

Sirs, I say that this dead blank of the arts that I more than dread is difficult even now to imagine; yet I fear that I must say that if it does not come about, it will be owing to some turn of events which we cannot at present foresee: but I hold that if it does happen, it will only last for a time, that it will be but a burning up of the gathered weeds, so that the field may bear more abundantly. I hold that men would wake up after a while, and look round and find the dullness unbearable, and begin once more inventing, imitating, and imagining, as in earlier days.

That faith comforts me, and I can say calmly, if the blank space must happen, it must, and amidst its darkness the new seed must sprout. So it has been before: first comes birth, and hope scarcely conscious of itself; then the flower and fruit of mastery, with hope more than conscious enough, passing into insolence, as decay follows ripeness; and then —the new birth again.

Meantime it is the plain duty of all who look seriously on the arts to do their best to save the world from what at the best will be a loss, the result of ignorance and unwisdom; to prevent, in fact, that most discouraging of all changes, the supplying the place of an extinct brutality by a new one; nay, even if those who really care for the arts are so weak and few that they can do nothing else, it may be their business to keep alive some tradition, some memory of the past, so that the new life when it comes may not waste itself more than enough in fashioning wholly new forms for its new spirit.

To what side then shall those turn for help, who really understand the gain of a great art in the world, and the loss of peace and good life that must follow from the lack of it? I think that they must begin by acknowledging that the ancient art, the art of unconscious intelligence, as one should call it, which began without a date, at least so long ago as those strange and masterly scratchings on mammoth-bones and the like found but the other day in the drift—that this art of unconscious intelligence is all but dead; that what little of it is left lingers among half-civilised nations, and is growing coarser, feebler, less intelligent year by year; nay, it is mostly at the mercy of some commercial accident, such as the arrival of a few shiploads of European dye-stuffs or a few dozen orders from European merchants: this they must recognise, and must hope to see in time its place filled by a new art of conscious intelligence, the birth of wiser, simpler, freer ways of life than the world leads now, than the world has ever led.

I said, *to see* this in time; I do not mean to say that our own eyes will look upon it: it may be so far off, as indeed it seems to some, that many would scarcely think it worth while thinking of: but there are some of us who cannot turn our faces to the wall, or sit deedless because our hope seems somewhat dim; and, indeed, I think that while the signs of the last decay of the old art with all the evils that must follow in its train are only too obvious about us, so on the other hand there are not wanting signs of the new dawn beyond that possible night of the arts, of which I have before spoken; this sign chiefly, that there are some few at least, who are heartily discontented with things as they are, and crave for something better, or at least some promise of it—this best of signs: for I suppose that if some half-dozen men at any time earnestly set their hearts on something coming about which is not discordant with nature, it will come to pass one day or other; because it is not by accident that an idea comes into the heads of a few; rather they are pushed on, and forced to speak or act by something stirring in the heart of the world which would otherwise be left without expression.

By what means then shall those work who long for reform in the arts, and who shall they seek to kindle into eager desire for possession of beauty, and better still, for the development of the faculty that creates beauty?

People say to me often enough: If you want to make your art succeed and flourish, you must make it the fashion: a phrase which I confess annoys me; for they mean by it that I should spend one day over my work to two days in trying to convince rich, and supposed influential people, that they care very much for what they really do not care in the least, so that it may happen according to the proverb: *Bell-wether took the leap, and we all went over*. Well, such advisers are right if they are content with the thing lasting but a little while; say till you can make a little money—if you don't get pinched by the door shutting too quickly: otherwise they are wrong: the people they are thinking of have too many strings to their bow, and can turn their backs too easily on a thing that fails, for it to be safe work trusting to their whims: it is not their fault, they cannot help it, but they have no chance of spending time enough over the arts to know anything practical of them, and they must of necessity be in the hands of those who spend their time in pushing fashion this way and that for their own advantage.

Sirs, there is no help to be got out of these latter, or those who let themselves be led by them: the only real help for the decorative arts must come from those who work in them; nor must they be led, they must lead.

You whose hands make those things that should be works of art, you must be all artists, and good artists too, before the public at large can take real interest in such things; and when you have become so, I promise you that you shall lead the fashion; fashion shall follow your hands obediently enough.

That is the only way in which we can get a supply of intelligent popular art: a few artists of the kind so-called now, what can they do working in the teeth of difficulties thrown in their way by what is called Commerce, but which should be called greed of money? working helplessly among the crowd of those who are ridiculously called manufacturers, *i.e.* handicraftsmen, though the more part of them never did a stroke of hand-work in their lives, and are nothing better than capitalists and salesmen. What can these grains of sand do, I say, amidst the enormous mass of work turned out every year which professes in some way to be decorative art, but the decoration of which no one heeds except the salesmen who have to do with it, and are hard put to it to supply the cravings of the public for something new, not for something pretty?

The remedy, I repeat, is plain if it can be applied; the handicraftsman, left behind by the artist when the arts sundered, must come up with him, must work side by side with him: apart from the difference between a great master and a scholar, apart from the differences of the natural bent of men's minds, which would make one man an imitative, and another an architectural or decorative artist, there should be no difference between those employed on strictly ornamental work; and the body of artists dealing with this should quicken with their art all makers of things into artists also, in proportion to the necessities and uses of the things they would make.

I know what stupendous difficulties, social and economical, there are in the way of this; yet I think that they seem to be greater than they are: and of one thing I am sure, that no real living decorative art is possible if this is impossible.

It is not impossible, on the contrary it is certain to come about, if you are at heart desirous to quicken the arts; if the world will, for the sake of beauty and decency, sacrifice some of the things it is so busy over (many of which I think are not very worthy of its trouble), art will begin to grow again; as for those difficulties above mentioned, some of them I know will in any case melt away before the steady change of the relative conditions of men; the rest, reason and resolute attention to the laws of nature, which are also the laws of art, will dispose of little by little: once more, the way will not be far to seek, if the will be with us.

Yet, granted the will, and though the way lies ready to us, we must not be discouraged if the journey seem barren enough at first, nay, not even if things seem to grow worse for a while: for it is natural enough that the very evil which has forced on the beginning of reform should look uglier, while on the one hand life and wisdom are building up the new, and on the other folly and deadness are hugging the old to them.

In this, as in all other matters, lapse of time will be needed before things seem to straighten, and the courage and patience that does not despise small things lying ready to be done; and care and watchfulness, lest we begin to build the wall ere the footings are well in; and always through all things much humility that is not easily cast down by failure, that seeks to be taught, and is ready to learn.

For your teachers, they must be Nature and History: as for the first, that you must learn of it is so obvious that I need not dwell upon that now: hereafter, when I have to speak more of matters of detail, I may have to speak of the manner in which you must learn of Nature. As to the second I do not think that any man but one of the highest genius could do anything in these days without much study of ancient art, and even he would be much hindered if he lacked it. If you think that this contradicts what I said about the death of that ancient art, and the necessity I implied for an art that should be characteristic of the present day, I can only say that, in these times of plenteous knowledge and meagre performance, if we do not study the ancient work directly and learn to understand it, we shall find ourselves influenced by the feeble work all round us, and shall be copying the better work through the copyists and *without* understanding it, which will by no means bring about intelligent art. Let us therefore study it wisely, be taught by it, kindled by it; all the while determining not to imitate or repeat it; to have either no art at all, or an art which we have made our own.

Yet I am almost brought to a stand-still when bidding you

to study nature and the history of art, by remembering that this is London, and what it is like: how can I ask working-men passing up and down these hideous streets day by day to care about beauty? If it were politics, we must care about that; or science, you could wrap yourselves up in the study of facts, no doubt, without much caring what goes on about you—but beauty! do you not see what terrible diffi-culties beset art, owing to a long neglect of art—and neglect of reason, too, in this matter? It is such a heavy question by what effort, by what dead-lift, you can thrust this difficulty from you, that I must perforce set it aside for the present, and must at least hope that the study of history and its monuments will help you somewhat herein. If you can really fill your minds with memories of great works of art, and great times of art, you will, I think, be able to a certain extent to look through the aforesaid ugly surround-ings, and will be moved to discontent of what is careless and brutal now, and will, I hope, at last be so much dis-contented with what is bad, that you will determine to bear no longer that shortsighted, reckless brutality of squalor that so disgraces our intricate civilisation.

Well, at any rate, London is good for this, that it is well off for museums,—which I heartily wish were to be got at seven days in the week instead of six, or at least on the only day on which an ordinarily busy man, one of the taxpayers who support them, can as a rule see them quietly,—and certainly any of us who may have any natural turn for art must get more help from frequenting them than one can well say. It is true, however, that people need some pre-liminary instruction before they can get all the good possible to be got from the prodigious treasures of art possessed by the country in that form: there also one sees things in a piecemeal way: nor can I deny that there is something melancholy about a museum, such a tale of violence, des-truction, and carelessness, as its treasured scraps tell us.

But moreover you may sometimes have an opportunity of studying ancient art in a narrower but a more intimate, a more kindly form, the monuments of our own land. Some-times only, since we live in the middle of this world of brick and mortar, and there is little else left us amidst it, except the ghost of the great church at Westminster, ruined as its exterior is by the stupidity of the restoring architect, and insulted as its glorious interior is by the pompous undertakers' lies, by the vainglory and ignorance of the last two centuries and a half—little besides that and the matchless Hall near it: but when we can get beyond that smoky world, there, out in the country we may still see the works of our fathers yet alive amidst the very nature they were wrought into, and of which they are so completely a part: for there indeed if anywhere, in the English country, in the days when people cared about such things, was there a full sympathy between the works of man and the land they were made for: —the land is a little land; too much shut up within the narrow seas, as it seems, to have much space for swelling into hugeness: there are no great wastes overwhelming in their dreariness, no great solitudes of forests, no terrible untrodden mountain-walls: all is measured, mingled, varied, gliding easily one thing into another: little rivers, little plains, swelling, speedily-changing up-lands, all beset with handsome orderly trees; little hills, little mountains, netted over with the walls of sheep-walks: all is little; yet not foolish and blank, but serious rather, and abundant of meaning for such as choose to seek it: it is neither prison nor palace, but a decent home.

All which I neither praise nor blame, but say that so it is: some people praise this homeliness overmuch, as if the land were the very axle-tree of the world; so do not I, nor any unblinded by pride in themselves and all that belongs to them: others there are who scorn it and the tameness of it: not I any the more: though it would indeed be hard if there were nothing else in the world, no wonders, no terrors, no unspeakable beauties: yet when we think what a small part of the world's history, past, present, and to come, is this land we live in, and how much smaller still in the history of the arts, and yet how our forefathers clung to it, and with what care and pains they adorned it, this unromantic, uneventful-looking land of England, surely by this too our hearts may be touched, and our hope quickened.

For as was the land, such was the art of it while folk yet troubled themselves about such things; it strove little to impress people either by pomp or ingenuity: not unseldom it fell into commonplace, rarely it rose into majesty; yet was it never oppressive, never a slave's nightmare nor an insolent boast: and at its best it had an inventiveness, an individuality that grander styles have never overpassed: its best too, and that was in its very heart, was given as freely to the yeoman's house, and the humble village church, as to the lord's palace or the mighty cathedral: never coarse, though often rude enough, sweet, natural and unaffected, an art of peasants rather than of merchant-princes or courtiers, it must be a hard heart, I think, that does not love it: whether a man has been born among it like ourselves, or has come wonderingly on its simplicity from all the grandeur overseas. A peasant art, I say, and it clung fast to the life of the people, and still lived among the cottagers and yeomen in many parts of the country while the big houses were being built "French and fine": still lived also in many a quaint pattern of loom and printing-block, and embroiderer's needle, while over-seas stupid pomp had extinguished all nature and freedom, and art was become, in France especially, the mere expression of that successful and exultant rascality, which in the flesh no long time afterwards went down into the pit for ever.

Such was the English art, whose history is in a sense at your doors, grown scarce indeed, and growing scarcer year by year, not only through greedy destruction, of which there is certainly less than there used to be, but also through the attacks of another foe, called nowadays "restoration."

I must not make a long story about this, but also I cannot quite pass it over, since I have pressed on you the study of these ancient monuments. Thus the matter stands: these old buildings have been altered and added to century after century, often beautifully, always historically; their very value, a great part of it, lay in that: they have suffered almost always from neglect also, often from violence (that latter a piece of history often far from uninteresting), but ordinary obvious mending would almost always have kept them standing, pieces of nature and of history.

But of late years a great uprising of ecclesiastical zeal, coinciding with a great increase of study, and consequently of knowledge of mediæval architecture, has driven people into spending their money on these buildings, not merely with the purpose of repairing them, of keeping them safe,

clean, and wind- and water-tight, but also of "restoring" them
to some ideal state of perfection; sweeping away if possible
all signs of what has befallen them at least since the Re-
formation, and often since dates much earlier: this has
sometimes been done with much disregard of art and entirely from ecclesiastical zeal, but oftener it has been well
meant enough as regards art: yet you will not have listened
to what I have said to-night if you do not see that from my
point of view this restoration must be as impossible to bring
about, as the attempt at it is destructive to the buildings so
dealt with: I scarcely like to think what a great part of them
have been made nearly useless to students of art and history:
unless you knew a great deal about architecture you perhaps would scarce understand what terrible damage has
been done by that dangerous "little knowledge" in this
matter: but at least it is easy to be understood, that to deal
recklessly with valuable (and national) monuments which,
when once gone, can never be replaced by any splendour of
modern art, is doing a very sorry service to the State.

You will see by all that I have said on this study of ancient art that I mean by education herein something much
wider than the teaching of a definite art in schools of design,
and that it must be something that we must do more or less
for ourselves: I mean by it a systematic concentration of
our thoughts on the matter, a studying of it in all ways,
careful and laborious practice of it, and a determination to
do nothing but what is known to be good in workmanship
and design.

Of course, however, both as an instrument of that study
we have been speaking of, as well as of the practice of the
arts, all handicraftsmen should be taught to draw very
carefully; as indeed all people should be taught drawing
who are not physically incapable of learning it: but the art
of drawing so taught would not be the art of designing,
but only a means towards *this* end, *general capability in
dealing with the arts.*

For I wish specially to impress this upon you, that
designing cannot be taught at all in a school: continued practice will help a man who is naturally a designer, continual
notice of nature and of art: no doubt those who have some
faculty for designing are still numerous, and they want from

a school certain technical teaching, just as they want tools: in these days also, when the best school, the school of successful practice going on around you, is at such a low ebb, they do undoubtedly want instruction in the history of the arts: these two things schools of design can give: but the royal road of a set of rules deduced from a sham science of design, that is itself not a science but another set of rules, will lead nowhere;—or, let us rather say, to beginning again.

As to the kind of drawing that should be taught to men engaged in ornamental work, there is only *one best* way of teaching drawing, and that is teaching the scholar to draw the human figure: both because the lines of a man's body are much more subtle than anything else, and because you can more surely be found out and set right if you go wrong. I do think that such teaching as this, given to all people who care for it, would help the revival of the arts very much: the habit of discriminating between right and wrong, the sense of pleasure in drawing a good line, would really, I think, be education in the due sense of the word for all such people as had the germs of invention in them; yet as aforesaid, in this age of the world it would be mere affectation to pretend to shut one's eyes to the art of past ages: that also we must study. If other circumstances, social and economical, do not stand in our way, that is to say, if the world is not too busy to allow us to have Decorative Arts at all, these two are the *direct* means by which we shall get them; that is, general cultivation of the powers of the mind, general cultivation of the powers of the eye and hand.

Perhaps that seems to you very commonplace advice and a very roundabout road; nevertheless 'tis a certain one, if by any road you desire to come to the new art, which is my subject to-night: if you do not, and if those germs of invention, which, as I said just now, are no doubt still common enough among men, are left neglected and undeveloped, the laws of Nature will assert themselves in this as in other matters, and the faculty of design itself will gradually fade from the race of man. Sirs, shall we approach nearer to perfection by casting away so large a part of that intelligence which makes us *men*?

And now before I make an end, I want to call your attention to certain things, that, owing to our neglect of the arts for other business, bar that good road to us and are such an hindrance, that, till they are dealt with, it is hard even to make a beginning of our endeavour. And if my talk should seem to grow too serious for our subject, as indeed I think it cannot do, I beg you to remember what I said earlier, of how the arts all hang together. Now there is one art of which the old architect of Edward the Third's time was thinking—he who founded New College at Oxford, I mean—when he took this for his motto: "Manners maketh man": he meant by manners the art of morals, the art of living worthily, and like a man. I must needs claim this art also as dealing with my subject.

There is a great deal of sham work in the world, hurtful to the buyer, more hurtful to the seller, if he only knew it, most hurtful to the maker: how good a foundation it would be towards getting good Decorative Art, that is ornamental workmanship, if we craftsmen were to resolve to turn out nothing but excellent workmanship in all things, instead of having, as we too often have now, a very low average standard of work, which we often fall below.

I do not blame either one class or another in this matter, I blame all: to set aside our own class of handicraftsmen, of whose shortcomings you and I know so much that we need talk no more about it, I know that the public in general are set on having things cheap, being so ignorant that they do not know when they get them nasty also; so ignorant that they neither know nor care whether they give a man his due: I know that the manufacturers (so called) are so set on carrying out competition to its utmost, competition of cheapness, not of excellence, that they meet the bargain-hunters half way, and cheerfully furnish them with nasty wares at the cheap rate they are asked for, by means of what can be called by no prettier name than fraud. England has of late been too much busied with the counting-house and not enough with the workshop: with the result that the counting-house at the present moment is rather barren of orders.

I say all classes are to blame in this matter, but also I say that the remedy lies with the handicraftsmen, who are not ignorant of these things like the public, and who have no call to be greedy and isolated like the manufacturers or middlemen; the duty and honour of educating the public lies with them, and they have in them the seeds of order and organisation which make that duty the easier.

When will they see to this and help to make men of us all by insisting on this most weighty piece of manners; so that we may adorn life with the pleasure of cheerfully *buying* goods at their due price; with the pleasure of *selling* goods that we could be proud of both for fair price and fair workmanship: with the pleasure of working soundly and without haste at *making* goods that we could be proud of?— much the greatest pleasure of the three is that last, such a pleasure as, I think, the world has none like it.

You must not say that this piece of manners lies out of my subject: it is essentially a part of it and most important: for I am bidding you learn to be artists, if art is not to come to an end amongst us: and what is an artist but a workman who is determined that, whatever else happens, his work shall be excellent? or, to put it in another way: the decoration of workmanship, what is it but the expression of man's pleasure in successful labour? But what pleasure can there be in *bad* work, in *un*successful labour; why should we decorate *that*? and how can we bear to be always unsuccessful in our labour?

As greed of unfair gain, wanting to be paid for what we have not earned, cumbers our path with this tangle of bad work, of sham work, so that heaped-up money which this greed has brought us (for greed will have its way, like all other strong passions), this money, I say, gathered into heaps little and big, with all the false distinction which so unhappily it yet commands amongst us, has raised up against the arts a barrier of the love of luxury and show, which is of all obvious hindrances the worst to overpass: the highest and most cultivated classes are not free from the vulgarity of it, the lower are not free from its pretence. I beg you to remember both as a remedy against this, and as explaining exactly what I mean, that nothing can be a work of art which is not useful; that is to say, which does not minister to the body when well under command of the mind, or which does not amuse, soothe, or elevate the mind in a healthy state. What tons upon tons of unutterable rubbish pretending to be works of art in some degree would this maxim clear out of our London houses, if it were understood and acted upon! To my mind it is only here and there (out of the kitchen) that you can find in a well-to-do house things that are of any use at all: as a rule all the decoration (so called) that has got there is there for the sake of show, not because anybody likes it. I repeat, this stupidity goes through all classes of society: the silk curtains in my Lord's drawing-room are no more a matter of art to him than the powder in his footman's hair; the kitchen in a country farmhouse is most commonly a pleasant and homelike place, the parlour dreary and useless.

Simplicity of life, begetting simplicity of taste, that is, a love for sweet and lofty things, is of all matters most necessary for the birth of the new and better art we crave for; simplicity everywhere, in the palace as well as in the cottage.

Still more is this necessary, cleanliness and decency everywhere, in the cottage as well as in the palace: the lack of that is a serious piece of *manners* for us to correct: that lack and all the inequalities of life, and the heaped-up thoughtlessness and disorder of so many centuries that cause it: and as yet it is only a very few men who have begun to think about a remedy for it in its widest range: even in its narrower aspect, in the defacements of our big towns by all that commerce brings with it, who heeds it? who tries to control their squalor and hideousness? there is nothing but thoughtlessness and recklessness in the matter: the helplessness of people who don't live long enough to do a thing themselves, and have not manliness and foresight enough to begin the work, and pass it on to those that shall come after them.

Is money to be gathered? cut down the pleasant trees among the houses, pull down ancient and venerable buildings for the money that a few square yards of London dirt will fetch; blacken rivers, hide the sun and poison the air with smoke and worse, and it's nobody's business to see to it or mend it: that is all that modern commerce, the counting house forgetful of the workshop, will do for us herein.

And Science—we have loved her well, and followed her diligently, what will she do? I fear she is so much in the pay of the counting-house, the counting-house and the drill-sergeant, that she is too busy, and will for the present do nothing. Yet there are matters which I should have

s

thought easy for her; say for example teaching Manchester how to consume its own smoke, or Leeds how to get rid of its superfluous black dye without turning it into the river, which would be as much worth her attention as the production of the heaviest of heavy black silks, or the biggest of useless guns. Anyhow, however it be done, unless people care about carrying on their business without making the world hideous, how can they care about Art? I know it will cost much both of time and money to better these things even a little; but I do not see how these can be better spent than in making life cheerful and honourable for others and for ourselves; and the gain of good life to the country at large that would result from men seriously setting about the bettering of the decency of our big towns would be priceless, even if nothing specially good befell the arts in consequence: I do not know that it would; but I should begin to think matters hopeful if men turned their attention to such things, and I repeat that, unless they do so, we can scarcely even begin with any hope our endeavours for the bettering of the arts.

Unless something or other is done to give all men some pleasure for the eyes and rest for the mind in the aspect of their own and their neighbours' houses, until the contrast is less disgraceful between the fields where beasts live and the streets where men live, I suppose that the practice of the arts must be mainly kept in the hands of a few highly cultivated men, who can go often to beautiful places, whose education enables them, in the contemplation of the past glories of the world, to shut out from their view the everyday squalors that the most of men move in. Sirs, I believe that art has such sympathy with cheerful freedom, openheartedness and reality, so much she sickens under selfishness and luxury, that she will not live thus isolated and exclusive. I will go further than this and say that on such terms I do not wish her to live. I protest that it would be a shame to an honest artist to enjoy what he had huddled up to himself of such art, as it would be for a rich man to sit and eat dainty food amongst starving soldiers in a beleaguered fort.

I do not want art for a few, any more than education for a few, or freedom for a few.

No, rather than art should live this poor thin life among a few exceptional men, despising those beneath them for an ignorance for which they themselves are responsible, for a brutality that they will not struggle with,—rather than this, I would that the world should indeed sweep away all art for awhile, as I said before I thought it possible she might do; rather than the wheat should rot in the miser's granary, I would that the earth had it, that it might yet have a chance to quicken in the dark.

I have a sort of faith, though, that this clearing away of all art will not happen, that men will get wiser, as well as more learned; that many of the intricacies of life, on which we now pride ourselves more than enough, partly because they are new, partly because they have come with the gain of better things, will be cast aside as having played their part, and being useful no longer. I hope that we shall have leisure from war,—war commercial, as well as war of the bullet and the bayonet; leisure from the knowledge that darkens counsel; leisure above all from the greed of money, and the craving for that overwhelming distinction that money now brings: I believe that as we have even now partly achieved LIBERTY, so we shall one day achieve EQUALITY, which, and which only, means FRATERNITY, and so have leisure from poverty and all its griping, sordid cares.

Then having leisure from all these things, amidst renewed simplicity of life we shall have leisure to think about our work, that faithful daily companion, which no man any longer will venture to call the Curse of labour: for surely then we shall be happy in it, each in his place, no man grudging at another; no one bidden to be any man's *servant*, every one scorning to be any man's *master*: men will then assuredly be happy in their work, and that happiness will assuredly bring forth decorative, noble, *popular* art.

That art will make our streets as beautiful as the woods, as elevating as the mountain-sides: it will be a pleasure and a rest, and not a weight upon the spirits to come from the open country into a town; every man's house will be fair and decent, soothing to his mind and helpful to his work: all the works of man that we live amongst and handle will be in harmony with nature, will be reasonable and beautiful: yet all will be simple and inspiriting, not childish nor enervating; for as nothing of beauty and splendour that man's mind and hand may compass shall be wanting from our public buildings, so in no private dwelling will there be any signs of waste, pomp, or insolence, and every man will have his share of the *best*.

It is a dream, you may say, of what has never been and never will be; true, it has never been, and therefore, since the world is alive and moving yet, my hope is the greater that it one day will be: true, it is a dream; but dreams have before now come about of things so good and necessary to us, that we scarcely think of them more than of the daylight, though once people had to live without them, without even the hope of them.

Anyhow, dream as it is, I pray you to pardon my setting it before you, for it lies at the bottom of all my work in the Decorative Arts, nor will it ever be out of my thoughts: and I am here with you to-night to ask you to help me in realising this dream, this *hope*.

THE ART OF THE
PEOPLE

"And the men of labour spent their strength in daily struggling for bread to maintain the vital strength they labour with: so living in a daily circulation of sorrow, living but to work, and working but to live, as if daily bread were the only end of a wearisome life, and a wearisome life the only occasion of daily bread."—DANIEL DEFOE.

I KNOW that a large proportion of those here present are either already practising the Fine Arts, or are being specially educated to that end, and I feel that I may be expected to address myself specially to these. But since it is not to be doubted that we are *all* met together because of the interest we take in what concerns these arts, I would rather address myself to you *all* as representing the public in general. Indeed, those of you who are specially studying Art could learn little of me that would be useful to yourselves only. You are already learning under competent masters—most competent, I am glad to know—by means of a system which should teach you all you need, if you have been right in making the first step of devoting yourselves to Art; I mean if you are aiming at the right thing, and in some way or another understand what Art means, which you may well do without being able to express it, and if you are resolute to follow on the path which that inborn knowledge has shown to you; if it is otherwise with you than this, no system and no teachers will help you to produce real art of any kind, be it never so humble. Those of you who are real artists know well enough all the special advice I can give you, and in how few words it may be said—follow nature, study antiquity, make your own art, and do not steal it, grudge no expense of trouble, patience, or courage, in the striving to accomplish the hard thing you have set yourselves to do. You have had all that said to you twenty times, I doubt not; and twenty times twenty have said it to yourselves, and now I have said it again to you, and done neither you nor me good nor harm thereby. So true it all is, so well known, and so hard to follow.

But to me. and I hope to you, Art is a very serious thing, and cannot by any means be dissociated from the weighty matters that occupy the thoughts of men; and there are principles underlying the practice of it, on which all serious-minded men, may—nay, must—have their own thoughts. It is on some of these that I ask your leave to speak, and to address myself, not only to those who are consciously interested in the arts, but to all those also who have considered what the progress of civilisation promises and threatens to those who shall come after us: what there is to hope and fear for the future of the arts, which were born with the birth of civilisation and will only die with its death—what on this side of things, the present time of strife and doubt and change is preparing for the better time, when the change shall have come, the strife be lulled, and the doubt cleared: this is a question, I say, which is indeed weighty, and may well interest all thinking men.

Nay, so universally important is it, that I fear lest you should think I am taking too much upon myself to speak to you on so weighty a matter, nor should I have dared to do so, if I did not feel that I am to-night only the mouthpiece of better men than myself, whose hopes and fears I share; and that being so, I am the more emboldened to speak out, if I can, my full mind on the subject, because I am in a city where, if anywhere, men are not contented to live wholly for themselves and the present, but have fully accepted the duty of keeping their eyes open to whatever new is stirring, so that they may help and be helped by any truth that there may be in it. Nor can I forget, that, since you have done me the great honour of choosing me for the President of your Society of Arts for the past year, and of asking me to speak to you to-night, I should be doing less than my duty if I did not, according to my lights, speak out straightforwardly whatever seemed to me might be in a small degree useful to you. Indeed, I think I am among friends, who may forgive me if I speak rashly, but scarcely if I speak falsely.

The aim of your Society and School of Arts is, as I understand it, to further those arts by education widely spread. A very great object is that, and well worthy of the reputation of this great city; but since Birmingham has also, I rejoice to know, a great reputation for not allowing things to go about shamming life when the brains are knocked out of them, I think you should know and see clearly what it is you have undertaken to further by these institutions, and whether you really care about it, or only languidly acquiesce in it—whether, in short, you know it to the heart, and are indeed part and parcel of it, with your own will, or against it; or else have heard say that it is a good thing if any one care to meddle with it.

If you are surprised at my putting that question for your consideration, I will tell you why I do so. There are some of us who love Art most, and I may say most faithfully, who see for certain that such love is rare nowadays. We cannot help seeing, that besides a vast number of people, who (poor souls!) are sordid and brutal of mind and habits, and have had no chance or choice in the matter, there are many high-minded, thoughtful, and cultivated men who inwardly think the arts to be a foolish accident of civilisation—nay, worse perhaps, a nuisance, a disease, a hindrance to human progress. Some of these, doubtless, are very busy about other sides of thought. They are, as I should put it, so *artistically* engrossed by the study of science, politics, or what not, that they have necessarily narrowed their minds by their hard and praiseworthy labours. But since such men are few, this does not account for a prevalent habit of thought that looks upon Art as at best trifling.

What is wrong, then, with us or the arts, since what was once accounted so glorious, is now deemed paltry?

The question is no light one; for, to put the matter in its clearest light, I will say that the leaders of modern thought do for the most part sincerely and single-mindedly hate and despise the arts; and you know well that as the leaders are, so must the people be; and that means that we who are met together here for the furthering of Art by wide-spread education are either deceiving ourselves and wasting our time, since we shall one day be of the same opinion as the best men among us, or else we represent a small minority that is right, as minorities sometimes are, while those upright men aforesaid, and the great mass of civilised men, have been blinded by untoward circumstances.

That we are of this mind—the minority that is right—is, I hope, the case. I hope we know assuredly that the arts we have met together to further are necessary to the life of man, if the progress of civilisation is not to be as causeless as the turning of a wheel that makes nothing.

How, then, shall we, the minority, carry out the duty which our position thrusts upon us, of striving to grow into a majority?

If we could only explain to those thoughtful men, and the millions of whom they are the flower, what the thing is that we love, which is to us as the bread we eat, and the air we breathe, but about which they know nothing and feel nothing, save a vague instinct of repulsion, then the seed of victory might be sown. This is hard indeed to do; yet if we ponder upon a chapter of ancient or mediæval history, it seems to me some glimmer of a chance of doing so breaks in upon us. Take for example a century of the Byzantine Empire, weary yourselves with reading the names of the pedants, tyrants, and tax-gatherers to whom the terrible chain which long-dead Rome once forged, still gave the power of cheating people into thinking that they were necessary lords of the world. Turn then to the lands they governed, and read and forget a long string of the causeless murders of Northern and Saracen pirates and robbers. That is pretty much the sum of what so-called history has left us of the tale of those days—the stupid languor and the evil deeds of kings and scoundrels. Must we turn away then, and say that all was evil? How then did men live from day to day? How then did Europe grow into intelligence and freedom? It seems there were others than those of whom history (so called) has left us the names and the deeds. These, the raw material for the treasury and the slave-market, we now call "the people," and we know that they were working all that while. Yes, and that their work was not merely slaves' work, the meal-trough before them and the whip behind them; for though history (so called) has forgotten them, yet their work has not been forgotten, but has made another history—the history of Art. There is not an ancient city in the East or the West that does not bear some token of their grief, and joy, and hope. From Ispahan to Northumberland, there is no building built between the seventh and seventeenth centuries that does not show the influence of the labour of that oppressed and neglected herd of men. No one of them, indeed, rose high above his fellows. There was no Plato, or Shakespeare, or Michael Angelo amongst them. Yet scattered as it was among many men, how strong their thought was, how long it abided, how far it travelled!

And so it was ever through all those days when Art was so vigorous and progressive. Who can say how little we should know of many periods, but for their art? History (so called) has remembered the kings and warriors, because they destroyed; Art has remembered the people, because they created.

I think, then, that this knowledge we have of the life of past times gives us some token of the way we should take in meeting those honest and single-hearted men who above all things desire the world's progress, but whose minds are, as it were, sick on this point of the arts. Surely you may say to them: When all is gained that you (and we) so long for, what shall we do then? That great change which we are working for, each in his own way, will come like other changes, as a thief in the night, and will be with us before we know it; but let us imagine that its consummation has come suddenly and dramatically, acknowledged and hailed by all right-minded people; and what shall we do then, lest we begin once more to heap up fresh corruption for the woeful labour of ages once again? I say, as we turn away from the flagstaff where the new banner has been just run up; as we depart, our ears yet ringing with the blare of the heralds' trumpets that have proclaimed the new order of things, what shall we turn to then, what *must* we turn to then?

To what else, save to our work, our daily labour?

With what, then, shall we adorn it when we have become wholly free and reasonable? It is necessary toil, but shall it be toil only? Shall all we can do with it be to shorten the hours of that toil to the utmost, that the hours of leisure may be long beyond what men used to hope for? and what then shall we do with the leisure, if we say that all toil is irksome? Shall we sleep it all away?—Yes, and never wake up again, I should hope, in that case.

What shall we do then? what shall our necessary hours of labour bring forth?

That will be a question for all men in that day when many wrongs are righted, and when there will be no classes of degradation on whom the dirty work of the world can be shovelled; and if men's minds are still sick and loathe the arts, they will not be able to answer that question.

Once men sat under grinding tyrannies, amidst violence and fear so great, that nowadays we wonder how they lived through twenty-four hours of it, till we remember that then, as now, their daily labour was the main part of their lives, and that daily labour was sweetened by the daily creation of Art; and shall we who are delivered from the evils they bore, live drearier days than they did? Shall men, who have come forth from so many tyrannies, bind themselves to yet another one, and become the slaves of nature, piling day upon day of hopeless, useless toil? Must this go on worsening till it comes to this at last—that the world shall have come into its inheritance, and with all foes conquered and nought to bind it, shall choose to sit down and labour for ever amidst grim ugliness? How, then, were all our hopes cheated, what a gulf of despair should we tumble into then?

In truth, it cannot be; yet if that sickness of repulsion to the arts were to go on hopelessly, nought else would be, and the extinction of the love of beauty and imagination would prove to be the extinction of civilisation. But that sickness the world will one day throw off, yet will, I believe, pass through many pains in so doing, some of which will look very like the death-throes of Art, and some, perhaps, will be grievous enough to the poor people of the world; since hard necessity, I doubt, works many of the world's changes, rather than the purblind striving to see, which we call the foresight of man.

Meanwhile, remember that I asked just now, what was

amiss in Art or in ourselves that this sickness was upon us. Nothing is wrong or can be with Art in the abstract—that must always be good for mankind, or we are all wrong together: but with Art, as we of these latter days have known it, there is much wrong; nay, what are we here for to-night if that is not so? were not the schools of art founded all over the country some thirty years ago because we had found out that popular art was fading—or perhaps had faded out from amongst us?

As to the progress made since then in this country—and in this country only, if at all—it is hard for me to speak without being either ungracious or insincere, and yet speak I must. I say, then, that an apparent external progress in some ways is obvious, but I do not know how far that is hopeful, for time must try it, and prove whether it be a passing fashion or the first token of a real stir among the great mass of civilised men. To speak quite frankly, and as one friend to another, I must needs say that even as I say those words they seem too good to be true. And yet—who knows?—so wont are we to frame history for the future as well as for the past, so often are our eyes blind both when we look backward and when we look forward, because we have been gazing so intently at our own days, our own lines. May all be better than I think it!

At any rate let us count our gains, and set them against less hopeful signs of the times. In England, then—and as far as I know, in England only—painters of pictures have grown, I believe, more numerous, and certainly more conscientious in their work, and in some cases—and this more especially in England—have developed and expressed a sense of beauty which the world has not seen for the last three hundred years. This is certainly a very great gain, which is not easy to over-estimate, both for those who make the pictures and those who use them.

Furthermore, in England, and in England only, there has been a great improvement in architecture and the arts that attend it—arts which it was the special province of the afore-mentioned schools to revive and foster. This, also, is a considerable gain to the users of the works so made, but I fear a gain less important to most of those concerned in making them.

. Against these gains we must, I am very sorry to say, set the fact not easy to be accounted for, that the rest of the civilised world (so called) seems to have done little more than stand still in these matters; and that among ourselves these improvements have concerned comparatively few people, the mass of our population not being in the least touched by them; so that the great bulk of our architecture —the art which most depends on the taste of the people at large—grows worse and worse every day.

I must speak also of another piece of discouragement before I go further. I daresay many of you will remember how emphatically those who first had to do with the movement of which the foundation of our art-schools was a part, called the attention of our pattern-designers to the beautiful works of the East. This was surely most well judged of them, for they bade us look at an art at once beautiful, orderly, living in our own day, and above all, popular. Now, it is a grievous result of the sickness of civilisation that this art is fast disappearing before the advance of western conquest and commerce—fast, and every day faster. While we are met here in Birmingham to further the spread of education in art, Englishmen in India are, in their short-sightedness, actively destroying the very sources of that education—jewellery, metal-work, pottery, calico-printing, brocade-weaving, carpet-making—all the famous and historical arts of the great peninsula have been for long treated as matters of no importance, to be thrust aside for the advantage of any paltry scrap of so-called commerce; and matters are now speedily coming to an end there. I daresay some of you saw the presents which the native Princes gave to the Prince of Wales on the occasion of his progress through India. I did myself, I will not say with great disappointment, for I guessed what they would be like, but with great grief, since there was scarce here and there a piece of goods among these costly gifts, things given as great treasures, which faintly upheld the ancient fame of the cradle of the industrial arts. Nay, in some cases, it would have been laughable, if it had not been so sad, to see the piteous simplicity with which the conquered race had copied the blank vulgarity of their lords. And this deterioration we are now, as I have said, actively engaged in forwarding. I have read a little book, a handbook[1] to the Indian Court of last year's Paris Exhibition, which takes the occasion of noting the state of manufactures in India one by one. "Art manufactures," you would call them; but, indeed, all manufactures are, or were, "art manufactures" in India. Dr. Birdwood, the author of this book, is of great experience in Indian life, a man of science, and a lover of the arts. His story, by no means a new one to me, or others interested in the East and its labour, is a sad one indeed. The conquered races in their hopelessness are everywhere giving up the genuine practice of their own arts, which we know ourselves, as we have indeed loudly proclaimed, are founded on the truest and most natural principles. The often-praised perfection of these arts is the blossom of many ages of labour and change, but the conquered races are casting it aside as a thing of no value, so that they may conform themselves to the inferior art, or rather the lack of art, of their conquerors. In some parts of the country the genuine arts are quite destroyed; in many others nearly so; in all they have more or less begun to sicken. So much so is this the case, that now for some time the Government has been furthering this deterioration. As for example, no doubt with the best intentions, and certainly in full sympathy with the general English public, both at home and in India, the Government is now manufacturing cheap Indian carpets in the Indian gaols. I do not say that it is a bad thing to turn out real work, or works of art, in gaols; on the contrary, I think it good if it be properly managed. But in this case, the Government, being, as I said, in full sympathy with the English public, has determined that it will make its wares cheap, whether it make them nasty or not. Cheap and nasty they are, I assure you; but, though they are the worst of their kind, they would not be made thus, if everything did not tend the same way. And it is the same everywhere and with all Indian manufactures, till it has come to this—that these poor people have all but lost the one distinction, the one glory that conquest had left them. Their famous wares, so praised by those who thirty years ago

---

[1] Now incorporated in the *Handbook of Indian Art*, by Dr. (now Sir George) Birdwood, published by the Science and Art Department.

began to attempt the restoration of popular art amongst
ourselves, are no longer to be bought at reasonable prices in
the common market, but must be sought for and treasured
as precious relics for the museums we have founded for our
art education. In short, their art is dead, and the commerce
of modern civilisation has slain it.

What is going on in India is also going on, more or less,
all over the East; but I have spoken of India chiefly because
I cannot help thinking that we ourselves are responsible for
what is happening there. Chance-hap has made us the
lords of many millions out there; surely, it behoves us to
look to it, lest we give to the people whom we have made
helpless scorpions for fish and stones for bread.

But since neither on this side, nor on any other, can art
be amended, until the countries that lead civilisation are
themselves in a healthy state about it, let us return to the
consideration of its condition among ourselves. And again
I say, that obvious as is that surface improvement of the
arts within the last few years, I fear too much that there is
something wrong about the root of the plant to exult over
the bursting of its February buds.

I have just shown you for one thing that lovers of Indian
and Eastern Art, including as they do the heads of our
institutions for art education, and I am sure many among
what are called the governing classes, are utterly powerless to stay its downward course. The general tendency of civilisation is against them, and is too strong for
them.

Again, though many of us love architecture dearly, and
believe that it helps the healthiness both of body and soul
to live among beautiful things, we of the big towns are
mostly compelled to live in houses which have become a
by-word of contempt for their ugliness and inconvenience.
The stream of civilisation is against us, and we cannot
battle against it.

Once more those devoted men who have upheld the
standard of truth and beauty amongst us, and whose
pictures, painted amidst difficulties that none but a painter
can know, show qualities of mind unsurpassed in any age—
these great men have but a narrow circle that can understand their works, and are utterly unknown to the great

mass of the people: civilisation is so much against them, that they cannot move the people.

Therefore, looking at all this, I cannot think that all is well with the root of the tree we are cultivating. Indeed, I believe that if other things were but to stand still in the world, this improvement before mentioned would lead to a kind of art which, in that impossible case, would be in a way stable, would perhaps stand still also. This would be an art cultivated professedly by a few, and for a few, who would consider it necessary—a duty, if they could admit duties—to despise the common herd, to hold themselves aloof from all that the world has been struggling for from the first, to guard carefully every approach to their palace of art. It would be a pity to waste many words on the prospect of such a school of art as this, which does in a way, theoretically at least, exist at present, and has for its watchword a piece of slang that does not mean the harmless thing it seems to mean—art for art's sake. Its fore-doomed end must be, that art at last will seem too delicate a thing for even the hands of the initiated to touch; and the initiated must at last sit still and do nothing—to the grief of no one.

Well, certainly, if I thought you were come here to further such an art as this I could not have stood up and called you *friends*; though such a feeble folk as I have told you of one could scarce care to call foes.

Yet, as I say, such men exist, and I have troubled you with speaking of them, because I know that those honest and intelligent people, who are eager for human progress, and yet lack part of the human senses, and are anti-artistic, suppose that such men are artists, and that this is what art means, and what it does for people, and that such a narrow, cowardly life is what we, fellow-handicraftsmen, aim at. I see this taken for granted continually, even by many who, to say truth, ought to know better, and I long to put the slur from off us; to make people understand that we, least of all men, wish to widen the gulf between the classes, nay, worse still, to make new classes of elevation, and new classes of degradation—new lords and new slaves; that we, least of all men, want to cultivate the "plant called man" in different ways—here stingily, there wastefully: I wish people to understand that the art we are striving for is a good thing which all can share, which will elevate all; in good sooth, if all people do not soon share it there will soon be none to share; if all are not elevated by it, mankind will lose the elevation it has gained. Nor is such an art as we long for a vain dream; such an art once was in times that were worse than these, when there was less courage, kindness, and truth in the world than there is now; such an art there will be hereafter, when there will be more courage, kindness, and truth than there is now in the world.

Let us look backward in history once more for a short while, and then steadily forward till my words are done: I began by saying that part of the common and necessary advice given to Art students was to study antiquity; and no doubt many of you, like me, have done so; have wandered, for instance, through the galleries of the admirable museum of South Kensington, and, like me, have been filled with wonder and gratitude at the beauty which has been born from the brain of man. Now, consider, I pray you, what these wonderful works are, and how they were made; and indeed, it is neither in extravagance nor without due meaning that I use the word "wonderful" in speaking of them. Well, these things are just the common household goods of those past days, and that is one reason why they are so few and so carefully treasured. They were common things in their own day, used without fear of breaking or spoiling—no rarities then—and yet we have called them "wonderful."

And how were they made? Did a great artist draw the designs for them—a man of cultivation, highly paid, daintily fed, carefully housed, wrapped up in cotton wool, in short, when he was not at work? By no means. Wonderful as these works are, they were made by "common fellows," as the phrase goes, in the common course of their daily labour. Such were the men we honour in honouring those works. And their labour—do you think it was irksome to them? Those of you who are artists know very well that it was not; that it could not be. Many a grin of pleasure, I'll be bound—and you will not contradict me—went to the carrying through of those mazes of mysterious beauty, to the invention of those strange beasts and birds and flowers that we ourselves have chuckled over at South Kensington. While they were at work, at least, these men were not unhappy, and I suppose they worked most days, and the most part of the day, as we do.

Or those treasures of architecture that we study so carefully nowadays—what are they? how were they made? There are great minsters among them, indeed, and palaces of kings and lords, but not many; and, noble and awe-inspiring as these may be, they differ only in size from the little grey church that still so often makes the commonplace English landscape beautiful, and the little grey house that still, in some parts of the country at least, makes an English village a thing apart, to be seen and pondered on by all who love romance and beauty. These form the mass of our architectural treasures, the houses that everyday people lived in, the unregarded churches in which they worshipped.

And, once more, who was it that designed and ornamented them? The great architect, carefully kept for the purpose, and guarded from the common troubles of common men? By no means. Sometimes, perhaps, it was the monk, the ploughman's brother; oftenest his other brother, the village carpenter, smith, mason, what not—"a common fellow," whose common everyday labour fashioned works that are to-day the wonder and despair of many a hard-working "cultivated" architect. And did he loathe his work? No, it is impossible. I have seen, as we most of us have, work done by such men in some out-of-the-way hamlet—where to-day even few strangers ever come, and whose people seldom go five miles from their own doors; in such places, I say, I have seen work so delicate, so careful, and so inventive, that nothing in its way could go further. And I will assert, without fear of contradiction, that no human ingenuity can produce work such as this without pleasure being a third party to the brain that conceived and the hand that fashioned it. Nor are such works rare. The throne of the great Plantagenet, or the great Valois, was no more daintily carved than the seat of the village mass-john, or the chest of the yeoman's good-wife.

So, you see, there was much going on to make life

endurable in those times. Not every day, you may be sure, was a day of slaughter and tumult, though the histories read almost as if it were so; but every day the hammer chinked on the anvil, and the chisel played about the oak beam, and never without some beauty and invention being born of it, and consequently some human happiness.

That last word brings me to the very kernel and heart of what I have come here to say to you, and I pray you to think of it most seriously—not as to my words, but as to a thought which is stirring in the world, and will one day grow into something.

That thing which I understand by real art is the expression by man of his pleasure in labour. I do not believe he can be happy in his labour without expressing that happiness; and especially is this so when he is at work at anything in which he specially excels. A most kind gift is this of nature, since all men, nay, it seems all things too, must labour; so that not only does the dog take pleasure in hunting, and the horse in running, and the bird in flying, but so natural does the idea seem to us, that we imagine to ourselves that the earth and the very elements rejoice in doing their appointed work; and the poets have told us of the spring meadows smiling, of the exultation of the fire, of the countless laughter of the sea.

Nor until these latter days has man ever rejected this universal gift, but always, when he has not been too much perplexed, too much bound by disease or beaten down by trouble, has striven to make his work at least happy. Pain he has too often found in his pleasure, and weariness in his rest, to trust to these. What matter if his happiness lie with what must be always with him—his work?

And, once more, shall we, who have gained so much, forego this gain, the earliest, most natural gain of mankind? If we have to a great extent done so, as I verily fear we have, what strange foglights must have misled us; or rather let me say, how hard pressed we must have been in the battle with the evils we have overcome, to have forgotten the greatest of all evils. I cannot call it less than that. If a man has work to do which he despises, which does not satisfy his natural and rightful desire for pleasure, the greater part of his life must pass unhappily and without self-respect. Consider, I beg of you, what that means, and what ruin must come of it in the end.

If I could only persuade you of this, that the chief duty of the civilised world to-day is to set about making labour happy for all, to do its utmost to minimise the amount of unhappy labour—nay, if I could only persuade some two or three of you here present—I should have made a good night's work of it.

Do not, at any rate, shelter yourselves from any misgiving you may have behind the fallacy that the art-lacking labour of to-day is happy work: for the most of men it is not so. It would take long, perhaps, to show you, and make you fully understand that the would-be art which it produces is joyless. But there is another token of its being most unhappy work, which you cannot fail to understand at once—a grievous thing that token is—and I beg of you to believe that I feel the full shame of it, as I stand here speaking of it; but if we do not admit that we are sick, how can we be healed? This hapless token is, that the work done by the civilised world is mostly dishonest work. Look now: I admit that civilisation does make certain things well, things which it knows, consciously or unconsciously, are necessary to its present unhealthy condition. These things, to speak shortly, are chiefly machines for carrying on the competition in buying and selling, called falsely commerce; and machines for the violent destruction of life—that is to say, materials for two kinds of war; of which kinds the last is no doubt the worst, not so much in itself perhaps, but because on this point the conscience of the world is beginning to be somewhat pricked. But, on the other hand, matters for the carrying on of a dignified daily life, that life of mutual trust, forbearance, and help, which is the only real life of thinking men—these things the civilised world makes ill, and even increasingly worse and worse.

If I am wrong in saying this, you know well I am only saying what is widely thought, nay widely said too, for that matter. Let me give an instance, familiar enough, of that wide-spread opinion. There is a very clever book of pictures[1] now being sold at the railway bookstalls, called

[1] These were originally published in *Fun*.

"The British Working Man, by one who does not believe in him,"—a title and a book which make me both angry and ashamed, because the two express much injustice, and not a little truth in their quaint, and necessarily exaggerated way. It is quite true, and very sad to say, that if any one nowadays wants a piece of ordinary work done by gardener, carpenter, mason, dyer, weaver, smith, what you will, he will be a lucky rarity if he get it well done. He will, on the contrary, meet on every side with evasion of plain duties, and disregard of other men's rights; yet I cannot see how the "British Working Man" is to be made to bear the whole burden of this blame, or indeed the chief part of it. I doubt if it be possible for a whole mass of men to do work to which they are driven, and in which there is no hope and no pleasure, without trying to shirk it—at any rate, shirked it has always been under such circumstances. On the other hand, I know that there are some men so right-minded, that they will, in despite of irksomeness and hopelessness, drive right through their work. Such men are the salt of the earth. But must there not be something wrong with a state of society which drives these into that bitter heroism, and the most part into shirking, into the depths often of half-conscious self-contempt and degradation? Be sure that there is, that the blindness and hurry of civilisation, as it now is, have to answer a heavy charge as to that enormous amount of pleasureless work—work that tries every muscle of the body and every atom of the brain, and which is done without pleasure and without aim—work which everybody who has to do with tries to shuffle off in the speediest way that dread of starvation or ruin will allow him.

I am as sure of one thing as that I am living and breathing, and it is this: that the dishonesty in the daily arts of life, complaints of which are in all men's mouths, and which I can answer for it does exist, is the natural and inevitable result of the world in the hurry of the war of the counting-house, and the war of the battlefield, having forgotten—of all men, I say, each for the other, having forgotten, that pleasure in our daily labour, which nature cries out for as its due.

Therefore, I say again, it is necessary to the further

progress of civilisation that men should turn their thoughts to some means of limiting, and in the end of doing away with, degrading labour.

I do not think my words hitherto spoken have given you any occasion to think that I mean by this either hard or rough labour; I do not pity men much for their hardships, especially if they be accidental; not necessarily attached to one class or one condition, I mean. Nor do I think (I were crazy or dreaming else) that the work of the world can be carried on without rough labour; but I have seen enough of that to know that it need not be by any means degrading. To plough the earth, to cast the net, to fold the flock—these, and such as these, which are rough occupations enough, and which carry with them many hardships, are good enough for the best of us, certain conditions of leisure, freedom, and due wages being granted. As to the bricklayer, the mason, and the like—these would be artists, and doing not only necessary, but beautiful, and therefore happy work, if art were anything like what it should be. No, it is not such labour as this which we need to do away with, but the toil which makes the thousand and one things which nobody wants, which are used merely as the counters for the competitive buying and selling, falsely called commerce, which I have spoken of before—I know in my heart, and not merely by my reason, that this toil cries out to be done away with. But, besides that, the labour which now makes things good and necessary in themselves, merely as counters for the commercial war aforesaid, needs regulating and reforming. Nor can this reform be brought about save by art; and if we were only come to our right minds, and could see the necessity for making labour sweet to all men, as it is now to very few—the necessity, I repeat; lest discontent, unrest, and despair should at last swallow up all society. If we, then, with our eyes cleared, could but make some sacrifice of things which do us no good, since we unjustly and uneasily possess them, then indeed I believe we should sow the seeds of a happiness which the world has not yet known, of a rest and content which would make it what I cannot help thinking it was meant to be: and with that seed would be sown also the seed of real art, the expression of man's happiness in his labour,—an art made by the people, and for the people, as a happiness to the maker and the user.

That is the only real art there is, the only art which will be an instrument to the progress of the world, and not a hindrance. Nor can I seriously doubt that in your hearts you know that it is so, all of you, at any rate, who have in you an instinct for art. I believe that you agree with me in this, though you may differ from much else that I have said. I think assuredly that this is the art whose welfare we have met together to further, and the necessary instruction in which we have undertaken to spread as widely as may be.

Thus I have told you something of what I think is to be hoped and feared for the future of art; and if you ask me what I expect as a practical outcome of the admission of these opinions, I must say at once that I know, even if we were all of one mind, and that what I think the right mind on this subject, we should still have much work and many hindrances before us; we should still have need of all the prudence, foresight, and industry of the best among us; and, even so, our path would sometimes seem blind enough. And, to-day, when the opinions which we think right, and which one day will be generally thought so, have to struggle sorely to make themselves noticed at all, it is early days for us to try to see our exact and clearly mapped road. I suppose you will think it too commonplace of me to say that the general education that makes men think, will one day make them think rightly upon art. Commonplace as it is, I really believe it, and am indeed encouraged by it, when I remember how obviously this age is one of transition from the old to the new, and what a strange confusion, from out of which we shall one day come, our ignorance and half-ignorance is like to make of the exhausted rubbish of the old and the crude rubbish of the new, both of which lie so ready to our hands.

But, if I must say, furthermore, any words that seem like words of practical advice, I think my task is hard, and I fear I shall offend some of you whatever I say; for this is indeed an affair of morality, rather than of what people call art.

However, I cannot forget that, in my mind, it is not

possible to dissociate art from morality, politics, and religion. Truth in these great matters of principle is of one, and it is only in formal treatises that it can be split up diversely. I must also ask you to remember how I have already said, that though my mouth alone speaks, it speaks, however feebly and disjointedly, the thoughts of many men better than myself. And further, though when things are tending to the best, we shall still, as aforesaid, need our best men to lead us quite right; yet even now surely, when it is far from that, the least of us can do some yeoman's service to the cause, and live and die not without honour.

So I will say that I believe there are two virtues much needed in modern life, if it is ever to become sweet; and I am quite sure that they are absolutely necessary in the sowing the seed of an *art which is to be made by the people and for the people, as a happiness to the maker and the user*. These virtues are honesty, and simplicity of life. To make my meaning clearer I will name the opposing vice of the second of these—luxury to wit. Also I mean by honesty, the careful and eager giving his due to every man, the determination not to gain by any man's loss, which in my experience is not a common virtue.

But note how the practice of either of these virtues will make the other easier to us. For if our wants are few, we shall have but little chance of being driven by our wants into injustice; and if we are fixed in the principle of giving every man his due, how can our self-respect bear that we should give too much to ourselves?

And in art, and in that preparation for it without which no art that is stable or worthy can be, the raising, namely, of those classes which have heretofore been degraded, the practice of these virtues would make a new world of it. For if you are rich, your simplicity of life will both go towards smoothing over the dreadful contrast between waste and want, which is the great horror of civilised countries, and will also give an example and standard of dignified life to those classes which you desire to raise, who, as it is indeed, being like enough to rich people, are given both to envy and to imitate the idleness and waste that the possession of much money produces.

Nay, and apart from the morality of the matter, which

I am forced to speak to you of, let me tell you that though simplicity in art may be costly as well as uncostly, at least it is not wasteful, and nothing is more destructive to art than the want of it. I have never been in any rich man's house which would not have looked the better for having a bonfire made outside of it of nine-tenths of all that it held. Indeed, our sacrifice on the side of luxury will, it seems to me, be little or nothing: for, as far as I can make out, what people usually mean by it, is either a gathering of possessions which are sheer vexations to the owner, or a chain of pompous circumstance, which checks and annoys the rich man at every step. Yes, luxury cannot exist without slavery of some kind or other, and its abolition will be blessed, like the abolition of other slaveries, by the freeing both of the slaves and of their masters.

Lastly, if, besides attaining to simplicity of life, we attain also to the love of justice, then will all things be ready for the new springtime of the arts. For those of us that are employers of labour, how can we bear to give any man less money than he can decently live on, less leisure than his education and self-respect demand? or those of us who are workmen, how can we bear to fail in the contract we have undertaken, or to make it necessary for a foreman to go up and down spying out our mean tricks and evasions? or we the shopkeepers—can we endure to lie about our wares, that we may shuffle off our losses on to some one else's shoulders? or we the public—how can we bear to pay a price for a piece of goods which will help to trouble one man, to ruin another, and starve a third? Or, still more, I think, how can we bear to use, how can we enjoy something which has been a pain and a grief for the maker to make?

And now, I think, I have said what I came to say. I confess that there is nothing new in it, but you know the experience of the world is that a thing must be said over and over again before any great number of men can be got to listen to it. Let my words to-night, therefore, pass for one of the necessary times that the thought in them must be spoken out.

For the rest I believe that, however seriously these words may be gainsayed, I have been speaking to an audience in whom any words spoken from a sense of duty and in hearty good-will, as mine have been, will quicken thought and sow some good seed. At any rate, it is good for a man who thinks seriously to face his fellows, and speak out whatever really burns in him, so that men may seem less strange to one another, and misunderstanding, the fruitful cause of aimless strife, may be avoided.

But if to any of you I have seemed to speak hopelessly, my words have been lacking in art; and you must remember that hopelessness would have locked my mouth, not opened it. I am, indeed, hopeful, but can I give a date to the accomplishment of my hope, and say that it will happen in my life or yours?

But I will say at least, Courage! for things wonderful, unhoped-for, glorious, have happened even in this short while I have been alive.

Yes, surely these times are wonderful and fruitful of change, which, as it wears and gathers new life even in its wearing, will one day bring better things for the toiling days of men, who, with freer hearts and clearer eyes, will once more gain the sense of outward beauty, and rejoice in it.

Meanwhile, if these hours be dark, as, indeed, in many ways they are, at least do not let us sit deedless, like fools and fine gentlemen, thinking the common toil not good enough for us, and beaten by the muddle; but rather let us work like good fellows trying by some dim candle-light to set our workshop ready against to-morrow's daylight—that to-morrow, when the civilised world, no longer greedy, strifeful, and destructive, shall have a new art, a glorious art, made by the people and for the people, as a happiness to the maker and the user.

THE BEAUTY OF LIFE

"——propter vitam vivendi perdere causas."—*Juvenal.*

I STAND before you this evening weighted with a disadvantage that I did not feel last year;—I have little fresh to tell you; I can somewhat enlarge on what I said then; here and there I may make bold to give you a practical suggestion, or I may put what I have to say in a way which will be clearer to some of you perhaps; but my message is really the same as it was when I first had the pleasure of meeting you.

It is true that if all were going smoothly with art, or at all events so smoothly that there were but a few malcontents in the world, you might listen with some pleasure, and perhaps advantage, to the talk of an old hand in the craft concerning ways of work, the snares that beset success, and the shortest road to it, to a tale of workshop receipts and the like: that would be a pleasant talk surely between friends and fellow-workmen; but it seems to me as if it were not for us as yet; nay, maybe we may live long and find no time fit for such restful talk as the cheerful histories of the hopes and fears of our workshops: anyhow to-night I cannot do it, but must once again call the faithful of art to a battle wider and more distracting than that kindly struggle with nature, to which all true craftsmen are born; which is both the building-up and the wearing-away of their lives.

As I look round on this assemblage, and think of all that it represents, I cannot choose but be moved to the soul by the troubles of the life of civilised man, and the hope that thrusts itself through them; I cannot refrain from giving you once again the message with which, as it seems, some chance-hap has charged me: that message is, in short, to call on you to face the latest danger which civilisation is threatened with, a danger of her own breeding: that men in

struggling towards the complete attainment of all the
luxuries of life for the strongest portion of their race should
deprive their whole race of all the beauty of life: a danger
that the strongest and wisest of mankind, in striving to
attain to a complete mastery over nature, should destroy
her simplest and widest-spread gifts, and thereby enslave
simple people to them, and themselves to themselves, and
so at last drag the world into a second barbarism more
ignoble, and a thousandfold more hopeless, than the first.

Now of you who are listening to me, there are some, I
feel sure, who have received this message, and taken it to
heart, and are day by day fighting the battle that it calls
on you to fight: to you I can say nothing but that if any
word I speak discourage you, I shall heartily wish I had
never spoken at all: but to be shown the enemy, and the
castle we have got to storm, is not to be bidden to run from
him; nor am I telling you to sit down deedless in the desert
because between you and the promised land lies many a
trouble, and death itself maybe: the hope before you you
know, and nothing that I can say can take it away from
you; but friend may with advantage cry out to friend in
the battle that a stroke is coming from this side or that:
take my hasty words in that sense, I beg of you.

But I think there will be others of you in whom vague
discontent is stirring: who are oppressed by the life that
surrounds you; confused and troubled by that oppression,
and not knowing on which side to seek a remedy, though
you are fain to do so: well, we, who have gone further into
those troubles, believe that we can help you: true we cannot at once take your trouble from you; nay, we may at
first rather add to it; but we can tell you what we think of
the way out of it; and then amidst the many things you
will have to do to set yourselves and others fairly on that
way, you will many days, nay most days, forget your trouble
in thinking of the good that lies beyond it, for which you
are working.

But, again, there are others amongst you (and to speak
plainly, I daresay they are the majority), who are not by
any means troubled by doubt of the road the world is going,
nor excited by any hope of its bettering that road: to them
the cause of civilisation is simple and even commonplace:

wonder, hope, and fear no longer hang about it; it has be-come to us like the rising and setting of the sun; it cannot err, and we have no call to meddle with it, either to com-plain of its course, or to try to direct it.

There is a ground of reason and wisdom in that way of looking at the matter: surely the world will go on its ways, thrust forward by impulses which we cannot understand or sway: but as it grows in strength for the journey, its necessary food is the life and aspirations of *all* of us: and we discontented strugglers with what at times seems the hurrying blindness of civilisation, no less than those who see nothing but smooth, unvarying progress in it, are bred of civilisation also, and shall be used up to further it in some way or other, I doubt not: and it may be of some service to those who think themselves the only loyal sub-jects of progress to hear of our existence, since their not hearing of it would not make an end of it: it may set them a-thinking not unprofitably to hear of burdens that they do not help to bear, but which are nevertheless real and weighty enough to some of their fellow-men, who are helping, even as they are, to form the civilisation that is to be.

The danger that the present course of civilisation will destroy the beauty of life—these are hard words, and I wish I could mend them, but I cannot, while I speak what I believe to be the truth.

That the beauty of life is a thing of no moment, I suppose few people would venture to assert, and yet most civilised people act as if it were of none, and in so doing are wrong-ing both themselves and those that are to come after them; for that beauty, which is what is meant by *art*, using the word in its widest sense, is, I contend, no mere accident to human life, which people can take or leave as they choose, but a positive necessity of life, if we are to live as nature meant us to; that is, unless we are content to be less than men.

Now I ask you, as I have been asking myself this long while, what proportion of the population in civilised coun-tries has any share at all in that necessity of life?

I say that the answer which must be made to that ques-tion justifies my fear that modern civilisation is on the road to trample out all the beauty of life, and to make us less than men.

Now if there should be any here who will say: It was always so; there always was a mass of rough ignorance that knew and cared nothing about art; I answer first, that if that be the case, then it was always wrong, and we, as soon as we have become conscious of that wrong, are bound to set it right if we can.

But moreover, strange to say, and in spite of all the suffering that the world has wantonly made for itself, and has in all ages so persistently clung to, as if it were a good and holy thing, this wrong of the mass of men being regardless of art was *not* always so.

So much is now known of the periods of art that have left abundant examples of their work behind them, that we can judge of the art of all periods by comparing these with the remains of times of which less has been left us; and we cannot fail to come to the conclusion that down to very recent days everything that the hand of man touched was more or less beautiful: so that in those days all people who made anything shared in art, as well as all people who used the things so made: that is, *all* people shared in art.

But some people may say: And was that to be wished for? would not this universal spreading of art stop progress in other matters, hinder the work of the world? Would it not make us unmanly? or if not that, would it not be intrusive, and push out other things necessary also for men to study?

Well, I have claimed a necessary place for art, a natural place, and it would be in the very essence of it, that it would apply its own rules of order and fitness to the general ways of life: it seems to me, therefore, that people who are overanxious of the outward expression of beauty becoming too great a force among the other forces of life, would, if they had had the making of the external world, have been afraid of making an ear of wheat beautiful, lest it should not have been good to eat.

But indeed there seems no chance of art becoming universal, unless on the terms that it shall have little self-consciousness, and for the most part be done with little effort; so that the rough work of the world would be as

little hindered by it, as the work of external nature is by
the beauty of all her forms and moods: this was the case
in the times that I have been speaking of: of art which was
made by conscious effort, the result of the individual striving
towards perfect expression of their thoughts by men very
specially gifted, there was perhaps no more than there is
now, except in very wonderful and short periods; though
I believe that even for such men the struggle to produce
beauty was not so bitter as it now is. But if there were not
more great thinkers than there are now, there was a countless multitude of happy workers whose work did express,
and could not choose but express, some original thought,
and was consequently both interesting and beautiful: now
there is certainly no chance of the more individual art becoming common, and either wearying us by its over-
abundance, or by noisy self-assertion preventing highly
cultivated men taking their due part in the other work of
the world; it is too difficult to do: it will be always but the
blossom of all the half-conscious work below it, the fulfilment of the shortcomings of less complete minds: but it will
waste much of its power, and have much less influence on
men's minds, unless it be surrounded by abundance of that
commoner work, in which all men once shared, and which,
I say, will, when art has really awakened, be done so easily
and constantly, that it will stand in no man's way to hinder
him from doing what he will, good or evil. And as, on the
one hand, I believe that art made by the people and for
the people as a joy both to the maker and the user would
further progress in other matters rather than hinder it, so
also I firmly believe that that higher art produced only by
great brains and miraculously gifted hands cannot exist
without it: I believe that the present state of things in which
it does exist, while popular art is, let us say, asleep or sick,
is a transitional state, which must end at last either in utter
defeat or utter victory for the arts.

For whereas all works of craftsmanship were once beautiful, unwittingly or not, they are now divided into two
kinds, works of art and non-works of art: now nothing made
by man's hand can be indifferent: it must be either beautiful and elevating, or ugly and degrading; and those things
that are without art are so aggressively; they wound it by

their existence, and they are now so much in the majority that the works of art we are obliged to set ourselves to seek for, whereas the other things are the ordinary companions of our everyday life; so that if those who cultivate art intellectually were inclined never so much to wrap themselves in their special gifts and their high cultivation, and so live happily, apart from other men, and despising them, they could not do so: they are as it were living in an enemy's country; at every turn there is something lying in wait to offend and vex their nicer sense and educated eyes: they must share in the general discomfort—and I am glad of it.

So the matter stands: from the first dawn of history till quite modern times, art, which nature meant to solace all, fulfilled its purpose; all men shared in it; that was what made life romantic, as people call it, in those days; that and not robber-barons and inaccessible kings with their hierarchy of serving-nobles and other such rubbish: but art grew and grew, saw empires sicken and sickened with them; grew hale again, and haler, and grew so great at last, that she seemed in good truth to have conquered everything, and laid the material world under foot. Then came a change at a period of the greatest life and hope in many ways that Europe had known till then: a time of so much and such varied hope that people call it the time of the New Birth: as far as the arts are concerned I deny it that title; rather it seems to me that the great men who lived and glorified the practice of art in those days, were the fruit of the old, not the seed of the new order of things: but a stirring and hopeful time it was, and many things were newborn then which have since brought forth fruit enough: and it is strange and perplexing that from those days forward the lapse of time, which, through plenteous confusion and failure, has on the whole been steadily destroying privilege and exclusiveness in other matters, has delivered up art to be the exclusive privilege of a few, and has taken from the people their birthright; while both wronged and wrongers have been wholly unconscious of what they were doing.

Wholly unconscious—yes, but we are no longer so: there lies the sting of it, and there also the hope.

When the brightness of the so-called Renaissance faded,

and it faded very suddenly, a deadly chill fell upon the arts: that New-birth mostly meant looking back to past times, wherein the men of those days thought they saw a perfection of art, which to their minds was different in kind, and not in degree only, from the ruder suggestive art of their own fathers: this perfection they were ambitious to imitate, this alone seemed to be art to them, the rest was childishness: so wonderful was their energy, their success so great, that no doubt to commonplace minds among them, though surely not to the great masters, that perfection seemed to be gained: and, perfection being gained, what are you to do?—you can go no further, you must aim at standing still —which you cannot do.

Art by no means stood still in those latter days of the Renaissance, but took the downward road with terrible swiftness, and tumbled down at the bottom of the hill, where as if bewitched it lay long in great content, believing itself to be the art of Michael Angelo, while it was the art of men whom nobody remembers but those who want to sell their pictures.

Thus it fared with the more individual forms of art. As to the art of the people; in countries and places where the greater art had flourished most, it went step by step on the downward path with that: in more out-of-the-way places, England for instance, it still felt the influence of the life of its earlier and happy days, and in a way lived on a while; but its life was so feeble, and, so to say, illogical, that it could not resist any change in external circumstances, still less could it give birth to anything new; and before this century began, its last flicker had died out. Still, while it was living, in whatever dotage, it did imply something going on in those matters of daily use that we have been thinking of, and doubtless satisfied some cravings for beauty: and when it was dead, for a long time people did not know it, or what had taken its place, crept so to say into its dead body—that pretence of art, to wit, which is done with machines, though sometimes the machines are called men, and doubtless are so out of working hours: nevertheless long before it was quite dead it had fallen so low that the whole subject was usually treated with the utmost contempt by every one who had any pretence of being a sensible man, and in short the whole civilised world had forgotten that there had ever been an art *made by the people for the people as a joy for the maker and the user*.

But now it seems to me that the very suddenness of the change ought to comfort us, to make us look upon this break in the continuity of the golden chain as an accident only, that itself cannot last: for think how many thousand years it may be since that primæval man graved with a flint splinter on a bone the story of the mammoth he had seen, or told us of the slow uplifting of the heavily-horned heads of the reindeer that he stalked: think I say of the space of time from then till the dimming of the brightness of the Italian Renaissance! whereas from that time till popular art died unnoticed and despised among ourselves is just but two hundred years.

Strange too, that very death is contemporaneous with new-birth of something at all events; for out of all despair sprang a new time of hope lighted by the torch of the French Revolution: and things that have languished with the languishing of art, rose afresh and surely heralded its new birth: in good earnest poetry was born again, and the English Language, which under the hands of sycophantic verse-makers had been reduced to a miserable jargon, whose meaning, if it have a meaning, cannot be made out without translation, flowed clear, pure, and simple, along with the music of Blake and Coleridge: take those names, the earliest in date among ourselves, as a type of the change that has happened in literature since the time of George II.

With that literature in which romance, that is to say humanity, was re-born, there sprang up also a feeling for the romance of external nature, which is surely strong in us now, joined with a longing to know something real of the lives of those who have gone before us; of these feelings united you will find the broadest expression in the pages of Walter Scott: it is curious as showing how sometimes one art will lag behind another in a revival, that the man who wrote the exquisite and wholly unfettered naturalism of the Heart of Midlothian, for instance, thought himself continually bound to seem to feel ashamed of, and to excuse himself for, his love of Gothic Architecture: he felt that it was romantic, and he knew that it gave him pleasure, but somehow he had not found out that it was art, having been taught in

T

many ways that nothing could be art that was not done by a named man under academical rules.

I need not perhaps dwell much on what of change has been since: you know well that one of the master-arts, the art of painting, has been revolutionised. I have a genuine difficulty in speaking to you of men who are my own personal friends, nay my masters: still, since I cannot quite say nothing of them I must say the plain truth, which is this: never in the whole history of art did any set of men come nearer to the feat of making something out of nothing than that little knot of painters who have raised English art from what it was, when as a boy I used to go to the Royal Academy Exhibition, to what it is now.

It would be ungracious indeed for me who has been so much taught by him, that I cannot help feeling continually as I speak that I am echoing his words, to leave out the name of John Ruskin from an account of what has happened since the tide, as we hope, began to turn in the direction of art. True it is, that his unequalled style of English and his wonderful eloquence would, whatever its subject-matter, have gained him some sort of a hearing in a time that has not lost its relish for literature; but surely the influence that he has exercised over cultivated people must be the result of that style and that eloquence expressing what was already stirring in men's minds; he could not have written what he has done unless people were in some sort ready for it; any more than those painters could have begun their crusade against the dullness and incompetency that was the rule in their art thirty years ago unless they had some hope that they would one day move people to underst and them.

Well, we find that the gains since the turning-point of the tide are these: that there are some few artists who have, as it were, caught up the golden chain dropped two hundred years ago, and that there are a few highly cultivated people who can understand them; and that beyond these there is a vague feeling abroad among people of the same degree, of discontent at the ignoble ugliness that surrounds them. That seems to me to mark the advance that we have made since the last of popular art came to an end amongst us, and I do not say, considering where we then were, that it is not a great advance, for it comes to this, that though the battle is still to win, there are those who are ready for the battle.

Indeed it would be a strange shame for this age if it were not so: for as every age of the world has its own troubles to confuse it, and its own follies to cumber it, so has each its own work to do, pointed out to it by unfailing signs of the times; and it is unmanly and stupid for the children of any age to say: We will not set our hands to the work; we did not make the troubles, we will not weary ourselves seeking a remedy for them: so heaping up for their sons a heavier load than they can lift without such struggles as will wound and cripple them sorely. Not thus our fathers served us, who, working late and early, left us at last that seething mass of people so terribly alive and energetic, that we call modern Europe; not thus those served us, who have made for us these present days, so fruitful of change and wondering expectation.

The century that is now beginning to draw to an end, if people were to take to nicknaming centuries, would be called the Century of Commerce; and I do not think I undervalue the work that it has done: it has broken down many a prejudice and taught many a lesson that the world has been hitherto slow to learn: it has made it possible for many a man to live free, who would in other times have been a slave, body or soul, or both: if it has not quite spread peace and justice through the world, as at the end of its first half we fondly hoped it would, it has at least stirred up in many fresh cravings for peace and justice: its work has been good and plenteous, but much of it was roughly done, as needs was; recklessness has commonly gone with its energy, blindness too often with its haste: so that perhaps it may be work enough for the next century to repair the blunders of that recklessness, to clear away the rubbish which that hurried work has piled up; nay even we in the second half of its last quarter may do something towards setting its house in order.

You, of this great and famous town, for instance, which has had so much to do with the Century of Commerce, your gains are obvious to all men, but the price you have paid for them is obvious to many—surely to yourselves most of all: I do not say that they are not worth the price; I know that England and the world could very ill afford to exchange the Birmingham of to-day for the Birmingham of the year 1700: but surely if what you have gained be more than a mockery, you cannot stop at those gains, or even go on always piling up similar ones. Nothing can make me believe that the present condition of your Black Country yonder is an unchangeable necessity of your life and position: such miseries as this were begun and carried on in pure thoughtlessness, and a hundredth part of the energy that was spent in creating them would get rid of them: I do think if we were not all of us too prone to acquiesce in the base byword "after me the deluge," it would soon be something more than an idle dream to hope that your pleasant midland hills and fields might begin to become pleasant again in some way or other, even without depopulating them; or that those once lovely valleys of Yorkshire in the "heavy woollen district," with their sweeping hill-sides and noble rivers, should not need the stroke of ruin to make them once more delightful abodes of men, instead of the dog-holes that the Century of Commerce has made them.

Well, people will not take the trouble or spend the money necessary to beginning this sort of reforms, because they do not feel the evils they live amongst, because they have degraded themselves into something less than men; they are unmanly because they have ceased to have their due share of art.

For again I say that therein rich people have defrauded themselves as well as the poor: you will see a refined and highly educated man nowadays, who has been to Italy and Egypt, and where not, who can talk learnedly enough (and fantastically enough sometimes) about art, and who has at his fingers' ends abundant lore concerning the art and literature of past days, sitting down without signs of discomfort in a house, that with all its surroundings is just brutally vulgar and hideous: all his education has not done more for him than that.

The truth is, that in art, and in other things besides, the laboured education of a few will not raise even those few above the reach of the evils that beset the ignorance of the great mass of the population: the brutality of which such a huge stock has been accumulated lower down, will often show without much peeling through the selfish refinement of those who have let it accumulate. The lack of art, or rather the murder of art, that curses our streets from the sordidness of the surroundings of the lower classes, has its exact counterpart in the dullness and vulgarity of those of the middle classes, and the double-distilled dullness, and scarcely less vulgarity of those of the upper classes.

I say this is as it should be; it is just and fair as far as it goes; and moreover the rich with their leisure are the more like to move if they feel the pinch themselves.

But how shall they and we, and all of us, move? What is the remedy?

What remedy can there be for the blunders of civilisation but further civilisation? You do not by any accident think that we have gone as far in that direction as it is possible to go, do you?—even in England, I mean?

When some changes have come to pass, that perhaps will be speedier than most people think, doubtless education will both grow in quality and in quantity; so that it may be, that as the nineteenth century is to be called the Century of Commerce, the twentieth may be called the Century of Education. But that education does not end when people leave school is now a mere commonplace; and how then can you really educate men who lead the life of machines, who only think for the few hours during which they are not at work, who in short spend almost their whole lives in doing work which is not proper for developing them body and mind in some worthy way? You cannot educate, you cannot civilise men, unless you can give them a share in art.

Yes, and it is hard indeed as things go to give most men that share; for they do not miss it, or ask for it, and it is impossible as things are that they should either miss or ask for it. Nevertheless everything has a beginning, and many great things have had very small ones; and since, as I have said, these ideas are already abroad in more than one form, we must not be too much discouraged at the seemingly boundless weight we have to lift.

After all, we are only bound to play our own parts, and

do our own share of the lifting; and as in no case that share can be great, so also in all cases it is called for, it is necessary. Therefore let us work and faint not; remembering that though it be natural, and therefore excusable, amidst doubtful times to feel doubts of success oppress us at whiles, yet not to crush those doubts, and work as if we had them not, is simple cowardice, which is unforgivable. No man has any right to say that all has been done for nothing, that all the faithful unwearying strife of those that have gone before us shall lead us nowhither; that mankind will but go round and round in a circle for ever: no man has a right to say that, and then get up morning after morning to eat his victuals and sleep a-nights, all the while making other people toil to keep his worthless life a-going.

Be sure that some way or other will be found out of the tangle, even when things seem most tangled, and be no less sure that some use will then have come of our work, if it has been faithful, and therefore unsparingly careful and thoughtful.

So once more I say, if in any matters civilisation has gone astray, the remedy lies not in standing still, but in more complete civilisation.

Now whatever discussion there may be about that often used and often misused word, I believe all who hear me will agree with me in believing from their hearts, and not merely in saying in conventional phrase, that the civilisation which does not carry the whole people with it, is doomed to fall, and give place to one which at least aims at doing so.

We talk of the civilisation of the ancient peoples, of the classical times: well, civilised they were no doubt, some of their folk at least: an Athenian citizen for instance led a simple, dignified, almost perfect life; but there were drawbacks to happiness perhaps in the lives of his slaves: and the civilisation of the ancients was founded on slavery.

Indeed that ancient society did give a model to the world, and showed us for ever what blessings were freedom of life and thought, self-restraint and a generous education: all those blessings the ancient free peoples set forth to the world —and kept them to themselves.

Therefore no tyrant was too base, no pretext too hollow, for enslaving the grandsons of the men of Salamis and

Thermopylæ: therefore did the descendants of those stern and self-restrained Romans, who were ready to give up everything, and life as the least of things, to the glory of their commonweal, produce monsters of license and reckless folly. Therefore did a little knot of Galilean peasants overthrow the Roman Empire.

Ancient civilisation was chained to slavery and exclusiveness, and it fell; the barbarism that took its place has delivered us from slavery and grown into modern civilisation; and that in its turn has before it the choice of never-ceasing growth, or destruction by that which has in it the seeds of higher growth.

There is an ugly word for a dreadful fact, which I must make bold to use—the residuum: that word since the time I first saw it used, has had a terrible significance to me, and I have felt from my heart that if this residuum were a necessary part of modern civilisation, as some people openly, and many more tacitly, assume that it is, then this civilisation carries with it the poison that shall one day destroy it, even as its elder sister did: if civilisation is to go no further than this, it had better not have gone so far: if it does not aim at getting rid of this misery and giving some share in the happiness and dignity of life to *all* the people that it has created, and which it spends such unwearying energy in creating, it is simply an organised injustice, a mere instrument for oppression, so much the worse than that which has gone before it, as its pretensions are higher, its slavery subtler, its mastery harder to overthrow, because supported by such a dense mass of commonplace well-being and comfort.

Surely this cannot be: surely there is a distinct feeling abroad of this injustice: so that if the residuum still clogs all the efforts of modern civilisation to rise above mere population-breeding and money-making, the difficulty of dealing with it is the legacy, first of the ages of violence and almost conscious brutal injustice, and next of the ages of thoughtlessness, of hurry and blindness; surely all those who think at all of the future of the world are at work in one way or other in striving to rid it of this shame.

That to my mind is the meaning of what we call National Education, which we have begun, and which is doubtless already bearing its fruits, and will bear greater, when all people are educated, not according to the money which they or their parents possess, but according to the capacity of their minds.

What effect that will have upon the future of the arts, I cannot say, but one would surely think a very great effect; for it will enable people to see clearly many things which are now as completely hidden from them as if they were blind in body and idiotic in mind: and this, I say, will act not only upon those who most directly feel the evils of ignorance, but also upon those who feel them indirectly,— upon us, the educated: the great wave of rising intelligence, rife with so many natural desires and aspirations, will carry all classes along with it, and force us all to see that many things which we have been used to look upon as necessary and eternal evils are merely the accidental and temporary growths of past stupidity, and can be escaped from by due effort, and the exercise of courage, goodwill, and fore-thought.

And among those evils, I do, and must always, believe will fall that one which last year I told you that I accounted the greatest of all evils, the heaviest of all slaveries; that evil of the greater part of the population being engaged for by far the most part of their lives in work, which at the best cannot interest them, or develop their best faculties, and at the worst (and that is the commonest, too) is mere unmiti-gated slavish toil, only to be wrung out of them by the sternest compulsion, a toil which they shirk all they can— small blame to them. And this toil degrades them into less than men: and they will some day come to know it, and cry out to be made men again, and art only can do it, and redeem them from this slavery; and I say once more that this is her highest and most glorious end and aim; and it is in her struggle to attain to it that she will most surely purify herself, and quicken her own aspirations towards perfection.

But we—in the meantime we must not sit waiting for obvious signs of these later and glorious days to show them-selves on earth, and in the heavens, but rather turn to the commonplace, and maybe often dull work of fitting our-selves in detail to take part in them if we should live to see one of them; or in doing our best to make the path smooth for their coming, if we are to die before they are here.

What, therefore, can we do, to guard traditions of time past that we may not one day have to begin anew from the beginning with none to teach us? What are we to do, that we may take heed to, and spread the decencies of life, so that at the least we may have a field where it will be possible for art to grow when men begin to long for it: what finally can we do, each of us, to cherish some germ of art, so that it may meet with others, and spread and grow little by little into the thing that we need?

Now I cannot pretend to think that the first of these duties is a matter of indifference to you, after my experience of the enthusiastic meeting that I had the honour of addressing here last autumn on the subject of the (so called) restoration of St. Mark's at Venice; you thought, and most justly thought, it seems to me, that the subject was of such moment to art in general, that it was a simple and obvious thing for men who were anxious on the matter to address themselves to those who had the decision of it in their hands; even though the former were called Englishmen, and the latter Italians; for you felt that the name of lovers of art would cover those differences: if you had any misgivings, you remembered that there was but one such building in the world, and that it was worth while risking a breach of etiquette, if any words of ours could do anything towards saving it; well, the Italians were, some of them, very naturally, though surely unreasonably, irritated, for a time, and in some of their prints they bade us look at home; that was no argument in favour of the wisdom of wantonly rebuilding St. Mark's façade: but certainly those of us who have not yet looked at home in this matter had better do so speedily, late and over late though it be: for though we have no golden-pictured interiors like St. Mark's Church at home, we still have many buildings which are both works of ancient art and monuments of history: and just think what is happening to them, and note, since we profess to recognise their value, how helpless art is in the Century of Commerce!

In the first place, many and many a beautiful and ancient building is being destroyed all over civilised Europe as well as in England, because it is supposed to interfere with the convenience of the citizens, while a little forethought might save it without trenching on that convenience[1]; but even apart from that, I say that if we are not prepared to put up with a little inconvenience in our lifetimes for the sake of preserving a monument of art which will elevate and educate, not only ourselves, but our sons, and our sons' sons, it is vain and idle of us to talk about art—or education either. Brutality must be bred of such brutality.

The same thing may be said about enlarging, or otherwise altering for convenience' sake, old buildings still in use for something like their original purposes: in almost all such cases it is really nothing more than a question of a little money for a new site: and then a new building can be built exactly fitted for the uses it is needed for, with such art about it as our own days can furnish; while the old monument is left to tell its tale of change and progress, to hold out example and warning to us in the practice of the arts: and thus the convenience of the public, the progress of modern art, and the cause of education, are all furthered at once at the cost of a little money.

Surely if it be worth while troubling ourselves about the works of art of to-day, of which any amount almost can be done, since we are yet alive, it is worth while spending a little care, forethought, and money in preserving the art of bygone ages, of which (woe worth the while!) so little is left, and of which we can never have any more, whatever good-hap the world may attain to.

No man who consents to the destruction or the mutilation of an ancient building has any right to pretend that he cares about art; or has any excuse to plead in defence of his crime against civilisation and progress, save sheer brutal ignorance.

[1] As I corrected these sheets for the press, the case of two such pieces of destruction is forced upon me: first, the remains of the Refectory of Westminster Abbey, with the adjacent Ashburnham House, a beautiful work, probably by Inigo Jones; and second, Magdalen Bridge at Oxford. Certainly this seems to mock my hope of the influence of education on the Beauty of Life; since the first scheme of destruction is eagerly pressed forward by the authorities of Westminster School, the second scarcely opposed by the resident members of the University of Oxford.

But before I leave this subject I must say a word or two about the curious invention of our own days called Restoration, a method of dealing with works of bygone days which, though not so degrading in its spirit as downright destruction, is nevertheless little better in its results on the condition of those works of art; it is obvious that I have no time to argue the question out to-night, so I will only make these assertions:

That ancient buildings, being both works of art and monuments of history, must obviously be treated with great care and delicacy: that the imitative art of to-day is not, and cannot be the same thing as ancient art, and cannot replace it; and that therefore if we superimpose this work on the old, we destroy it both as art and as a record of history: lastly, that the natural weathering of the surface of a building is beautiful, and its loss disastrous.

Now the restorers hold the exact contrary of all this: they think that any clever architect to-day can deal off-hand successfully with the ancient work; that while all things else have changed about us since (say) the thirteenth century, art has not changed, and that our workmen can turn out work identical with that of the thirteenth century; and, lastly, that the weather-beaten surface of an ancient building is worthless, and to be got rid of wherever possible.

You see the question is difficult to argue, because there seem to be no common grounds between the restorers and the anti-restorers: I appeal therefore to the public, and bid them note, that though our opinions may be wrong, the action we advise is not rash: let the question be shelved awhile: if, as we are always pressing on people, due care be taken of these monuments, so that they shall not fall into disrepair, they will be always there to "restore" whenever people think proper and when we are proved wrong; but if it should turn out that we are right, how can the "restored" buildings be restored? I beg of you therefore to let the question be shelved, till art has so advanced among us, that we can deal authoritatively with it, till there is no longer any doubt about the matter.

Surely these monuments of our art and history, which, whatever the lawyers may say, belong not to a coterie, or to a rich man here and there, but to the nation at large, are worth this delay: surely the last relics of the life of the "famous men and our fathers that begat us" may justly claim of us the exercise of a little patience.

It will give us trouble no doubt, all this care of our possessions: but there is more trouble to come; for I must now speak of something else, of possessions which should be common to all of us, of the green grass, and the leaves, and the waters, of the very light and air of heaven, which the Century of Commerce has been too busy to pay any heed to. And first let me remind you that I am supposing every one here present professes to care about art.

Well, there are some rich men among us whom we oddly enough call manufacturers, by which we mean capitalists who pay other men to organise manufacturers; these gentlemen, many of whom buy pictures and profess to care about art, burn a deal of coal: there is an Act in existence which was passed to prevent them sometimes and in some places from pouring a dense cloud of smoke over the world, and, to my thinking, a very lame and partial Act it is: but nothing hinders these lovers of art from being a law to themselves, and making it a point of honour with them to minimise the smoke nuisance as far as their own works are concerned; and if they don't do so, when mere money, and even a very little of that, is what it will cost them, I say that their love of art is a mere pretence: how can you care about the image of a landscape when you show by your deeds that you don't care for the landscape itself? or what right have you to shut yourself up with beautiful form and colour when you make it impossible for other people to have any share in these things?

Well, and as to the smoke Act itself: I don't know what heed you pay to it in Birmingham,[1] but I have seen myself what heed is paid to it in other places; Bradford for instance: though close by them at Saltaire they have an example which I should have thought might have shamed them; for the huge chimney there which serves the acres of weaving and spinning sheds of Sir Titus Salt and his brothers is as

---

[1] Since perhaps some people may read these words who are not of Birmingham, I ought to say that it was authoritatively explained at the meeting to which I addressed these words, that in Birmingham the law is strictly enforced.

guiltless of smoke as an ordinary kitchen chimney. Or Manchester: a gentleman of that city told me that the smoke Act was a mere dead letter there: well, they buy pictures in Manchester and profess to wish to further the arts: but you see it must be idle pretence as far as their rich people are concerned: they only want to talk about it, and have themselves talked of.

I don't know what you are doing about this matter here; but you must forgive my saying, that unless you are beginning to think of some way of dealing with it, you are not beginning yet to pave your way to success in the arts.

Well, I have spoken of a huge nuisance, which is a type of the worst nuisances of what an ill-tempered man might be excused for calling the Century of Nuisances, rather than the Century of Commerce. I will now leave it to the consciences of the rich and influential among us, and speak of a minor nuisance which it is in the power of every one of us to abate, and which, small as it is, is so vexatious, that if I can prevail on a score of you to take heed to it by what I am saying, I shall think my evening's work a good one. Sandwich-papers I mean—of course you laugh: but come now, don't you, civilised as you are in Birmingham, leave them all about the Lickey hills and your public gardens and the like? If you don't I really scarcely know with what words to praise you. When we Londoners go to enjoy ourselves at Hampton Court, for instance, we take special good care to let everybody know that we have had something to eat: so that the park just outside the gates (and a beautiful place it is) looks as if it had been snowing dirty paper. I really think you might promise me one and all who are here present to have done with this sluttish habit, which is the type of many another in its way, just as the smoke nuisance is. I mean such things as scrawling one's name on monuments, tearing down tree boughs, and the like.

I suppose 'tis early days in the revival of the arts to express one's disgust at the daily increasing hideousness of the posters with which all our towns are daubed. Still we ought to be disgusted at such horrors, and I think make up our minds never to buy any of the articles so advertised.

I can't believe they can be worth much if they need all that shouting to sell them.

Again, I must ask what do you do with the trees on a site that is going to be built over? do you try to save them, to adapt your houses at all to them? do you understand what treasures they are in a town or a suburb? or what a relief they will be to the hideous dog-holes which (forgive me!) you are probably going to build in their places? I ask this anxiously, and with grief in my soul, for in London and its suburbs we always[1] begin by clearing a site till it is as bare as the pavement: I really think that almost anybody would have been shocked, if I could have shown him some of the trees that have been wantonly murdered in the suburb in which I live (Hammersmith to wit), amongst them some of those magnificent cedars, for which we along the river used to be famous once.

But here again see how helpless those are who care about art or nature amidst the hurry of the Century of Commerce.

Pray do not forget, that any one who cuts down a tree wantonly or carelessly, especially in a great town or its suburbs, need make no pretence of caring about art.

What else can we do to help to educate ourselves and others in the path of art, to be on the road to attaining an *Art made by the people and for the people as a joy to the maker and the user*?

Why, having got to understand something of what art was, having got to look upon its ancient monuments as friends that can tell us something of times bygone, and whose faces we do not wish to alter, even though they be worn by time and grief: having got to spend money and trouble upon matters of decency, great and little; having made it clear that we really do care about nature even in the suburbs of a big town—having got so far, we shall begin to think of the houses in which we live.

For I must tell you that unless you are resolved to have good and rational architecture, it is, once again, useless your thinking about art at all.

I have spoken of the popular arts, but they might all be

[1] Not *quite* always: in the little colony at Bedford Park, Chiswick, as many trees have been left as possible, to the boundless advantage of its quaint and pretty architecture

summed up in that one word Architecture; they are all parts of that great whole, and the art of house-building begins it all: if we did not know how to dye or to weave; if we had neither gold, nor silver, nor silk; and no pigments to paint with but half-a-dozen ochres and umbers, we might yet frame a worthy art that would lead to everything, if we had but timber, stone, and lime, and a few cutting tools to make these common things not only shelter us from wind and weather, but also express the thoughts and aspirations that stir in us.

Architecture would lead us to all the arts, as it did with earlier men: but if we despise it and take no note of how we are housed, the other arts will have a hard time of it indeed.

Now I do not think the greatest of optimists would deny that, taking us one and all, we are at present housed in a perfectly shameful way, and since the greatest part of us have to live in houses already built for us, it must be admitted that it is rather hard to know what to do, beyond waiting till they tumble about our ears.

Only we must not lay the fault upon the builders, as some people seem inclined to do: they are our very humble servants, and will build what we ask for; remember, that rich men are not obliged to live in ugly houses, and yet you see they do; which the builders may be well excused for taking as a sign of what is wanted.

Well, the point is, we must do what we can, and make people understand what we want them to do for us, by letting them see what we do for ourselves.

Hitherto, judging us by that standard, the builders may well say that we want the pretence of a thing rather than the thing itself; that we want a show of petty luxury if we are unrich, a show of insulting stupidity if we are rich: and they are quite clear that as a rule we want to get something that shall look as if it cost twice as much as it really did.

You cannot have Architecture on those terms: simplicity and solidity are the very first requisites of it: just think if it is not so. How we please ourselves with an old building by thinking of all the generations of men that have passed through it! do we not remember how it has received their joy, and borne their sorrow, and not even their folly has left sourness upon it? it still looks as kind to us as it did to them. And the converse of this we ought to feel when we look at a newly-built house if it were as it should be: we should feel a pleasure in thinking how he who had built it had left a piece of his soul behind him to greet the new-comers one after another long and long after he was gone:— but what sentiment can an ordinary modern house move in us, or what thought—save a hope that we may speedily forget its base ugliness?

But if you ask me how we are to pay for this solidity and extra expense, that seems to me a reasonable question; for you must dismiss at once as a delusion the hope that has beeñ sometimes cherished, that you can have a building which is a work of art, and is therefore above all things properly built, at the same price as a building which only pretends to be this: never forget when people talk about cheap art in general, by the way, that all art costs time, trouble, and thought, and that money is only a counter to represent these things.

However, I must try to answer the question I have supposed put, how are we to pay for decent houses?

It seems to me that, by a great piece of good luck, the way to pay for them is by doing that which alone can produce popular art among us: living a simple life, I mean. Once more I say that the greatest foe to art is luxury, art cannot live in its atmosphere.

When you hear of the luxuries of the ancients, you must remember that they were not like our luxuries, they were rather indulgences in pieces of extravagant folly than what we to-day call luxury; which perhaps you would rather call comfort: well I accept the word, and say that a Greek or Roman of the luxurious time would stare astonished could he be brought back again, and shown the comforts of a well-to-do middle-class house.

But some, I know, think that the attainment of these very comforts is what makes the difference between civili-sation and uncivilisation, that they are the essence of civilisation. Is it so indeed ? Farewell my hope then!— I had thought that civilisation meant the attainment of peace and order and freedom, of goodwill between man and man, of the love of truth and the hatred of injustice,

and by consequence the attainment of the good life which
these things breed, a life free from craven fear, but full of
incident: that was what I thought it meant, not more stuffed
chairs and more cushions, and more carpets and gas, and
more dainty meat and drink—and therewithal more and
sharper differences between class and class.

If that be what it is, I for my part wish I were well out
of it, and living in a tent in the Persian desert, or a turf
hut on the Iceland hill-side. But however it be, and I
think my view is the true view, I tell you that art abhors
that side of civilisation, she cannot breathe in the houses
that lie under its stuffy slavery.

Believe me, if we want art to begin at home, as it must,
we must clear our houses of troublesome superfluities that
are for ever in our way: conventional comforts that are
no real comforts, and do but make work for servants and
doctors: if you want a golden rule that will fit everybody,
this is it:

*"Have nothing in your houses that you do not know to be useful,
or believe to be beautiful."*

And if we apply that rule strictly, we shall in the first
place show the builders and such-like servants of the public
what we really want, we shall create a demand for real
art, as the phrase goes; and in the second place, we shall
surely have more money to pay for decent houses.

Perhaps it will not try your patience too much if I lay
before you my idea of the fittings necessary to the sitting-
room of a healthy person: a room, I mean, which he
would not have to cook in much, or sleep in generally,
or in which he would not have to do any very litter-making
manual work.

First a book-case with a great many books in it: next
a table that will keep steady when you write or work at it:
then several chairs that you can move, and a bench that
you can sit or lie upon: next a cupboard with drawers:
yext, unless either the book-case or the cupboard be very
beautiful with painting or carving, you will want pictures
or engravings, such as you can afford, only not stopgaps,
but real works of art on the wall; or else the wall itself must
be ornamented with some beautiful and restful pattern:
we shall also want a vase or two to put flowers in, which

latter you must have sometimes, especially if you live in a town. Then there will be the fireplace of course, which in our climate is bound to be the chief object in the room.

That is all we shall want, especially if the floor be good; if it be not, as, by the way, in a modern house it is pretty certain not to be, I admit that a small carpet which can be bundled out of the room in two minutes will be useful, and we must also take care that it is beautiful, or it will annoy us terribly.

Now unless we are musical, and need a piano (in which case, as far as beauty is concerned, we are in a bad way), that is quite all we want: and we can add very little to these necessaries without troubling ourselves, and hindering our work, our thought, and our rest.

If these things were done at the least cost for which they could be done well and solidly, they ought not to cost much; and they are so few, that those that could afford to have them at all, could afford to spend some trouble to get them fitting and beautiful: and all those who care about art ought to take great trouble to do so, and to take care that there be no sham art amongst them, nothing that it has degraded a man to make or sell. And I feel sure, that if all who care about art were to take this pains, it would make a great impression upon the public.

This simplicity you may make as costly as you please or can, on the other hand: you may hang your walls with tapestry instead of whitewash or paper; or you may cover them with mosaic, or have them frescoed by a great painter: all this is not luxury, if it be done for beauty's sake, and not for show: it does not break our golden rule: *Have nothing in your houses which you do not know to be useful or believe to be beautiful.*

All art starts from this simplicity; and the higher the art rises, the greater the simplicity. I have been speaking of the fittings of a dwelling-house—a place in which we eat and drink, and pass familiar hours; but when you come to places which people want to make more specially beautiful because of the solemnity or dignity of their uses, they will be simpler still, and have little in them save the bare walls made as beautiful as may be. St. Mark's at Venice has very little furniture in it, much less than most Roman

Catholic churches: its lovely and stately mother St. Sophia of Constantinople had less still, even when it was a Christian church: but we need not go either to Venice or Stamboul to take note of that: go into one of our own mighty Gothic naves (do any of you remember the first time you did so?) and note how the huge free space satisfies and elevates you, even now when window and wall are stripped of ornament: then think of the meaning of simplicity, and absence of encumbering gew-gaws.

Now after all, for us who are learning art, it is not far to seek what is the surest way to further it; that which most breeds art is art; every piece of work that we do which is well done, is so much help to the cause; every piece of pretence and half-heartedness is so much hurt to it. Most of you who take to the practice of art can find out in no very long time whether you have any gifts for it or not: if you have not, throw the thing up, or you will have a wretched time of it yourselves, and will be damaging the cause by laborious pretence: but if you have gifts of any kind, you are happy indeed beyond most men; for your pleasure is always with you, nor can you be intemperate in the enjoyment of it, and as you use it, it does not lessen, but grows: if you are by chance weary of it at night, you get up in the morning eager for it; or if perhaps in the morning it seems folly to you for a while, yet presently, when your hand has been moving a little in its wonted way, fresh hope has sprung up beneath it and you are happy again. While others are getting through the day like plants thrust into the earth, which cannot turn this way or that but as the wind blows them, you know what you want, and your will is on the alert to find it, and you, whatever happens, whether it be joy or grief, are at least alive.

Now when I spoke to you last year, after I had sat down I was half afraid that I had on some points said too much, that I had spoken too bitterly in my eagerness; that a rash word might have discouraged some of you; I was very far from meaning that: what I wanted to do, what I want to do to-night, is to put definitely before you a cause for which to strive.

That cause is the Democracy of Art, the ennobling of daily and common work, which will one day put hope and pleasure in the place of fear and pain, as the forces which move men to labour and keep the world a-going.

If I have enlisted any one in that cause, rash as my words may have been, or feeble as they may have been, they have done more good than harm; nor do I believe that any words of mine can discourage any who have joined that cause or are ready to do so: their way is too clear before them for that, and every one of us can help the cause whether he be great or little.

I know indeed that men, wearied by the pettiness of the details of the strife, their patience tried by hope deferred, will at whiles, excusably enough, turn back in their hearts to other days, when if the issues were not clearer, the means of trying them were simpler; when, so stirring were the times, one might even have atoned for many a blunder and backsliding by visibly dying for the cause. To have breasted the Spanish pikes at Leyden, to have drawn sword with Oliver: that may well seem to us at times amidst the tangles of to-day a happy fate: for a man to be able to say, I have lived like a fool, but now I will cast away fooling for an hour, and die like a man—there is something in that certainly: and yet 'tis clear that few men can be so lucky as to die for a cause, without having first of all lived for it. And as this is the most that can be asked from the greatest man that follows a cause, so it is the least that can be taken from the smallest.

So to us who have a Cause at heart, our highest ambition and our simplest duty are one and the same thing: for the most part we shall be too busy doing the work that lies ready to our hands, to let impatience for visibly great progress vex us much; but surely since we are servants of a Cause, hope must be ever with us, and sometimes perhaps it will so quicken our vision that it will outrun the slow lapse of time, and show us the victorious days when millions of those who now sit in darkness will be enlightened by an *Art made by the people and for the people, a joy to the maker and the user.*

HOW WE LIVE
& HOW WE MIGHT LIVE

THE word Revolution, which we Socialists are so often forced to use, has a terrible sound in most people's ears, even when we have explained to them that it does not necessarily mean a change accompanied by riot and all kinds of violence, and cannot mean a change made mechanically and in the teeth of opinion by a group of men who have somehow managed to seize on the executive power for the moment. Even when we explain that we use the word revolution in its etymological sense, and mean by it a change in the basis of society, people are scared at the idea of such a vast change, and beg that you will speak of reform and not revolution. As, however, we Socialists do not at all mean by our word revolution what these worthy people mean by their word reform, I can't help thinking that it would be a mistake to use it, whatever projects we might conceal beneath its harmless envelope. So we will stick to our word, which means a change of the basis of society; it may frighten people, but it will at least warn them that there is something to be frightened about, which will be no less dangerous for being ignored; and also it may encourage some people, and will mean to them at least not a fear, but a hope.

Fear and Hope—those are the names of the two great passions which rule the race of man, and with which revolutionists have to deal; to give hope to the many oppressed and fear to the few oppressors, that is our business; if we do the first and give hope to the many, the few *must* be frightened by their hope; otherwise we do not want to frighten them; it is not revenge we want for poor people, but happiness; indeed, what revenge can be taken for all the thousands of years of the sufferings of the poor?

However, many of the oppressors of the poor, most of them, we will say, are not conscious of their being oppressors (we shall see why presently); they live in an orderly, quiet way themselves, as far as possible removed from the feelings of a Roman slave-owner or a Legree; they know that the poor exist, but their sufferings do not present themselves to them in a trenchant and dramatic way; they themselves have troubles to bear, and they think doubtless that to bear trouble is the lot of humanity; nor have they any means of comparing the troubles of their lives with those of people lower in the social scale; and if ever the thought of those heavier troubles obtrudes itself upon them, they console themselves with the maxim that people do get used to the troubles they have to bear, whatever they may be.

Indeed, as far as regards individuals at least, that is but too true, so that we have as supporters of the present state of things, however bad it may be, first those comfortable unconscious oppressors who think that they have everything to fear from any change which would involve more than the softest and most gradual of reforms, and secondly those poor people who, living hard and anxiously as they do, can hardly conceive of any change for the better happening to them, and dare not risk one tittle of their poor possessions in taking any action towards a possible bettering of their condition; so that while we can do little with the rich save inspire them with fear, it is hard indeed to give the poor any hope. It is, then, no less than reasonable that those whom we try to involve in the great struggle for a better form of life than that which we now lead should call on us to give them at least some idea of what that life may be like.

A reasonable request, but hard to satisfy, since we are living under a system that makes conscious effort towards reconstruction almost impossible: it is not unreasonable on our part to answer, "There are certain definite obstacles to the real progress of man; we can tell you what these are; take them away, and then you shall see."

However, I purpose now to offer myself as a victim for the satisfaction of those who consider that as things now go we have at least got something, and are terrified at the idea of losing their hold of that, lest they should find they are worse off than before, and have nothing. Yet in the course of my endeavour to show how we might live, I must more or less deal in negatives. I mean to say I must point out where in my opinion we fall short in our present attempt at decent life. I must ask the rich and well-to-do what sort of a position it is which they are so anxious to preserve at any cost? and if, after all, it will be such a terrible loss to them to give it up? and I must point out to the poor that they, with capacities for living a dignified and generous life, are in a position which they cannot endure without continued degradation.

How do we live, then, under our present system? Let us look at it a little.

And first, please to understand that our present system of Society is based on a state of perpetual war. Do any of you think that this is as it should be? I know that you have often been told that the competition, which is at present the rule of all production, is a good thing, and stimulates the progress of the race; but the people who tell you this should call competition by its shorter name of *war* if they wish to be honest, and you would then be free to consider whether or no war stimulates progress, otherwise than as a mad bull chasing you over your own garden may do. War, or competition, whichever you please to call it, means at the best pursuing your own advantage at the cost of some one else's loss, and in the process of it you must not be sparing of destruction even of your own possessions, or you will certainly come by the worse in the struggle. You understand that perfectly as to the kind of war in which people go out to kill and be killed; that sort of war in which ships are commissioned, for instance, "to sink, burn, and destroy"; but it appears that you are not so conscious of this waste of goods when you are only carrying on that other war called *commerce*; observe, however, that the waste is there all the same.

Now let us look at this kind of war a little closer, run through some of the forms of it, that we may see how the "burn, sink, and destroy" is carried on in it.

First, you have that form of it called national rivalry, which in good truth is nowadays the cause of all

gunpowder and bayonet wars which civilized nations wage.
For years past we English have been rather shy of them,
except on those happy occasions when we could carry them
on at no sort of risk to ourselves, when the killing was all on
one side, or at all events when we hoped it would be We
have been shy of gunpowder war with a respectable enemy
for a long while, and I will tell you why: It is because we
have had the lion's share of the world-market; we didn't
want to fight for it as a nation, for we had got it; but now
this is changing in a most significant, and, to a Socialist,
a most cheering way; we are losing or have lost that lion's
share; it is now a desperate "competition" between the
great nations of civilization for the world-market, and to-
morrow it may be a desperate war for that end. As a
result, the furthering of war (if it be not on too large a
scale) is no longer confined to the honour-and-glory kind
of old Tories, who if they meant anything at all by it meant
that a Tory war would be a good occasion for damping
down democracy; we have changed all that, and now it is
quite another kind of politician that is wont to urge us on
to "patriotism" as 'tis called. The leaders of the Progressive Liberals, as they would call themselves, long-headed
persons who know well enough that social movements are
going on, who are not blind to the fact that the world will
move with their help or without it; these have been the
Jingoes of these later days. I don't mean to say they know
what they are doing: politicians, as you well know, take
good care to shut their eyes to everything that may happen
six months ahead; but what is being done is this: that the
present system, which always must include national rivalry,
is pushing us into a desperate scramble for the markets on
more or less equal terms with other nations, because, once
more, we have lost that command of them which we once
had. Desperate is not too strong a word. We shall let this
impulse to snatch markets carry us whither it will, whither
it must. To-day it is successful burglary and disgrace, to-
morrow it may be mere defeat and disgrace.

Now this is not a digression, although in saying this I
am nearer to what is generally called politics than I shall
be again. I only want to show you what commercial war
comes to when it has to do with foreign nations, and that

even the dullest can see how mere waste must go with it. That is how we live now with foreign nations, prepared to ruin them without war if possible, with it if necessary, let alone meantime the disgraceful exploiting of savage tribes and barbarous peoples on whom we force at once our shoddy wares and our hypocrisy at the cannon's mouth.

Well, surely Socialism can offer you something in the place of all that. It can; it can offer you peace and friendship instead of war. We might live utterly without national rivalries, acknowledging that while it is best for those who feel that they naturally form a community under one name to govern themselves, yet that no community in civilization should feel that it had interests opposed to any other, their economical condition being at any rate similar; so that any citizen of one community could fall to work and live without disturbance of his life when he was in a foreign country, and would fit into his place quite naturally; so that all civilized nations would form one great community, agreeing together as to the kind and amount of production and distribution needed; working at such and such production where it could be best produced; avoiding waste by all means. Please to think of the amount of waste which they would avoid, how much such a revolution would add to the wealth of the world! What creature on earth would be harmed by such a revolution? Nay, would not everybody be the better for it? And what hinders it? I will tell you presently.

Meantime let us pass from this "competition" between nations to that between "the organizers of labour," great firms, joint-stock companies; capitalists in short, and see how competition "stimulates production" among them: indeed it does do that; but what kind of production? Well, production of something to sell at a profit, or say production of profits: and note how war commercial stimulates that: a certain market is demanding goods; there are, say, a hundred manufacturers who make that kind of goods, and every one of them would if he could keep that market to himself, and struggles desperately to get as much of it as he can, with the obvious result that presently the thing is overdone, and the market is glutted, and all that fury of manufacture has to sink into cold ashes. Doesn't that seem something like war to you? Can't you see the waste of it—waste of labour, skill, cunning, waste of life in short? Well you may say, but it cheapens the goods. In a sense it does; and yet only apparently, as wages have a tendency to sink for the ordinary worker in proportion as prices sink; and at what a cost do we gain this appearance of cheapness! Plainly speaking, at the cost of cheating the consumer and starving the real producer for the benefit of the gambler, who uses both consumer and producer as his milch cows. I needn't go at length into the subject of adulteration, for every one knows what kind of a part it plays in this sort of commerce; but remember that it is an absolutely necessary incident to the production of profit out of wares, which is the business of the so-called manufacturer; and this you must understand, that, taking him in the lump, the consumer is perfectly helpless against the gambler; the goods are forced on him by their cheapness, and with them a certain kind of life which that energetic, that aggressive cheapness determines for him: for so far-reaching is this curse of commercial war that no country is safe from its ravages; the traditions of a thousand years fall before it in a month; it overruns a weak or semi-barbarous country, and whatever romance or pleasure or art existed there, is trodden down into a mire of sordidness and ugliness; the Indian or Javanese craftsman may no longer ply his craft leisurely, working a few hours a day, in producing a maze of strange beauty on a piece of cloth: a steam-engine is set a-going at Manchester, and that victory over nature and a thousand stubborn difficulties is used for the base work of producing a sort of plaster of china-clay and shoddy, and the Asiatic worker, if he is not starved to death outright, as plentifully happens, is driven himself into a factory to lower the wages of his Manchester brother worker, and nothing of character is left him except, most like, an accumulation of fear and hatred of that to him most unaccountable evil, his English master. The South Sea Islander must leave his canoe-carving, his sweet rest, and his graceful dances, and become the slave of a slave: trousers, shoddy, rum, missionary, and fatal disease—he must swallow all this civilization in the lump, and neither himself nor we can help him now till social order displaces the hideous tyranny of gambling that has ruined him.

Let those be types of the consumer: but now for the producer; I mean the real producer, the worker; how does this scramble for the plunder of the market affect him? The manufacturer, in the eagerness of his war, has had to collect into one neighbourhood a vast army of workers, he has drilled them till they are as fit as may be for his special branch of production, that is, for making a profit out of it, and with the result of their being fit for nothing else: well, when the glut comes in that market he is supplying, what happens to this army, every private in which has been depending on the steady demand in that market, and acting, as he could not choose but act, as if it were to go on for ever? You know well what happens to these men: the factory door is shut on them; on a very large part of them often, and at the best on the reserve army of labour, so busily employed in the time of inflation. What becomes of them? Nay, we know that well enough just now. But what we don't know, or don't choose to know, is that this reserve army of labour is an absolute necessity for commercial war; if *our* manufacturers had not got these poor devils whom they could draft on to their machines when the demand swelled, other manufacturers in France, or Germany, or America, would step in and take the market from them.

So you see, as we live now, it is necessary that a vast part of the industrial population should be exposed to the danger of periodical semi-starvation, and that, not for the advantage of the people in another part of the world, but for their degradation and enslavement.

Just let your minds run for a moment on the kind of waste which this means, this opening up of new markets among savage and barbarous countries which is the extreme type of the force of the profit-market on the world, and you will surely see what a hideous nightmare that profit-market is: it keeps us sweating and terrified for our livelihood, unable to read a book, or look at a picture, or have pleasant fields to walk in, or to lie in the sun, or to share in the knowledge of our time, to have in short either animal or intellectual pleasure, and for what? that we may go on living the same slavish life till we die, in order to provide for a rich man what is called a life of ease and luxury; that is to say, a life so empty, unwholesome, and degraded, that perhaps, on the whole, he is worse off than we the workers are: and as to the result of all this suffering, it is luckiest when it is nothing at all, when you can say that the wares have done nobody any good; for oftenest they have done many people harm, and we have toiled and groaned and died in making poison and destruction for our fellow-men.

Well, I say all this is war, and the result of war, the war this time, not of competing nations, but of competing firms or capitalist units: and it is this war of the firms which hinders the peace between nations which you surely have agreed with me in thinking is so necessary; for you must know that war is the very breath of the nostrils of these fighting firms, and they have now, in our times, got into their hands nearly all the political power, and they band together in each country in order to make their respective governments fulfil just two functions: the first is at home to act as a strong police force, to keep the ring in which the strong are beating down the weak; the second is to act as a piratical body-guard abroad, a petard to explode the doors which lead to the markets of the world: markets at any price abroad, uninterfered-with privilege, falsely called *laissez-faire*,[1] at any price at home, to provide these is the sole business of a government such as our industrial captains have been able to conceive of. I must now try to show you the reason of all this, and what it rests on, by trying to answer the question, Why have the profit-makers got all this power, or at least why are they able to keep it?

That takes us to the third form of war commercial: the last, and the one which all the rest is founded on. We have spoken first of the war of rival nations; next of that of rival firms: we have now to speak of rival men. As nations under the present system are driven to compete with one another for the markets of the world, and as firms or the captains

---

[1]Falsely; because the privileged classes have at their back the force of the Executive by means of which to compel the unprivileged to accept the terms; if this is "free competition" there is no meaning in words.

of industry have to scramble for their share of the profits of the markets, so also have the workers to compete with each other—for livelihood; and it is this constant competition or war amongst them which enables the profit-grinders to make their profits, and by means of the wealth so acquired to take all the executive power of the country into their hands. But here is the difference between the position of the workers and the profit-makers: to the latter, the profit-grinders, war is necessary; you cannot have profit-making without competition, individual, corporate, and national; but you may work for a livelihood without competing; you may combine instead of competing.

I have said war was the life-breath of the profit-makers; in like manner, combination is the life of the workers. The working-classes or proletariat cannot even exist as a class without combination of some sort. The necessity which forced the profit-grinders to collect their men first into workshops working by the division of labour, and next into great factories worked by machinery, and so gradually draw them into the great towns and centres of civilization, gave birth to a distinct working-class or proletariat: and this it was which gave them their *mechanical* existence, so to say. But note, that they are indeed combined into social groups for the production of wares, but only as yet mechanically; they do not know what they are working at, nor whom they are working for, because they are combining to produce wares of which the profit of a master forms an essential part, instead of goods for their own use: as long as they do this, and compete with each other for leave to do it, they will be, and will feel themselves to be, simply a part of those competing firms I have been speaking of; they will be in fact just a part of the machinery for the production of profit; and so long as this lasts it will be the aim of the masters or profit-makers to decrease the market value of this human part of the machinery; that is to say, since they already hold in their hands the labour of dead men in the form of capital and machinery, it is their interest, or we will say their necessity, to pay as little as they can help for the labour of living men which they have to buy from day to day: and since the workmen they employ have nothing but their labour-power, they are compelled to underbid one another for employment and wages, and so enable the capitalist to play his game.

I have said that, as things go, the workers are a part of the competing firms, an adjunct of capital. Nevertheless, they are only so by compulsion; and, even without their being conscious of it, they struggle against that compulsion and its immediate results, the lowering of their wages, of their standard of life: and this they do, and must do, both as a class and individually: just as the slave of the great Roman lord, though he distinctly felt himself to be a part of the household, yet collectively was a force in reserve for its destruction, and individually stole from his lord whenever he could safely do so. So, here, you see, is another form of war necessary to the way we live now, the war of class against class, which, when it rises to its height, and it seems to be rising at present, will destroy those other forms of war we have been speaking of; will make the position of the profit-makers, of perpetual commercial war, untenable; will destroy the present system of competitive privilege, or commercial war.

Now observe, I said that to the existence of the workers it was combination, not competition, that was necessary, while to that of the profit-makers combination was impossible, and war necessary. The present position of the workers is that of the machinery of commerce, or in plainer words its slaves; when they change that position and become free, the class of profit-makers must cease to exist; and what will then be the position of the workers? Even as it is they are the one necessary part of society, the life-giving part; the other classes are but hangers-on who live on them. But what should they be, what will they be, when they, once for all, come to know their real power, and cease competing with one another for livelihood? I will tell you: they will be society, they will be the community. And being society—that is, there being no class outside them to contend with—they can then regulate their labour in accordance with their own real needs.

There is much talk about supply and demand, but the supply and demand usually meant is an artificial one; it is under the sway of the gambling market; the demand is forced, as I hinted above, before it is supplied; nor, as each producer is working against all the rest, can the producers hold their hands, till the market is glutted and the workers, thrown out on the streets, hear that there has been over-production, amidst which over-plus of unsaleable goods they go ill-supplied with even necessaries, because the wealth which they themselves have created is "ill-distri-buted," as we call it—that is, unjustly taken away from them.

When the workers are society they will regulate their labour, so that the supply and demand shall be genuine, not gambling; the two will then be commensurate, for it is the same society which demands that also supplies; there will be no more artificial famines then, no more poverty amidst over-production, amidst too great a stock of the very things which should supply poverty and turn it into well-being. In short, there will be no waste and therefore no tyranny.

Well, now, what Socialism offers you in place of these artificial famines, with their so-called over-production, is, once more, regulation of the markets; supply and demand commensurate; no gambling, and consequently (once more) no waste; not overwork and weariness for the worker one month, and the next no work and terror of starvation, but steady work and plenty of leisure every month; not cheap market wares, that is to say, adulterated wares, with scarcely any *good* in them, mere scaffold-poles for building up profits; no labour would be spent on such things as these, which people would cease to want when they ceased to be slaves. Not these, but such goods as best fulfilled the real uses of the consumers would labour be set to make; for, profit being abolished, people could have what they wanted, instead of what the profit-grinders at home and abroad forced them to take.

For what I want you to understand is this: that in every civilized country at least there is plenty for all—is, or at any rate might be. Even with labour so misdirected as it is at present, an equitable distribution of the wealth we have would make all people comparatively comfortable; but that is nothing to the wealth we might have if labour were not misdirected.

Observe, in the early days of the history of man he was

the slave of his most immediate necessities; Nature was mighty and he was feeble, and he had to wage constant war with her for his daily food and such shelter as he could get. His life was bound down and limited by this constant struggle; all his morals, laws, religion, are in fact the outcome and the reflection of this ceaseless toil of earning his livelihood. Time passed, and little by little, step by step, he grew stronger, till now after all these ages he has almost completely conquered Nature, and one would think should now have leisure to turn his thoughts towards higher things than procuring to-morrow's dinner. But, alas! his progress has been broken and halting; and though he has indeed conquered Nature and has her forces under his control to do what he will with, he still has himself to conquer, he still has to think how he will best use those forces which he has mastered. At present he uses them blindly, foolishly, as one driven by mere fate. It would almost seem as if some phantom of the ceaseless pursuit of food which was once the master of the savage was still hunting the civilized man; who toils in a dream, as it were, haunted by mere dim unreal hopes, borne of vague recollections of the days gone by. Out of that dream he must wake, and face things as they really are. The conquest of Nature is complete, may we not say? and now our business is and has for long been the organization of man, who wields the forces of Nature. Nor till this is attempted at least shall we ever be free of that terrible phantom of fear of starvation which, with its brother devil, desire of domination, drives us into injustice, cruelty, and dastardliness of all kinds: to cease to fear our fellows and learn to depend on them, to do away with competition and build up co-operation, is our one necessity.

Now, to get closer to details; you probably know that every man in civilization is worth, so to say, more than his skin; working, as he must work, socially, he can produce more than will keep himself alive and in fair condition; and this has been so for many centuries, from the time, in fact, when warring tribes began to make their conquered enemies slaves instead of killing them; and of course his capacity of producing these extras has gone on increasing faster and faster, till to-day one man will weave, for instance, as much cloth in a week as will clothe a whole village for years; and the real question of civilization has always been what are we to do with this extra produce of labour—a question which the phantom, fear of starvation, and its fellow, desire of domination, has driven men to answer pretty badly always, and worst of all perhaps in these present days, when the extra produce has grown with such prodigious speed. The practical answer has always been for man to struggle with his fellow for private possession of undue shares of these extras, and all kinds of devices have been employed by those who found themselves in possession of the power of taking them from others to keep those whom they had robbed in perpetual subjection; and these latter, as I have already hinted, had no chance of resisting this fleecing as long as they were few and scattered, and consequently could have little sense of their common oppression. But now that, owing to the very pursuit of these undue shares of profit, or extra earnings, men have become more dependent on each other for production, and have been driven, as I said before, to combine together for that end more completely, the power of the workers—that is to say, of the robbed or fleeced class— has enormously increased, and it only remains for them to understand that they have this power. When they do that they will be able to give the right answer to the question what is to be done with the extra products of labour over and above what will keep the labourer alive to labour: which answer is, that the worker will have all that he produces, and not be fleeced at all: and remember that he produces collectively, and therefore he will do effectively what work is required of him according to his capacity, and of the produce of that work he will have what he needs; because, you see, he cannot *use* more than he needs—he can only *waste* it.

If this arrangement seems to you preposterously ideal, as it well may, looking at our present condition, I must back it up by saying that when men are organized so that their labour is not wasted, they will be relieved from the fear of starvation and the desire of domination, and will have freedom and leisure to look round and see what they really do need.

U

Now something of that I can conceive for my own self, and I will lay my ideas before you, so that you may compare them with your own, asking you always to remember that the very differences in men's capacities and desires, after the common need of food and shelter is satisfied, will make it easier to deal with their desires in a communal state of things.

What is it that I need, therefore, which my surrounding circumstances can give me—my dealings with my fellowmen—setting aside inevitable accidents which co-operation and forethought cannot control, if there be such?

Well, first of all I claim good health; and I say that a vast proportion of people in civilization scarcely even know what that means. To feel mere life a pleasure; to enjoy the moving one's limbs and exercising one's bodily powers; to play, as it were, with sun and wind and rain; to rejoice in satisfying the due bodily appetites of a human animal without fear of degradation or sense of wrong-doing: yes, and therewithal to be well-formed, straight-limbed, strongly knit, expressive of countenance—to be, in a word, beautiful—that also I claim. If we cannot have this claim satisfied, we are but poor creatures after all; and I claim it in the teeth of those terrible doctrines of asceticism, which, born of the despair of the oppressed and degraded, have been for so many ages used as instruments for the continuance of that oppression and degradation.

And I believe that this claim for a healthy body for all of us carries with it all other due claims: for who knows where the seeds of disease which even rich people suffer from were first sown: from the luxury of an ancestor, perhaps; yet often, I suspect, from his poverty. And for the poor: a distinguished physicist has said that the poor suffer always from one disease—hunger; and at least I know this, that if a man is overworked in any degree he cannot enjoy the sort of health I am speaking of; nor can he if he is continually chained to one dull round of mechanical work, with no hope at the other end of it; nor if he lives in continual sordid anxiety for his livelihood, nor if he is ill-housed, nor if he is deprived of all enjoyment of the natural beauty of the world, nor if he has no amusement to quicken the flow of his spirits from time to time: all these things, which touch

more or less directly on his bodily condition, are born of
the claim I make to live in good health; indeed, I suspect
that these good conditions must have been in force for
several generations before a population in general will be
really healthy, as I have hinted above; but also I doubt not
that in the course of time they would, joined to other conditions, of which more hereafter, gradually breed such a
population, living in enjoyment of animal life at least,
happy therefore, and beautiful according to the beauty of
their race. On this point I may note that the very varia-
tions in the races of men are caused by the conditions under
which they live, and though in these rougher parts of the
world we lack some of the advantages of climate and surroundings, yet, if we were working for livelihood and not
for profit, we might easily neutralize many of the disad-
vantages of our climate, at least enough to give due scope
to the full development of our race.

Now the next thing I claim is education. And you must
not say that every English child is educated now; that sort
of education will not answer my claim, though I cheerfully
admit it is something: something, and yet after all only
class education. What I claim is liberal education; opportunity, that is, to have my share of whatever knowledge
there is in the world according to my capacity or bent of
mind, historical or scientific; and also to have my share
of skill of hand which is about in the world, either in the
industrial handicrafts or in the fine arts; picture-painting,
sculpture, music, acting, or the like: I claim to be taught,
if I can be taught, more than one craft to exercise for the
benefit of the community. You may think this a large
claim, but I am clear it is not too large a claim if the community is to have any gain out of my special capacities, if
we are not all to be beaten down to a dull level of medi-
ocrity as we are now, all but the very strongest and toughest
of us.

But also I know that this claim for education involves
one for public advantages in the shape of public libraries,
schools, and the like, such as no private person, not even
the richest, could command: but these I claim very con-
fidently, being sure that no reasonable community could
bear to be without such helps to a decent life.

Again, the claim for education involves a claim for abundant leisure, which once more I make with confidence; because when once we have shaken off the slavery of profit, labour would be organized so unwastefully that no heavy burden would be laid on the individual citizens; every one of whom as a matter of course would have to pay his toll of some obviously useful work. At present you must note that all the amazing machinery which we have invented has served only to increase the amount of profit-bearing wares; in other words, to increase the amount of profit pouched by individuals for their own advantage, part of which profit they use as capital for the production of more profit, with ever the same waste attached to it; and part as private riches or means for luxurious living, which again is sheer waste—is in fact to be looked on as a kind of bonfire on which rich men burn up the product of the labour they have fleeced from the workers beyond what they themselves can use. So I say that, in spite of our inventions, no worker works under the present system an hour the less on account of those labour-saving machines, so-called. But under a happier state of things they would be used simply for saving labour, with the result of a vast amount of leisure gained for the community to be added to that gained by the avoidance of the waste of useless luxury, and the abolition of the service of commercial war.

And I may say that as to that leisure, as I should in no case do any harm to any one with it, so I should often do some direct good to the community with it, by practising arts or occupations for my hands or brain which would give pleasure to many of the citizens; in other words, a great deal of the best work done would be done in the leisure time of men relieved from any anxiety as to their livelihood, and eager to exercise their special talent, as all men, nay, all animals are.

Now, again this leisure would enable me to please myself and expand my mind by travelling if I had a mind to it; because, say, for instance, that I were a shoemaker; if due social order were established, it by no means follows that I should always be obliged to make shoes in one place; a due amount of easily conceivable arrangement would enable me to make shoes in Rome, say, for three months, and to come back with new ideas of building, gathered from the sight of the works of past ages, amongst other things which would perhaps be of service in London.

But now, in order that my leisure might not degenerate into idleness and aimlessness, I must set up a claim for due work to do. Nothing to my mind is more important than this demand, and I must ask your leave to say something about it. I have mentioned that I should probably use my leisure for doing a good deal of what is now called work; but it is clear that if I am a member of a Socialist Community I must do my due share of rougher work than this— my due share of what my capacity enables me to do, that is; no fitting of me to a Procrustean bed; but even that share of work necessary to the existence of the simplest social life must, in the first place, whatever else it is, be reasonable work; that is, it must be such work as a good citizen can see the necessity for; as a member of the community, I must have agreed to do it.

To take two strong instances of the contrary, I won't submit to be dressed up in red and marched off to shoot at my French or German or Arab friend in a quarrel that I don't understand; I will rebel sooner than do that.

Nor will I submit to waste my time and energies in making some trifling toy which I know only a fool can desire; I will rebel sooner than do that.

However, you may be sure that in a state of social order I shall have no need to rebel against any such pieces of unreason; only I am forced to speak from the way we live to the way we might live.

Again, if the necessary reasonable work be of a mechanical kind, I must be helped to do it by a machine, not to cheapen my labour, but so that as little time as possible may be spent upon it, and that I may be able to think of other things while I am tending the machine. And if the work be specially rough or exhausting, you will, I am sure, agree with me in saying that I must take turns in doing it with other people; I mean I mustn't, for instance, be expected to spend my working hours always at the bottom of a coal-pit. I think such work as that ought to be largely volunteer work, and done, as I say, in spells. And what I say of very rough work I say also of nasty work. On the other hand, I should think very little of the manhood of a stout and healthy man who did not feel a pleasure in doing rough work; always supposing him to work under the conditions I have been speaking of—namely, feeling that it was useful (and consequently honoured), and that it was not continuous or hopeless, and that he was really doing it of his own free will.

The last claim I make for my work is that the places I worked in, factories or workshops, should be pleasant, just as the fields where our most necessary work is done are pleasant. Believe me there is nothing in the world to prevent this being done, save the necessity of making profits on all wares; in other words, the wares are cheapened at the expense of people being forced to work in crowded, unwholesome, squalid, noisy dens: that is to say, they are cheapened at the expense of the workman's life.

Well, so much for my claims as to my *necessary* work, my tribute to the community. I believe people would find, as they advanced in their capacity for carrying on social order, that life so lived was much less expensive than we now can have any idea of, and that, after a little, people would rather be anxious to seek work than to avoid it; that our working hours would rather be merry parties of men and maids, young men and old enjoying themselves over their work, than the grumpy weariness it mostly is now. Then would come the time for the new birth of art, so much talked of, so long deferred; people could not help showing their mirth and pleasure in their work, and would be always wishing to express it in a tangible and more or less enduring form, and the workshop would once more be a school of art, whose influence no one could escape from.

And, again, that word art leads me to my last claim, which is that the material surroundings of my life should be pleasant, generous, and beautiful; that I know is a large claim, but this I will say about it, that if it cannot be satisfied, if every civilized community cannot provide such surroundings for all its members, I do not want the world to go on; it is a mere misery that man has ever existed. I do not think it possible under the present circumstances to speak too strongly on this point. I feel sure that the time will come when people will find it difficult to believe that a rich community such as ours, having such command over external Nature, could have submitted to live such a mean, shabby, dirty life as we do.

And once for all, there is nothing in our circumstances save the hunting of profit that drives us into it. It is profit which draws men into enormous unmanageable aggregations called towns, for instance; profit which crowds them up when they are there into quarters without gardens or open spaces; profit which won't take the most ordinary precautions against wrapping a whole district in a cloud of sulphurous smoke; which turns beautiful rivers into filthy sewers; which condemns all but the rich to live in houses idiotically cramped and confined at the best, and at the worst in houses for whose wretchedness there is no name.

I say it is almost incredible that we should bear such crass stupidity as this; nor should we if we could help it. We shall not bear it when the workers get out of their heads that they are but an appendage to profit-grinding, that the more profits that are made the more employment at high wages there will be for them, and that therefore all the increditable filth, disorder, and degradation of modern civilization are signs of their prosperity. So far from that, they are signs of their slavery. When they are no longer slaves they will claim as a matter of course that every man and every family should be generously lodged; that every child should be able to play in a garden close to the place his parents live in; that the houses should by their obvious decency and order be ornaments to Nature, not disfigurements of it; for the decency and order above-mentioned when carried to the due pitch would most assuredly lead to beauty in building. All this, of course, would mean the people—that is, all society—duly organised, having in its own hands the means of production, to be *owned* by no individual, but used by all as occasion called for its use, and can only be done on those terms; on any other terms people will be driven to accumulate private wealth for themselves, and thus, as we have seen, to waste the goods of the community and perpetuate the division into classes, which means continual war and waste.

As to what extent it may be necessary or desirable for

people under social order to live in common, we may differ pretty much according to our tendencies towards social life. For my part I can't see why we should think it a hardship to eat with the people we work with; I am sure that as to many things, such as valuable books, pictures, and splendour of surroundings, we shall find it better to club our means together; and I must say that often when I have been sickened by the stupidity of the mean idiotic rabbit warrens that rich men build for themselves in Bayswater and elsewhere, I console myself with visions of the noble communal hall of the future, unsparing of materials, generous in worthy ornament, alive with the noblest thoughts of our time, and the past, embodied in the best art which a free and manly people could produce; such an abode of man as no private enterprise could come anywhere near for beauty and fitness, because only collective thought and collective life could cherish the aspirations which would give birth to its beauty, or have the skill and leisure to carry them out. I for my part should think it much the reverse of a hardship if I had to read my books and meet my friends in such a place; nor do I think I am better off to live in a vulgar stuccoed house crowded with upholstery that I despise, in all respects degrading to the mind and enervating to the body to live in, simply because I call it my own, or my house.

It is not an original remark, but I make it here, that my home is where I meet people with whom I sympathise, whom I love.

Well, that is my opinion as a middle-class man. Whether a working-class man would think his family possession of his wretched little room better than his share of the palace of which I have spoken, I must leave to his opinion, and to the imaginations of the middle class, who perhaps may sometimes conceive the fact that the said worker is cramped for space and comfort—say on washing-day.

Before I leave this matter of the suroundings of life, I wish to meet a possible objection. I have spoken of machinery being used freely for releasing people from the more mechanical and repulsive part of necessary labour; and I know that to some cultivated people, people of the artistic turn of mind, machinery is particularly distasteful, and they will be apt to say you will never get your surroundings pleasant so long as you are surrounded by machinery. I don't quite admit that; it is the allowing machines to be our masters and not our servants that so injures the beauty of life nowadays. In other words, it is the token of the terrible crime we have fallen into of using our control of the powers of Nature for the purpose of enslaving people, we careless meantime of how much happiness we rob their lives of.

Yet for the consolation of the artists I will say that I believe indeed that a state of social order would probably lead at first to a great development of machinery for really useful purposes, because people will still be anxious about getting through the work necessary to holding society together; but that after a while they will find that there is not so much work to do as they expected, and that then they will have leisure to reconsider the whole subject; and if it seems to them that a certain industry would be carried on more pleasantly as regards the worker, and more effectually as regards the goods, by using hand-work rather than machinery, they will certainly get rid of their machinery, because it will be possible for them to do so. It isn't possible now; we are not at liberty to do so; we are slaves to the monsters which we have created. And I have a kind of hope that the very elaboration of machinery in a society whose purpose is not the multiplication of labour, as it now is, but the carrying on of a pleasant life, as it would be under social order—that the elaboration of machinery, I say, will lead to the simplification of life, and so once more to the limitation of machinery.

Well, I will now let my claims for decent life stand as I have made them. To sum them up in brief, they are: First, a healthy body; second, an active mind in sympathy with the past, the present, and the future; thirdly, occupation fit for a healthy body and an active mind; and fourthly, a beautiful world to live in.

These are the conditions of life which the refined man of all ages has set before him as the thing above all others to be attained. Too often he has been so foiled in their pursuit that he has turned longing eyes backward to the days before civilization, when man's sole business was getting himself food from day to day, and hope was dormant in him, or at least could not be expressed by him.

Indeed, if civilization (as many think) forbids the realization of the hope to attain such conditions of life, then civilization forbids mankind to be happy; and if that be the case, then let us stifle all aspirations towards progress— nay, all feelings of mutual good-will and affection between men—and snatch each one of us what we can from the heap of wealth that fools create for rogues to grow fat on; or better still, let us as speedily as possible find some means of dying like men, since we are forbidden to live like men.

Rather, however, take courage, and believe that we of this age, in spite of all its torment and disorder, have been born to a wonderful heritage fashioned of the work of those that have gone before us; and that the day of the organization of man is dawning. It is not we who can build up the new social order; the past ages have done the most of that work for us; but we can clear our eyes to the signs of the times, and we shall then see that the attainment of a good condition of life is being made possible for us, and that it is now our business to stretch out our hands to take it.

And how? Chiefly, I think, by educating people to a sense of their real capacities as men, so that they may be able to use to their own good the political power which is rapidly being thrust upon them; to get them to see that the old system of organizing labour *for individual profit* is becoming unmanageable, and that the whole people have now got to choose between the confusion resulting from the break up of that system and the determination to take in hand the labour now organized for profit, and use its organization for the livelihood of the community: to get people to see that individual profit-makers are not a necessity for labour but an obstruction to it, and that not only or chiefly because they are the perpetual pensioners of labour, as they are, but rather because of the waste which their existence as a class necessitates. All this we have to teach people, when we have taught ourselves; and I admit that the work is long and burdensome; as I began by saying, people have been made so timorous of change by the terror of starvation that even the unluckiest of them are stolid and hard to move.

Hard as the work is, however, its reward is not doubtful. The mere fact that a body of men, however small, are banded together as Socialist missionaries shows that the change is going on. As the working-classes, the real organic part of society, take in these ideas, hope will arise in them, and they will claim changes in society, many of which doubtless will not tend directly towards their emancipation, because they will be claimed without due knowledge of the one thing necessary to claim, *equality of condition*; but which indirectly will help to break up our rotten sham society, while that claim for equality of condition will be made constantly and with growing loudness till it *must* be listened to, and then at last it will only be a step over the border, and the civilised world will be socialised; and, looking back on what has been, we shall be astonished to think of how long we submitted to live as we live now.

THE AIMS OF ART

IN considering the Aims of Art, that is, why men toil-
somely cherish and practise Art, I find myself compelled
to generalize from the only specimen of humanity of
which I know anything; to wit, myself. Now, when I think of
what it is that I desire, I find that I can give it no other
name than happiness. I want to be happy while I live;
for as for death, I find that, never having experienced it,
I have no conception of what it means, and so cannot
even bring my mind to bear upon it. I know what it is to
live; I cannot even guess what it is to be dead. Well, then,
I want to be happy, and even sometimes, say generally,
to be merry; and I find it difficult to believe that that is
not the universal desire: so that, whatever tends towards
that end I cherish with all my best endeavour. Now, when
I consider my life further, I find out, or seem to, that it
is under the influence of two dominating moods, which
for lack of better words I must call the mood of energy
and the mood of idleness: these two moods are now one,
now the other, always crying out in me to be satisfied.
When the mood of energy is upon me, I must be doing
something, or I become mopish and unhappy; when the
mood of idleness is on me, I find it hard indeed if I cannot
rest and let my mind wander over the various pictures,
pleasant or terrible, which my own experience or my
communing with the thoughts of other men, dead or alive,
have fashioned in it; and if circumstances will not allow
me to cultivate this mood of idleness, I find I must at the
best pass through a period of pain till I can manage to
stimulate my mood of energy to take its place and make
me happy again. And if I have no means wherewith to

588

rouse up that mood of energy to do its duty in making me happy, and I have to toil while the idle mood is upon me, then am I unhappy indeed, and almost wish myself dead, though I do not know what that means.

Furthermore, I find that while in the mood of idleness memory amuses me, in the mood of energy hope cheers me; which hope is sometimes big and serious, and sometimes trivial, but that without it there is no happy energy. Again, I find that while I can sometimes satisfy this mood by merely exercising it in work that has no result beyond the passing hour—in play, in short—yet that it presently wearies of that and gets languid, the hope therein being too trivial, and sometimes even scarcely real; and that on the whole, to satisfy my master the mood, I must either be making something or making believe to make it.

Well, I believe that all men's lives are compounded of these two moods in various proportions, and that this explains why they have always, with more or less of toil, cherished and practised art.

Why should they have touched it else, and so added to the labour which they could not choose but do in order to live? It must have been done for their pleasure, since it has only been in very elaborate civilizations that a man could get other men to keep him alive merely to produce works of art, whereas all men that have left any signs of their existence behind them have practised art.

I suppose, indeed, that nobody will be inclined to deny that the end proposed by a work of art is always to please the person whose senses are to be made conscious of it. It was done *for* some one who was to be made happier by it; his idle or restful mood was to be amused by it, so that the vacancy which is the besetting evil of that mood might give place to pleased contemplation, dreaming, or what you will; and by this means he would not so soon be driven into his workful or energetic mood: he would have more enjoyment, and better.

The restraining of restlessness, therefore, is clearly one of the essential aims of art, and few things could add to the pleasure of life more than this. There are, to my knowledge, gifted people now alive who have no other vice than this of restlessness, and seemingly no other curse in their lives to make them unhappy: but that is enough; it is "the little rift within the lute." Restlessness makes them hapless men and bad citizens.

But granting, as I suppose you all will do, that this is a most important function for art to fulfil, the question next comes, at what price do we obtain it? I have admitted that the practice of art has added to the labour of mankind, though I believe in the long run it will not do so; but in adding to the labour of man has it added, so far, to his pain? There always have been people who would at once say yes to that question; so that there have been and are two sets of people who dislike and contemn art as an embarrassing folly. Besides the pious ascetics, who look upon it as a worldly entanglement which prevents men from keeping their minds fixed on the chances of their individual happiness or misery in the next world; who, in short, hate art, because they think that it adds to man's earthly happiness—besides these, there are also people who, looking on the struggle of life from the most reasonable point that they know of, contemn the arts because they think that they add to man's slavery by increasing the sum of his painful labour: if this were the case, it would still, to my mind, be a question whether it might not be worth the while to endure the extra pain of labour for the sake of the extra pleasure added to rest; assuming, for the present, equality of condition among men. But it seems to me that it is not the case that the practice of art adds to painful labour; nay more, I believe that, if it did, art would never have arisen at all, would certainly not be discernible, as it is, among peoples in whom only the germs of civilization exist. In other words, I believe that art cannot be the result of external compulsion; the labour which goes to produce it is voluntary, and partly undertaken for the sake of the labour itself, partly for the sake of the hope of producing something which, when done, shall give pleasure to the user of it. Or, again, this extra labour, when it *is* extra, is undertaken with the aim of satisfying that mood of energy by employing it to produce something worth doing, and which, therefore, will keep before the worker a lively hope while he is working; and also by giving it work to do in which there is absolute immediate pleasure. Perhaps it is difficult to explain to the non-artistic capacity that this definite sensuous pleasure is always present in the handiwork of the deft workman when he is working successfully, and that it increases in proportion to the freedom and individuality of the work. Also you must understand that this production of art, and consequent pleasure in work, is not confined to the production of matters which are works of art only, like pictures, statues, and so forth, but has been and should be a part of all labour in some form or other: so only will the claims of the mood of energy be satisfied.

Therefore the Aim of Art is to increase the happiness of men, by giving them beauty and interest of incident to amuse their leisure, and prevent them wearying even of rest, and by giving them hope and bodily pleasure in their work; or, shortly, to make man's work happy and his rest fruitful. Consequently, genuine art is an unmixed blessing to the race of man.

But as the word "genuine" is a large qualification, I must ask leave to attempt to draw some practical conclusions from this assertion of the.Aims of Art, which will, I suppose, or indeed hope, lead us into some controversy on the subject; because it is futile indeed to expect any one to speak about art, except in the most superficial way, without encountering those social problems which all serious men are thinking of; since art is and must be, either in its abundance or its barrenness, in its sincerity or its hollowness, the expression of the society amongst which it exists.

First, then, it is clear to me that, at the present time, those who look widest at things and deepest into them are quite dissatisfied with the present state of the arts, as they are also with the present condition of society. This I say in the teeth of the supposed revivification of art which has taken place of late years: in fact, that very excitement about the arts amongst a part of the cultivated people of to-day does but show on how firm a basis the dissatisfaction above mentioned rests. Forty years ago there was much less talk about art, much less practice of it, than there is now; and that is specially true of the architectural arts, which I shall mostly have to speak about now. People have consciously striven to raise the dead in art since that time, and with some superficial success. Nevertheless, in spite of this conscious effort, I must tell you that England, to a person who can feel and understand beauty, was a less grievous place to live in then than it is now; and we who feel what art means know well, though we do not often dare to say so, that forty years hence it will be a more grievous place to us than it is now if we still follow up the road we are on. Less than forty years ago—about thirty—I first saw the city of Rouen, then still in its outward aspect a piece of the Middle Ages: no words can tell you how its mingled beauty, history, and romance took hold on me; I can only say that, looking back on my past life, I find it was the greatest pleasure I have ever had: and now it is a pleasure which no one can ever have again: it is lost to the world for ever. At that time I was an undergraduate of Oxford. Though not so astounding, so romantic, or at first sight so mediæval as the Norman city, Oxford in those days still kept a great deal of its earlier loveliness: and the memory of its grey streets as they then were has been an abiding influence and pleasure in my life, and would be greater still if I could only forget what they are now—a matter of far more importance than the so-called learning of the place could have been to me in any case, but which, as it was, no one tried to teach me, and I did not try to learn. Since then the guardians of this beauty and romance so fertile of education, though professedly engaged in "the higher education" (as the futile system of compromises which they follow is nick-named), have ignored it utterly, have made its preservation give way to the pressure of commercial exigencies, and are determined apparently to destroy it altogether. There is another pleasure for the world gone down the wind; here, again, the beauty and romance have been uselessly, causelessly, most foolishly thrown away.

These two cases are given simply because they have been fixed in my mind; they are but types of what is going on everywhere throughout civilization: the world is everywhere growing uglier and more commonplace, in spite of the conscious and very strenuous efforts of a small group of people towards the revival of art, which are so obviously out of joint with the tendency of the age that, while the uncultivated have not even heard of them, the mass of the cultivated look upon them as a joke, and even that they are now beginning to get tired of.

Now, if it be true, as I have asserted, that genuine art is an unmixed blessing to the world, this is a serious matter; for at first sight it seems to show that there will soon be no art at all in the world, which will thus lose an unmixed blessing; it can ill afford to do that, I think.

For art, if it has to die, has worn itself out, and its aim will be a thing forgotten; and its aim was to make work happy and rest fruitful. Is all work to be unhappy, all rest unfruitful, then? Indeed, if art is to perish, that will be the case, unless something is to take its place—something at present unnamed, undreamed of.

I do not think that anything will take the place of art; not that I doubt the ingenuity of man, which seems to be boundless in the direction of making himself unhappy, but because I believe the springs of art in the human mind to be deathless, and also because it seems to me easy to see the causes of the present obliteration of the arts.

For we civilized people have not given them up consciously, or of our free will; we have been *forced* to give them up. Perhaps I can illustrate that by the detail of the application of machinery to the production of things in which artistic form of some sort is possible. Why does a reasonable man use a machine? Surely to save his labour. There are some things which a machine can do as well as a man's hand, *plus* a tool, can do them. He need not, for instance, grind his corn in a hand quern; a little trickle of water, a wheel, and a few simple contrivances will do it all perfectly well, and leave him free to smoke his pipe and think, or to carve the handle of his knife. That, so far, is unmixed gain in the use of a machine—always, mind you, supposing equality of condition among men; no art is lost, leisure or time for more pleasurable work is gained. Perhaps a perfectly reasonable and free man would stop there in his dealings with machinery; but such reason and freedom are too much to expect, so let us follow our machine-inventor a step farther. He has to weave plain cloth, and finds doing so dullish on the one hand, and on the other that a power-loom will weave the cloth nearly as well as a hand-loom: so, in order to gain more leisure or time for more pleasureable work, he uses a power-loom, and foregoes the small advantage of the little extra art in the cloth. But so doing, as far as the art is concerned, he has not got a pure gain; he has made a bargain between art and labour, and got a makeshift as a consequence. I do not say that he may not be right in so doing, but that he has lost as well as gained. Now, this is as far as a man who values art and is reasonable would go in the matter of machinery *as long as he was free*— that is, was not *forced* to work for another man's profit; so long as he was living in a society *that had accepted equality of condition*. Carry the machine used for art a step farther, and he becomes an unreasonable man, if he values art and is free. To avoid misunderstanding, I must say that I am thinking of the modern machine, which is as it were alive, and to which the man is auxiliary, and not of the old machine, the improved tool, which is auxiliary to the man, and only works as long as his hand is thinking; though I will remark, that even this elementary form of machine has to be dropped when we come to the higher and more intricate forms of art. Well, as to the machine proper used for art, when it gets to the stage above dealing with a necessary production that has accidentally some beauty about it, a reasonable man with a feeling for art will only use it when he is *forced* to. If he thinks he would like ornament, for instance, and knows that the machine cannot do it properly, and does not care to spend the time to do it properly, why should he do it at all? He will not diminish his leisure for the sake of making something he does not want unless some man or band of men force him to it; so he will either go without the ornament, or sacrifice some of his leisure to have it genuine. That will be a sign that he wants it very much, and that it will be worth his trouble: in which case, again, his labour on it will not be mere trouble, but will interest and please him by satisfying the needs of his mood of energy.

This, I say, is how a reasonable man would act if he were free from man's compulsion; not being free, he acts very differently. He has long passed the stage at which machines are only used for doing work repulsive to an average man, or for doing what could be as well done by a machine as a man, and he instinctively expects a machine to be invented whenever any product of industry becomes sought after. He is the slave to machinery; the new machine *must* be invented, and when invented he *must*—I will not say use it, but be used by it, whether he likes it or not.

But why is he the slave to machinery? Because he is the slave to the system for whose existence the invention of machinery was necessary.

And now I must drop, or rather have dropped, the assumption of the equality of condition, and remind you that, though in a sense we are all the slaves of machinery, yet that some men are so directly without any metaphor at all, and that these are just those on whom the great body of the arts depends—the workmen. It is necessary for the system which keeps them in their position as an inferior class that they should either be themselves machines or be the servants to machines, in no case having any interest in the work which they turn out. To their employers they are, so far as they are workmen, a part of the machinery of the workshop or the factory; to themselves they are proletarians, human beings working to live that they may live to work: their part of craftsmen, of makers of things by their own free will, is played out.

At the risk of being accused of sentimentality, I will say that since this is so, since the work which produces the things that should be matters of art is but a burden and a slavery, I exult in this at least, that it cannot produce art; that all it can do lies between stark utilitarianism and idiotic sham.

Or indeed is that merely sentimental? Rather, I think, we who have learned to see the connection between industrial slavery and the degradation of the arts have learned also to hope for a future for those arts; since the day will certainly come when men will shake off the yoke, and refuse to accept the mere artificial compulsion of the gambling market to waste their lives in ceaseless and hopeless toil, and when it does come, their instincts for beauty and imagination set free along with them, will produce such art as they need; and who can say that it will not as far surpass the art of past ages as that does the poor relics of it left us by the age of commerce?

A word or two on an objection which has often been made to me when I have been talking on this subject. It may be said, and is often, You regret the art of the Middle Ages (as indeed I do), but those who produced it were not free, they were serfs, or gild-craftsmen surrounded by brazen walls of trade restrictions; they had no political rights, and were exploited by their masters, the noble caste, most grievously. Well, I quite admit that the oppression and violence of the Middle Ages had its effect on the art of those days, its shortcomings are traceable to them; they repressed art in certain directions, I do not doubt that; and for that reason I say, that when we shake off the present oppression as we shook off the old, we may expect the art of the days of real freedom to rise above that of those old violent days. But I do say that it was possible then to have social, organic, hopeful progressive art; whereas now such poor scraps of it as are left are the result of individual and wasteful struggle, are retrospective and pessimistic. And this hopeful art was possible amidst all the oppression of those days, because the instruments of that oppression were grossly obvious, and were external to the work of the craftsman. They were laws and customs obviously intended to rob him, and open violence of the highway-robbery kind. In short, industrial production was not the instrument used for robbing the "lower classes"; it is now the main instrument used in that honourable profession. The mediæval craftsman was free on his work, therefore he made it as amusing to himself as he could; and it was his pleasure and not his pain that made all things beautiful that were made, and lavished treasures of human hope and thought on everything that man made, from a cathedral to a porridge-pot. Come, let us put it in the way least respectful to the mediæval craftsman, most polite to the modern "hand": the poor devil of the fourteenth century, his work was of so little value that he was allowed to waste it by the hour in pleasing himself—and others; but our highly-strung mechanic, his minutes are too rich with the burden of perpetual profit for him to be allowed to waste one of them on art; the present system will not allow him—cannot allow him—to produce works of art.

So that there has arisen this strange phenomenon, that there is now a class of ladies and gentlemen, very refined indeed, though not perhaps as well informed as is generally supposed, and of this refined class there are many who do really love beauty and incident—*i.e.*, art—and would make sacrifices to get it; and these are led by artists of great manual skill and high intellect, forming altogether a large body of demand for the article. And yet the supply does not come. Yes, and moreover, this great body of enthusiastic demanders are no mere poor and helpless people, ignorant fisher-peasants, half-mad monks, scatter-brained sansculottes—none of those, in short, the expression of whose needs has shaken the world so often before, and will do yet again. No, they are of the ruling classes, the masters of men, who can live without labour, and have abundant leisure to scheme out the fulfilment of their desires; and yet I say they cannot have the art which they so much long for, though they hunt it about the world so hard, sentimentalizing the sordid lives of the miserable peasants of Italy and the starving proletarians of her towns, now that all the picturesqueness has departed from the poor devils of our own country-side, and of our own slums. Indeed, there is little of reality left them anywhere, and that little is fast fading away before the needs of the manufacturer and his ragged regiment of workers, and before the enthusiasm of the archæological restorer of the dead past. Soon there will be nothing left except the lying dreams of history, the miserable wreckage of our museums and picture-galleries, and the carefully guarded interiors of our æsthetic drawing-rooms, unreal and foolish, fitting witnesses of the life of corruption that goes on there, so pinched and meagre and cowardly, with its concealment and ignoring, rather than restraint of, natural longings; which does not forbid the greedy indulgence in them if it can but be decently hidden.

The art then is gone, and can no more be "restored" on its old lines than a mediæval building can be. The rich and refined cannot have it though they would, and though we will believe many of them would. And why? Because those who could give it to the rich are not allowed by the rich to do so. In one word, slavery lies between us and art.

I have said as much as that the aim of art was to destroy the curse of labour by making work the pleasurable satisfaction of our impulse towards energy, and giving to that energy hope of producing something worth its exercise.

Now, therefore, I say, that since we cannot have art by striving after its mere superficial manifestation, since we can have nothing but its sham by so doing, there yet remains for us to see how it would be if we let the shadow take care of itself and try, if we can, to lay hold of the substance. For my part I believe, that if we try to realize the aims of art without much troubling ourselves what the aspect of the art itself shall be, we shall find we shall have what we want at last: whether it is to be called art or not, it will at least be *life*; and, after all, that is what we want. It may lead us into new splendours and beauties of visible art; to architecture with manifolded magnificence free from the curious incompleteness and failings of that which the older times have produced—to painting, uniting to the beauty which mediæval art attained the realism which modern art aims at; to sculpture, uniting the beauty of the Greek and the expression of the Renaissance with some third quality yet undiscovered, so as to give us the images of men and women splendidly alive, yet not disqualified from making, as all true sculpture should, architectural ornament. All this it may do; or, on the other hand, it may lead us into the desert, and art may seem to be dead amidst us; or feebly and uncertainly to be struggling in a world which has utterly forgotten its old glories.

For my part, with art as it now is, I cannot bring myself to think that it much matters which of these dooms awaits it, so long as each bears with it some hope of what is to come; since here, as in other matters, there is no hope save in Revolution. The old art is no longer fertile, no longer yields us anything save elegantly poetical regrets; being barren, it has but to die, and the matter of moment now is, as to how it shall die, whether *with* hope or *without* it.

What is it, for instance, that has destroyed the Rouen, the Oxford of *my* elegant poetic regret? Has it perished for the benefit of the people, either slowly yielding to the growth of intelligent change and new happiness? or has it been, as it were, thunderstricken by the tragedy which mostly accompanies some great new birth? Not so. Neither phalangstere nor dynamite has swept its beauty away, its destroyers have not been either the philanthropist or the Socialist, the co-operator or the anarchist. It has been sold, and at a cheap price indeed: muddled away by the greed and incompetence of fools who do not know what life and pleasure mean, who will neither take them themselves nor let others have them. That is why the death of that beauty wounds us so: no man of sense or feeling would dare to regret such losses if they had been paid for by new life and happiness for the people. But there is the people still as it was before, still facing for its part the monster who destroyed all that beauty, and whose name is Commercial Profit.

I repeat, that every scrap of genuine art will fall by the same hands if the matter only goes on long enough, although a sham art may be left in its place, which may very well be carried on by *dilettanti* fine gentlemen and ladies without any help from below; and, to speak plainly, I fear that this gibbering ghost of the real thing would satisfy a great many of those who now think themselves lovers of art; though it is not difficult to see a long vista of its degradation till it shall become at last a mere laughing-stock; that is to say, if the thing were to go on: I mean, if art were to be for ever the amusement of those whom we now call ladies and gentlemen.

But for my part I do not think it will go on long enough to reach such depths as that; and yet I should be hypocritical if I were to say that I thought that the change in the basis of society, which would enfranchise labour and make men practically equal in condition, would lead us by a short road to the splendid new birth of art which I have mentioned, though I feel quite certain that it would not leave what we now call art untouched, since the aims of that revolution do include the aims of art—viz., abolishing the curse of labour.

I suppose that this is what is likely to happen; that machinery will go on developing, with the purpose of saving men labour, till the mass of the people attain real leisure enough to be able to appreciate the pleasure of life; till, in fact, they have attained such mastery over Nature that they no longer fear starvation as a penalty for not working more than enough. When they get to that point they will doubtless turn themselves and begin to find out what it is that they really want to do. They would soon find out that the less work they did (the less work unaccompanied by art, I mean), the more desirable a dwelling-place the earth would be; they would accordingly do less and less work, till the mood of energy, of which I began by speaking, urged them on afresh: but by that time Nature, relieved by the relaxation of man's work, would be recovering her ancient beauty, and be teaching men the old story of art. And as the Artificial Famine, caused by men working for the profit of a master, and which we now look upon as a matter of course, would have long disappeared, they would be free to do as they chose, and they would set aside their machines in all cases where the work seemed pleasant or desirable for handiwork; till in all crafts where production of beauty was required, the most direct communication between a man's hand and his brain would be sought for. And there would be many occupations also, as the processes of agriculture, in which the voluntary exercise of energy would be thought so delightful, that people would not dream of handing over its, pleasure to the jaws of a machine.

In short, men will find out that the men of our days were wrong in first multiplying their needs, and then trying, each man of them, to evade all participation in the means and processes whereby those needs are satisfied; that this kind of division of labour is really only a new and wilful form of arrogant and slothful ignorance, far more injurious to the happiness and contentment of life than the ignorance of the processes of Nature, of what we sometimes call *science*, which men of the earlier days unwittingly lived in.

They will discover, or rediscover rather, that the true secret of happiness *lies in the taking a genuine interest in all the details of daily life*, in elevating them by art instead of handing the performance of them over to unregarded drudges, and ignoring them; and that in cases where it was impossible either so to elevate them and make them interesting, or to lighten them by the use of machinery, so as to make the labour of them trifling, that should be taken as a token that the supposed advantages gained by them were not worth the trouble and had better be given up. All this to my mind would be the outcome of men throwing off the burden of Artificial Famine, supposing, as I cannot help supposing, that the impulses which have from the first glimmerings of history urged men on to the practice of Art were still at work in them.

Thus and thus only *can* come about the new birth of Art, and I think it *will* come about thus. You may say it is a long process, and so it is; but I can conceive of a longer. I have given you the Socialist or Optimist view of the matter. Now for the Pessimist view.

I can conceive that the revolt against Artificial Famine or Capitalism, which is now on foot, may be vanquished. The result will be that the working class—the slaves of society—will become more and more degraded; that they will not strive against overwhelming force, but, stimulated by that love of life which Nature, always anxious about the perpetuation of the race, has implanted in us, will learn to bear everything—starvation, overwork, dirt, ignorance, brutality. All these things they will bear, as, alas! they bear them too well even now; all this rather than risk sweet life and bitter livelihood, and all sparks of hope and manliness will die out of them.

Nor will their masters be much better off: the earth's surface will be hideous everywhere, save in the uninhabitable desert; Art will utterly perish, as in the manual arts so in literature, which will become, as it is indeed speedily becoming, a mere string of orderly and calculated ineptitudes and passionless ingenuities; Science will grow more and more one-sided, more incomplete, more wordy and useless, till at last she will pile herself up into such a mass of superstition, that beside it the theologies of old time will seem mere reason and enlightment. All will get lower and lower till the heroic struggles of the past to realize hope from year to year, from century to century, will be utterly forgotten, and man will be an indescribable being—hopeless, desireless, lifeless.

And will there be deliverance from this even? Maybe man may, after some terrible cataclysm, learn to strive towards a healthy animalism, may grow from a tolerable animal into a savage, from a savage into a barbarian, and so on; and some thousands of years hence he may be beginning once more those arts which we have now lost, and be carving interlacements like the New Zealanders, or scratching forms of animals on their cleaned blade-bones, like the pre-historic men of the drift.

But in any case, according to the Pessimist view, which looks upon revolt against Artificial Famine as impossible to succeed, we shall wearily trudge the circle again, until some accident, some unforeseen consequence of arrangement, makes an end of us altogether.

That pessimism I do not believe in, nor, on the other hand, do I suppose that it is altogether a matter of our wills as to whether we shall further human progress or human degradation; yet, since there are those who are impelled towards the Socialist or Optimistic side of things, I must conclude that there is some hope of its prevailing, that the strenuous efforts of many individuals imply a force which is thrusting them on. So that I believe that the "Aims of Art" will be realized, though I know that they cannot be, so long as we groan under the tyranny of Artificial Famine. Once again I warn you against supposing, you who may specially love art, that you will do any good by attempting to revivify art by dealing with its dead exterior. I say it is the *aims of art* that you must seek rather than the *art itself;* and in that search we may find ourselves in a world blank and bare, as the result of our caring at least this much for art, that we will not endure the shams of it.

Anyhow, I ask you to think with me that the worst which can happen to us is to endure tamely the evils that we see; that no trouble or turmoil is so bad as that; that the necessary destruction which reconstruction bears with it must be taken calmly; that everywhere—in State, in Church, in the household—we must be resolute to endure no tyranny, accept no lie, quail before no fear, although they may come before us disguised as piety, duty, or affection, as useful opportunity and good-nature, as prudence or kindness. The world's roughness, falseness, and injustice will bring about their natural consequences, and we and our lives are part of those consequences; but since we inherit also the consequences of old resistance to those curses, let us each look to it to have our fair share of that inheritance also, which, if nothing else come of it, will at least bring to us courage and hope; that is, eager life while we live, which is above all things the Aim of Art.

USEFUL WORK
VERSUS
USELESS TOIL

THE above title may strike some of my readers as strange. It is assumed by most people nowadays that all work is useful, and by most *well-to-do* people that all work is desirable. Most people, well-to-do or not, believe that, even when a man is doing work which appears to be useless, he is earning his livelihood by it—he is "employed," as the phrase goes; and most of those who are well-to-do cheer on the happy worker with congratulations and praises, if he is only "industrious" enough and deprives himself of all pleasure and holidays in the sacred cause of labour. In short, it has become an article of the creed of modern morality that all labour is good in itself—a convenient belief to those who live on the labour of others. But as to those on whom they live, I recommend them not to take it on trust, but to look into the matter a little deeper.

Let us grant, first, that the race of man must either labour or perish. Nature does not give us our livelihood gratis; we must win it by toil of some sort or degree. Let us see, then, if she does not give us some compensation for this compulsion to labour, since certainly in other matters she takes care to make the acts necessary to the continuance of life in the individual and the race not only endurable, but even pleasurable.

You may be sure that she does so, that it is of the nature of man, when he is not diseased, to take pleasure in his work under certain conditions. And, yet, we must say in the teeth of the hypocritical praise of all labour, whatsoever it may be, of which I have made mention, that there is some labour which is so far from being a blessing that it is a curse; that it would be better for the community and for

603

the worker if the latter were to fold his hands and refuse to work, and either die or let us pack him off to the workhouse or prison—which you will.

Here, you see, are two kinds of work—one good, the other bad; one not far removed from a blessing, a lightening of life; the other a mere curse, a burden to life.

What is the difference between them, then? This: one has hope in it, the other has not. It is manly to do the one kind of work, and manly also to refuse to do the other.

What is the nature of the hope which, when it is present in work, makes it worth doing?

It is threefold, I think—hope of rest, hope of product, hope of pleasure in the work itself; and hope of these also in some abundance and of good quality; rest enough and good enough to be worth having; product worth having by one who is neither a fool nor an ascetic; pleasure enough for all for us to be conscious of it while we are at work; not a mere habit, the loss of which we shall feel as a fidgety man feels the loss of the bit of string he fidgets with.

I have put the hope of rest first because it is the simplest and most natural part of our hope. Whatever pleasure there is in some work, there is certainly some pain in all work, the beast-like pain of stirring up our slumbering energies to action, the beast-like dread of change when things are pretty well with us; and the compensation for this animal pain in animal rest. We must feel while we are working that the time will come when we shall not have to work. Also the rest, when it comes, must be long enough to allow us to enjoy it; it must be longer than is merely necessary for us to recover the strength we have expended in working, and it must be animal rest also in this, that it must not be disturbed by anxiety, else we shall not be able to enjoy it. If we have this amount and kind of rest we shall, so far, be no worse off than the beasts.

As to the hope of product, I have said that Nature compels us to work for that. It remains for *us* to look to it that we *do* really produce something, and not nothing, or at least nothing that we want or are allowed to use. If we look to this and use our wills we shall, so far, be better than machines.

The hope of pleasure in the work itself: how strange that

hope must seem to some of my readers—to most of them! Yet I think that to all living things there is a pleasure in the exercise of their energies, and that even beasts rejoice in being lithe and swift and strong. But a man at work, making something which he feels will exist because he is working at it and wills it, is exercising the energies of his mind and soul as well as of his body. Memory and imagination help him as he works. Not only his own thoughts, but the thoughts of the men of past ages guide his hands; and, as a part of the human race, he creates. If we work thus we shall be men, and our days will be happy and eventful.

Thus worthy work carries with it the hope of pleasure in rest, the hope of the pleasure in our using what it makes, and the hope of pleasure in our daily creative skill.

All other work but this is worthless; it is slaves' work—mere toiling to live, that we may live to toil.

Therefore, since we have, as it were, a pair of scales in which to weigh the work now done in the world, let us use them. Let us estimate the worthiness of the work we do, after so many thousand years of toil, so many promises of hope deferred, such boundless exultation over the progress of civilization and the gain of liberty.

Now, the first thing as to the work done in civilization and the easiest to notice is that it is portioned out very unequally amongst the different classes of society. First, there are people—not a few—who do no work, and make no pretence of doing any. Next, there are people, and very many of them, who work fairly hard, though with abundant easements and holidays, claimed and allowed; and lastly, there are people who work so hard that they may be said to do nothing else than work, and are accordingly called "the working classes," as distinguished from the middle classes and the rich, or aristocracy, whom I have mentioned above.

It is clear that this inequality presses heavily upon the "working" class, and must visibly tend to destroy their hope of rest at least, and so, in that particular, make them worse off than mere beasts of the field; but that is not the sum and end of our folly of turning useful work into useless toil, but only the beginning of it.

For first, as to the class of rich people doing no work, we

all know that they consume a great deal while they produce nothing. Therefore, clearly, they have to be kept at the expense of those who do work, just as paupers have, and are a mere burden on the community. In these days there are many who have learned to see this, though they can see no further into the evils of our present system, and have formed no idea of any scheme for getting rid of this burden; though perhaps they have a vague hope that changes in the system of voting for members of the House of Commons, may, as if by magic, tend in that direction. With such hopes or superstitions we need not trouble ourselves. Moreover, this class, the aristocracy, once thought most necessary to the State, is scant of numbers, and has now no power of its own, but depends on the support of the class next below it—the middle class. In fact, it is really composed either of the most successful men of that class, or of their immediate descendants.

As to the middle class, including the trading, manufacturing, and professional people of our society, they do, as a rule, seem to work quite hard enough, and so at first sight might be thought to help the community, and not burden it. But by far the greater part of them, though they work, do not produce, and even when they do produce, as in the case of those engaged (wastefully indeed) in the distribution of goods, or doctors, or (genuine) artists and literary men, they consume out of all proportion to their due share. The commercial and manufacturing part of them, the most powerful part, spend their lives and energies in fighting amongst themselves for their respective shares of the wealth which they *force* the genuine workers to provide for them; the others are almost wholly the hangers-on of these; they do not work for the public, but a privileged class: they are the parasites of property, sometimes, as in the case of lawyers, undisguisedly so; sometimes, as the doctors and others above mentioned, professing to be useful, but too often of no use save as supporters of the system of folly, fraud, and tyranny of which they form a part. And all these we must remember have, as a rule, one aim in view; not the production of utilities, but the gaining of a position either for themselves or their children in which they will not have to work at all. It is their ambition and the end of their whole lives to gain, if not for themselves yet at least for their children, the proud position of being obvious burdens on the community. For their work itself, in spite of the sham dignity with which they surround it, they care nothing: save a few enthusiasts, men of science, art or letters, who, if they are not the salt of the earth, are at least (and oh, the pity of it!) the salt of the miserable system of which they are the slaves, which hinders and thwarts them at every turn, and even sometimes corrupts them.

Here then is another class, this time very numerous and all-powerful, which produces very little and consumes enormously, and is therefore in the main supported, as paupers are, by the real producers. The class that remains to be considered produces all that is produced, and supports both itself and the other classes, though it is placed in a position of inferiority to them; real inferiority, mind you, involving a degradation both of mind and body. But it is a necessary consequence of this tyranny and folly that again many of these workers are not producers. A vast number of them once more are merely parasites of property, some of them openly so, as the soldiers by land and sea who are kept on foot for the perpetuating of national rivalries and enmities, and for the purposes of the national struggle for the share of the product of unpaid labour. But besides this obvious burden on the producers and the scarcely less obvious one of domestic servants, there is first the army of clerks, shop-assistants, and so forth, who are engaged in the service of the private war for wealth, which, as above said, is the real occupation of the well-to-do middle class. This is a larger body of workers than might be supposed, for it includes amongst others all those engaged in what I should call competitive salesmanship, or, to use a less dignified word, the puffery of wares, which has now got to such a pitch that there are many things which cost far more to sell than they do to make.

Next there is the mass of people employed in making all those articles of folly and luxury, the demand for which is the outcome of the existence of the rich non-producing classes; things which people leading a manly and uncorrupted life would not ask for or dream of. These things, whoever may gainsay me, I will for ever refuse to call wealth: they are not wealth, but waste. Wealth is what Nature gives us and what a reasonable man can make out of the gifts of Nature for his reasonable use. The sunlight, the fresh air, the unspoiled face of the earth, food, raiment and housing necessary and decent; the storing up of knowledge of all kinds, and the power of disseminating it; means of free communication between man and man; works of art, the beauty which man creates when he is most a man, most aspiring and thoughtful—all things which serve the pleasure of people, free, manly and uncorrupted. This is wealth. Nor can I think of anything worth having which does not come under one or other of these heads. But think, I beseech you, of the product of England, the workshop of the world, and will you not be bewildered, as I am, at the thought of the mass of things which no sane man could desire, but which our useless toil makes—and sells?

Now, further, there is even a sadder industry yet, which is forced on many, very many, of our workers—the making of wares which are necessary to them and their brethren, *because they are an inferior class*. For if many men live without producing, nay, must live lives so empty and foolish that they *force* a great part of the workers to produce wares which no one needs, not even the rich, it follows that most men must be poor; and, living as they do on wages from those whom they support, cannot get for their use the *goods* which men naturally desire, but must put up with miserable makeshifts for them, with coarse food that does not nourish, with rotten raiment which does not shelter, with wretched houses which may well make a town-dweller in civilization look back with regret to the tent of the nomad tribe, or the cave of the pre-historic savage. Nay, the workers must even lend a hand to the great industrial invention of the age—adulteration, and by its help produce for their own use shams and mockeries of the luxury of the rich; for the wage-earners must always live as the wage-payers bid them, and their very habits of life are *forced* on them by their masters.

But it is waste of time to try to express in words due contempt of the productions of the much-praised cheapness of our epoch. It must be enough to say that this cheapness is necessary to the system of exploiting on which modern manufacture rests. In other words, our society includes a great mass of slaves, who must be fed, clothed, housed and amused as slaves, and that their daily necessity compels them to make the slave-wares whose use is the perpetuation of their slavery.

To sum up, then, concerning the manner of work in civilized States, these States are composed of three classes—a class which does not even pretend to work, a class which pretends to work but which produces nothing, and a class which works, but is compelled by the other two classes to do work which is often unproductive.

Civilization therefore wastes its own resources, and will do so as long as the present system lasts. These are cold words with which to describe the tyranny under which we suffer; try then to consider what they mean.

There is a certain amount of natural material and of natural forces in the world, and a certain amount of labour-power inherent in the persons of the men that inhabit it. Men urged by their necessities and desires have laboured for many thousands of years at the task of subjugating the forces of Nature and of making the natural material useful to them. To our eyes, since we cannot see into the future, that struggle with Nature seems nearly over, and the victory of the human race over her nearly complete. And, looking backwards to the time when history first began, we note that the progress of that victory has been far swifter and more startling within the last two hundred years than ever before. Surely, therefore, we moderns ought to be in all ways vastly better off than any who have gone before us. Surely we ought, one and all of us, to be wealthy, to be well furnished with the good things which our victory over Nature has won for us.

But what is the real fact? Who will dare to deny that the great mass of civilized men are poor? So poor are they that it is mere childishness troubling ourselves to discuss whether perhaps they are in some ways a little better off than their forefathers. They are poor; nor can their poverty be measured by the poverty of a resourceless savage, for he knows of nothing else than his poverty; that he should be cold, hungry, houseless, dirty, ignorant, all that is to him as natural as that he should have a skin. But for us, for the

x

most of us, civilization has bred desires which she forbids us to satisfy, and so is not merely a niggard but a torturer also.

Thus then have the fruits of our victory over Nature been stolen from us, thus has compulsion by Nature to labour in hope of rest, gain, and pleasure been turned into compulsion by man to labour in hope—of living to labour!

What shall we do then, can we mend it?

Well, remember once more that it is not our remote ancestors who achieved the victory over Nature, but our fathers, nay, our very selves. For us to sit hopeless and helpless then would be a strange folly indeed: be sure that we can amend it. What, then, is the first thing to be done?

We have seen that modern society is divided into two classes, one of which is *privileged* to be kept by the labour of the other—that is, it forces the other to work for it and takes from this inferior class everything that it *can* take from it, and uses the wealth so taken to keep its own members in a superior position, to make them beings of a higher order than the others: longer lived, more beautiful, more honoured, more refined than those of the other class. I do not say that it troubles itself about its members being *positively* long lived, beautiful or refined, but merely insists that they shall be so *relatively* to the inferior class. As also it cannot use the labour-power of the inferior class fairly in producing real wealth, it wastes it wholesale in the production of rubbish.

It is this robbery and waste on the part of the minority which keeps the majority poor; if it could be shown that it is necessary for the preservation of society that this should be submitted to, little more could be said on the matter, save that the despair of the oppressed majority would probably at some time or other destroy Society. But it has been shown, on the contrary, even by such incomplete experiments, for instance, as Co-operation (so called), that the existence of a privileged class is by no means necessary for the production of wealth, but rather for the "government" of the producers of wealth, or, in other words, for the upholding of privilege.

The first step to be taken then is to abolish a class of men privileged to shirk their duties as men, thus forcing others to do the work which they refuse to do. All must work according to their ability, and so produce what they consume—that is, each man should work as well as he can for his own livelihood, and his livelihood should be assured to him; that is to say, all the advantages which society would provide for each and all of its members.

Thus, at last, would true Society be founded. It would rest on equality of condition. No man would be tormented for the benefit of another—nay, no one man would be tormented for the benefit of Society. Nor, indeed, can that order be called Society which is not upheld for the benefit of every one of its members.

But since men live now, badly as they live, when so many people do not produce at all, and when so much work is wasted, it is clear that, under conditions where all produced and no work was wasted, not only would every one work with the certain hope of gaining a due share of wealth by his work, but also he could not miss his due share of rest. Here, then, are two out of the three kinds of hope mentioned above as an essential part of worthy work assured to the worker. When class robbery is abolished, every man will reap the fruits of his labour, every man will have due rest—leisure, that is. Some Socialists might say we need not go any further than this; it is enough that the worker should get the full produce of his work, and that his rest should be abundant. But though the compulsion of man's tyranny is thus abolished, I yet demand compensation for the compulsion of Nature's necessity. As long as the work is repulsive it will still be a burden which must be taken up daily, and even so would mar our life, even though the hours of labour were short. What we want to do is to add to our wealth without diminishing our pleasure. Nature will not be finally conquered till our work becomes a part of the pleasure of our lives.

That first step of freeing people from the compulsion to labour needlessly will at least put us on the way towards this happy end; for we shall then have time and opportunities for bringing it about. As things are now, between the waste of labour-power in mere idleness and its waste in unproductive work, it is clear that the world of civilization is supported by a small part of its people; when *all* were working *usefully* for its support, the share of work which each would have to do would be but small, if our standard of life were about on the footing of what well-to-do and refined people now think desirable. We shall have labour-power to spare, and shall in short, be as wealthy as we please. It will be easy to live. If we were to wake up some morning now, under our present system, and find it "easy to live," that system would force us to set to work at once and make it hard to live; we should call that "developing our resources," or some such fine name. The multiplication of labour has become a necessity for us, and as long as that goes on no ingenuity in the invention of machines will be of any real use to us. Each new machine will cause a certain amount of misery among the workers whose special industry it may disturb; so many of them will be reduced from skilled to 'unskilled workmen, and then gradually matters will slip into their due grooves, and all will work apparently smoothly again; and if it were not that all this is preparing revolution, things would be, for the greater part of men, just as they were before the new wonderful invention.

But when revolution has made it "easy to live," when all are working harmoniously together and there is no one to rob the worker of his time, that is to say, his life; in those coming days there will be no compulsion on us to go on producing things we do not want, no compulsion on us to labour for nothing; we shall be able calmly and thoughtfully to consider what we shall do with our wealth of labour-power. Now, for my part, I think the first use we ought to make of that wealth, of that freedom, should be to make all our labour, even the commonest and most necessary, pleasant to everybody; for thinking over the matter carefully I can see that the one course which will certainly make life happy in the face of all accidents and troubles is to take a pleasurable interest in all the details of life. And lest perchance you think that an assertion too universally accepted to be worth making, let me remind you how entirely modern civilization forbids it; with what sordid, and even terrible, details it surrounds the life of the poor, what a mechanical and empty life she forces on the rich; and how rare a holiday it is for any of us to feel ourselves a part of Nature, and unhurriedly, thoughtfully, and happily to note the course of our lives amidst all the little links of events which connect them with the lives of others, and build up the great whole of humanity.

But such a holiday our whole lives might be, if we were resolute to make all our labour reasonable and pleasant. But we must be resolute indeed; for no half measures will help us here. It has been said already that our present joyless labour, and our lives scared and anxious as the life of a hunted beast, are forced upon us by the present system of producing for the profit of the privileged classes. It is necessary to state what this means. Under the present system of wages and capital the "manufacturer" (most absurdly so called, since a manufacturer means a person who makes with his hands) having a monopoly of the means whereby the power to labour inherent in every man's body can be used for production, is the master of those who are not so privileged; he, and he alone, is able to make use of this labour-power, which, on the other hand, is the only commodity by means of which his "capital," that is to say, the accumulated product of past labour, can be made productive to him. He therefore buys the labour-power of those who are bare of capital and can only live by selling it to him; his purpose in this transaction is to increase his capital, to make it breed. It is clear that if he paid those with whom he makes his bargain the full value of their labour, that is to say, all that they produced, he would fail in his purpose. But since he is the monopolist of the means of productive labour, he can *compel* them to make a bargain better for him and worse for them than that; which bargain is that after they have earned their livelihood, estimated according to a standard high enough to ensure their peaceable submission to his mastership, the rest (and by far the larger part as a matter of fact) of what they produce shall belong to him, shall be his *property* to do as he likes with, to use or abuse at his pleasure; which property is, as we all know, jealously guarded by army and navy, police and prison; in short, by that huge mass of physical force which superstition, habit, fear of death by starvation—IGNORANCE, in one word, among the propertyless masses enables the propertied classes to use for the subjection of—their slaves.

Now, at other times, other evils resulting from this system may be put forward. What I want to point out now is the impossibility of our attaining to attractive labour under this system, and to repeat that it is this robbery (there is no other word for it) which wastes the available labour-power of the civilized world, forcing many men to do nothing, and many, very many more to do nothing useful; and forcing those who carry on really useful labour to most burdensome over-work. For understand once for all that the "manufacturer" aims primarily at producing, by means of the labour he has stolen from others, not goods but profits, that is, the "wealth" that is produced over and above the livelihood of his workmen, and the wear and tear of his machinery. Whether that "wealth" is real or sham matters nothing to him. If it sells and yields him a "profit" it is all right. I have said that, owing to there being rich people who have more money than they can spend reasonably, and who therefore buy sham wealth, there is waste on that side; and also that, owing to there being poor people who cannot afford to buy things which are worth making, there is waste on that side. So that the "demand" which the capitalist "supplies" is a false demand. The market in which he sells is "rigged" by the miserable inequalities produced by the robbery of the system of Capital and Wages.

It is this system, therefore, which we must be resolute in getting rid of, if we are to attain to happy and useful work for all. The first step towards making labour attractive is to get the means of making labour fruitful, the Capital, including the land, machinery, factories, etc., into the hands of the community, to be used for the good of all alike, so that we might all work at "supplying" the real "demands" of each and all—that is to say, work for livelihood, instead of working to supply the demand of the profit market—instead of working for profit—*i.e.*, the power of compelling other men to work against their will.

When this first step has been taken and men begin to understand that Nature wills all men either to work or starve, and when they are no longer such fools as to allow some the alternative of stealing, when this happy day is come, we shall then be relieved from the tax of waste, and consequently shall find that we have, as aforesaid, a mass of labour-power available, which will enable us to live as we please within reasonable limits. We shall no longer be hurried and driven by the fear of starvation, which at present presses no less on the greater part of men in civilized communities than it does on mere savages. The first and most obvious necessities will be so easily provided for in a community in which there is no waste of labour, that we shall have time to look round and consider what we really do want, that can be obtained without over-taxing our energies; for the often-expressed fear of mere idleness falling upon us when the force supplied by the present hierarchy of compulsion is withdrawn, is a fear which is but generated by the burden of excessive and repulsive labour, which we most of us have to bear at present.

I say once more that, in my belief, the first thing which we shall think so necessary as to be worth sacrificing some idle time for, will be the attractiveness of labour. No very heavy sacrifice will be required for attaining this object, but some *will* be required. For we may hope that men who have just waded through a period of strife and revolution will be the last to put up long with a life of mere utilitarianism, though Socialists are sometimes accused by ignorant persons of aiming at such a life. On the other hand, the ornamental part of modern life is already rotten to the core, and must be utterly swept away before the new order of things is realized. There is nothing of it—there is nothing which could come of it that could satisfy the aspirations of men set free from the tyranny of commercialism.

We must begin to build up the ornamental part of life—its pleasures, bodily and mental, scientific and artistic, social and individual—on the basis of work undertaken willingly and cheerfully, with the consciousness of benefiting ourselves and our neighbours by it. Such absolutely necessary work as we should have to do would in the first place take up but a small part of each day, and so far would not be burdensome; but it would be a task of daily recurrence, and therefore would spoil our day's pleasure unless it were made at least endurable while it lasted. In other words, all labour, even the commonest, must be made attractive.

How can this be done?—is the question the answer to which will take up the rest of this paper. In giving some hints on this question, I know that, while all Socialists will agree with many of the suggestions made, some of them may seem to some strange and venturesome. These must be considered as being given without any intention of dogmatizing, and as merely expressing my own personal opinion.

From all that has been said already it follows that labour, to be attractive, must be directed towards some obviously useful end, unless in cases where it is undertaken voluntarily by each individual as a pastime. This element of obvious usefulness is all the more to be counted on in sweetening tasks otherwise irksome, since social morality, the responsibility of man towards the life of man, will, in the new order of things, take the place of theological morality, or the responsibility of man to some abstract idea. Next, the day's work will be short. This need not be insisted on. It is clear that with work unwasted it *can* be short. It is clear also that much work which is now a torment, would be easily endurable if it were much shortened.

Variety of work is the next point, and a most important one. To compel a man to do day after day the same task, without any hope of escape or change, means nothing short of turning his life into a prison-torment. Nothing but the tyranny of profit-grinding makes this necessary. A man might easily learn and practise at least three crafts, varying sedentary occupation with outdoor—occupation calling for the exercise of strong bodily energy for work in which the mind had more to do. There are few men, for instance, who would not wish to spend part of their lives in the most necessary and pleasantest of all work—cultivating the earth. One thing which will make this variety of employment possible will be the form that education will take in a socially ordered community. At present all education is directed towards the end of fitting people to take their places in the hierarchy of commerce—these as masters, those as workmen. The education of the masters is more ornamental than that of the workmen, but it is commercial still; and even at the ancient universities learning is but little regarded, unless it can in the long run be made *to pay*. Due education is a totally different thing from this, and concerns itself in finding out what different people are fit for, and helping them along the road which they are inclined to take. In a duly ordered society, therefore, young people would be taught such handicrafts as they had a turn for as a part of their education, the discipline of their minds and bodies; and adults would also have opportunities of learning in the same schools, for the development of individual capacities would be of all things chiefly aimed at by education, instead, as now, the subordination of all capacities to the great end of "money-making" for oneself—or one's master. The amount of talent, and even genius, which the present system crushes, and which would be drawn out by such a system, would make our daily work easy and interesting.

Under this head of variety I will note one product of industry which has suffered so much from commercialism that it can scarcely be said to exist, and is, indeed, so foreign from our epoch that I fear there are some who will find it difficult to understand what I have to say on the subject, which I nevertheless must say, since it is really a most important one. I mean that side of art which is, or ought to be, done by the ordinary workman while he is about his ordinary work, and which has got to be called, very properly, Popular Art. This art, I repeat, no longer exists now, having been killed by commercialism. But from the beginning of man's contest with Nature till the rise of the present capitalistic system, it was alive, and generally flourished. While it lasted, everything that was made by man was adorned by man, just as everything made by Nature is adorned by her. The craftsman, as he fashioned the thing he had under his hand, ornamented it so naturally and so entirely without conscious effort, that it is often difficult to distinguish where the mere utilitarian part of his work ended and the ornamental began. Now the origin of this art was the necessity that the workman felt for variety in his work, and though the beauty produced by this desire was a great gift to the world, yet the obtaining variety and pleasure in the work by the workman was a matter of more importance still, for it stamped all labour with the impress of pleasure. All this has now quite disappeared from the work of civilization. If you wish to have ornament, you must pay specially for it, and the workman is compelled to produce ornament, as he is to produce other wares. He is compelled to pretend happiness in his work, so that the beauty produced by man's hand, which was once a solace to his labour, has now become an extra burden to him, and ornament is now but one of the follies of useless toil, and perhaps not the least irksome of its fetters.

Besides the short duration of labour, its conscious usefulness, and the variety which should go with it, there is another thing needed to make it attractive, and that is pleasant surroundings. The misery and squalor which we people of civilization bear with so much complacency as a necessary part of the manufacturing system, is just as necessary to the community at large as a proportionate amount of filth would be in the house of a private rich man. If such a man were to allow the cinders to be raked all over his drawing-room, and a privy to be established in each corner of his dining-room, if he habitually made a dust and refuse heap of his once beautiful garden, never washed his sheets or changed his tablecloth, and made his family sleep five in a bed, he would surely find himself in the claws of a commission *de lunatico*. But such acts of miserly folly are just what our present society is doing daily under the compulsion of a supposed necessity, which is nothing short of madness. I beg you to bring your commission of lunacy against civilization without more delay.

For all our crowded towns and bewildering factories are simply the outcome of the profit system. Capitalistic manufacture, capitalistic land-owning, and capitalistic exchange force men into big cities in order to manipulate them in the interests of capital; the same tyranny contracts the due space of the factory so much that (for instance) the interior of a great weaving-shed is almost as ridiculous a spectacle as it is a horrible one. There is no other necessity for all this, save the necessity for grinding profits out of men's lives, and of producing cheap goods for the use (and subjection) of the slaves who grind. All labour is not yet driven into factories; often where it is there is no necessity for it, save again the profit-tyranny. People engaged in all such labour need by no means be compelled to pig together in close city quarters. There is no reason why they should not follow their occupations in quiet country homes, in industrial colleges, in small towns, or, in short, where they find it happiest for them to live.

As to that part of labour which must be associated on a large scale, this very factory system, under a reasonable order of things (though to my mind there might still be drawbacks to it), would at least offer opportunities for a full and eager social life surrounded by many pleasures. The factories might be centres of intellectual activity also, and work in them might well be varied very much: the tending of the necessary machinery might to each individual be but a short part of the day's work. The other work might vary from raising food from the surrounding country to the study and practice of art and science. It is a matter of course that people engaged in such work, and being the masters of their own lives, would not allow any hurry or want of foresight to force them into enduring dirt, disorder, or want of room. Science duly applied would enable them to get rid of refuse, to minimize, if not wholly to destroy, all the inconveniences which at present attend the use of elaborate machinery, such as smoke, stench and noise; nor would they endure that the buildings in which they worked or lived should be ugly blots on the fair face of the earth. Beginning by making their factories, buildings, and sheds decent and convenient like their homes, they would infal-libly go on to make them not merely negatively good, inoffensive merely, but even beautiful, so that the glorious art of architecture, now for some time slain by commercial greed, would be born again and flourish.

So, you see, I claim that work in a duly ordered com-munity should be made attractive by the consciousness of usefulness, by its being carried on with intelligent interest, by variety, and by its being exercised amidst pleasurable surroundings. But I have also claimed, as we all do, that the day's work should not be wearisomely long. It may be said, "How can you make this last claim square with the others? If the work is to be so refined, will not the goods made be very expensive?"

I do admit, as I have said before, that some sacrifice will

be necessary in order to make labour attractive. I mean that, if we *could* be contented in a free community to work in the same hurried, dirty, disorderly, heartless way as we do now, we might shorten our day's labour very much more than I suppose we shall do, taking all kinds of labour into account. But if we did, it would mean that our new-won freedom of condition would leave us listless and wretched, if not anxious, as we are now, which I hold is simply impossible. We should be contented to make the sacrifices necessary for raising our condition to the standard called out for as desirable by the whole community. Nor only so. We should, individually, be emulous to sacrifice quite freely still more of our time and our ease towards the raising of the standard of life. Persons, either by themselves or associated for such purposes, would freely, and for the love of the work and for its results—stimulated by the hope of the pleasure of creation—produce those ornaments of life for the service of all, which they are now bribed to produce (or pretend to produce) for the service of a few rich men. The experiment of a civilized community living wholly without art or literature has not yet been tried. The past degradation and corruption of civilization may force this denial of pleasure upon the society which will arise from its ashes. If that must be, we will accept the passing phase of utilitarianism as a foundation for the art which is to be. If the cripple and the starveling disappear from our streets, if the earth nourish us all alike, if the sun shine for all of us alike, if to one and all of us the glorious drama of the earth—day and night, summer and winter—can be presented as a thing to understand and love, we can afford to wait awhile till we are purified from the shame of the past corruption, and till art arises again amongst people freed from the terror of the slave and the shame of the robber.

Meantime, in any case, the refinement, thoughtfulness, and deliberation of labour must indeed be paid for, but not by compulsion to labour long hours. Our epoch has invented machines which would have appeared wild dreams to the men of past ages, and of those machines we have as yet *made no use*.

They are called "labour-saving" machines—a commonly used phrase which implies what we expect of them; but we do not get what we expect. What they really do is to reduce the skilled labourer to the ranks of the unskilled, to increase the number of the "reserve army of labour"—that is, to increase the precariousness of life among the workers and to intensify the labour of those who serve the machines (as slaves their masters). All this they do by the way, while they pile up the profits of the employers of labour, or force them to expend those profits in bitter commercial war with each other. In a true society these miracles of ingenuity would be for the first time used for minimizing the amount of time spent in unattractive labour, which by their means might be so reduced as to be but a very light burden on each individual. All the more as these machines would most certainly be very much improved when it was no longer a question as to whether their improvement would "pay" the individual, but rather whether it would benefit the community.

So much for the ordinary use of machinery, which would probably, after a time, be somewhat restricted when men found out that there was no need for anxiety as to mere subsistence, and learned to take an interest and pleasure in handiwork which, done deliberately and thoughtfully, could be made more attractive than machine work.

Again, as people freed from the daily terror of starvation find out what they really wanted, being no longer compelled by anything but their own needs, they would refuse to produce the mere inanities which are now called luxuries, or the poison and trash now called cheap wares. No one would make plush breeches when there were no flunkies to wear them, nor would anybody waste his time over making oleomargarine when no one was *compelled* to abstain from real butter. Adulteration laws are only needed in a society of thieves—and in such a society they are a dead letter.

Socialists are often asked how work of the rougher and more repulsive kind could be carried out in the new condition of things. To attempt to answer such questions fully or authoritatively would be attempting the impossibility of constructing a scheme of a new society out of the materials of the old, before we knew which of those materials would disappear and which endure through the evolution which is leading us to the great change. Yet it is not difficult to conceive of some arrangement whereby those who did the roughest work should work for the shortest spells. And again, what is said above of the variety of work applies specially here. Once more I say, that for a man to be the whole of his life hopelessly engaged in performing one repulsive and never-ending task, is an arrangement fit enough for the hell imagined by theologians, but scarcely fit for any other form of society. Lastly, if this rougher work were of any special kind, we may suppose that special volunteers would be called on to perform it, who would surely be forthcoming, unless men in a state of freedom should lose the sparks of manliness which they possessed as slaves.

And yet if there be any work which cannot be made other than repulsive, either by the shortness of its duration or the intermittency of its recurrence, or by the sense of special and peculiar usefulness (and therefore honour) in the mind of the man who performs it freely,—if there be any work which cannot be but a torment to the worker, what then? Well, then, let us see if the heavens will fall on us if we leave it undone, for it were better that they should. The produce of such work cannot be worth the price of it.

Now we have seen that the semi-theological dogma that all labour, under any circumstances, is a blessing to the labourer, is hypocritical and false; that, on the other hand, labour is good when due hope of rest and pleasure accompanies it. We have weighed the work of civilization in the balance and found it wanting, since hope is mostly lacking to it, and therefore we see that civilization has bred a dire curse for men. But we have seen also that the work of the world might be carried on in hope and with pleasure if it were not wasted by folly and tyranny, by the perpetual strife of opposing classes.

It is Peace, therefore, which we need in order that we may live and work in hope and with pleasure. Peace so much desired, if we may trust men's words, but which has been so continually and steadily rejected by them in deeds. But for us, let us set our hearts on it and win it at whatever cost.

What the cost may be, who can tell? Will it be possible

to win peace peaceably? Alas, how can it be? We are so hemmed in by wrong and folly, that in one way or other we must always be fighting against them: our own lives may see no end to the struggle, perhaps no obvious hope of the end. It may be that the best we can hope to see is that truggle getting sharper and bitterer day by day, until it breaks out openly at last into the slaughter of men by actual warfare instead of by the slower and crueller methods of "peaceful" commerce. If we live to see that, we shall live to see much; for it will mean the rich classes grown conscious of their own wrong and robbery, and consciously defending them by open violence; and then the end will be drawing near.

But in any case, and whatever the nature of our strife for peace may be, if we only aim at it steadily and with singleness of heart, and ever keep it in view, a reflection from that peace of the future will illumine the turmoil and trouble of our lives, whether the trouble be seemingly petty, or obviously tragic; and we shall, in our hopes at least, live the lives of men: nor can the present times give us any reward greater than that.

ART AND SOCIALISM

M Y friends, I want you to look into the relation of Art to Commerce, using the latter word to express what is generally meant by it; namely, that system of competition in the market which is indeed the only form which most people now-a-days suppose that Commerce can take.

Now whereas there have been times in the world's history when Art held the supremacy over Commerce; when Art was a good deal, and Commerce, as we understand the word, was a very little; so now on the contrary it will be admitted by all, I fancy, that Commerce has become of very great importance and Art of very little.

I say this will be generally admitted, but different persons will hold very different opinions not only as to whether this is well or ill, but even as to what it really means when we say that Commerce has become of supreme importance and that Art has sunk into an unimportant matter.

Allow me to give you my opinion of the meaning of it; which will lead me on to ask you to consider what remedies should be applied for curing the evils that exist in the relations between Art and Commerce.

Now to speak plainly it seems to me that the supremacy of Commerce (as we understand the word) is an evil, and a very serious one; and I should call it an unmixed evil—but for the strange continuity of life which runs through all historical events, and by means of which the very evils of such and such a period tend to abolish themselves.

For to my mind it means this: that the world of modern civilisation in its haste to gain a very inequitably divided material prosperity has entirely suppressed popular Art; or in other words that the greater part of the people have no share in Art—which as things now are must be kept in the hands of a few rich or well-to-do people, who we may fairly say need it less and not more than the laborious workers.

Nor is that all the evil, nor the worst of it; for the cause of this famine of Art is that whilst people work throughout the civilised world as laboriously as ever they did, they have lost—in losing an Art which was done by and for the people—the natural solace of that labour; a solace which they once had, and always should have, the opportunity of expressing their own thoughts to their fellows by means of that very labour, by means of that daily work which nature or long custom, a second nature, does indeed require of them, but without meaning that it should be an unrewarded and repulsive burden.

But, through a strange blindness and error in the civilisation of these latter days, the world's work almost all of it—the work some share of which should have been the helpful companion of every man—has become even such a burden, which every man, if he could, would shake off. I have said that people work no less laboriously than they ever did; but I should have said that they work more laboriously.

The wonderful machines which in the hands of just and foreseeing men would have been used to minimise repulsive labour and to give pleasure—or in other words added life—to the human race, have been so used on the contrary that they have driven all men into mere frantic haste and hurry, thereby destroying pleasure, that is life, on all hands: they have instead of lightening the labour of the workmen, intensified it, and thereby added more weariness yet to the burden which the poor have to carry.

Nor can it be pleaded for the system of modern civilisation that the mere material or bodily gains of it balance the loss of pleasure which it has brought upon the world; for as I hinted before those gains have been so unfairly divided that the contrast between rich and poor has been fearfully intensified, so that in all civilised countries, but most of all in England, the terrible spectacle is exhibited of two peoples, living street by street, and door by door—people of the same blood, the same tongue, and at least nominally living under the same laws—but yet one civilised and the other uncivilised.

All this I say is the result of the system that has trampled down Art, and exalted Commerce into a sacred religion; and it would seem is ready, with the ghastly stupidity which is its principal characteristic, to mock the Roman satirist for his noble warning by taking it in inverse meaning, and now bids us all "for the sake of life to destroy the reasons for living."

And now in the teeth of this stupid tyranny I put forward a claim on behalf of labour enslaved by Commerce, which I know no thinking man can deny is reasonable, but which if acted on would involve such a change as would defeat Commerce; that is, would put Association instead of Competition, Social order instead of Individualist anarchy.

Yet I have looked at this claim by the light of history and my own conscience, and it seems to me so looked at to be a most just claim, and that resistance to it means nothing short of a denial of the hope of civilisation.

This then is the claim:—

It is right and necessary that all men should have work to do which shall be worth doing, and be of itself pleasant to do; and which should be done under such conditions as would make it neither over-wearisome nor over-anxious.

Turn that claim about as I may, think of it as long as I can, I cannot find that it is an exorbitant claim; yet again I say if Society would or could admit it, the face of the world would be changed; discontent and strife and dishonesty would be ended. To feel that we were doing work useful to others and pleasant to ourselves, and that such work and its due reward *could* not fail us! What serious harm could happen to us then? And the price to be paid for so making the world happy is Revolution: Socialism instead of *Laissez faire.*

How can we of the middle classes help to bring such a state of things about; a state of things as nearly as possible the reverse of the present state of things?

The reverse; no less than that. For first, *The work must be worth doing*: think what a change that would make in the world! I tell you I feel dazed at the thought of the immensity of work which is undergone for the making of useless things.

It would be an instructive day's work for any one of us who is strong enough to walk through two or three of the principal streets of London on a week-day, and take accurate note of everything in the shop windows which is embarrassing or superfluous to the daily life of a serious man. Nay, the most of these things no one, serious or unserious, wants at all; only a foolish habit makes even the lightest-minded of us suppose that he wants them, and to many people even of those who buy them they are obvious encumbrances to real work, thought and pleasure. But I beg you to think of the enormous mass of men who are occupied with this miserable trumpery, from the engineers who have had to make the machines for making them, down to the hapless clerks who sit day-long year after year in the horrible dens wherein the wholesale exchange of them is transacted, and the shopmen, who not daring to call their souls their own, retail them amidst numberless insults which they must not resent, to the idle public which doesn't want them but buys them to be bored by them and sick to death of them.

I am talking of the merely useless things; but there are other matters not merely useless, but actively destructive and poisonous which command a good price in the market; for instance, adulterated food and drink. Vast is the number of slaves whom competitive Commerce employs in turning out infamies such as these. But quite apart from them there is an enormous mass of labour which is just merely wasted; many thousands of men and women making *nothing* with terrible and inhuman toil which deadens the soul and shortens mere animal life itself.

All these are the slaves of what is called luxury, which in the modern sense of the word comprises a mass of sham wealth, the invention of competitive Commerce, and enslaves not only the poor people who are compelled to work at its production, but also the foolish and not over happy people who buy it to harass themselves with its encumbrance.

Now if we are to have popular Art, or indeed Art of any kind, we must at once and for all be done with this *luxury*; it is the supplanter, the changeling of Art; so much so that by those who know of nothing better it has even been taken for Art, the divine solace of human labour, the romance of each day's hard practice of the difficult art of living.

But I say Art cannot live beside it, nor self-respect in any class of life. Effeminacy and brutality are its companions on the right hand and the left. This, first of all, we of the well-to-do classes must get rid of if we are serious in desiring the new birth of Art: and if not then corruption is digging a terrible pit of perdition for society, from which indeed the new birth may come, but surely from amidst of terror, violence and misery.

Indeed if it were but ridding ourselves, the well-to-do people, of this mountain of rubbish that would be something worth doing: things which everybody knows are of no use; the very capitalists know well that there is no genuine healthy demand for them, and they are compelled to foist them off on the public by stirring up a strange feverish desire for petty excitement, the outward token of which is known by the conventional name of fashion—a strange monster born of the vacancy of the lives of rich people, and the eagerness of competitive Commerce to make the most of the huge crowd of workmen whom it breeds as unregarded instruments for what is called the making of money.

Do not think it a little matter to resist this monster of folly; to think for yourselves what you yourselves really desire, will not only make men and women of you so far, but may also set you thinking of the due desires of other people, since you will soon find when you get to know a work of Art, that slavish work is *un*desirable.

And here furthermore is at least a little sign whereby to distinguish between a rag of fashion and a work of Art: whereas the toys of fashion when the first gloss is worn off them do become obviously worthless even to the frivolous— a work of Art, be it never so humble, is long lived; we never tire of it; as long as a scrap hangs together it is valuable and instructive to each new generation. All works of Art in short have the property of becoming venerable amidst decay: and reason good, for from the first there was a soul in them, the thought of man, which will be visible in them so long as the body exists in which they were implanted.

And that last sentence brings me to considering the other side of the necessity for labour only occupying itself in making goods that are worth making. Hitherto we have been thinking of it only from the user's point of view; even so looked at it was surely important enough; yet from the other side—as to the producer—it is far more important still.

For I say again that in buying these things

" 'Tis the lives of men you buy!"

Will you from mere folly and thoughtlessness make yourselves partakers of the guilt of those who compel their fellow men to labour uselessly?

For when I said it was necessary for all things made to be worth making, I set up that claim chiefly on behalf of *Labour*; since the waste of making useless things grieves the workman doubly. As part of the public he is *forced* into buying them, and the more part of his miserable wages are squeezed out of him by an universal kind of truck system; as one of the producers he is *forced* into making them, and so into losing the very foundations of that pleasure in daily work which I claim as his birthright; he is compelled to labour joylessly at making the poison which the truck system compels him to buy. So that the huge mass of men who are compelled by folly and greed to make harmful and useless things are sacrificed to Society. I say that this would be terrible and unendurable even though they were sacrificed to the good of Society—if that were possible; but if they are sacrificed not for the welfare of Society but for its whims, to add to its degradation, what do luxury and fashion look like then? On one side ruinous and wearisome waste leading through corruption to corruption on to complete cynicism at last, and the disintegration of all Society; and on the other side implacable oppression destructive of all pleasure and hope in life, and leading—whitherward?

Here then is one thing for us of the middle-classes to do before we can clear the ground for the new birth of Art, before we can clear our own consciences of the guilt of enslaving men by their labour. One thing; and if we *could* do it perhaps that one thing would be enough, and all other healthy changes would follow it: but can we do it? Can we escape from the corruption of Society which threatens us? Can the middle-classes regenerate themselves?

At first sight one would say that a body of people so powerful, who have built up the gigantic edifice of modern Commerce, whose science, invention and energy have

subdued the forces of nature to serve their every-day purposes, and who guide the organisation that keeps these
natural powers in subjection in a way almost miraculous;
at first sight one would say surely such a mighty mass of
wealthy men could do anything they please.

And yet I doubt it: their own creation, the Commerce
they are so proud of, has become their master; and all we of
the well-to-do classes—some of us with triumphant glee,
some with dull satisfaction, and some with sadness of heart—
are compelled to admit not that Commerce was made for
man, but that man was made for Commerce.

On all sides we are forced to admit it. There are of the
English middle-class to-day, for instance, men of the highest
aspirations towards Art, and of the strongest will; men who
are most deeply convinced of the necessity to civilisation of
surrounding men's lives with beauty; and many lesser men,
thousands for what I know, refined and cultivated, follow
them and praise their opinions: but both the leaders and
the led are incapable of saving so much as half a dozen
commons from the grasp of inexorable Commerce: they are
as helpless in spite of their culture and their genius as if they
were just so many over-worked shoemakers: less lucky than
King Midas, our green fields and clear waters, nay the very
air we breathe are turned not to gold (which might please
some of us for an hour may be) but to dirt; and to speak
plainly we know full well that under the present gospel of
Capital not only there is no hope of bettering it, but that
things grow worse year by year, day by day. Let us eat and
drink, for to-morrow we die—choked by filth.

Or let me give you a direct example of the slavery to
competitive Commerce, in which we hapless folk of the
middle-classes live. I have exhorted you to the putting away
of luxury, to the stripping yourselves of useless encumbrances, to the simplification of life, and I believe that there
are not a few of you that heartily agree with me on that
point. Well, I have long thought that one of the most
revolting circumstances that cling to our present class-
system, is the relation between us, of the well-to-do, and
our domestic servants: we and our servants live together
under one roof, but are little better than strangers to each
other, in spite of the good nature and good feeling that often

exists on both sides: nay strangers is a mild word; though we are of the same blood, bound by the same laws, we live together like people of different tribes. Now think how this works on the job of getting through the ordinary day's work of a household, and whether our lives can be simplified while such a system lasts. To go no further, you who are housekeepers know full well (as I myself do, since I have learned the useful art of cooking a dinner) how it would simplify the day's work, if the chief meals could be eaten in common; if there had not got to be double meals, one upstairs, another down stairs. And again, surely we of this educational century, cannot be ignorant of what an education it would be for the less refined members of a household to meet on common easy terms the more refined once a day, at least; to note the elegant manners of well-bred ladies, to give and take in talk with learned and travelled men, with men of action and imagination: believe me that would beat elementary education.

Furthermore this matter cleaves close to our subject of Art: for note, as a token of this stupidity of our sham civilisation, what foolish rabbit warrens our well-to-do houses are obliged to be; instead of being planned in the rational ancient way which was used from the time of Homer to past the time of Chaucer, a big hall, to wit, with a few chambers tacked on to it for sleeping or sulking in. No wonder our houses are cramped and ignoble when the lives lived in them are cramped and ignoble also.

Well, and why don't we who have thought of this, as I am sure many of us have, change this mean and shabby custom, simplifying our lives thereby and educating our *friends*, to whose toil we owe so many comforts? Why do not you—and I—set about doing this to-morrow?

Because we *cannot*; because our servants wouldn't have it, knowing, as we know, that both parties would be made miserable by it.

The civilisation of the nineteenth century forbids us to share the refinement of a household among its members!

So you see, if we middle-class people belong to a powerful folk, and in good sooth we do, we are but playing a part played in many a tale of the world's history: we are great but hapless; we are important dignified people, but bored to death; we have bought our power at price of our liberty and our pleasure.

So I say in answer to the question Can we put luxury from us and live simple and decent lives? Yes, when we are free from the slavery of Capitalist-Commerce; but not before.

Surely there are some of you who long to be free; who have been educated and refined, and had your perceptions of beauty and order quickened only that they might be shocked and wounded at every turn, by the brutalities of competitive Commerce; who have been so hunted and driven by it that, though you are well-to-do, rich even may be, you have now nothing to lose from social revolution: love of Art, that is to say of the true pleasure of life, has brought you to this, that you must throw in your lot with that of the wage-slave of competitive Commerce; you and he must help each other and have one hope in common, or you at any rate will live and die hopeless and unhelped. You who long to be set free from the oppression of the money grubbers, hope for the day when you will be *compelled* to be free!

Meanwhile if otherwise that oppression has left us scarce any work to do worth doing, one thing at least is left us to strive for, the raising of the standard of life where it is lowest, where it is low: that will put a spoke in the wheel of the triumphant car of competitive Commerce.

Nor can I conceive of anything more likely to raise the standard of life than the convincing some thousands of those who live by labour, of the necessity of their supporting the second part of the claim I have made for Labour; namely *That their work should be of itself pleasant to do.* If we could but convince them that such a strange revolution in Labour as this would be of infinite benefit not to them only, but to all men; and that it is so right and natural that for the reverse to be the case, that most men's work should be grievous to them, is a mere monstrosity of these latter days, which must in the long run bring ruin and confusion on the Society that allows it—If we could but convince them, then indeed there would be chance of the phrase *Art of the People* being something more than a mere word.

At first sight, indeed, it would seem impossible to make

men born under the present system of Commerce understand that labour may be a blessing to them: not in the sense
in which the phrase is sometimes preached to them by those
whose labour is light and easily evaded: not as a necessary
task laid by nature on the poor for the benefit of the rich;
not as an opiate to dull their sense of right and wrong, to
make them sit down quietly under their burdens to the end
of time, blessing the squire and his relations: all this they
could understand our saying to them easily enough, and
sometimes would listen to it I fear with at least a show of
complacency—if they thought there were anything to be
made out of us thereby. But the true doctrine that labour
should be a real tangible blessing in itself to the working
man, a pleasure even as sleep and strong drink are to him
now: this one might think it hard indeed for him to understand, so different as it is to anything which he has found
labour to be.

Nevertheless though most men's work is only borne as a
necessary evil like sickness, my experience as far as it goes is,
that whether it be from a certain sacredness in handiwork
which does cleave to it even under the worst circumstances,
or whether it be that the poor man who is driven by necessity to deal with things which are terribly real, when he
thinks at all on such matters, thinks less conventionally than
the rich; whatever it may be, my experience so far is that
the working man finds it easier to understand the doctrine of
the claim of Labour to pleasure in the work itself than the
rich or well-to-do man does. Apart from any trivial words of
my own, I have been surprised to find, for instance, such a
hearty feeling toward John Ruskin among working-class
audiences: they can see the prophet in him rather than the
fantastic rhetorician, as more superfine audiences do.

That is a good omen, I think, for the education of times
to come. But we who somehow are so tainted by cynicism,
because of our helplessness in the ugly world which surrounds and presses on us, cannot we somehow raise our own
hopes at least to the point of thinking that what hope glim-
mers on the millions of the slaves of Commerce is something
better than a mere delusion, the false dawn of a cloudy midnight with which 'tis only the moon that struggles? Let us
call to mind that there yet remain monuments in the world

which show us that all human labour was not always a grief and a burden to men. Let us think of the mighty and lovely architecture, for instance, of mediæval Europe: of the buildings raised before Commerce had put the coping stone on the edifice of tyranny by the discovery that fancy, imagination, sentiment, the joy of creation and the hope of fair fame are marketable articles too precious to be allowed to men who have not the money to buy them, to mere handicraftsmen and day labourers. Let us remember there was a time when men had pleasure in their daily work, but yet as to other matters hoped for light and freedom even as they do now: their dim hope grew brighter, and they watched its seeming fulfilment drawing nearer and nearer, and gazed so eagerly on it that they did not note how the ever watchful foe, oppression, had changed his shape and was stealing from them what they had already gained in the days when the light of their new hope was but a feeble glimmer; so they lost the old gain, and for lack of it the new gain was changed and spoiled for them into something not much better than loss.

Betwixt the days in which we now live and the end of the middle ages, Europe has gained freedom of thought, increase of knowledge, and huge talent for dealing with the material forces of nature; comparative political freedom withal and respect for the lives of *civilised* men, and other gains that go with these things: nevertheless I say deliberately that if the present state of Society is to endure, she has bought these gains at too high a price in the loss of the pleasure in daily work which once did certainly solace the mass of men for their fears and oppressions: the death of Art was too high a price to pay for the material prosperity of the middle classes.

Grievous indeed it was, that we could not keep both our hands full, that we were forced to spill from one while we gathered with the other: yet to my mind it is more grievous still to be unconscious of the loss; or being dimly conscious of it to have to force ourselves to forget it and to cry out that all is well.

For, though all is not well, I know that men's natures are not so changed in three centuries that we can say to all the thousands of years which went before them; You were wrong to cherish Art, and now we have found out that all men need is food and raiment and shelter, with a smattering of knowledge of the material fashion of the universe. Creation is no longer a need of man's soul, his right hand may forget its cunning, and he be none the worse for it.

Three hundred years, a day in the lapse of ages, has not changed man's nature thus utterly, be sure of that: one day we shall win back Art, that is to say the pleasure of life; win back Art again to our daily labour. Where is the hope then, you may say; Show it us.

There lies the hope, where hope of old deceived us. We gave up Art for what we thought was light and freedom, but it was less than light and freedom which we bought: the light showed many things to those of the well-to-do who cared to look for them: the freedom left the well-to-do free enough if they cared to use their freedom; but these were few at the best: to the most of men the light showed them that they need look for hope no more, and the freedom left the most of men free—to take at a wretched wage what slave's work lay nearest to them or starve.

There is our hope, I say. If the bargain had been really fair, complete all round, then were there nought else to do but to bury Art, and forget the beauty of life: but now the cause of Art has something else to appeal to: no less than the hope of the people for the happy life which has not yet been granted to them. There is our hope: the cause of Art is the cause of the people.

Think of a piece of history, and so hope! Time was when the rule of Rome held the whole world of civilisation in its poisonous embrace. To all men—even the best, as you may see in the very gospels—that rule seemed doomed to last for ever: nor to those who dwelt under it was there any world worth thinking of beyond it: but the days passed and though none saw a shadow of the coming change, it came none the less, like a thief in the night, and the *Barbarians*, the world which lay outside the rule of Rome, were upon her; and men blind with terror lamented the change and deemed the world undone by the Fury of the North. But even that fury bore with it things long strange to Rome, which once had been the food its glory fed on: hatred of lies, scorn of riches, contempt of death, faith in the fair fame won by steadfast endurance, honourable love of women—all these things the

Northern Fury bore with it, as the mountain torrent bears the gold; and so Rome fell and Europe rose, and the hope of the world was born again.

To those that have hearts to understand, this tale of the past is a parable of the days to come; of the change in store for us hidden in the breast of the Barbarism of civilisation—the Proletariat; and we of the middle class, the strength of the mighty but monstrous system of competitive Commerce, it behoves us to clear our souls of greed and cowardice and to face the change which is now once more on the road; to see the good and the hope it bears with it amidst all its threats of violence, amidst all its ugliness, which was not born of itself but of that which it is doomed to destroy.

Now once more I will say that we well-to-do people, those of us who love Art, not as a toy, but as a thing necessary to the life of man, as a token of his freedom and happiness, have for our best work the raising of the standard of life among the people; or in other words establishing the claim I made for Labour—which I will now put in a different form, that we may try to see what chiefly hinders us from making that claim good and what are the enemies to be attacked.

Thus then I put the claim again:—

Nothing should be made by man's labour which is not worth making; or which must be made by labour degrading to the makers.

Simple as that proposition is, and obviously right as I am sure it must seem to you, you will find, when you come to consider the matter, that it is a direct challenge to the death to the present system of labour in civilised countries. That system, which I have called competitive Commerce, is distinctly a system of war; that is of waste and destruction: or you may call it gambling if you will, the point of it being that under it whatever a man gains he gains at the expense of some other man's loss. Such a system does not and cannot heed whether the matters it makes are worth making; it does not and cannot heed whether those who make them are degraded by their work: it heeds one thing and only one, namely, what it calls making a profit; which word has got to be used so conventionally that I must explain to you what it really means, to wit the plunder of the weak by the strong! Now I say of this system, that it is of its very nature destructive of Art, that is to say of the happiness of life. Whatever consideration is shown for the life of the people in these days, whatever is done which is worth doing, is done in spite of the system and in the teeth of its maxims; and most true it is that we do, all of us, tacitly at least, admit that it is opposed to all the highest aspirations of mankind.

Do we not know, for instance, how those men of genius work who are the salt of the earth, without whom the corruption of society would long ago have become unendurable? The poet, the artist, the man of science, is it not true that in their fresh and glorious days, when they are in the heyday of their faith and enthusiasm, they are thwarted at every turn by Commercial War, with its sneering question "Will it pay?" Is it not true that when they begin to win worldly success, when they become comparatively rich, in spite of ourselves they seem to us tainted by the contact with the commercial world?

Need I speak of great schemes that hang about neglected; of things most necessary to be done, and so confessed by all men, that no one can seriously set a hand to because of the lack of money; while if it be a question of creating or stimulating some foolish whim in the public mind, the satisfaction of which will breed a profit, the money will come in by the ton. Nay, you know what an old story it is of the wars bred by Commerce in search of new markets, which not even the most peaceable of statesmen can resist; an old story and still it seems for ever new, and now become a kind of grim joke, at which I would rather not laugh if I could help it, but am even forced to laugh from a soul laden with anger.

And all that mastery over the powers of nature which the last hundred years or less has given us: what has it done for us under this system? In the opinion of John Stuart Mill, it was doubtful if all the mechanical inventions of modern times have done anything to lighten the toil of labour: be sure there is no doubt, that they were not made for that end, but to "make a profit." Those almost miraculous machines, which if orderly forethought had dealt with them might even now be speedily extinguishing all irksome and unintelligent labour, leaving us free to raise the standard of skill of hand and energy of mind in our workmen, and to produce afresh that loveliness and order which only the hand of man guided by his soul can produce—what have they done for us now? Those machines of which the civilized world is so proud, has it any right to be proud of the *use* they have been put to by Commercial war and waste?

I do not think exultation can have a place here: Commercial war has made a profit of these wonders; that is to say it has by their means bred for itself millions of unhappy workers, unintelligent machines as far as their daily work goes, in order to get cheap labour, to keep up its exciting but deadly game for ever. Indeed that labour would have been cheap enough—cheap to the Commercial war generals, and deadly dear to the rest of us—but for the seeds of freedom which valiant men of old have sowed amongst us to spring up in our own day into Chartism and Trades Unionism and Socialism, for the defence of order and a decent life. Terrible would have been our slavery, and not of the working classes alone, but for these germs of the change which must be.

Even as it is, by the reckless aggregation of machine-workers and their adjoints in the great cities and the manufacturing districts, it has kept down life amongst us, and keeps it down to a miserably low standard; so low that any standpoint for improvement is hard to think of even. By the means of speedy communication which it has created, and which should have raised the standard of life by spreading intelligence from town to country, and widely creating modest centres of freedom of thought and habits of culture—by the means of the railways and the like it has gathered to itself fresh recruits for the reserve army of competing lack-alls on which its gambling gains so much depend, stripping the country side of its population, and extinguishing all reasonable hope and life in the lesser towns.

Nor can I, an artist, think last or least of the outward effects which betoken this rule of the wretched anarchy of Commercial war. Think of the spreading sore of London swallowing up with its loathsomeness field and wood and heath without mercy and without hope, mocking our feeble efforts to deal even with its minor evils of smoke-laden sky and befouled river: the black horror and reckless squalor of our manufacturing districts, so dreadful to the senses which are unused to them that it is ominous for the future of the race that any man can live among it in tolerable cheerfulness: nay in the open country itself the thrusting aside by miserable jerry-built brick and slate of the solid grey dwellings that are still scattered about, fit emblems in their cheery but beautiful simplicity of the yeomen of the English field, whose destruction at the hands of yet young Commercial war was lamented so touchingly by the high-minded More and the valiant Latimer. Everywhere in short the change from old to new involving one certainty, whatever else may be doubtful, a worsening of the aspect of the country.

This is the condition of England: of England the country of order, peace and stability, the land of common sense and practicality; the country to which all eyes are turned of those whose hope is for the continuance and perfection of modern progress. There are countries in Europe whose aspect is not so ruined outwardly, though they may have less of material prosperity, less wide-spread middle-class wealth to balance the squalor and disgrace I have mentioned: but if they are members of the great Commercial whole, through the same mill they have got to go, unless something should happen to turn aside the triumphant march of War Commercial before it reaches the end.

That is what three centuries of Commerce have brought that hope to which sprung up when feudalism began to fall to pieces. What can give us the day-spring of a new hope? What, save general revolt against the tyranny of Commercial War? The palliatives over which many worthy people are busying themselves now are useless: because they are but unorganised partial revolts against a vast wide-spreading grasping organisation which will, with the unconscious instinct of a plant, meet every attempt at bettering the condition of the people with an attack on a fresh side; new machines, new markets, wholesale emigration, the revival of grovelling superstitions, preachments of thrift to lack-alls, of temperance to the wretched; such things as these will baffle at every turn all partial revolts against the monster we of the middle-classes have created for our own undoing.

I will speak quite plainly on this matter, though I must say an ugly word in the end if I am to say what I think. The one thing to be done is to set people far and wide to think it possible to raise the standard of life. If you think of it, you will see clearly that this means stirring up *general discontent*.

And now to illustrate that I turn back to my blended claim for Art and Labour, that I may deal with the third clause in it: here is the claim again:—

It is right and necessary that all men should have work to do:
First, *Work worth doing:*
Second, *Work of itself pleasant to do:*
Third, *Work done under such conditions as would make it neither over-wearisome nor over-anxious.*

With the first and second clauses, which are very nearly related to each other, I have tried to deal already. They are as it were the soul of the claim for proper labour; the third clause is the body without which that soul cannot exist. I will extend it in this way, which will indeed partly carry us over ground already covered:

No one who is willing to work should ever fear want of such employment as would earn for him all due necessaries of mind and body.

All due necessaries—what are the due necessaries for a good citizen?

First, *honourable and fitting work*: which would involve giving him a chance of gaining capacity for his work by due education; also, as the work must be worth doing and pleasant to do, it will be found necessary to this end that his position be so assured to him that he cannot be compelled to do useless work, or work in which he cannot take pleasure.

The second necessity is *decency of surroundings*: including (*a*) good lodging; (*b*) ample space; (*c*) general order and beauty. That is (*a*) our houses must be well built, clean and healthy; (*b*) there must be abundant garden space in our towns, and our towns must not eat up the fields and natural features of the country; nay I demand even that there be left waste places and wilds in it, or romance and poetry—that is Art—will die out amongst us. (c) Order and beauty means, that not only our houses must be stoutly and properly built, but also that they be ornamented duly: that the fields be not only left for cultivation, but also that they be not spoilt by it any more than a garden is spoilt: no one for instance to be allowed to cut down, for mere profit, trees whose loss would spoil a landscape: neither on any pretext should people be allowed to darken the daylight with smoke, to befoul rivers, or to degrade any spot of earth with squalid litter and brutal wasteful disorder.

The third necessity is *leisure*. You will understand that in using that word I imply first that all men must work for some portion of the day, and secondly that they have a positive right to claim a respite from that work: the leisure they have a right to claim, must be ample enough to allow them full rest of mind and body: a man must have time for serious individual thought, for imagination—for dreaming even—or the race of men will inevitably worsen. Even of the honourable and fitting work of which I have been speaking, which is a whole heaven asunder from the forced work of the Capitalist system, a man must not be asked to give more than his fair share; or men will become unequally developed, and there will still be a rotten place in Society.

Here then I have given you the conditions under which work worth doing, and undegrading to do, can be done: under no other conditions can it be done: if the general work of the world is not worth doing and undegrading to do it is a mockery to talk of civilisation.

Well then can these conditions be obtained under the present gospel of Capital, which has for its motto "The devil take the hindmost"?

Let us look at our claim again in other words:

> In a properly ordered state of Society every man willing to work
>   should be ensured—
> First—*Honourable and fitting work;*
> Second—*A healthy and beautiful house;*
> Third—*Full leisure for rest of mind and body.*

Now I don't suppose that anybody here will deny that it would be desirable that this claim should be satisfied: but what I want you all to think is that it is *necessary* that it be

Y

satisfied; that unless we try our utmost to satisfy it, we are but part and parcel of a society founded on robbery and injustice, condemned by the laws of the universe to destroy itself by its own efforts to exist for ever. Furthermore, I want you to think that as on the one hand it is possible to satisfy this claim, so on the other hand it is impossible to satisfy it under the present plutocratic system, which will forbid us even any serious attempt to satisfy it: the beginnings of Social Revolution must be the foundations of the re-building of the Art of the People, that is to say of the Pleasure of Life.

To say ugly words again. Do we not *know* that the greater part of men in civilised societies are dirty, ignorant, brutal— or at best, anxious about the next week's subsistence—that they are in short *poor*? And we know, when we think of it, that this is unfair.

It is an old story of men who have become rich by dishonest and tyrannical means, spending in terror of the future their ill-gotten gains liberally and in charity as 'tis called: nor are such people praised; in the old tales 'tis thought that the devil gets them after all. An old story— but I say "*De te fabula*"—of *thee* is the story told: *thou* art the man!

I say that we of the rich and well-to-do classes are daily doing in likewise: unconsciously, or half consciously it may be, we gather wealth by trading on the hard necessity of our fellows, and then we give driblets of it away to those of them who in one way or other cry out loudest to us. Our poor laws, our hospitals, our charities, organised and unorganised, are but tubs thrown to the whale; blackmail paid to lame-foot justice, that she may not hobble after us too fast.

When will the time come when honest and clear-seeing men will grow sick of all this chaos of waste, this robbing of Peter to pay Paul, which is the essence of Commercial war? When shall we band together to replace the system whose motto is "The devil take the hindmost" with a system whose motto shall be really and without qualification "One for all and all for one."

Who knows but the time may be at hand, but that we now living may see the beginning of that end which shall extinguish luxury and poverty? when the upper, middle,

and lower classes shall have melted into one class, living
contentedly a simple and happy life.

That is a long sentence to describe the state of things
which I am asking you to help to bring about: the abolition
of slavery is a shorter one and means the same thing. You
may be tempted to think the end not worth striving for on
one hand; or on the other to suppose, each one of you, that
it is so far ahead, that nothing serious can be done towards
it in our own time, and that you may as well therefore sit
quiet and do nothing: let me remind you how only the other
day in the life-time of the youngest of us many thousand
men of our own kindred gave their lives on the battle-field
to bring to a happy ending a mere episode in the struggle
for the abolition of slavery: they are blessed and happy, for
the opportunity came to them, and they seized it and did
their best, and the world is the wealthier for it; and if such
an opportunity is offered to us shall we thrust it from us
that we may sit still in ease of body, in doubt, in disease of
soul? These are the days of combat: who can doubt that
as he hears all round him the sounds that betoken discontent
and hope and fear in high and low, the sounds of awakening
courage and awakening conscience? These, I say, are the
days of combat, when there is no external peace possible to
an honest man; but when for that very reason the internal
peace of a good conscience founded on settled convictions is
the easier to win, since action for the cause is offered us.

Or, will you say that here in this quiet, constitutionally
governed country of England there is no opportunity for
action offered to us: if we were in gagged Germany, in
gagged Austria, in Russia where a word or two might
land us in Siberia or the prison or fortress of Peter and
Paul—why then, indeed—

Ah! my friends, it is but a poor tribute to offer on the
tombs of the martyrs of liberty, this refusal to take the torch
from their dying hands! Is it not of Goëthe it is told, that
on hearing one say he was going to America to begin life
again, he replied, "Here is America, or nowhere!" So for
my part I say, "Here is Russia, or nowhere."

To say the governing classes in England are not afraid of
freedom of speech, *therefore* let us abstain from speaking
freely, is a strange paradox to me. Let us on the contrary

press in through the breach which valiant men have made for us: if we hang back we make their labours, their sufferings, their deaths of no account.

Believe me we shall be shown that it is all or nothing: or will anyone here tell me that a Russian moujik is in a worse case than a sweating tailor's wage-slave? Do not let us deceive ourselves, the class of victims exists here as in Russia. There are fewer of them? May be—then are they of themselves more helpless, and so have more need of our help.

And how can we of the middle-classes, we the capitalists, and our hangers-on, help them? By renouncing our class, and on all occasions when antagonism rises up between the classes casting in our lot with the victims: with those who are condemned at the best to lack of education, refinement, leisure, pleasure and renown; and at the worst to a life lower than that of the most brutal of savages—in order that the system of competitive Commerce may endure.

There is *no* other way: and this way I tell you plainly, will in the long run give us plentiful occasion for self-sacrifice without going to Russia. I feel sure that in this assembly there are some who are steeped in discontent with the miserable anarchy of the century of Commerce: to them I offer a means of renouncing their class by supporting a Socialist propaganda in joining the Democratic Federation, which I have the honour of representing before you, and which I believe is the only body in this country which puts forward constructive Socialism as its program.

This to my mind is opportunity enough for those of us who are discontented with the present state of things and long for an opportunity of renunciation; and it is very certain that in accepting the opportunity you will have at once to undergo some of the inconveniences of martyrdom, though without gaining its dignity at present. You will at least be mocked and laughed at by those whose mockery is a token of honour to an honest man; but you will, I don't doubt it, be looked on coldly by many excellent people, not *all* of whom will be quite stupid. You will run the risk of losing position, reputation, money, friends even: losses which are certainly pin pricks to the serious martyrdom I have spoken of; but which none the less do try the stuff a man is made of—all the more as he can escape them with little other reproach of cowardice than that which his own conscience cries out at him.

Nor can I assure you that you will for ever escape scot-free from the attacks of open tyranny. It is true that at present Capitalist Society only looks on Socialism in England with dry grins. But remember that the body of people who have for instance ruined India, starved and gagged Ireland, and tortured Egypt, have capacities in them—some ominous signs of which they have lately shown—for openly playing the tyrants' game nearer home.

So on all sides I can offer you a position which involves sacrifice; a position which will give you your "America" at home, and make you inwardly sure that you are at least of some use to the cause: and I earnestly beg you, those of you who are convinced of the justice of our cause, not to hang back from active participation in a struggle which—who ever helps or who ever abstains from helping—must beyond all doubt end at last in Victory!

A FACTORY AS IT
MIGHT BE

WE socialists are often reproached with giving no details of the state of things which would follow on the destruction of that system of waste and war which is sometimes dignified by the lying title of the harmonious combination of capital and labour. Many worthy people say: "We admit that the present system has produced unsatisfactory results, but at least it is a system; you ought to be able to give us some definite idea of the results of that reconstruction which you call Socialism."

To this Socialists answer, and rightly, that we have not set ourselves to build up a system to please our tastes, nor are we seeking to impose it on the world in a mechanical manner, but rather that we are assisting in bringing about a development of history which would take place without our help, but which, nevertheless, compels us to help it; and that, under these circumstances, it would be futile to map out the details of life in a condition of things so different from that in which we have been born and bred. Those details will be taken care of by the men who will be so lucky as to be born into a society relieved of the oppression which crushes us, and who surely will be, not less, but more prudent and reasonable than we are. Nevertheless, it seems clear that the economical changes which are in progress must be accompanied by corresponding developments of men's aspirations; and the knowledge of their progress cannot fail to rouse our imaginations into picturing for ourselves that life at once happy and manly which we *know* social revolution will put within the reach of all men.

Of course, the pictures so drawn will vary according to the turn of mind of the picturer, but I have already tried to show in *Justice* that healthy and undomineering individuality will be fostered and not crushed out by Socialism. I will, therefore, as an artist and handicraftsman venture to develop a little the hint contained in *Justice*, of April 12th, 1884, on the conditions of pleasant work in the days when we shall work for livelihood *and pleasure* and not for "profit."

Our factory, then, is in a pleasant place—no very difficult matter when, as I have said before, it is no longer necessary to gather people into miserable, sweltering hordes for profit's sake—for all the country is in itself pleasant, or is capable of being made pleasant with very little pains and forethought. Next, our factory stands amidst gardens as beautiful (climate apart) as those of Alcinoüs, since there is no need of stinting it of ground, profit rents being a thing of the past, and the labour on such gardens is like enough to be purely voluntary, as it is not easy to see the day when 75 out of every 100 people will not take delight in the pleasantest and most innocent of all occupations, and our working people will assuredly want open-air relaxation from their factory work. Even now, as I am told, the Nottingham factory hands could give many a hint to professional gardeners in spite of all the drawbacks of a great manufacturing town. One's imagination is inclined fairly to run riot over the picture of beauty and pleasure offered by the thought of skilful co-operative gardening for beauty's sake, which beauty would by no means exclude the raising of useful produce for the sake of livelihood.

Impossible I hear an anti-Socialist say. My friend, please to remember that most factories sustain to-day large and handsome gardens, and not seldom parks and woods of many acres in extent; with due appurtenances of highly-paid Scotch professional gardeners, wood reeves, bailiffs, gamekeepers, and the like, the whole being managed in the most wasteful way conceivable; *only* the said gardens, etc., are, say, twenty miles away from the factory, *out of the smoke*, and are kept up for *one member of the factory only*, the sleeping partner to wit, who may, indeed, double that part by organising its labour (for his own profit), in which case he receives ridiculously disproportionate pay additional.

Well, it follows in this garden business that our factory

must make no sordid litter, befoul no water, nor poison the air with smoke. I need say nothing more on that point, as, "profit" apart, it would be easy enough.

Next, as to the buildings themselves, I must ask leave to say something, because it is usually supposed that they must of necessity be ugly, and truly they are almost always at present mere nightmares; but it is, I must assert, by no means necessary that they should be ugly, nay, there would be no serious difficulty in making them beautiful, as every building might be which serves its purpose duly, which is built generously as regards material, and which is built with pleasure by the builders and designers; indeed, as things go, those nightmare buildings aforesaid sufficiently typify the work they are built for, and look what they are: temples of over-crowding and adulteration and over-work, of unrest, in a word; so it is not difficult to think of our factory buildings, showing on their outsides what they are for, reasonable and light work, cheered at every step by hope and pleasure. So in brief, our buildings will be beautiful with their own beauty of simplicity as workshops, not bedizened with tomfoolery as some are now, which do not any the more for that hide their repulsiveness; but, moreover, besides the mere workshops, our factory will have other buildings which may carry ornament further than that, for it will need dining-hall, library, school, places for study of various kinds, and other such structures; nor do I see why, if we have a mind for it, we should not emulate the monks and craftsmen of the Middle Ages in our ornamentation of such buildings; why we should be shabby in housing our rest and pleasure and our search for knowledge, as we may well be shabby in housing the shabby life we have to live now.

And, again, if it be doubted as to the possibility of getting these beautiful buildings on the score of cost, let me once again remind you that every great factory does to-day sustain a palace (often more than one) amidst that costly garden and park aforesaid out of the smoke, but that this palace, stuffed as it is with all sorts of costly things, is for one member of the factory only, the sleeping partner— useful creature! It is true that the said palace is mostly, with all it contains, beastly ugly; but this ugliness is but a part of the bestial waste of the whole system of profit-mongering, which refuses cultivation and refinement to the workers, and, therefore, can have no art, not even for all its money.

So we have come to the outside of our factory of the future, and seen that it does not injure the beauty of the world, but adds to it rather. I will try to give a picture of how the work goes on there.

We have in previous pages tried to look through the present into the future, and see a factory as it might be, and got as far as the surroundings and outside of it; but those externals of a true palace of industry can be only realised naturally and without affectation by the work which is to be done in them being in all ways reasonable and fit for human beings; I mean no mere whim of some one rich and philanthropic manufacturer will make even one factory permanently pleasant and agreeable for the workers in it; he will die or be sold up, his heir will be poorer or more single-hearted in his devotion to profit, and all the beauty and order will vanish from the short-lived dream; even the external beauty in industrial concerns must be the work of society and not of individuals.

Now as to the work, first of all it will be useful, and, therefore, honourable and honoured; because there will be no temptation to make mere useless toys, since there will be no rich men cudgelling their brains for means for spending superfluous money, and consequently no "organisers of labour" pandering to degrading follies for the sake of profit, wasting their intelligence and energy in contriving snares for cash in the shape of trumpery which they themselves heartily despise. Nor will the work turn out trash; there will be no millions of poor to make a market for wares which no one would choose to use if he were not driven to do so; everyone will be able to afford things good of their kind, and, as will be shown hereafter, will have knowledge of goods enough to reject what is not excellent; coarse and rough wares may be made for rough or temporary purposes, but they will openly proclaim themselves for what they are; adulteration will be unknown.

Furthermore, machines of the most ingenious and best-approved kinds will be used when necessary, but will be used simply to save human labour; nor, indeed, could they be used for anything else in such well-ordered work as we are thinking about; since, profit being dead, there would be no temptation to pile up wares whose apparent value as articles of *use*, their conventional value as such, does not rest on the necessities or reasonable desires of men for such things, but on artificial habits forced on the public by the craving of the capitalists for fresh and ever fresh profit; these things have no real value as things to be used, and their conventional (let us say sham) utility value has been the breed of their value, as articles of exchange for profit, in a society founded on profit-mongering.

Well, the manufacture of useless goods, whether harmful luxuries for the rich or disgraceful make-shifts for the poor, having come to an end, and we still being in possession of the machines once used for mere profit-grinding, but now used only for saving human labour, it follows that much less labour will be necessary for each workman; all the more as we are going to get rid of all non-workers, and busy-idle people; so that the working time of each member of our factory will be very short, say, to be much within the mark, four hours a day.

Now, next it may be allowable for an artist—that is, one whose ordinary work is pleasant and not slavish—to hope that in no factory will all the work, even that necessary four hours' work, be mere machine-tending; and it follows from what was said above about machines being used to save labour, that there would be no work which would turn man into mere machines; therefore, at least some portion of the work, the necessary and in fact compulsory work I mean, would be pleasant to do; the machine-tending ought not to require a very long apprenticeship, therefore in no case should any one person be set to run up and down after a machine through all his working hours every day, even so shortened as we have seen; now the attractive work of our factory, that which was pleasant in itself to do, would be of the nature of art; therefore all slavery of work ceases under such a system, for whatever is burdensome about the factory would be taken turn and turn about, and so distributed, would cease to be a burden—would be, in fact, a kind of rest from the more exciting or artistic work.

Thus, then, would the sting be taken out of the factory system, in which, as things now are, the socialisation of labour, which ought to have been a blessing to the community, has been turned into a curse by the appropriation of the products of its labour by individuals, for the purpose of gaining for them the very doubtful advantages of a life of special luxury, and often of mere idleness; the result of which, to the mass of the workers, has been a dire slavery, of which long hours of labour, ever-increasing strain of labour during those hours, and complete repulsiveness in the work itself have been the greatest evils.

It remains for me to set forth my most sanguine hopes of the way in which the gathering together of people in such social bodies as properly-ordered factories might be, may be utilised for increasing the general pleasure of life, and raising its standard, material and intellectual; for creating, in short, that life rich in incident and variety, but free from the strain of mere sordid trouble, the life which the individualist vainly babbles of, but which the Socialist aims at directly, and will one day attain to.

In a duly ordered society, in which people would work for a livelihood, and not for the profit of another, a factory might not only be pleasant as to its surroundings, and beautiful in its architecture, but even the rough and necessary work done in it might be so arranged as to be neither burdensome in itself nor of long duration for each worker; but, furthermore, the organisation of such a factory, that is to say of a group of people working in harmonious co-operation towards a useful end, would of itself afford opportunities for increasing the pleasure of life.

To begin with, such a factory will surely be a centre of education; any children who seem likely to develop gifts towards its special industry would gradually and without pain, amidst their book-learning be drawn into technical instruction which would bring them at last into a thorough apprenticeship for their craft; therefore, the bent of each child having been considered in choosing its instruction and occupation, it is not too much to expect that children so educated will look forward eagerly to the time when they will be allowed to work at turning out real useful wares; a child whose manual dexterity has been developed without undue forcing side by side with its mental intelligence would surely be as eager to handle shuttle, hammer, or what not for the first time as a real workman, and begin making, as a young gentleman now is to get hold of his first gun and begin killing.

This education so begun for the child will continue for the grown man, who will have every opportunity to practise the niceties of his craft if he be so minded, to carry it to the utmost degree of perfection, not for the purpose of using his extra knowledge and skill to sweat his fellow-workman, but for his own pleasure and honour as a good artist. Similar opportunities will be afforded him to study, as deeply as the subject will bear, the science on which his craft is founded; besides, a good library and help in studying it will be provided by every productive group (or factory), so that the worker's other voluntary work may be varied by the study of general science or literature.

But, further, the factory could supply another educational want by showing the general public how its goods are made. Competition being dead and buried, no new process, no detail of improvements in machinery would be hidden from the first inquirer; the knowledge which might thus be imparted would foster a general interest in work, and in the realities of life, which would surely tend to elevate labour and create a standard of excellence in manufacture, which in its turn would breed a strong motive towards exertion in the workers.

A strange contrast such a state of things would be to that now existing! For to-day the public, and especially that part of it which does not follow any manual occupation, is grossly ignorant of crafts and processes, even when they are carried on at their own doors; so that most of the middle class are not only defenceless against the most palpable adulterations, but, also, which is far more serious, are of necessity whole worlds removed from any sympathy with the life of the workshop.

So managed, therefore, the factory, by co-operation with other industrial groups will both provide an education for its own workers, and contribute its share to the education of citizens outside, but, further, it will, as a matter of course, find it easy to provide for mere restful amusements, as it will have ample buildings for library, school-room, dining-hall, and the like; social gatherings, musical or dramatic entertainments will obviously be easy to manage under such conditions.

One pleasure—and that a more serious one—I must mention, a pleasure which is unknown at present to the workers, and which, even for the classes of ease and leisure, only exists in a miserably corrupted and degraded form, I mean the practice of the fine arts. People living under the conditions of life above-mentioned, having manual skill, technical and general education, and leisure to use these advantages, are quite sure to develop a love of art, that is to say, a sense of beauty and an interest in life, which in the long run must stimulate them to the desire for artistic creation, the satisfaction of which is of all pleasures the greatest.

I have started by supposing our group of social labour busying itself in the production of bodily necessaries; but we have seen that such work will only take a small part of each worker's time; their leisure, beyond mere bodily rest and recreation, I have supposed some would employ in perfecting themselves in the niceties of their craft, or in research as to its principles; some would stop there, others would take to studying more general knowledge, but some —and I think most—would find themselves impelled towards the creation of beauty, and would find their opportunities for this under their hands as they worked out their due quota of necessary work for the common good; these would *amuse* themselves by ornamenting the wares they made, and would only be limited in the quantity and quality of such work by artistic considerations as to how much or what kind of work really suited the wares; nor, to meet a possible objection, would there be any danger of such ornamental work degenerating into mere amateur twaddle, such as is now being inflicted on the world by the ladies and gentlemen in search for a refuge from boredom; because our workers will be thoroughly educated as workers and will know well what good work and true finish (not trade finish) means, and because the public, being a body of workers also, everyone in some line or other, will well understand what real work means. Our workers, therefore, will do their artistic work under keen criticism of themselves, their workshop comrades, and a public composed of intelligent workmen.

To add beauty to their necessary daily work will furnish outlet for the artistic aspirations of most men; but, further, our factory which is externally beautiful, will not be inside like a clean jail or workhouse; the architecture will come inside in the form of such ornament as may be suitable to the special circumstances. Nor can I see why the highest and most intellectual art, pictures, sculpture, and the like should not adorn a true palace of industry. People living a manly and reasonable life would have no difficulty in refraining from over-doing both these and other adornments; here then would be opportunities for using the special talents of the workers, especially in cases where the daily necessary work affords scanty scope for artistic work.

Thus our Socialistic factory, besides turning out goods useful to the community, will provide for its own workers work light in duration, and not oppressive in kind, education in childhood and youth. Serious occupation, amusing relaxation, and more rest for the leisure of the workers, and withal that beauty of surroundings, and the power of producing beauty which are sure to be claimed by those who have leisure, education, and serious occupation.

No one can say that such things are not desirable for the workers; but we Socialists are striving to make them seem not only desirable but necessary, well knowing that under the present system of society they are impossible of attainment—and why? Because we cannot afford the time, trouble, and thought necessary to obtain them. Again, why cannot we? *Because we are at war*, class against class, and man against man; all our time is taken up with that; we are forced to busy ourselves not with the arts of peace, but with the arts of war, which are, briefly, trickery and oppression. Under such conditions of life, labour can but be a terrible burden, degrading to the workers, more degrading to those who live upon their work.

This is the system which we seek to overthrow and supplant by one in which labour will no longer be a burden.

HOW I BECAME A
SOCIALIST

I AM asked by the Editor to give some sort of a history of the above conversion, and I feel that it may be of some use to do so, if my readers will look upon me as a type of a certain group of people, but not so easy to do clearly, briefly and truly. Let me, however, try. But first, I will say what I mean by being a Socialist, since I am told that the word no longer expresses definitely and with certainty what it did ten years ago. Well, what I mean by Socialism is a condition of society in which there should be neither rich nor poor, neither master nor master's man, neither idle nor overworked, neither brain-sick brain workers, nor heart-sick hand workers, in a word, in which all men would be living in equality of condition, and would manage their affairs unwastefully, and with the full consciousness that harm to one would mean harm to all—the realisation at last of the meaning of the word COMMON-WEALTH.

Now this view of Socialism which I hold to-day, and hope to die holding, is what I began with; I had no transitional period, unless you may call such a brief period of political radicalism during which I saw my ideal clear enough, but had no hope of any realisation of it. That came to an end some months before I joined the (then) Democratic Federation, and the meaning of my joining that body was that I had conceived a hope of the realisation of my ideal. If you ask me how much of a hope, or what I thought we Socialists then living and working would accomplish towards it, or when there would be effected any change in the face of society, I must say, I do not know. I can only say that I did not measure my hope, nor the joy that it brought me at the time. For the rest, when I took that step I was blankly ignorant of economics; I had never so much as opened Adam Smith, or heard of Ricardo, or of Karl Marx. Oddly enough, I *had* read some of Mill, to wit, those posthumous papers of his (published, was it in the *Westminster Review* or the *Fortnightly*?) in which he attacks Socialism in its Fourierist guise. In those papers he put the arguments, as far as they go, clearly and honestly, and the result, so far as I was concerned, was to convince me that Socialism was a necessary change, and that it was possible to bring it about in our own days. Those papers put the finishing touch to my conversion to Socialism. Well, having joined a Socialist body (for the Federation soon became definitely Socialist), I put some conscience into trying to learn the economical side of Socialism, and even tackled Marx, though I must confess that, whereas I thoroughly enjoyed the historical part of *Capital*, I suffered agonies of confusion of the brain over reading the pure economics of that great work. Anyhow, I read what I could, and will hope that some information stuck to me from my reading; but more, I must think, from continuous conversation with such friends as Bax and Hyndman and Scheu, and the brisk course of propaganda meetings which were going on at the time, and in which I took my share. Such finish to what of education in practical Socialism as I am capable of I received afterwards from some of my Anarchist friends, from whom I learned, quite against their intention, that Anarchism was impossible, much as I learned from Mill against *his* intention that Socialism was necessary.

But in this telling how I fell into *practical* Socialism I have begun, as I perceive, in the middle, for in my position of a well-to-do man, not suffering from the disabilities which oppress a working man at every step, I feel that I might never have been drawn into the practical side of the question if an ideal had not forced me to seek towards it. For politics as politics, *i.e.*, not regarded as a necessary if cumbersome and disgustful means to an end, would never have attracted me, nor when I had become conscious of the wrongs of society as it now is, and the oppression of poor people, could I have ever believed in the possibility of a *partial* setting right of those wrongs. In other words,

I could never have been such a fool as to believe in the happy and "respectable" poor.

If, therefore, my ideal forced me to look for practical Socialism, what was it that forced me to conceive of an ideal? Now, here comes in what I said of my being (in this paper) a type of a certain group of mind.

Before the uprising of *modern* Socialism almost all intelligent people either were, or professed themselves to be, quite contented with the civilisation of this century. Again, almost all of these really were thus contented, and saw nothing to do but to perfect the said civilisation by getting rid of a few ridiculous survivals of the barbarous ages. To be short, this was the *Whig* frame of mind, natural to the modern prosperous middle-class men, who, in fact, as far as mechanical progress is concerned, have nothing to ask for, if only Socialism would leave them alone to enjoy their plentiful style.

But besides these contented ones there were others who were not really contented, but had a vague sentiment of repulsion to the triumph of civilisation, but were coerced into silence by the measureless power of Whiggery. Lastly, there were a few who were in open rebellion against the said Whiggery—a few, say two, Carlyle and Ruskin. The latter, before my days of practical Socialism, was my master towards the ideal aforesaid, and, looking backward, I cannot help saying, by the way, how deadly dull the world would have been twenty years ago but for Ruskin! It was through him that I learned to give form to my discontent, which I must say was not by any means vague. Apart from the desire to produce beautiful things, the leading passion of my life has been and is hatred of modern civilisation. What shall I say of it now, when the words are put into my mouth, my hope of its destruction—what shall I say of its supplanting by Socialism?

What shall I say concerning its mastery of and its waste of mechanical power, its commonwealth so poor, its enemies of the commonwealth so rich, its stupendous organisation —for the misery of life! Its contempt of simple pleasures which everyone could enjoy but for its folly? Its eyeless vulgarity which has destroyed art, the one certain solace of labour? All this I felt then as now, but I did not know why it was so. The hope of the past times was gone, the struggles of mankind for many ages had produced nothing but this sordid, aimless, ugly confusion; the immediate future seemed to me likely to intensify all the present evils by sweeping away the last survivals of the days before the dull squalor of civilisation had settled down on the world. This was a bad look-out indeed, and, if I may mention myself as a personality and not as a mere type, especially so to a man of my disposition, careless of metaphysics and religion, as well as of scientific analysis, but with a deep love of the earth and the life on it, and a passion for the history of the past of mankind. Think of it! Was it all to end in a counting-house on the top of a cinder-heap, with Podsnap's drawing-room in the offing, and a Whig committee dealing out champagne to the rich and margarine to the poor in such convenient proportions as would make all men contented together, though the pleasure of the eyes was gone from the world, and the place of Homer was to be taken by Huxley? Yet, believe me, in my heart, when I really forced myself to look towards the future, that is what I saw in it, and, as far as I could tell, scarce anyone seemed to think it worth while to struggle against such a consummation of civilisation. So there I was in for a fine pessimistic end of life, if it had not somehow dawned on me that amidst all this filth of civilisation the seeds of a great change, what we others call Social-Revolution, were beginning to germinate. The whole face of things was changed to me by that discovery, and all I had to do then in order to become a Socialist was to hook myself on to the practical movement, which, as before said, I have tried to do as well as I could.

To sum up, then the study of history and the love and practice of art forced me into a hatred of the civilisation which, if things were to stop as they are, would turn history into inconsequent nonsense, and make art a collection of the curiosities of the past, which would have no serious relation to the life of the present.

But the consciousness of revolution stirring amidst our hateful modern society prevented me, luckier than many others of artistic perceptions, from crystallising into a mere railer against "progress" on the one hand, and on the other from wasting time and energy in any of the numerous schemes by which the quasi-artistic of the middle classes hope to make art grow when it has no longer any root, and thus I became a practical Socialist.

A last word or two. Perhaps some of our friends will say, what have we to do with these matters of history and art? We want by means of Social-Democracy to win a decent livelihood, we want in some sort to live, and that at once. Surely any one who professes to think that the question of art and cultivation must go before that of the knife and fork (and there are some who do propose that) does not understand what art means, or how that its roots must have a soil of a thriving and unanxious life. Yet it must be remembered that civilisation has reduced the workman to such a skinny and pitiful existence, that he scarcely knows how to frame a desire for any life much better than that which he now endures perforce. It is the province of art to set the true ideal of a full and reasonable life before him, a life to which the perception and creation of beauty, the enjoyment of real pleasure that is, shall be felt to be as necessary to man as his daily bread, and that no man, and no set of men, can be deprived of this except by mere opposition, which should be resisted to the utmost.

COMMUNISM

WHILE I think that the hope of the new-birth of society is certainly growing, and that speedily, I must confess myself puzzled about the means toward that end which are mostly looked after now; and I am doubtful if some of the measures which are pressed, mostly, I think, with all honesty of purpose, and often with much ability, would, if gained, bring us any further on the direct road to a really new-born society, the only society which can be a new birth, a society of practical equality. Not to make any mystery about it, I mean that the great mass of what most non-socialists at least consider at present to be socialism, seems to me nothing more than a *machinery* of socialism, which I think it probable that socialism *must* use in its militant condition; and which I think it *may* use for some time after it is practically established; but does not seem to me to be of its essence. Doubtless there is good in the schemes for substituting business-like administration in the interests of the public for the old Whig muddle of *laissez faire* backed up by coercion and smoothed by abundant corruption, which, worked all of it in the interest of successful business men, was once thought such a wonderful invention, and which certainly was the very cement of society as it has existed since the death of feudalism. The London County Council, for instance, is not merely a more useful body for the administration of public business than the Metropolitan Board of Works was: it is instinct with a different spirit; and even its general *intention* to be of use to the citizens and to heed their wishes, has in it a promise of better days, and has already done something to raise the dignity of life in London amongst a certain part of the population, and down to certain classes. Again, who can quarrel with the attempts to relieve the sordidness of civilized town life by the public acquirement of parks and other open spaces, planting of trees, establishment of free

660

libraries and the like? It is sensible and right for the public to push for the attainment of such gains; but we all know very well that their advantages are very unequally distributed, that they are gains rather for certain portions of the middle-classes than for working people. Nay, this socialist machinery may be used much further: it may gain higher wages and shorter working hours for the working men themselves: industries may be worked by municipalities for the benefit both of producers and consumers. Working-people's houses may be improved, and their management taken out of the hands of commercial speculators. More time might be insisted on for the education of children; and so on, and so on. In all this I freely admit a great gain, and am glad to see schemes tried which would lead to it. But great as the gain would be, the ultimate good of it, the amount of progressive force that might be in such things would, I think, depend on *how* such reforms were done; in what spirit; or rather what else was being done, while these were going on, which would make people long for equality of condition; which would give them faith in the possibility and workableness of socialism; which would give them courage to strive for it and labour for it; and which would do this for a vast number of people, so that the due impetus might be gained for the sweeping away of all privilege. For we must not lose sight of the very obvious fact that these improvements in the life of the larger public can only be carried out at the expense of some portion of the freedom and fortunes of the proprietary classes. They are, when genuine, one and all attacks I say on the "liberty and property" of the non-working or useless classes, as some of those classes see clearly enough. And I admit that if the sum of them should become vast and deep reaching enough to give to the useful or working classes intelligence enough to conceive of a life of equality and co-operation; courage enough to accept it and to bring the necessary skill to bear on working it; and power enough to force its acceptance on the stupid and the interested, the war of classes would speedily end in the victory of the useful class, which would then become the new Society of Equality.

Intelligence enough to conceive, courage enough to will, power enough to compel. If our ideas of a new Society are anything more than a dream, these three qualities must animate the due effective majority of the working-people; and then, I say, the thing will be done.

Intelligence, courage, power *enough*. Now that *enough* means a very great thing. The effective majority of the working people must I should think be something as great in numbers as an actual mechanical majority; because the non-working classes (with, mind you, their sworn slaves and parasites, men who can't live without them) are even numerically very strong, and are stronger still in holding in their hand the nine points of the law, possession to wit; and as soon as these begin to think there is any serious danger to their privilege—i.e., their livelihood—they will be pretty much unanimous in defending it, and using all the power which they possess in doing so. The necessary majority therefore of intelligence, courage, and power is such a big thing to bring about, that it will take a long time to do so; and those who are working for this end must clearly not throw away time and strength by making more mistakes than they can possibly help in their efforts for the conversion of the working people to an ardent desire for a society of equality. The question then, it seems to me, about all those partial gains above mentioned, is not so much as to what advantage they may be to the public at large in the passing moment, or even to the working people, but rather what effect they will have towards converting the workers to an understanding of, and ardent desire for Socialism; true and complete Socialism I mean, what I should call Communism. For though making a great many poor people, or even a few, somewhat more comfortable than they are now, somewhat less miserable, let us say, is not in itself a light good; yet it would be a heavy evil, if it did anything towards dulling the efforts of the whole class of workers towards the winning of a real society of equals. And here again come in those doubts and the puzzlement I began by talking about. For I want to know and to ask you to consider, how far the betterment of the working people might go and yet stop at last without having made any progress on the *direct* road to Communism. Whether in short the tremendous organization of civilized commercial society is not playing the cat and mouse game with us socialists. Whether the Society of Inequality might not accept the quasi-socialist machinery above mentioned, and work it for the purpose of upholding that society in a somewhat shorn condition, maybe, but a safe one. That seems to me possible, and means the other side of the view: instead of the useless classes being swept away by the useful, the useless classes gaining some of the usefulness of the workers, and *so* safeguarding their privilege. The workers better treated, better organized, helping to govern themselves, but with no more pretence to equality with the rich, nor any more hope for it than they have now. But if this be possible, it will only be so on the grounds that the working people have ceased to desire real socialism and are contented with some outside show of it joined to an increase in prosperity enough to satisfy the cravings of men who do not know what the pleasures of life might be if they treated their own capacities and the resources of nature reasonably with the intention and expectation of being happy. Of course also it could not be possible if there be, as we may well hope, an actual necessity for new development of society from out of our present conditions: but granting this necessity, the change may and will be exceedingly slow in coming if the working people do not show their sense of the necessity by being overtaken by a longing for the change and by expressing that longing. And moreover it will not only be slow in coming but also in that case it can only come through a period of great suffering and misery, by the ruin of our present civilization: and surely reasonable men must hope that if the Socialism be necessary its advent shall both be speedy and shall be marked by the minimum of suffering and by ruin not quite complete. Therefore, I say, what we have to hope for is that the inevitable advance of the society of equality will speedily make itself felt by the consciousness of its necessity being impressed upon the working people, and that they will consciously and not blindly strive for its realization. That in fact is what we mean by the education into Socialism of the working classes. And I believe that if this is impossible at present, if the working people refuse to take any interest in Socialism, if they practically reject it, we must accept that as a sign that the necessity for an essential change in society is so far distant, that we need scarcely trouble ourselves about it. This is the test; and for this reason it is so deadly serious for us to find out whether those democratic tendencies and the schemes of new administration they give birth to are really of use in educating the people into *direct* Socialism. If they are not, they are of use for nothing else; and we had best try if we can't make terms with intelligent Tories and benevolent Whigs, and beg them to unite their intelligence and benevolence, and govern us as kindly and wisely as they can, and to rob us in moderation only. But if they are of use, then in spite of their sordid and repellent details, and all the sickness of hope deferred that the use of such instruments assuredly brings us, let us use them as far as they will go, and refuse to be disappointed if they will not go very far: which means if they will not in a decade turn into a united host of heroes and sages a huge mass of men living under a system of society so intricate as to look on the surface like a mere chance-hap muddle of many millions of necessitous people, oppressed indeed, and sorely, not by obvious individual violence and ill-will, but by an economic system so far reaching, so deeply seated, that it may well seem like the operation of a natural law to men so uneducated that they have not even escaped the reflexion of the so-called education of their masters, but in addition to their other mishaps are saddled also with the superstitions and hypocrisies of the upper classes, with scarce a whit of the characteristic traditions of their own class to help them: an intellectual slavery which is a necessary accompaniment of their material slavery. That as a mass is what revolutionists have got to deal with: such a mass indeed I think could and would be vivified by some spark of enthusiasm, some sudden hopeful impulse towards aggression, if the necessity for sudden change were close at hand. But is it? There are doubtless not a few in this room, myself perhaps amongst them (I say *perhaps* for one's old self is apt to grow dim to one)—some of us I say once believed in the inevitableness of a sudden and speedy change. That was no wonder with the new enlightenment of socialism gilding the dullness of civilization for us. But if we must now take soberer views of our hopes, do not reproach us with that. Remember how hard other tyrannies have died.

though to the economical oppression of them was added obvious violent individual oppression, which as I have said is lacking to the heavy tyranny of our times; and can we hope that it will be speedier in its ending than they? I say that the time is not now for the sudden kindling of the impulse of direct aggression amongst the mass of the workmen. But what then! are we to give up all hope of educating them into Socialism? Surely not. Let us use all means possible for drawing them into socialism, so that they may at last find themselves in such a position that they understand themselves to be face to face with false society, themselves the only possible elements of true society.

So now I must say that I am driven to the conclusion that those measures I have been speaking of, like everything that under any reasonable form does tend towards socialism (present conditions being understood) *are* of use toward the education of the great mass of the workers; that it is necessary in the present to give form to vague aspirations which are in the air about them, and to raise their aims above the mere businesslike work of the old trades unions of raising wages with the consent (however obtained) of the employers; of making the workers see other employers[1] than those who live on the profit wrung out of their labour. I think that taking up such measures, directly tending towards Socialism, is necessary also in getting working people to raise their standard of livelihood so that they may claim more and yet more of the wealth produced by society, which as aforesaid they can only get at the expense of the nonproducing classes who now rob them. Lastly, such measures, with all that goes towards getting them carried, will train them into organization and administration; and I hope that no one here will assert that they do not need such training, or that they are not at a huge disadvantage from the lack of it as compared with their masters who have been trained in these arts.

But this education by political and corporate action must, as I hinted above, be supplemented by instilling into the minds of the people a knowledge of the aims of socialism, and a longing to bring about the complete change which

---

[1] The public to wit, i.e., the workers themselves in their other position of consumers.

will supplant civilization by communism. For the Social-democratic measures above mentioned are all of them either make-shift alleviations to help us through the present days of oppression, or means for landing us in the new country of equality. And there is a danger that they will be looked upon as ends in themselves. Nay it is certain that the greater number of those who are pushing for them will at the time be able to see no further than them, and will only recognize their temporary character when they have passed beyond them, and are claiming the next thing. But I must hope that we can instil into the mass of people some spirit of expectation, however vague, beyond the needs of the year; and I know that many who are on the road to socialism will from the first and habitually look toward the realization of the society of equality, and try to realize it for themselves—I mean they will at least try to think what equality will turn out to be, and will long for it above all things. And I look to this spirit to vivify the striving for the mere machinery of Socialism; and I hope and believe that it will so spread as the machinery is attained that however much the old individualist spirit may try to make itself master of the corporate machinery, and try by means of the public to govern the public in the interests of the enemies of the public, it may be defeated.

All this however is talking about the possible course of the Socialist movement; but since, as you have just heard, it seems to me necessary that in order to make any due use of socialist machinery one should have some sort of idea as to the life which is to be the result of it, let me now take up the often told tale of what we mean by communism or socialism; for between complete Socialism and Communism there is no difference whatever in my mind. Communism is in fact the completion of Socialism: when that ceases to be militant and becomes triumphant, it will be communism.

The Communist asserts in the first place that the resources of nature, mainly the land and those other things which can only be used for the reproduction of wealth and which are the effect of social work, should not be owned in severalty, but by the whole community for the benefit of the whole. That where this is not the case the owners of these means of production must of necessity be the masters of those who

do not own a sufficiency of them to free them from the need
of paying with a portion of their labour for the use of the
said means of production; and that the masters or owners of
the means of production do practically own the workers;
very practically, since they really dictate to them the kind
of life they shall lead, and the workers cannot escape from
it unless by themselves becoming owners of the means of
production, i.e. of other men. The resources of nature therefore, and the wealth used for the production of further
wealth, the plant and stock in short, should be communized.
Now if that were done, it would at once check the accumulation of riches. No man can become immensely rich by the
storing up of wealth which is the result of the labour of his
own brain and hands: to become very rich he must by
cajolery or force deprive others of what their brains or hands
have earned for them: the utmost that the most acquisitive
man could do would be to induce his fellow citizens to pay
him extra for his special talents, if they specially longed for
his productions. But since no one could be very rich, and
since talent for special work is never so very rare, and would
tend to become less rare as men were freer to choose the
occupations most suitable for them, producers of speciali-
ties could not exact *very* exorbitant payment, so that the
aristocracy of talent, even if it appeared, would tend to disappear, even in this first state of incomplete Communism.
In short there would be no very rich men: and all would be
well off: all would be far above the condition of satisfaction
of their material necessities. You may say how do I know
that? The answer is because there could not be so much
waste as there is now. Waste would tend to disappear. For
what is waste? First, the causeless destruction of raw
material; and secondly, the diverting of labour from useful
production. You may ask me what is the standard of usefulness in wares? It has been said, and I suppose the common view of that point is, that the price in the market gives
us the standard; but is a loaf of bread or a saw less useful
than a Mechlin lace veil or a diamond necklace? The truth
is that in a society of inequality, a society in which there
are very rich people and very poor ones, the standard of
usefulness is utterly confused: in such a society the market
price of an article is given us by the necessities of the poor

and the inordinate cravings of the rich; or rather indeed *their* necessity for spending their wealth—or rather their riches—somehow: by no means necessarily in pleasure. But in a society of equality the demand for an article *would* be a standard of its usefulness in one way or other. And it would be a matter of course that until everybody had his absolute necessities and his reasonable comforts satisfied, there would be no place for the production of luxuries; and always labour would be employed in producing things that people (all the people, since classes would have disappeared) really want.

Remember what the waste of a society of inequality is: 1st: The production of sordid makeshifts for the supply of poor folk who cannot afford the real article. 2nd: the production of luxuries for rich folk, the greater part of which even their personal folly does not make them want. And 3rdly: the wealth wasted by the salesmanship of competitive commerce, to which the production of wares is but a second-ary object, its first object being the production of a profit for the individual manufacturer. You understand that the necessary distribution of goods is not included in this waste; but the endeavour of each manufacturer to get as near as he can to a monopoly of the market which he supplies.

The minimization of waste therefore, which would take place in the incomplete 1st stages of a society of equality—a society only *tending* to equality—would make us wealthy: labour would not be wasted: workmen would not be employed in producing either slave wares, or toys for rich men: their genuine well-made wares would be made for other workmen who would know what they wanted. When the wares were of such a kind as required very exquisite skill and long training to produce, or when the material used was far fetched and dear bought, they would not cease to be produced, even though private citizens could not acquire them: they would be produced for the public use, and their real value be enormously increased thereby, and the natural and honest pride of the workman duly satisfied. For surely wealthy people will not put up with sordid surroundings or stinginess in public institutions: they will assuredly have schools, libraries, museums, parks and all the rest of it real and genuine, not makeshifts for such things: especially as being no longer oppressed by fears for their livelihood, and all the dismal incidents of the battle for mere existence, they will be able to enjoy these things thoroughly: they will be able in fact to use them, which they cannot do now. But in all I have been saying about this new society hitherto I have been thinking I must remind you of its inchoate and incomplete stages. The means of production communized but the resulting wealth still private property. Truth to tell, I think that such a state of things could only embrace a very short period of transition to complete communism: a period which would only last while people were shaking down into the new Society; for if there were no poor people I don't see how there could be any rich. There would indeed be a natural compulsion, which would prevent any man from doing what he was not fitted for, because he could not do it usefully; and I need not say that in order to arrive at the wealth I have been speaking of we must all work usefully. But if a man does work usefully you can't do without him; and if you can't do without him you can only put him into an inferior position to another useful citizen by means of compulsion; and if you compel him to it, you at once have your privileged classes again. Again, when all people are living comfortably or even handsomely, the keenness of the strife for the better positions, which will then no longer involve a life of idleness or power over one's neighbours, will surely tend to abate: men get rich now in their struggles not to be poor, and because their riches shield them from suffering from the horrors which are a necessary accompaniment of the existence of rich men; e.g., the sight of slums, the squalor of a factory country, the yells and evil language of drunken and brutalized poor people and so forth. But when all private life was decent and, apart from natural accident, happy; and when public institutions satisfied your craving for splendour and completeness; and when no one was allowed to injure the public by defiling the natural beauty of the earth, or by forbidding men's cravings for making it more beautiful to have full sway, what advantage would there be in having more nominal wealth than your neighbour? Therefore, as on the one hand men whose work was acknowledged as useful would scarcely subject themselves to a new system of caste; and, on the other, people living happily with all their reasonable needs easily satisfied would hardly worry themselves with worrying others into giving them extra wealth which they could not use, so I think the communization of the means of industry would speedily be followed by the communization of its product: that is that there would be complete equality of condition amongst all men. Which again does not mean that people would (all round) use their neighbours' coats, or houses or tooth brushes, but that every one, whatever work he did, would have the opportunity of satisfying all his reasonable needs according to the admitted standard of the society in which he lived: i.e., without robbing any other citizen. And I must say it is in the belief that this is possible of realization that I continue to be a socialist. Prove to me that it is not; and I will not trouble myself to do my share towards altering the present state of society, but will try to live on, as little a pain to myself and a nuisance to my neighbour as I may. But yet I must tell that I shall be more or less both a pain to myself (or at least a disgrace) and a nuisance to my neighbour. For I do declare that any other state of society but communism is grievous and disgraceful to all belonging to it.

Some of you may expect me to say something about the machinery by which a communistic society is to be carried on. Well, I can say very little that is not merely negative. Most anti-socialists and even some socialists are apt to confuse, as I hinted before, the co-operative machinery towards which modern life is tending with the essence of socialism itself; and its enemies attack it, and sometimes its friends defend it on those lines; both to my mind committing a grievous error, especially the latter. E.g. An anti-socialist will say How will you sail a ship in a socialist condition? How? Why with a captain and mates and sailing master and engineer (if it be a steamer) and ABs and stokers and so on and so on. *Only* there will be no 1st, 2nd and 3rd class among the passengers: the sailors and stokers will be as well fed and lodged as the captain or passengers; and the Captain and the stoker will have the same pay.

There are plenty of enterprises which will be carried on then, as they are now (and, to be successful, must probably remain) under the guidance of one man. The only difference between then and now will be, that he will be chosen because he is fit for the work, and not because he must have a job found for him; and that he will do his work for the benefit of each and all, and not for the sake of making a profit. For the rest, time will teach us what new machinery may be necessary to the new life; reasonable men will submit to it without demur; and unreasonable ones will find themselves compelled to by the nature of things, and can only I fear console themselves, as the philosopher did when he knocked his head against the door post, by damning the Nature of things.

Well, since our aim is so great and so much to be longed for, the substituting throughout all society of peace for war, pleasure and self-respect for grief and disgrace, we may well seek about strenuously for some means for starting our enterprise; and since it is just these means in which the difficulty lies, I appeal to all socialists, while they express their thoughts and feelings about them honestly and fearlessly, not to make a quarrel of it with those whose aim is one with theirs, because there is a difference of opinion between them about the usefulness of the details of the means. . It is difficult or even impossible not to make mistakes about these, driven as we are by the swift lapse of time and the necessity for doing something amidst it all. So let us forgive the mistakes that others make, even if we make none ourselves, and be at peace amongst ourselves, that we may the better make War upon the monopolist.

PRINTED IN GREAT BRITAIN
BY ROBERT MACLEHOSE AND CO. LTD.
THE UNIVERSITY PRESS, GLASGOW